A Course of Love

A of Love

COMBINED VOLUME

Mari Perron, First Receiver

A Course of Love (Book One) was first published by New World Library, Novato, California. A Course of Love (Book One), A Course of Love: The Treatises (Book Two), and A Course of Love: The Dialogues (Book Three) were subsequently published as separate volumes by The Center for A Course of Love, St. Paul, Minnesota.

The union of which this Course speaks inspired the
cover emblem, which is modeled after the Angel's Trumpet,
a large flower with five petals that spiral as they unfurl.
It hangs downward, facing the earth. By day its beauty is fully
displayed, but it is at night that its exquisite, delicate
perfume is released. This act of creation,
equally embracing both light and dark,
suggests the joining of heaven and earth.

TAKE HEART PUBLICATIONS
12402 Bitney Springs Road
Nevada City, California 95959
www.takeheartpublications.com

ISBN 1-978-58469-503-5

Book design and computer production by
Patty Arnold, *Menagerie Design & Publishing*

Manufactured in the United States of America
First Printing, July, 2014

You are, as you read these words, as much a "receiver" of this dialogue as she who first hears these words and transfers them to paper. Is a piece of music not received by you even when you may be one of thousands or millions who hear it? Does it matter who is first to hear the music? This is, in truth, a dialogue between me and you. Wish not that the "way" of the transcriber of these words were the way for everyone, and think not that to hear "directly" from the Source is different than what you do here. (D:1.18–19)

Mari Perron was, in Jesus's words, the "first receiver" of this Course. (C:12.7, 11) Accordingly that term has been adopted for this Combined Volume.

Table of Contents

FOREWORD xiii

A COURSE OF LOVE: BOOK ONE

INTRODUCTION 1

THE PRELUDE 5

CHAPTER 1: *A Course of Love* 16

CHAPTER 2: *What Love Is* 21

CHAPTER 3: *The First Lesson* 26

CHAPTER 4: *Love's Equity* 31

CHAPTER 5: *Relationship* 37

CHAPTER 6: *Forgiveness/Joining* 45

CHAPTER 7: *Withholding* 51

CHAPTER 8: *The Separation from the Body* 58

CHAPTER 9: *The Prodigal's Return* 65

CHAPTER 10: *Use and Understanding* 79

CHAPTER 11: *Free Will and Willingness* 88

CHAPTER 12: *Origin of Separation* 93

CHAPTER 13: *Observation and Experience* 99

CHAPTER 14: *Special Relationships, Earthly and Human* 102

CHAPTER 15: *The Special Self* 110

CHAPTER 16: *What You Choose Instead* 114

CHAPTER 17: *Conscious Non-Planning* 120

CHAPTER 18: *The Mind Engaged* 124

CHAPTER 19: *Oneness and Duality* 130

CHAPTER 20: *The Embrace* 137

CHAPTER 21: *Love Is* 146

CHAPTER 22: *The Intersection* 149

CHAPTER 23: *The Freedom of the Body* 154

CHAPTER 24: *The Time of Tenderness* 160

CHAPTER 25: *Devotion as a Type of Participation* 161

CHAPTER 26: *The Full Life* 167

CHAPTER 27: *Being* 172

CHAPTER 28: *Bearing Witness* 176

CHAPTER 29: *Attention* 179

CHAPTER 30: *Being Present* 184

CHAPTER 31: *The Nature of the Mind* 187

CHAPTER 32: *Love Returned to Love* 194

THE TREATISES OF A COURSE OF LOVE: BOOK TWO

A TREATISE ON THE ART OF THOUGHT: THE FIRST TREATISE

CHAPTER 1: *The First Instruction* 200

CHAPTER 2: *The Art of Thought* 203

CHAPTER 3: *The Call to the Miracle* 207

CHAPTER 4: *The Center of the Universe* 212

CHAPTER 5: *The Choice for Love* 218

CHAPTER 6: *The Act of Prayer* 221

CHAPTER 7: *Suffering and the New Learning* 223

CHAPTER 8: *Incarnation and Resurrection* 225

CHAPTER 9: *Giving and Receiving* 228

CHAPTER 10: *Peace* 232

A TREATISE ON THE NATURE OF UNITY AND ITS RECOGNITION: THE SECOND TREATISE

CHAPTER 1: *Treasure* 238

CHAPTER 2: *To Hear the Call* 241

CHAPTER 3: *To Answer the Call* 241

CHAPTER 4: *The Call to Who You Are* 245

CHAPTER 5: *The Source of Your Call* 250

CHAPTER 6: *The Belief: Accomplishment* 252

CHAPTER 7: *The Belief: Giving and Receiving As One* 255

CHAPTER 8: *The Belief: No Relationships Are Special* 260

CHAPTER 9: *The Belief: There Is No Loss But Only Gain* 262

CHAPTER 10: *The Belief: We Only Learn in Unity* 266

CHAPTER 11: *The Belief: We Exist in Relationship and Unity* 270

CHAPTER 12: *The Belief: Correction and Atonement* 274

CHAPTER 13: *The Final Call* 277

A TREATISE ON THE PERSONAL SELF: THE THIRD TREATISE

CHAPTER 1: *True and False Representation* 280

CHAPTER 2: *The Purpose of Representation* 283

CHAPTER 3: *The True Self* 287

CHAPTER 4: *The Dismantling of Illusion* 290

CHAPTER 5: *Original Purpose* 292

CHAPTER 6: *The Desire for Reward* 294

CHAPTER 7: *The Explosion of Belief* 296

CHAPTER 8: *The House of Truth* 298

CHAPTER 9: *To Dwell in the House of Truth* 302

CHAPTER 10: *An Exercise in Forgetting* 302

CHAPTER 11: *The Temptations of the Human Experience* 308

CHAPTER 12: *The Physical Self in the House of Truth* 311

CHAPTER 13: *The Practice: No Loss But Only Gain* 314

CHAPTER 14: *Not Other Than Who You Are* 317

CHAPTER 15: *The New Beginning* 321

CHAPTER 16: *Willingness, Temptation, and Belief* 325

CHAPTER 17: *A Mistake in Learning* 329

CHAPTER 18: *Observation* 332

CHAPTER 19: *Physical Reality* 334

CHAPTER 20: *Suffering and Observance* 338

CHAPTER 21: *The Identity of the True Self* 343

CHAPTER 22: *The True Self in Observable Form* 348

A TREATISE ON THE NEW: THE FOURTH TREATISE

CHAPTER 1: *All Are Chosen* 354

CHAPTER 2: *Shared Vision* 361

CHAPTER 3: *Natural Vision* 369

CHAPTER 4: *The Inheritance of Everlasting Life* 372

CHAPTER 5: *The Energy of Creation and the Body of Christ* 376

CHAPTER 6: *A New Choice* 380

CHAPTER 7: *An End to Learning* 382

CHAPTER 8: *To Come to Know* 385

CHAPTER 9: *Beyond Learning* 390

CHAPTER 10: *Creating Anew* 392

CHAPTER 11: *The End of Learning and the Sustainability of
Christ-Consciousness* 395

CHAPTER 12: *A Prelude to The Dialogues* 396

THE DIALOGUES OF A COURSE OF LOVE: BOOK THREE

CHAPTER 1: *Acceptance of the State of Grace of the Newly Identified
Child of God* 407

CHAPTER 2: *Acceptance and Denial* 413

CHAPTER 3: *The Covenant of the New* 418

CHAPTER 4: *The New You* 423

CHAPTER 5: *True Representation* 430

CHAPTER 6: *The Body and the Elevation of Form* 435

CHAPTER 7: *Time and the Experience of Transformation* 442

CHAPTER 8: *The Territory of Conscious Awareness* 448

CHAPTER 9: *Awareness that Does Not Come from Thought* 452

CHAPTER 10: *The Goal and the Accomplishment of the Elevated Self of Form* 455

CHAPTER 11: *The Return to Unity and the End of Thought As You Know It* 457

CHAPTER 12: *The Body and Your Thoughts* 461

CHAPTER 13: *Sharing and a Refinement of Your Means of Expressing What You Know* 466

CHAPTER 14: *New Frontiers Beyond the Body and Mind, Form and Time* 470

CHAPTER 15: *Becoming and the Principles of Creation* 474

CHAPTER 16: *From Image to Presence* 479

CHAPTER 17: *The Secret of Succession* 484

THE FORTY DAYS AND FORTY NIGHTS

DAY 1: *Accept Me* 490

DAY 2: *Accept Your Self* 495

DAY 3: *Accept Abundance* 500

DAY 4: *The New Temptations* 512

DAY 5: *Access to Unity* 523

DAY 6: *The Time In Between* 528

DAY 7: *Conditions of the Time of Acceptance* 534

DAY 8: *Accept the Present* 538

DAY 9: *Freedom* 545

DAY 10: *Power* 551

DAY 11: *Christ-Consciousness* 559

DAY 12: *The Spacious Self Joined in Relationship* 561

DAY 13: *Union with the Spacious Self* 563

DAY 14: *Healing* 565

DAY 15: *Entering the Dialogue* 568

DAY 16: *Paradise Re-Found* 575

DAY 17: *The Fulfillment of the Way of Jesus* 579

Day 18: *The Way to Paradise* 583

Day 19: *The Way of Mary* 587

Day 20: *The First Transition* 591

Day 21: *The Reversal* 593

Day 22: *Channeling* 595

Day 23: *Carrying* 599

Day 24: *Potential* 601

Day 25: *Tending Your Garden* 603

Day 26: *Self-Guidance* 605

Day 27: *The Apprehension of Levels of Experience* 607

Day 28: *From Externally to Internally Directed Life Experience* 611

Day 29: *The Common Denominator of Experience* 615

Day 30: *Yielding to Wholeness* 617

Day 31: *Joining* 619

Day 32: *The Experience of the Self and the Power of God* 621

Day 33: *Being in Relationship* 625

Day 34: *Saying Yes to Power* 628

Day 35: *Being a Creator in Unity and Relationship* 630

Day 36: *Who You Are in Unity and Relationship* 634

Day 37: *A New Idea of God* 639

Day 38: *Who I Am* 646

Day 39: *Who I Am to You* 648

Day 40: *Who You Are to Me* 655

Epilogue : *A Note on Being* 661

Addendum: *Learning in the Time of Christ* 665

Referencing Guide 675

Related Works.. .677

Resources .... .677

Foreword

For almost three years Mari Perron heard an inner voice, as if dictating. She transcribed what she heard. The result, unedited, is *A Course of Love*. It explicitly states that it is a "continuation" of *A Course in Miracles*, although there is no formal connection between the two courses. Both courses were received in an identical manner. In both courses Jesus is entirely forthright about his identity as the Source.

The two courses were received approximately 30 years apart. Helen Schucman received *A Course in Miracles* over a period of seven years in the late 1960s and early 1970s; Mari received *A Course of Love* from December, 1998 through October, 2001. Both courses present themselves with a rare degree of authority and intelligence. Their spiritually pioneering nature is far beyond what either woman could have written on her own. Those familiar with *A Course in Miracles* will recognize the distinctive and brilliant style, although most people will probably find the language of *A Course of Love* considerably less complicated and more accessible than its predecessor.

The dictation Mari scribed specifically referred to this Course as a "continuation of the coursework provided in *A Course in Miracles*." (A.4) It also stated:

> Where the original Course in Miracles was a course in thought reversal and mind training, a course to point out the insanity of the identity crisis and dislodge the ego's hold, this is a course to establish your identity and to end the reign of the ego. (C:P.8)

Mari Perron grew up in a working class family in St. Paul, Minnesota. At the University of Minnesota she majored in English; as a returning adult student with three children she won the notable Jean Keller-Bouvier Award for literary accomplishment. A practicing Catholic, she felt deeply about her faith and had no particular interest in other approaches to spirituality. "I wanted to write mystery novels and smoke cigarettes and be an intellectual." She describes herself as an "ordinary" woman.

It was a deeply personal joining together in relationship with two other women that paved the way for the transmission of *A Course of Love*. (Similarly, those familiar with the history of *A Course in Miracles* will recall that it was Helen's colleague, Bill Thetford's "speech" that "there must be another way" out of their conflict, and Helen's wholehearted agreement, that signaled the events leading to the transmission through Helen.) In 1993 Mari was one of three administrators conducting an off-site adult-study program for the university's health services department. The nature of their jobs required all three women—Mari, Mary, and Julieanne—to work together closely. At about the same time, Julieanne and Mary each discovered that they were pregnant, and that their babies were due to be born on nearly the same date. Julieanne gave birth to a healthy baby. Mary's baby, Grace, had a serious heart malformation. Five weeks after her birth and following multiple surgeries, Grace died. Although the stark contrast in the situations of the two women could easily have torn the group apart, instead it intensified their closeness. Through Grace's life and death the three women bonded together in a deeply personal quest for meaning. They read many spiritual books. They each had significant experiences and insights. Most importantly, they actively shared their feelings and discoveries with their "spirit sisters."

One of the readings the women shared suggested it was possible to contact one's "angel." Mari was skeptical. Nevertheless, on May 1, 1995, she decided to try by typing a little letter. Her favorite way of expressing herself is through writing. She was "ready to ask" even though she did not expect an answer. The following is how she recounts what happened next:

"Dearest Angel,

"I think I have felt you with me since my earliest childhood, certainly in my most tormented times when you would tell me I was special and a part of me believed you. Thank you. That voice that said I was special kept me living as much as I could live. Feeling as much as I could feel. . . . It is this of me that is willing to believe I can talk to you. It is this part of me that says it makes sense. Will you talk to me?"

The answer came immediately, my fingers responding and typing the words almost before the thoughts had entered my mind. . . . I did not hear a voice distinct from my own. But I knew the words were not my own.

Smell the sweetness. You are sweet. Don't try to force it, to will it, just let it come. It is there in the in-between, between thought and feeling. Breathe. Feel your heart.

So began the receiving of messages from a voice that identified itself as an angel going by the name of "Peace." Mari later wrote, "I look back now and think how simple this communication was. How childlike. How innocent. . . . It was given through the act of asking." In 1995, Mari, Mary, and Julieanne decided to share their story with the world through publication of *The Grace Trilogy* (Hazelden, 1997; available as an ebook through Take Heart Publications). Her experiences with receiving messages from the angel Peace turned out to be a prelude, or perhaps an exercise, for things to come.

Mari discovered *A Course in Miracles* in 1996.

> I read about ACIM in a newspaper article that did not name it as a book that came in the voice of Jesus. When I started reading it, I still didn't realize that it was, and when I became aware of it I didn't believe it. But by then I wasn't about to put the book down because I felt everything in it was Truth with a capital T. . . . After a while I started to figure maybe it really was Jesus.

She was enthralled. Although usually Mari voraciously read many books, for two years she read little other than *A Course in Miracles*, many times through, especially the Text. Well over a year before she actually heard the voice, preparation had begun. Mari says:

> *A Course of Love* began with a dream. The dream came to me in July of 1997. In the dream, I heard, You can no longer sell your mind for money. Your mind now belongs to God.

Months of soul-searching followed. Eventually Mari left her job and held herself ready—for what, she had no idea. After nine months and much financial uncertainty she considered going back to work, but an inner knowing kept telling her that she "had work to do for God." Then her friend Mary shared a dream in which she saw "a new course in miracles." Mari felt that somehow Mary's dream was an announcement of the work to come—a work so monumental that Mari had been unable to accept signs that now, looking back, had pointed toward this scribing work all along. A week later, on December 1, 1998, Mari began to "hear" the voice.

> As soon as I heard the familiar voice of Jesus, not as I remembered it from my youth or the Bible, but as I remembered it from many readings of *A Course in Miracles*, I was awestruck by the task set before me. For the next three years, I dedicated myself to receiving the three books that combine to deliver this new message.

Referring to Mari, Jesus said that "the first receiver of these words can 'hear' these words as thoughts. Keep in mind that she has thoughts she is not thinking." (D:12.7)

In 2001, Mari, along with friend and former literary agent Dan Odegard, worked to bring forth the first edition of *A Course of Love*, published by New World Library. Several decisions made at that time were later reversed. Because of ongoing litigation over the copyright to *A Course in Miracles*, language was removed that referred directly to *A Course of Love* as a continuation of *A Course of Miracles*. This language was later restored. Similarly, the misleading subtitle "The Complete Course" was later deleted—it contained the first volume only.

Once published, Mari felt "it wasn't really calling me to do anything with it. Instead I felt called to solitude and spent most of the next couple of years embracing that way of life." Outwardly, then, Mari may seem an unlikely person through whom Jesus would extend monumentally to the world. But when New World Library decided not to publish the other volumes, she promptly went about making them available on her own.

Mari brought out The Treatises and The Dialogues. In 2003, as she worked on these volumes, Mari received an additional message, "Learning in the Time of Christ," in the same manner as the rest of the material. It anticipated future discussion groups and was clearly meant as an aid to both individuals and groups who would be studying this Course. It is presented at the end of this Combined Volume as an Addendum—although those so inclined may find it illuminating at any time.

Finally, when New World Library let the so-called "Complete Course" go out of print, Mari prepared to self-publish all three volumes as a coherent series. Once again, as she was preparing the volumes on Valentine's Day, 2006, she received yet another message evidently intended to introduce this Course. It is included in this Combined Edition as the Introduction.

Even as a self-publisher, Mari was not naturally inclined to campaign on behalf of *A Course of Love*, but she took to heart the message that "you can only be who you are by sharing who you are." (C:31.17) She decided that not only was she willing to ask, to listen, and to transcribe, but also to share—and not just the beautiful consoling words of Jesus. Mari shares her own humanity, her challenges and struggles as a mom, her lack of resources, the problems of addiction in her own family, and a perspective on healing that is not a sentimental view of love or life. In her blog, her books, and her abundant private correspondence, Mari speaks of the acceptance that love can draw to those with "imperfect" pasts and how "knowing and being known" can invite justice, equality, and dignity, as well as peace.

In her first printing of all three books of this Course, Mari wrote the following as a Foreword:

> In *A Course of Love*, as well as in *A Course in Miracles*, Jesus says that love cannot be taught. What can't be taught is a mystery. These messages from Jesus are both mystery and revelation of mystery.

> In 1998, I was reading *A Course in Miracles* and seeking my own heart's calling when I heard a Voice tell me that I would receive a new course in miracles. As you might imagine, my part in this mystery–having this Course of Love come to me and through me–raised a number of questions.

> How did it happen? How was this guidance made possible? What did it feel like? What did I actually experience?

> Receiving Jesus and his guidance was easy. I loved the relationship and the process by which I wrote. The words arose from within, more or less as thoughts I didn't think. This writing practice lasted three years. The work of it was effortless, uncomplicated, and awe-inspiring.

> There was a way I made it difficult, though. This is what I want to tell you about so that I might save you from the same unnecessary suffering.

> It was when each day's writing was done that difficulty would arise. That was when I would begin to think about it. Thinking about it, I felt overwhelmed. My mind struggled and grew painfully frustrated by its inability to comprehend what was happening and even what was being said. My mind could not accept the new experience. I couldn't understand it, explain it, or compare it to anything else.

> My feelings fared little better. As soon as I stood back from the work I was doing, I felt like a peon on an iceberg enveloped by immensity. I felt surrounded by the most powerful force in the universe, as if I was in the eye of a hurricane.

> Yet I was just sitting at my desk. A mere moment away from dinner. I'd find it hard to believe I could still eat. I'd hear the sound of the television or the phone ringing and I'd be whisked back from my iceberg in a nano-second. The shift in atmosphere felt as if it would just about kill me.

> This is how sharp the contrast was between union and separation. I knew I couldn't continue to feel union only when I was actively engaged in the work. I couldn't continue to feel miserable as soon as it stopped. I knew

that Jesus didn't leave me when I left my desk, but I felt unable to extend my awareness of union much beyond it.

This didn't stop me from trying. I felt that if I tried hard enough, I could learn how to do it. If I could only get a clear grasp, a definitive understanding of what was going on, then I would "have it." I could "achieve" union. I kept trying to make it be like other experiences I had learned from and learned to duplicate – experiences from which I had always stood back – a mind, or a self, observing.

It wasn't by the effort of my mind, but through stillness of mind, that I eventually realized that it wasn't something miraculous about "the work" that made union possible and separation intolerable. Union was what arose naturally when the blocks to my awareness of love's presence were removed. This was what happened as I received the Course. The barrier of my separate thoughts melted away and Jesus was with me without being "other than me." We were in relationship without being separate.

In union there is no "self" standing back, observing the experience. Without a separate consciousness, there is no thought. Without thought there is oneness of being.

When I saw this, I knew that I could experience oneness in life, that I'd had these experiences in the past, and that I continue to have them. They just weren't experiences of my thinking mind.

It would only be after such an experience that an awareness that "something happened" would come. Then I'd think, "Oh my God, that was the greatest thing ever. I want to have that again." Once more the work would begin toward realizing unity wasn't something I could "have" and that it's who I am when I'm not being an "other" to myself; when I'm not being separate.

When I'm thinking, I'm present to this "other" who is the self I think I am. "She" is there in my thoughts just like any other person, thing, or situation taking up space in my mind. I am not alone with God and not in unity.

Having an "I," and all that is not "I," is the way of thinking. This is not the way of the heart that Jesus calls us to. He ends this Course (Book One) by saying, "Think not." (C:32.4)

To move from the experience of separation to the experience of union is to experience the power of God and the force of love. It is an unthinkable experience.

Jesus says: "Start with this idea: You will allow for the possibility of a new truth to be revealed to your waiting heart. Hold in your heart the idea that as you read these words—and when you finish reading these words—their truth will be revealed to you. Let your heart be open to a new kind of evidence of what constitutes the truth." (C:7.23)

Revelation is what this Course is, as well as the new way of knowing that it invites. When I received the Course I received revelation. When I thought about it, I blocked my ability to recognize what I received.

You are about to receive this Course. As you open your heart to it, don't rely on your mind to recognize what you receive. When you close the book and go about your day, don't do as I did and bring it to your mind. Hold it in your heart. Stay in love's presence. Don't step back into separation. Do everything you can to quit standing back from life. Start at the beginning, with who you truly are. Don't think too much. Let your heart lead the way.

Then you will see that in the beginning, and before the beginning, and before the before, there was only love.

Being a first receiver can be challenging. For both Helen Schucman—whose story of receiving *A Course in Miracles* is well known—and Mari Perron, their new, uninvited status brought with it an odd mixture of isolation, uncertainty, even notoriety. Just what were they to do with the material, and with their lives? Yet despite bouts of inner conflict, both Helen and Mari vigorously protected the integrity of the text and knew that they had received a rare and precious gift.

A Course of Love gives enormous importance to its predecessor. It says: "The world as a state of being, as a whole, has entered a time, brought on largely by *A Course in Miracles*, in which readiness for miracle-mindedness is upon it." It did so "by threatening the ego." (C:P.5)

A Course of Love is decidedly non-threatening, at least in its style. Jesus carefully and methodically progresses from The Course to The Treatises to The Dialogues—using logic, developing sometimes-radical ideas, yet speaking gently and always to the heart. Unlike *A Course in Miracles*, this Course presents few exercises, but rather offers a "mountaintop" experience in The Forty Days and Forty Nights. It speaks as much to "she" as to "he," to sisters as to brothers, and strongly validates feminine ways of knowing. It reveals a "Way of Mary" that exists in symbiotic relationship to the "Way of Jesus" now ending. It emphasizes "being who you are" in a way that does not negate the personal self or the body. It reveals how the human form can be transformed into "the elevated Self of form," and how an illusory world will be made "new"—divine—through relationship and unity.

Understandably, those familiar with *A Course in Miracles* may initially be skeptical of *A Course of Love's* authenticity, but they will recognize its

‚continuity. And although familiarity with *A Course in Miracles* offers valuable preparation and perspective, *A Course of Love* stands alone. Regardless of religious or spiritual background, those called to it will find treasure.

With this Combined Volume, *A Course of Love* ends its relative obscurity. Since originally transcribed, no concerted effort was made to promote it. Nevertheless, an "underground" of keen interest developed, including translations in foreign languages. Its time has come because so many yearn for connectivity of the heart and are bursting with passion to be who they really are.

This is not an ordinary spiritual book. "Something different is going on here." (D:12.5) Let it wash over you. As Jesus says near the end of The Forty Days and Forty Nights:

> This Course requires no thought and no effort. There is no prolonged study and the few specific exercises are not required. This Course has succeeded in ways you do not yet understand and have no need to understand. These words have entered your heart and sealed the rift between your mind and heart. (C:32.4)

This Course speaks as if it were written just for you. So it was. (D:Day40.31)

Glenn Hovemann, editor
May, 2014

The text of this Combined Volume has been carefully compared with the original transcription and is presented as originally received, edited for minor matters such as spelling and punctuation only. To make it easily referenced, each paragraph has been numbered. A standard form of referencing is suggested on page 675.

A COURSE OF LOVE

BOOK ONE

Introduction

1.1 This course was written for the mind—but only to move the mind to appeal to the heart. To move it to listen. To move it to accept confusion. To move it to cease its resistance to mystery, its quest for answers, and to shift its focus to the truth and away from what can be learned only by the mind.

1.2 What is learned by the mind only rearranges reality. The mind then holds to the new reality as a new set of rules without change. It sees reality through these new mental constructs and calls this way of seeing new. In order to support its new reality it must insist that others follow these new rules. Truth, it says, has been found, and it is "here" in these new rules and not in those of old. The mind will then tell you how to feel according to its rules and will resist all ways of feeling, all ways of being, that appear to run counter to these rules, as if it knows, because of these rules, how things are.

1.3 The mind will speak of love and yet hold the heart prisoner to its new rules, new laws, and still say "this is right" and "this is wrong." It will speak of love and not see its intolerance or judgment. It will speak of love to be helpful and with all sincerity, and yet the very logic that it uses, though new, wounds the heart of the most tender, of those most called to love and its sweetness. "I am wrong to feel the way I do" the tender-hearted says to herself and, convinced that another knows what she does not, covers-over her tenderness with protection.

1.4 You think that in order to share you must be able to speak the same language and so you regress to the language of the mind with its precision. The mind so hates to be confused, to be open, to remain open, and to not know. It desires anchors to hold it in one spot, and held there suffers the pounding of the sea of change, resists the current, fortifies itself against the storm. The mind will return always to where it feels safe and sure of itself and so it goes nowhere and sees not transformation, or creation, or the new horizon that would defy its reality.

1.5   The mind cannot hold open the doors of the heart and yet we turn within, turn to the mind, and show it where its openness lies, where sweetness abides, where love's knowing is found. All the mind can do is rearrange reality and hold it still and captive and rule bound. The laws of love are not laws such as these. The laws of love are not rules, facts, or right answers. The laws of love bring spiritual freedom, the freedom that lies beyond belief, beyond thought, beyond adherence to any authority other than one's own heart.

1.6   The heart is needed to guide the mind in a way that it does not desire to be guided, a way that is one of joining, a way that does not allow the mind's separate stance, its rules, or its right answers. The heart is needed because it is who and where you are and responds in love to what is one with it. We are one heart.

1.7   We are one mind. The route to oneness and union, to life in form that accepts oneness and union, to a humanity restored to wholeness, is through the heart of the mind.

1.8   This Course will seem remedial to some, easy to some, complex to some. The mind may say, "Yes, yes, I know. Tell me something I don't know." The mind may reel at contradictions, cling to known truths, compare this wisdom to other wisdom. The mind will attempt to understand with its own logic and fight the logic of the heart. The mind will seek new rules and perhaps be willing to rearrange its reality once again.

1.9   The mind is its own reality. You cannot escape the mind's reality with the mind. You cannot learn how to escape the reality of the mind with the mind's pattern of learning or of logic. You cannot live in a new and fresh world and retain the mind's reality.

1.10   There is no "everyone" to whom I speak, to whom I give these words. There is no single, no solitary, no separate mind to whom these words are spoken. These words are spoken heart to heart, from One Heart to One Heart.

1.11   "Everyone" is just a concept. These words are given to each One. They are heard only by each "alone" by which I mean in the sanctity of the One Heart. We are one heart. We are one mind. Joined in wholeheartedness we are the heaven of the world. We replace bitterness with sweetness. We dwell in the reality of the One Heart, creation's birthplace, birthplace of the new.

1.12   The new is not that which has always existed. It is not that which can be predicted. It is not that which can be formed and held inviolate. The new is creation's unfolding love. The new is love's expression. The new is the true replacement of the false, illusion's demise, joy birthed amongst sorrow. The new is yet to be created, One Heart to One Heart.

I.13   This is a course for the heart. The birthplace of the new.

The Prelude

P.1   This is a course in miracles. It is a required course. The time for you to take it is now. You are ready and miracles are needed.

P.2   Pray for all those in need of miracles. To pray is to ask. But for what are you asking? This is the first instruction in this Course of Love. All are in need of miracles. This is the first step in miracle readiness: asking for all to be included in what we do here. By praying for all those in need of miracles you are praying for all to learn as you learn, you are asking to link your mind with all minds. You are asking to end your separated state and learn in a state of unity. This is a basic recognition that this is the only way you learn.

P.3   The separated self or the ego does not learn. Even when the ego has taken many courses and received many teachings, the ego has not learned but has merely become threatened. Spirit does not need to take a course of love. If the ego cannot learn and the spirit does not need to, then who is this Course of Love and all other such courses for? Learning our true identity, the identity of the Self that is capable of learning, is something everyone must do. Can the ego learn this? Never. Does spirit need to? No. Who, then, is this Course for?

P.4   This is a basic question that was not adequately answered in *A Course in Miracles*. While a course in miracles is meaningless to the ego and unnecessary to spirit it would seem to have no audience at all if these are the only two states that exist. Since it is impossible to be part spirit and part ego, assuming there would be such a state in which learning could take place would be meaningless.

P.5   The world as a state of being, as a whole, has entered a time, brought on largely by *A Course in Miracles*, in which readiness for miracle-mindedness is upon it. *A Course in Miracles* opened a door by threatening the ego. All those who, with egos weakened, walked this world with the hope of leaving ego behind, with miracle-minded intent, have awakened human beings to a new identity. They have ushered in a time of ending our identity crisis. Not since Jesus walked the earth has such a time been upon humankind.

P.6   What is it in you that is capable of learning? What is it in you that recognizes that ego is not what you are? What is it in you that recognizes your spirit? What is it in you that hovers between two worlds, the world of the ego's dominion and that of spirit? What recognizes the difference? The Christ in you.

P.7   It is easy to imagine how the Christ in you differs from your ego but not as easy to recognize how the Christ in you differs from spirit. The Christ in you is that which is capable of learning in human form what it means to be a child of God. The Christ in you is that which is capable of bridging the two worlds. This is what is meant by the second coming of Christ.

P.8   The ego is what you made. Christ is what God made. The ego is your extension of who you think you are. Christ is God's extension of who He is. In order to end the need for learning, you must know who you are and what this means. Where the original Course in Miracles was a course in thought reversal and mind training, a course to point out the insanity of the identity crisis and dislodge the ego's hold, this is a course to establish your identity and to end the reign of the ego.

P.9   There are still few who dare to believe in the glory of who they are, few who can lay aside the idea that to think of themselves in the light of God's thought of them rather than their own is arrogance. This is only because the ego is not yet and finally gone. You are right not to desire to glorify the ego in any way. You know that the ego cannot be glorified and that you would not want it to be. This is why, while the ego remains, you cannot know who you are. The only glory is of God and His creations. That you are among the creations of God cannot be disputed. Thus all glory is due you. All glory is yours, and your efforts to protect it from the ego's reach are valiant but unnecessary. The ego cannot claim the glory that is yours.

P.10   Many of you desire to be "foot soldiers," to just live the good life without claiming glory, without having any grand ideas about yourselves. It is possible to do much good without recognizing who you are, but it is impossible to be who you are, and you are what the world is for. Your recognition of your Self and your recognition of your brothers and sisters is what the world is for. To stop before this is accomplished when it is in reach is every bit as insane as belief in the ego. Ask yourself what it is that stops you. As humble as you seem to be in your choice, you are still letting ego make your choice. This is not humility but fear.

P.11   The further teachings of the original Course were designed to turn fear into love. When you think you can go only so far and no further in your acceptance of the teachings of the Course and the truth of your Self as God created you, you are abdicating love to fear. You are perhaps making this world a better place but you are not abolishing it. In your acceptance of doing good works and being a good person, you are accepting ministry to those in hell rather than choosing heaven. You accept what you view as possible and reject what you perceive as impossible. You thus cling to the laws of man and reject the laws of God. You claim your human nature and reject your divine nature.

P.12   What is this rejection but rejection of your Self? What is this rejection but fear masquerading as humility? What is this rejection but rejection of God? What is this but a rejection of miracles?

P.13   You who have rejected your Self are likely to feel increasingly burdened. Although an initial burst of energy may have followed your reading of the Course or your discoveries of other forms of the truth, although you may even have experienced what seemed to be miracles happening "to" you, as you continued to reject your Self this energy and these experiences that lightened your heart would have begun to recede and to seem as distant and unreal as a mirage. All that you retain is a belief in effort and a struggle to be good and to do good, a belief that clearly demonstrates that you have rejected who you are.

P.14   Oh, Child of God, you have no need to try at all, no need to be burdened or to grow tired and weary. You who want to accomplish much good in the world realize that only you can be accomplished. You are here to awaken from your slumber. You are here not to awaken to the same world, a world that seems a little more sane than before but still governed by insanity, a world in which it seems possible to help a few others but certainly not all others, but to awaken to a new world. If all that you see changed within your world is a little less insanity than before, then you have not awakened but still are caught in the nightmare your ego has made. By choosing to reject yourself you have chosen to try to make sense of the nightmare rather than to awaken from it. This will never work.

P.15   By rejecting who you are, you are demonstrating that you think you can believe in some of the truth but not all of it. Many of you have accepted, for instance, that you are more than your body while retaining your belief in the body. You thus have confused yourself further by accepting that you are two selves—an ego self represented by the body—and a spirit self that represents to you an invisible world in which you can believe but not take part. You thus have placed the ego at odds with spirit, giving the ego an internal and invisible foe to do battle with. This was hardly the purpose of any teachings of the truth that have as their aim the exact opposite of this conflict-inducing situation. The truth unites. It does not divide. The truth invites peace, not conflict. Partial truth is not only impossible, it is damaging. For sooner or later in this lopsided battle, the ego will win out. The spirit as you have defined it is too amorphous, too lacking in definition and believability to win this battle against what you perceive as your reality.

P.16   You who have come close to truth only to turn your back and refuse to see it, turn around and look once again. You have traveled your path and the end of the journey is in sight. You stand at the precipice with a view of the new world glittering with all the beauty of heaven set off at just a little distance in a golden light. When you could have seen this sight you turned your back and sighed, looking back on a world familiar to you, and choosing it instead. You do not see that this choice, even made with every good intention of going back and making a difference, is still a choice for hell when you could instead have chosen heaven. Yet you know that choosing heaven is the only true way to change the world. It is the exchange of one world for another. This is what you fear to do. You are so afraid to let go of the world that you have known that, even though it is a world of conflict, sickness, and death, you will not exchange it, will not relinquish it.

P.17   While God remains unknown to you and you remain unknown to your Self, so too does heaven remain concealed. Thus, in turning your back on heaven, you turn your back on your Self and God as well. Your good intentions will not overcome the world and bring an end to hell. In all the history of the world, many have done good, heroic, and at times miraculous deeds without the world changing from a place of misery and despair. What is more arrogant? To believe that you alone can do what millions of others have not been able to do? Or to believe that you, in union with God, can?

What makes more sense? To choose to try again what others have tried and failed to accomplish? Or to choose to leave behind the old and choose a new way, a way in which you become the accomplished, and in your accomplishment bring the new into being?

P.18 What is the difference between your good intentions and willing with God? The difference is in who you think you are and who God knows you to be. While this difference remains you cannot share your will with God or do what God has appointed you to do. Who you think you are reveals the choice that you have made. It is either a choice to be separate from God or a choice to be one with God. It is a choice to know yourself as you always have, or a choice to know your Self as God created you. It is the difference between wanting to know God now, and wanting to wait to know God until you have decided you are worthy or until some other designated time, such as at death.

P.19 What are good intentions but a choice to do what you can, alone, by yourself, against great odds? This is why good intentions so often fail to come to be at all, and why, when every effort has been made, the outcome seldom seems worth the effort. You cannot earn your way to heaven or to God with your effort or your good intentions. You cannot earn, and will not ever feel as if you have earned, the designation of a person of such worth that you are deserving of all that God would freely give. Give up this notion.

P.20 You have decided that you know how to do good works but that you do not know how to do what God asks of you. You think, if God asked me to build a bridge I would build a bridge, and this is likely true. Yet you will not become the bridge. You refuse to recognize that the Christ in you provides the bridge that you need only walk across to bridge the distance between heaven and hell, between your separated self and union with God and all your brothers and sisters. You prefer to think a good deed here, a bit of charity there, is more important. You prefer to give up on yourself and to help others, without realizing that you can help no others until you have helped yourself. You prefer selflessness to self because this is your chosen way to abolish ego and to please God. This is not unlike the attitude of a good mother who decides to sacrifice herself for her children, without realizing that her sacrifice is not only unnecessary but undesirable.

P.21   Your good intentions neither please nor displease God. God simply waits for your return to heaven, for your acceptance of your birthright, for you to be who you are.

P.22   Another failure to accomplish lies at the other end of the spectrum, with a concentration on self that seems to have no end point and no limit to the interest it generates. While forgiveness and the release of guilt are necessary, and while recognition of gifts and what leads to joy cannot be done without, they are the point only to the extent of making one ready for a new choice. Prolonged interest in self can be as damaging as the selflessness of those intent on doing good works. Rather than leading to knowledge of God, prolonged interest in self can further entrench the ego.

P.23   Seekers are but another category of those who at the precipice act as if they have hit a wall rather than come across a bridge. It is precisely the place at which you stopped that you must return to. Those who continue to seek may have left teachings of the Course or of one or another spiritual or religious tradition only to find another and still another. For those intent on seeking there is always more to seek, but those who find must stop to realize what they have found and to realize that they seek no more.

P.24   The Course speaks of patience that is infinite. God is patient, but the world is not. God is patient for God sees you only as you are. The Christ in you is also still and ever present. But the weakening done your ego by whatever learning you have done has left room for strength, a strength that entered as if by a little hole made in your ego's armor, a strength that grows, and grows impatient with delay. It is not your ego that grows impatient for change, for your ego is highly invested in things remaining the same. It is, rather, a spirit of compassion that reels at the senselessness of misery and suffering. A spirit that seeks to know what to do, a spirit that does not believe in the answers it has been given.

P.25   The way to overcome the dualism that threatens even the most astute of learners is through the Christ in you, through the One who knows what it is to be God's child and also to walk the earth as child of man. This is not your helper, as the Holy Spirit is, but your identity. While the Holy Spirit was properly called upon to change your perception and show you the false from the true, your recognition of the Christ in you is proper in this time of identification of your undivided Self.

P.26 Let us, for the moment, speak of the family of God in terms of the family of man, in terms, in short, that you will recognize. In the family of man, there are many families but it is called one family, the family of man. It is called one species, the human species. Within this family of man are individual families, and among them, that which you call "your" family. A family has many members but it is called one family. All of its members are descended from the same ancestors, the same bloodline. Within that bloodline are genes that carry particular traits and predispositions. A child of one family may resemble the child of another distant relative or a relative who lived and died many years previously. You see nothing odd or foreign in this. This is the nature of family, as you understand family. And beyond the physical nature of families, the bloodlines and the ancestors, what holds the family together as one is love. The family is, in fact, the only place where unconditional love is seen as acceptable. Thus, no matter how good one child is perceived to be and how bad another is perceived to be, the love of the parent for the child is the same. A son or daughter does not earn the love that is given him or her, and this too is seen as acceptable and even "right."

P.27 Obviously the nature of God is different than the nature of man. God does not have physical form and does not produce physical offspring. God does, however, have a son, a child, an offspring, who must exist in some form like unto the Father. Within the story of the human race there is a story about the coming of God's son, Jesus Christ, who was born, grew into a man, died and rose again to live on in some form other than that of a man. Those who believe the story have accepted that Jesus was God's son before he was born, while he walked the earth, and after he died and resurrected. Whether this is your belief or not, it comes close to the truth in a form that you can understand. Jesus is simply the example life, the life that demonstrated what it means to be God's child.

P.28 Just as there is part of you that thinks that you are undeserving and made for suffering and strife, there is another part of you that knows this is not true. Think back, and you will remember that, from the earliest of ages you have known that life is not as it is meant to be; that you are not as you are meant to be. The part of you that rages against injustice, pain, and horror does so from a place that does not accept and will never accept that these things are what are meant for you or for those who walk this world with you. And yet your history, in which you so believe, will tell you that the world has always been thus and that there is no escape from it. In such a world the question should not be why do so many take their lives, but why do so few.

P.29   There are many forms of pain and horror, from physical illnesses to torture to loss of love, and in between these many frightful occurrences is the equally distressing life of the purposeless, where hours pass endlessly in toil that is the cost of your survival here. Even those who have studied much and learned the lessons of the Course well, leave their learning and their teaching sit idly by while they earn their living until the dust that has collected upon it obscures it from their sight. This is the cost of turning back when heaven could have been reached, the cost in continuing to believe in the laws of the world that govern the survival of the body. This is the way of those who know this is not the way it is meant to be and then doubt their knowing. This is the way it has always been, they cry. They lament that they see but one real world while heaven waits just beyond their willingness to proceed.

P.30   You are the creation like unto your Father and the family of man is like unto the family of God. Just as children grow in your "real world" and leave their family, separate from their family to begin their "own" life, so have you done as part of God's family. In the human family the separateness and independence that come with age are seen as the way that things should be, and yet a return to the "family of origin" is also seen as natural. Children go away for a time, eager to assert their independence, only later to return. The return is the symbol of maturity, acceptance, and often of forgiveness.

P.31   What does it mean to believe in God? You recognize that you cannot know God in the same way in which you know another human being, and yet you keep seeking this type of knowing. Even with another human being, knowing what they stand for, what their truth is, what rules they obey, how they think and how what they think aligns with what they do is the essence of knowing them. God gave you the Word to know him by. God gave you the Word made flesh as an example to live by—an example of a living God. What more than this is necessary? You seek form when you already have content. Does this make any sense?

P.32   You read what authors write and feel that you know not only their characters, but them as well. Yet you meet an author face to face and you can seldom see in them what you saw in their writing. When you meet an author face to face, you view their form. When you read their words, you view their content. When you quit seeing with the ego's eyes, you quit seeing form and quit searching for it. You begin seeing content.

P.33   Content is all you have of God. There is no form to see, yet in the content is the form revealed. This is true seeing. For content is all and form is nothing.

P.34   The content of God is love. Jesus embodied God by embodying love. He came to reverse the way God was thought of, to put an end to seeing God in human terms of vengeance, punishment, and judgment.

P.35   Jesus did this not only by embodying God in human form, but by giving a true rather than a false picture of power. Before the coming of the word made flesh, the incarnation, the only idea humankind could draw of an all-powerful being was a being whose power resembled the powerful among them. Jesus took such a stand against those with this kind of power that he was put to death. But Jesus did not abdicate for a powerless people. Jesus taught true power, the power of love, a power proven by the resurrection.

P.36   Jesus, united with the Christ in you, is he who can teach you who you are and how to live as who you are in a new world. He can open heaven to you and walk you through its gates, there to exchange this world at last for your true home. But it is not your body that will pass through heaven's gates, nor your body's eyes that will view the new world you will behold and take with you. To view a physical world of dimension, shape, and scope like unto the old and hope to transport it from one place to another would be delusional. The new world does not have to do with form, but with content. A content that is as transferable as an author's words upon a page.

P.37   How many would not travel to heaven if they could get on a bus and be transported there? Yet each of you holds within you the power to reach heaven. Knowing your Self as who you really are is the only thing that will allow you to quit fearing your power. Jesus accepted his power and so brought the power of heaven to earth. This is what the Christ in you can teach you to do. This is miracle-mindedness. This is love.

P.38   This is oneness. The Christ in you teaches only in the sense of imparting knowledge that you already have and once again have access to as you join with your own real Self. Once this is accomplished, you are accomplished. Because you are complete. But if your joining with Christ is the accomplishment and completion of all lessons, who is he who provides the lessons? This is Jesus.

P.39　The Christ in you is your shared identity. This shared identity made Jesus one with Christ. The two names mean the same thing, as oneness is what was always shared and always will be. You are eternally one with Christ. The only way you can identify Jesus differently is to relate to the Jesus who was a man, the Jesus who existed in history. This is the same way in which you are able to see yourself—as man or woman, as a being existing in a particular time in history. This one- or at best three-dimensional nature of your seeing is the nature of the problem. If you cannot see yourself "other than" as man or woman living in a particular place in a particular time, you cannot see your Self. Thus Jesus comes to you again, in a way that you can accept, to lead you beyond what you can accept to what is true.

P.40　To tell someone, even a young child, that a caterpillar becomes a butterfly is seemingly unbelievable. This does not make it any less true. The butterfly, although some perceive it as being lovelier to behold, is still the same being as the caterpillar. The caterpillar did not cease to exist; it simply transformed into what it always was. Thus it would seem as if the butterfly is both butterfly and caterpillar, two separate things becoming one. You are well aware of the fact that if you could not see the transformation take place "with your own two eyes," you would not believe that the two seemingly disparate creatures were the same. Someone telling you this story of transformation without being able to show you proof that you could see would be accused of making up a fairytale for your amusement.

P.41　How many of you see the story of your own self in this same frame of mind? It is a nice fairytale, an acceptable myth, but until your body's eyes can behold the proof, this is what it will remain. This is the insanity of the nightmare you choose not to awaken from. It is as if you have said, I will not open my eyes until someone proves to me that they will see when they are opened. You sit in darkness awaiting proof that only your own light will dispel.

P.42　Your willingness to learn is evident or you would not be here. You have been told and told again that a little willingness is all that is necessary. Why do you seem then to have not advanced or to have advanced only a little bit, when your willingness is mighty? Only because you have not vanquished the ego. You learn and then you let the ego come and take all you have learned from you again and still again. It is ingenious in its ways of getting you to turn back again and still again, until you feel as if you are going in and out through a revolving door.

P.43   You were your Self before you began your learning, and the ego cannot take your Self from you but can only obscure it. Thus the teachings you need now are to help you separate the ego from your Self, to help you learn to hear only one voice.

P.44   This time we take a direct approach, an approach that seems at first to leave behind abstract learning and the complex mechanisms of the mind that so betray you. We take a step away from intellect, the pride of the ego, and approach this final learning through the realm of the heart. This is why, to end confusion, we call this course *A Course of Love*.

CHAPTER 1

A Course of Love

1.1   Every living being has a heart. Let us define heart as the center of being, that place from which all feeling arises. All true feeling is love. All love praises God. All love is recognition of the glory of God and all God created. Love is the only pure response of the created for the Creator, the only response of the Creator to the created. Your recognition of what love is will return you to God and your Self.

1.2   You learned in *A Course in Miracles* that all knowledge is generalizable. So is all feeling. All feeling results from love or lack of love. There are no other reasons for the feelings that you experience. All feelings are generated by the heart and have nothing to do with the body. The heart of the body is the altar at which all your offerings to God are made. All offerings are love or lack of love. Lack of love is nothing. Thus, all offerings made from a place other than love are nothing. All offerings made from a place of fear or guilt are nothing.

1.3   Love is the condition of your reality. In your human form your heart must beat for the life of your self to take place. This is the nature of your reality. Love is as essential to your being as the heart to the body. You would not exist without love. It is there even if you are as unaware of it as you are of the beating of your heart. A baby is no less alive because it does not realize its heart is beating. You are no less your Self even though you do not realize that without love you would not exist.

1.4   God's only thought is love. It is a thought without limit, endlessly creating. Because of the extension of God's thought of love, you exist. I exist with you in this selfsame thought. You do not understand this only because you do not understand the nature of your own thoughts. You have placed them inside your body, conceptualizing them in a form that makes no sense.

1.5   Yet when you apply your thought to learning you learn. Let this encourage you. This is an ability we can use together to learn anew.

1.6   You should be in a hurry only to hear the truth. And of course all of the ways that you act when you want to hurry are backward to what you would achieve. Let your worries come and let your worries go. Remember always that they simply do not matter except in terms of time, and that you will save time by letting them go. Remember that your worries affect nothing. You think if your worries affect time this is an effect, but time is an illusion. It too does not matter. Remind yourself of this as well. This is part of letting go of the old world to make way for the new. Realize these things do not matter and will not be carried with you to the new world. So you might as well let them go now.

1.7   It is as if you have carried your heavy luggage with you everywhere just in case you might need something. Now you are beginning to trust that you will not need these things you have carried. Ah, no heavy coat. For you trust the sun will shine, that warmth will surround you. You are an immigrant coming to a New World with all your possessions in hand. But as you glimpse what was once a distant shore and now is near, you realize none of what you formerly possessed and called your treasures are needed. How silly you feel to have carted them from one place to the next. What a waste of time and energy to have been slowed down by such a heavy burden. What a relief to realize that you need carry it no more. How you wish you would have believed they were not needed when you began. How happy you are to leave them behind.

1.8   You do not realize as yet how heavy was your burden. Had you literally carried a heavy and useless trunk from one world to another when you had been told by someone wiser that it would not be needed, you would upon realizing the truth ask yourself what else you had been told and disregarded. You might try one more thing and then another that you previously would not have tried when you were so convinced that you were right and the other wrong. And as each new step is tried and found to work, your confidence in the wisdom of this teacher would continue to grow. You might consider that you could still learn from your mistakes and find the learning in the end to be the same, and this you surely might do from time to time. But eventually you would realize that it would be quicker and easier to learn without mistakes, and eventually you would realize also that the wisdom of your teacher had become your own.

1.9   The urge to test another's wisdom is the urge to find your own way and have it be a better way. It is the urge not to trust the teacher in all things but only in certain things. It is the desire to find your way on your own so that you can take pride in your accomplishment, as if by following another's map the sense of accomplishment in your arrival would be diminished. This wanting to do things on your own is a trick of the ego, your pride a gift the ego demands. These are the magic thoughts that oppose miracle-mindedness. These are the thoughts that say *on my own* I am everything, rather than *on my own* I am nothing. A true leader follows until she is ready to lead. She does not strike out on her own at the beginning, before she knows the way. There is no shame in learning. No shame in following the course another has put forth. Each true course changes in application. Fifty students may sit in a classroom being taught the same lessons and not one will learn in exactly the same way as another. This is true with the teaching and learning of information, and true with the teaching and learning of the truth as well. The only way that you can fail to learn the truth is to demand to learn it on you own. For on your own it is impossible to learn.

1.10   Resign as your own teacher. Accept me as your teacher and accept that I will teach you the truth. Find no shame in this. You cannot learn what I would teach you without me. You have tried in countless ways and can try still again. But you will not succeed. Not because you are not smart enough. Not because you will not try hard enough. But because it is impossible. It is impossible to learn anything on your own. Your determination to do so only blocks your learning. It is only through union with me that you learn because it is only in union with me that you are your Self. All your effort is based on disbelief of this truth, and your attempts to prove that this truth is not the truth. All that this effort brings you is frustration. All your seeming success from this effort brings you is pride to offer to your ego. This gift your ego demands is not worth the price you pay. The price of this gift is everything.

1.11   A teacher always has a role in the learning of the student. This does not diminish the student's achievement. You must realize it is your desire to make of yourself your own creator that has caused all your problems. This is the authority problem. It is pervasive in the life of your physical form and in the life of your mind. It is only your heart that does not consider this an issue of concern. This is another reason we appeal to the heart.

1.12   The heart cares not where love comes from, only that it comes. This is useful to us in several ways. By this I do not mean that there are not particular objects of your affection. This is not the love of which we speak. The heart yearns for what is like itself. Thus love yearns for love. To think of achieving love "on one's own" is ludicrous. This is why love is your greatest teacher. To yearn for what is like yourself is to yearn for your Creator and, when perception is healed, to create like your Creator. This yearning exists naturally within you and cannot be diminished or satiated.

1.13   Those who are seen as loveless and alone in the world are those you find to be the objects of your pity. Yet you do not realize that this is the state your ego has you endlessly striving to achieve. Your ego would have you believe that only when you need no one to achieve all you desire, only when you are satisfied with what you are and with what you can do *on your own*, only then will your autonomy and your learning be complete, for this is all your learning has been for. The goal of this world is for you to stand on your own, complete within yourself. This goal will never be reached, and only when you give up trying to reach it can you begin to learn anything of value. You are complete only within God, where you endlessly abide. Striving to be that which you can never be is the hell you have created.

1.14   Lack of striving is seen as a settling for less. This would be true if what you were striving for had value. To strive mightily for nothing is still to have nothing and to end up with nothing. Striving, however, must be distinguished from struggle. To strive for that which has value is what this Course is about. It has nothing to do with struggle. You think also that to leave struggle behind, to disengage from the conflict of this world that causes it, is to turn your back on the real world and all that has meaning in it. In this you think correctly. And yet you do not choose this option, thinking that to do so you turn your back on responsibility and on duty, thus counting this action as a noble one. This desire to engage in struggle has nothing to do with what you are responsible for. It is merely your ego's attempt to involve you in distractions that keep you from your real responsibility. Think again about your attraction to struggle. It is your attraction to the game, a game you hope to win, another chance to show your stamina and your strength, your quick wits and your cunning mind. It is another chance to prevail against the odds so stacked against you that you can once again convince yourself that you alone have succeeded against mighty adversaries. It is the only way you see to prove your power and control over a world of chaos. To not engage in the chaos at all is seen not as desirable, but as a sort of abdication, a loss through failure to engage. Although you are well aware you will not win the game you play here, you see the effort to do so, no matter how futile, as being that which makes up your life. To not engage is to not prove your own existence.

1.15   This is what you have made this world for: to prove your separate existence in a world apart from your Creator. This world does not exist. And you do not exist apart from your Creator. Your yearning for love is what tells you this is so. It is the proof you do not recognize.

1.16   What could cause you to yearn for love in a loveless world? By what means do you continue to recognize that love is at the heart of all things even while it is not valued here? Here is a fine example that means and end are the same. For love is what you are as well as what you strive for. Love is means and end.

1.17   All the symbols of your physical life reflect a deeper meaning that, while hidden to you, you still know exists. The union of two bodies joined in love create a child, the union of man and woman joined in marriage create oneness.

1.18   Love is at the heart of all things. How you feel but reflects your decision to accept love or to reject it and choose fear. Both cannot be chosen. All feelings you label joyous or compassionate are of love. All feelings you label painful or angry are of fear. This is all there is. This is the world you make. Love or fear is your reality by your choice. A choice for love creates love. A choice for fear creates fear. What choice do you think has been made to create the world you call your home? This world was created by your choice, and a new world can be created by a new choice. But you must realize that this is all there is. Love or lack of love. Love is all that is real. A choice for love is a choice for heaven. A choice of fear is hell. Neither are a place. They are a further reflection of means and end being the same. They are but a further reflection of your power.

Chapter 2

What Love Is

2.1 What love is cannot be taught. It cannot be learned. But it can be recognized. Can you pass love by and not know that it is there? Oh, yes. You do it constantly by choosing to see illusion rather than the truth. You cannot be taught love but you can be taught to see love where it already exists. The body's eyes are not the eyes with which love can be recognized. Christ's vision is. For only Christ's vision beholds the face of God.

2.2 While you look for a God with a physical form you will not recognize God. Everything real is of God. Nothing unreal exists. Each person passing from this life to the next learns no great secret. They simply realize love is all there is. Nothing unreal exists. Think for yourself: If you were going to die tomorrow what would you today find meaningful? Only love. This is salvation's key.

2.3 Because love has no physical form you cannot believe that love could be what you are, what you strive to be, what you seek to return to. Thus you believe you are something other than love and separate from love. You label love a feeling, and one of many. Yet you have been told there are but two from which you choose: love and fear. Because you have chosen fear so many times and labeled it so many things you no longer recognize it as fear. The same is true of love.

2.4 Love is the name you give to much you fear. You think that it is possible to choose it as a means to buy your safety and security. You thus have defined love as a reaction to fear. This is why you can understand love as fear's opposite. This is true enough. But because you have not properly recognized fear as nothing, you have not properly recognized love as everything. It is because of the attributes you have given fear that love has been given attributes. Only separate things have attributes and qualities that seem to complement or oppose. Love has no attributes, which is why it cannot be taught.

2.5   If love cannot be taught but only recognized, how is this recognition made possible? Through love's effects. For cause and effect are one. Creation is love's effect, as are you.

2.6   To believe that you are able to act in love in one instance and act in anger in another, and that both actions originate from the same place, is an error of enormous proportions. You again label love a "sometimes" component and think that to act in love more frequently is an achievement. You label acting from love "good" and acting out of anger "bad." You feel you are capable of loving acts of heroic proportions and fearful actions of horrific consequence, acts of bravery and acts of cowardice, acts of passion you call love and acts of passion you call violence. You feel unable to control the most extreme of these actions that arise from these extremes of feeling. Both "ends" of feelings are considered dangerous and a middle ground is sought. It is said that one can love too much and too little but never enough. Love is not something you do. It is what you are. To continue to identify love incorrectly is to continue to be unable to identify your Self.

2.7   To continue to identify love incorrectly is to continue to live in hell. As much as highs and lows of intense feeling are sought by some to be avoided, it is in the in-between of passionless living that hell is solidified and becomes quite real. You can label joy heaven and pain hell and seek the middle ground for your reality thinking there are more than these two choices. A life of little joy and little pain is seen as a successful life, for a life of joy is seen as nothing more than a daydream, a life of pain a nightmare.

2.8   Into this confusion of love's reality you add the contents of your history, the learned facts and the assumed theories of your existence. Although your purpose here remains obscure, you identify some things you call progress and others that you call evolution and you hope you have some miniscule role to play in advancing the status of humankind. This is the most you have any hope of doing, and few of you believe you will succeed. Others refuse to think of life in terms of purpose and thereby condemn themselves to purposeless lives, convinced one person among billions makes no difference and is of no consequence. Still others put on blinders to the world and seek only to make their corner of it more safe and secure. Some shift from one option to the next, giving up on one and hoping that the other will bring them some peace. To think that these are the only options available to creatures of a loving God is insane. Yet you believe that to think the opposite is true insanity. Given even your limited view of who you are, could this really be true?

2.9   The insanity of your thought process and the world you perceive must be made known to you before you are willing to give it up. You do know this, and yet you constantly *forget*. This forgetting is the work of your ego. Your true Self does not want to forget, and cannot for even the tiniest fraction of a second. It is precisely the inability of your true Self to forget that gives you hope of learning to recognize love, and, with that recognition, of ending the insanity you now perceive.

2.10   Your real Self is the Christ in you. How could it be anything but love, or see with eyes other than those of love? Would you expect any decent human being to look on a loveless world, on misery and despair, and not be moved? Think not that those who seem to add to the world's misery are any exception. There is not a soul that walks this earth that does not weep at what it sees. Yet the Christ in you does not weep, for the Christ in you sees with eyes of love. The difference is the eyes of love see not the misery or despair. They are not there! This is the miracle. The miracle is true seeing. Think not that love can look on misery and see love there. Love looks not on misery at all.

2.11   Compassion is not what you have made of it. The Bible instructs you to be compassionate as God is compassionate. You have defined it unlike the compassion of God. To believe God looks upon misery and responds with sympathy and concern and does not end the misery is to believe in a God who is compassionate as you are compassionate. You think you would end misery if you could, beginning with your own, and yet you could no more end misery by making it real than could God. There is no magic here of turning misery into delight and pain into joy. These acts would indeed be magic, an illusion on top of an illusion. You have but accepted illusion as the truth, and so seek other illusions to change what never was into something that never will be.

2.12   To be compassionate as God is compassionate is to see as God sees. Again, I stress to you, this is not about looking upon misery and saying to yourself you see it not. I am not an advocate of heartlessness but whole-heartedness. If you believe even the tiniest fraction of what is true, if you but believe you are a small part of God no bigger than a pinprick of light in a daunting sun, you still cannot believe in the reality of misery and despair.

If you do, you believe this is the state of God as well. And if this were true, what hope would there be for misery's end? What light would there be in the universe that could end the darkness?

2.13 Reverse this thought and see if it makes any more sense than it did before. In this scenario a benevolent and loving God who has extended His being into the creation of the universe has somehow managed to extend what is not of Him, to create what is unlike to His being in every way. Would even you attempt such folly? Would you conceive of the inconceivable?

2.14 What answer then is left but that you do not see reality for what it is? What benefit is left to you in seeing incorrectly? What risk in attempting to see anew? What would a world without misery be but heaven?

2.15 Look not to figures from the past to show you the way beyond illusions to the present. Look within to the one in you who knows the way. Christ is within you and you rest within God. I vowed to never leave you and to never leave you comfortless. The Holy Spirit has brought what comfort you would accept to your troubled mind. Now turn to me to comfort your troubled heart.

2.16 You have not sufficiently reversed your thinking, or your heart would not still be troubled. The reversal has not occurred because you separate mind and heart and think you can involve one without involving the other. You believe that to know with your mind is a learning process that stands apart from all else that you are. Thus you can know without that knowing being who you are. You think you can love without love being who you are. Nothing stands apart from your being. Nothing stands alone. All your attempts to keep things separate are but a reenactment of the original separation made to convince yourself that the separation actually occurred.

2.17 You do not stand separate and alone. At these words your heart rejoices and your mind rebels. Your mind rebels because it is the stronghold of the ego. Your thought system is what has made the world you see, the ego its constant companion in its construction.

2.18 Yet your mind too rejoiced in the learning of all the teachings that have brought you here, congratulating itself on a feat that brought it rest. It is from this rest that the heart begins to be heard.

2.19 Just as the Holy Spirit can use what the ego has made, the ego can use what the mind has learned but has not integrated. Until you are what you have learned, you leave room for the ego's machinations. Once you are what you have learned, there is no room in which the ego can exist and, banished from the home you made for it, it slowly dies. Until this happens, the ego takes pride in what the mind has acquired, even unto the greater peace and contentment offered by your learning. It can and does see itself as better and stronger and more capable of worldly success. It would use all you have learned for its own motivations and pat you on the back for your new abilities. Without your vigilance it may even seem to have become stronger than before and fiercer in its criticism. It pretends to hold you to new standards, only to use what you have learned to increase your guilt. Thus it wins in daily battles and works for your final abdication, the day that you give up and admit defeat. It challenges your right to happiness and love and miracles, and seeks only to have you claim that living with such fantasies does not work and will not ever be possible here.

2.20 Into this battlefield you have bravely marched. The war rages by day and by night and you have grown weary. Your heart cries out for solace and does not go unheard. Help is here.

2.21 Do not believe that all that you have learned will not do what it was given you to do. Do not believe in your failure or the ego's success. All you have learned is still with you regardless of your perception of the outcome of your learning. Your perception of an outcome within your control is all that needs to change. Remember that cause and effect are one. What you want to learn you cannot fail to learn.

2.22 We will begin by working on a state of neutrality in which the war is no longer fought, the daily battles cease. Who wins and who loses is not of concern to us here. Peace has not yet come. But the white flag of surrender has been waved and dropped upon a hallowed ground where neutrality will for a short time reign before peace breaks out with glad rejoicing.

2.23 There are no plunders to be treasured. No victors of this war. All that has been learned and learned again is that this is what you do not want. Freedom to return home, away from cries of agony, defeat, and vainglory is all that now is sought. A state of neutrality is where the return begins. Armies may not yet be marching home, but their preparation is underway.

CHAPTER 3

The First Lesson

3.1   Love is. It teaches by being what it is. It does not do anything. It does not strive. It neither succeeds nor fails. It is neither alive nor dead. And thus it always was and always will be. It is not particular to you as human beings. It *is* in relationship to everything. All to all.

3.2   Just as true knowledge cannot be learned, love cannot be learned and you cannot be learned. All that you desire and cannot learn is already accomplished. It is accomplished in you. It is you. Imagine the ocean or the cheetah, the sun or the moon or God Himself, attempting to learn what they are. They are the same as you. All exist within you. You are the universe itself.

3.3   It is a shared universe with no divisions. There are no sections, no parts, no inside and no outside, no dreams and no illusions that can escape or hide, disappear, or cease to be. There is no human condition that does not exist in all humans. It is completely impossible for one to have what another does not have. All is shared. This has always been true and is endlessly true. Truth is truth. There are no degrees of truth.

3.4   You are not form, nor is your real world. You seek the face of God in form as you seek for love in form. Both love and God are there, but they are not the form that your body's eyes see. Just as these words you see upon this page are symbols only of meaning far beyond what the symbols can suggest, so too is everything and everyone around you, those you see and those you only can imagine. To seek the "face" of God, even in the form of Christ, is to seek for what is forever without form. To truly see is to begin to see the formless. To begin to see the formless is to begin to understand what you are.

3.5   All that you now see are but symbols of what is really there before you, in glory beyond your deepest imaginings. Yet you persist in wanting only what your eyes can see and hands can hold. You call these things real and all else unreal. You can close your eyes and believe that you are in the dark, but you will not believe that you are no longer real. Close your eyes on all that you have become accustomed to seeing. And you will see the light.

3.6   In the light that comes only to eyes that no longer see, you will find the Christ who abides in you. In Jesus Christ, the Son of God became the son of the man. He walked the world with a face much like your own, a body with two legs and two arms, ten fingers and ten toes. And yet you know this was not Jesus, nor is this a picture of the Christ. Jesus gave a face to love, as you do here as well. But love did not attach itself to form and say, "This is what I am." How can anything have a form except in symbols? A family crest, a mother's ring, a wedding band are all the same: They but represent what they symbolize in form.

3.7   There is no form that is not thus. A form is but a representation. You see a thousand forms a day with different names and different functions and you think not that they are all the same. You place values on each one based on usefulness or pleasant appearance, on popularity or on reputation. Each one you place in relationship to yourself, and so you do not even see the form as it is but only as what it will do for you. You imprison form within your meaning, and still your meaning is truer than its form. You give all meaning to everything, and thus you populate your world with angels and with demons, their status determined by who would help you and who would thwart you. Thus do you determine your friends and your enemies, and thus you have friends who become enemies and enemies who become friends. While a pencil may essentially remain a pencil in your judgment, at least as long as it has all the qualities that you have determined that a pencil should have, few people can exhibit the qualities you have predetermined that they should possess at all times and in all places. And so one disappoints and another enthralls, one champions your cause and another denigrates you. In all scenarios you remain the maker of your world, giving it its causes and effects. If this can be so, how can the world be anything but symbolic, with each symbol's meaning chosen by you and for you. Nothing is what it is, but only what it is to you.

3.8   Into this rank confusion is brought a simple statement: *Love is.* Never changing, symbolizing only itself, how can it fail to be everything or to contain all meaning? No form can encompass it for it encompasses all form. Love is the light in which form disappears and all that is, is seen as it is.

3.9   You who are looking for help wonder now how this would help you. What is there left to say that has not been said? What are these words but symbols, by my own admission? It is in what they symbolize that help arrives. You do not need to believe in the words nor the potential of the exercises to change your life, for these words enter you as what they are, not the symbols that they represent. An idea of love is planted now, in a garden rich with what will make it grow.

3.10   Everything has birth in an idea, a thought, a conception. Everything that has been manifested in your world was first conceived within the mind. While you know this is true, you continue to believe you are the effect and not the cause. This is partially due to your concept of the mind. What you conceive it to be, it will be to you. While many teachings have attempted to dislodge this concept that you hold so dear, because you use the mind to deal in concepts, you have been unable to let new learning have its effect. This is because you believe your mind is in control of what it thinks. You believe in a process of input and output, all completely human and scientifically provable. The birth of an idea is thus the result of what has come before, of seeing something old as new, of improving on a former idea, of taking various information and collecting it into a new configuration.

3.11   What has this meant for learning that is not of this world? It means that you filter it through the same lens. You think of it in the same way. You seek to gather it together so that it will provide an improvement to what has been before. You look for evidence that shows that if you behave in a certain way certain things will happen as a result. Like a child learning not to touch a stove because it is hot and a burn will result, or learning that a warm blanket is comforting, you subject it to a thousand tests dependent on your senses and your judgment. While you believe you know what will hurt you and what you will find comforting, you subject what cannot be compared to the comparable.

3.12   Think not that your mind as you conceive of it learns without comparison. Everything is true or false, right or wrong, black or white, hot or cold, based solely on contrast. One chemical reacts one way and one reacts another, and it is only in the study of the two that you believe learning takes place.

3.13   You have not given up the idea that you are in control of what you learn, nor have you accepted that you can learn in a way that you have not learned before. Thus we move from head to heart to take advantage of your concepts of the heart, concepts much more in line with learning that is not of this world.

3.14   These words of love do not enter your body through your eyes and take up residence in your brain, there to be distilled into a language that you can understand. As you read, be aware your heart, for this is where this learning enters and will stay. Your heart is now your eyes and ears. Your mind can remain within your concept of the brain, for we bypass it now and send it no information to process, no data for it to compute. The only change in thinking you are asked to make is to realize that you do not need it.

3.15   What this will mean to you goes far beyond the learning of this Course. One such concept, given up and not replaced, will free you beyond your deepest imaginings and free your sisters and brothers as well. Once one such concept is felled, others follow quickly. But none is more entrenched than this one, the one we begin today to let fall away.

3.16   You who have been unable to separate mind from body, brain from head, and intelligence from knowledge, take heart. We give up trying. We simply learn in a new way and in our learning realize that our light shines from within our heart, our altar to the Lord. Here the Christ in us abides and here we concentrate our energies and our learning, soon to learn that what we would know cannot be computed in the databanks of an over-worked and over-trusted brain, a mind we cannot separate from where we believe it to be.

3.17   Our hearts, in contrast, go out to the world, to the suffering, to the weak of body and of mind. Our hearts are not so easily contained within the casing of our flesh and bone. Our hearts take wing with joy and break with sadness. Not so the brain that keeps on registering it all, a silent observer, soon to tell you that the feelings of your heart were foolishness indeed. It is to our hearts that we appeal for guidance, for there resides the one who truly guides.

3.18   You who think this idea is rife with sentiment, sure to lead you to abandoning logic, and thereafter certainly to cause your ruin, I say to you again: take heart. Such foolishness as your heart's desires will save you now. Remember it is your heart that yearns for home. Your heart that yearns for love remembered. Your heart that leads the way that, should you follow, will set you certainly on the path for home.

3.19   What pain has your heart endured that it has failed to treasure for its source? Its source is love, and what greater proof need you of love's strength? Such pain as has your heart endured would surely be a knife to cut through tissue, a blow that to the brain would stop all functioning, an attack upon the cells far greater than any cancer. The pain of love, so treasured that it cannot be let go, can and does indeed attack the tissue, brain, and cells. And then you call it illness and allow the body to let you down, still and always holding love unto yourself.

3.20   Must pain accompany love and loss? Is this the price you pay, you ask, for opening up your heart? And yet, should you be asked if you would have other than the love you would not answer yes. What else is worth such cost, such suffering, so many tears? What else would you not let go when pain comes near, as a hand would drop a burning ember? What other pain would you hold closely, a grief not to be given up? What other pain would you be so unwilling to sacrifice?

3.21   Think not that these are senseless questions, made to bring love and pain together and there to leave you unaided and unhelped, for pain and love kept together in this way makes no sense, and yet makes the greatest sense of all. These questions merely prove love's value. What else do you value more?

3.22   Your thoughts might lead you to a dozen answers now, more for some and less for others, your answers depending on the tenacity of your thoughts, which, led by your ego, would throw logic in love's way. Some others might use their thoughts in yet another manner, claiming to choose love and not pain when what they really choose is safety at love's expense. No one here believes they can have one without the other and so they live in fear of love, all the while desiring it above all else.

3.23   Think you not that love can be kept apart from life in any way. But we begin now to take life's judgment from it, the judgments gained by your experience, judgment based on how much love you have received and how much love has been withheld from you. We begin by simply accepting the proof we have been given of love's strength. For this we will return to again and again as we learn to recognize what love is.

CHAPTER 4

Love's Equity

4.1 Do you have to love God to know what love is? When you love purely, you know God whether you realize it or not. What does it mean to love purely? It means to love for love's sake. To simply love. To have no false idols.

4.2 False idols must be brought to light and there seen as the nothing that they are before you can love for love's sake. What is a false idol? What you think love will get you. You are entitled to all that love would give but not to what you think love will provide for you through its acquisition. This is a classic example of not recognizing that *love is*.

4.3 Love and longing are so intimately attached because they joined together at the moment of separation when a choice to go away from love and a choice to return were birthed in unison. Love was thus not ever lost but shadowed over by longing that, placed between you and your Source, both obscured Its light and alerted you of Its eternal presence. Longing is your proof of love's existence, for even here you would not long for what is not remembered.

4.4 All your long search for proof of God's existence ends here when you recognize what love is. And with this proof is proof of your existence established as well. For in your longing for love, you recognize as well your longing for your Self. Why would you wonder who you are and what your purpose here is all about, if not for your recognition, given witness by your longing, of what you fear you are not, but surely are?

4.5 All fear ends when proof of your existence is established. All fear is based on your inability to recognize love and thus who you are and who God is. How could you not have been fearful with doubt as powerful as this? How can you not rejoice when doubt is gone and love fills all the space that doubt once occupied? No shadows linger when doubt is gone. Nothing stands between the child of God and the child's own Source. There remain no clouds to block the sun, and night gives way to day.

4.6 Child of God, you are alien here but need not be alien to your Self. In your knowledge of your Self, all threat of time and space and place dissolves. You may still walk an alien land, but not in a fog of amnesia that obscures what would be a brief adventure and replaces it with dreams of terror and confusion so rampant that no toehold of security is possible, and day turns endlessly into night in a long march toward death. Recognize who you are and God's light goes before you, illuminating every path and shining away the fog of dreams from which you waken undisturbed.

4.7 Love alone has the power to turn this dream of death into a waking awareness of life eternal.

4.8 Yearning, learning, seeking, acquiring, the need to own, the need to keep, the grasping call, the driving force, the chosen passion—all these things that you have made to replace what you already have will lead you back as surely as they can lead you astray. Where what you have made will lead rests only on your decision. Your decision, couched in many forms, is simply this: to proceed toward love or to withdraw from it, to believe it is given or withheld.

4.9 Love is all that follows the law of God in your world. All else assumes that what one has is denied another. While love cannot be learned nor practiced, there is a practice we must do in order to recognize love's presence. We practice living by the law of love, a law of gain not loss, a law that says the more you give the more you gain.

4.10 There are no losers and no winners under God's law. Not one is given more than another. God cannot love you more than your neighbor, nor can you earn more of God's love than you have, or a better place in Heaven. The mind, under the ego's direction, has thrived on winners and on losers, on striving for and earning a better place. The heart knows not these distinctions, and those who think their hearts have learned them by being battered and abused by their experience here, rejoice in knowing that it is not so. This seeming illusion is believed in because your mind has made it so. Your thoughts have reviewed and reviewed again all the pain that love has brought. It dwells on those occasions when love has failed because it does not recognize that love cannot fail.

4.11 Your expectations and false perceptions of your brothers and sisters are what have caused you to believe that love can fail, be lost, withdrawn, or turned to hate. Your false perception of your Father is what has caused all other perceptions to be false, including the one you hold of your own Self.

4.12   When you think of acting out of love, your thoughts of love are based on sentiment and must be challenged. Love is not being nice when you are feeling surly. Love is not doing good deeds of charity and service. Love is not throwing logic to the wind and acting in foolish ways that pass as gaiety but cannot masquerade as joy. You each have an image in your mind of someone you believe knows what love is. This is perhaps an elderly person who is always kind and gentle, with no cross word for anyone, and no concern for his or her own self. This is perhaps a mother whose love is blind and self-sacrificing. Still others of you might imagine a couple long married in which each person is devoted to the other's happiness, or a father whose love is unconditional, or a priest or minister who guides unfailingly. For each or any one of these that you admire, you give attributes that you do not have and that you might one day acquire when the time is right. For that kind and gentle stance you do not believe will serve you now, that blindness and self-sacrifice is something to be gained at too high a price, that devotion you might think is fine for one whose partner is more loving than your own, that unconditional love is great, but must it not be tempered by good judgment? And surely that ability to guide others must be earned through the acquisition of wisdom not within your reach.

4.13   Thus, your image of love is based upon comparison. You have chosen one who demonstrates that which in you is most lacking and you use that image to chastise yourself while saying this is what you want.

4.14   Your ideas of being in love are quite another category all together. In this context love is not only full of sentiment but of romance. This stage of love is seldom seen as lasting or as something that can be maintained. It is the purview of the young, and the daydream of the aging. It is synonymous with passion and an overflow of feelings that defy all common sense. To be in love is to be vulnerable, for once common sense has failed to keep you acting as expected, you might forget to guard your heart or to keep your real Self in hiding. How dangerous indeed is such an act in a world where trust can turn to treachery.

4.15   Each one of you has held an ideal of what the perfect mate would mean, an ideal that changed over time. Those most bound by the ego might think of stature and of wealth, of physical beauty and the trappings of good upbringing. Those most insecure will believe in a partner who would shower him or her with praise and gifts, with attention never wavering. Another who prizes independence seeks a partner in good health, not too demanding, a companion and a lover who will be convenient within a busy life.

4.16　You believe you can fall in love with the wrong person and make a better choice based upon criteria more important than love. You thus believe love is a choice, something to be given to some and not to others. You hope to be a winner in this game you play, a chosen one who will have each ounce of love that is given returned in kind. This is a balancing act you play with God's most holy gift, resenting giving love that gains you little in return. And yet in this resentment you recognize the truth of what love is.

4.17　In no other area of life do you expect such fairness, such exchange of equal value. You give your mind to an idea, your body to a job, your days to activities that do not interest or fulfill you. You accept what you are paid within certain boundaries you have set; you expect that a certain amount of prestige will follow certain accomplishments; you accept that some tasks have to be done for survival's sake. You hope there will be some fairness here in what you give and what you are given back. You hope your hard work will produce results, the dinner you prepared be eaten with delight, your ideas greeted as inspired. But this you do not expect. You often, in fact, expect the reverse to be the case, and are grateful for each acknowledgment the world gives you for the ways in which you spend your days. For spend your days you do, and soon that spending will deplete the limited number of days in store for you and you will die. Life is not fair, nor meant to be, you claim. But love is something else.

4.18　In this you are correct, for love is nothing like your image of your life and has no resemblance to how you spend your days or the way your days will end. Love is all that is set apart in your perception from what you do here. You think this setting apart gives love little relevance to other areas of your life. Love is seen as personal, something another gives in a special way to you alone, and you to him or her. Your love life has nothing to do with your work life, your issues of survival here, your ability to achieve success, or the state of your health and general welfare.

4.19   Even you who do not recognize what love is protect what you call love from the illusions you have made.

4.20   A thing set apart from the madness of the world is useful now. It may not be what love is, but what love is has guided you in choosing to set love apart from what you call the *real world*, from that which is, in fact, the sum total of what you have made. The world you struggle so to navigate is what you have made it, a place where love fits not and enters not in truth. But love has entered you and leaves you not, and so you too must have no place in this world that you have made but must have another where you are at home and can abide within love's presence.

4.21   The lucky ones among you have made a place resembling home within your world. It is where you keep love locked away behind closed doors. It is where you return after your forays into the world that you have made and upon entering believe you leave the world's madness outside your door. Here you feel safe and gather those you love around you. Here you share your day's adventures, making sense of what you can and leaving out the rest, and here you gain the strength you need to walk outside those doors again another day. You spend your life intent upon retiring to this safe place you have made of love in a world of madness, and hope that you will live to see the day when you can leave the madness behind, and that you will still find love behind the doors you have passed through so many times in a journey spent earning your right to leave it no more.

4.22   Some would call such a life selfish and wonder how the occupants of this semi-happy dream have earned the right to turn their backs upon the world even for the scanty hours that they make believe they can do so. Full-scale interaction with the world of madness is all that some are willing to accept of others or themselves. These are the angry ones who would demand that others bring what love they have into the madness to take responsibility for the mess that has been made, to attempt to restore order to chaos, anything so that the angry ones feel less alone with what their anger shows them. Love, they say, cannot be set apart, and so they feel love not, nor see it either. Yet they too recognize love for what it is when they scream, "You cannot have it while all of these do not. You cannot hoard it to yourself when so many are in need."

4.23   Everywhere you look is proof of love's difference found. This difference is your salvation. Love is not like anything or everything else that goes on here. And so your places to worship love have been built, your sacraments protect love's holiness, your homes host those you love most dearly.

4.24 Thus has your perception of love prepared you for what love is. For within you is the altar for your worship, within you has love's holiness been protected, within you abides the Host who loves all dearly. Within you is the light that will show you what love is and keep it not set apart from life any longer. Love cannot be brought to the world of madness, nor the world of madness brought to love. But love can allow a new world to be seen, a world that will allow you to abide within love's presence.

4.25 Take all the images of love set apart that you have made and extend them outside love's doors. What difference would a world of love make to those who lock their doors upon the world? How vast the reaches where their world of love could extend once love joined the world. How little need for the angry ones to retain their anger when love has joined the world. For love does join the world, and it is within this joining that love abides, holy as itself.

4.26 The world is but a reflection of your inner life, the reality unseen and unprepared for by all your strategy and defenses. You prepare for everything that goes on outside yourself and nothing that occurs within. Yet it is a joining that occurs within that brings about the joining of all the world for all the world to see. This joining of the world within is but your recognition of what love is, safe and secure within you and your brother, as you join together in truth. Think you not that this joining is a metaphor, a string of pleasant words that will bring you comfort if you heed them, one more sentiment in a world where lovely words replace what they would mean. This joining is the goal you seek, the only goal worthy of love's call.

4.27 This goal is set apart from all others as love is here, a goal that touches not on what you perceive to be a loveless world. It has no relation to the world outside of you, but every relation to the world within, where in love's presence both outer and inner worlds become as one and leave beyond your vision the world that you have seen and called your home. This foreign world where you have been so lonely and afraid will linger for a while where it can terrify you no longer, until finally it will fade away into the nothingness from which it came as a new world rises up to take its place.

Chapter 5

Relationship

5.1   The Christ in you is wholly human and wholly divine. As the wholly divine, nothing is unknown. As the wholly human, everything has been forgotten. Thus we begin to relearn the known as the One who already possesses all. It is this joining of the human and divine that ushers in love's presence, as all that caused you fear and pain falls away and you recognize again what love is. It is this joining of the human and divine that is your purpose here, the only purpose worthy of your thought.

5.2   You who have so filled your mind with senseless wanderings and thoughts that think of nothing that is real, rejoice that there is a way to end this chaos. The world you see is chaos and nothing in it, including your thoughts, are trustworthy. This is why your thoughts must be newly dedicated, dedicated to the only purpose worthy of your thought: the purpose of joining with your real Self, the Christ in you.

5.3   I said earlier, it is only through union with me that you learn, because it is only in union with me that you are your Self. Now we must expand your understanding of union and of relationship as well as your understanding of me.

5.4   Union is impossible without God. God is union. Is this not like saying God is Love? Love is impossible without union. The same is true of relationship. God creates all relationship. When you think of relationship, you think of one relationship and then another. The one you share with this friend or that, with husband or wife, with child or employer or parent. In thinking in these specific terms you lost the meaning of the holy relationship. Relationship itself is holy.

5.5   Relationship exists apart from particulars. This is what you can't conceive of and what your heart must newly learn. All truth is generalizable because truth is not concerned with any of the specific details or forms of your world. You think relationship exists between one body and another, and while you think this is so, you will not understand relationship or union or come to recognize love as what it is.

5.6   Relationship is what exists between one thing and another. It is not one thing or another thing. It is not a third thing in terms of being a third object, but it is something separate, a third something. You realize that a relationship exists between your hand and a pencil when you go to write something down, but it is a relationship you take so completely for granted that you have forgotten that it exists. All truth lies in relationship, even one so simple as this. The pencil is not real, nor the hand that grasps it. Yet the relationship between the two is quite real. "When two or more are joined together" is not an injunction for bodies to unite. It is a statement that describes the truly real, the only reality that exists. It is the joining that is real and that causes all creation to sing a song of gladness. No one thing exists without another. Cause and effect are one. Thus, one thing cannot cause another without their being one or joined in truth.

5.7   We are beginning now to paint you a new picture, a picture of things unseen before but visible to your heart if not your eyes. Your heart knows love without a vision of it. You give it form and say, "I love this one" or "I love that," yet you know that love exists apart from the object of your affection. Love is set apart in a frame not of this world. You hold objects up to capture it, to put a frame around love's vision and say, "This is it." Yet once you have it captured and hanging for all to look at and behold, you realize this is not love at all. You then begin your building of defenses, your evidence to cite to say, "Yes indeed, this is love and I have it here. It hangs upon my wall and I gaze upon it. It is mine to own and keep and cherish. As long as it is where I can look upon it, it is real to me and I am safe."

5.8   "Ah," you think when you find love, "now my heart is singing; now I know what love is all about." And you attach the love you have found to the one in whom you found it and seek immediately to preserve it. There are millions of museums to love, far more than there are altars. Yet your museums cannot preserve love. You have become collectors rather than gatherers. Your fear has grown so mighty that all that would combat it is collected for safekeeping. Like the frame of love upon your wall, the collections that fill your shelves, whether they are of ideas or money or things to look at, are your desperate attempts to keep something for yourself away from all the rest. In setting love apart, you recognized it had no place here; but you went on to set yourself apart and all else that you could find to define as valuable. You build your banks as well as your museums as palaces to your love and no longer see the golden calves hiding within the palace walls.

5.9   This urge to preserve things is but your urge to leave a mark upon the world, a mark that says, "I have acquired much in my time here. These things I love are what I leave the world, what I pass down; they declare that I was here." Again you have the right idea, yet it is so sadly displaced as to make a mockery of who you are. Love does mark your place—but in eternity, not here. What you leave behind is never real.

5.10   Love gathered together is a celebration. Love collected is but a mockery of love. This difference must be recognized and understood, as must the urge to set love apart from all the rest, for with understanding, these urges can be made to make sense. With understanding they can begin to bring sanity to an insane world.

5.11   You do not yet believe nor understand that the urges that you feel are real, and neither good nor bad. Your feelings in truth come from love, your response to them is what is guided by fear. Even feelings of destruction and violence come from love. You are not bad, and you have no feelings that can be labeled so. Yet you are misguided concerning what your feelings mean and how they would bring love to you and you to love.

5.12   It is in understanding the relationship that exists between what you feel and what you do that love's lessons are learned. Each feeling requires that you enter into a relationship with it, for it is there you will find love. It is in every joining, every entering into, that love exists. Every joining, every entering into, is preceded by a suspension of judgment. Thus what is judged cannot be joined nor entered into where it can be understood. What is judged remains outside of you, and it is what remains outside that calls you to do what love would call you not to do. What remains outside is all that has not joined with you. What has joined with you becomes real in the joining, and what is real is only love.

5.13   Do you see the practicality of this lesson? What terror can be caused by an urge to violence that, once joined with love, becomes something else? An urge to violence may mean many things, but always lurking behind it is an overwhelming desire for peace. Peace may mean destruction of the old, and love can facilitate the rise and fall of many armies. What armies of destruction will rock the world when they are brought to love?

5.14　Within you is all the world safe, sure, and secure. No terror reigns. No nightmares rule the night. Let me give you once again the difference between what is within and what is without: Within is all that has joined with you. Without is all that you would keep separate. Within you is every relationship you have ever had with anything. Outside of you is all that you have kept apart, labeled, judged, and collected on your shelves.

5.15　This is all the two worlds are made up of. The one you see as real is the one you keep outside of yourself, making it possible to look upon it with your body's eyes. The one you do not see and do not believe in is the one you cannot look outward to see, but is the one that nonetheless is truly real. To look inward at the real world requires another kind of vision: the vision of your heart, the vision of love, the vision of the Christ in you.

5.16　You look outside the doors of your home and, whether you see suburban streets bathed in lamplight, streets that steam with garbage and crime, or cornfields growing, you say that is the real world. It is the world you go out into in order to earn your living, receive your education, find your mate. But the home in which you stand, much like your inner world, is where you live the life that makes the most sense. It is where your values are formed, your decisions are made, your safety found. This comparison is not idly drawn. Your home is within and it is real, as real as the home you have made within the world seems to be. You can say the real world is somewhere outside yourself, as you picture the real world being beyond your doors, but saying this cannot make it so.

5.17　It is your continuing desire to have a relationship only with the world without that causes such a world to remain. This is because your definition of relationship is not one of joining. What you join with becomes real. As you take it into your Self you thereby make it real because you make it one with your real Self. This is reality. All you do not join with remains outside and is illusion, for what is not one with you does not exist.

5.18　You thus become a body moving through a world of illusion where nothing is real and nothing is happening in truth. This illusionary world is full of things you have told yourself and been instructed that you have to do, but that you do not want to do. The more your life consists of such things, the smaller your reality becomes. All that would join with you and become part of the real world of your creation remains beyond your reach.

5.19   There is nothing in your world that cannot be made holy through relationship with you, for you are holiness itself. You do not know this only because you fill your mind and leave your heart empty. Your heart becomes full only through relationship or union. A full heart can overshadow a full mind, leaving no room for senseless thoughts but only for what is truly real.

5.20   The first and only exercise for your mind within this Course has already been stated: Dedicate your thought to union. When senseless thoughts fill your mind, when resentments arise, when worry comes, repeat the thought that comes to open your heart and clear your mind: "I dedicate all thought to union." As often as you need to replace senseless thoughts, think of this and say it to yourself not once but a hundred times a day if needed. You do not need to worry about what to replace your senseless thoughts with, as your heart will intercede by fulfilling its longing for union as soon as you have expressed your willingness to let it do so.

5.21   You do not yet understand the strength of your resistance to the union that would turn hell into heaven, insanity to peace. You do not yet understand your ability to choose that which you make real in your creation of the world. The only meaning possible for free will is this: what you choose to join with you, and what you choose to leave outside of yourself.

5.22   Your desire to be separate is the most insane desire of which you have conceived. Over all your longing for union you place this desire to be separate and alone. Your entire resistance to God is based on this. You think you have chosen to be separate from God so that you can make it on your own, and while you long to return to God and the heaven that is your home, you do not want to admit that you cannot get there on your own. You thus have made of life a test, believing that you can pass or fail through your own effort. Yet the more you struggle to do so on your own, the more you realize the futility of your efforts, even though you do not want to admit that your efforts are futile. You cling to effort as if it is the way to God, not wanting to believe all effort is in vain or that a simple solution exists. A simple solution within your world, a solution that requires no exertion on your part, is seen to be of little value. The individual, you reason, is made through all this effort and struggle and without it would not be. In this you are correct, for as you make of yourself an individual, you deny yourself your union with all others.

5.23   All your efforts to be an individual are concentrated on the life of your body. Your concentration on the life of your body is meant to keep your body separate. "Overcoming" is your catch phrase here as you struggle to overcome all the adversity and obstacles that would keep you from having what you think you want to have. This is your definition of life, and while it remains it defines the life you see as real. It presents you with a thousand choices to make, not once but many times, until you believe that your power of choice is a fantasy and that you are powerless indeed. You thus narrow what you want and go after it with single-minded determination, believing the only choice within your control is what to work hard to obtain. If you let all the world recede and concentrate on this one choice, you reason that you are bound to eventually succeed. This is the extent of your faith in your own ability to maneuver this world that you have made; and if you finally do succeed, your faith is seen as justified. The cost is not examined nor acknowledged, yet when this faith is realized the cost becomes quite real. Rather than feeling as if you have gained, feelings of loss will now be what you fight to overcome. What have you done wrong, you wonder? Why are you not satisfied with all you have achieved?

5.24   This *getting what you want* that drives your life is proven time and time again to not be what you want once you have achieved it. Yet you think when this occurs that you have simply chosen the wrong thing and so choose another and another, not stopping to realize that you choose among illusions. You are so surprised that you have not found happiness in what you seek! You continue living life as a test, driving yourself to follow one accomplishment with another, sure that the next one or the next will be the one to do the trick.

5.25   A trick this is indeed, for what has once failed to work will surely fail again. Stop now and give up what you think you want.

5.26   Stop now and realize your reaction to these words, the strength of your resistance. Give up what you want? This is surely what you have expected God to ask of you and what you have spent your lifetime guarding against. Why should you make this sacrifice? What then would your life be for? You want so little really. How can you be asked to give this up?

5.27 You do want little, and only when you realize this can you proceed to claiming everything that is yours.

5.28 For every joining, every union that you enter into, your real world is increased and what is left to terrify you decreased. This is the only loss that union generates, and it is a loss of what was merely illusion. As union begins to look more attractive to you, you are beginning to wonder how it comes about. There must be some secret you do not know. What is the difference, you ask, between setting a goal and achieving it and joining with something?

5.29 These do not have to be two separate things, but are made so by your choice, the choice to achieve what you will on your own. This is all the difference there is between union and separation. Separation is all you perceive on your own. Union is all that you invite me into and share with God. You cannot be alone nor without your Father, yet your invitation is necessary for your awareness of this presence. As I once was, you are both human and divine. What your human self has forgotten, your real Self retains for you, waiting only for your welcome to make it known to you once more.

5.30 God is known to you within relationships, as this is all that is real here. God cannot be seen in illusion nor known to those who fear him. All fear is fear of relationships and thus fear of God. You can accept terror that reigns in another part of the world because you feel no relationship to it. It is only in relationship that anything becomes real. This you realize and so you strive to keep far from you all that in relationship with you would add to your discomfort and your pain. To think that any relationship can cause terror, discomfort, or pain is where you err in thinking of relationship.

5.31 You think that to come in contact with violence is to have a relationship with it. This is not so. If this were so, you would be joined to all you come in contact with and the world would be heaven indeed, as all you see became blessed by your holiness. That you move through your world without relating to it in any way is what causes your alienation from the heaven it can be.

5.32 Remember now one lovely day, for each of you has had at least one that was a shining light in a world of darkness. A day in which the sun shone on your world and you felt part of everything. Every tree and every flower welcomed you. Every drop of water seemed to refresh your soul, every breeze to carry you to heaven. Every smile seemed meant for you, and your feet hardly seemed to touch the soft ground on which you walked. This is what awaits you as you join with what you see. This awaits you as you place no judgment on the world, and in so doing join with everything and extend your holiness across a world of grief, causing it to become a world of joy.

CHAPTER 6

Forgiveness/Joining

6.1 Joining rests on forgiveness. This you have heard before without understanding what it is you would forgive. You must forgive reality for being what it is. Reality, the truly real, is relationship. You must forgive God for creating a world in which you cannot be alone. You must forgive God for creating a shared reality before you can understand it is the only one you would want to have. You have to forgive this reality for being different than you have always imagined it to be. You have to forgive yourself for not being able to make it on your own, because you have realized the impossibility of doing so. You have to forgive yourself for being what you are, a being who exists only in relationship. You have to forgive all others for being as you are. They too cannot be separate, no matter how hard they try. Forgive them. Forgive yourself. Forgive God. Then you will be ready to begin learning just how different it really is to live in the reality of relationship.

6.2 Your brother does not exist apart from you, nor you from your brother. This is reality. Your mind is not contained within your body but is one with God and shared equally with all alike. This is reality. The heart that is the center of your being is the center of everything that exists. This is reality. None of these things make you less than what you have perceived yourself to be, but they do make it impossible for you to be separate. You can desire what is impossible until the end of your days but you cannot make it possible. Why not forgive the world for being other than what you have thought it to be and begin to learn what it really is? This is what the world is here for. And when you have learned what it would teach you, you will have need of it no more, and you will gently let it go and find heaven in its place.

6.3 This is all that the words and symbols and forms and structures of your world have come to teach you, stated as simply and directly as is possible. You are neither separate nor alone and never were and never can be. All your illusions were created in order to obscure this fact of your existence because you would rather it not be so. Only when you quit wishing for what cannot be, can you begin to see what is.

6.4   I was least accepted as prophet and savior by those who were most like me, those who watched me grow, worked alongside my parents, and lived in the same town. This was because they knew I was not different from them, and they could not accept that they were the same as me. They were then, and you are now, no different than I. We are all the same because we are not separate. God created the universe as an interrelated whole. That the universe is an interrelated whole is no longer disputed even by science. What you have made to hide your reality has been, with the help of the Holy Spirit, being turned into that which will help you learn what your reality really is. Yet you still refuse to listen and to learn. You still prefer things to be other than what they are and, through your preference, choose to keep it so.

6.5   Make a new choice! The choice that your heart yearns to make for you and that your mind is finding increasingly difficult to deny. When you choose unity over separation, you choose reality over illusion. You end opposition by choosing harmony. You end conflict by choosing peace.

6.6   All this forgiveness can do for you. Forgiveness of the original error—the choice to believe that you are separate despite the fact that this is not so and cannot ever be. What loving creator would create a universe in which such a thing could be? A thing alone would be a thing created without love, for love creates like itself and is forever one with everything that has been created. This simple realization will start you on the path to learning what your heart would have you learn.

6.7   The fact that you are not alone in the world shows you that you are not meant to be alone. Everything here is to help you learn to perceive correctly, and from there to go beyond perception to the truth.

6.8   What is the opposite of separation but being joined in relationship? Everything joined with you in relationship is holy because of what you are. Every contrast that you see here but points to this truth. Evil is only seen in relation to good. Chaos is only seen in relation to peace. While you see these as separate things you do not see what the relationship would show you. Contrast demonstrates, which is why it is a favorite teaching device of the Holy Spirit. Contrast demonstrates only to reveal the relationship that exists between truth and illusion. When you chose to deny relationship, you chose a thought system based on the opposite of your reality. Thus each choice to deny union reveals its opposite. What is separate from peace is chaos. What is separate from good is evil. What is separate from the truth is insane. Since you cannot be separate, all these factors that oppose your reality exist only in opposition to it. This is what you chose to create when you chose to pretend you can be what you cannot be. You chose to live in opposition to the truth, and the opposition is of your making.

6.9   Choose again! And let go your fear of what the truth will bring. What could be more insane than that which you now call sanity? What loss can there be in joining with what is so like yourself? It is only a small step away from where you currently stand, so helpless and alone.

6.10   Yet fear you do, and the maintenance of your fear keeps you very busy. You stoke its fire lest it go out and leave you to a warmth not of this world. This is the warmth that you would have, warmth so all-pervasive no chill of winter need ever arise again. And yet, still you choose the fire. You choose the fires of hell to the light of heaven. Only you can stoke those fires, and this is what makes them desirable to you. A warmth not of this world, given freely, with no work involved, causes you to shake your head. How can it be for you if you cannot put in effort to attain it? And even if it were so, what then? Some, you think, might choose to live near the equator, to have the sun shine every day and the need to stoke the fire put behind them. But not you. You, you think, prefer the seasons, the cold as well as the warmth, the snow as well as the rain, the dark of night and the clouds that block the sun. Without all of these, what would life be? Perpetual sunshine would be too easy, too lacking in imagination, too sterile. To have every day the same would be uninteresting now. Perhaps later. Maybe when you are old and have grown weary of the world. Then perhaps you will sit in the sun.

6.11   This is the heaven of your mind, the meaning you give to joining, the face you put on eternal peace. With such a vision in your mind it is no wonder that you choose it not, or that you put it off until the end of your days. A heaven such as this would be for the old and the infirm, the ones ready to leave the world, those who have already grown worn out from it. What fun would such a heaven be for those of you still young and full of vigor? Those still willing to face another battle? Those who have not yet faced every challenge? If there is a mountain left to climb, why choose heaven? Surely it can be chosen later when disease has taken your limbs' use from your control and your mind no longer races forward to what is next.

6.12 Eagerness for life and eagerness for heaven are seen to be in opposition. Heaven and its milieu of eternal peace is rightly kept, you think, for the end of life, and so you scream at the unfairness when a young one leaves the world. Heaven is not for the young, you say. How unfair that those who die young have not had a chance at life, a chance to face the struggle and the challenge, the coming of the new day and the dying of the old. How sad they have not had the opportunity to stand separate and alone and to become what they would become. What they are is no more valued than what you are. What is still to come is what you live for, with the undying hope that it will not be that which came before. For every challenge faced is but a call to face the next. And each one comes to replace the old with hope that this one will be the one—and equal hope that it will not.

6.13 To succeed is but a little death from which you must hurry on to where the challenge of a new success and new reason to exist awaits. The carrot of fulfillment you hold before yourself when grasped is quickly eaten and life feeds on itself once again. Just as you eat to still your hunger only to become hungry again, so does the rest of your life need this constant maintenance to retain the reality you have given it. "Struggle to succeed and succeed to struggle yet another day" is the life you have made, and the life you fear heaven would replace. To give up the idea that this is where meaning is found, fulfillment attained, happiness birthed amongst sorrow, is seen as giving up. Heaven's help is most called upon for just this time, this time when giving up is close, for never do you feel more in need of help than when all your plans have failed and giving up becomes an alternative more attractive than carrying on.

6.14 Few ask for the grace to give up what has been for what could be. For giving up is seen as failure, and here is what you fear the most. To not succeed at life would indeed be a failure if it were possible for it to be so. Yet even this possibility you would cling to, for with no chance of failure is no chance of success, or so you reason. The contrast that you have come to see in your separated state makes only either/or situations possible. While a choice for heaven is indeed a choice to renounce hell, while truth is indeed a choice to renounce illusion, these are the only real choices that exist, and they do not extend into your illusions but only into truth. For in truth are all illusions gone, in heaven is all thought of hell forever vanquished.

6.15   How can I convince you that peace is what you want when you do not know what peace is? Those who once worshiped golden calves did so because they knew of no other choice. A god of love was as foreign a concept to them as is a life of peace to you. What is foreign to the world has changed, but the world has not. Those who live with war seek peace. Those who live with failure seek success. Put another way, both are saying this: you seek to make sense of an insane world, to find meaning within meaninglessness, purpose among the purposeless.

6.16   How can I make peace attractive to you who know it not? The Bible says, "The sun shines and the rain falls on the good and evil alike." Why then do you think that peace is endless sunshine? Peace is merely enjoyment of the rain and sun, night as well as day. Without judgment cast upon it, peace shines on all that you would look upon, as well as every situation you would face.

6.17   Situations too are relationships. When peace enters your relationships, situations, too, are what they are meant to be and seen in heaven's holy light. No longer do situations pit one against another, making it impossible for anyone to achieve what they would achieve. The challenge now is in creation rather than accomplishment. With peace, accomplishment is achieved in the only place where it makes any sense to desire it. With your accomplishment comes the freedom and the challenge of creation. Creation becomes the new frontier, the occupation of those too young to rest, too interested in living still to welcome the peace of dying. Those who could not change the world one iota through their constant effort, in peace create the world anew.

6.18   Here they find the loveliest of answers to their questions. It takes not time nor money nor the sweat of their brow to change the world: it takes only love. A forgiven world is whole, and in its wholeness one with you. It is here, in wholeness, that peace abides and heaven is. It is from wholeness that heaven waits for you.

6.19   Think about this now—for how could heaven be a separate place? A piece of geography distinct from all the rest? How could it not encompass everything and still be what it is: home to God's beloved son and dwelling place of God Himself? It is because God is not separate from anything that you cannot be. It is because God is not separate from anything that heaven is where you are. It is because God is love that all your relationships are holy, and from them you can find the way to Him and to your holy Self.

6.20   Are your relationships with those you love severed when they leave this world? Do you not still think of them? And do you not still think of them as who they were in life? What is the difference, in your mind, between who they were and who they are after death? In honesty will you admit an envy, an awareness that they still exist, but without the pain and burden of the body, without the limits placed upon those who remain? You imagine them still in bodily form, perhaps, yet you imagine them happy and at peace. Even those who claim not to believe in God or an afterlife of any sort will, when prompted to be truthful, admit this is an image that lights their mind with peace and hope. This image is as ancient as the earth and sky and all that lies beyond it. It did not arise from fantasy, nor did it pass from one mind to the next as stories often will. It is but part of your awareness of who you are, an awareness you would deny in favor of thoughts of death so grim they make of life a nightmare.

6.21   It is your denial of all your happy thoughts that has led you to a life of such unhappiness. Thoughts of terror and of sin you will embrace, but thoughts of resurrection and new life you still before they have a chance at birth and call them wishful thinking. What harm do you expect happy thoughts to do to you? At best you see them as delusional. But what you fear is disappointment. All that you have wished for and have not acquired within your life is the evidence you would use to deny yourself hope of any kind. You do not understand the difference between wishing for what can never be and accepting what is.

6.22   The world cannot fail to disappoint you, for your conception of it is based upon deception. You have deceived only yourself, and your deception has not changed what is nor will it ever succeed in doing so. Only God and His appointed helpers can lead you from this self-deception to the truth. You have been so successful at deception that you no longer can see the light unaided. But join your brother and the light begins to shine, for all are here to aid you. This is the purpose of the world and of love most kind: to end your self-deception and return you to the light.

CHAPTER 7

Withholding

7.1 A major thought reversal is required now before we can go on. It has been stated and emphasized countless times before, and it will be here as well: What you give you will receive in truth. What you do not receive is a measure of what you withhold. Your heart is accustomed to giving in a way that your mind is not. Your mind would hold on to every idea for what it might bring you, and is resentful of those whose ideas do come to fruition and succeed in getting desirable things within this world. "I had that idea," you lament when another succeeds where you have failed. "I could have been where that person is if not for the unfairness of life," you wail. Your mind dwells in a world of its own made up largely of *if onlys*. Your heart, on the other hand, knows of giving and of a return not based on the world of your mind or of physical circumstance. Despite disappointments most severe, your heart knows that what you give you receive in truth.

7.2 And yet you would withhold a piece of yourself even from love, and this is what we must correct. For what you withhold you cannot receive, and you cannot receive a piece of heaven nor know a piece of God or your own Self. Your giving must be total for you to receive in truth. We will concentrate more now, however, on withholding than on giving for you do not yet understand what you would give, for you do not recognize what you have to give. You do, however, recognize what you withhold and can begin to recognize this in every situation. As the awareness of your withholding dawns upon your heart, you will begin to realize what you do not give, and with that realization, what you have to give.

7.3 Comparison of one thing to another—a comparison that seeks out differences and magnifies them and names one thing this and one thing that—is the basis of all learning in your world. It is based on contrast and opposites and on separating into groups and species. Not only is each individual distinct and separate, but so too are groups of individuals, pieces of land, systems and organizations, the natural world and the mechanistic world, heaven and earth, divine and human.

7.4   In order to identify yourself in this world, you have had to withhold a piece of yourself and say of this piece, "This is what makes me uniquely who I am." Without this piece of yourself that you have determined to be unique, your existence would seem to serve even less purpose than it does now. Thus that which is most separate, or that which you have determined separates you the most, is that which you value most highly.

7.5   This one thought constitutes a thought system in and of itself, for it is the primary thought by which you live your life. Your effort goes into maintaining this illusion that what you are must be protected, and that your protection rests on holding this piece of yourself separate. Like the love you set aside from this world, this thought too is one that can be used, for it recognizes that you are as apart from this world as love is. The harsh realities of the world may claim your body and your time, but this one piece of yourself that you have set aside you allow it not to claim. This piece is held within your heart, and it is this piece with which we now will work.

7.6   This is the piece that screams *never* to that which would beat you down. Life is seen as a constant taking away and this, you claim, will *never* be taken from you. For those whose lives are threatened, it is called the will to live. For those whose identity is threatened, it is called the cry of the individual. For others it is the call to create, and for still others the call to love. Some will not give up hope to cynicism. Others label it ethics, morals, values, and say this is the line I will *never* cross. It is the cry that says, "I will not sell my soul."

7.7   Rejoice that there is something in this world that you will not bargain with, something you hold sacrosanct. This is your Self. Yet this Self that you hold so dear that you will never let it go is precisely what you must be willing to freely give away. This is the only Self that holds the light of who you are in truth, the Self that is joined with the Christ in you.

7.8   To this Self is this appeal put forth. Let it be heard and held within your heart. Hold it joyously alongside what already occupies your heart— the love you set aside and the piece of yourself that you won't let go. As you learn that what you give you will receive in truth, you will see that what abides within your heart is all that is worthy of your giving and all you would receive.

7.9   Let us return now to what you would withhold, and see the effects that this withholding has upon yourself and the world that seems to hold you separate. This is, indeed, the first and most general lesson in regard to withholding: The world does not keep you separate. You keep yourself separate from the world. This is what has made the world the world it is. What you withhold allows illusion to rule and truth to be locked away in a vault so impenetrable and so long secured that you have thought it forgotten. You have not realized the vault is your own heart, or that the truth is what you have chosen to keep secure and set aside there. When you believe that this is so and that what you give away you will receive in truth, you will throw open the doors to this safe house, and all the joy you have kept from yourself will return. A great exchange will happen as a powerful wind sweeps through your heart, and all the love you have denied the world will be released. It will flow in every direction, leaving not a corner of the universe untouched. In an instant the eternal will be upon you. Death will be a dream as the wind of life reunited with itself gathers from directions that are beyond direction and breathes life back into what has so long been locked away. After this a gentle breeze will come, never again to leave you, as life breathes as one.

7.10   Your withholding takes on many forms that nonetheless are merely effects of the selfsame cause that keeps truth separate from illusion. Where truth has come illusion is no more. Truth has no need of your protection, for truth brought to illusion shines its light into the darkness, causing it to be no more.

7.11   There are but two forms of withholding: what you withhold *of* yourself from the world and what you withhold *for* yourself from the world. A grievance is something you have chosen for yourself, a piece of a relationship separated off and held in contempt and righteousness. You are unaware that you choose this form of withholding, sometimes dozens or even hundreds of times a day. An unreturned phone call, a bit of traffic, a harsh word spoken, an unremembered errand—all can be resentments you hold to yourself and refuse to let go. By the time you begin your day you may hold several of these in your mind, and there you build them into reasons for even further withholding. Now you have an excuse—or several excuses—for a *bad day*. Why should you give anything to anyone when your day has already treated you so badly? You withhold even a smile, because you have chosen grievances over love.

7.12   You might choose to tell those you encounter of your bad day, and if they are properly sympathetic you may feel that you have gotten something in exchange for the resentments you carry, and if the exchange is determined to be of equal value you might let them go. A response of less than sympathetic proportions, however, is simply added to your list of grievances until the burden of what you hang onto becomes more than you can bear. Now you look for one upon whom you can unload your burdens, hoping you can pass your grievances en mass to someone else. If you succeed through anger, spite, or meanness, you simply take on guilt and withdraw still further into your own misery.

7.13   What you do not realize is that every situation is a relationship—even those as simple as unreturned phone calls and snarled traffic. You relate to someone or something in every situation you encounter, and what you hold against them you withhold from them. You have taken a piece of them and hold it unkindly to yourself, not in joining but in separation. Totally unaware, you too are subject to these whims of your brothers and sisters, and find at times pieces of yourself scattered hither and yon, knowing they are lost to you but not knowing how this loss came about or where to retrieve these missing pieces, not knowing that you can prevent the loss entirely by being one. What is joined cannot be parceled out and scattered, but must remain in wholeness. What is joined resides in peace and knows no grievance. What is joined resides in love inviolate.

7.14   There is another way in which you withhold pieces of relationships for yourself. This withholding is not of the form of grievances but of the form of specialness. You withhold in order to make yourself special, always at another's expense. All your efforts to *best* your brothers and sisters are thus: all competition, all envy, all greed. These all relate to your image of yourself and your efforts to reinforce it. This is your desire not to be intelligent, but to be *more* intelligent than your colleague. This is your desire not to be generous, but to be *more* generous than your relative. This is your desire for wealth that is *greater* than your neighbors, attractiveness *greater* than that of your friends, success *greater* than that of the average man or woman. You pit yourself not only against individuals but groups and nations, teams and organizations, religions and neighbors and family members. This is the desire to be right, or in control, or to have more or be more. This is life based on comparison of illusion to illusion.

7.15   You do not see this as withholding, but what you claim for yourself at another's expense is indeed withholding, and in your world you know not how to claim anything for yourself without withholding it from someone else. You have now set yourself up in a position to withhold your intelligence from others lest they profit from it. You want your intelligence known and recognized, but you want it known and recognized as *yours*. If someone wants the intelligence you have to offer, something must be given in return. What you demand can range from admiration to money, but it is all the same and the demand is always there. It is the ransom that you insist be paid, the homage you claim is due, that without which you will withhold what you have. And you are thankful for these things with which you can demand ransom of the world, for without them you would be the one called upon to pay.

7.16   These are examples of what you withhold from the world *for* yourself. But what of that which you withhold from the world *of* yourself? Both these things are much the same in truth, for what you hold away from all the rest, what you hold for ransom and do not freely give, you do not have the use of for yourself. Those ideas that you save up, that creativity that only you would benefit from, that wealth you would amass —these things are as useless to you when saved for yourself alone as they would be if they did not exist. They bring you not to truth or happiness, nor can they buy you love or the success you seek. What you withhold from the world you withhold from yourself, for you are not separate from the world. In every situation what you would keep is what you will not have, because you keep it only from yourself.

7.17   We must return now to relationship and correct as quickly as possible any erroneous ideas you have, especially those that might make of this a trivial point or one that is specific and not generalizable. All relationship exists in wholeness. The small examples used earlier were meant to help you recognize relationship itself, relationship as something different from the objects, persons, or situations related to. Now we must expand on this idea.

7.18   Broadening your view from the specific to the general is one of the most difficult tasks of the curriculum. It is easy to see why this is so when you recognize how bound your thinking is to specifics. Again this is why we call on love and the hidden knowledge of your heart. Your heart already sees in a manner much more whole than the perception of your split mind. Even your language and images reflect this truth, this difference between the wisdom of your heart and that of your mind. Your heart may be said to break, but the image that these words call forth is of a heart cracked open, not of a heart in separate pieces. Your brain, on the other hand, is separated into right and left hemispheres. One side has one function, one side another. While your brain and your mind are not the same, your image of your mind and what it does and does not do is linked with your image of your brain. Let this image go and concentrate on the wholeness of your heart, no matter how you view its current condition. Be it wounded, bleeding, broken or full, it rests in wholeness within you at the center of who you are.

7.19   It is from this center that truth will light your way.

7.20   It is from this center that you will come to understand that relationship exists in wholeness. We have begun to dislodge your idea that you stand separate and alone, a being broken off from all the rest. Your forgiveness of all that has led to this misperception is not yet complete, nor will it be until your understanding is greater than it is now. For you cannot give up the only reality you know without believing in and having at least some elementary understanding of what the truth of your reality actually is.

7.21   If you cannot be alone you must be continuously in relationship. Thus, relationship must not depend on interaction as you understand it. It is easy to see the relationship between a pencil and your hand, your body and another, the actions that you do and the effects they seem to cause. All of these relationships are based on what your senses tell you, the evidence you have relied upon to make sense of your world. Those who have developed reliance on ways of knowing not governed by the acceptable senses are seen as suspect. And yet you accept many causes for your feelings, from variations in the weather to unseen and unverifiable diseases. You have given others, whom you see as having more authority than you, license to provide you with their version of the truth, and for consistency's sake you choose to believe in the version of the truth most predominate in your society. Thus the *truth* is different in one place than it is in another and it even appears to be in conflict. You cling to known truths, even though you are aware of their instability in time as well as place, and so you live with constant denial that even what is known to you is not known at all. You thus cling to the one sure thing that permeates your existence: the knowledge that death will claim you and all of those you love.

7.22   Realize that when you are asked to give this up, you are asked to give up an existence so morbid that anyone with any sanity would gladly toss it to the wind and ask for an alternative. An alternative exists. Not in dreams of fantasy but in truth. Not in changing form and circumstance but in eternal consistency.

7.23   Accept a new authority, even if only for the little while that it will take you to read these words. Start with this idea: You will allow for the possibility of a new truth to be revealed to your waiting heart. Hold in your heart the idea that as you read these words—and when you finish reading these words—their truth will be revealed to you. Let your heart be open to a new kind of evidence of what constitutes the truth. Think of no other outcomes than your happiness, and when happiness comes deny it not, nor its source. Remind yourself that when love comes to fill your heart, you will deny it not, nor its source. You do not need to believe that this will happen, but only to allow for the possibility of it happening. Do not turn your back on the hope offered here, and when new life flows in to release the old, forget not from where it came.

CHAPTER 8

The Separation from the Body

8.1   The thoughts of your heart you have defined as your emotions. These thoughts stand apart from the wisdom of your heart that we have already discussed—the wisdom that knows to set love apart, as well as your own Self. Emotions, the thoughts of your heart, are what we will now work with, separating as we do the truth from your perception of it.

8.2   This curriculum aims to help you see that your emotions are not the real thoughts of your heart. What other language might your heart speak? It is a language spoken so quietly and with such gentleness that those who cannot come to stillness know it not. The language of your heart is the language of communion.

8.3   Communion is union that we will speak of here as being of the highest level, though in truth, no levels separate union at all. As a learning being, the idea of levels is helpful to you and will aid you in seeing that you progress from one step, or one level of learning, to another. This is more a process of remembering than learning, and this you will understand as memory begins to return to you. Your heart will aid you in replacing thinking with remembering. In this way, remembering can be experienced as the language of the heart.

8.4   This remembering is not of former days spent upon this earth, but of remembering who you really are. It comes forth from the deepest part of you, from the center in which you are joined with Christ. It speaks of no experiences here, wears no faces, and bears no symbols. It is a memory of wholeness, of all to all.

8.5   Many emotions as well as thoughts would seem to block your way to the stillness in which this memory can be found. Yet as you have seen again and yet again, the Holy Spirit can use what you made for a higher purpose when your purpose is in union with that of spirit. We will thus examine a new way of looking at emotions, a way that will allow them to assist you in your learning rather than block you from it.

8.6   You think of the heart as the place of feeling, and thus you associate emotions with your heart. Emotions, however, are really reactions of your body to stimuli that arrive through your senses. Thus, the sight of a lovely sunset can bring tears to your eyes. The slightest contact between your hand and the skin of a baby can cause you to feel as if your heart overflows with love. Harsh words that enter through your ears can cause your face to redden and your heart to beat with a heaviness you label anger or a sting you would call shame. Problems that mount up and seem too much to bear can cause what you call emotional turmoil or even a nervous breakdown. In these situations either too many feelings are going on all at once or all feeling is shut down all at once. As with everything else in this world, you strive for a balance that allows your heart to beat at one steady pace, for one emotion to surface at a time, for feelings that you can control. And yet you feel controlled by your feelings, emotions that seem to have a life of their own, and a body that reacts to all of it in ways that make you uncomfortable, anxious, ecstatic, or terrified.

8.7   None of this speaks of what your heart would say to you, but masks the language of the heart and buries stillness deep beneath an ever-changing milieu of life lived on the surface, as if your own skin were the playground for all the angels and demons that would dance there. What you would remember is replaced by memories of these emotions—so many that they could not be counted even for one day, even by those who claim to have them not. It is not your thoughts to which you turn to bring you evidence for your resentment, ammunition for your vengeance, pain for your remembering. It is to your emotions, those feelings that you would say come from your own heart.

8.8   What foolishness to think love could abide with companions such as these. If these be in your heart, where is love? If these illusions were real there would be no place for love at all, but love abides where illusion cannot enter. These illusions are like barnacles upon your heart, adhering to its surface, but keeping it not from fulfilling its function or carrying within itself that which keeps you safe upon this raging sea.

8.9   Safe within your heart lies love's reality, a reality so foreign to you that you think you remember it not. Yet it is to this reality we head as we travel deep within you to the center of your Self.

8.10   Even those of you whose perceptions remain quite faulty know that there is a difference between what lies on the surface and what lies beneath. Often the surface of a situation is all that is seen, the surface of a problem all that is recognized, the surface of a relationship all that is known to you. You speak openly of these levels of seeing, recognizing, and knowing, saying often, "On the surface it would seem that..." and this observation is often followed by attempts to see beneath the surface to find causes, motivations, or reasons for a situation, problem, or relationship. Often this search is called seeking for the truth. While the way in which you go about seeking for the truth in places it is not causes it to remain hidden from you, your recognition that a truth is available in a place other than on the surface is useful to us now, as is your recognition that something other than what appears *on the surface* exists.

8.11   What do you mean to do when you attempt to look beneath the surface? Do you mean to look beneath the skin, or into the hidden recesses of a heart or mind? Without union all your seeking will not reveal the truth. And while there is a part of you that knows this, you prefer instead of union a game of speculation, conjecture, and probable cause. You look for explanations and information rather than the truth you claim to seek. You look in judgment rather than in forgiveness. You look from separation's stance rather than from the grace-filled place of union. Perhaps you are thinking now that if you knew how this union worked you would surely use it to find the truth, and for other objectives as well. You would like to be a problem solver, a person who could, as in a court of law, separate right from wrong, truth from lies, fact from fiction. You do not even see that what you desire is further separation, and that separation cannot bring about the truth nor arise from unity.

8.12   Even your loftiest desires are fraught with righteousness that is still righteousness no matter what the noble cause you deem yourself willing to address. You would see into another's mind and heart in order perhaps to help them, but also to have power over them. Whatever you might come to know you would deem your property and its disposition your purview. How dangerous would you be if union were such as this? How rightly you would fight it to protect your own secrets from revelation. This faulty perception of union would keep you from the goal you seek, the goal that is no goal but your only reality, the natural state in which you would exist but for your decision to reject your reality and your true nature.

8.13   Do you see now why unity and wholeness go hand in hand? Why you cannot withhold a piece of yourself and realize the unity that is your home? Were it possible to exist in unity and still withhold, unity would be a mockery. Who would you withhold for? And whom would you withhold from? Unity is wholeness. All for all.

8.14   We have talked now of what is on the surface. Let us try an experiment.

8.15   Think of your body now as the surface of your existence and look upon it. Stand back from it, for it is not your home. The heart we speak of does not abide in it and nor do you. Separate bodies cannot unite in wholeness. They were made to keep wholeness from you and to convince you of the illusion of your separateness. Step back. See your body as just the surface layer of your existence. It is what appears to be and no more. Let it not keep you from seeing the truth, as you do not let other surface conditions hide the truth from you. Even if you have not formerly found the truth, you have recognized what is not the truth. Your body is not the truth of who you are, no matter how much it appears to be. For now, let's consider it the surface aspect of your existence.

8.16   We will go one step further as well, for many of you are thinking still that it is what is within the body that is real: your brain and heart, your thoughts and emotions. If your body contained what was real, it too would be real. Just as if a surface situation contained the truth, it would be the truth. If your body and what lies within it are not who you are, you feel as if you are left homeless. This feeling of homelessness is necessary for your return to your real home, for were you locked up and contained within your body, and were you to accept this container as your home, you would not accept another.

8.17   Your "other" home is the home you feel as if you have left and the home you feel the desire to return to. Yet it is where you are, and you could not be anywhere else. Your home is here. You think this is incongruous with the truth as I'm revealing it, the truth that heaven is your home, but it is not. There is no *here* in the terms that you would think of it, the terms that set your reality in a location, on a planet, in a body. *God is here* and you belong to God. This is the only sense in which you can or should accept the notion that you belong here. When you realize God is here, then and only then can you truthfully say *here* is where I belong.

8.18   Now that you are standing back from your body, participating in this experiment to recognize the surface element of your existence, you are perhaps more aware than ever before of being in a particular place and time. As you stand back and observe your body, this is what you will see: a form moving through time and place. You may be more aware than ever of its actions and complaints, its sturdiness or lack thereof. You may be realizing how it governs your existence and wondering how you could spend even a moment without awareness of it.

8.19   This moment without awareness of the body was beautifully described in *A Course in Miracles* as the Holy Instant. You may not think observation of your body is a good way to achieve this, but as you observe you learn to hold yourself apart from what you see. A reminder is needed here, however, a reminder to not observe with your mind, but with your heart. This observance will contain a holiness, a gift of sight beyond that of your normal vision.

8.20   You may begin by feeling compassion toward this body that you have long viewed as your home. There it goes again, one more time, sleeping and waking. One more time fueling itself with energy. One more time expending that energy. One more time growing weary. One more day is greeted, and its greeting lies upon your heart. Each day tells you all things come to pass. At times this is cause for rejoicing. At other times a cause for sorrow. But never can it be evaded that each day is a beginning and an ending both. Night is as certain as day.

8.21   Into these days that come to pass move many other bodies such as yours. Each one is distinct—and there are so many! As you become an observer you may well be overwhelmed by what you observe, by the sheer magnitude of all that with you occupies the world. Some days this will make you feel like one of many, a tiny peon of little significance. On other days you will feel quite superior, the ultimate achievement of the world and all its years of evolution. There are days you will feel quite of the earth, as if this is your natural home and heaven to your soul. On other days your feeling will be quite the opposite, and you will wonder where you are. Yes, there your body is, but where are you?

8.22   Although you cannot observe it, you will become aware of how the past walks through your days with you, and the future too. Both are like companions who for a little while are welcome distractions but are loathe to leave you when you would have them gone.

8.23   Where lives this past and future? Where does day go when it is night? What are you to make of all these forms that wander through your days with you? What is it, really, that you are observing?

8.24   This is your reenactment of creation, begun each morning and completed each night. Each day is your creation held together by the thought system that gave it birth. To observe this is to see its reality. To see this reality is to see the image of God you have created in God's likeness. This image is based on your memory of the truth of God's creation and your desire to create like your Father. It is the best, in your forgetfulness, that you could do; but still it tells you much.

8.25   Everything is held together by the thought system that gave birth to it. There are but two thought systems: the thought system of God, and the thought system of the ego or the separated self. The thought system of the separated self sees everything in separation. The thought system of God sees everything in unity. God's thought system is one of continuous creation, rebirth and renewal. The ego's thought system is one of continuous destruction and disassembly, of decay and death. And yet how like they are one to the other!

8.26   How like to memory it is to think a thing remembered in every smallest detail and yet to have no idea what the memory is about! All memory is twisted and distorted by what you would have it be. Everyone can think of at least one long remembered incident that when given to the light of truth revealed a lie of outlandish proportions. These are the memories of loved ones you were sure were trying to hurt you when in truth they were only trying to help. The memories of situations you deemed meant to embarrass or destroy you that were in truth meant to teach you what you needed to learn to lead you to a success you now enjoy.

8.27   Thus your memory of God's creation is a memory you retain to the smallest detail, and yet the details mask the truth so thoroughly that all truth is given over to illusion.

8.28   How can it be that you move through the same world day by day in the same body, observing many situations like onto each other, awakening to the same sun rising and setting, and yet can experience each day so differently that one day you feel happy and one day you feel sad, one day you feel hope and one day you feel despair? How can it be that what was created so like to God's creation can be so opposite to it? How can memory so deceive the eyes, and yet fail to deceive the heart?

8.29   This is the truth of your existence, an existence in which your eyes deceive you but your heart believes not in the deception. Your days are but evidence of this truth. What your eyes behold will one day deceive you while what your heart beholds will the next day see through the deception. And so one day lived in your world is misery incarnate and the next a thing of joy.

8.30   Rejoice that your heart is not deceived, for herein lies your path to true remembering.

CHAPTER 9

The Prodigal's Return

9.1 You wonder how it can be said that your heart is not deceived when it seems so often to deceive you. It seems as fickle as your mind, telling you one thing one day and one thing the next. Even more so than your mind it seems to lead you astray, forcing you to walk through paths full of danger and treachery into the deepest darkness instead of toward the light. It is your emotions rather than your heart that would do this to you.

9.2 Emotions speak the language of your separated self rather than the language of your heart. They are the forward guard of your defense system, always on the lookout for what might hurt or slight the *little you* that they deem under their protection, or the other little selves you deem under yours. But remember now how like to creation in form if not in substance what you have made is. Creation needs no protection. It is only your belief in the need for protection that has caused what you feel to become so clouded by illusion. If you felt no need to protect your heart, or any of those bodies that you love, your feelings would retain their innocence and could not hurt you in any way.

9.3 The desire to protect is a desire that arises from distrust and is based totally on fear. If there were no fear, what would there be to protect? Thus, all of your love—the love that you imagine you keep within yourself, and the love that you imagine you receive and give—is tainted by your fear and cannot be real love. It is because you remember love as that which kept you safe, that which kept you happy, that which bound all those you love to you, that you attempt to use love here. This is a real memory of creation that you have distorted. Your faulty memory has caused you to believe love can be used to keep you safe, to make you happy and bind to you those you choose to love. This is not the case, for love cannot be used.

9.4 This is how you have distorted all relationship as well, making of it something that only becomes real in its use by you or to you. In your memory of creation you have remembered that all things exist in relationship, and that all things happen in relationship. Thus you have chosen to use relationship to prove your existence and to make things happen. This use of relationship will never provide the proof or the action you seek, because relationship cannot be used.

9.5   Look around the room in which you sit and take away the usefulness from each thing you see in it. How many items would you keep that you now look upon? Your body too was created for its usefulness. It sets you apart, just as each item in your room is set apart by what it is useful for. Ask yourself now: To whom is your body useful? This question does not apply to those for whom you cook or clean, those whose bodies you would repair or minds improve. The question is, really, who might have seen a use for a body such as yours before it was created? What kind of creator would create it and for what purpose?

9.6   You did not create your Self, but your body you did create. It was created for its usefulness just like every other object that shares the space you occupy. Think for a moment of what the creator of such a body would have intended the body to be. The body is a finite entity, created to be self-contained but also to self-destruct. It was created with a need for constant maintenance, a maintenance that requires toil and struggle. Every inch of its surface is a receiver and transmitter of information yet it carries additional tools such as eyes and ears to enhance its communication and to control what goes in and what goes out. It is as susceptible to pain as to pleasure. It contains the means for joining, but for joining that is of a temporary nature. It is as capable of violence as gentleness. It is born and dies in a state of helplessness.

9.7   The body could not help but be thus, as it was made with dual purposes in mind. It was made to make real and then glorify a separated self, and it was made to punish that separated self for the separation. Its creator had in mind what is reflected in the body: self-aggrandizement and self-effacement, pleasure and pain, violence and gentleness. A desire to know everything but only through its own effort, a desire to see everything but only through its own eyes, a desire to be known but only through what it would choose to share. Alongside these desires it is easy to see how a world such as that of the body developed. Alongside the desire to know was the desire not to know. Alongside the desire to see was the desire not to see. Alongside the desire to share was the desire to be hidden. Alongside the desire to live was the desire to live no more.

9.8   You have always been as you were created, but this is what you chose to make from that with which you started. In other words, you took what you are and made this of yourself. You did not create something from nothing and you did not usurp the power of God. You took what God created and turned it into an illusion so powerful that you believe it is what you are, rather than believing in the truth. But just as you have done this, you can undo this. This is the choice set before you—to go on believing in the illusion you have made, or to begin to see the truth.

9.9   Now you seek to know how to escape what you have made. To do so you must withdraw all faith from it. This you are not ready yet to do, but this is what your heart will now prepare you for. As you are prepared, you walk alongside he who has waited for you with a single purpose instead of alongside the conflicting desires you chose to let lead you to this strange world. You travel lightly now where before you walked in chains. You travel now with a companion who knows you as you are and would show your Self to you.

9.10   Look upon your body now as you earlier looked upon the space you occupy. Take away the body's usefulness. Would you keep that which you now look upon? As you stand back and observe your body, always with the vision of your heart, think about just what it is that you would use it for. What God created cannot be used, but what you have made can, for its only purpose is your use. Choose to use it now to return you to your real Self, and the new purpose you establish will change its conditions as well as its usefulness to you.

9.11   All use is predicated on the simple idea that you do not have what you need. You will continue to believe this while your allegiance remains split. Until you have withdrawn all faith in what you have made, you will believe that what you made remains useful to you. Since this is the case, and since it cannot be changed without your total willingness to change it—a willingness not yet complete—we will, instead of trying to ignore what you have made, use it in a new way. Keep in mind, however, that we are merely saving time, and that your real Self has no need to use anything at all.

9.12   As stated before, what is most useful to us now is your perception of your heart. Your illusions concerning it, when undone, will quickly reveal to you the truth because your misperceptions concerning your heart remain closer to the truth than any that you hold. The memories of your heart are the strongest and purest that exist, and their remembrance will help to still your mind and reveal the rest.

9.13 We thus return to your perception of your emotions and all that causes you to feel. In your feelings, especially those you cannot name, lies your connection to all that is. This is useful because what you have named and classified is harder to dislodge and bring to light. Even those feelings you attempt to name and keep cleverly in a box that you have labeled this or that often are not content to stay where you would place them. They seem to betray you, when it is you who betray them by not allowing them to be what they are. This could be used as a capsule definition of your entire problem: You do not allow anything that exists in your world, including yourself, to be what it is.

9.14 Feelings that on their own seem to rebel against this insane situation are guided by memories trying to reveal the truth to you. They call to you from a place that you know not. The difficulty is that the only self that is listening to this call is your separated self. It is in the attempts of the separated self to interpret what feelings would say that they become as distorted as all the rest. It is the separated self that feels impelled to label feelings good and bad, some worthy of acknowledgment and the rest worthy only of denial or contempt. It is your language that gives emotion its place, one step behind fear, in your battle to control or protect what you have made.

9.15 Fear always lies one step beneath the surface of a situation because it lies one step beneath the surface of your self. Peel back the first level of what your eyes allow you to observe and you will find fear lurking there. The next level, depending on your disposition, is either the desire to control or the desire to protect. They are really the same but they wear different faces to the world. If, for the purposes of our discussion, the body is the surface aspect of your self, and if beneath that surface what is first encountered is fear, it is from fear that all the rest proceeds. Surely it is easy to see that neither the desire to control nor to protect would exist without the layer of fear that comes before it.

9.16 Fear, like all the rest of your emotions, comes in many guises and is given many names, but there are really only two emotions: one is fear, the other love. Fear is thus the source of all illusion, love the source of truth.

9.17   How could one separated off from all the rest not be fearful? It matters not at all that all whom you observe seem to be separate as well. No one really believes another to be as separate as he is. It always seems as if others have what you lack and what you are looking for. You seem to be alone in your frailty, loneliness, and lack of love. Others misunderstand you and know you not, and neither can you make any sense of them.

9.18   This need not be, for you are not separate! The relationships you seek to end your loneliness can do so if you but learn to see relationship differently. As with all your problems in perception, fear is what blocks the vision of your heart, the light the Christ in you would shine upon the darkness. Can you not see that when you chose to make yourself separate and alone you also make the choice for fear? Fear is nothing but a choice, and it can be replaced by choice of another kind.

9.19   It has been said often that cause and effect are one in truth. The world you see is the effect of fear. Each one of you would have compassion for a child tormented by nightmares. Each parent's most fervent wish would be to tell a child truthfully there is no cause for fear. Age has not taken fear from any of you nor made your dream of life any less of a nightmare. Yet you spare few moments of compassion for yourself, and when such chance occurrences come about you quickly override compassion with practicality. While it makes sense to you to attempt to dispel a child's nightmare, you see no way to dispel your own. You hide fear beneath the surface, and behind each alternate label you would give it, in a desperate attempt to see it not. To live in fear is, indeed, a curse, and one that you would try to tell yourself is not present in your life. You look to others to feel compassion for, to those living in countries torn by war or neighborhoods steeped in violence. There is cause for fear, you say. But not here.

9.20   This is the only way you have been able to see to bring relief to the nightmare of a life of fear. You project fear outward and away from yourself, seeing not that you keep that which you would project. Seeing not that outward signs of fear are but reflections of what you keep within.

9.21   Think now of one of those you have identified as living the life of fear you deny yourself. And imagine that you could bring this one in from that dark and dangerous place. She is cold, and you prepare a fire and give her a warm blanket for her knees. He is hungry and you prepare a feast for him fit to serve a king. This one exists in the violence you would keep outside your doors, and from your inner sanctum you give this one a respite from the war that rages beyond it. All of your behavior and even your fantasies testify that you believe an absence of cold makes for warmth. That the absence of hunger is fullness. The absence of violence peace. You think that if you but provide these things that are opposite to what you would not want to have, you have accomplished much. But a warm fire will only provide warmth as long as it is stoked. A meal will provide fullness only until the next is needed. Your closed door only keeps you safe while its boundary is respected. To replace the temporary with the temporary is not an answer.

9.22 You may be thinking now that what I have just told you is not an answer is precisely what the Bible has instructed you to do. I am recorded as telling you to feed the hungry, to quench the thirst of the thirsty, to welcome and give rest to the stranger. I have said when you do this unto others you do this to me. Do you think that I am in need of a meal, a cup of water, a warm bed? While you are trapped in the illusion of need surely these acts of charity are of some value, but again I tell you that this value is temporary. My words call you to the eternal, to nourishment and rest of the spirit rather than the body. That your sights are set on the care of the body alone is another example of choosing an opposite for replacement.

9.23 Is this not your way of solving all the problems that you face? You see what you do not want and try to replace it with its opposite. Your life is thus spent in struggling against what you have for what you have not. Only one example is needed to clarify the predicament in which you have placed yourself. You feel lacking and so you want. You want and want and want. You truly believe you do not have what you need, and so make yourself continuously needy. You thus spend your life trying to fulfill your needs. For most of you, this trying takes on the form of work and you spend your entire life working to meet your needs and those of the ones you love. What would you do with your life if you had no needs to meet? What would you do with your life if you had no fear? These questions are the same.

9.24 The only replacement that can occur that will accomplish what you seek is the replacement of illusion with the truth, the replacement of fear with love, the replacement of your separated self with your real Self, the

Self that rests in unity. It is your knowledge that this must occur that leads you to attempt every other kind of replacement. You can continue on in this fashion, always hoping that the next replacement will be the one that succeeds in bringing you what you desire, or you can choose instead the only replacement that will work.

9.25   All that you are asked to give up is your insane notion that you are alone. We speak much of your body here only because it is your proof of this insane idea's validity. It is your proof as well that a life of fear is warranted. How could you not fear for the safety of a home as fragile as the body? How could you fail to provide the next meal for yourself and those within your care? You do not see all that these distractions of meeting needs would keep you from.

9.26   And yet the very reality that you have set up—the reality of not being able to succeed in what you must constantly strive to do—is a situation set up to provide relationship. Like everything else you have remembered of creation and made in its image, so too is this. While making yourself separate and alone you have also made it necessary to be in relationship to survive. Without relationship your *species* itself would cease to be, in fact, all life would end. Of course you must help your sister and brother, for they are yourself, and they are your only means to grasp eternity even within this false reality you have made.

9.27   Let us return to the example of feeding your sister's hunger and quenching your brother's thirst. This is not only a lesson in feeding and quenching spiritual hunger and thirst, but a lesson in relationship as well. It is the relationship inherent in meeting another's need that makes the meeting of the need a thing of lasting value. It is your willingness to say, "Brother, you are not alone" that is the benefit of such situations, not only to your brother but also to you. It is in saying, "Sister, you are not alone" that spiritual hunger and thirst is met with the fullness of unity. It is in realizing that you are not alone that you realize your unity with me and begin to turn from fear toward love.

9.28   You are not your own creator. This is your salvation. You did not create something from nothing, and what you started with is what God created and remains as God created it. You do not have to ask yourself to stretch your belief beyond these simple statements. Are they really so implausible as to be beyond your acceptance? Is it so impossible to imagine that what God created was distorted by your desire to have your reality be other than what it is? Have you not seen this kind of distortion take place within the reality you do see? Is this not the story of the gifted son or daughter who squanders all the gifts he or she possesses by seeing them not or by sadly distorting what they might be useful for?

9.29   You are the prodigal sons and daughters welcomed constantly to return home to your Father's safe embrace.

9.30   Think of your automobile or computer or any other *thing* you use. Without a user, would it have any function at all? Would it be anything? An automobile abandoned and without a user might become the home to a family of mice. A computer might be covered with a cloth, a flowerpot placed on top of it. Someone not knowing what it is for would make of it what he or she would have it be, but never would the user seek to exchange roles with it. When an accident happens, an automobile cannot be seen to be at fault for mistakes made by its user. Yet in a way this exchange of roles is similar to what you have attempted to do and it is like placing the blame for a car accident on the automobile. You have attempted to change places with the body, claiming that it is using you rather than that you are using it. You do so out of guilt in an attempt to place your guilt outside yourself. "My body made me do it" is like the cry of the child with an imaginary friend. With his claim of an imaginary friend, the child announces that his body is not within his control. What is your ego but an imaginary friend to you?

9.31   Child of God, you need no imaginary friend when you have beside you he who is your friend always and would show you that you have no needs at all. What you truly are cannot be used, not even by God. See you not that it is only in illusion that you can use others who are like yourself?

9.32   You learn your concept of using others from the reality you have made in which you use the body that you call your home and identify as your own self. How can the user and the object of use be one and the same? This insanity makes the purpose of your life seem to be one of usefulness. The more your body can be of use to others and to yourself, the more worthwhile you see it as being. Ages have passed since creation began, and still you have not learned the lesson of the birds of the air or the flowers of the field. Two thousand years have passed since you were told to observe this lesson. The lilies of the field neither sow nor reap and yet they are provided for. The birds of the air live to sing a song of gladness. So do you.

9.33   God's will for you is happiness, and never has it been otherwise. God's creation is for eternity and has no use for time. Time too is of your making, an idea of use gone mad, as once again you have taken something made for your own use and allowed it to become the user. With your own two hands you give away all your happiness and power to that which you have made! It matters little now that in so doing you once again imitated what your faulty memory would tell you that your Creator did. God alone can give free will. In giving your power to things like your body and to ideas like time your imitation of the gift of free will is so falsely placed in illusion that you cannot see this madness for what it truly is. Your body has no use for your power, and time was not made for happiness.

9.34   The free will that God gave you is what has allowed you to make of yourself and your world what you will. Now you look upon this world with guilt and see it as evidence of your evil nature. It reinforces your belief that you have changed too much from what you were to ever again be worthy of your true inheritance. You fear that this, too, you would squander and lay to ruin. The only thing that might succeed in proving your place as that of royal inheritor would be if you could fix yourself and the world, restoring it to a previous condition that you imagine you know. In this scenario God is like unto your banker rather than your Father. You would prove to God that you can "make a go of it" before you would ask Him for His help.

9.35   As long as you do not want to be forgiven you will not feel the gentle touch of forgiveness upon you and your world. While there is no need in truth for this forgiveness, as there is no truth to this big change that you believe you have undergone, your desire to be forgiven is a first step away from your belief that you can fix things by yourself and in so doing earn your way back into your Father's home. Being willing to be forgiven is the precursor of atonement, the state in which you allow your errors to be corrected for you. These errors are not the sins you hold against yourself, but merely your errors in perception. Correction, or atonement, returns you to your natural state where true vision lies and error and sin disappear.

9.36   Your natural state is one of union, and each joining that you do in holy relationship returns a little of the memory of union to you. This memory of your divinity is what you seek in truth from each special relationship you enter into, but your true quest is hidden by the concept of use that gets in its way. While your heart seeks for union, your separated self seeks for what it can use to fill the emptiness and ease the terror of its separation. What your heart seeks in love it attains, but your separated self would keep this attainment from you by turning every situation into a means to serve its ends. As long as union is seen as a means only to keep loneliness from you it is not seen for what it truly is.

9.37 You have placed limits on all things in your world, and it is these limits of usefulness that would block your memory's return. A love relationship, while seen as the ultimate achievement in terms of the closeness you can acquire with a brother or sister, is still limited by what you would have it do. Its purpose, simply stated, is to supply a lack. This is your definition of completion. What is missing in you is found in another and together a sense of wholeness is achieved.

9.38 Again this is but a distortion of creation. You remember that wholeness is achieved through union, but not how to accomplish it. You have forgotten that only you can be accomplished. You believe that by putting various parts together a whole can be achieved. You speak of balance, and try to find something for one part of yourself in one place and something for another somewhere else. This one fulfills your need for friendship and that one for intellectual stimulation. In one activity you express your creativity and in another your prayerfulness. Like a diversified investment portfolio, you think this parceling out of different aspects of yourself protects your assets. You fear "putting all your eggs in one basket." You seek to balance the things you label drudgery and the things you label exciting. In doing so you see yourself as "spending your time" wisely, and you call yourself a "well-rounded individual." As long as more than this is not sought, more than this will not be realized.

9.39 Seeking what you have lost in other people, places, and things is but a sign that you do not understand that what you have lost still belongs to you. What you have lost is missing, not gone. What you have lost is hidden to you but has not disappeared nor ceased to be. What you have lost is valuable indeed, and this you know. But you know not what this valuable something is. One thing alone is sure: When you have found it you will know that it has been found. This is what will bring you happiness and peace, contentment and a sense of belonging. This is what will cause you to feel as if your time here has not been in vain. You know that whatever else your life seems to be for, if on your deathbed you have not found what you have sought, you will not leave in deepest peace but in dark despair and fear. You will have no hope for what lies *beyond* life, for you will have found no hope *in* life.

9.40   Your quest for what is missing thus becomes the race you run against death. You seek it here, you seek it there, and scurry on to the next thing and the next. Each person runs this race alone, with hope only of victory for himself. You realize not that if you were to stop and take your brother's hand, the racecourse would become a valley full of lilies, and you would find yourself on the other side of the finish line, able at last to rest.

9.41   The injunction to rest in peace is for the living, not the dead. But while you run the race you will know it not. Competition that leads to individual achievement has become the idol you would glorify, and you need not look far for evidence that this is so. This idolatry tells you that glory is for the few, and so you take your place in line at the starting gate and make your bid for glory. You run the race as long as you can and, win or lose, your participation in the race was but the required offering to the idol you have made. And at some point, when you can run the race no more, you bow down to those who have achieved glory; they become your idols and you become their subjects, watching what they do with envy and with awe. To these you make your sacrifices and pay your homage. To these you say, "I would be like you." To these you look for a vicarious fulfillment, having given up any hope for real fulfillment. Here you are entertained, shocked, excited, or repelled. Here you watch the gladiators kill one another for your amusement. Here is your notion of use displayed in all its most horrific detail.

9.42   What is this but a demonstration, on a larger scale, of what you live each day? This is all that anything larger than yourself demonstrates to you. All society, groups, teams, and organizations are but a collective portrayal of individual desire. Slaves and masters but use one another and the same laws bind both. Who is master and who is slave in this body you would call your home? What freedom would you have without the demands your body places upon you? The same question can be asked of this world you see as home to the body. Which is master and which is slave when both are held in bondage? The glory you give idols is but bondage as well. Without your idolatry their glory would be no more, and so they live in fear no less than that of those who idolize them.

9.43   Use, in any form, leads to bondage, and so to perceive a world based on use is to see a world where freedom is impossible. What you think you need your sister for is thus based upon this insane premise that freedom can be purchased and that master is freer than slave. Although this is illusion, it is the illusion that is sought. The purchase price is usefulness. And so each joining is seen as a bartering in which you trade your usefulness for that of another. An employer has use for your skills and you have use for the salary and benefits the employer offers. A spouse is useful in many ways that complement your areas of usefulness. A store provides you with goods that you would use, and you supply a store with capital that its owner will use. If you are gifted with beauty or athletic or artistic talent that can be used, how lucky you think you are. A beautiful face and a fit body can be traded for so much. It is no secret that you live in a world of supply and demand. From the simple concept of individuals needing to be in relationship to survive has grown this complex web of use and abuse.

9.44   Abuse is but improper use—use on a scale that makes the insanity of use obvious to both the user and the usee, and so has its proper place in our discussion here. Look at patterns of abuse, in everything from drugs and alcohol to physical or emotional mistreatment. These, like the larger examples of your daily life gone awry, are but demonstrations of internal desires taken to a greater extreme; only these, rather than being reflected by the group, are reflected within the individual. The individual with issues of abuse would do a service to the world if the people in it were to understand what that abuse is a reflection of. Like any extreme, it merely points out what in less extreme instances is still the same: Use is improper.

9.45   It is its purpose that makes use improper. The Holy Spirit can guide you to use the things that you have made in ways that benefit the whole, and this is the distinction between proper and improper use, or use and abuse. You would use for the benefit of the separated self. When magnified, the destructive force of such abuse is easily apparent. Again you would place the blame outside yourself and label drugs, alcohol, tobacco, gambling, and even food as destructive forces. Like the automobile you would blame for an accident, user and usee have become confused. All such confusion stems from the initial confusion of the use you think your body would put you to. All such confusion stems from your displacement of yourself and your abdication of your power to the things that you have made.

9.46 Let me say again that this is your misguided attempt to follow in creation's way. God gave all power to his creations, and you would choose to do this as well. Your intent is not evil, but guided by the guilt and false remembering of the separated self. As much as you have desired anonymity and autonomy from God, still you blame God for creating a situation in which you think you have been allowed to hurt yourself. How could God allow all this suffering, you ask? Why does He tempt you with such destructive forces? Forces beyond your control? Why did not God create a world benign and unable to harm you?

9.47 Such is the world that God did create: A world so lovely and so peaceful that when you see it once again you will cry with joy and forget your sadness in an instant. There will be no long remembering of regrets, no feeling badly for all the years in which you saw this not. There will merely be a glad "Aha!" as what was long forgotten is returned to you. You will but smile at the childish games you played, and have no more regrets than you would have for your childhood. Your innocence will stand out clearly here, and never again will you doubt that the world that God created belongs to you and you to it.

9.48 All your vast wanderings will be seen for what they are. All that you desired will be revealed as only two desires, the desire to love and the desire to be loved. Why wait to see that these desires are all that call you to the strange behavior you display? Those who give in to abuse are merely calling louder for the selfsame love that all are in search of. Judgment is not due them, for all here are abusers—starting with their own selves.

9.49 Attempts to modify the behavior of abuse are near to useless in a world based on use. The foundation of the world must change, and the stimulus for this change lies within you. All use ends with joining, for use is what you have traded joining for. Instead of recognizing your union, a state in which you are whole and complete because you are joined with all, you have determined to stand separate and use the rest to support your separate stance. Do you see you the difference in these two positions? In what way is your

way better than the way God created for you, a way that is completely free
of conflict? Despite your bravest attempts to remain separate, you must use
your brothers and sisters in order to even maintain the illusion of your separation. Would it not simply be better to end this charade? To admit that you
were not created for separation but for union? To begin to let go of your fear
of joining, and as you do let go of use as well?

9.50 How different would the world be if you would but attempt for one day
to replace use with union! Before you can begin, however, we must expand
on the lessons you are learning by observing your own self. Now we seek
to uncover the illusion that you can be used by your body, for your own
seeming use by such as this leads to all other ideas of use.

CHAPTER 10
Use and Understanding

10.1   First let us consider what it is the body would use. Although you feel slave to it and under the weight of its control, who is the *you* it would control? How can it make you do other than you choose to do? Learn this lesson well, for herein lies the cure to all disease and the hope of all healing. While the body seems to tell you what you feel and bid you act in accordance with its feelings, how can this be so? The body by itself is neutral. But as long as you attribute the body with bringing you pleasure, the body will bring you pain as well. You cannot choose one without the other, because the choice is the same. The body is a tool made for your use in maintaining the illusion of your separation. That it has seeming power can only be because you think you put your power there. If this were true, much power indeed would it wield. But what you have made cannot be invested with the power of creation without your joining with it. How, you think, could you be more linked with anything than you are with your own body? If you are not even joined with this presence that you call your home, how can you be expected to join with others?

10.2   Now we must return to the concept of relationship, for the thought of bodies joined in union closer than the union that you feel with the body you call your own is indeed ridiculous. Joining happens in relationship, not in physical form. Joining is not the obliteration of one thing to make another—joining makes each one whole, and in this wholeness one with all. This union has never really ceased to be, but as long as you do not realize that it exists its benefits are unavailable to you. As much as I would like it to be so, my telling you the truth of your existence is not enough of itself to make you aware of what you have for so long hidden from yourself. I can merely tell you where to look, and save you countless years of seeking where the truth is not, if you will but seek where I bid you find.

10.3   There are aspects of what I am telling you that you readily embrace and others that you do not understand and would wait awhile before implementing. What you truly do not understand is wholeness. All things exist in wholeness, including the thought system that you made to protect the illusion you hold so dear. Your thought system is completely alien to the truth, but completely consistent as a system. You cannot abandon one tenet and retain another because by retaining part you retain all. This will lead to seeming failure to learn what I would have you learn. What God would have me teach, you cannot fail to learn, but neither can you learn of it in parts. The thought system of truth is as wholly consistent as the thought system of illusion, and you cannot take what you will and leave the rest. Thus we will continue to point out the differences in the two thought systems so that your ideas can begin to change, until finally your heart takes over and makes the one choice you are bound to make. Your heart—not to be confused with the pump that runs the body, but identified as the center of yourself—has no thought system separate from your own and must exist in the reality where you think you are.

10.4　The beginning of all transformation is at the source, and this is as true of illusion as of the truth. You see your body as your self, and your self as "source" of all that you have done and felt in all your days upon this earth. Yet your real Source is at the center of your Self, the altar to your Creator, the Self you share in unity with Christ. Christ is the "part" of God that resides in you, not in separation but in the eternal wholeness in which God and you together exist in truth.

10.5　For those of you who have been journeying long, as well as those of you just beginning, this abandonment of the body as your home and source of all you are is the greatest hurdle to overcome. As you observe the body and dare to think of life without it, you again and again encounter its reality. When its awareness begins to leave you is just when you may be beset by headaches, back pain, and other seeming maladies. This is the separated self that you have made calling you back to the body to prove to you that it is insurmountable. Many people at this point try to think these maladies away, and when they do not succeed they see this as further evidence of their entrenchment in the body. Beware all attempts to think the body away and to think miracles into existence. This desire merely shows you know not the source of healing and are not ready to be healed.

10.6　That you are not ready yet does not mean you will not be ready, just as having lost something does not mean it no longer exists. Yet your separated self would cite all evidence of its failure to be other than separate and be quick to point out to you the impossibility of being other than what you are—a body. This is the "fact" it whispers constantly in your ear, the lie that it would have you believe makes all else you would learn here as impossible as this. You listen to this voice because it has been your constant companion and teacher in your separation, not realizing that what it has taught you is to be separate. Be warned that it will constantly try to interfere as long as you place any merit in what it tells you.

10.7   Think of another, a teacher or a parent, whose "voice" you hear as you go through your days. Whether you want to hear this voice or not, whether this voice was wise or foolish, the very repetition of this voice keeps it in your memory. This may be the voice that says, "Stand up straight," or "You're special," or "You will never amount to anything." Many of you may have used therapy to still the negative messages that you hear, and after much effort succeeded at replacing what was negative with messages of a more positive nature. And these are but messages of an outside source! Your own thoughts are much more persistent and insistent than these. They have been with you longer and more constantly. Vigilance is needed to dislodge them.

10.8   I tell you this not to discourage you, but to encourage you not to give up. Your purpose now is the holiest possible and all of heaven is with you. All that is needed is your continuing willingness. All that can cause you to fail is giving up. I give you these examples that will make you say, "It will not be easy," but I tell you neither will it be hard if you but remember this: your willingness is all that is needed. When your separated self whispers to you, "Your body is but a fact," all you need tell yourself is, "I am still willing to believe otherwise."

10.9   Be aware also of your desire for reward. As you feel yourself becoming closer to God and your true Self, as you gain more awareness of yourself as a "good" person and one trying to be better still, you will begin to look for your rewards. Later you will look back upon this time and smile and laugh out loud at the innocence of these desires that but reveal that you stand merely at the beginning of the curriculum. To want a reward for goodness, for trying harder, for being closer to God than your brother or sister, are all desires of your separated self wanting something for itself and all its effort. This is but a stage you will pass through, though some may linger long here.

You will stay until you realize that all are good and that you cannot earn more of God's good graces than your brother. You will stay until you realize that God has given everything already to everyone.

10.10 Again but state your willingness. A willingness to believe that you have everything you need despite the "fact" that it does not seem so. Your willingness is all that is needed to move you through this stage and to the next. Be encouraged rather than discouraged that God does not grant all your desires here. For these are not yet your true desires, and the rewards you would choose here are as dust to those you will become aware of as you proceed.

10.11 Let us talk a moment here of miracles. Simply stated, miracles are a natural consequence of joining. Magic is your attempt to do miracles *on your own*. In the early stages of your learning, you will be tempted to play a game of make believe. You will not believe that you are not your body, but you would make believe that you are not. You may then be tempted to believe that because you are pretending you are not a body, you can pretend you do not feel the pain of a headache or the cold of a winter day, and this pretending may even make you feel a little less pain or a little less cold. But this attempt to fool yourself is welcomed by your separated self who knows pretending will not make it so.

10.12 These attempts to fool yourself are based on your lack of understanding rather than your lack of belief. You would not still be reading if you believed you were your body and that alone. Long have you known that there is more to you than flesh and bones. Belief is not your problem. Understanding is. While you believe in God, you do not understand God. While you believe in me, you do not understand how these words have come from me. While you believe in heaven and an afterlife, you do not understand what or where they are. And to believe in something that you do not understand makes you feel peculiar at the least and delusional at the worst. You want to believe and so you believe. But you also want to be "right" about what you believe. The convenient thing about your belief in God, in me, in heaven and in an afterlife is that you do not think you will be proven wrong here. If you are wrong, you will merely rot away after you have died and no one will know how wrong you were! If you are wrong, at least you believed in something that brought you comfort and in the end did you no harm.

10.13 This is not as easily said about the concept of not being separate, however. The only thing you find really difficult to believe is that you are in union with your brothers and sisters, right now, today. To believe in God without understanding God is one thing. To believe in your union with your neighbor without understanding either union or your neighbor is something else. This belief will not necessarily bring you comfort or do you no harm. What if you believe in the goodness of your neighbor and that belief is unwarranted? What if you are trusting and find that trust to be misplaced? What if you are simply naïve and are taken for a fool? What if you are wrong?

10.14 A similar fear strikes your heart when you consider giving up your belief in the body. To believe you are not your body while you walk around within it is something quite different than believing in God. Here all the proof available would say that you are wrong. All the proof of your eyes and ears, as well as that of science, would say you are your body. Even history would seem to prove this fact as you look back and say even Jesus died before he could rise again as spirit.

10.15 I am here to teach you once again because I was the example life. Do you believe that when I walked the earth I was a body, or do you believe that I was the Son of God before I was born into human form, during the time I existed in human form, and after I rose again? This is rightly called the mystery of faith: Christ has died, Christ has risen, Christ will come again. What is missing from this recitation? Christ was born. Nowhere in the mystery of faith is it stated that Christ became a body.

10.16 You have not been told that the body does not exist, only that it is not you. Like all tools you made, it is illusion because you have no need of tools. But while you believe you do, it is quite real to you. To give up the body entirely is a choice you need not make. As your learning advances you will see that this is possible, but there may be reasons not to choose this. At this point, however, all that is asked is that your body is seen as what it is—both in terms of what you made it for and in terms of the way in which you can now be guided to use it for the benefit of all.

10.17 The choice for many has seemed to be "Would you rather be right or happy?" Only the ego would choose being right over happiness. As you observe your body, also observe its actions in terms of the choices it makes. Ask yourself, "What choice may have led to this situation or event?" For choice is always involved *before* the fact. Nothing happens to the Son of God by accident. This observation will help to put the responsibility of your life back into your hands, where it belongs. You are not helpless, nor are you at the whim of forces beyond your control. The only force beyond your control is your own mind, and this need not be. When you begin to ask yourself, What choice might lead to happiness instead of this, you will begin to see a difference in your body's response to what appear to be external events, and then a change in the external events themselves.

10.18 Your mind might still prefer to be right rather than happy, so it is important that you let your heart lead in making this new choice. When you find yourself in a situation you do not like, again offer your willingness to find some happiness within it. These instructions to your heart will begin to make a difference to your state of mind.

10.19 What you would call your state of mind is more like a general atmosphere, an ambiance, a mood—and this setting is determined with your heart. The thoughts of your separated self care little for such as this and would call such concerns irrelevant to its well-being. Its survival *as it is* is its only concern. This is not just concern for needs such as food and shelter, but for survival of the thought system of the separated self. Happiness is not a priority here, but being right is quite important to it. It would prefer to be serious and heavy-hearted rather than light-hearted and gay. Being serious about life is a major strategy of the separated self, which recognizes its own seriousness as necessary to maintain its separation. Joy is truly the greatest threat to the separated self, for it comes from union and reinforces union's appeal at the expense of the appeal of separation.

10.20 You do not realize how quickly the separated self rushes in to sabotage all movement away from separation and toward union. Many of you have recognized that you seem to minimize your chances for happiness and maximize your chances for unhappiness through the choices you would make. You look back longingly at times of happiness and wonder what went wrong and why you could not maintain that happy state. There might be many practical reasons to cite for your happiness' demise, but in the loneliness that comes with its loss you will wonder, at least briefly, why the choice for practicality needed to be made. Yet if the separated self can look back and see that it chose being right over being happy, it will congratulate itself despite its unhappiness and say, "I did the right thing." It will see itself as victor over the foolish dreams of happiness and say how glad it is that it came to its senses before it was too late.

10.21   Each of you is aware of a threshold you would cross that leaves no route open for return. That threshold is often a happiness so fulfilling that once you have experienced it you say, "I will take this despair no more." For others this threshold is the opposite, an experience of pain so great that they would rather die than continue on in such a way. Addicts too but choose a different threshold wherein after experiencing the oblivion of the separated self through drugs, alcohol, or even constant work or shopping, they refuse to return to the separated self's reality. If they cannot leave it, they will block it out. Some, at this threshold, turn back. They deny themselves the joy or the pain or the oblivion that would make return impossible and count themselves lucky for not going to the place from which change would become inevitable.

10.22   The separated self is so ensconced in fear that the known fears of its existence seem preferable to the unknown fears of any other kind of existence. That an option could be chosen that leaves no room for fear at all does not occur to it, for the absence of fear is something it has never known.

10.23   If the body is the surface aspect of your existence and fear lies beneath the surface, see the advantage of this exercise: Place your body out in front of yourself where you can be its silent observer. As you watch your hands go about their work or the shadow form on the ground as you walk to and fro, you will be learning the only separation that can be useful to you.

10.24   Your first realization of significance will be that all you hear does not come through your ears. You will find that you are full of thoughts— thoughts *about* your body, the same kind of thoughts you might have of someone else's body. The difference will be that these thoughts will not seem to have originated in your head. You may realize for the first time or in a different way that you have always heard your thoughts without the benefit of your ears. You may be saying now, "Of course that is the way we hear our thoughts—it is the nature of thought." But have you ever before considered the nature of your thoughts, or have you merely taken them for granted?

10.25   Thoughts are not seen nor heard and yet they are with you constantly, and never more so than as you conduct your experiment in detachment from the body. This is why we conduct this experiment. Whether you term yourself successful or a hopeless failure at conducting this experiment, you will realize anew that your thoughts more accurately define who you are than your body does. Whether they wander aimlessly or are quite focused, your thoughts are more the source of all you are and all you do than is the body you observe.

10.26 You may laugh at yourself for taking part in this silly experiment, but you will realize the desire to laugh at yourself is quite genuine and not conceived from meanness. There will be a happier self who seems to think this game is rather fun, and who is not at all concerned with the game's success. This laughter too, as well as the sense of fun that prompted it, will come without the body's participation.

10.27 You will soon develop an ability to see without your body's eyes. This, too, will seem like a silly game at first, a trick of your imagination. You will, at first, observe only that which you can "see"— your arms and legs, your shadow falling as you walk—but more and more you will come to see the body as a whole. You will see it from behind as you follow it about its day, without, at first even being aware that this is happening. And you will find that as you observe, you are more aware of your surroundings, and more aware that your body is part of everything that is happening. There is your body and six more crossing the street. There is your body sitting at a desk in a building with many others. You will realize how seldom before you were aware of the street you walked down, of the buildings it traveled between, of the open sky above, of all the "others" traveling it with you. You will feel more a part of everything rather than less, and be surprised by this feeling.

10.28 Keep going now for this is but a beginning. Experiment, just for the fun of it, without allowing room for discouragement. This is not a test and you cannot fail. You are merely playing. Play at observing yourself from above. Can you look "down" upon yourself? And can you skip along and get in front to see your body coming toward you?

10.29 This body that you claim to be your "self" is but a form—how can it be that you can see it not?

10.30 What you will be feeling as you proceed is the feeling of the tunnel vision of the separated self giving way to the expanded vision of the unified Self. As you *feel* this happening, you will begin to be aware of feelings too that are not bound to the body. Like the thoughts you neither see nor hear with your body's eyes or ears, these feelings too will not depend upon your body's senses.

10.31 You will find quite a bit of resistance to this experiment. You will find you are too serious to play this game and that you have better things to do. Yet as much as you resist, the idea has been planted and you will find yourself, at times that seem to be "against your will," participating in it despite your determination not to do so. Once you begin to feel the effects of the experiment you will also encounter fear, especially if you take the game too seriously. There will be times when you will not want to laugh when the urge to do so comes upon you, and other times that after the slightest moment of expanded vision you will welcome back your tunnel vision with gratitude. You will feel relieved that your feet still touch the ground and that the boundary of your body is still intact. But you will remember the urge to laugh gently at yourself and the expanded vision as well. You will remember that for a moment your body did not seem to be a boundary that kept you contained within its limitations. Then you will remember that this is but a Course in remembering and that memory is the language of the heart.

10.32 Many of you will rebel here thinking this is not what you signed on for. You just want to read about this Course, perhaps, and not be required to take it. You will want to keep it theoretical and not apply it. You will ask for the information, and say you would really rather not have the experience. You wanted but the travelers' guide and not the actual journey. This is what too many of you sought, and many of you still resist realizing that you got more than you bargained for. A door has been reached, a threshold crossed. What your mind still would deny your heart cannot. A tiny glimmering of memory has returned to you and will not leave you to the chaos you seem to prefer. It will keep calling you to acknowledge it and let it grow. It will tug at your heart in the most gentle of ways. Its whisper will be heard within your thoughts. Its melody will play within your mind. "Come back, come back," it will say to you. "Come home, come home," it will sing. You will know there is a place within yourself where you are missed and longed for and safe and loved. A little peace has been made room for in the house of your insanity.

CHAPTER 11
Free Will and Willingness

11.1   The exercises in this Course of Love are few, and they are contained within the Course itself rather than separated from it. There are but a few reasons for this method. The first is your attitude toward instruction, and the fact that you do not really desire it. What you desire is what cannot be given from anywhere but your own Source. Again you realize this aspect of creation, and it has helped to solidify your stance against union and your lack of desire for instruction. This is due to your confusion about your source. All of your fierce determination to hang on to your individuality stems from this confusion. If your "source" were truly your body and the brain that causes it to function, then you would indeed be required to learn things *on your own*, for all true learning must come from your Source.

11.2   You think your source and your Creator are two separate things, and too seldom remember even that you are not your own creator. You have made this separation based on the idea that what created you cannot be one with you. Again this only points to your lack of recognition of what creation really is. And yet when you would practice creativity you realize it is a celebration of the creator—and when you honor artists of all kinds you honor but this fact. Every poem bears the mark of its creator, as does each work of art you would gaze upon and call a masterpiece, as well as those creations of little hands you hang on refrigerator doors or office walls. You did not create your Self, and yet you make of life a re-creation of yourself and in so doing try to prove that "you" are your own source.

11.3   This is one reason you do not like the idea that those who would instruct you know more than you now know, and why you begin each new course of learning by feeling as if you have less. You then begin your attempts to acquire what you lack, so that you no longer have less than anyone else. Some of you may be confident in your learning skills and rush in to conquer this new territory as you have others that have come before. These would read each book as quickly as they can, with highlighter in tow, and when they have turned the last page be done with learning what this book would have to teach and rush on to the next. Those of you less confident may quit before you begin in order to keep from failing one more time. Even those who feel the power of these words within their hearts and vow to go slowly and carefully through each page and section, giving total dedication to what this text would have them do, are at risk of trying too hard to be earnest rather than simply desiring to learn.

11.4   Each one of these risks I have sought to limit by limiting the exercises to a simple few that will stay with you when all hurrying, fear of failing, and earnest attempts at trying hard have long been past. Each exercise is but an idea, and ideas leave not their source. All ideas here are but ideas of union come to replace ideas of separation. This will happen of its own without your understanding as long as you remain willing for the ideas to dwell within you, and you do not try to shut them out. Realize that the ideas of both success and failure are detrimental here. To feel you have achieved success in learning what love is all about is as ridiculous as feeling as if you have failed to learn what love is. Neither can happen. And your perception that either can will shut out all ideas of union.

11.5   What love is cannot be taught. Remember that your task here is to remove the barriers that keep you from realizing what love is. That is the learning goal of this Course—your awareness of what love is—and no earthly course can take you beyond this goal. It is only your willingness that is required.

11.6   Willingness must thus be talked about and separated from what you would have it be. Willingness and faith go together. What you have faith in, you will see. This Course asks for your willingness to have faith in something new. You have placed your faith in what you have made, and while it remains there you remain unwilling to relinquish illusion's hold on you. You can be faithful to but one thought system. One is the thought system of the separated self and is based on separation. The other is the thought system of creation and is based on union. Your faith in what you have made has been shaken now, and you realize you would like to place your faith elsewhere. You would like to, but you have your doubts, and this is where you become confused on the issue of willingness.

11.7   Willingness does not arise from conviction but brings conviction. Willingness is your declaration of openness, not necessarily of firm belief. You see free will and willingness together and while they are the same, their application is quite different.

11.8   Your free will you guard most closely, knowing this is what made the separation possible. You regard it as your one protection from God, the one thing that allows you to be other than what God would have you be. It is your "God given" right of independence, that which allowed you to leave God's side the way a child reaching the age of adulthood has the right to leave her parents' home.

11.9   To think you must protect anything from God is insane, and you know that this is so. But because you view free will as all you have that God cannot take away from you, you have not yet given up its protection. It does not matter to you that it is insane to think that He who has given you everything seeks to take anything away from you. While you still view yourself as a body, you cannot help but think of God as a vengeful God whose final vengeance is your own death. While you still think of your self as a body, it is easier to accept that your banishment from paradise was God's decision, not your own. You think you can be grateful to Him for some things and blame Him for others. Yes, perhaps this God you think you know has given you everything, but He can also take it all away, and in the end He surely will. He then will judge you and determine if you should be rewarded for a life of goodness or punished for a life of evil. He might accept you back, but He might not. A God such as this would seem to have little faith in you and to deserve little of your faith in return.

11.10   And so you give to God a little faith and cherish your free will, the true god of the separated self. You think at times that this was God's mistake, the one weakness in His plan, and one that you would use. At other times you think that this was but God's curse on you, a thing to tempt you to the life of desperation that you live. But your strongest perception of your free will is of its power. No matter what God wants of you, you can use your free will to rebel and to make your own choices, choices different than those your Creator would make for you. This right to make your own decisions, and the power to flaunt them before God, is all that makes your little separated self feel powerful at all.

11.11 You do not see that what you choose to do with your free will matters not to God at all, for what you have chosen to use it for is the one thing that it cannot provide —your separation from your Creator. He remains as He is, as you remain as you are.

11.12 It is true that your free will is powerful as it is part, but only part, of what has allowed you to believe in your separated state. While you could have used your free will to create like unto your Father, by choosing to make yourself separate from Him—something that could never truly occur—you have chosen instead to do nothing at all with your free will but make this one insane choice. Your willingness to make a new choice is what will once again make your free will like unto your Father's will, which is one with it in truth.

11.13 Your protectiveness of your free will is why we must separate willingness from your perception of free will. Your free will is the last bastion of your separate army, the final line of defense, the site where the final battle will take place. Before this final battle is reached your willingness to change your mind about its need to be fought is what is desired by your Father and this Course.

11.14 God will never wrestle your free will from you, or fight battles to win it for Himself. This final battle is in your own mind, and it is a figment of the illusions you have made. Let this prophecy you have made go, and realize that willingness does not negate free will. Yet even while you cannot yet quite give up your guardianship of it, it is sufficient to begin with a temporary choice, though a lasting choice will be required before you will feel the shift of cause and quit worrying about effect. For now what you desire are effects, without realizing cause must shift to change the effects you would have come about. This matters not at this point. You are offered the opportunity to make a temporary decision that can be rescinded at any time. Your temporary willingness will be enough to begin to effect cause and in so doing bring some sanity to your restless mind and heart.

11.15 What willingness is it that you are asked to give? It can come in many manners and be given many forms. It can be called a willingness to change your mind, or to allow yourself to be open to new possibilities. It can be called a change of heart, or a willingness but to, for a little while, withdraw your fear and your protection from it. But what this willingness really does is allow your call to be sounded, your call to love and to be loved. It is a willingness to receive love from your Source and to be loved for who you are. Is this so much to ask?

11.16 It is a call that comes not from weakness but from strength, and that goes out to truth and not illusion. It is a call whose answer will come to you quickly on the wings of angels, a fluttering your heart will feel, for angels too are one with you. It may feel like loneliness compounded for the brief instant you await its coming and feel the emptiness that has been opened for its coming.

11.17 This is a call that requires you to do nothing but to remain faithful to it. You do not need to think about it, but only let it be. You need put no words on it, for words cannot express it any more than words can teach you what love is—or that love is. You need not concentrate on where to find love, for love will find you. You need not concentrate on giving love, for you cannot give what you do not yet know, and when you know it you need not give it, for it will extend from you naturally in miracles called love. Love is all that will fill your emptiness, and all that will never leave you empty again as it extends from you to your brothers and sisters. Love is all that will not leave you wanting. Love is all that will replace use with unity.

11.18 You exist, quite simply, because of your relationship with love. Love is the unity you seek. In having chosen separation over unity, you but chose fear over love. When you let go of fear and invite unity to return, you but send out an invitation to love and say *you are welcome here*. What is a dinner party where love is not? It is merely a social obligation. But a dinner party where love is welcomed to take its place becomes a celebration. Your table becomes an altar to the Lord and grace is upon it and the Lord is with you.

CHAPTER 12

Origin of Separation

12.1 The word *love* is part of your problem with this Course. If I were to take the word love and change it to some sophisticated-sounding technical term, and say this is the stuff that binds the world together in unity, it would be easier for you to accept. If I were to say you know not of this sophisticated term and this is why you have believed in your separation rather than in your unity with all things, you would be far more likely to nod your head and say, "I was but ignorant of this, as was everyone else." If a scientist were to tell you that a benign energy had been found that proved your connection to everything in the universe, and gave it some fancy name, you would say, "A new discovery has been found and I am willing to believe it may be true, especially if others are also going to believe it to be true."

12.2 You feel a little duped at being told love is the answer. You feel a little chastised to be told you know love not. You feel a little deceived to think that love may not be limited to what you have thought it to be. You think it is typical of a spiritual text to tell you love is the answer, as if it has not been said before. This message was preached long ago and still the world remains the same. How could this be the correct answer when this is so? Life is too complicated to be solved by love.

12.3 How quickly you would return to cynicism and to believing you have already tried and failed. For all of you believe that you have tried this idea called love, and all of you believe you have evidence that it is not the answer at all. What is your evidence? Your own failure to be happy and the unhappiness of the world you see.

12.4 We have said before the only meaning possible for your free will is your choice of what to join with and your choice of what to leave outside of yourself. Yet you must understand that nothing that is not part of God is worthy of joining, nor *can* join with you. What you have sought to join with is the reason for your unhappiness. For you seek to join with what cannot be joined, and you seek separation from all that could be joined with you and all that would fill your dark and lonely places with the happiness you seek.

12.5   This Course may seem to have come far astray from what you would have it do, for you are looking for something specific from it, though you know it not. You are looking for the rest and quiet joy that only comes from love. You are looking for the safety and security of a loving home, even if it is one only of philosophy. You look for the soft assurance of certainty, not of your mind but of your heart. There is a part of you that thinks, *"If I could just be sure..."* and stops there, for you are not even sure of what it is you seek assurance. And yet you know what tires you most is your inability to be certain of anything. And you are tired indeed.

12.6   God's will for you is happiness, and of this you can be certain. To align your will with God's is but to make this certain state your home. This is but a wish come true, and when it is all you wish for it will come to be. And in the granting of this wish will come your rest and the laying down of every heavy burden you have carried.

12.7   Admit now your desire to rest, a desire that could make you weep and make you wish to sleep an endless sleep. If you but understood the energy required to keep the world of your illusion in its place, you would understand the rest that will simply come of giving up your need to do so. Your desire for certainty is part of your resistance to any ideas that seem to be about change. What little that you think you know you would strive to keep, and yet deep down you realize that you know nothing with the certainty you seek.

12.8   Uncertainty of any kind is doubt about your self. This is why this Course aims to establish your identity, for from it all the rest will come. As such, this Course seems to ask for change at every level, and yet from one change alone will all the others follow—and through no effort on your part at all. And even this one change is not a change at all, for it merely seeks to remove all the changes you but think that you have made to God's creation. This change seeks but to restore you to your Self.

12.9   Your Self rests totally unchanged within the Christ in you. Re-establishing your relationship with your brother is what will show your Self to you. You have one brother who wears but many faces in your perception of who he is, and while you know him not you cannot know your Self. This one brother can unite you with all whom you perceive as others, for all others are one with him as well as you. This is the one joining that needs to occur to bring about all the rest.

12.10 This is the one disjoining that your choice for separation brought about, and it is but a separation from your Self. This is the most difficult point to get across, because in it lies a contradiction, the one contradiction that has created the world you see and the life you live. Although it is impossible for something to have gone wrong in God's creation, something has gone wrong! All you need do is look about you to know that this is so—and, rather than be discouraged by this news, you breathe a sigh of relief because you knew this to be true and yet have felt as if this is the secret that has been kept from you. It is as if you are told endlessly "everything is fine" while you know this is not true. And if "everything" is fine, it must just be you who are all wrong.

12.11 All of creation seems to hum along in perfect harmony. The stars light up the sky, the sun and moon do what they were appointed to do, the animals of the sea, ground, and air are but what their Creator bade them be, the mountains stand in all their majesty, rivers flow and desert sands countless in number are blown endlessly about. Everything seems to be what it is and what it has always been, but for, perhaps, the mark of man upon it. Yet the moon remains the moon despite man's landing on it. The earth remains the earth despite your highways, roads and bridges. And somewhere you know not, peace remains peace despite your wars, and happiness remains happiness despite your despair.

12.12 Yet what of you? You, too, seem to have remained the same for countless ages. Perhaps you believe that long ago you evolved from a form different than that which you inhabit now; but certainly within the laws of evolution, you have changed as little as the birds of the air or fish of the sea. Yet somehow you know that in all of creation, it is humanity alone that somehow is not what it was meant to be. On a lovely day and in a lovely place you can see that creation's paradise still exists, but nowhere can you find the being God created in His image.

12.13 Does it make any sense at all that this would come to be? Or that once upon a time there walked upon the earth those who did reveal God's image, and that when they ceased to be seen here God's image was lost to earth forever? Could even one have come and gone and left this void forever more unfilled? A gaping hole within the universe itself?

12.14 But one was needed to end the separation, and in this one are all the rest joined. For what alone in all creation could be affected by your free will but your own self? But one was needed to, of his own free will, join his will with his Father's for it to be done for all. This is all correction or atonement means, and all that is in need of your acceptance. Join your brother who made this choice for all, and you are reunited with the Christ in you.

12.15 Joined minds cannot think separately and have no hidden thoughts. They are, in fact, not minds in the plural at all, but all-one-mind. What this Course is saying is that at some point that does not exist in time, God's son made the choice for separation. Whether God's son had one form or many at that time matters not, for one form or many, there was still one mind, the mind of God's son joined in unity with that of his Father. Many of you have been taught this mystery of faith. Father, Son, and Holy Spirit are One. If you had indeed learned what you were taught, the separation would be no more.

12.16 These words, *Father, Son, and Holy Spirit*, like the word *love*, are but symbols representing ideas that represent what is. That you have made of the Father a singular figure, somehow greater than the Son, and accepted the Holy Spirit as something largely not within your understanding, only exemplifies the nature of the error in need of correction. While words, as symbols, cannot fully explain what cannot be symbolized, a beginning is made that must be completed through the memories of your heart. So we continue, realizing that these words can express the truth only within their ability as symbols, and that farther than where these symbols can take you, the truth lies within your Self.

12.17 You have all seen the way a thought that seems to arise out of nowhere can affect you. An idea, birthed one day, does not seem to have been there the day before. Perhaps it is the idea of taking a trip or having a baby, of returning to school, or quitting a job. This idea, newly birthed, may seem to come and go, or may grow into an obsession, but either way, it leaves not its source. And without the birth of the idea, the results of the idea would not come to be. You may have a thousand ideas one day and ten thousand the next, so many that you could never keep track of them all, and yet they still exist within you and do not splinter off and become something on their own apart from you. Imagine this occurring and you will see how senseless this situation would be. Could a trip happen on its own? To whom would it happen?

12.18 You may very well say, however, that an idea seemed to take on a life of its own and compel you to do things you might have never dreamed of doing. People often look back upon their lives and wonder how they got from here to there, and some may see that one idea took root and changed what seemed to be a destiny already written.

12.19 As near as words can describe the separation, this is what occurred: An idea of separation entered the mind of God's son. Like any idea of yours, this idea did not leave its Source nor change the essence of its Source in any way. While the idea of taking an adventurous vacation when brought to fruition might reshape the life of the one participating in it, it would not change who that person was, or who his father was, or the nature of the family he was born into. All that would change would be the shape of his life, the things that would happen within it, perhaps the places in which it would occur or the people that would be part of it. In short, the external aspects of the life.

12.20 From the idea of separation came the idea of an external aspect of life. Before the idea of the separation, there was no such thing—and there still is no such thing except as an extension of the original idea. Just as we discussed your desire to protect or to control proceeding from the concept of fear, and realized that without fear they would not exist, so too is it with the external aspect of life. Without the original idea of separation, the external aspect of life would not exist. Just as fear is not real although it seems to be, separation is not real although it seems to be.

12.21 The Father did not prevent the idea of separation from taking place, and could not any more than you could prevent an idea from occurring to you. Just as an idea of yours, once born, continues to exist, so too, did this idea of separation. But just as your ideas do not take on a life of their own even though they at times seem to, this idea as well had no ability to be more than what it was, *except* for as the son chose to participate in it.

12.22 Thus, the son's participation in the idea of separation seemed to bring about a completely reshaped life, a destiny different than that which had already been written. Yet this participation could not but proceed from the original idea and could not proceed in reality but only in the external aspect of life that preceded it. The idea of separation changed nothing in reality, but became a drama acted out upon a stage so real that it seemed to be reality.

12.23 Separation is painful only to those who believe it can occur in truth. What would a child's rejection or a parent's death mean to those who did not believe in separation? Do you believe that God believes in separation? He knows it not, and because He knows it not, it does not exist. Because He knows it not, He has not been hurt by it. He knows no rejection and no death. He knows no pain or sorrow. His son remains with him in his eternal home, joined with him as always in eternal completion.

12.24 Yet while the son's extension into an external world is quite real, it is all that is truly real within it. The son could not create unlike the Father who created everything by extension of Himself. Neither the Father's extension, nor the Son's, lessened Father or Son in any way. Replace the word Father with the word Creation and see if this does not help to make this concept clear. Could Creation's continuing extension of itself, its continuing creation, make less of it than what it started out to be? What we call Father is but creation's heavenly face, a personification of what cannot truly be personified. You find it hard to believe Creation itself can be benevolent and kind, or just another name for love, but such it is. God is but creation's starting point, the creator of creation and yet Creation itself. The Son and Holy Spirit, like unto Creation, proceeded from the starting point of God. God is the Son and Holy Spirit's starting point as well, the Creator of the Son and Holy Spirit, yet He also *is* the Son and Holy Spirit.

12.25 Now, carry this pattern forward, for the pattern of God's extension is the pattern of creation and thus the pattern of the universe. The Son extended himself into creation, and you are that extension and as holy as is he. The idea of separation only seems to have made God's son susceptible to division, and these word symbols are all that seem to separate Father, Son, and Holy Spirit from Creation or from each other.

CHAPTER 13

Observation and Experience

13.1   You will never fully *understand* what unity means, but you will come to *feel* what unity means, and this I promise you. This is what we work toward in this Course, for once you have experienced the *feeling* of unity, you will need no understanding of it. This is all the exercises that call you to observe your body are for. They are the preparation for what is to come: the preparation for feeling that which is not of your body. Our next exercise takes this one step further, and is merely an extension of the first. In this exercise you will begin to realize that your brothers and sisters are not their bodies, any more than you are yours. This is a natural extension of observing your body in action, because as your body seems to interact with others and as you observe this interaction, you will "see" yourself and others in a new light. Your body will seem more connected with those of the others it interacts with, for they will be grouped together in your observation of them. It will not be only others you observe but yourself and others, placing you and "them" together where you belong. This seeming togetherness of bodies is just a first step that will take you beyond the illusion of bodies to togetherness of spirit.

13.2   As you observe, always with your heart and not your mind, and begin to include others in your observation, I ask you to concentrate on one thing only. This is a simple exercise, and enjoyable too. It but calls for you to ask one thing: Ask yourself what you already know of the spirit of the person you observe. You will be amazed at the knowledge you already have and the joy it brings you to remember it.

13.3   These are but exercises in memory recollection, and the more you practice them the more true memory will return to you. Do not apply any effort to these exercises, particularly not that of recalling spirit. Just let impressions come to you, and when they make you feel like smiling know that you are feeling memory return. If, when trying to call up memory of spirit, you find your brow knitting in concentration, you are applying effort and need to cease attempting the exercise at that time. If you give this exercise just the tiniest bit of consistent practice, however, it will soon become routine to you, for you will want to continuously experience the pleasure that it brings.

13.4   While you may desire to put what you feel into words, this exercise is not about putting words on feelings or using them to describe spirit. It is best to leave words off this experience as, if you do not, you will soon be ascribing some attributes to one spirit and not to another, just to differentiate between them. The purpose here is to show you that they cannot be differentiated or compared or defined in the same way you have defined their bodies in the past.

13.5   You will soon find that what you recall of spirit is love. You will want to give it many names at first, and might not even recognize it as love, for it will come without all the longing and sadness you so often associate with it. While the feeling of love that washes over you from one may feel like courage, and from another like gentleness, and while this is all part of what you are encouraged to feel, it is simply asked that you let the feelings come and with them the realization that while no two spirits will seem exactly the same, they also are not "different." The love from each will fill you with happiness because it is already complete and has no needs and so no sense of longing or sadness of any kind. Because it is complete, it will ask nothing of you, but will seem to offer you a warm welcome, as if you are a long lost friend returning home.

13.6   And so you are. This is the new "proof" that, while not scientific or verifiable, will offer you the evidence you seek to confirm the truth of what you are being told here. All that is required to gather this new evidence is to trust in your own heart. Are you willing to believe what your heart would tell you?

13.7   This exercise should take no time nor break your stride or the flow of your conversation. All it asks you to do is to become aware of spirit and to allow this awareness to abide within you. If you feel resistance to attempting this exercise, remember that you already know that you are more than your body, and ask yourself if it makes sense to not do all you can to become aware of the "more" you know you are.

13.8   While you will not realize it at first, because you have no experience but only memory of feeling yourself in such a way, you will eventually realize that the memories you recall of the spirit of others include memories that are your own, memories that are of your own Self. For no spirit exists that is not part of you, or you of it. If you find yourself distracted by these memories, do not push them aside as interruptions in your day, but know that anything that distracts you from the little self you think you are is worth the minutes you would give to its contemplation.

13.9   What further objections can you have, for here we ask you not to follow any instruction other than that of your own Self? We invite the return of what you know, and let your real Self guide you gently back to where you want to be and already are in truth.

13.10 Your ego will strongly resist your attempts to listen to your heart, and will call this every kind of foolishness, a waste of time that could be spent on better things. Yet time is not required, nor is money or the use of any other thing you value. And there is not even the slightest chance of being made to look foolish by what you are asked to do.

13.11 Might some of your preconceived notions of others and yourself be shattered? Oh yes, and rightly so. Gladly will you let them go and, if you trust yourself, all the evidence against your brother that you have stored up in your lifetime will be let go as well.

13.12 Each of you will initially find it difficult to accept the innocence and sinlessness of others and yourself, for your memory will contain no hint of past misdeeds, errors or mistakes. No one will have leveled any hurts on you or anyone else. No reason for guilt will exist within this memory. No shame or fear is here, and no grievances of any kind. For here forgiveness is already accomplished—and when memory of forgiveness returns to you, can memory of your Father or your own Self be far behind?

Chapter 14

Special Relationships, Earthly and Human

14.1   The purpose of the life you share here with your brothers and your sisters has been to challenge God's creation. Now your united purpose must change to that of remembering who you are *within* God's creation, rather than in the world that you have made. Think but a minute of this, and you will begin to see the enormity of the difference in these two purposes.

14.2   Is it not true that you have made an enemy of creation? Do you feel part of it and at one with all within it? If not, you have made yourself creation's enemy. You seek to be different from all the rest, and in this seeking proclaim that one part of creation is better than another part. You thus seek to fragment creation as you have fragmented your own self. And from the vantage point you have established in which you view yourself as the epitome of God's creation, you see the rest of creation as being meant to serve your ends. And since your *end* or goal is that of separation and being different from all the rest, this is the goal you ask creation to bow down to, a goal that never can be achieved any more than can your separation from what you think is unlike you.

14.3   You cannot have feelings of superiority and not an enemy make. The same occurs when you would make yourself inferior, and you are always making for yourself a place at one of these extremes. And all this effort and conflict arises simply from your insistence upon being separate. He who is your enemy you cannot help but be at war with. Where there is war there can be no peace. War is not simply the existence of external activity. External activity is but the effect of a cause that remains internal, and all war is but war upon yourself.

14.4   Do you not see how your notion of heaven being an attainment you can reach only after death fits your goal of separation? If your belief in heaven were true, your challenge to creation would be real and only your death would prove the victor. For if after death your creator God provided you with a paradise not of this world, a separate place to honor your specialness and separation from all else that He created, then would you be vindicated and the purpose of your war made holy. You would be proven right and creation wrong.

14.5 Would this make sense? What creator would create a world in which the highest achievement of the life upon it would be to leave it in order to gain life? What creator would create a world not meant to exist in harmony? Harmony is life. What creator would create a temporary life and hold eternal life as a reward for death?

14.6 If you can see the senselessness of a creator and a creation such as this and still believe in it, then you must believe in a god who is insane. You— who pride yourself on reason and practicality—think if a creation such as this could contain any reason whatsoever. Why then do you believe in it?

14.7 You who have made a god of reason and of intellect, think carefully now of what your reason and your intellect have made for you. How terrible would it really be to realize that although you have tried mightily, a creation such as this cannot be made to make any sense at all? Those who have turned their backs on God and refused to believe in such nonsense have simply refused to make reason try to fit the unfitable without seeing that an alternative exists.

14.8 You are not asked to believe the unbelievable, or to disregard all that reason would say to you. Only the opposite is true. You are asked rather to give up the laws of chaos for the laws of reason. The laws of illusion for the laws of truth.

14.9 Think you not that reason opposes love, for love gives reason its foundation. The foundation of your insane world is fear. The foundation of Heaven, your true home, is love. The same world based upon these different foundations could not help but look quite different.

14.10 Your ideas of love, however, fit your goal of separation as neatly and conveniently as does your idea of heaven. For what you require of love is that it set you apart and make you special. Much more is demanded of those you love than of any of your other brothers and sisters. The *more* that is required is all to feed your idea of your own specialness. You look for constant verification that this one you love loves you in return, and if this attention is not provided you feel you have cause for claiming wounds that cannot be healed and reparations that cannot be paid. You thus hold the one you love the most in the greatest bondage, and call that bondage a relationship.

14.11 This can be most clearly seen in relationships that were once "everything" to you and have since failed you. This can be a memory of any relationship, and each of you has one. It can be of parent and child, of best friends, of a marriage or a partnership, or even that of a mentor or student. Whatever the relationship's configuration, it was one that truly brought you joy. Within it you were happy and felt as if you needed nothing more than this. It was a relationship so intense that at its peak you would have begun to see its continuation without change as the major goal of your life. Without it, life would not be worth living, and so it was necessary to retain it at all cost.

14.12 This is a classic example that reveals much to you about yourself and the world you have made if you are but willing to look at it with eyes that truly see. It is the magnifying glass that will allow you to see your world in all its mad confusion. For what caused you such great joy seemed to come at the cost of pain and to leave you more alone and comfortless than before. How could this be said of love? And how could it have failed you so? And how, if it were real—as it surely felt as if it was—could it prove anything but that love is no answer, and surely not for you?

14.13 We must begin with what is obvious, a simple point that some of you have denied and that some of you could not. What makes this relationship stand out in your mind and feel so painful in your memory of it is that it was quite real in a way that is different from your relationships before or since. No other relationship affected you in such a way. Never were you more sure of a relationship's value to you. Anything that could make you feel so joyous, so safe and warm and loved, could not help but hold a value quite beyond compare. In this you were correct. It was no illusion that caused you to feel this way. This was not the love that passes for love in this world, but something else entirely. For at least one brief moment, this was true love, for nothing but love can be the cause of joy, nor offer a haven of safety in an insane world.

14.14 It is your response to love that concerns us now, for the return of love is coming and you do not want to make the same response again.

14.15 Everything that you consider valuable you want to keep. This makes perfect sense to you because the foundation of your world is fear. Were the foundation of your world love, everything that you consider valuable you could not wait to share. Perhaps you think the desire to keep things for yourself stems from something other than fear. You might call this desire pride or security, or even accept that it is vanity, before you would call it fear. But fear is what it is.

14.16 Only fear breeds the feelings of lack that stand with it, the cornerstone of the foundation of your separate world. You do not realize that you have created a universe for yourself, a universe that you are required to maintain, and that without your effort would dissolve. This universe is yourself and you are everything in it. Do you not believe that were you to perish something quite unique would be lost to the world? You are alone and irreplaceable: one of a kind. Within you lie all that you would hope to contribute and create. Within the actions and interactions of your lifetime lie all the effects you would hope to have on what remains here. Without you, the people and the events that you would influence, would behave quite differently and bring about different results than are somehow meant to occur. Although you know not your purpose, at least a part of you believes that this is true, for there must be some reason for your existence—although you cannot quite imagine what that reason might be. You must be meant to be because you are, and you cannot fathom that you would exist at all if there were not a reason for you to do so.

14.17 Is this not a description of a universe? What is a universe but itself and everything in it? Nothing would seem to exist outside of it, and so it must be unique. Everything that would happen within the universe would depend upon it.

14.18 You think that you are quite aware of your small space within the universe, and that it is foolishness to say that you think otherwise. Yet, since only what you know is part of your universe, do you not see that it depends on you, and if it depends on you that it is you? Only what you are aware of exists in the universe that is you. Only what happens to you affects your universe. Your universe is completely different than anyone else's and completely self-contained. The laws of your universe are for the maintenance of your body, because without it you would not exist. And when you cease to exist, so does your universe. The lights will be turned out upon it and it will be no more.

14.19 What a big job you have assigned yourself! It is no small wonder that you live in fear when so much is dependent upon you. And no wonder that when you find a respite, a place of rest and beauty and of love, you want to claim it for your own lest it get away! It too must be maintained within your universe, or you will know it not and its benefits will escape and be lost to you. You wish that you could join with it and make it one with you, but since you know not that this can be done or how to do it, you try to accomplish the "next best thing" and keep it close to you, a twin universe still existing separately, but close enough that you can gaze upon it and feel the benefit of its warmth because of its proximity. More than this you cannot do, but still you try. With chains you would bind this separate universe to your own, for as long as it maintains its autonomy, which it must, even its nearness is not enough. And so what you attempt next is an exchange of sorts. Like two countries, one rich in oil, another in grain, you set up dependencies that will keep you linked. Some of you do this quite obviously, and over years and years create a web of intricate design, a snare or trap that seems impossible to dismantle because of its interconnections. Others experience this plan of entrapment solely in their mind as they plot and plan for what they never have the opportunity to put into place. Still others are more coy in their design, and dress it up to look like sacrifice and gifts given, but all with the same purpose in mind. What none realize is that fear has replaced love.

14.20 Some may realize that they are afraid of losing love, and even speak of it and try to alleviate the fear with official commitments, pledges and promises made. Others may deny their fear, and say they trust in what they have and the faithfulness of the one they love. Fewer than these are those who do not need to voice their faith and trust, for their feelings remain strong despite their fear. For even those who fear no deception must remain afraid of the great deceiver. Whether they call it life or death, it is still the same. It is the chance that cannot be foreseen but is always there: death may take their loved one prematurely, and if not prematurely certainly eventually.

14.21 And all of these, those who would admit to fear, and those who would not, would still believe that love exists despite fear's claim upon it, and think that they are lucky to have found a love to shield them for a little while from all the other things they fear. And yet the greatest fear of all is that of loss of love. You who have given everything to be alone and separate fear most of all that which you have given everything to attain. For what is loss of love but confirmation of your separate state? What is loss of love but being left alone?

14.22 Loss of love comes from only one source. Call it fear or call it separation but it is still the same. For in your separated state you ask that love make you special to someone else, and that one special to you. You think this is what love is for, and so you make of it something it is not and only call it love.

14.23 Heaven can only be made to seem to fit your goal of separation, and the same is true of love. You cannot change what love is or what heaven is. All that seems to make it change is the function or purpose you would give it. It is but you who gave heaven the purpose of giving you something to look forward to, a reward for a life lived according to your own rules, a reward to be gained by some and not by others, a pinnacle of achievement that will prove your rightness and your success after you are gone. Love you give the same purpose, but bid it do the job of rewarding you here and now. It, like heaven, is your proof that you are good and worthy, special and to be rewarded for your specialness.

14.24 You have thus placed love and heaven together in a parody of creation's meaning of each. Yes, they go together, and this you know; but the purpose of neither is what you have ascribed it to be. The purpose you give each thing within your world is what makes it what it is to you. And as each purpose you have ascribed to anything proceeds from the foundation of fear that built your world, each purpose is as senseless and as reversed from the truth as is the next.

14.25 This is why this Course cannot just talk of love and bring you any closer to it than you are. While you realize not the purpose of anything in truth, you cannot know love or your own Self.

14.26 While your purpose remains to make yourself and others special, you will not put an end to the separation. And you cannot just let go of your own specialness. For as long as you hold on to the specialness of others you hold on to your own. There is no reason to hold on to another's specialness unless you hold onto your own. And what you give to others you keep for yourself. Give another specialness, and you keep it for yourself as well as see it in them instead of seeing their glory. Specialness keeps them separate, and therefore susceptible to loss. How can you lose what is one with you? You cannot. You can only lose that which is separate. And specialness does make separate.

14.27 This is the problem compounded in your "special" love relationships of having experienced real specialness, which is not specialness at all but glory. Your joining caused this, for each joining brings you in touch with your brother. Each joining returns you to your holy relationship with your brother, which is the only one you have in truth. Only this relationship is real, and in it are included all others. One does not discard or replace the other. What is real is all-inclusive. What is unreal is nothing.

14.28 You who do not know how to trade your separated state for that of union have still done so when you have loved freely and without fear. In this state your memory returns to you of who you are, and you are innocent and joyous and one with love itself. That this memory does not last, and these feelings seem unsustainable, is the result only of that which does discard and replace. As we have said before, there are but two emotions. One is love, the other fear. Fear, through your own choice, replaces and discards love. Fear is always strongest when you value something that you feel may be threatened. Love threatens most your specialness. Before your conscious mind has any awareness of what is happening, your memory of love, of innocence and of joy, threatens your specialness, your ego, your separated self who quickly rushes in with love's replacement. Nothing but fear could take the memory of love from you, or replace so quickly the glory that is your nature with the specialness that is not.

14.29 You think love is what you value most, and so resist any notion that what you view as love is not what you think it is. But as long as you equate love with the special ones on whom you choose to bestow it, you will know love not. What you will know is specialness, raised to the level of the Almighty and set upon His throne in a crown of jewels.

14.30 In your world love has no meaning unless it is attached to a partic- ular thing. And as soon as love is attached to a particular, love's opposite is brought into existence. While you refuse to look upon this simple fact, you have no hope of change, nor does your world. You who think, *"What harm can come of loving this one above all others?"* think again. For you are choosing not to love but to make special. And you are choosing but to make love's opposite real to you and those you claim to love, as well as those you claim not to love.

14.31 Let us ask instead how loving all as one can bring harm? If you love all the same, what loss is there to anyone, including the one you would choose to make special? All that is lost is specialness. This is the view of life you cannot imagine bringing about, or bringing joy in its coming. But this is what you must begin to imagine if you desire to accept love's coming instead of to reject it once again. For your refusal to give up specialness is your refusal of the Christ in you and a refusal of love itself.

CHAPTER 15

The Special Self

15.1   We have talked much now of your special love for others, but what of the specialness you desire for yourself? Do you not see how intricately linked these two desires are? The desire to give and receive specialness is the driving desire of your life, and the world you see but reflects this desire. Love's opposite would not exist but for your invitation of it. All hate, guilt, shame, and envy are but the result of your creation of an opposite to love through specialness. All the maladies of the current time as well as those of history would give way to love without the interference of all that would make special. You think issues of survival rule the world—and so they do, but they would not if it were not for your need to be special. Transportation would be transportation rather than a status symbol. Without a desire for specialness, a person would have no need for status at all. Beauty would be what it is and not what products would make it. Without a desire for specialness, a person would have no need for products at all. Wealth would be the happy state of everyone, for without specialness to feed, there would be neither want nor hunger. Without a desire for specialness there would be no war, for there would be no reason to break the peace. No land would be considered more sacred to some than others, no resources withheld, no people deemed subservient.

15.2   What harm is there in specialness? Only all the harm you see within the world.

15.3   While you desire specialness for yourself, your true Self will remain hidden and unknown, and since this is a Course that seeks to reveal your true identity, specialness must be seen for what it is so that you will desire it no longer. You can have specialness or your true Self, but never both. The desire for specialness is what calls your little self into being. This is the self that is easily wounded, the self that takes on grievances and refuses to give them up, the self that is prone to pettiness and bitterness, resentment and deception.

Be truthful as you examine yourself and you will see that this is so.

15.4   It is more difficult to see that this desire for specialness does not stop with what would bring misery to your own mind and heart. Perhaps the leader of some impoverished country brings misery to others with his desire for specialness, but not you. Yes, taken on a grand scale, you can see that this desire can wreak havoc; but still you would not believe that your own desire for specialness or to make another special could make a difference to many—or possibly even to anyone. You just want to love your mate and children, your parents or your friends, and would be quite content to have them think you special and to make them special to you. Out in the wider world you think you are anonymous and so are they. If within the small sphere of those they love they cannot be made to feel special—and you along with them —then what is the point of being here at all? For this is indeed the point you have made of your life.

15.5   And so within this small sphere you do what is necessary to maintain your specialness and that of the others within it. Depending on your culture what is necessary may mean few things, or many and different things for each one. From this sphere of influence comes your notions of success, your ideas of what is necessary to be good, your notions of what it means to treat others well. You would not be special to this one if you did not look a certain way, and you would not be special to that one if you did not earn a certain amount of money. You would not be special if you did not give this one certain gifts and opportunities, nor would you fulfill your responsibility of making this one special if you did not do so. To make one small change in this culture is difficult to impossible, because if you were to go your own way and choose your own look, lifestyle, or attitude, you might risk being seen as special within this group, and your choices might affect your ability to make others feel special in the way in which they have become accustomed to your doing so.

15.6   How many rest within this sphere of influence? Twenty, fifty, one hundred? And how many times is this multiplied by each of them? And yet this is but a fraction of who your specialness influences. In truth, your specialness affects everyone.

15.7   Your desire for specialness makes of you a slave to others and others to you. It diminishes your freedom, and for no end. For what others think of you does not make you special, nor does what you think or do for others make them special. All notions of popularity, success, and competition begin here. All notions of loyalty as well.

15.8 For now we come upon a linchpin in your plan for specialness—one of great necessity to overcome if you are to reach the learning goal this Course has set. Loyalty stems from faith, and where you set your faith is as much a determiner of your perception as is your concept of separation. All change seems to question your loyalty to others and all choices are made with this loyalty in mind. Loyalty stems here from your faith in fear and all from which you need protection. To belong to a loyal group, a family or community of supporters, is seen as necessary for your safety. While many of you do not have this, you strive for it, and its attainment has been the cause of much suffering in your world. This banding together for support against fear simply makes fear real, and the seeming cause for loyalty essential.

15.9 Your concept of loyalty is what makes it difficult for you to entertain withdrawing your effort to manifest the specialness of others and yourself. *Making special* seems to be a responsibility you have undertaken, and a refusal to *make special* an act of disloyalty. What's more, when all is said and done, you are loyal not only to your group but to humanity itself. Despite the many ills that have made you and those you love suffer, to call into question humanity's right to specialness seems the ultimate act of disloyalty to your own kind. To even think that you could change and be unlike others of your kind, you would call an act of treachery. To give your allegiance to your Father and to the learning goals this Course has set is but an act of treason upon the world as you know it.

15.10 And so it is. And so must your faith and loyalty be placed in something new, something worthy of your diligence and something that will not leave behind your brothers and your sisters to a life of suffering and of sin.

15.11 All suffering and sin comes from specialness, and so it is but specialness you must leave behind. And there is a way to do so, a way that will not harm any of those you love even while betraying all they would hold dear. But which would you rather betray? The truth or illusion? You cannot be loyal to both, and herein lies your problem. For at the turning point you look back and see one other you cannot betray, and one other whose special treatment of yourself you cannot live without or abandon hope of receiving. And so you choose illusion over truth and betray all that you are and the hope your brother has placed in you as savior of the world.

15.12 You who still fantasize that you can have it both ways, give up your fantasy and realize that real choice lies before you. No, this is not an easy choice, or it would have been chosen long ago and saved much suffering and put an end to hell. But it also is not a difficult choice, nor one that is in truth yours alone to make. This choice cannot be made without your brother and is indeed your brother's holy choice, as well as his birthright and your own. You only need be open to the place that no specialness can enter, and bid your brother choose for you. For in his choice you join with him and with your Father. In this choice lies one united will for glory that knows neither specialness nor separation. In this choice lies life eternal.

Chapter 16

What You Choose Instead

16.1   The glory that you felt from love only seemed to be available from one and not from another. Love is not available *from* anyone in the way you think it is. Love has but one source! That this source lies within each of you does not make it many sources, for the many of you have but one source as well. This common source does not make any of you special, but all of you the same.

16.2   You may ask now why it doesn't seem so, and the only answer is that you do not want it to. You perceive but what you wish for, and your wish for specialness leads you not to see sameness anywhere at all, for what is the same cannot be special.

16.3   You all are familiar with the "problem" child who seeks love and attention in ways deemed inappropriate. You know this child is no less than any other child, and what he seeks the same as any other. Yet if this child grows up with behavior that remains unchanged you call him deviant or criminal, and claim that it is not love he seeks, and that he is now less than those who once were the same as he. What is the same does not change and become different. Innocence is not replaced by sin.

16.4   What you do to criminals you do but to yourself and to those you claim to love with a special love. For you do not see them in the changeless innocence in which they were created and remain, but with the eyes of judgment. That you have judged and found the ones you love good and worthy of your love makes not your judgment justified any more than the judgment that condemns a body to death or to "life" in prison.

16.5   Life in prison and a body condemned to death is what judgment does to all of you who believe that what is the same can be made different. This is as true of the love you reserve for special ones as it is of the condemnation you reserve for others you have singled out. For judgment is what is required to make one special and another not.

16.6   Without judgment there would be no separation, for you would see no difference between yourself and your brothers and sisters. Your judgment began with your own self, and from it was all conflict born. Without differences there is no cause for conflict. Judgment makes different. It looks past what is the same and sees it not and sees instead what it is looking for. What you are looking for is what you will find, but finding it does not make it the truth, except as it is the truth about what you choose to see. Your choice lies with God or with the self you believe you have succeeded in separating from Him, and based on this choice alone is how you see determined.

16.7   Judgment is the function the separated mind has given itself. This is where all of its energy is expended, for constant judgment is required to maintain the world you see. The Holy Spirit can replace your specialness with a special function; but this function cannot be yours while you choose judgment itself as your proper role.

16.8   Only your heart can lead you to the forgiveness that must overcome judgment. A forgiven world is a world whose foundation has changed from fear to love. Only from this world can your special function be fulfilled and bring the light to those who still live in darkness.

16.9   Child of God, see you how important it is that you listen to your heart! Your heart does not want to see with judgment or with fear. It calls to you to accept forgiveness that you may give it and henceforth look upon the forgiven world with love.

16.10   I repeat again that reason does not oppose love, as your split mind would have you believe it does. For your split mind judges even love and opposes it on the basis that it uses no judgment! Here you can see the value that you place on judgment, even to the ridiculous notion that you can judge judgment itself. You deem yourself capable of making good judgments and poor judgments, and you deem love as being capable of neither. Love seems to operate on its own apart from what your mind would bid it do, and this is why you fear it even while you yearn for it. This is what the split mind would call reason—a world in which there are two sides to everything and two sides that oppose each other. How can this be reason? The truth opposes nothing, nor does love.

16.11   Again your memory of creation serves you, even if it has not served you well. It is this memory that tells you that love does not judge, and only your split mind that has made of this memory what will serve its purpose. What it calls a deficiency is your saving grace. Letting go of what your mind would tell you in favor of what your heart already knows is but the purpose of this Course.

16.12 Only forgiveness replaces judgment, but true forgiveness is as foreign to you as is true love. You think forgiveness looks upon another in judgment and pardons the wrongs you would enumerate. True forgiveness simply looks past illusion to the truth where there are no sins to be forgiven, no wrongs to be pardoned. Forgiveness looks on innocence and sees it where judgment would see it not.

16.13 This form of forgiveness seems impossible to you because you look upon an unforgiven world where evil walks, danger lurks, and nowhere is safety to be found. Each separated one is out for his or her own self, and if you do not watch out for your own safety, surely you will perish. Yet while you watch vigilantly you know that you cannot protect yourself and that you are not safe. There is only one of you and so many of "them." Never can you keep your guard up quite enough or secure a final guarantee against disaster. And yet you cling to all attempts to do so even while knowing they are ineffective.

16.14 You think you cannot give up your vigilance because you know no other way to ensure your safety, and even if you cannot guarantee your safety against everything all of the time, you believe you can guarantee your safety against some things some of the time. And for this occasional protection that has no validity and no proof you give up love!

16.15 While you claim you need proof before you can believe or accept something as a fact or as the truth, and certainly before you can act upon it, you live as if you believe that what has never worked before will somehow miraculously work in the future. You have nothing but evidence of a life of unhappiness and despair, where occasional moments of joy or the few people that you love out of the many that you do not are all that make your life worth living. You think that to be asked to give up the caution, protection, and vigilance that protects these moments of joy and people you love as well as your own self is to be asked to live a life of even greater risk than that which you live now.

16.16 Your judgment has not made the world a better place! If history proves anything, it proves the opposite of what you would care to believe. The more the individual, society, and culture indulge in the desire to judge, the more godlike they think they make themselves. For all of you here know that judgment is not your place, and that it belongs to God and God alone. This is firmly attached to your memory of creation. To wrestle the right to judge away from God is an act against God, and like a child who has dared to defy his parents, the act of defiance fills the defiant one with boldness. Something dangerous has been tried and has seemingly succeeded. The order of the universe has flipped. The child believes she has "stolen" the role of parent away from the parent without having become a parent. God has become the enemy to those who judge just as the parent of a defiant child becomes the enemy in the child's perception.

16.17 But the child is wrong. The child has made a mistake. And with this mistake, the child believes that the relationship with the parent has been severed. It is this belief in a severed relationship with God that seems to replace the holy relationship that cannot be replaced. Judgment thus reinforces the idea of separation, making of it something even darker than it started out as being. It no longer seems like a choice that the child has made, but seems to be an irreparable rift that a new choice cannot mend.

16.18 Child of God, this is not so and cannot ever be, for the right to judge is but the right of the Creator who judges all of creation as it was created and remains. You only think that you have changed the unchangeable.

16.19 Judgment does not make you safe, and defining evil does not abolish it, but only makes it real to you. Yet you believe judgment to be based on justice, and justice to include the punishment of those you have defined as evil. You have thus made justice one with vengeance, and in doing so have robbed justice of its meaning.

16.20 Those who sit in judgment call upon their power to do what it cannot do. All power comes from love, as does all justice. Any basis other than love for power or for justice makes a mockery of both. *Might makes right* is a saying that is known to many of you, and even those who know the saying not believe in the tenets it represents. This, you will claim, you have evidence for. It is all around you. The strong survive and the weak perish. The mighty prevail, and so define what is right for all those over whom they prevail. Those in power are those who make the laws, and those who have no power must obey them.

16.21 And yet you are as frightened of those who have no power as those who do. Criminals are feared and shunned, and yet they have no power but that which they make from their own selves. You want power to come only through legitimate channels and do not want those who have no power to possess it through the same weapons or might that you claim make those in authority powerful. While you want those you have given power to protect you, you also fear them, and they in turn fear the powerless who might take away their power or rise up against them. What kind of power is it that needs to be constantly defended? What is it about the powerless that frightens you, except that they might not accept their powerless state? And what does this say but what history has shown you—that who is powerful and who is not is not determined by might or any authority that can be given and taken away. Power is possessed by those who claim it. By those who cry *I am*. For the beginning of power comes from the rejection of powerlessness. The rejection of powerlessness is but a step toward your identity achieved through the awakening of love of Self.

16.22 What misery the world has suffered in the name of judgment, power, and justice. What misery can be avoided by finding the true power inherent in your identity. For you are not powerless. Those of you who think you have traditional means of power on your side turn not to your own power, and then you wonder why those most spiritual, both currently and historically, seem to suffer hardship. Yet it is often only those who suffer hardship who will rise up and claim the power that is their own instead of looking for it elsewhere. Your perception but looks at power backward and wonders why God has forsaken a people who seem to be so godly.

16.23 God forsakes no people, but people forsake God when they give away their power and claim not their birthright. Your birthright is simply the right to be who you are, and there is nothing in the world that has the power to take this right from you. The only way you lose it is by giving it away. And this you do.

16.24 God wants no sacrifice from you, yet when you give away your power you make of yourself a sacrificial lamb, an offering onto God that God does not want. You look back on stories of sacrifice from the Bible and think what a barbaric time that was, and yet you repeat the same history but in different form. If a talented physician were to give up his power to heal you would surely call it a waste, and yet you give up your power to be who you are and think it is just the way life is. You give away your power and then bow down to those whom you have given it to, for you are afraid of nothing more than your own power.

16.25 This fear but stems from what you have used your power for. You know your power created the world of illusion in which you live, and so you think another must be able to do it better. You no longer trust yourself with your own power, and so you have forgotten it and realize not how important it is for it to be reclaimed. As good as you may want to be, you would still go meekly through your life trying to comply with rules of God and man with thought of some greater good in mind. If everyone did what he or she wanted to do, you reason, society would collapse and anarchy would rule. You think you are only fair in deciding that if everyone cannot do what they would want, then you, too, must abdicate your wishes for the common good. You thus behave in "noble" ways that serve no purpose.

16.26 If you cannot claim at least a small amount of love for your own Self, then neither can you claim your power, for they go hand-in-hand. There is no "common good" as you perceive of it, and you are not here to assure the continuance of society. The worries that would occupy you can be let go if you but work instead for the return of heaven and the return of your own Self.

CHAPTER 17

Conscious Non-Planning

17.1 Being who you are is no luxury reserved for the idle rich, or the very young or old. Being who you are is necessary for the completion of the universe. Without the real you in it, there would be a void within the universe—and this would be impossible. And yet there is a way in which you are missing.

17.2 This has to do with consciousness and what you are aware of. Let's just say the space that you would fill as your own Self is held for you by another part of your consciousness that has never left it. It is the reunion of these two selves that will bring about the completion of the universe and the return of heaven. *Where two are joined together* can be used rightly here as well as in regard to relationship. Your choice to separate from God is but a separation from your own Self, and this is truly the separation that needs to be healed to return you to God.

17.3 You shy away from thoughts of a consciousness beyond that which you are aware because of fear. And yet you know you cannot claim that you are aware of all that exists within the universe, or even that you fully know your own Self. What is fearful about the unknown is simply that it is unknown. Coming to know what was previously unknown to you can remove the fear, if you will let it.

17.4 Consciousness of which you are unaware is not magic, superstition, or insanity. Yet you shield yourself from knowledge of it as if it would change the nature of the universe itself. It will change your perception of it. This is both what you desire and what you fear just as you both desire and fear knowing yourself.

17.5 There is an underlying assumption that you know all that is good for you to know, and that to know more is going to mean that things you would rather not know, and therefore must be *bad*, are what will be revealed. And yet all the evidence of your own thoughts will reveal to you your willingness to accept the *bad* about yourself and your world. And so this assumption that what is unknown must be bad cannot be valid, even by your own standards of evidence. Yet, in your estimation, the unknown cannot be fully good or worthy of your knowing because the reason that you use is loyal to the world you see. This is why even Heaven, which you would label good, is not wholly good in your estimation of it. Why is it not wholly good? Because you have defined it as lacking much of what you have judged to be good in the world you now perceive.

17.6   You have, however, willingly entered many unknown states. Some of you have gotten married, had children, taken mind-altering drugs, or attempted strenuous or even terrifying physical feats. But all of you without exception have willingly entered the unknown state of sleep and experienced the loss of consciousness that it brings. Each of you has had the experience of dreaming during the time of sleep. Some may claim they know everything there is to know about sleep and dreaming, being married, using drugs, or having children; but even those of you who would listen to what the experts have to say believe this not.

17.7   Each day is an unknown you enter into, despite your every attempt to anticipate what it might hold. And yet, while it would seem you would grow quite used to this phenomenon, you do not. You still make your plans and rail against everything that interferes with them, even knowing in advance that your greatest efforts at organization are often to no avail. A Course in Miracles asks you to "receive instead of plan," and yet few of you understand the meaning of this simple instruction or what it says to you of the unknown.

17.8   What it says is that the unknown is benevolent. What it says is that what you cannot anticipate can be anticipated for you. What it says is that you could be receiving constant help if you would but let it come. What it says is that you are not alone.

17.9   Receiving implies that something is being given. Receiving implies a willingness to accept what is given. This willingness is what you do not offer. Yet this is due to your lack of understanding about the nature of creation, and can be corrected.

17.10 Sin is simply the belief that correction cannot be made. This is the mistake that has happened in creation. This is how the impossible has become possible. If you were not so determined to believe correction cannot be made, correction would have occurred. This is the original error that is so in need of correction: your belief in sin—or in other words, your belief that what you have chosen is not reversible.

17.11   Is this not evident in the judgment you rely upon and in your treatment of criminals as well as of your own self and those you love? You believe mistakes must be paid for, not once but many times, and no matter how heavy the payment is, it only "pays for" what was done and cannot ever be undone. What does payment do but purchase something that is then yours to keep? What have you purchased with all your effort to make amends for your wrongdoing? You have but purchased guilt, and hold it to yourself—a constant companion and a judgment on your own self.

17.12   See you now why those who judge cannot enter heaven? Judgment proceeds from the belief in sin and the irreversibility of all errors. If you do not believe you can reverse or "turn back" to the state in which you existed before the original error, then you never shall.

17.13   And yet all you need do is turn back. Being an observer of your body has prepared you for this. Step back now to the place that has been held for you. You have not lost "your place in line" because you wandered. It has been held for you by the most loving of brothers, a brother united with your own Self.

17.14   This space you can turn back to holds no judgment and no fear, and so it is the repository of all that has proceeded from love. There it keeps all love's gifts safe for you. Love's gifts are gifts of creation or extension, gifts you have both given and received. Each act of love is added to the space in the universe that is yours and has become part of the whole along with you. All that has proceeded from fear is nothing, and has no existence apart from your own thoughts.

17.15   Your thoughts, however, have become quite harsh, and quite entrenched in the belief in their right to judge. Many of you have let go your belief in sin and still held onto your belief in judgment, thinking one is different from the other. They are not different, and while you do not see this your thoughts remain based on fear and fear thus remains your foundation. For judgment is but the belief that what God created can be changed, and has been.

17.16   Forgiveness, which replaces judgment, must come from your heart. To forgive based on the logic of your mind rather than the compassion of your heart is to only give thought to forgiveness. This many of you will give, even to deciding to forgive despite your better judgment. See you not how little sense this makes, how insincere this even sounds?

17.17   Sincerity is synonymous with wholeheartedness—a concept you do not understand for it is beyond concepts. But now we begin to integrate your learning as we move to wholeness. The first move toward wholeness is but to understand this: heart and mind are not separate. A united mind and heart is a whole heart, or wholeheartedness. You may ask then why this Course has treated them as separate parts of you. This is simply because this is the way you see them, and because it has allowed me to address the different functions you have given them.

17.18   What is the same cannot have different functions. And now your mind and heart must work together in the united function we have established—returning to you your identity within God's creation.

CHAPTER 18

The Mind Engaged

18.1   Many of you believe God's creation included the fall from paradise as described in the biblical story of Adam and Eve and in the creation stories of many cultures and religions. When you accept this, even in non-literal terms, as the story of the separation, you accept separation itself. This story is, rather than a story of an actual event, a story that describes the problem. It is but the story of perception's birth. And your perception of the fall makes of the fall a curse. This interpretation would be inconsistent, however, with a benevolent God and a benevolent universe. This interpretation accepts that separation can occur. It cannot. Belief in the fall is belief in the impossible.

18.2   Imagine that you are part of a chain of bodies holding hands and encircling the globe. I am among those whose hand you hold. All are linked, even if each one is not holding the hand of every other one. If one link in the chain were to be removed, the chain would no longer form a circle but would *fall*, each end suspended in space. The chain would now be a line seeming to go from here to there, instead of enclosing and encompassing everything. The separation assumes that you can break the chain. This would be as impossible as it would be for me to let go of your hand.

18.3   Now imagine further that this chain is keeping the Earth in its orbit. It is obvious that the Earth falling out of orbit would cause dire consequences of a universal nature. It is simply less obvious that you are part of what has established and keeps a universal order, part of a whole that would be a completely different whole without your presence, just as the universe would be a completely different universe without the presence of the Earth.

18.4   Yet this is, in effect, what you think you have done. You think that you have changed the nature of the universe and made it possible for life to exist separately and alone with no relationship, no connection, no unity with the whole. This you have not done. You have not *fallen* from unity. You have not *fallen* from God.

18.5   This chain I have described helps you to imagine the place I hold for you, as you held mine when I entered the world in physical form. Even if it is just an illustration, it illustrates that none of us leave wholeness or each other.

18.6   While you have been taught that you are not your body, it is impossible for you to deny the body here. Yet you can change the function you have ascribed to it, and so its way of functioning. If you do not see it as the result of a fall, as a curse, as a punishment from God, or as your home, a dwelling place that keeps you separate, then you can begin to see it as what it is, a learning device given you by a loving creator. Before the idea of separation, there was no need for learning. But a loving creator creates not that which can have a need go unfulfilled. As soon as the need for learning arose, the perfect means to fulfill that need was established. You have simply failed to see it as such.

18.7   This is the error birthed by perception, before which there was no possibility of misinterpretation, because there was no external world to be perceived. A learning device, when not perceived as such, holds not much hope of fulfilling the function it was created to fulfill. But when perception changes and a thing is seen as what it is, then it cannot fail to accomplish what it was created to accomplish.

18.8   An external world is but a projection that cannot take you away from the internal world where you exist in wholeness, a link in the chain of creation. Imagine again this chain and your Self among those who comprise it, and imagine the life that you experience now taking place much like that you would see projected on a movie screen. You have not left your place as you view this movie and experience its sights and sounds, joys and sorrows. And yet you are also part of the projection, and this is where your awareness now abides, seemingly trapped upon the screen, viewing everything from the two eyes of the one projected there. Again, this is but what this Course's exercises have attempted to help you see: a world you can observe and learn in and from, for as long as you would choose to learn what the idea of separation would teach you. Making a new choice, a choice to learn from unity, is what this Course prepares you for.

18.9   Learning from unity requires an integrated mind and heart, or whole-heartedness. A half-hearted approach to this learning will not work, nor will the attention of a split mind. It cannot be emphasized strongly enough that you learn what you choose to learn. For proof of this all you need do is look at the world that was created from your wish to learn what the idea of separation would teach you. When you resided in unity, you could not imagine what this world would be like any more than you can now imagine what a united world will be like. You did not understand, from unity's standpoint, what it was that you were asking for, or the extent of involvement this learning would require. In order to learn what the idea of separation would teach you, you needed to believe that you existed in a separated state. Thus, "forgetting" that you actually reside in unity was a requirement of this condition you wished to experience. This condition was thus made available.

18.10 While this explanation makes perfect sense, you find it quite unbelievable on the basis of your perception of yourself and the limited range of power you believe your decision making to have. The only way to make the unbelievable believable is to alter what you experience. The state in which you now exist was not only unbelievable but also inconceivable to you in your natural state. Experience was required in order to alter your belief system and is required now as well.

18.11 The experience of unity will alter your belief system and that of others, for what you learn in unity is shared. Because you are currently learning from separation, however, each must experience unity individually before their belief system can be changed, even when what is learned is shared at another level.

18.12 Perception of levels is a function of time, and thus it seems that great amounts of time are needed before change of a lasting nature can occur. This is why miracles save time, for they integrate all levels, temporarily collapsing time. Time is actually a measurement of learning, or the "time" it takes for learning to pass from one level to another through experience, for here learning is experienced in time.

18.13 In order for your experience base to change from that of learning in separation to that of learning in unity, learning from what unity can teach you must be birthed as an idea. To hear or learn of another's idea is not to give birth to it. You thus must each experience the birth of the idea of learning from unity in order for it to come from within and leave not its source. An idea of mine can only become an idea of yours through your relationship with it. You need only to experience this idea in your own way, from the desire to know from which all ideas are born, in order to give it life.

18.14   Once an idea is born, it exists in relationship to its creator. All that remains now is a choice of participation. In unity, all that you desired was participated in fully by a mind and heart combined in wholeheartedness. You knew your Self to be the creator, and loved all that you created. You did not desire and fear something at the same time, and your desires did not change from moment to moment. What you desired you experienced fully with your whole being, making it one with you. That you keep yourself from desiring anything fully here is what makes this existence so chaotic and erratic. A mind and heart in conflict is what keeps you from desiring anything fully, and thus from creating.

18.15   Thus the integration of mind and heart must be our goal in order for you to create the state in which unity can be experienced. Obviously, this is up to you. As you chose to create a state of separation, you must choose to create a state of unity.

18.16   It can come as no surprise to you that your mind has ruled your heart. What this Course has thus far attempted to do is to briefly change your orientation from mind to heart. This is a first step in what will seem now like an attempt to balance two separate things, but is really an attempt to unite what you have only perceived as separate. If the heart is the center of your Self, where then is the mind? The center is but the Source in which all exist as one mind. To say this to you before we loosened some of your perceptions about the supremacy of the mind, however, would have been folly. The one mind is not as you have perceived *your* mind. The one mind is but a mind in which love rules, and mind and heart are one. We will proceed by calling this wholeheartedness rather than mind or heart.

18.17   A wandering mind is seen as quite the norm, and thoughts that dart about in a chaotic fashion are as acceptable and seemingly as inevitable to you as breathing. A split mind is seen as not much less normal although it is recognized that a split mind makes decision making difficult. You were already told that the only exercise for your mind that would be included in this Course of Love is that you dedicate all thought to union. This now must be seen in two dimensions rather than one. In addition to dedicating thought to unity with the whole, you must dedicate yourself to unifying thought itself.

18.18 You do not realize what a wholehearted choice in regards to experiencing separation did. Wholeheartedness is but a full expression of your power. A full expression of your power is creation. What has been created cannot be uncreated. What has been created can, however, be transformed. Transformation occurs in time. Thus transformation and miracles need to work hand-in-hand.

18.19 The transformation from a state of separation to a state of unity is a miracle indeed, for this transformation requires recognition of a state that you cannot recognize in separation. While this is a paradox, it is not impossible for the simple reason that you never left the state of unity that you do not recognize. Your lack of recognition can thus be overcome by remembering the truth of what you are.

18.20 Unifying thought is more than a matter of focus or single-mindedness, although these are both steps in the right direction. Unifying thought is also a matter of integrating the thought or language of your heart with that which you more naturally perceive as thought, the words and images that "go through" your mind.

18.21 We talked briefly here of emotions, doing so only to differentiate your feelings of love from your feelings of lack of love or fear. What we have as yet talked even less of, however, is what emotion covers up, and the stillness that lies beneath. I have referred to the true language of the heart as communion, or union of the highest level, and of remembrance of who you are being the means by which communion can return to you. So what we speak of now is integrating remembrance and thought.

18.22 While we spoke of what you think of as emotion being reactions of the body to stimulus, we did not speak of this stimulus itself. Before we do so, we must clarify further the function of the body as a learning device. Your body seems to experience both pleasure and pain, yet as a learning device, it is neutral. It does not experience, but only conveys that which can be experienced to you. You then relay a reaction back to it. This circular relationship between you and the body is the perfect relationship for the purpose of learning, since both the experience and the reaction to the experience can then be learned from, and because the learner can choose both. It is not, however, the perfect relationship when you have misperceived the body as your home rather than as a learning device. Because you have misperceived the body as your home, there is, in a sense, no "you" to which the body can send its signals. And so the body seems to be in charge and to be both the experiencer and the interpreter of experience. In addition, this misperception has allowed the body's function to go unrecognized. You thus have not recognized the truth of what causes pain nor that you can reject the experience of it. The same is true of pleasure.

18.23 Determination of pleasure and pain is made with the judgment of the separated self who not only believes it is the body, but that it is at the body's mercy. Yet the body has no mercy to offer the separated self. It is only a learning device. But you have not recognized this and have failed to learn that all you experience as painful is the result of feelings of lack of love, and that all you have experienced as pleasurable are feelings of love. This would seem to contradict what was said earlier about the pain experienced from love and your willingness to cling to it despite the pain you are experiencing. Yet the pain comes not from your feelings of love, but feelings of love lost.

18.24 Having no one to receive and reject feelings of pain and replace them with feelings of love causes all your distress. Think not that you react to pain of any kind with the love from your real Self that would dispel it. The Self you have taken out of the learning loop is the Self of love.

CHAPTER 19

Oneness and Duality

19.1   There was no evil intent in the creation of the body as a learning device, and as a learning device it was perfectly created. The problem lies in what you have, in your forgetfulness, made of the body. Only from thinking of the body as yourself did ideas of glorifying the body arise. To glorify a learning device makes no sense. And yet in creating the perfect device from which you could experience separation, all such problems were anticipated and corrective devices created alongside them. You could not fully experience separation without a sense of self as separate, and you could not fully experience anything without your free will. A separate self with a free will operating in an external world, as well as a spirit self desiring the experience of separation, would naturally lead to a situation where the whole range of experiences available to a separate being would exist.

19.2   The complex set of criteria needed to create a world of separation was, in the instant of creation, anticipated and provided in a form consistent with creation's laws. While this world was created with love, as all of creation was, it was also created to provide the desired experience. Thus was fear born, for a separate self is a fearful self by its nature. How could it not be?

19.3   You who have grown weary of this experience rejoice, for you can choose a new experience. Your free will has not been taken from you, nor has the power of creation abandoned you. Within creation's own laws does the solution rest.

19.4   The solution lies in transformation, and that is why you are still needed here. Beneath the world of illusion that you have made to glorify the separated self lies the world that was created for your learning, and that so exists in truth. It is not the only world by any means, but it is still heaven because heaven must be where you are. A wholehearted choice to abandon all ideas of glorifying the separated self and to let the world be what it is will begin the transformation. This requires the first unification, the unification of mind and heart, after which unification with God is naturally returned to your awareness, for this unification returns you to the Christ in you and the one mind united with God which you have never left. Creation's power then returns to you to help all the separated ones remember union.

19.5 Although this all may sound like science fiction to you, realize that you accept much in all areas of your life, from that of religion to science itself, that sounds like fiction. You are not, however, expected to believe all I have told you on faith alone. Experience is needed to change your beliefs and place your faith securely in them. The first step in leading you to experience of another kind is your willingness to accept that you are here to learn, and that your body can provide the means.

19.6 Your saving grace is that even a separated self yearns for union and knowledge of its Creator. Thus along with this yearning was a means provided for its fulfillment, and with this fulfillment lies the end of the separation.

19.7 I was part of this means, but only part. Fulfillment can be provided by each and every one of your brothers and sisters, for in each is the Christ available to be seen and experienced as it was from me. It is in your holy relationships that union can be found and experienced, and thus from these that you fuel your desire for union with all and for knowledge of your Creator. This yearning must but be a pure yearning —untainted by fear and judgment and approached with wholeheartedness—for it to be fulfilled. It is not the means that are lacking but the wholehearted desire.

19.8 Let me speak briefly of the role I played so that you can better understand the role that waits for you. I came in the fulfillment of scripture. All this really means is that a certain community had been led to expect my arrival. They awaited me with expectation and so found in me what they hoped to find. What my brothers and sisters saw in me allowed me to be who I was, even while in human form. I tell you truly if you were to see any of your brothers and sisters today as those who awaited my birth saw me, they too would remember who they are. This is the role I ask you to accept so that you can provide for others what was provided for me.

19.9 Each one of your brothers and sisters is as holy as I and as beloved to God. Can you not witness to their belovedness as those long ago witnessed to mine? You have not been able to do this thus far because you have desired specialness for yourself and a few others rather than belovedness for all. But now, perhaps, you are ready.

19.10 The separated self cannot relearn unity except through union. Here, union is achieved in relationship. To see your brothers and sisters as those of long ago saw me is the way to achieve relationship of the highest order and relearn communion, the language of the heart. This is why you have been asked to experience the spirit of your brothers and sisters rather than simply relating to their bodies as you always have. I was not seen as a body by those who believed in me, although I had a body to help me learn just as you do.

19.11 My testimony witnessed to your arrival just as the scriptures witnessed to mine. Even while some of my words were distorted or misinterpreted, you can still revisit them and see that this is so. I did not proclaim myself to be above or different from the rest, but called each of you brother and sister and reminded you of our Father's love and of our union with Him.

19.12 Your belief in your brothers and sisters will not be total, however, without the reunion of mind and heart that produces the state of wholeheartedness. This state was not achieved at all times by all those who believed in me—and perfection is not asked of you. As can be clearly seen from the records left to you, the apostles did not, in fact, achieve this state during my life-time, for they looked at me as different and looked to me for power. Only after my resurrection did the Holy Spirit come upon them and reveal their own power to them by uniting mind and heart with belief. They were then reunited with me as they were united with the Christ. You thus must learn to see yourself as you see your brothers and sisters, and place your belief not in differences but in sameness.

19.13 In order to do this there is still one more layer to the unification of thought, and this brings up another reason for our reliance on the heart. Thought, as you know it, is an aspect of duality. It cannot be otherwise in your separated state. You must think in terms of "I" and "them," "death and life," "good and evil." This *is* thought. Thought occurs in words, and words separate. It is only in combining mind and heart with a focus on letting the heart lead that love can be combined with thought in such a way as to actually transcend thought as you know it. This transcendence is a function of wholeheartedness.

19.14 This is, in essence, why the greatest thinkers have not been able to deci-pher the riddle, the mystery, of the divine, and why they conclude that God is unknowable. God *is* knowable from within the mystery of non-duality itself. It would be impossible for you to be a being that can yearn for knowledge of your Creator without this knowledge being available. In creation, all needs are fulfilled the instant they become needs, which is why there are no needs. If everything you need has been provided, having needs makes no sense.

19.15 Philosophy applies thought to mystery and that is why philosophy becomes such a muddle of words. It is difficult for you to accept that what you most need to know cannot be achieved through the same methods you have used in order to know about other things. And, increasingly, you are willing to exchange experience for second-hand knowledge and to believe you can come to know through the experiences of others. Yet, in the case of coming to know what lies before you now—coming to know your own Self— it is obvious that another's experience will not bring this knowledge to you, not even my experience. If this were so, all of those who read of my life and words would have learned what I learned from my experience. While many have learned much of others, this type of learning is but a starting point, a gateway to experience.

19.16 To think without thought or know without words are ideas quite foreign to you, and truly, while you remain here, even experiences beyond thoughts and words you will apply word and thought to. Yet love has often brought you close to a "thought-less" and "word-less" state of being, and it can do so again. As you join with your own Self in unity, all that in love you have created and received returns to its home in you, and leaves you in a state of love in which the wordless and formless is very near.

19.17 Your only concept of oneness is of a single form, a single entity. There is either one chair or two. One table or four. Your emphasis has been on quantity, and one is seen as less than any other number. Yet, on the other hand, when only one of anything exists it is highly prized. God is thus "God" due, at least in part, to what you view as His singularity. You view those who worship many gods as primitive, although those who believe in a god synonymous with creation are closer to a true picture of God than those who view God as a solitary figure. Still, oneness and unity go together, the unity of creation being part of the oneness of God, and the oneness of God part of the unity of creation. A mind trained by separation can have no concept of this, as all concepts are born from the mind's separate thoughts. Yet this same mind could still conceive of a creator. A mind that can conceive of a creator combined with a heart that yearns for knowledge of, and union with, that creator, can bypass the need for the separate thoughts of the separated one's thought system. But you must be trained to do this. Thus your training begins. And begins with prayer.

19.18 As was said in the beginning, praying is asking. You but asked for your separated state and it was made so. Now you need to but ask for unity to return for it to be so. The condition or state of being from which you ask is what is in need of adjustment and thus of training before you can be aware of the answer you will receive. It is clear you can ask for what you know not. This is not the problem. The problem is in who is doing the asking. The separated self, while capable of asking, is hardly capable of believing in or accepting the response. It is this non-belief in a response that makes it capable of asking. Now that you are beginning to shed the concept of the separate self and to believe in the possibility of response, you will find yourself more afraid to ask. All your asking or prayer awaits is but your belief in the love without fear that has always responded.

19.19 Out of the deepest, darkest chaos of your mind comes the possibility of light. It is a bit like traveling backward, or the review of life that some experience after death. In order to remember unity you must, in a sense, travel back to it, undoing as you go all you have learned since last you knew it, so all that remains is love. This undoing, or atonement, has begun—and once begun is unstoppable and thus already inevitably accomplished.

19.20 My brothers and sisters in Christ, do not become impatient now. We are on the home stretch and all you long for is nearer than ever before. To talk of going "back" will undoubtedly make you feel impatient, but this is not a going back that will in any way resemble the "going back" that you have tried to do before. While it is, in a sense, a request to review your life, it is the last such review that will be required before letting the past go completely. All your previous attempts to go back have been like attempts to pay a debt that will never go away. This going back will leave you debt free and thus free in truth.

19.21 This going back is the journey without distance. You need not go in search of it, and in truth, cannot, for the past does not abide in you. What you need rather do is strive for a place of stillness from which what needs review can arise as if it were a reflection arising from a deep pool. Here what is in need of healing will but briefly come to the surface and leave the hidden depths where light could not reach it and healing could not come. What comes forth for healing needs but a nod of love from your heart, a passing glance of compassion, the merest moment of reflection, before it will dissipate and show a new reflection.

19.22 This going back is, in reality, more in the way of reflection than review, although if you were to think of this as a re-viewing of your self, you would be quite accurate. It is like unto the final judgment as it has been described, a sorting of the real from the unreal, of truth from illusion. Despite the similarity between what this will call forth and the description of the final judgment, judgment is not the means or end of this reckoning.

19.23 The loftiest aim of which you are currently capable is that of changing your perception. Although our ultimate goal is to move beyond perception to knowledge, a first step in doing this is changing your means of perception to that of right-mindedness. Your willingness to accept me as your teacher will help you to accept my sight as your own and thus to be right-minded. The way you have perceived of yourself and your world until now has not been right-minded, and you are beginning to realize this. Thus it is now appropriate for the realization to come to you that your mind, and your perception, can be changed. This is necessary before you can look back in a new way and not simply cover the same ground you have covered a million times, seeing causes for recriminations, blame, and guilt. Looking back in judgment is not what is required here. Only the opposite will advance our aim of uniting mind and heart.

19.24 The Holy Spirit exists in your right mind, and is the bridge to exchanging perception for knowledge. Knowledge is light, and the only light in which you can truly see. You will not truly desire to unite your mind and heart in wholeheartedness until you see clearly. One purpose of the distinctions you have made between mind and heart are their ability to keep one part of yourself blameless. Whatever happens, your divided notion of yourself allows you to both protect and conceal. Fault always lies elsewhere. The guiltless part of you is always free to redeem the guilt-filled self. This idea of self-redemption has long been a culprit that has kept union, even with your own Self, undesirable to you. The concept that in oneness there is no need for blame or guilt or even for redemption is inconceivable to the separate mind. But not to the heart.

CHAPTER 20

The Embrace

20.1 Your longing now has reached a fever pitch, a burning in your heart quite different from that which you have felt before. Your heart may even feel as if it is stretching outward, straining heavenward, near to bursting with its desire for union, a desire you do not understand but can surely feel.

20.2 This is a call to move now into my embrace and let yourself be comforted. Let the tears fall and the weight of your shoulders rest upon mine. Let me cradle your head against my breast as I stroke your hair and assure you that it will be all right. Realize that this is the whole world, the universe, the all of all in whose embrace you literally exist. Feel the gentleness and the love. Drink in the safety and the rest. Close your eyes and begin to see with an imagination that is beyond thought and words.

20.3 You are no longer the object viewing the subjects of the kingdom. You are the heart of the kingdom. The kingdom's beauty revealed. The beloved child suckled at the breast of the queen mother earth, one child of one mother, nameless and beyond naming. No "I" resides here. You have given up the vision of your eyes and the "I" of your ego. You are loosed of bounds, no longer a thing of beauty, but beauty itself.

20.4 "Thingness" is over, and your identity no longer stands in form but flows from life itself. Your beauty is the gathering of the atoms, the order in chaos, the silence in solitude, the grace of the cosmos. Our heart is the light of the world.

20.5 We are one heart.

20.6 We are one mind. One creative force gathering the atoms, establishing the order, blessing the silence, gracing the cosmos, manifesting the light of the heart. Here we live as one body, experiencing communion, the soul's delight, rather than otherness. It is a seamless world, a tapestry where each thread is vibrant and strong. A canticle where each tone is pure and indivisible.

20.7   We have returned to the embrace. And now your arms cradle me as well, for an embrace, although it may begin with one reaching out to another, concludes with mutuality, shared touch, a melding of one into another. The embrace makes one of two.

20.8   And now we begin to see with the eyes of our heart. We are no longer looking *out* but looking *in*. All landscapes and horizons form within the embrace. All beauty resides there. All light is fused and infused within the embrace. Within the embrace our sight clears and what we see is known rather than understood.

20.9   Here, rest comes to weariness and gently lays it aside. Time has ended and there is nothing you must do. Being replaces identity and you say, *I am. I am*, and there is nothing outside of me. Nothing outside of the embrace.

20.10   From here your life becomes imaginal, a dream that requires you not to leave your home, your place of safety and of rest. You are cradled gently while your spirit soars, dreaming happy dreams at last. With love surrounding you in arms that hold you close, you feel the heartbeat of the world just beneath your resting head. It thunders in your ears and moves through you until there is no distinction. We are the heartbeat of the world.

20.11   This is creation. This is God. This is our home.

20.12   We exist in the embrace of love like the layers of light that form a rainbow, indivisible and curved inward upon each other. Love grows from within as a child grows within its mother's womb. Inward, inward, into the embrace, the source of all beginnings, the kernel and the wholeness of all life. The whole exists untroubled by what it will be. It is.

20.13   The time of parables has ended. A new time of no time awaits. Nothing is like unto anything else. Likeness, like thingness, has been overcome with oneness. Oneness prevails. The reign of Christ is at hand.

20.14   I am alive and you do believe this or you would not be here. Yet you think not of me living and imagine it not. Christ reigns in the kingdom in which I live just as Christ reigned within me on earth. In the cave on this earth where my dead body was laid, the Christ in me returned me to the embrace. The singular heartbeat of the man Jesus no longer sounded. My heartbeat was the heartbeat of the world.

20.15   Imagine a body in a cave, a cave in the earth, the earth in the planet, the planet in the universe. Each cradles the other. None are passive. None are dead. All share the heartbeat of the world and are at rest within each other, within each other's embrace and the embrace of God's love, God's creation, God's heartbeat. God's heartbeat is the Source of the world, the Soul of the world, the Sound of the world in harmony, existence with no beginning and no end. One embrace. All in all. None lesser and none greater for all is all. One is one.

20.16 There is no longer cause for alienation, nor for the feeling of abandonment so many of you have felt. You are now within the embrace where all such hurts are healed.

20.17 The world does not exist apart from you, and so you must realize your compassionate connection. The world is not a collection of cement buildings and paved streets nor of cold, heartless people who would as soon do you harm as good. It is but the place of your interaction with all that lives within you, sharing the one heartbeat. The heartbeat of the world does not exist apart from God. The heartbeat of the world is thus alive and part of you. This heart connection is what we seek to return you to. This realization that the world is not a *thing*, as you are not a *thing*. Your identity is shared and one in Christ. A shared identity is a quality of oneness. A shared identity is one identity. When you identify with Christ you identify with the one identity. When you realize the oneness of your identity you will be one with Christ. Christ is synonymous with oneness.

20.18 Who could be left out of the embrace? And who from within the embrace could be separate and alone?

20.19 Have you never felt as if you would wrap your arms around the world and bring it comfort if you could? This you can do. Not with physical arms, but with the arms of love. Have you never cried for the state of the world as you would for one small child in need of love? Has the world then not lost its thingness? And has it not as well lost its personalness? Are your tears not shed for what lives and breathes and exists along with you? And is the you who shed such tears a personal being? A thing? A mass of flesh and bone? Or are you, like the world you cry for, devoid of thingness and a personal self? And when you have leapt for joy at the world's beauty, has it not leapt with you, returning grace for grace?

20.20 Is it possible to have a concept of wholeness, of *all*, and for it not to exist? And how could it exist apart from you? Oneness with Christ, dear brother and sister, is nothing more than this concept realized. And also nothing less.

20.21 This lesson is only as complicated as the most complex among you needs it to be. But for some it can be simple, as simple as realizing the oneness of the embrace. Within the embrace you can let all thought go. Within the embrace, you can quit thinking even of holy things, holy men and women, and even divine beings, even the one God. Is not the embrace itself holy? Is not the sunrise and sunset? Is not the least of the birds of the air as holy as the mighty eagle? The blade of grass, the fleck of sand, the wind and air, the ocean and her surf, all live by the universal heartbeat and exist within the embrace. Is not all you can imagine holy when you imagine with love? Is not all you cannot imagine holier still?

20.22 Sanctity is all that exists within the embrace. How could you be less than sacred? You exist in holiness.

20.23 The first step in remembering this holiness is forgetting. Let yourself forget that you do not feel holy and that the world does not appear to be sacred. Let your heart remember that you are holy and that the world is sacred. A thousand things can pull you from your remembrance. Forgetting "things" can free you to remember.

20.24 Forget yourself and memory will return to you. Beyond your personal self and the identity you have given your personal self is your being. This is the face of Christ where all being resides. This is your true identity.

20.25 Thankfulness is the nature of your being. It could not be otherwise when awe and magnificence encompass you in the embrace. Your heart sings in gratitude for the all that you are. You are the beauty of the world and peace abides within you.

20.26 Peace is the foundation of your being. Not a peace that implies an absence but a peace that implies a fullness. Wholeness is peaceful. Only separation creates conflict.

20.27 Love is the source of your being. You flow from love, an outpouring without end. You are thus eternal. You are pure and innocent because you flow from love. What flows from love is changeless and boundless. You are without limit.

20.28 Power is the expression of who you are. Because you are changeless and boundless, you are all-powerful. Only lack of expression leads to power-lessness. No true expression is possible until you know who you are. To know who you are and not to express who you are with your full power is the result of fear. To know the safety and love of the embrace is to know no cause for fear, and thus to come into your true power. True power is the power of miracles.

20.29 Miracles are expressions of love. You might think of them as acts of cooperation. Holiness cannot be contained, and it is not within your power to limit it. To feel the holiness of the embrace is to release its power. While expression and action are not the same, understanding their relationship to each other is essential.

20.30 Expressions of love are as innumerable as the stars in the universe, as bountiful as beauty, as many-faceted as the gems of the earth. I say again that sameness is not a sentence to mediocrity or uniformity. You are a unique expression of the selfsame love that exists in all creation. Thus your expression of love is as unique as your Self. It is in the cooperation between unique expressions of love that creation continues and miracles become natural occurrences.

20.31 This cooperation is natural when fear has been rejected. You have long embraced fear and rejected love. Now the reverse is true. This reversal of truth has changed the nature of your universe and the laws by which it operates. The laws of fear were laws of struggle, limits, danger, and competitiveness. The laws of love are laws of peace, abundance, safety, and cooperation. Your actions and the results of your actions in a universe of love will naturally be different from your actions and the results of your actions in a universe of fear. You set the laws of the universe when you chose fear. The laws of the universe of love are God-given.

20.32 Acceptance of your true power is acceptance of your God-given authority via your free will. When I beseeched my Father, saying, *"They know not what they do,"* I was expressing the nature of my brothers and sisters as caused by fear. To accept your power and your God-given authority is to know what you do. Let the fear be taken from this area of your thought so that you can see the application of cooperative action. As long as you fear your own ability to know what you do, you cannot be fully cooperative.

20.33 The rest of the universe, existing in a state of compassionate free will devoid of fear, knows what it does. There are no opposing forces that are not in agreement about their opposing force. No atoms do battle. No molecules compete for dominance. The universe is a dance of cooperation. You are but asked to rejoin the dance.

20.34 The embrace has returned you to attunement with the heartbeat, the music of the dance. You have not known what you do or what to do only because of fear, only because you have been out of accord with the one heartbeat. The world, the universe, is your partner—and only now do you hear the music that brings grace to all your movements, all your actions, all your expressions of love. While this may seem to be metaphorical language it is not. Listen and you will hear. Hear, and you cannot help but rejoice in the dance.

20.35 You have not before now been able to even imagine knowing what you do. You hope to have moments of clarity concerning what you are doing in a given moment, what you have done, what you hope to do in the future. But even these moments of clarity are fractional. They seldom have any relation to the whole. Knowing what you do comes from existing within the embrace. You know you do the will of God because you are at one with that will.

20.36 Bitterness and uncertainty are replaced by hope. Hope is the condition of the initiate, new to the realization of having a home within the embrace. It is the response that says to all you have just read, "Ah, if only it were true. If only it could be true." Notice the complete change in this "if only" from those we have spoken of earlier—the "if onlys" of fear. If you put half as much faith in these "if onlys" as you have in the "if onlys" of fear, all the certainty I have spoken of will be yours.

20.37 Knowing what you do is a present moment knowing. It is not about plans. It is about moment-by-moment knowing exactly who you are and acting out of that loving identity, and it is about knowing that as you do so you are in accord and enjoying the full cooperation of the entire universe.

20.38 Hope is a manner of acting as if the best possible outcome you can imagine could truly occur. Hope is a willingness to accept love and the grace and cooperation that flow from love. Hope is a willingness to ask for help, believing it will come. Hope is the reason and the outcome for which we pray. Hope acknowledges the kindliness of the universe and has no use for things. The inanimate as well as the animate is called upon, depended upon for service. All use is replaced with service, and appreciation replaces the callousness with which use once occurred.

20.39 All service is cooperative and depends on a belief in mutuality. All fear that what is good for one may not be good for the whole is replaced by an understanding that each one is worthy of his or her desires. *Eachness* replaces *thingness* but not oneness. All fear that what one gets means that less is available for another is replaced with an understanding of abundance. Receiving replaces all notions of taking or getting. All that is received is for the mutual benefit of all and takes nothing away from anyone. There is no limit to love and so there are no limits to anything that flows from love. What one benefits from everyone benefits from.

20.40 Receiving is an act of mutuality. It stems from a basic law of the universe expressed in the saying that the sun shines and the rain falls on the good and evil alike. All gifts of God are given equally and distributed equally. It is your belief that this is not so that causes judgment. All who believe they have "more" fall prey to righteousness. All who believe they have "less" fall victim to envy. Both "fall" from grace and limit their ability to receive. No gifts are received when all gifts are judged. While the gift is still given, the judgment changes the nature of the gift by limiting its ability to be of service. A gift one feels one cannot "use" is discarded. Thus have many of your treasures lain fallow.

20.41 What you each have been given is that which will serve your purpose. You could have no more perfect gifts, for your gifts are expressions of your Father's perfect love for you. Look deep inside and feel your heart's gladness. Your construction was no mistake. You are not flawed. You are not wanting. You would not be other than you are except when you give in to making judgments. Look deeply and you will see that what you would call your imperfections are as chosen and as dear to you as all the rest.

20.42 You would not be other than who you are. You may know that this is true or you may dwell in fantasies, desiring what another has or some success, fame, or riches that seem impossible for you to attain. And yet, whether you know it is true or not, it is true: You would not be other than who you are. Herein lie your peace and your perfection. If you would not be other than you are, then you must be perfect. This is a conclusion both logical to the mind and believable to the heart, and its acceptance is a step toward wholeheartedness.

20.43 To believe in your perfection and the equality of your gifts is peaceful because it releases you from trying to acquire that which you previously believed you were lacking. It releases you from judgment because you know that your brothers and sisters are also beings of perfection. When you begin to see them as such, what you will receive from them is far grander than anything you would before have wished to take from them.

20.44 Your thinking will begin to change to reflect your recognition of reception. Reception and welcome are highly linked. You will find you are welcome to all the gifts you recognize in your brothers and sisters just as you freely will offer yours to serve them. To serve rather than to use is an enormous change in thinking, feeling, and acting. It will immediately make the world a kinder, gentler place. And it is only a beginning.

20.45 To serve is different from your ideas of service, however. Your ideas of service are bound to your ideas of charity. Your idea of charity is based on some having more and some having less. Thus, you must remain cognizant of this distinction between serving and service. It will be helpful if you keep in mind that the idea of *to serve* is being used to replace the idea of *to use* and is its opposite. It replaces the thought of *taking* with the thought of *receiving*. It implies that you are welcome to all the gifts of the universe and that they can be given, through you, to others as well. It implies willingness rather than resistance. To change your thinking and your feelings from expecting resistance to expecting willingness is another key change that will lead toward wholeheartedness. When you change your actions from those of resistance and use to those of being willing to serve and be served, it will assist not only you and your peacefulness, but will bring peacefulness to the world as well.

20.46 Before you begin to resist the notion that you could have anything to do with world peace, realize that you naturally have reacted with resistance. You must replace your willingness to believe in your inadequacy and smallness with your willingness to believe in your ability and mightiness. Remember not your ego concerns and remember instead the warmth of the embrace. Remember not your personal identity but remember instead your shared identity.

20.47 Your personal concerns are concerns you have been taught to believe you have. They are small concerns and they are among the reasons for your belief in your inability to effect change within your own life and certainly within the greater life of the universe. You must understand that when you think of your personal life, personal concerns, personal relationships, you are separating yourself from the whole. These concerns are a matter of perception, and are things your mind has been trained to see as being within its scope. It is as if you have cordoned off a little section of life and said, "These are the things that relate to my existence and to me and they are all I need concern myself with." Even when you think of expanding your view, you deem that expansion unrealistic. You cannot do everything. You cannot effect world peace. You can barely keep your personal concerns in order. Your effort to do so is all that stands between you and chaos.

20.48 Your heart has a different scope, a different view. It is the view from within the embrace, the view from love's angle. It is the view of the dying who realize nothing matters but love. This realization is not one of sentiment, regrets, or wishful thinking. It is the view from the embrace, the return to one heartbeat, the return to what is known. This knowing you might call wisdom and think of as an attainable ideal of thought. Yet it is not about thought at all, but is beyond thought. It is not wisdom but the truth. The truth is that which exists. The false is illusion. Love is all that matters because love is all that is.

CHAPTER 21

Love Is

21.1   Love is.

21.2   Love is eternal, and you do not as yet grasp its meaning or the meaning of eternity. This is because, as a particular being, you are time-bound. You can realize the eternal even in your temporary form if you can let go of your particularity. Particularity has to do with mass, substance, form. Your being is far beyond your imagined reliance on the particular. The particular is about parts and parts are all you see. I remind you of what was said earlier concerning relationships existing apart from particulars. I repeat that relationship exists *between* one thing and another and that it is in the intersection of parts that the holiness of what is in-between is found. This will be discussed in more detail later, but for now, I return you, through the embrace, to the holy relationship but in a broadened form.

21.3   The holy relationship in its broadened form is eternity, the eternity of the embrace. If the embrace is the source of all, the one heartbeat, then it is eternity itself. It is the face of love, its texture, taste, and feel. It is love conceptualized. It is an abstract rather than a particular concept, even while having a seeming structure that your heart can feel. Concepts that cannot be felt with your heart are of no use to you now, for they are meant for their usefulness rather than for their service. Concepts that touch your heart serve you through this touch. They also begin to help break you away from the need for comparisons, for there is no need to compare what your heart can feel. When your heart can feel, you need no judgment to tell you the difference between one thing and another. You thus can begin to quit relying on your body's eyes to distinguish the true from the false, the real from the unreal.

21.4   Love appeals to you through the heart. God appeals to you through your heart. Your heart has not been open to the appeals of love partially because of your use of concepts. Concepts have been used to order your world and to assist your mind in keeping track of all that is in it. Your mind does not need this assistance. To begin to conceptualize in ways that touch your heart will free your mind of its reliance on thought concepts, thus allowing heart and mind to *speak the same language or to be communicated with in the same way.*

21.5 · There has been a division between the language of your mind and heart. Your mind insists on thinking and learning in a certain way, a way contrary to the language of your heart, and so, like two people from different countries speaking different languages, there has been little communication and much misunderstanding. Occasionally the problems associated with a lack of a common language have been set aside when the actions needed in a certain circumstance have demanded cooperation. You see this in times of emergency or crisis of every kind. And like the two people from different countries who do not understand each other, working together momentarily diminishes the boundaries of language, and a temporary solidarity is formed through like action. At such times two strangers who are foreign to one another might recognize that the other's "heart is in the right place." The "right place" with two people—as with mind and heart—is the place of no division. The unification of mind and heart that produces right action currently occurs primarily in crisis situations because of a lack of shared language. The formation of a shared language can thus be seen to aid in unification.

21.6   *The embrace* can now be likened to the starting point of a shared language, a language shared by mind and heart and by all people. It is a language of images and concepts that touch the one heart and serve the one mind.

21.7   Conflict between mind and heart occurs for an additional reason as well, although this conflict has at its root the problem of language as determined by perception. This is a problem of meaning. Mind and heart interpret meaning in different ways. You do not even begin to understand the enormity of this conflict or what it means to you, but I assure you that as long as mind and heart interpret meaning in different ways you will not find peace. You have, in the past, accepted these different interpretations as natural. You see that there are two ways of viewing a situation, even if you do not label one way of viewing or perceiving being of the mind and the other of the heart. And you *accept* this conflict-inducing situation. You accept that your mind sees one truth and your heart another, and you act anyway! You act without agreement or resolution. You act without unity. And, just as if you were two people acting on different truths in the same situation, conflict cannot help but continue. No matter which path you follow, the path of the mind or the path of the heart, you will not get where you are wanting to go until they are joined. You might imagine three paths—one path representing mind, one path representing heart, and one path representing wholeheartedness. The path of neither mind nor heart alone will take you where the path of unity will take you, and the journey will not be the same.

21.8   The major cause of the conflict that arises between mind and heart is the perception of internal and external differences in meaning. In extreme instances this is considered moral conflict, an example being the individual knowing the "right" thing to do but acting instead on what is the accepted thing to do within his or her community. In such an instance the external and internal meanings of the same situation are considered to be different. This is fairly easy to see in extreme circumstances, but it is a situation that exists constantly and in every instance until unity is achieved. Until unity is achieved you do not understand that you give meaning to all things, and that there is nothing and no one external to you who can determine meaning for you.

21.9   The final thing you must understand is that meaning does not change. While only you can determine meaning, and while only a wholehearted approach will determine true meaning, the truth is the truth and does not change. Only unity, however, allows you to see the truth and to claim it as your discovery and your truth as well as universal truth. Seeing the truth returns you to unity and to true communication or communion with your brothers and sisters in Christ. *Your brothers and sisters in Christ* is an expression that has always been meant to symbolize the unity of those who know the one truth.

21.10   Knowing the one truth is not about knowing a certain dogma or a set of facts. Those who know the truth do not see themselves as right and others as wrong. Those who know the truth find it for themselves by joining mind and heart. Those who know the truth become beings of love and light and see the same loving truth in all.

CHAPTER 22

The Intersection

22.1   We will talk much more of imagining now, and you may, at first, be resistant to this instruction. To imagine is too often associated with daydreaming, fiction, or make-believe, and these functions are all prescribed to be for certain parts of your life and for certain times that you deem appropriate. Please assure yourself, as I assure you, that now is an appropriate time, an essential time, for such activity. Your thoughts regarding imagining and imagination will change with your change in perspective on use. You will no longer be using your imagination but letting your imagination be of service to you.

22.2   We will be letting images serve as learning devices. They will enhance our use of language so that our language becomes one for both head and heart. We will begin by discussing the concept of *intersection* and look at it as a passing-*through* that establishes a partnership or relationship. While we have previously discussed relationship as not being one thing or the other but a third something, we have not as yet discussed how this relationship is provided in form. Now we will do so.

22.3   A prime image of this idea is provided by the axis. A line passes through a circle and the circle revolves around the line, or axis. Imagine a globe spinning around its axis. You know that the globe is representative of the Earth. What you less frequently picture is the relationship between the globe and the axis, even though you realize the axis allows the globe to spin.

22.4   A second and equally worthy image is that of a needle passing through material. Of itself, it can hold two pieces of material together. With the addition of thread passed through the eye of the needle, it can bind many parts in many different configurations.

22.5   A needle can also pass through something like an onion, piercing many layers. While such a piercing has no intrinsic value in terms of purpose, it provides an image of a straight line passing through not one, but many layers of another substance.

22.6 Intersection is often seen as a division between rather than as a relationship among. The illustrations used here, however, concentrate upon a passing through rather than upon an idea of division, and they help to show that even what is divided by intersection remains whole.

22.7 The image of intersection is simply meant to represent the point where the world intersects with you—where your path crosses that of others, where you encounter situations in your daily life, where you experience those things that cause you to feel or believe in a certain way—and it is at this point of intersection that not only relationship, but partnership is found. The partnership of axis to globe, and of needle and thread to material, is easily seen. In these two examples, the partnership creates something that did not previously exist by providing a function and a purpose for each. In the case of the needle and the onion, partnership is less apparent because function and purpose are not apparent. Partnership is thus equated with productive intersection rather than intersection itself.

22.8 Meaning is similarly interpreted. Intersections that create function and purpose are deemed meaningful. Intersections that seem to have no function or purpose are deemed meaningless. The act of passing through is, of itself, seen as of little consequence.

22.9 Yet it is the passing through that creates the intersection. Everything within your world and your day must pass through you in order to gain reality. While you might think of this as everything outside of yourself, please, when thinking of this, use the words I have provided: *everything within your world*. In the act of pass-through you assign meaning to everything within your world. The meaning you assign becomes the reality of the object you have assigned meaning to. You have seen your purpose as one of assigning meaning to that which intersects with you in a given way that you deem as purposeful. Yet it is in the passing through that meaning occurs of itself.

22.10 Further, it is the part of you through which everything within your world passes and your awareness of it that determines the meaning you give it. You are much more like unto the layers of the onion than the globe, with everything within your world needing to pass through layers with a seeming lack of purpose for the passing through.

22.11 You might think of the axis for a moment as a funnel through which eternity is poured and a whole heart as that which can allow free pass-through of all that is provided.

22.12 In contrast, the layered approach to intersection causes you to feel as if external forces are bombarding you. These forces must pass through one or another of your five senses—which you might think of collectively as layers—and are allowed no other access. These forces must then be directed. Often great effort is expended keeping these forces from piercing your heart, the center of yourself. You instead deflect them, using your mind, which might be considered another layer, to send them to various compartments—or, continuing with the onion theme, to one of the various layers of yourself. These layers protect your heart, and a great percentage of them are involved with denial, with creating places where things enter and simply sit. These "things" are not really things, but are all that you have found no meaning for. Since your function is seen as assigning meaning rather than receiving meaning, that which you consider meaningless sits, and that which you consider beyond meaning sits. You might imagine yourself as the creator of an unfinished dictionary, and all that is sitting as that to which you have determined you will, at some later date, get around to assigning meaning.

22.13 The "meaningless" category might include such things as the happenings of your daily routine, chance encounters, illness, or accidents, while in the "beyond meaning" category exists the relationship that broke your heart, grief, poverty, war, the events that seemed to alter your destiny, the search for God. By using the word *sit*, I mean to imply that these things have not passed through you and in the act of passing through formed a relationship and a partnership with you.

22.14 While passing through would seem to imply an entry and exit point, the relationship developed during the pass-through continues. Just as wind or water passing through an entry and exit point has an impact and a motion, so does what passes through you provide the movement of your journey. What passes through you is transformed by the relationship with you just as surely as you are transformed by the relationship with it.

22.15 When you remove yourself from the self-held position of "meaning-giver," you let things be what they are and, allowed to be what they are, their meaning is naturally revealed. What this takes is a pass-through approach and a relinquishment of the idea of bringing things to a stop where they can be examined under a microscope quite apart from their relationship to you or to anything else.

22.16 Imagine yourself brought to such a halt and examined apart from everything else within your world. Anyone wanting to learn anything about you would be wiser to observe you as you are within your world. Would you still be the same person in a laboratory? Are you still who you are when another takes you into his or her mind and assigns meaning to you?

22.17 You have made of yourself a laboratory where you bring everything for examination, categorization, testing, and filing away. This is the scenario that separates you from everything else within your world. Everything has meaning only according to what it means to you and not as what it is.

22.18 Obviously two kinds of meaning are being talked about. The first we talked of earlier as the finding of truth. The second is what we are talking of here, the finding of a definition, a personal meaning. Can you see the difference?

22.19 The personal and individual is the "I" we are dispelling. Think a moment of how you tell a story or report on events that have taken place within your life. You personalize. You are likely to report on what a certain set of circumstances meant "to you." This kind of thinking is thinking with the small "I." "I saw." "I felt." "I thought." "I did." The individual, personal, separated self is at the center of all such stories. One quite literally cannot conceive of the story without the "I." Yet this you must learn to do, and this task is given you as an exercise.

22.20 Begin to imagine life passing through you rather than getting stopped for examination at its intersection with you. Begin to imagine seeing the world without the emphasis on your personal self. Begin to form sentences and eventually to tell stories without the use of the "I" pronoun. This will seem, at first, as if it is depersonalizing the world and making it less intimate. It will seem as if you are shirking some primal responsibility to assign meaning to everything. Rather than resisting this, strive to cease giving meaning. Start quite simply. Go from the broad to the specific. For example, when you walk out your door in the morning you might generally think, *What a lovely day.* What this sentence says is that you have immediately taken in your surroundings and judged them. It is a lovely day "to you." The day has all or most of the requirements you find pleasing in a day. Replace such a thought with: "The grass is green. The birds are singing. The sun is warm." Simple reporting.

22.21 When you are asked questions such as, "How was your day?" respond as much as possible without using the word *I* or *my*. Quit referring to people and things in terms of ownership, saying "my boss," "my husband," "my car."

22.22 This removal of the personal "I" is but a first step to returning you to the consciousness of unity, a first step in going beyond meaning as definition to meaning as truth. As odd and impersonal as it will seem at first, I assure you the feeling of impersonality will be replaced quickly with an intimacy with your surroundings that you never felt before.

22.23 This intimacy itself will allow you to see your "self" as an integral part of all that exists within your world rather than as the small and insignificant personal self you generally accept as your "self." By eliminating the personal, the universal becomes available. As the universal becomes available, you will have no desire for the personal. Even so, you will find that what you consider your individuality or uniqueness is very much intact, but that it is different than you have always imagined it to be. You will find that you fulfill a grand purpose, and have a wonderful part to play in a grand design. You will not feel cheated by losing your separated self. You will feel free.

CHAPTER 23
The Freedom of the Body

23.1 Knowing and love are inseparable. When this is realized, it is obvious that love is the only true wisdom, the only true understanding, the only true knowing. Love is the great teacher. And your loving relationships the means of learning love.

23.2 The lessons learned from love will go a long way in assuaging your remaining fears about the loss of your individuality that you believe will accompany the loss of your separated self. For, as each of you has found as you have loved another, the more you love and long to possess a loved one, the more you realize that your loved one cannot be possessed. While in a love relationship the greatest knowing is sought and, with willing partners, attained; one's partner in such a relationship still transcends complete knowing. The relationship becomes the known. While it is your nature to seek for more, it is also the nature of life to exist in relationship and to become known through relationship. This is how knowing comes to be. Knowing through relationship is not a "second best" situation. It is how life is. It is how love is.

23.3 Thus, while your partner in love transcends total knowing, this too is "how it is." How it is meant to be. Love inviolate. Each of you is love inviolate. Yet relationally, you may be able to "read each other's thoughts," be cognizant of the slightest switch in mood, finish each other's sentences. You know the other would lay down his or her life for you, rise to any occasion of your need, share your every fear and joy.

23.4 Non-partnered love also shares a knowing through relationship. The loved one may be on the other side of the country, separated by distance, or previous choices, or past hurts, and yet a relationship continues.

23.5 In both partnered and non-partnered love relationships, the one you come to know, the only one who does not transcend total knowing, is your Self.

23.6   The same is true of your relationship with God. As in any love relationship, the desire to know God can be all consuming. Yet, while God
transcends knowing, your relationship with God is how you know both God
and your Self.

23.7   Let me remind you of a key learning aid discussed some pages back:
You would not be other than you are. No matter how much you grow to love
another, that love does not cause you to want to *be* the other person. That
love causes you to want to have a *relationship* with the other person. This
should tell you something about the nature of love.

23.8   When obsessively in love you may want the other person to be *you*, but
rarely the other way around. This is what has caused you to make God over
in your own image and to try to do the same to others. This comes of seeing
oneself as an image rather than as a being existing in relationship. This
comes from ego rather than from the true Self.

23.9   What you long for is re-union. Yet reunion too is relationship, because
union is relationship. Imagine a crowd of people in a small room. This is not
relationship. When you are tempted to think of relationship having to do
with physical proximity, think of this example. Now imagine communities of
faith. Around the world, people are united in belief, and not only in religious
beliefs. Ideology, politics, profession unite people. "Parties" and "associations" are formed to foster the idea of unity through shared belief. They are
not necessary, as is seen by the reality that they only form after the fact. The
belief fosters the form and the form is then meant to foster the belief.

23.10   This is true of the body as well. Think of the way in which the word
body is used and this will be clear. The *body* politic. A *body* of knowledge.
Belief fostered the form and the form was meant to foster the belief. Thus
belief and form have a symbiotic relationship. Understanding of this *loving*
relationship can help you to experience freedom of the body, which is an
extension, in form, of your belief in the personal "I."

23.11   Belief fosters union. Union does not foster belief, because in unity belief
is no longer required. Belief fostered the union of atoms and cells into the
form required by the belief in the separated self. Belief of another kind can
foster the creation of form of another kind.

23.12   If form is an extension of belief you can see why what you believe is
critical to how you live with form. We are speaking here of ways of thinking

similar to those which you term induction and deduction. In the past, exercises have most often begun with an alteration of beliefs regarding form. Here we have taken an opposite approach, beginning with exercises to alter your belief in your identity and concluding with exercises to alter your belief in form. This is consistent with our primary focus on learning from the heart. The mind goes from the small to the large, the heart from the large to the small. Only the wholehearted see the connection of all.

23.13 I repeat: *Belief of another kind can foster the creation of form of another kind.* A wholehearted belief in the truth about your Self is what is required to cause this to be so. It is what is necessary now. It will change the world.

23.14 *Belief of another kind* is what miracles are all about. It is what you are all about as a miracle worker. For you to change your beliefs is the miracle that we are after, the result we seek from this Course.

23.15 Obviously, your belief in who and what you are is the basis for your entire foundation, a foundation previously built on fear. Clearly, belief in the body was easily translated into a belief in the validity of fear. When you are free of this misperception, this inaccurate belief, your body will be freed. It will no longer be an object of use but a means of service.

23.16 Freeing your perception from your nearly immutable belief in form will allow for all changes in form required by the miracle. Form is not a constant but a result. While you believe that belief is the result of form, it is not. Form is the result of belief. Thus belief is not only capable of changing form but also is necessary in order to do so.

23.17 History has shown you that what you believe is possible becomes possible. Science has proven the link between researcher and research findings. Still you find it difficult to believe that what is possible depends upon what you can imagine being possible. You must cease to see the difficulty and begin to see the ease with which what you can imagine becomes reality.

23.18 You have no capabilities that do not serve you, because they were created to serve you. The ability to imagine is such a capability, freely and equally given to all. Imagination is linked to true vision, for it exercises the combined capabilities of mind and heart. It is akin to perception, and can lead the way in changing how you perceive of yourself and the world around you.

23.19 Beyond imagination is the spark that allows you to conceive of what never was conceived of before. This spark is inspiration, the infusion of spirit. Taking the creation of form backward, it leads to this conclusion: Spirit precedes inspiration, inspiration precedes imagination, imagination precedes belief, and belief precedes form.

23.20 Spirit is your more direct link with the one Source. Spirit is directly from the Source, while form is a by-product of spirit. Thus form is once removed, or further away from the Source. Again working backward, however, the form you have created is still a step necessary in the return to the Source. The necessary step is that of moving beyond form—recognizing and acknowledging form for what it is and then continuing on, working backward to change your belief, to allow imagination to serve you and spirit to fill you.

23.21 You then can move forward again, taking form beyond its given parameters and becoming a miracle worker.

23.22 The body encompasses or holds the belief. It is the composite of your beliefs, the totality. It will continue to hold former beliefs as well as new beliefs until old beliefs are purged. The purging of old beliefs frees space for the new. It allows your form to reflect what and who you are now in terms that coincide with the "you" whom you have always been.

23.23 There is no quick route to this purging, as it is the most individual of accomplishments. As you learned your beliefs, you must unlearn your beliefs. As you begin the process of unlearning you may feel tested. You are not being tested but given opportunities for unlearning. To learn that a previously held belief is no longer valid is the only way to truly purge that belief.

23.24 These learning opportunities call for a period of engagement with life. Many of you will have begun to experience unlearning opportunities even while your study of this Course may have led you to turn inward and attempt to disengage from life. A period of engagement with life cannot be avoided, however, and your attempts to avoid it will only cause an increase in feelings generated by experiences of duality. While you hold conflicting beliefs within you, you will be conflicted and affected by polarity. Unlearning allows you to purge old beliefs so that only one set of beliefs is operative within you. This is the only route to the certainty you seek, and leads to true conviction. True conviction cannot be attained without this experience of unlearning and purging.

23.25 All unlearning opportunities are opportunities for miracle readiness. There is no trick to identifying unlearning opportunities. From this point forward, I assure you, all experiences will be thus until unlearning is no longer needed. If you will remember that the one exercise for your mind is dedicating all thought to union, you will keep your mind engaged and less resistant to unlearning. When you feel resistance—and of course your mind will resist unlearning what it has striven to learn—return your dedication to union. Acknowledge your mind's resistance as a sign that unlearning is going on. Acknowledge it but do not engage it.

23.26 What will happen when you look at each situation as a challenge to your beliefs? If you do not remember that you are involved in a process of unlearning that will lead to the conviction you have so long sought, you will indeed feel tested and will try to take control of the learning situation. Not taking control, however, is the key to unlearning. What you term as *being in control* is simply another way of saying *acting on old beliefs.* As long as you attempt to remain in control, old beliefs will not be purged.

23.27 Attempting to exert control over learning situations is a reflection of belief that you have nothing to learn. An attitude of openness is required for unlearning and new learning both. Control opposes openness. Mastery comes through the process of both unlearning and learning anew. This is but another way of stating that which was stated in *A Course in Miracles*: Resign as your own teacher. The desire to control is the desire to remain your own teacher and/or to choose your teachers and learning situations. Neither can occur if you would truly choose to change your beliefs and move on to the new or the truth.

23.28 Looked at in another way, this process has much in common with forgiveness. The action associated with it raises it to a level similar to that of atonement. It is an undoing accompanied by a new means of doing. In the process of unlearning, both forgiveness and atonement occur. You recognize that your false beliefs were the result of faulty learning. As unlearning is replaced by new learning, judgment falls away as your innocence is established. Can a child be found guilty when the child has not yet learned that which is needed for right action?

23.29 You might ask, how do you learn what you have failed to learn previously? What are the lessons? What is the curriculum? How will you know when you have achieved a learning objective? Yet how can you become a master of what another would teach? Of lessons another would select? Your life must become your teacher, and you its devoted pupil. Here is a curriculum designed specifically for you, a curriculum only you can master. Only your own life experiences have led to the learning you have accumulated and translated into beliefs. Only your own life experiences will reverse the process.

Chapter 24

The Time of Tenderness

24.1   Where you learned to hate, you will learn to love. Where you learned to fear, you will learn safety. Where you learned to distrust, you will learn trust. And each learning experience will be a learning experience *because* it will touch your heart. It may be as simple as a smile from a child that melts away all the resentment you held from your childhood—*because* you allow that smile to touch your heart. It may be a time of weepiness and what you would term emotionalism. You may feel as if everything makes you want to cry because everything will touch you, each lesson will feel tender. Unlearning has no harshness about it. If you simply allow it to come, it will reward you constantly with what can best be described as tenderness.

24.2   The time to resist tenderness is over. The time to resist the tears of weariness is over. This is the time of the embrace.

24.3   These feelings of tenderness can be seen as a sign. Let them alert you that unlearning is taking place. Welcome them as harbingers of this good news. Know that the time of tenderness is a sure path on the way home.

24.4   The time of tenderness precedes the time of peace and is the forerunner of compassion. The time of tenderness is thus the final learning ground before accomplishment is complete. The learning that occurs during the time of tenderness is learning from love. No lessons learned without love touch your heart. No lessons that do not touch your heart will accomplish anything. The purpose of the final lessons are both unlearning and moving through unlearning to new learning. These lessons must be accomplished in life and require an engagement with life. This engagement is a promise, a commitment. It requires participation, involvement, attention, being present. These are the lessons with which we will conclude.

Devotion as a Type of Participation

25.1 To devote oneself to an objective is a vow to accomplish. To be devoted is to be prayerful. As we said in the beginning, to pray is to ask for all to be included in what you do. Devotion is thus our first lesson in learning how to be engaged in life during the time of tenderness.

25.2 Devotion is the outcome of love and in this instance is an action word, a verb, a means of serving and being served by love. Devotion is a particular type of participation. It cannot be faked. But it can be practiced.

25.3 You, dear children, have faked your way through much of life. You have faked confidence when you are uncertain, interest where you feel indifference, knowledge of things about which you know nothing. But those who have tried to fake love cannot do it. The same is true of devotion, because there is no real devotion without love.

25.4 Love cannot be faked because you know love. Because you know it, imitations of love are immediately felt. You may choose to deny the feeling, but you cannot prevent it from occurring. You can attempt to earn the love of those from whom you desire it, you can attempt to buy it, change for it, or capture it. This you cannot do. Yet, love is always present. Let us spend a moment considering this contradiction.

25.5 How can love always be present when you can undeniably feel each and every absence of love? The problem is in the perceiver rather than the perceived. Each time you feel a lack of love, it comes from within yourself. This lack of love, or "faked" love of which you cannot help but be aware, is a signal to you that you want something. When you become aware that you want something, you are also becoming aware that you feel you lack something. All feelings of lack are synonymous with feelings of fear. Where there is fear, love is hidden. Love is rejected when a choice for fear is made. You cannot be without love, but you can reject love. When you reject love, it is hidden from you, because receiving completes giving. Each of your brothers and sisters are love inviolate. What each gives is incomplete until it is received.

25.6   When you feel a lack of love in others, you have projected your fear onto them. Only when you cease to do this will you feel true devotion.

25.7   When you feel lack of love, you feel as if the "other" gives you nothing. Yet it is your lack of ability to receive that causes this feeling. The practice of devotion is a means by which you can purify your engagement with life and all you encounter within it. Devotion is synonymous with true service. True service does not look for what another has to give or what another has that you might use. True service recognizes God's law of giving and receiving, and the practice of devotion is, in effect, the practice of allowing giving and receiving to be one. It is, during the time of tenderness, a true practice that, like vigilance, is a means to a desired end. You must practice recognizing your feelings of lack of love, and realize these feelings come from your inability to receive. Do this practice until it is no longer needed.

25.8   Devotion is inclusive. It implies a subject and an object: One who is devoted and one who is an object of devotion. While we are moving away from subject/object relationships to the relationship of unity, the idea of one who is devoted, and of those for whom devotion is practiced, is useful during the time of tenderness. It will lead to the understanding of oneness as completion, an understanding of giving and receiving as one.

25.9   Devotion leads to harmony through action. This is possible for you now only if you have integrated the most basic teaching of this Course and no longer feel duped by life. All of your contests of will are supported by your contention that you have been misled. It is as if you have paid for your ticket, arrived for the concert, and been told your ticket is not valid. This makes you angry. This anger is reenacted in thousands of different scenarios in your life day after day and year after year until you realize and truly believe the basic tenets this Course has put forward.

25.10   To be in concert, just as to perform a concert, is contingent on harmony. It is being in agreement about the purpose for which you are here and your entitlement to be fully present here. If you still believe you are here to acquire some perceived ideal separated state, then all action will be out of harmony. If, however, you have accepted the basic tenets of this Course and believe you are here to realize unity, then all action will be in harmony. If you believe you and your brothers and sisters are here in a state of reprisal, having fallen from grace, then all action will be out of harmony. If you believe you and all other living things are here in a state of grace, then all action will be in harmony. If you believe one living thing is more important than any other, then all action will be out of harmony. If you believe all are essential, then all action will be in harmony.

25.11 While one special relationship continues, all special relationships continue because they are given validity. The holy relationship of unity depends on the release of the beliefs that foster special relationships.

25.12 To believe you are in concert with the universe is to believe that you have no need for struggle, to believe you have no lack, to believe in your state of grace. While you believe even one person is against you, you are not in concert with God. While you believe fate works against you, you are not in concert with the universe. These attitudes confirm a continuing belief in your separated and vulnerable state. During the time of tenderness, you will learn, through the practice of devotion, to identify and reject all such attitudes and to adopt an attitude of invulnerability.

25.13 An attitude of invulnerability is necessary now. It is not arrogance or a means by which to flirt with risk and danger. It is simply your reality. During the time of tenderness you may feel vulnerable. But the time of tenderness is a time of healing, and as you are healed you will realize you are no longer vulnerable to being wounded. Fear of being wounded—physically, mentally, emotionally, and spiritually—has kept you from engaging with life. Being healed and recognizing your own state of being healed is a key purpose of the time of tenderness. You cannot realize your true identity while you hang on to wounds of any kind. All wounds are evidence of your belief that you can be attacked and hurt. You have not necessarily seen disappointment as attack or hopelessness as hurt, but you do feel these emotions as wounds. While you think you can remain disappointed or disillusioned, you will not be invulnerable. There is always, behind every disappointment or disillusion, every attack and every hurt, a person you believe acted toward you without love. While you believe feelings of lack of love come from anywhere but within, you will not be invulnerable.

25.14 A realization of your invulnerability is not necessary in terms of use but in terms of service. Those who claim invulnerability and use it as a test of fate, or an excuse to challenge the mighty forces of humanity or nature, will eventually lose the game they play. True invulnerability can only be claimed by those who recognize it as part of their true identity. Invulnerability will then serve you and your brothers and sisters. Its service is one of conquering fear and allowing love to reign.

25.15 Involvement flows from participation and engagement. While it may conjure up notions of joining movements or parties, or of making social contributions, pure joining is its objective. The first joining comes from within and it is putting into practice the lessons of joining mind and heart in wholeheartedness.

25.16 This first joining is a choice made from love without regard for the personal self. You begin to live from love when the personal self gets out of the way. And when the personal self gets out of the way in any instance, it is the turning point. It is the signal that you are ready to live from love. This is what this Course is about. Living from love. Living from love is what will reverse the lessons of the past. Reversing the lessons of the past is what will allow you to live in love in every instance.

25.17 Living in love in every instance is what occurs when the whole Self is involved in the love of life. There are no "parts" of the Self fractioned off and holding resentments. There are no "parts" of Self living in the past or the future. There is not a "mindful" Self living separately from a "soulful" Self. There is not a "worker" Self living separately from a "prayerful" Self. All Selves are joined in wholeheartedness. The one Self is solely involved in living love.

25.18 As you begin to live love, a reverse of what you might expect to happen will happen. While you may expect that everything will take on greater importance, the reverse will at first be true. You will see little in what you do that matters. You will wonder why you are unconcerned about many of the things you have been concerned about previously. Your life may actually seem to have less purpose. You may begin to wonder what to do. You will almost certainly question what you do for a "living." You will question many patterns and habits.

25.19 This is unlearning taking place. It may feel frustrating and be tinged with anxiety, anger, confusion, perplexity, even rage. You will doubt that these are the proper feelings of a person living love. Yet they are common feelings of unlearning, and should be accepted as such. You will learn that while some things you have done and will continue to do may not matter, they may still be done with patience, grace, and love. You will learn that other things you have done, beliefs you have held, patterns and habits that have occupied you, will not accompany you into your life of love. These you will leave behind.

25.20 You may also notice a growth in your desire to take credit for what you have created, and a desire to create anew. At this stage, this desire will come from a feeling of needing to reassert the self. This need will arise as you realize that you can take no credit for your life. Wanting to take credit is of the ego, and at this stage the desire to create may be linked with ego as well. Your personal self will be looking for a place in which to reside. It will be looking for identity. It will want to say: *"This is who I am."* This is an exciting sign, for it means the old identity is losing hold. Be patient during this time, and your new identity will emerge. If the urge to create is strong, certainly let it serve you. But do not seek for praise or acknowledgement of your creations at this time. You will soon realize that creation is not of, or for, the personal self.

25.21 This will be a time of discernment. You may feel it as a time of decision making, but the less you attempt to make conscious decisions the quicker your unlearning will take place and the lessons of discernment occur. Discernment is needed only until you are better able to comprehend the whole. Comprehension of the whole is aided by a return to wholeness of the Self. Until wholeness of the Self is complete, discernment is necessary.

25.22 Practice discernment by being still and awaiting wisdom. Your feeling of being identity-less will make decision-making and choices of all kinds appear to be difficult during this time. You must realize decisions and choices are made by relying upon the very lessons you are in the process of unlearning. At the same time, however, decisions and choices will seem to need to be made with increasing frequency. Your feeling of needing to make new choices, while strong, will not necessarily reflect real need but rather an impatience with the way things are and were. You will want to force change rather than wait for it to arrive. If you acknowledge your impatience as a sign of readiness for change that does not necessarily require action on your part, you will feel some relief.

25.23 When action is seen to be necessary, this is exactly when a time of stillness is needed. You might think of this time of stillness as a time of consulting with your new identity. Simply sitting quietly, and posing the question or concern that is in need of appropriate action will suffice. When an answer comes to you, acknowledge that it is an answer from your new identity and express appreciation for it. While you will at times doubt that you have received an answer or that the answer you have received is correct, you will soon learn to trust this quiet process of discernment. You will know you have succeeded when you truly feel as if you have "turned the question or concern over" and allowed it to be responded to in a new way.

25.24 When you are guided to act in ways that are contrary to usual patterns of action you have taken in the past, you will often meet resistance. Try to be lighthearted at such times and to remember that if it "doesn't matter," you might as well try the new way. Remind yourself that you have nothing to lose. You will soon learn that this is so. You will also soon realize why this time of engagement with life is necessary. Experience is necessary to complete the cycle of unlearning and learning.

25.25 Being fully engaged with life while taking the time for discernment is uncommon. Putting action before stillness, activity before rest, is seen as synonymous with a full life. We must, therefore, speak a bit of what a full life is.

Chapter 26

The Full Life

26.1 It is often spoken of with some amazement that I lived a short life, preached for only a small part of it, traveled not very far, had few possessions or influential friends. We have talked before of the tragedy you feel when anyone dies young. You each have some notion of what you believe a full life to be. For some of you it would include marriage and children, for others career, religious commitment, or creative endeavors. Some would think of travel and adventure, friendships, or financial security. Most of you will think of having a long life.

26.2 Many of you question the line between fate and accomplishment. Are some chosen for greatness? Others for mediocrity?

26.3 Few recognize the tragedy in the *life* of a person, except in instances of great dichotomy, perhaps best expressed in the life of the tragic hero. This observance of tragedy *in life* occurs only when the observation is also made of the greatness, the glory, *in the life*. Without the recognition of the glory of life, there is no recognition of tragedy until the life has ended. In contrast, in the life of the tragic hero, excluding those who are posthumously given such a title, the tragedy is most often considered a fall from greatness. It is seen in the allure of myths where those who associate themselves too closely with the gods are punished for such folly. Such fear of greatness and glory, of the possibility of a fall from greatness and glory, results in many tragedy-less lives. "Nothing ventured, nothing gained," is an axiom for such lives. Fear of the "fall" is a primal fear, the first fear, the fear behind all such axioms.

26.4 Again I offer my life as the example life and reiterate the message expressed in *A Course in Miracles:* The true meaning of the crucifixion is that it was the last and final end to all such fears and myths. All such fears were taken to the cross with me and banished in the resurrection of the glory that is ours.

26.5 Do not be afraid. My brothers and sisters in Christ, realize that there is no cause for fear. You cannot fly too closely to the sun. You cannot be deceived any longer by tales of woe or of fallen heroes. Your story is one of glory. Your greatness can no longer be denied, unless *you* deny it.

26.6 Do you feel beautiful and prized and worthy? Then so shall you be.

26.7 No fear is greater than the fear of meaninglessness. And, as stated before, the quest for meaning is how you have described your purpose here. To have no meaning to attach to your life is the tragedy you see within it and attempt to keep hidden from yourself. This fear goes hand in hand with your fear of the fall, for if you were to attempt to assign the meaning to your life that you think it should have, a fall would surely await you, at least in your imaginings. You are thus caught in a double bind, living a life you feel is devoid of meaning and letting fear keep you from seeking the meaning you would give it. You feel no inherent sense of purpose, no grace, no meaning beyond what you would give to your own endeavors.

26.8 This is what we now leave behind as we seek to become involved with life. I say *we* because I am with you and will not leave your side. I say *we* because your first involvement is involvement with Christ, an involvement that links us in oneness and glory once again. I say *we* because *we are* life. I say *we* because we cannot live love apart from one another.

26.9 You do not yet, but will soon realize the happiness that is ours. Your mind can just not accept that happiness as well as meaning is due you through no effort of your own. Scenes of your life play through your mind that "prove" that you are neither inherently happy, nor your life inherently meaningful. Your reliance on these scenes and memories must be broken before my words can reach your mind and begin to replace these scenes with new ones. Until that time is upon you, let my words touch your heart.

26.10 You who struggle to understand what these words say and what they might mean, who strive to find the clues to what they ask you to do, will find it difficult to cease your struggle and your striving. You find it almost impossible still to believe effort is not called for—that what your heart but wishes for could simply come true through your acceptance of these words. But I am prepared to make it easy for you.

26.11 You who have so sought happiness without finding it, rejoice. It is not lost. It does not require you to define it or put a name to it before it can be yours. Is this not what you have cried about in frustration? Have you not long sought to put a name on happiness? Have you not long lamented that if you knew what would bring you happiness you would surely pursue it? Have you not long stated that if you knew what would bring meaning to your life you would surely do it? Have you not long wished to know your purpose? To be given a goal that would fulfill the longing in you? Have you not prayed for signs? Read books that have promised you a series of steps to take to get where you want to go, only to realize you know not where that is?

26.12 And have you not become impatient with advice, with teachers and with courses of study? Have you not felt at the limit of your patience with instruction? Have you not felt the call to live growing stronger in you by the day? Are you not anxious to say: *"Tell me what to do and I will do it?"* Are you not ready for certainty above all else? Are you not ready to be done with studying and to begin with living? Have you not become increasingly convinced that you have not been living, and wondered what it is you have been doing? Have you not grown weary of what passes for life in your world? Have you not wished you could throw out all the thoughts and worries that fill your mind and begin anew?

26.13 Are you not simply ready to be done with the way things have been and to begin a new way? Are you not ready to listen to a new voice?

26.14 All this frustration and impatience has been building. This buildup has been necessary. Now, like an explosion waiting to happen, it only needs a trigger to be released. With its release the new can begin.

26.15 This Course is but a trigger. These words the prelude to the explosion. It is as if you have been waiting for someone to whisper: *Now!* The whisper has come. The time is now.

26.16 Can you let the worries of today leave your mind? Can you let the disappointments of yesterday go and be no more? Can you let the planning for the future cease? Can you be still and know your Self?

26.17 This is perhaps disappointing to you, but it is all that is required. If you could truly succeed at doing this for one instant, you would experience all that is holy and be forever new.

26.18 You may experience disappointment at these words, and feel as if you have been waiting to be invited to a party and that the invitation hasn't come. This is because you are ready for the next step, the step of being engaged with life. The step of living from love. And I assure you, there is no need to sit about and wait for the time of the celebration to come. This is the invitation to the celebration. This is the invitation to greet this day with no worry, disappointment, or planning. This is the invitation to greet your Self and to find your Self within this day.

26.19 It requires no new plans. It asks not that you make any decisions. It asks not that you *do* anything new. This is an invitation from love to love. It asks only that you be open and allow giving and receiving as one to take place. It asks only that you be unoccupied with the old so that the new may arrive. It asks only that you listen to your heart and let your Self be heard.

26.20 I cannot tell you here what you will hear. How can I, when each of you will hear the answer of your heart? The calling of love to love inviolate? The answer that only you can hear. There is no mold, no form, no stock answer. This is why all answers have disappointed you in the past. Your answer is not the same as any other. No matter how filled with wisdom one person's answer may be, it is not yours.

26.21 You are a thought of a God. An idea. This thought, or idea, is what you seek. It can be found only at its source. Its source is love, and its location is your own heart.

26.22 Think a moment of a novel or movie with no plot. This would be the same as saying that there was no idea brought to completion within the pages or on the film. In God's idea of you is all that is known about you. God's idea of you is perfect, and until now your form has been but an imperfect representation of God's idea. In God's idea of you is the pattern of the universe, much as within a novel, movie, piece of music, invention or artistic idea is the completion of the pattern that will make that idea a masterpiece. An idea is irrevocably linked with its source and one with its source. There was no God separate from you to have this idea of you. You were birthed in unison with God's idea of you.

26.23 This does not need to be understood, but only accepted to the extent you can accept it. This is necessary because of your reliance on a God who is "other" than you for the provision of your answers. Acceptance of your birth in unison with God's idea of you is acceptance of your Self as co-creator of the pattern of the universe, acceptance of the idea or the story that is you. Can you not see that you were birthed into a place in the pattern of

God's creation? Or that you not only can know but have always known of this place?

26.24 This is not a place of physical form but a place of holiness, an integral place in the pattern that is oneness with God. It is a place you have never left but that you long for, believing that you know it not. Your life here is much like a search for your story. Where will this chapter lead? What will the end be like? Was one event a mistake and another a blessing in disguise? You seek to know your story's table of contents, or at least a brief outline. Where does your life fit in the larger picture? And yet, you realize that—like reading a story—when the end is reached and all is known, the story is over except in memory and reflection and perhaps in speculation. What might a sequel reveal?

26.25 This viewing of your life as a story is what you do. You spend each day in review or speculation. What has happened and what will happen next? You attempt to rewrite previous chapters and to cast all the parts and plan all the events of the next. This is, in effect, your attempt to control what you do not believe you created, and what you feel deprived of creating. As a being birthed by a thought of God, you grew simultaneously with God's thought. You knew your place in the pattern of creation from the outset. A full life is quite simply a fulfillment of that thought and that pattern. The only way to know it is to think it once again. The only way to think it once again is to be wholehearted, for a split mind and heart do not think clearly.

26.26 Being whole is being present. Being whole is being all you are. Being whole is being present as all you are. When this occurs you are All in All, One in being with your Father.

26.27 I fulfilled my story, my pattern, the idea of me that came from the thought of God. In doing so, I restored unity, oneness with God. I ushered in the new way that you are now longing to adopt. I ushered in a time of being.

CHAPTER 27

Being

27.1   We return now to what your being is. Being is. As love is. You have attached being to being *human*. In your quest to identify yourself, you simply narrowed yourself to the visible and describable. Thus you have identified death as the only means by which to reach oneness with your Father, knowing that such oneness is not compatible with the human nature you ascribe to yourself. In this one error do all errors lie. For what quest can be fulfilled when the only answer to life seems to be death? This is why and how my death and resurrection provided an answer and an end to the need for answers.

27.2   Your *being* here is not futile or without purpose. Your *being* is itself all purpose, all honor, all glory. There is no being apart from being. There is no being *alive* and being *dead*, being *human* or being *divine*. There is only being. Being is.

27.3   Yet being, like love, *is* in relationship. Thus, your purpose here, rather than being one of finding meaning, is one of coming to know through relationship. It is in coming to know through relationship that you come to know your Self.

27.4   The purpose of this Course has been stated in many ways and is stated again here: The purpose of this Course is to establish your identity. The importance of this purpose cannot be underestimated. Let us address the question of why this is so important.

27.5   You have been caught in a cycle of seeing the self as important for a period of time and then seeing the self as unimportant for a period of time. Seeing the self as important seems at one time like a function of the ego, and at another as a function of the divine. You become confused between the personal self and a true Self only because you have not as yet identified your true Self. Once you have identified your true Self all such confusion will end.

27.6   We have already stated that relationship is the only "known" in an unknowable world. We have already stated that the only being who is not beyond the limits of total knowing is the Self. Thus it is in knowing the Self that all is known.

27.7   When you fully realize that the only way to know the Self is through relationship, your concerns about concentration on the self will end. Life is not a matter of self versus other. Life is a matter of relationship. Life is not a matter of human versus divine, but a matter of relationship between the human and the divine. Life is not a matter of one living thing versus another, but of the relationship between all living things.

27.8   If you can only come to know your Self through relationship, you can only come to know God through relationship. Christ *is* the holy relationship that exists between all and God, providing the bridge that spans the very concept of *between* and provides for the connection of unity. Thus your relationship with Christ always was and always will be. Your task here is to come to know that relationship once again.

27.9   The thought of God by which you were created is synonymous with the Christ in you. It is your relationship with your Source and all that He created.

27.10   Can you begin to visualize or perceive your true identity as relationship itself? And what of God? Can you unlearn all concepts and free your mind to accept all relationship instead? If all meaning and all truth lies in relationship, can you be other than relationship itself? Can God? Can you imagine relationship rather than singular objects and bodies, as *all* that exists, and thus who you are and who God is? Is it such a huge leap to go from saying you only exist in relationship to you only exist *as* relationship? You think it is, and feel yourself further diminished and lacking in identity just by contemplating such an idea. And so you must be reassured of the Self you are.

27.11   This establishment of your identity that we seek to do here is not just so that you can better understand yourself or your world, or even so that you can bring Heaven to Earth. Although these are complementary goals, as stated before, these are goals that you cannot accomplish "on your own" or with the concept you now hold of yourself. Just as you can look about and see that no two bodies on this earth are exactly the same, the Self you are is a unique Self. A Self of relationship does not imply a Self that is the same as all the rest. But it does imply a Self that is integral to all the rest. You matter, and you matter as an interactive part of the relationship that is life. You are already accomplished as who you are. All is accomplished in unity. In separation you merely strive for all that is yours in relationship. Relationship *is* unity, and relationship is your natural state. It is who you are.

27.12   Because you do not understand does not mean that you are not learning the truth. You do not understand because you think in terms of singularity rather than in terms of unity. This is why this Course has not concentrated on your thinking. Again you are bidden to turn to your heart for the truth that is hidden there yet waiting to be revealed. Your heart knows of unity and knows not any desire to be alone and separate. Your heart understands relationship as its source of being. You are not separate from your Source.

27.13   Living in relationship is living in love and is living as who you are. Living in relationship is living in the present. How do you learn to move from living in separation to living in relationship?

27.14   To live in relationship is to accept all that is happening in the present as your present reality, and as a call to be in relationship with it. It is the willingness to set aside judgment so that you are not contemplating what "should" be happening rather than what *is* happening. It looks past perception of "others" to relationship and wholeness. To live in relationship is to live in harmony even with conflict. It is an understanding that if conflict arises in your present there is something to be learned from your relationship with conflict.

27.15   Living in relationship is living from your center, the heart of your Self. It is complete reliance on relationship itself rather than on the mind. Thus your actions reflect the proper response to the relationship that is occurring in the present rather than to your preconceived notions of others, the previous judgments your mind once made and relies upon out of habit, or your considerations of what the situation might mean to your future. It is not the individual "you" that dictates your responses to situations based on surface interpretations of what those situations entail. It is rather the you in and within the relationship that responds out of the knowledge gained through relationship.

27.16   How often have you, even with the best of intentions, not known the proper response to make? You even wonder as you pray whether you should pray for specific outcomes or for God's Will to be done. You fear being a miracle worker because you do not think that you will ever know what is called for.

27.17 As you learn to live in relationship in the present, this confusion will pass. Your relationship will guide you surely to the proper response. I use the term "proper" here not as a measure of judgment, but as an indication that there is a *way* in which those who live in relationship become certain, and their willingness to act unimpeded by uncertainty. All uncertainty is fear. All fear is doubt about one's self. How can you not know how to respond when doubt is gone and certainty has come? How can certainty ever come without an understanding of the relationship of all things?

27.18 Does an understanding of the relationship of all things mean that you will have power that is not of this world? Will you see the future and the past, be cognizant of destiny and of fate? You do have power that is not of this world, but this does not mean power as you see it here, the power of details and the information of which you think when desiring or fearing a fate of prophecy. The power we speak of is the power of *knowing*.

27.19 How often have you known the "right" thing to do without knowing the details of what came before and what was to come? Sometimes you have acted on this knowing, and at other times not. Living in relationship provides a constant knowing of this sort, a simple knowing of a *way* things are meant to be. It is a knowing felt within the heart for which there still will be no proof, but for which there will be the certainty you heretofore have lacked. The typical fears you have experienced in the past will not arise within this knowing.

27.20 How will you know when you have achieved the state of grace in which you were created, and that you are living in relationship? You will know by the certainty you feel. If you do not feel this certainty, what can you do?

27.21 You are ready now, and all that will you prevent you from living a life of love is unwillingness to do so. There is only one remaining source of such unwillingness. Your willingness will now depend on whether or not you trust. Do you trust these words? Do you trust in God? Can you trust in your Self?

CHAPTER 28

Bearing Witness

28.1   We must speak about bearing witness to what you have learned. As this Course bears witness to the truth, thus must your lives bear witness. Lest this too be distorted, it must be discussed.

28.2   This is not a contest. Bearing witness has become a spectator sport and it is not meant to be thus. How, then, you might ask, is the truth brought to those still living in illusion?

28.3   Because inner knowing is both individual and collective, both personal and universal, this is the source of all proof. And so you believe coming together to share common testimony validates the proof of inner and collective knowing. You think shared beliefs amass, like a congregation around a pulpit, and even believe in a theory of mass that purports that when a certain magnitude of belief occurs, evolutionary steps are brought about. This, however, is not about evolutionary steps, and so a process intent upon bringing the collective to a fever pitch of belief through common testimony is not our aim.

28.4   Trust and bearing witness go together, as the validation sought through bearing witness is a symptom of distrust. Few are chosen to be prophets, and the plethora of testimony taking place is brought about by innocence more so than by wisdom. This sharing of personal testimony has reached its zenith and will no longer be as welcomed or appreciated, so even were the intent of this Course to bring testimony together in such a way as to cause an evolutionary step, it would not work. Thus we must concentrate on wisdom, the wisdom of the heart.

28.5   There is a trust that goes beyond proof, and beyond the need for any witnessing at all. This is the trust of knowing. Knowing is of the heart, and holds a consistency and certainty that the dawn of innocence does not contain. The dawn of innocence is but a recognition of the most common denominator of existence. As such, it is a beginning only, a true dawn that must, as the sun rises, give way to day and the brilliance and clarity of the wisdom of which we speak.

28.6 This daytime of your journey is approaching. It is the time for the sun to cut through the mists of dawn. It is the middle of the journey, a time of teaching and of learning both. It is the time of planting and of harvest that comes before the time of rest. It is the time of celebration that comes before the quiet and the settling of the dusk.

28.7 You would think of this as the time of work being done. This it is, but without the drudgery of time *spent*. It is your time to shine, to be a light to those who live in darkness.

28.8 And yet it is a time of great humility. Of wearing the face of Christ for all to see. For here is wisdom gained and shared.

28.9 Do you not see that any attempt to turn bearing witness into a convincing argument for your point of view, no matter what that point of view may be, makes what you have come to know pointless to you as well as to those you would convince? You think that when you are enlightened enough to know, you are also enlightened enough to know what to do with what you know. While you continue to think of a separation in terms of *doing* and of *knowing*, it is obvious this cannot be the case.

28.10 As the dawn is unrestrained in its bursting forth, so has been your time of innocence. Not so the approach of day as the sun slowly rises and as slowly sets. This is a time of being both guided and restrained. A time of realizing that you can *know* without knowing what to *do*, and that this is not a mistake. Many reach this stage and, not knowing what to do with what they know, begin to doubt their knowing. This is a human response to a knowing that is not human in origin. Knowing is alien to you, and that is why you seek validation. Each validation is seen and felt as a reward, a prize, a confirmation that you believe allows your conviction to grow. Because you believe it, this is, at first, quite true. But now it is no longer the time to rely on conviction that comes from the witnesses you find along your way. They serve a limited purpose for a limited time. Now is the time to step beyond the validation that your teachers can give you. When this step is not taken, gatherings of witnesses abound, and what they bear witness to stops short of what they would see.

28.11 Witnesses are for the mind and fall short of devotion, which is the natural response of those who know and worry not of what to do. This is a difficult stage as you feel obligated and inspired to act and yet awkward in your actions. We have spoken before of the desire to create that may arise as you begin to enter this stage of your journey. This is often compounded by a feeling of wondering what is next as you wait in anticipation for a calling of some kind, so certain are you of an impending challenge to action, of some necessary form to be given to what you carry within.

28.12 Again, as when you feel the need to convince others of your belief, the need to give form to what is beyond form misses the point of what you have gained. You may be asking now, "Are you saying to do nothing?" At the thought of this you will be aghast and, what is more, bitterly disappointed. Again, as in the beginning, you seek a task to accomplish, forgetting that only you can be accomplished.

28.13 When one thinks, "There is so much to say," one forgets to listen. Be guided in your going out. Be restrained in what you say. Be attentive in your listening. Where you are is where you are supposed to be. The path to follow to all changes will be shown to you if you will but be attentive. If you follow the way that is shown to you, all uncertainty will end. Uncertainty is where difficulty lies. Certainty and ease as surely go together. There are no more decisions for you to make. There is only a call for a dedicated and devoted will, a will dedicated to the present moment, to those who are sent to you and to how you are guided to respond to them. One will be a teacher, another a student. The difference will be clear if you listen with your heart.

CHAPTER 29

Attention

29.1 To attend is to be present and to be of service. This is the meaning of which we speak when we ask for a commitment to life that requires your attention. It is both a request for focus and readiness and a request for service that can only be given in the present by a mind and heart available to the requirements of the present. It is the appropriate attitude for the time of tenderness, as it is an attitude of ministry.

29.2 Your function cannot be known to you while you shy away from the idea of service. Whether you realize it or not, you associate service with subjugation, particularly the idea of service to a higher Will or higher Cause. Some of you associate it with a lack of free will, a lack of choice, a course that will lead you to a subservient stature. Others think of it in terms of charity, and continue to see a difference between those who would serve and those who would be served. Few of you have as yet integrated this Course's definition of service into your lives. But now you shall. For you cannot bring the learning you have done here into an engagement with life and not realize the true meaning of service, or in contrast, the true meaning of use.

29.3 You who have so worried over what to do have both welcomed and feared the idea of some kind of service being required of you. There is no mystery to this, as the idea of service in your society is one of enforced duty, as exemplified by your military service. You have no notion, as did people of the past, of being of service to God. This is a symptom of the reign of the ego and its ability to both aggrandize your notion of yourself, and to minimize it. To be of service to God is not to be a slave to God but to attend to God. To give God your attention and your care. You who would cry, *God make use of me,* only need to give to God your devotion and your willingness to serve instead of use.

29.4 Further, you need to let the universe be of service to you rather than trying to use the universe to accomplish your goals. These adjustments in your attitude toward service will bring about the completion of the cycle of giving and receiving, and the beginning of wholeness.

29.5   This is as true for your own goal of wholeheartedness as it is for any wider goal of unity, for they are the same goal. Wholeheartedness is unity regained. Your return to unity is your return to your full power and your ability to be of quite literal service to God and your brothers and sisters.

29.6   If God were to speak to you Himself and tell you of what means your service would be to Him, He would but tell you this: *My child, return to me.* God has no Will apart from yours. Your return to unity is all God seeks for you, for Himself, and for all His children. The return to unity was my accomplishment, and all that is meant by what I have often repeated here: Only you can be accomplished. Your service is but dedication to this goal.

29.7   My return to unity accomplished this goal for all, for all are one in me and one in unity. This is why you have no need to concern yourself with anything other than this goal. Your realization of this goal's accomplishment is your realization of your divinity, a state unaltered and yet in need of your recognition and return.

29.8   While this goal may at first appear to be one of selfish intent and individual gain, it is not. A return to unity is a return to unity. From within the center, the core of unity, your accomplishment goes out to the world, as mine once did.

29.9   The time of tenderness is the time of your approach to unity. The atonement that is accomplished here is the means of opening the gate to your approach. No one has closed this gate to you, but you by your own hand pulled it shut as you departed your heavenly home, and you do not remember that your own hand can open it once again. It is a gate of illusion, of mist, of clouds before the sun. Your hand is outstretched now and your light is clearing away the mist. The gateway to unity stands before you, an arch of golden light beneath a rainbow vibrant with the colors of life. Life, not death, assures your approach. God Himself will guide your entry.

29.10 Many of you have noticed the consistency with which you have glorified falsely that which you would imitate from creation. In work too you will find an example of this. For you all know that work and service somehow go together. In many cultures has work thus been glorified and made to seem as if it is the proper use of a life. And yet, as your Father's child, your work is as His. Your work is that of creation. Your creation is your service to the world as your Father's work is his service to you. As you cannot imagine God toiling, so you should cease to imagine your Self doing thus.

29.11 Many of you think of life itself as toil. There is much you need to do just to stay alive, and if a thing is required, expected, necessary, your tendency is to rebel against it and to seek for ease in getting it done or ways to avoid doing it at all. Thus have your paper plates and dishwashers taken the ritual from a meal, your mass-manufacturing the satisfaction of the hand-made. While this is neither good nor bad, this attitude of life as toil is part of your rebellion against ideas of service. You have no time for more than you do now, and you think of service, if you think of it at all, as something to be fit in here or there where it is convenient in your busy schedule.

29.12 It is extremely important for you to realize that God's work takes place outside of time, as do all acts of true service or creation. This is not a readily understandable concept, but one that is necessary for you to have faith in. It is essential to your release of the concept of toil and your acceptance of your function here.

29.13 No matter how busy your schedule, it is only a schedule in terms of your perception of it. Your *schedule* is just another way of saying your *life*, and an alternative view of how you look at your life, when seen thus, is absolutely necessary.

29.14 No wholeness will be possible for you while you look at life in terms of schedules, plans, time-tables, or things to get done. No wholeness will be possible for you while you compartmentalize your life into designated pieces giving yourself time for work and time for leisure and seeing them not as the same thing. Life is life. Life is. As love is.

29.15 Life is service to God. God is service to life. You are God in life. Thus you are both life and service to life, both God and service to God. All of the vast universe was created the same: to live and to serve life, to be of God and be of service to God. To be served and to serve. To be provided for and to provide. To have needs met and to meet needs. This circular nature of the universe leaves no one unattended. Yet you realize this not.

29.16 The separation but accentuated this manner of functioning and made of it something difficult and challenging, something to be changed. The separation accentuated this manner of functioning and made of it, as of the rest of creation, something that it is not. The separation accentuated this manner of functioning, but it did not create it. Life exists in service to itself. This could also be stated thus: Life exists in relationship. Relationship is the interaction within which service occurs. The replacement of the idea of service with the idea of use made for the existence of special relationships. The idea of use created all ideas of toil as the only means of having needs met. The idea of use created all notions of distrust, starting with—as we have stated before—your ideas of using the very body you call your home rather than allowing it to serve you.

29.17 The universe exists in reciprocal relationship or holy relationship, rather than special relationship. This is the nature of existence, as unity is the nature of existence and cannot be changed and has not changed, although you believe it not. It is a joyful relationship, as the nature of relationship is joy. Once you have given up your belief in separation this will be known to you.

29.18 The choice to change your belief is before you. Are you not ready to make it?

29.19 As you once chose separation you can now choose unity. Not knowing that unity was a choice prevented you from making this choice before now. Now I tell you clearly, the choice is yours. Choose once again.

29.20 As you make your choice, remember your choice must be wholehearted, for it is in wholeheartedness that the power of choice exists. A split mind and heart can prevent you from utilizing the power of choice, but it cannot prevent you from claiming this choice as your own. Choose anew and let the power of heaven come together to seal the rift between your mind and heart, and make you whole once again.

29.21 Claiming your identity and your power to make choices is an act that comes from an entirely different place than decision-making. Claiming is akin to prayer and is but an asking, an asking for your true inheritance. You have felt that you need to know for what it is you ask. And yet you cannot know until you inherit. Can you have faith that your true inheritance is what you truly desire, even knowing not exactly what that inheritance is? Can you not follow me in my choice and accept it as your own?

29.22 You who have so long been afraid to claim your smallest gifts, look again at claiming with the definition I have provided. Claiming is also contrary to how you have perceived of it in terms of claiming something for your own:

You claim not to own or to separate what you have from what another has and then to call it special. You claim in order to reclaim your Self.

29.23 How can one's talent cause another to be less talented? How can one's service deprive anyone else of the right to serve? No two are alike. Only in God are all the same.

29.24 This is the great divide, the separation, between the visible and the invisible, the indivisible and the divisible. Only those reunited with God achieve the state of unity. Only the state of unity exists.

29.25 Your gifts, your talents, your uniqueness, are your service. Can you not look at them thus? And can you not come to understand the reciprocal nature of giftedness? That what God has given only needs to be received? That what you have received only needs to be given? The indivisibleness of God is simply this: an unbroken chain of giving and receiving. Thus is this a definition of unity as well.

29.26 Service is but another way of stating this law of creation, this unbroken chain of giving and receiving. All your worry over the future and the past is but a worry about the return of gifts given. What gift of opportunity did you not accept in the past, might you not recognize in the future? What gift of fortune, what chance encounter, what decision might have changed your life? What should you have done that you didn't? What might you do in the future if not for your fear of where the direction you choose might take you? What peace might you know if you realized, truly realized, that all gifts come but once and are forever? The past nor the future matter not. All is available in the here and now where giving and receiving occur.

29.27 No chance to learn or grow is ever missed. Each still exists, though not in time. Each still exists, but in the present. Can you replace your attention to the past and future with an attention to the present?

Being Present

30.1 How is being *present* different than *being*? Are they not the same thing? Should they not be? And yet how seldom are you fully present for your own life, your own Self, your own being. If you were fully aware of your own being, you would be in oneness with Your Father.

30.2 How can one be distracted from oneself? And yet you are. Many go through life searching for self-definition, self-actualization. Where are they as they search? Where is their being? If reaching a particular destination is all that is sought, the journey becomes but the means for getting there. All learning is seen as preparation for the future, or for some eventual outcome, rather than for your being. You attempt to learn for something other than your Self, for some purpose other than your Self. Thus was service given another route for being separated from the Self and your function here. When you learn in order to contribute something to your work and your world, you bypass your Self.

30.3 Your learning must take on a new focus. *Be like the little children,* and inhale the world around you in order to make it part of your Self. *Be like the little children,* and learn in order to claim your learning for your Self. Learn who you are through each experience rather than learning in order to find out who you are or what your contribution will eventually be.

30.4 Being in relationship is being present. Being present has nothing to do with time as you think of it. You think of this instruction to be present as an instruction that relates to time. You think of present time, past time, future time. We have spoken of these modes of *keeping* time as well, but as the word *keeping* illustrates, there is nothing about time that can be kept. The only thing real about time is its eternal nature.

30.5 You are headed toward what might be called universal consciousness, though you will not know it when it is at first achieved. For universal consciousness is knowing Self, while you think it is knowing all. Knowing

Self is knowing all, but this you do not as yet understand.

30.6 Universal consciousness is being in relationship. It is the true Self, the *known* Self, in all its glorious relationship with life. All matter is born and dies. All life is forever. The known Self realizes this and begins to act in accordance with this knowing.

30.7 This world as you perceive of it is built around the foundation of fear, a fear that stemmed from the belief in finite life, in being born into a body and dying to the body. The person who *knows*, truly *knows*, the simplest truth of the identity of the Self no longer lives in a dualistic position with God, but in a monistic state with Him. The difference is in realizing relationship with the infinite instead of the finite, with life as opposed to matter.

30.8 This huge difference is easily overlooked and rarely seen as the key that unlocks the door to universal consciousness, being present. There is no *being* and no *present* in matter. In matter, being must be attached to form. In the sense of time described by the word present, there is no infinitude, but only a vague concept of *now.* This is the key concept that I not only knew but demonstrated. This is the legacy, the inheritance, I left to you.

30.9 This discourse may seem to have traveled far from words of love, words promised and words given in truth. For no love is finite in nature. Love has no beginning and no end. Love is a demonstration and a description of universal consciousness, of being in relationship.

30.10 All relationship is relationship with God Who Is Love.

30.11 What the Course is speaking of now, in essence, is gain without loss. You will never be aware of gain without loss while you believe in what is finite in nature. The cycle of giving and receiving is thus never complete, and the certainty you seek always waiting for something you do not yet have—some information, some guarantee, some proof or validation. You might think if you are "right" you will be successful, if you are "successful" you will be secure, if you are "good" you will prosper. You do not see these ways of thinking as ideas associated with gain and loss, but they are. All thinking that is of a "if this, then that" nature is thinking in terms of gain and loss. This is why we have worked to leave thinking behind. This belief in gain and loss is a cornerstone of your system of perception viewed from a stance of "if this, then that." It rules the nature of your existence because you have made it ruler by abandoning the laws of God.

30.12 The laws of God are laws of Love. Within the laws of love there is no loss, but only gain.

30.13 The source of love and its location is your own heart. Think now of the created form, the body. When the heart stops beating, life is seen to be over. Are you thus your heart? Or can you not see that the created form was made in God's own image, as was all creation. You are God's image given form, as is all creation. We, all of us together, are the heartbeat of the world. Without unity we would not be. Without our Source, which is God, we would not be.

30.14 The laws of unity are God's laws and are simple indeed: giving and receiving are one. And thus giving and receiving as one is the only way in which God's laws are fulfilled. Since God's laws are the laws that rule the universe, they cannot go unfulfilled. Giving and receiving are thus one in truth. God's laws are generalizable and do not change, and thus the laws of man have not usurped the laws of God. It is only in your perception that the laws of man take precedence over the laws of God. Since perception arises from the mind, we must now discuss the mind.

CHAPTER 31

The Nature of the Mind

31.1 There is only one Mind, just as there is only one Will. This you are afraid of, as you believe this statement threatens your independence, something you consider a state of being to be highly prized. This statement, however, more rightly confirms your interdependence and your wholeness.

31.2 The idea of sharing one heart, one heartbeat, one love, is not so unacceptable to you as the idea of sharing one mind. Your thoughts, you feel, are your own, private and sacrosanct. These highly guarded and regarded thoughts are what *A Course in Miracles* calls body thoughts. Distinctions are made in many religions and philosophies that separate thought—as dictated by the body—from thought of a higher order, or spiritual thought. Thoughts related to your personal self and the "laws" of the body, such as those of survival, are not the thoughts of the true Self. This is the clarification that needs to be made for some of you to fully let go of your fear of the shared thought system of unity.

31.3 How silly is it to be afraid of the truth? Fear of the truth is like a fear of the impossible being possible. Like the fear of death, it is the product of upside-down thinking.

31.4 You do not understand that something can be inseparable and still not be the same. The miracle of turning water into wine illustrates, as all miracles do, the fallacy of this concept. You must understand this and all miracles correctly if you are to be a miracle worker. What is inseparable cannot be different, but this does not mean it must be the same. Inseparable does not mean replaceable. Water does not replace wine nor wine water, yet each are from the same source, and so they are not different even while they are not the same.

31.5 Your fear of sameness is your fear of oneness, and it is an unfounded fear, though understandable given your concept of what is the same and what is different. Yet, as your forms so readily illustrate, while all bodies are the same, they are also different. Form but imitates content.

31.6   This is the difficulty with studying the mind. The mind is your being and so you can study it not, no more than you can ever see the entirety of your body unaided, or remove your own brain to view it beneath a microscope. Yet you call your body your own and identify it as your self. Your body moves and breathes, your heart beats and your blood pumps, quite unaided by your conscious self. You know that if you had to consciously cause these functions to take place, you would surely die, for managing the workings of the body would be more than your conscious mind could handle. You could not possibly give all the commands necessary if such commands were needed. Thankfully, you have a brain that fulfills this function, yet this brain is also you. Does it work independently from you? Is it separate? Is it the same?

31.7   So too is it with mind. Mind *is* your being. It is no accident that it has become synonymous to many of you with brain, an interchangeable word that conveys the same idea. Mind is the control center, that which remembers and stores away knowledge, that which is both you and beyond your understanding of you. Form mimics content. Form mimics the truth, but does not replace it.

31.8   The rest of your world imitates truth as well. You live on one world, one planet, one Earth. You may live on different continents, different countries, various cities, but all of you rely on the one Earth as part of a sameness and interdependence you accept. You are aware that this Earth rests in a cosmos beyond your comprehension, and that the cosmos too is something that the Earth and all on the Earth are part of. You believe fully that you are inseparable from the Earth, the cosmos, gravity, the laws that rule the universe, just as you believe your brain and, erroneously, your mind, is inseparable from your body.

31.9   Thus your confusion is also your key to understanding. You need but look at creation's projection to understand the nature of perfection and your own Self as Creator and Created. Being part of the whole that is your known universe has made you and no other being less consequential. All over the world people of good faith fight to save even one life. Each life is irreplaceable and no one argues this point, yet you allow yourself to resist the whole idea of God because you believe that what is one cannot also be many.

31.10 Give up this notion of losing your Self to God, and you will be done for all time with resisting God. Only in God can you find your Self. This is known to you, and is the reason for man's quest for God throughout all time. Man may think he looks to God for answers, for release from pain, for reward, or for an after-life. But man has always looked to God for his own Self. Not looking to God to find your Self would be akin to searching everywhere but the Earth for humankind. If you do not seek where what you wish to find can be found, you seek in vain.

31.11 The purpose of the mind is extension. Thus, the upside-down perception that causes you to protect your private thoughts and see them as the seat of yourself calls for the exact opposite of extension. This is the only true source of conflict. And, yet again, your perception of your thoughts as yourself is the closest answer to the truth that you were able, in your limited view of yourself, to come up with. There is a part of you that *knows* that you have higher thoughts, and knows that these higher thoughts are your Self. Rather than discriminating between higher and lower thoughts, you have aggrandized all your thoughts and given them an identity we have called the ego. Without dislodging your belief in your ego as yourself you will never realize your true identity.

31.12 For some this dislodging occurs by coming to a better understanding of the mind, for others by coming to a better understanding of the heart, or love. How the ego becomes dislodged matters not. What matters is where you place your devotion.

31.13 Devotion cannot be split and must be total to be at all. Thus while you believe you are devoted to the thoughts of a split mind you are devoted to nothing. This is why so many attempts at understanding fail. Trying to come to understanding with a split mind is impossible. Impossible learning goals lead to depression. This is why we must learn anew with a mind and heart joined in wholeheartedness.

31.14 The ego is that part of yourself that clings to the idea of separation, and thus cannot grasp the basic truth of your existence: that giving and receiving are one in truth. Put another way, all this says is that in order to *be* your Self, you have to *share* your Self. What you keep you lose. This is the principle of giving and receiving that, being finally and totally understood, will free you to be wholehearted.

31.15 All that you would keep private and unshared is, in essence, who you think you are. I say who you think you are because it is important to distinguish who you *think* you are from who you truly are. On the one hand, you think that you are your past, your shame, your guilt; on the other that you are your future, your glory, your potential. You neither want to share your most negative nor your most positive thoughts about yourself. These are your great secrets, the secrets that fill your mind day-to-day with thoughts that *keep* you from your Self.

31.16 And so there is just a small portion of yourself you share, the portion that your ego has deemed safe, acceptable, presentable. The portion that your ego has deemed will cause you no risk. It is the ego that asks: Are you certain that if you share that feeling, you will still be loved? Are you certain that if you reveal that secret, you will still be safe? Are you certain that if you try something new, you will still be accepted? It is the ego that deems honesty a game; the ego that you let decide upon your truth. For what you live is what you believe is the truth about yourself. While you continue to live dishonestly, your notion of what your identity truly is cannot improve.

31.17 My dear brothers and sisters, what you truly are cannot be improved upon. But because you are in a state of unremembering, you must relearn who you are. You can only relearn who you are by being who you are. You can only be who you are by sharing who you are.

31.18 The truth is your identity. Honesty is being free of deception. You, who are already worrying about honesty and sharing being about some need to confess, think a moment about why you are worried. The idea of confessing is an idea of sharing. Rather than thinking of who you are being all tied up with sin and a need for forgiveness, think of this simply as a need to share. This would seem antithetical with what I have already said—that what you keep you lose, and what you share you gain. You think of confessing as a way of letting go and getting rid of that which you do not want. Some of you believe this can be done and others don't. Those who believe in it believe in sin, and that it can be replaced by forgiveness. Those who do not believe in it do not believe that sin can be forgiven and do not seek forgiveness, believing forgiveness is something that they do not deserve. Few truly believe in atonement or undoing. Few truly believe there is no sin. Few truly believe that they are not the sum of their behaviors. How, then, is confession good for the soul?

31.19 You cannot be honest while you do not know the truth about yourself. If you remembered your Self, notions such as confession being good for the soul would be no more. But in order to remember your Self, you need a means of learning who you are. Everything that has ever happened in your life has happened as a learning device to help you remember who you are. Those things about which you feel guilt and shame are simply the remnants of lessons unlearned. While you hang on to them by keeping them hidden, no learning occurs.

31.20 Who you are is love, and all things brought to love are seen in a new light, a light that keeps what you would learn to help you remember who you are, and in that remembrance transforms the rest, leaving with you nothing to be ashamed of, nothing to keep hidden, leaving you with nothing but the truth of who you are. Thus, what you give through sharing you gain *in truth*. No other type of gain is possible.

31.21 The same is true of your potentials, which brought to love are accomplished and simply become the truth that has always existed about who you are.

31.22 Sharing is thus not about who you think you are, but about who you truly are, and yet it is the way to learn the difference while learning is still necessary.

31.23 Sharing is the means through which the holy relationship you have with everything is revealed *in truth*. This truth lies within everything that exists, as it lies within you. As you learn that who you are is love, no deception is possible, and you can only be who you are *in truth*.

31.24 What you gain *in truth* is never lost or forgotten again, because it returns remembrance to your mind. What your mind remembers cannot *not* be shared.

31.25 Your ego thoughts can never share the truth with you nor with anyone else. The ego invented the idea of "telling" the truth and using it as an opposite to telling an untruth or lie. Thus were born ideas of being able to keep truth a secret, one of the most ridiculous ideas of the ego thought system.

31.26 Your past has nothing to do with the truth about who you are, except in the degree to which it has or has not helped you to remember who you are. What you have learned *in truth* resides in your mind as a part of you. What you have not yet learned from awaits your learning — or in other words, awaits the transfer of your feelings and experience to truth, and thus to your mind. Only the truth abides within your mind, for only it can enter the holy altar you share with me.

31.27 This altar is not a thing, but a devotion to the one truth, the whole truth. Being of one mind is being of one truth, and how can you be of anything less? Only the ego sprang from a lie, the lie of separation that created the illusion of separate minds and varying degrees of truth.

31.28 Just as you look to God for your Self, knowing not what it is you seek, so too do you look to your brothers and sisters and all else that lives along with you. But when you look, knowing not what you seek, what you find varies. Since there is only one truth, finding a variety of answers means nothing. If you but change what you look for, what you see and what you learn will also change.

31.29 If you can look for your Self within your brothers and sisters, however, they must also be able to look for their Selves in you. If you are constantly reflecting back what you think your brothers and sisters want to see, they can learn nothing from you. If your truth about who you think you are changes day-to-day, you are reflecting the very variety of answers they expect to find and have been finding elsewhere.

31.30 You do not think you are looking for yourself in others, but think instead that you are looking for something or someone other than yourself. At certain times of your life you state this seeking you are doing quite clearly, and it is always specific. You are looking for a friend, a spouse, a mentor. You believe you are seeking something other than you to complete yourself, because you are seeking to complete yourself. You are seeking wholeness. And you are even correct in seeking it from your brothers and sisters—just not in the way you perceive of it.

31.31 When you find the truth of any brother or sister, you find the truth about your Self, for the truth does not change. And if who you truly are *is* the truth, how can you be different? Thus it can be said that the truth and the mind are one in truth. The truth is what is. What is not the truth is illusion. Does this not make perfect sense?

31.32 It is in this perfect sense of the perfect sanity of truth that salvation lies. Salvation is simply your return to your Self.

31.33 If your sister and brother seek the truth, or salvation, from you, and you seek the truth, or salvation from them, what is truly occurring? How can this work? This is but another aspect of giving and receiving being one in truth. Giving and receiving are both taking place, both at the same time, as are seeking and finding, once you are aware of what it is you seek.

31.34 This aspect of giving and receiving as one is called relationship. It allows you to experience who you are and thus to know, or remember, who you are. It is in your recognition of the truth about your brother and sister that you recognize the truth about your Self. It is only in relationship that this occurs, because only in relationship are you experiencing anything.

31.35 You do not exist outside of relationship, just as your mind does not exist outside of oneness. Your experience here is but an extension of mind into a realm in which experience can occur. Your ego has made of this something different than it is. Rather than extension of mind, your experience has become a projection of ego. This can change.

31.36 As you interact with your brothers and sisters, you seek to get to know them. You do this so that you find what you have in common, and go on from there to shared experiences. You also seek to know your brothers and sisters so that you will come to know what to expect from them. Once you have determined a brother's or sister's usual mode of behavior, deviations from that usual mode concern you. You may determine someone is in a "mood," and see that the effects of that mood are either good or bad, for either you or them or both. Since you live in a world of such extreme uncertainty, one of your highest requirements of those you have relationships with is a mode of behavior that allows you to know what to expect. Thus, as you move from acquaintances to relationships of a deeper nature, you quickly determine the nature of those relationships and have an investment in them staying the same. Since this is most often true for them as well, you too become locked into the expected sameness.

31.37 One relationship in which this is not the case is the relationship of teacher and student. Another relationship that expects change and growth is that of parent to child. These two relationships have comprised your ideas of our Father and me as you have realized that you are here to learn. Now, with a clear learning goal in mind, these idealized relationships must be broadened so that they are seen in all rather than in a few, and so that they are seen clearly as what they really are.

CHAPTER 32

Love Returned to Love

32.1   Let us first consider the roles of teacher and learner. A teacher is first and foremost anything that aids your remembering. Thus look not at the form in which a teacher arrives. It can truly be said that all of life is your teacher. There is not one aspect of it that is not designed to help you to remember who you are. As we have stated repeatedly, the form of your world in many ways reflects the content of who you are. It also reflects the content of who you are not. It is in telling the difference between the two that you need guidance. You have previously looked to those who do not know the difference for your answers. Now you can see that you need to look to a different source.

32.2   That Source is Love, and it is available in every situation but for the asking: What would love have me do? What would love have me see? What would love have me say? When you call upon Love you call upon your Source. When you seek the wisdom of your heart you call upon me. When you seek the truth that is in your mind, you call upon the Holy Spirit. Thus is the Sacred Trinity always available in every situation, and for whichever learning mode you are most comfortable. All learning modes, however, will eventually return you to the Source, which is Love. The difference between Father, Son, and Holy Spirit is but the same difference of which we speak when we assure you that you are of one Mind and one Heart, and that regardless of this truth you will not, in coming to know and experience this, lose your Self. The way in which you experience relationship with each aspect of the Trinity is different despite the oneness of the Trinity. The same is true of all relationship with everything. The way in which you experience relationship with each aspect of creation is different despite the oneness of creation. It is in the different relationship of one aspect of creation with all the rest that the difference you so prize as your uniqueness exists. And only there. Only in relationship are you uniquely you. Only relationship exists. For Love *is* relationship.

32.3   Thus we end this Course with love given and love received in truth. You are the learner here until you realize that you are Love. You then become the teacher of what you are. Your mind and heart join in wholeheartedness in the embrace. You are home, and there you will forever stay.

32.4   And thus I say to you, Amen. You have returned to Love, and your relationship with Love has returned you to your Self. Think not. This Course requires no thought and no effort. There is no prolonged study and the few specific exercises are not required. This Course has succeeded in ways you do not yet understand and have no need to understand. These words have entered your heart and sealed the rift between your mind and heart. Be true to love and you cannot fail to be true to your Self.

32.5   If you do not think you are yet prepared, if you think you are not yet ready, cease to think. Read again these words of love and let the sound of love soothe your worries away. Give to me the thoughts that remain to trouble you and I will return them to you transformed by Love. Do not grieve your thoughts or believe in loss of anything of any kind. Thus will all you have already received be remembered in this time of the second coming of Christ.

32.6   And what of miracles? The last and final miracle has occurred, for what miracles are needed when mind and heart are one and you have returned to the embrace? This is the miracle to end all need of miracles, the only accomplishment of the only Son of God. For what your heart has shared with your mind is shared with all minds and what your heart has to share is only Love. Thus has Love returned to Love.

THE TREATISES OF
A COURSE OF LOVE

BOOK TWO

A Treatise on The Art of Thought

The First Treatise

CHAPTER 1

The First Instruction

1.1   A split mind does not learn for a split mind is incapable of giving and receiving as one. A split mind does not rest for it can find no peace. A state of peace is a prerequisite of giving and receiving as one. Any state other than that of peace is conflicted by the desire for peace and the ways in which peace is seen as being approachable. Peace is seen as being outside of one's being and the means are sought for the union of being with that which will provide for peace. Knowing not what this is, is the source of conflict and of all seeking. No one seeks for what they already know how to find or for what they already believe they possess.

1.2   While *A Course of Love* has led you to a state of wholeness of mind and heart, or wholeheartedness, your realization of this state of being requires further guidance. Thus this Treatise will attempt to give specific examples of what to look for as your learning continues, or how to identify wholehearted responses from those of a split mind. Its further purpose will be to identify the service that you can provide once your wholeheartedness is completely realized.

1.3   The first instruction I give to you is to seek no more. All that you are in need of knowing has been provided within *A Course of Love*. That your learning does not feel complete is not a failing of this Course or of yourself. That your learning does not feel complete is the result of forgetfulness, which is the opposite of mindfulness. Your further learning then is learning based on mindfulness or remembering.

1.4   *A Course of Love* has provided you with what you need to know, which is the function of all coursework. This does not mean that you have acquired the ability to live what you have learned, only that you are ready to. The very word "remember," as well as the concept of memory, implies mindfulness and the ability to reproduce or recall both what has been learned and what has been previously experienced. This reproducing and recollecting are acts of creation. They do not bring back a reality that once was but transform that reality into a present moment experience. It is in the present-moment experience memory provides that truth rather than illusion can now be experienced and learned from. It is in the present-moment experience that you will receive the blessing of being able to respond differently to love.

1.5   All that you have experienced in truth is love. All that illusion provided you with was nothing. Thus your first task as you remember and re-experience is that of separating illusion from the truth. This act will require no effort for what you have learned in this Course has prepared you for this. As each situation that re-enacts a previous learning experience arises, you will, if you trust your heart, be perfectly able to identify illusion and truth. This is a simple act of recognizing meaning. All that you believe you learned from illusion will have no meaning to you now and will allow you to give up any remnants of false learning you acquired. All that you learned in error from identifying love incorrectly will be relearned as love is properly identified.

1.6   Although I have just instructed you to trust in your heart, your reunited mind and heart will now be called to act in unison. That A Course of Love instructed you little in the mechanics of the mind was consistent with the theme and learning goals of this Course. The mechanics of the mind can in truth be left behind now as we concentrate rather on the art of thought.

1.7   The mechanics of the mind were what engaged you in so many daily battles that you became almost too weary to continue. The mechanics of the mind were what were in need of being overcome in order for you to listen once again to the wisdom of your heart. The mechanics of your over-worked and over-stimulated mind were what you were asked to leave behind as this act of leaving behind was the only means by which you could allow your mind to be restful enough for it to even contemplate union or the new learning required in order to facilitate your return to union. Your return to union is your return to love and it is accessed at the center or heart of your Self. Your mind was in need of silencing in order for you to hear the wisdom of your heart and begin your return. Now, in order to complete your return, mind and heart must work as one.

1.8   You are a thinking being. This cannot be denied nor should it be. Thus a Course that left you with an erroneous impression that relying on feeling alone would complete your learning would in actuality leave your learning incomplete. Without this "Treatise on the Art of Thought," too many of you would become muddled in your feelings and know not where to turn to explain the many riddles they would seem at times to represent.

1.9   A mind and heart joined in union abolishes the ego. The ego-mind was what was once in charge of all your thoughts. Since the ego is incapable of learning the ego-mind had to be circumvented in order for true learning to take place. This is what *A Course of Love* accomplished. This learning was accomplished in you, making you The Accomplished. As The Accomplished, you now are able to access universal mind.

1.10   The joy that will come to you from the thoughts of a mind joined in union will be unparalleled in your experience here. "Ah," you will say with a relief and joy that knows no bounds, "this is what it is to experience and know the truth. This is what it is to create, for this is what it is like to think as God thinks." Where once you recognized only illusion and called it reality, the mind joined in union will now, more and more, recognize only truth and experience only the truly real.

1.11   You can already imagine what an extensive change this will bring, and, as you are still experiencing change in time, without guidance, this change would be seen as quite difficult no matter how grand its outcome and even in spite of your recognition, at first in mere fleeting moments, that it is a change you would welcome.

1.12   Again your willingness is called upon. Be willing now to apply the art of thought to the experience of truth.

CHAPTER 2

The Art of Thought

2.1 The closing pages of *A Course of Love* instructed you to think no more. A break in time was needed for you to disengage the ego-mind that produced the type of thinking that needs to come to an end. This ending is but a beginning in truth and has led you to readiness to learn the art of thought.

2.2 We identified much for you to leave behind within the pages of *A Course of Love*. These many things which seemed so distinct and separate and which ranged from fear, to struggle, to effort, to control and protection, can all now be seen as the product of the thoughts of your ego-mind.

2.3 To experience the truth and apply to that experience the thoughts of the ego-mind, the same thoughts that were applied to former experiences of the truth, would be to respond to love the same way again. The questions you have asked concerning how love could be the answer when it has been preached by so many for so long is answered here. The answer lies in your response to love. To respond is to answer. You have sought your "answer" everywhere, but here is where it lies. It is yours to give and can only be given to love from love. Only in giving is it received.

2.4 Thus we have sought to uncover your Source, to provide you access to your heart, from which all responses flow. As your heart is the Source of your true Self, your thoughts, once removed from those of the ego-mind are the expression and extension of your true Self. They are the answer of the Created to the Creator, the answer of the Self to God.

2.5 Thoughts that were guarded by the ego-mind were in need of being set free. Appealing to your heart was the means or cause of this freedom being accomplished in you. What was spoken of within *A Course of Love* as unlearning has begun and continues here. What was spoken of within *A Course of Love* as new learning has begun and continues here as well. The difference is that you are now ready to learn a new means of response to this unlearning and learning. That response is the art of thought.

2.6   The so-called thinking of the ego-mind was so tyrannical that its use throughout your lifetime deadened many of your feelings. It led you so far from the truth that you no longer trust in it. It confused the smallest issues to such a degree that it left you unable to respond purely to anything. The so-called thinking of the ego-mind could be likened to chitchat, background noise, static. So little meaning did it have that all meaning became muddled.

2.7   Your only recourse to this situation in the past was focus. You thus applied your thoughts to learning subjects of a specific nature. Through this focus you believed you accomplished much. You congratulated yourself on having the discipline required to train your mind to focus and to learn, or shamed yourself when you were unable to do so. To those most skilled in this training of the ego-mind worldly rewards have long been given. These people attain degrees and skills and then further apply the discipline that they have learned by using their skills and knowledge in the world for even greater rewards. These rewards have further emphasized the importance of such focused thoughts and thus further entrenched the ego-mind. To think that you could learn the truth of who you are through these same means was the fallacy that the early teaching of *A Course of Love* sought to dispel.

2.8   But again, as was stated often throughout *A Course of Love,* an alternative exists. It did not exist when you knew not of it and so your attempts at learning have been valiant and are no cause for anxiety. But now this alternative is being revealed to you, and it does call for a change of thought so extensive that all thought as you once knew it does need to cease.

2.9   You have already succeeded in learning in this new way once or you would not be here. This is your proof that you can do so again and again until the new way totally replaces the old and the art of thought leaves behind forever the need for what the ego-mind once but seemed to offer you.

2.10   The thoughts of your ego-mind were ruled by the nature of the body. To exist as *creatures* whose only thoughts are of survival of the body is to exist in a lower order. The laws of the body have thus subjected you to conditions that invited the ego-mind to turn its attention to existence in this lower order. It is only *you* who can recognize and invite the higher order or subject *yourself* to its conditions. It is only your attention to the existence of this higher order that will reveal its laws to you. These are the laws of God or the laws of love.

2.11   The laws of God or the laws of love can be summarized by the simple statement of giving and receiving being one in truth. The implications of this statement are far broader than at first might seem indicated. All of these implications have been touched upon within *A Course of Love*. The most essential of these implications is that of relationship for giving and receiving cannot occur without relationship.

2.12   All relationship is but relationship between Creator and Created. The new means of thinking is referred to here as the "art" of thought in order to call your wholehearted attention to the continual act of creation that is the relationship between Creator and Created. Creation is but a dialogue to which you have not responded. The art of thought will free you to respond.

2.13   This response needs to at first be seen in two parts. An example illustrates. To look at a sunset is to see an object, the sun. It is also to see the sky, to see the variety of colors displayed, to see the horizon. It is to see the surrounding area, perhaps to see the play of clouds among the descending rays, perhaps to feel the warmth or chill of an evening. The whole experience might include the sound of birds or traffic, the rhythm of the ocean, or the pounding of your own heart. It might be a shared experience, one in which you share the feeling of awe inspired by this sight with one you love. It might be seen as you walk or drive, rake leaves or gaze from an office window. It might be a deathbed vision or the first sunset of which a young child is aware. It might be a scene taken totally for granted as you go about whatever business calls you at that hour.

2.14   The sunset is a gift of God. It is what it is. This is the first part of this example.

2.15   The second part is its reception. A gift has been given. What is your response?

2.16   The sunset is part of your human experience. In the lower order of that experience it speaks to your survival needs. It may signal many things ranging from a desire to get safely home before it is dark, to a desire to eat an evening meal. It signals change in the natural world around you. Birds and squirrels and flowers too have a reaction to the setting of the sun. They react to what is. This is their response, an altogether lovely response of created to Creator.

2.17   Yet to rise above this lower order of experience is to receive and to give back. First the sunset is experienced for what it is. It is acknowledged. It is a fact of your existence as a human being, a part of the natural world, a gift of the Creator. Secondly, it is experienced relationally. It speaks to you and you to it. It binds you to the natural world and to the present but also to the higher world and the eternal. It binds you to all those who have and will experience the sunset by being a shared experience. It is there not for you alone, but in listening to its call for a response, it becomes a gift for you that is in no way diminished by it being a gift for all.

2.18 Finally, the sunset becomes, through your experience of it, an opportunity to apply the art of thought.

2.19 Thus, these are the basic rules of the art of thought: First, to experience what is and to acknowledge what is, both as a fact of your existence as a human being and as a gift of the Creator. Second, to acknowledge the relationship inherent in the experience, the call for a response, and the nature of all gifts as being given to all.

2.20 While this may seem somewhat elementary in relation to a sunset, its application to all areas of life will at first seem quiet demanding. But what is elementary remains elementary once it is learned.

2.21 To experience what is and to acknowledge what is, one must be present, present as human being. To experience what *is* and to acknowledge what *is* as being a gift of God is to be present as a divine being having a human experience. No part of being is negated. All senses and feelings of the human being are called into awareness and yet there is also acknowledgment of the Creator behind the Created.

2.22 To acknowledge the relationship and the nature of the gift is to realize unity. To realize the call for a response is to hear the call to create like unto the Creator. This creating like unto the Creator may be used as a definition for the art of thought.

CHAPTER 3

The Call to the Miracle

3.1 The first opportunities for the art of thought to be applied relate to memory in terms of your experience here. In other words they will relate to the re-experiencing of all that you believe has shaped your life. These opportunities are but the forerunners of new learning. They are but opportunities to replace illusion with the truth so that the truth of who you are is all that remains.

3.2 Seeing how different from the experience of illusion is the experience of truth is the same as seeing how different the art of thought is from the thinking of the ego-mind! The art of thought is diametrically opposed to the thinking of the ego-mind.

3.3 The ego-mind sees nothing for what it is. The ego-mind sees not anything but what it *wants* as gifts and even these it sees not as gifts but as rewards. The ego-mind barters rather than giving and receiving as one, believing in a return only for effort. Because it sees only rewards and not gifts, it cannot see that gifts are shared. Because it cannot see that gifts are shared, it cannot afford to see relationship. Because it believes it is *on its own* it cannot see the higher order. Because of all of this, it cannot experience the truth and so exists in illusion.

3.4 The experience of truth dispels illusion and thus the ego-mind. The art of thought replaces the ego-mind with the wholehearted. The wholehearted is but the heart and mind joined in unity.

3.5 How can what is closely guarded extend? How can what is controlled create? How can what continues to give in to fear know love? All your reasons for fear-based living have been discounted one by one. And yet you dare not try to live without it. Why? Because of the thoughts of the ego-mind. The ego-mind is concerned only with its own survival but it has you convinced it is your survival that depends on it. How can you be convinced to live as if the truth were otherwise? For only if you begin to live as if the truth were otherwise can you see that it truly is otherwise, or based on a wisdom other than what has come before.

3.6 The only way for you to come to live in truth is through faith; not a faith in what might be, but a faith in what is. A faith in what is, is a faith in miracles. Miracles are what you are now asked to call upon. For calling upon miracles is an act of faith. You think the quest for miracles is a quest for proof that demonstrates a lack of faith but the reverse is true. What kind of miracle would lead to a lack of faith? There is no such kind of miracle.

3.7 I ask you now to request a miracle.

3.8 What kind of a miracle should you ask for? How big of a miracle should you request? How big is your faith? How much proof does it require? I speak not in jest but ask you to seriously consider just what kind of miracle is needed to get you to change your mind about who you are and thus about the nature of your thoughts.

3.9 Observe yourself as you think through this question. Can you remove all fear from it? Why should it be that fear is what you encounter? The bigger the miracle that occurs to you, the more you are likely to fear the consequences. These are not consequences for the world you fear, but consequences for yourself. If you requested a miracle, and it came true, what then? If you request a small miracle and it comes true, how awful you would feel that you had not requested a bigger miracle. You will almost feel panic at the thought of such a choice being put before you. If you will agree to choose a miracle at all, which many of you will balk at doing, you want to choose the "right" miracle. Some of you may think through just what kind of miracle would be most convincing to you since you see this exercise as what it is, an attempt to convince you to think otherwise about yourself. If you ask for a cure for a disease, how will you know that this cure is a miracle and not the result of scientific discovery or the natural course an illness was bound to take? What miracle could be seen as only miracle and not leave doubt as to its circumstances? Would you choose a miracle that would leave no room for doubt? Such a simple miracle might be the turning of water into wine. What harm could come from it? And yet even this you would fear for if you asked for such a miracle and it came to be, you would then have to contemplate your power to perform miracles. Here you find your greatest fear of all; fear of your power.

3.10   As was said within *A Course of Love*, willingness does not require conviction but leads to conviction. The apostles had no faith in their ability to perform miracles. The faith they showed was in their willingness to try. This little willingness gave way to conviction as miracles flowed through them as the blessings that they are.

3.11   I do not want to lose any of you here, but such is your fear that you can already see your own loss. As great as the fear of miracles is, the fear of not being able to perform is greater. You think of this as a test and one you can pass or fail. And what's more, not only would your passing of this test require you to contemplate your power, but your failure would require you to contemplate your lack of it. If you asked for a miracle and it did not come to be, wouldn't it negate all you have achieved thus far and send you back to a state of disbelief? Better not to try at all than to risk trying and failing when such consequences would seem to hang in the balance.

3.12   But again I tell you this is no idle request. Whatever is necessary to convince you now is what I will provide. Such is the urgency of the time, the urgency for the return to unity, the urgency of the need to leave fear behind. Can you not, from this one example of your fear of miracles, see the glaring reality of all you still would fear?

3.13   This too is a means of unlearning. How can you leave behind all you fear without seeing all you fear for what it is and choosing to lay it aside?

3.14   This does not have to be done right now if your fear is mightier than your willingness. But hold this thought within your mind. What is needed to convince you will be provided. Such is the urgency of your return to unity. If not now, then soon, you will be asked to make this final choice, this choice to leave fear behind for good and to become who you are.

3.15   Who you are is a miracle worker. This is not all that you are but is a measure of who you are. This is not all that you are but this is the quickest means of realizing who you are. As was said in *A Course in Miracles*, miracles are timesaving devices. Although asking you to choose a miracle would seem to violate one of the rules of miracle-readiness as described in *A Course in Miracles*, the extreme need of your return to love requires extreme measures.

3.16   Let us consider your objections to miracles one-by-one for in so doing we will uncover the source of all your fears as well as the Source of miracles.

3.17 First you will say you have no objections to miracles, only to having them performed through you. Your lack of willingness to perform miracles, you will say, stems from your unworthiness to perform miracles. Your unworthiness stems from your belief that you are "only" human. You are not God. You are not a holy person. Thus miracles should not flow through you.

3.18 Secondly you would object to being asked to choose a miracle. Surely you cannot know the consequences of what any miracle would have on the rest of the world. If you were to ask for a life to be spared, how would you know it was not that person's "time to die"? If you were to ask for the cure of a disease, how would you know that disease was not meant to be to further someone's learning? If you were to ask to win the lottery, how could such selfishness not be punished?

3.19 Thirdly, you might, at the suggestion that you need proof to shore up your faith, balk, even while you remain convinced that a failure of such proof would shake your faith.

3.20 Fourth, you might balk at the suggestion that God would grant miracles on such a whim, such a fanciful idea as that of your being convinced of your own power. How could this possibly be important? Even were you to possess such power, surely it is a power that is of God and needs not you for its accomplishment. Better not to mess with such things. Even the thought of it leads you to ideas of magic and power that is not of this world and thus that must have a dark side as well as a light. Here suspicion dawns and threatens all you have come to hold dear.

3.21 These thoughts border on the sacrilegious. Miracles are the realm of Jesus and of the saints and that is surely where they belong. To even implore them would be heresy.

3.22 You fear as well that you do not know what miracles are and thus cannot perform them. You want a definition first. What is an appropriate miracle? For whom should they be requested? What are the criteria? How are they done? Do they happen all at once? Or can they be for some future date? What about the correction of something that has already occurred? You have far too many questions without answers to choose a miracle.

3.23 Although many more fears might prevail upon you, we will consider only one further fear, the fear of making the wrong choice in your choice of miracles. This is the same as a fear of scarcity. For surely the working of one miracle would be a fluke anyway. Proof of nothing and easily discounted and explained away. Surely to believe that where one miracle worked another might be possible would be to have ideas of grandeur not meant for you. Here your thoughts might stray to the performing of many miracles. What a media circus that would be. You would be in demand to end so much suffering in so many places. Surely you wouldn't want that even if it could come to be. Indeed this would require the auspices of a saintly soul and not one such as you.

3.24 See you not the choices made in each of these scenarios and the reasoning or lack of reasoning behind them? You are not worthy. You are not saintly, godlike or even holy. You might choose incorrectly. You might invoke retribution. You might be selfish. You might be proved to have no faith. You might succumb to thoughts of grandeur.

3.25 In short, you are too afraid, for a variety of reasons, to try. In short, you are not willing and have many reasons for not being willing. What we have done here is bring your fears to light, fears that you did not even realize you held so closely or would be so terrified to let go.

3.26 Now we can address each of these fears, bringing to them the art of thought rather than the thinking of the ego-mind.

Chapter 4

The Center of the Universe

4.1 By asking you to request a miracle, I am honoring who you are and inviting you into the state of mind that is miracle-readiness. The art of thought *is* the expression of that state. The art of thought *is* the miracle.

4.2 Thus we must dispel, along with the illusion of fear, the illusion of specificity. You have not been asked to request a specific miracle. Although your thoughts have naturally gone to consideration of the specific, this is but an indication that you are still in the habit of thinking you learned under the instruction of the ego-mind. This Treatise must change that habit in order for all your thoughts to become the miracles that express the truth of who you are. This Treatise will put your instruction fully under my guidance and allow you to disregard the instruction of the ego-mind.

4.3 *A Course of Love* began with an injunction to pray. *A Course in Miracles* began with a definition of miracles. Both are the same. Prayer and the art of thought are the same. This should serve to make it clear that the request I have made of you is once again far more broad and generalizable than your old habit of thought has led you to see. Miracles are, in other words, a way of thinking, the new way that we are going to learn together. They are the state of giving and receiving as one. They are the state in which blessings flow. They are your natural state.

4.4 How can the rules of thought we have identified serve to bring about the miracle that you are? The first means identified was that of experiencing what is and acknowledging what *is* both as a fact of your existence as a human being and as a gift of the Creator. Now that we have more properly identified the miracle, you must see that your Self is what is in need of identification and acknowledgment. This identification and acknowledgment was the stated goal of *A Course of Love*. It does not negate your existence as a human being nor does it deny your existence as being a gift of the Creator. Recall the sunset. Are you any less the glory of God than the sun? This is a call to be as aware of your Self as you are capable of being aware of the sunset.

4.5   When the sun has remained but an object to you, no effect is possible from the sunset. The sun, even during the most blazing sunset, has at times remained no more than object to you. So too has your Self. When your Self is seen as no more than a body it is seen as little more than an object.

4.6   The second rule of the art of thought is to acknowledge relationship, the call for a response, and the nature of all gifts as being given to all. This is thus a call to realize that you exist in relationship, that your relationship calls for a response, and that you are given to all as all are given to you.

4.7   This is an enormous shift in your habit of thought as you become the center of the universe.

4.8   This is quite a different *you* than the self of the ego-mind. The ego-mind, in its imitation of creation, put the "you" of the ego or the body at the center of its thought system and from this central position developed all of its ideas of glorifying the separated self as well as of subjugating the separated self. This subjugation to the ego-mind is what led to the ego-mind being able to develop the "laws of man." These laws of man are the laws of the body's survival.

4.9   Your responsibilities shift completely under the laws of God. Your thoughts are released from their concentration on what exists outside of you as your responsibility is placed where it belongs, in the call to respond. This response is only yours to give and is all you are asked to give. This response comes from within the Self—the rightly identified and acknowledged Self.

4.10   Think of all you now feel responsible for and this lesson will become more clear. While your first thoughts will automatically go to a lengthy list of those concerns associated with the survival of the body, they will miss a whole aspect of concerns associated with keeping others other. You keep others other by attempting to respond for them rather than responding to them. You thus have thought it is your responsibility to care for the world outside of yourself rather than for your Self.

4.11   There is much play on the words response, responsible, and responsibility here. This is no accident. Your call is to respond and you have seen this call incorrectly as a call to be responsible. The idea of responsibility sprang from the ego-mind that would usurp the power of God. What kind of gift arrives with a demand for the receiver to be responsible for it?

4.12   You may answer that there are many, even within this Course's definition of gift, the most obvious of which might be your children. Another of
which might be your talents. It is the idea of your responsibility for these
gifts that has led to your oppression. Again I tell you, your call is to respond
rather than to be responsible. How can you be free to respond when your
thinking remains tied to responsibility?

4.13   Responsibility but implies a guardianship that is not needed. Responsibility implies needs that would not be met without you. Response is given
and thus genuine. It is a natural act of giving and receiving as one. Responsibility is a demanded response, a necessary response, an obligation. Response
happens from within. Responsibility is all about dealing with an outside
world. While both may result in the same or similar actions does not negate
the need for the difference to be realized. Charity is a responsibility. Love
is a response. See you not the difference? Can a father not be guided by
responsibility and still fail to give love? Can a dancer not struggle mightily
to perfect her talent without experiencing its joy?

4.14   Do you think the Creator is responsible for what was created? To think
of the Creator in this way is to think of the Creator with the upside-down
thinking of the ego-mind. Is this not the kind of thinking that has caused
you to blame God for what you have labeled "bad" as well as to praise God
for what you have labeled "good"? Would not this kind of a creator be at
odds with the concept of free will?

4.15   But for a creator not to respond to what has been created—this would
indeed be a travesty! This would be antithetical to the laws of creation! This
would be antithetical to love!

4.16   My request to you to choose a miracle is but a request to you to hear
Creation's response to who you are. What might such a response sound like?
Feel like? Look like? It is a response of pure appreciation and love. It is always
available. It is the gift given in everything you look upon and see without the
obstacle of the ego-mind's interpretation.

4.17   Let us speak a moment of this interpretation. That each of you interprets
what you see, read, hear, smell and touch differently must mean something.
What you have decided that this means is that you are an independent
thinker, something you have prized. Some of you will accept another's interpretation of meaning if it is helpful to you, saves you time, or seems in accord

with your own views. Others of you feel it necessary to interpret everything *on your own*. Without further discussion, you would see interpretation and response quite similarly and this would but lead to a continuation of the belief in different forms of the truth.

4.18   The art of thought is being taught here in order to prevent just such a conclusion. The truth is the truth and not dependent upon your definition of it. A response is not an interpretation. A response is an expression of who you are rather than of what you believe something else to be.

4.19   You who have thought that your interpretation of events and feelings has given them their meaning—think again. Their meaning exists already and is not up to you to determine. This is not your responsibility. You who have thought that your interpretation of situations and the feelings they have aroused have defined who you are, think again. Be willing to apply the art of thought rather than the thinking of the ego-mind. Interpretation but gives you opinions *about* those things that you experience. Response reveals the truth to you because it reveals the truth *of you*.

4.20   The joy you have thought has come to you from an interpretation that is uniquely your own is as nothing compared to the joy that will come to you from a response that is uniquely *you*. But you must give up your penchant for interpretation before you can learn to respond. I realize that this will concern you while you continue to not realize the difference between response and interpretation. The only way for this concern to have the chance to leave you is for you to begin to practice the art of thought and thus begin to learn the difference.

4.21   As was already stated, the first opportunities for you to learn the art of thought will be provided through what we have called the re-experiencing of memory. These are opportunities to re-experience the lessons your life has brought you. You will experience the same lessons in the same way, rather than in a *new* way, if you meet these experiences again with the attitude of interpreting them rather than responding to them. They do not require interpretation but response. Response was what was required in the first place and your inability to respond need not be repeated. You are being revisited with these lessons expressly for the purpose of *not* repeating your former reaction or interpretation of them. You are being revisited with these lessons so that you may apply to them the art of thought rather than the thinking of the ego-mind. The art of thought will reveal the truth to you. The thinking of the ego-mind would simply reinterpret the meaning you previously gave to these lessons.

4.22 This is a sticky distinction, for you are used to congratulating yourself on the maturity required to reinterpret previous lessons. To form a new opinion about something gives you a feeling of open-mindedness and growth. Lay aside your desire for reasons for self-congratulation in favor of Self-revelation. The saying, "The truth shall be revealed to you" is the same as saying "Your Self shall be revealed to you."

4.23 *Revelation* is a proper description of the mode by which the art of thought teaches and helps you learns. It is not through study, effort, or re-interpretation but through revelation.

4.24 Revelation is direct communication with God in the sense that it is direct communication from a Self you have known not, the Self that is one with the Creator.

4.25 We must backtrack a little here to do the same exposition that we did in regard to miracles in regard to revelation. By asking you to choose a miracle, you were provided a means through which your fears became clear to you. There are a few of you who would deny these fears. Fewer still are unafraid of miracles and eager to embrace them. As you may have surmised, we are getting at your final fears here, those most deeply buried and kept in secret from you. Some of you who would count yourselves least fearful are those of you whose fears are most deeply buried. So whether you count yourself among the fearful or not, please continue to give me your attention just a while longer as we uncover all that would still hold you back.

4.26 As was said within *A Course of Love*, all fear is doubt about your self. Now we must expand upon this thought, for doubt about your Self is doubt about God. While God is nothing but the Source of Love, you have, in your doubt, made of God the source of fear. Pause a moment here and let the enormity of this confusion sink in, for this is the reversal in thinking that will pave the way for all the rest. Because of this confusion you have responded to Creation with fear. Is it no wonder a new response is asked of you?

4.27 In the translations of the Bible and many other religious texts, the word or idea of awe has been confused with the word or idea of fear. *A Course in Miracles* told you that awe is the providence of God and not due miracles or any other thing or being. I bring up this point to assure you that this confusion is nothing new, but a confusion so deeply ingrained in you that it has become an aspect of yourselfas human being. From time immemorial, fear has been associated with God. This was the thinking I came to reverse. While I succeeded in revealing a God of love, this revelation has not been reconciled with your experience here. This is what we will now seek to do by putting an end to fear and ushering in, with this ending, the beginning of a time of miracles.

CHAPTER 5

The Choice for Love

5.1   Why, when a God of Love was revealed so long ago and in so many times and in so many forms since then that they remain forever countless, has fear of God remained? The only answer possible is because fear of the Self has remained.

5.2   This is a two-fold fear that must be looked at carefully now and with all the power of the art of thought. One aspect of this fear has to do with the human experience, the other aspect with the divine experience.

5.3   When it was said within *A Course of Love* that the great paradox of creation is that, while creation is perfect, something has gone wrong within it, this fear in relation to the human experience is of what it was I spoke. The choice for suffering that has been made within the human condition is what I speak of specifically here. While I can tell you suffering is illusion, you cannot still your fear of it nor tear your eyes away from it or remove from it the feelings of your heart. While I came to reveal the choice of Love to you, the choice that you each must make to end such suffering, the illusion of suffering has continued and in its continuation made the choice of Love seem all but impossible. If not for the suffering that you see all around you, the choice for Love would have been made. If the choice for Love had been made, the suffering you see around you would be no more. This is the paradox.

5.4   The second aspect of this fear is fear of the divine. A part of this fear of the divine is related to the fear of the human condition. How can you not be fearful of creation when such suffering occurs within it? But there is another aspect that relates to the fear of union we spent much time discussing within *A Course of Love*. It is a fear of the human mind that cannot comprehend the all or the nothingness, the eternal or the void. While your thought system here has been described often as insanity, this is the insanity you would fear that may actually grow stronger as you get closer to the truth. This is the part of you that believes this communication itself is insane, that believes that to contemplate miracles is insane, that both welcomes and fears visions and abilities you see as being currently beyond your capabilities.

5.5 This fear of all and nothingness is fear of God, fear of Life, fear of Creation, fear of Self. For there is only all and nothing.

5.6 A part of you is aware of this and as fearful of the all of everything as of the void of nothing. You feel as if you are headed toward "something" from somewhere but neither here nor there feel completely real to you. The lucky among you have made of this in-between place an adventure, and are happy in your seeking. You do not care to end this happy state and there is indeed much to be learned from the in-between. It is, however, a starting point only.

5.7 The whole of life could in fact be seen as the illusion of an *in-between* you have created between all and nothing. This in-between place is your comfort zone and, although you feel compelled to push at its edges, this pushing simply leaves the edges quite intact and causes them to be capable of offering resistance. Your search for "something" within the in-between, if it leads not beyond the in-between, but shields you from the recognition of the all you are capable of finding and the nothing in which you reside.

5.8 In order to experience the truth, you must move into a state that is real. *Nothing* is as real as *everything*, and is what some of you will or have experienced as a "dark night of the soul." To realize that you reside in nothingness is but the counterpart of realizing that there is an all to which you belong.

5.9 Again I tell you that it is only your body and the thinking of your ego-mind that make the in-between state of the illusion in which you now exist seem real. I must make a distinction here, between the seemingly real, and the aspect of your existence that *is* real. Your heart as we have defined it many times within this Course, must exist in the thought system that is real to you. The thought system of the ego-mind is what has been real to you and thus where your heart has been held captive. Thus, your real Self is not present in the realm of the truly real, but is actually present within the illusion. This is why all seeking must turn within, toward the heart where the real Self abides. There is nothing else that will free who you are but freedom from the ego's thought system. That the ego's thought system has kept you from this freedom is the seeming difficulty you experience in learning this course of study and the reason, when you have freed your self, that you will look back and see how easy this one choice really is.

5.10   The body, and thus the "you" whom you think you are, would not experience anything without the presence of the heart. The heart is the only cause of your *experience* here. When released from the ego thought system, the heart becomes the determiner of what you experience since you know it as the *cause*. This is what is meant by mind and heart being joined in union, or being wholehearted. It is the real you or center of your Self, being joined with the only thought system that is real, the thought system of the truth. How could a thought system based on anything but the truth lead to anything but illusion?

5.11   The "here" that you experience is the experience dictated by the ego-mind, and this experience is all that makes you believe you are other than who you are. Thus the abolishing of the ego-mind, as stated many times and in many ways, must now be brought to completion.

5.12   This is why I have asked you to choose the manner in which you would be once and finally convinced. You must *experience* the reality of the new thought system or it will remain forever theoretical. You must let go of the foundation of fear on which the old thought system was built in order to *experience* the new.

5.13   The art of thought *invites* the *experience* of the new thought system by being willing to replace the old with the new. While this will at first be a learned activity, and as such have its moments of seeming difficulty, it is learned only in the sense of practicing the mindfulness that will allow the memory of it to return to you.

5.14   Mindfulness and wholeheartedness are but different expressions of the union of mind and heart. Mindfulness will aid you in remembering. Wholeheartedness will aid you in reconciling the laws of God with the laws of man. Through mindfulness you will remember who you are. Through wholeheartedness you will be who are.

5.15   It is in this way that you will enter a time of miracles, put an end to suffering, and thus begin the return to love.

CHAPTER 6

The Act of Prayer

6.1　The thought system of the ego-mind is a learned system and this is why it can be unlearned. The thought system of the truth is always present as the truth is always present and can be neither learned nor unlearned. It will thus be revealed to you as soon as the learned thought system ceases to block its realization.

6.2　How is this revelation to take place? It will begin by learning the art of thought as the act of prayer. We have spoken already of memory here, and have presented the acts of reproducing and recollecting that are involved with memory as acts of creation. Prayer is but reproducing and recollecting a divine memory and divine memory cannot help but produce a divine outcome. Said in another way, prayer reproduces the truth and allows the truth to exist as it is. Prayer does this because it is the act of consciously choosing union. Choosing union moves you into the real state of "all" from the unreal state of the in-between. Only from within a state that is real can anything happen in truth.

6.3　Thus prayer must be redefined as the act of consciously choosing union. With this definition, you can see how your life can become a prayer. This does not negate the fact that a prayer is also a constant dialogue of asking, being answered, and responding. This is the aspect of prayer that makes of it an act of creation.

6.4　Prayer and miracles work hand-in-hand once both are seen for what they are. Do not forget what union is. Union is the mind and heart being joined in wholeheartedness. It is *your* union with your *Self.* Union with your Self is union with God. Thus your concentration must not stray back to old concepts of prayer or of reaching God through the intercession of prayer as if God were separate from you and accessible only through a specific means of communication. You can see, perhaps, how this attitude toward prayer came about, as it is, like much you have learned, close to the truth without being the truth.

6.5   To *use* prayer only as a means of reaching out to a god seen as separate is to attempt to use what cannot be used. Such ideas of prayer have had credence because this reaching out does at least recognize that there is something to reach out to. Such ideas of prayer have long been opening doors for those who are ready to walk through them to a real relationship with God and Self. But this is not the concept of prayer of which we speak nor one that can reasonably be called a way of life or likened to the art of thought. Prayers such as these emanate from either heart or mind and have not the power of the wholehearted. Prayers such as these emanate from the state of fear that is the reality of the separated self.

6.6   To pray out of fear is not to pray at all, because such prayer chooses not the union that is the prerequisite. To pray out of fear is to ask from an unreal state of lack for what is seen as missing or desired. In contrast, true prayer, formed in union, is a means of creating, recollecting, or recalling a divine memory and transforming that divine memory into a present moment experience.

6.7   Memory is valuable to us now because it relies not on perception. If perception were all that were available to you, each experience would begin and end and have no ability to relate to anything else at all. Without memory, what you learned one day would be gone the next. A person you met one day you would not know the next. Thus memory allows relationship. Memory, or how you relate to past experiences, is what makes each individual unique. A family can share many similar experiences without relating to them in the same way. It is the way experience is related to, through memory, which shapes the different personalities, paths, and thus future experiences of each of you.

6.8   So what happens when memories of past experiences are revisited under the all-encompassing umbrella of a new way of thought? The different personalities become one, the different paths become one path, the future experiences become one. And in this oneness is peace everlasting.

6.9   What happens when this oneness is accomplished is that divine memories arise to replace perception. This is miracle-mindedness. The accomplishment of this state of being is the reason for which you are here. It is your return to your Self. It heralds the return of heaven through the second coming of Christ, the energy that will bridge the two worlds.

Chapter 7

Suffering and the New Learning

7.1 Suffering is seen as a condition of this world because the world is seen as a world in which who you are can never be accomplished. You have perceived this inability to be who you are in terms of not being able to do as you would desire to do, live as you would desire to live, achieve what you would choose to achieve. The true way in which to see this prerequisite to the condition of suffering is as the perceived inability to be who you truly are, a being existing in union. Take away all, for the moment, that you would strive to be, and the feeling of not being able to be accomplished or complete will still be with you. Recall the many times you felt certain that a particular achievement would complete you and take away your feelings of lack. Even the most successful among you have found that your worldly success has been unable to bring you the satisfaction and the peace you desire.

7.2 Even the most spiritual and godly among you accept suffering. Even those who understand as completely as possible the truth of who they are accept suffering. My use of the word *accept* is important here, as these may not see suffering as pain but only as a natural part of being human that calls for acceptance. They thus find peace within suffering rather than abolishing suffering. This acceptance is due to the belief that spirit has chosen a form, and more accurately put a "lesser" form in which to exist, and that that choice includes the choice to suffer. This belief may accept suffering as a learning device rather than a punishment, but it still, in its acceptance of a false notion, invites suffering. This belief accepts learning through contrast, that evil is seen in relation to good, peace in relation to chaos, love in relation to fear. This belief exists in the in-between, where on the one hand there is darkness, and on the other hand there is light. One or the other must exist at a given time, but never both. Thus the absence of good health is disease; the absence of peace is conflict, the absence of truth illusion. This belief does not accept that there is only one reality and that it must exist where you are.

7.3   We are moving you now away from all such beliefs to a knowing that precludes the need for belief at all.

7.4   Yes, I have said that contrast is a favored teaching device of the Holy Spirit. But I have not yet said that the time of the Holy Spirit is ending even though I have stated that the time of the second coming of Christ is here. I have said that the time of parables has ended and asked you not to look to those historical figures that taught in such a way as your examples any longer. I have said a new way of learning is needed and is here. To continue to rely on the ways of old, *no matter how effective they were and no matter how much they spoke the truth* will be to not learn the new.

7.5   You have advanced, taken steps, climbed to a new level, and acquired an ability to perceive differently, in order to make this new learning possible. If you do not let what you have attained serve you, you will not realize what this new learning has been for. You may reach an ideal of human satisfaction and happiness, but you will not go beyond what is human.

7.6   This is why we must speak now of being human in a new way. We must reconcile the differences between the human and divine. We must, in other words, speak of incarnation.

CHAPTER 8

Incarnation and Resurrection

8.1 I was proclaimed to be the Word incarnate, the union of the human and the divine, the manifestation of the Will of God. I have told you that you are no different than I was. Now I call you to be no different than I am.

8.2 As a man, I suffered, died and was buried. As who I Am, I resurrected. "I am the resurrection and the life." What I was in life was the manifestation, in form, of the Will of God. Thus too have you been. God is the giver of life, thus life is God's Will. But with my resurrection, which was accomplished for all, the meaning of life, the reality of life, changed, though you have known this not. The great experiment in separation ended with the resurrection, though you have known this not. For the resurrection and life are now one and the same.

8.3 That they *are* the same has not meant the automatic realization of this change of enormous proportions. The very nature of change is one of slow realization. Change occurs all around you every day without your realization of it. Only in retrospect are the greatest of changes seen. Thus the understanding of the truth of an historical event changes over time and it may take a hundred or a thousand or even two thousand years for the *real* truth to be realized. Even though many versions of the truth have been accepted previously, there is only one truth. There was only one truth at the time the event or change took place, and there is only one truth in time or eternity regardless of the variety of interpretations of the truth.

8.4 I have come to you now to reveal the one truth that has existed for the past two thousand years without your comprehension of it. The nature of life changed with the resurrection. *I am the resurrection and the life. So are you.*

8.5 As I no longer suffer the separation, you need no longer suffer the separation. Even though the resurrection returned not life to the form I once occupied, it returned me to you in the form of the resurrected Christ who exists in all of you, bringing resurrection even unto your forms. I became the Word incarnate upon my resurrection rather than upon my birth. This will seem confusing given your definition of incarnation as the Word made flesh. You took this to mean that flesh took on the definition of the Word or the almighty when I became flesh and bone through birth. But neither my birth nor my death were consequent with the Word as the Word is I Am, the Word is Life Eternal. My resurrection brought about the Word made flesh in each of you. You who have come after me are not as I was but as I Am. Does this not make sense, even in your human terms of evolution? *You are the resurrected and the life.*

8.6 How does this relate to your thinking? You have been reborn as god-man, as God and man united. The resurrection is the cause and effect of the union of the human and divine. This is accomplished. This is *in effect* the way in which the man Jesus became the Christ. This is *in effect* the way.

8.7 Now, how could one man's resurrection be the way or even *a way.* How can resurrection provide a path or example for you to follow? You must see the link between resurrection and incarnation, the link between resurrection and the birth of the god-man.

8.8 The heart and mind joined in union accomplished the reunion of the separated self with God. The resurrection was evidence of this accomplishment. It laid aside death's claim and with it the claim of all that is temporary. The resurrection was witnessed as the proof required, much as proof has been offered to you now in the form of miracles. How could one rise from the dead and others not follow?

8.9 Illusion is the death you need but arise from. Arise and awaken to your resurrected self! There is no longer a *god-head* to follow into paradise. Take not the example of any of these and know instead the example of woman, of Mary, Mother of God.

8.10 What is a mother but she who incarnates, makes spirit flesh through her own flesh, makes spirit flesh through union. That you have, in your version of creation, made it necessary for woman to join with man in order for new life to come forth, is but another example of how your memory of creation was made to serve what you would have come to be. The separated self could not exist in separation and so created a way in which other separated forms could come into existence and live with you in separation. That you recognized union as a prerequisite to creation is proof of your memory's tenacity and the failure of illusion to completely rid you of what you know.

8.11 The virgin birth was thus a necessary step in the reclaiming of the real act of creation, the bringing forth of the new through union with the divine Self. Whether you believe the virgin birth was reality or myth matters not as myth and reality have no concrete distinction in the illusion within which you live. In other words you live as much by myth as by truth and myth often more accurately reflects the truth than what you would call real. This is not a call, however, to embrace myth, but to embrace the truth.

8.12 Mary is called upon now as the myth to end all myths for in this example life alone is the key to the riddle provided.

8.13 You are each called to return to your virgin state, to a state unaltered by the separation, a state in which what is begotten is begotten through union with God. It is from this unaltered state that you are free to resurrect, as I resurrected. It is through the Blessed Virgin Mary's resurrection *in form* that the new pattern of life is revealed.

8.14 The new pattern of life is the ability to resurrect in form. The ability to resurrect in life. The ability to resurrect now.

8.15 Thus is the glory that is yours returned to you *in life* rather than *in death*.

8.16 The male provided the manifestation or the effect of the cause created by the female in the virgin birth. My mother, Mary, was responsible for the incarnation of Christ in me as I am responsible for the incarnation of Christ in you. This union of the male and female is but union of the parts of yourself expressed in form and story, expressed, in other words, in a visual pattern that aides your understanding of the invisible. It is one more demonstration of the union that returns you to your natural state. It is one more demonstration of cause and effect being one in truth. It is one more demonstration of what needs to occur now, in this time, in order for the truth of the resurrection to be revealed and lived.

8.17 We have talked thus far of union of heart and mind. Lest you think that this union is not all encompassing, we will reflect a moment here on how the art of thought brings all you have seen as parts of the self, such as male and female, conception and action, inspiration and manifestation, together into the wholehearted.

CHAPTER 9

Giving and Receiving

9.1   The art of thought is not possible without a return to the virgin or unaltered self. The *practice* of the art of thought is what will complete the return begun through the coursework in *A Course of Love*. This will bring about the union of the male and female, of conception and action, of inspiration and manifestation. This is what we have been speaking of when speaking of miracle-mindedness or miracle-readiness. This *is* wholeheartedness and is achieved through mindfulness.

9.2   Whether you be male or female matters not, as you are in truth, the union of each. The end of separation that brought about the resurrection brought about this union and the separation of male and female continues to exist only in form.

9.3   However, we are talking now, in a certain sense, of an elevation of form. While this is actually an elevation beyond form, it must begin in the reality where you think you are. In other words, it must begin with form. You cannot await some changed state but must create the changed state you await.

9.4   You are used to creating in outward ways. One of the few exceptions to this outward creation is the act of giving birth. But birth, like all outward manifestations, but reflects inner change. The growth of a new being within the womb of another is a visible manifestation of gestation, which is the prelude to resurrection. What was once part of the mother and father, what would have died without the joining that occurred within, becomes new life.

9.5   Now you are asked to carry new life not in the womb but in the united mind and heart.

9.6   Let us consider why birth has been the purview of women and males have been incapable of giving birth. This is because, in your version of creation, there needed to be a giver and a receiver. You knew that giving and receiving makes one in truth. This is your recreation of this universal truth. You remembered that something does not come from nothing and that nothing is all that exists without relationship.

9.7   Yet you have not remembered that the first union is of mind and heart. The first union is union with the Self. This union with the Self is resurrection or rebirth. All are capable of this life-giving union. All are capable of birthing the Self.

9.8   But what then of the necessary act of giving and receiving? In this birth of the Self, who is the giver and who is the receiver? In order for the Self to be birthed, giving and receiving must be one in truth. Yet it seems there must be one to give and one to receive. You have long waited to receive what you have thought could come only from some *other*. Your churches are but evidence of this as you seek from religion an intercessor, one to facilitate for you this receiving or communion. Only through the Christ *within you* does this giving and receiving become one in truth.

9.9   As I awaited my death I was given the gift of knowing what would come to be through my resurrection. This I tried to pass on in the simplest of terms. I tried to make it known that while I would die and resurrect into a new form, you would also; that this new form would exist within you; that you would become the Body of Christ and giving and receiving would be complete.

9.10   You are the Body of Christ.

9.11   What will it mean to bring about the union of the male and female, of conception and action, of inspiration and manifestation? It will mean union and a time of miracles. It will mean that you are the living Body of Christ.

9.12   In the broadest of terms, this is already happening. As the ego has become threatened and allowed the coming of guidance, males and females both have begun to work with the parts of themselves over which the ego has the least control. For males this has most often meant a turning away from the intellectual realm, which was ruled by the ego, to the realm of feelings. For females this has most often meant a turning away from the feeling realm where their egos held most sway, toward the intellectual. This instinctual turning toward an opposite has been made to serve you through the intercession of the Holy Spirit. In turning within rather than without to find what you need to free you from the ego's reign, you have turned toward wholeness. In the same way that embracing both the male and female attributes within you causes a merging of both and a wholeness to be achieved, so too does a wholeness then come about with conception and action, inspiration and manifestation.

9.13   Lest you fight these ideas as stereotypical, I will give just a few brief examples. These I ask you to cull from your own recent experience. What has caused the ego to become more apparent to you as you have learned this Course? Has it not seemed to lie dormant for periods of time and then to suddenly be called back to life through some event or situation? What was this event or situation? Did it not threaten your self-image? And did this threat occur at what you would call the feeling level or at the intellectual level? Were your feelings hurt or your pride? Your feelings called into question or your ideas? And what guise did the ego take as it rallied to your aide? Did it require you to retreat or advance? Did it stir emotions or attempt to still them?

9.14   These may be difficult questions to answer as your initial reaction and your response will likely have taken on different forms. You may for instance, have reacted by being hurt or angry. Your response may then have been either an emotional one or an intellectual one. The point here is that the one that is most comfortable and that is likely your first reaction, is cognizant with your old pattern, or the pattern of the ego. What breaks the ego's hold will be the second reaction, or the turning away from the old.

9.15   One first reaction might be to puff oneself up with pride, bolster one's position, think one's way through, argue, manipulate, or chastise another so that you feel better in relationship to the other in the situation or event. Another's first reaction might be one of self-pity, of making oneself or another feel guilty, or of experiencing a sense of diminished self-esteem or worthiness. The first will feel like an intellectual position. The second like a feeling position. Turning away from the intellectual position to one of feeling will most readily and quickly solve the first. The second will be most readily and quickly overcome by a turn toward reason or the intellect. The perceived attack will have entered at the place where you have placed your highest value and are thus most vulnerable. In the past your response would have been to protect and use that which you have most valued. Now your response will have been changing. You will not see so much to value in what has called your ego into action and will turn away from it.

9.16   What "was" is being thrown out and the first step in this is embracing what you heretofore have not embraced. You are pulling forth sides of your selves that were previously undervalued rather than looking for an *other* to provide what you lack. This is important and universal in its impact. It would seem to be about balance but is about wholeness. Male and female are labels laden with attributes. When the different attributes are merged, male and female will be no more and wholeness will reign.

CHAPTER 10

Peace

10.1   Now let me address the issue of the peace you have been experiencing as well as your reactions to this peace. It is so foreign to each of you that you can't quite imagine that it is what you are supposed to be feeling. There is a core of peace at the center of your Self now and the issues that you choose to deal with will not affect that core of peace at all. While you may find this almost disturbing, you will not go to extremes to break this peace.

10.2   My peace is yours. You have asked for it and it has been given to you. To not have it, you will have to choose not to have it. And this will be tempting on occasion. You will wonder at the lack of extremes in your feelings and want to bring them back. You will experience this loss of extremes as a lack. You will think something is wrong. You will feel this particularly when others around you experience extremes. A friend is experiencing feelings on an extreme level and this will seem to tell you that this friend is really alive. Whether it be joy or sorrow, it will seem *real* in a way that peace does not. It will seem so *human* that a wave of desire to be fully human will wash over you. You will think that this human who has caught your attention is fully engaged and fully experiencing the moment. You will think this is what you want. And I say again that it will not matter whether it be joy or sorrow for you are, or have been, attracted by both for the same reason, the reason of wanting to be fully engaged in the human experience.

10.3   Here is this experience you have created and how often have you been fully engaged in it? How often have you given yourself over to those highs and lows? You will be tempted to give yourself over once again in this most human of ways. You will cry and laugh for the poignancy of the human experience. This is the *known* that you will be tempted not to give up. If you can't be moved from your peace by the greatest of these experiences, the most profound sorrow or the most all-encompassing joy, you will feel inhuman. You will think that this cannot be where you are meant to be, what you are meant to feel. You will wonder what is wrong with you.

10.4   This *is* temptation. The temptation of the human experience. This is what you continue to choose over the Peace of God. This is not a right or wrong choice but it is a choice. It is your free will to continue to make this choice.

10.5   You used your free will to choose the human experience. Now are you willing to use it to choose the Peace of God instead? Can you wholeheartedly choose peace? Can you choose peace long enough to become accustomed to joy without sorrow? If you cannot, you will continue to create hell as well as heaven and will continue the separation between the divine and the human. Is heaven worth enough to you to give up hell?

10.6   These extremes of the human experience have been learning devices. They have cracked open hearts and minds to the divine presence within. You have chosen them for just this reason. But you can now be an observer and look upon them as your brothers and sisters learning choice without choosing to return to learning in the same way again. You no longer need these experiences to alert you to the divine presence. Once you have learned to read you do not return to learning to read over and over again even while you may continue to read for a lifetime. You can continue to experience life and still carry the Peace of God within you. As you live in peace you can be an example to your brothers and sisters, an example that says there is another way.

10.7   Are you being asked to give up extremes? Yes. You are being asked to give up all that would take peace from you. But as you have been told before, you will be giving up nothing. It will seem as if it is so for a while perhaps. You will continue to be attracted to those living at the extremes and there is no reason not to take joy in observing another's happiness or to feel compassion at another's suffering. But you need not partake and you cannot partake if you are going to carry the Peace of God within you.

10.8   This is what has been meant by the many references that have been made to God not seeing suffering. God exists with you in peace. When you feel peace, you feel the Peace of God. There is no other peace. There is no other God. Whether you believe it now or not, I assure you, within the Peace of God is all the joy of what you have known as the human experience and none of the sorrow.

10.9 Each of you will have an experience you look back on, an experience of profound joy or grief that also became an experience of profound learning. You will think that you would not be who you are now without experiences such as this one. You will think that I cannot possibly be asking you to give up these types of experiences. But you have already had them! I ask you not to give them up. Only to make now a new choice.

10.10 It is your memory of these events that hold such sway over you that you would choose not the Peace of God. But look past what you have remembered to what was truly there. No moment of true learning ever arrived without the Peace of God for without the Peace of God no true learning is possible.

10.11 Let us separate experiences you might call peak experiences from experiences of extremes that served as learning devices. Peak experiences often follow occasions of happiness or trauma, but they do not happen within them. Peak experiences are what you can look forward to rather than back upon if you but choose the Peace of God.

10.12 The extremes that we are talking of leaving behind are extremes of reaction to a chosen lesson. What you are being asked to leave behind is the need for such lessons. If you have learned the curriculum, what further lessons are needed? What quiet knowing cannot come to you in peace? Why would you believe you can learn from the turmoil of extremes what you cannot learn in peace eternal?

10.13 This is what you have believed and why you have not chosen yet to accept your inheritance. Yet let the memory of the truth return to you now and you will see that peace is all you have sought learning to attain. If you do not pause now and accept that it is here, you will not know the Peace of God that is your own Self.

10.14 Peace, in whatever way you find it, in whatever expression it takes, no matter what words you use to describe it, is your answer to God and God's answer to you. Peace is the inheritance I left you. Peace of body, mind and heart. Peace is the realm of miracles, the condition of the wholehearted, the prerequisite to the art of thought, the description of heaven, the abode of Christ. Peace has come to you and you to Peace.

10.15 Now your final instruction is here. You who have found peace—live in peace. You have been given the Peace of God—go in Peace. Spread peace throughout the land. Go out in peace and love and service to all. For in this going out you come home and bring with you all the brothers and sisters you have brought to peace. Go in peace to love and serve with all your heart. Thus are we one heart, one mind, one unity. Thus are we one in a relationship of love and peace that is our eternal home. Welcome home my brothers and sisters in Christ. Welcome home.

A Treatise on
The Nature of Unity
and Its Recognition

The Second Treatise

CHAPTER 1

Treasure

1.1　You are all aware, at least at times, that there are treasures that lie within you. What was once regarded as treasure, such as a talent that was in need of developing, when realized, is often disregarded thereafter as a treasure and becomes instead something regarded as an ability and later as simply part of your identity. This is what we are going to explore in this Treatise. A treasure that you do not as yet recognize is going to be recognized. Once recognized it will begin to be regarded as an ability. And finally, through experience, it will become your identity. We will begin by discussing the nature of treasure.

1.2　Treasure is most often seen in one of two ways—as something valuable to be sought and found or as something found that is kept secure and cherished.

1.3　Treasure in the first sense is, first and foremost, something that you believe exists and have defined as being of value. As this Treatise is not concerned with material treasure, we will not explore the dimensions of physical treasure except to say that the feelings that cause one to think that any physical thing is capable of being a treasure or being treasured are of the ego. We will instead assume that you have moved beyond these ego concerns and explore the realm of internal treasures.

1.4　Those of you who have moved beyond the realm of the ego, in your fear of returning to it, often turn away from internal treasures that you believe, when realized, might feed the ego. Despite many observations within this Course regarding desire, you may still fear your desire. Despite many exhortations that your purpose here is to be who you are, you may have determined that exploring your internal treasure is now unnecessary. You may well be feeling a sense of relief in having learned that who you are right now is a being of perfection, and you may find in this a somewhat peaceful resting place to dwell in for a time. You may find that despite having learned much about the need to leave judgment behind, you judge your desire to be other than you are now, including any desires related to those internal treasures you had once hoped to have become abilities. You think this willingness to accept who you are now is what this Course has led you to and evidence of your accomplishment. You may view this as license to stay as you are and to cease striving for more.

1.5   This resting place is indeed hallowed ground and an earned respite, a demarcation even between the old way and the new way of living. But it is not the end that is sought. No matter how peaceful this place of rest may at first seem, it will soon become stagnant and unsatisfying. Left in such a place without further instruction, you would soon return to your old ideas of heaven and see peace as a state of being for those too weary to fully live. Done with the adventures of living, you would deem yourself no longer interested in the hunt for buried treasure and see it not.

1.6   This place is not life but neither is it death, for even death is not an eternal resting *place* in the sense that you have imagined it. Even rest, once truly learned, is simply rest. It is not a resting *place*, a *place* to stop along the journey of life anymore than it is a *place* at which life stops and death reigns. It is not a point at which you arrive, never to depart. Rest, when truly learned, is a state of being in which struggle has ceased and peace has triumphed over chaos, love has triumphed over fear.

1.7   You may still see but two choices: peace or struggle. But with such an attitude, you would soon be struggling to maintain your peace. There is another choice, and it lies within.

1.8   The treasure that lies within that you do not yet fully recognize is that of unity. As you have learned much of unity within the context of this Course, unity, like rest, may have come to be viewed as a place at which you can arrive. Like peace, it may feel like a bubble of protection, something that sets you apart from life and the chaos that seems to reign there. You must realize that you think in terms of place because you think in terms of form. Thus even I have often used the idea of place as a teaching aid. But you are ready now to begin to think without the need for form.

1.9   Even the desires you may have once identified as hoping to develop into abilities, are given a structure and form in your thinking of them. A desire to paint, in your thoughts becomes a completed painting that you hang upon your wall. The time of painting becomes a place. A room or studio is envisioned in which all the tools of the artist's trade are available. An aspiring pianist imagines a grand piano and performances in a magnificent concert hall or a little Spinet that will grace a living room and invite friends and family to gather round. A writer sees a book in print, a runner wins a race, a tennis player becomes a champion. These are all scenes of things and places, or in other words, of the external, of form.

1.10 Thinking without form is a harbinger of unity. Form is a product of the separation. Thought "forms" are the product of the separation. Unity is not a place or a thing but the realm of the one heart and one mind; the realm of the formless and timeless. But also the realm of connectedness, of what binds all that lives in creation with the Creator.

1.11 You are a creator but a creator who creates with thought unlike to any thoughts you have had before. Your thoughts of a grand piano will never create a grand piano. What kind of thoughts, then, would create a pianist?

1.12 Thoughts joined in unity. Thoughts joined in unity can be likened to thinking without thought. They can be likened to imagination. They can be likened to love.

1.13 Ego desires cause one to think of a grand piano. Thoughts joined in unity hear music. Ego desires cause one to think of an elaborately framed painting. Thoughts joined in unity see beauty. You are used to thinking that if you do not have a tangible goal, such as that of music lessons or the purchase of a piano, you will never reach the goals associated with those tangible steps. Thoughts joined in unity create without goals or planning, without effort or struggle. This does not make an instrument unnecessary for a musician or mean that a painter will not eventually put a brush to a canvas. But it does mean that the treasure exists without these "things" and that the treasure is already a fully realized creation. The treasure already is and it is already valuable and available.

1.14 This is a first step in the change in thinking that needs to occur. It is an elementary step and one easily accomplished with but a bit of willingness. This change in thinking in regards to treasures you do recognize will pave the way for recognition of treasures you heretofore have not recognized.

CHAPTER 2

To Hear the Call

2.1 Why would we begin "A Treatise on Unity" by talking of treasure? To pave the way for talking of calling. What is it in you that recognizes talents that lie fully realized within? The practical mind is not the source of such imagination. The practical mind makes of imagination a fantasy. It is the heart that sees with true imagination and the heart that speaks to you in terms that are consistent with the idea you currently hold of hearing a call or having a calling.

2.2 Having a calling is spoken of in lofty terms. Few outside of those who feel they have a calling for something beyond their ordinary, limited, view of the themselves use this phrase. But many recognize that they have a calling even unto things the world considers mundane.

2.3 How does a farmer explain that she or he cannot be other than a farmer? That rising and setting with the sun is in their blood, in the very nature of who they are. That being one with the land is essential to them.

2.4 What bravery it takes in today's world to follow a calling to teach. To set aside other careers that offer far more prestige and economic gain to instead be a sharer of knowledge, a shaper of minds.

2.5 What overriding kindness calls one to take care of another's body, to be a healer?

2.6 How does one explain a joy that is like no other and that comes from the simple act of caring for a child, preparing a meal, bringing grace and order to a home?

2.7 This list of different callings could be endless, and each could be considered unexplainable. Those who seek an explanation before following a calling, who look for reasons of a practical nature, who would seek guarantees of the rightness and outcome of following such a call, seek for proof they have already been given. The call itself is proof. It is proof of the heart's ability to be heard. Of the heart's ability to recognize the unseen and to imagine the existence of that which will reveal its true nature and its joy.

2.8   All of you are capable of hearing the truth of what the heart would tell you. All of you are just as capable of believing in that truth as of doubting it. All that prevents you from believing in truth is a mind and heart acting in separation rather than in union.

2.9   You think that what prevents you from being who you are is far broader than this simple idea of hearing and following a calling would indicate. You think what prevents you from being who you are is far broader than a division between mind and heart. Some of you would say you feel no calling, or that you feel many. Others would cite practical reasons for doing other than what they feel called to do. All of these ideas illustrate your belief that something other than your own willingness is necessary. Only in your own willingness does anything exist because only in your willingness is the power of creation expressed.

CHAPTER 3

To Answer the Call

3.1   Your life is already an act of creation. It *was* created. All of it. It exists, fully realized within you. Your work here is to express it. *You* are far more than your life here. *You* created your life here in union with the one mind and one heart, in union, in other words, with God. Everything you have ever wanted to be *is*. Everything you have ever thought or imagined *is* and is reflected in the world you see. The only difference between the life you are living and the life you want lies in your willingness to express who you are.

3.2   There would be no need for form if there had been no desire for expression. Life *is* the desire to express outwardly what exists within. What I refer to so often here as being within, as if "within" is a *place* in which something resides, is unity and it is the *place* where being resides. It is the *place* or *realm* of one heart and one mind. It is the place where everything already exists fully realized. It is like a trunk full of treasure. Like a menu of possibilities. All you must do is wholeheartedly recognize the treasure you have already chosen to bring to the world. Your heart speaks to you of this treasure and guides you to open the trunk and release it to the world—to your world—to the human world. As I have said, in the realm of unity where your being resides, this is already accomplished. Your link between the realm of unity and the realm of physicality is your heart. Your heart tells you of the *already accomplished* and bids you to express it with your physicality, thus uniting the two realms through expression.

3.3   Your mind exists in unity. Your heart exists *where you think you are*, thus providing the means for union between *where you think you are* and where your being actually resides. Remember always that your heart is where the Christ in you abides and that the Christ is your identity. Remember that it is the Christ in you that learns and raises learning to the holiest of levels. It is the Christ in you that learns to walk the earth as child of God, as who you really are.

3.4   This was stated early in *A Course of Love* and is returned to now for a specific reason. While the truth that it is the Christ in you that learns may have been given little attention as you began your learning, it cannot now be ignored. Now *you* have realized your learning. *You* have begun to see the changes that your learning is capable of bringing to your life. *You* have felt the peace and love of the embrace. *You* know that you are experiencing something real and learning something that is of relevance even within the daily life you currently move through. Now you must fully recognize the distinction between the ego-self that previously was the self of learning and experience, and the Christ-Self that is now the Self of learning and experience. You must take on the mantle of your new identity, your new Self.

3.5   It is this recognition that you are now acting and living in the world as your Christ-Self rather than as your ego-self that will aid you in expression. Without expression, the return to unity that has been accomplished will not be realized.

3.6   If you still balk at the idea that the Christ could be in need of learning, then your idea of the Christ is still based on an old way of thinking, as are your ideas of learning.

3.7   Learning and accomplishment are not linear as you have perceived them to be. If we return to the idea of talents this may be easier to explain. If the ability to create beautiful music already exists within you, you do not have to learn what beautiful music is, only how to express it. If you see beauty within, you do not have to learn what beauty is, only how to express it. Expression and creation are not synonymous. Creation is a continuous and on-going expansion of the same thought of love that brought life into existence. The seeds of creation exist in everything and provide for continuing creation. Thus the seeds of all that you can express exist "within" you, in the creation that is you. The power of creation is released through your choice, your willingness to express that aspect of creation. It is quite literally true that the seeds of much of creation lie dormant within you, already accomplished but awaiting expression in this realm of physicality.

3.8   In this same way, then, Christ can be seen as the seed of your identity. Christ is the continuous and on-going expansion of the same thought of love that brought life into existence. Christ is your identity in the broadest sense imaginable. Christ is your identity within the unity that is creation.

CHAPTER 4

The Call to Who You Are

4.1   Creation is not an aspect of this world alone. Creation is an aspect of the whole, the all of all, the alpha and the omega, eternity and infinity. It is not only life as you know it now, but life in all its aspects. It is life beyond death as well as life before birth and life during your time here. It is all one because it is all from the same Source.

4.2   You are not only part of creation, but as has been said many times, a creator, and as such a continuing act of creation. This does not mean that creation is acted out upon you but that you are acted out upon creation. The idea of creation as something static would be completely contrary to the meaning of creation. Yet you continue to think that you stand apart from it and affect it not. This is consistent to the thinking that would tell you that you are at the mercy of fate. Fate and creation are hardly the same thing. You are at the mercy only of your own ego and only until you willingly let it go.

4.3   *A Course in Miracles* and *A Course of Love* work hand-in-hand because the change of thinking taught within *A Course in Miracles* was a change of thinking about yourself. It attempted to dislodge the ego-mind that has provided you with an identity that you but *think* you are. *A Course of Love* then followed in order to reveal to you who you truly are. While you continue to act within the world as who you *think* you are rather than as who you are, you have not integrated these two pieces of learning.

4.4   This is the stage of learning that you are at and what this Treatise addresses. This Treatise is attempting to show you how to *live* as who you are, how to act within the world as the new Self you have identified. Just like learning how to swim, it is a new way of movement. Just as moving through water is a way of movement quite inconsistent with that of moving on land, so too is the new way of acting out or expressing who you are quite inconsistent with the way in which you have formerly acted out or expressed who you are. This is, of course, because you formerly acted out of a set of conditions that corresponded to who you *think* you are rather than who you truly are.

4.5   You will almost literally continue to "bump in" to who you think you are as you complete the process of unlearning. It might be best explained by continuing with the swimming metaphor. If acting in the world as who you truly are is like swimming, bumping in to who you think you are could be likened to trying to move within water as you would on land. Why, when moving freely through the water would you suddenly try to move as if on land? The explanation could be as simple as forgetting where you are, or as complex as a sudden panic or fear brought on by any number of factors. Either way, the result would always be the same; a sudden change from ease of movement to struggle, from going with the flow to resistance.

4.6   A first step then in learning to recognize when you are acting upon notions of who you think you are rather than on who you truly are, is the appearance of struggle or resistance. As a swimmer quickly learns, the only way to return to ease of movement is to cease to struggle or resist. The ability to let go of struggle is a learned ability for the swimmer and is a learned ability for you now as you journey back to your real Self. It requires remembrance, trust, and a wholehearted approach that allows the body, mind and heart to act in unison. This wholehearted approach is the condition from which unity is recognized. The water is not taken for granted but always recognized as the condition of the swimmer's environment. You are no longer confined to the conditions of separation, my dear brothers and sisters, and this is what it is time for you to learn.

4.7   This applies directly to your *reaction* to all that occurs within your life. Let us look now at your reaction to the idea put forth earlier of having a calling.

4.8   Despite whatever way you currently have of identifying calling as it relates to you there are few among you who have not reacted to the idea of calling with two sets of feelings and thoughts. One set of thoughts and feelings contain all that one might attribute to the glad acceptance of a gift of high value, or in other words, a treasure. One set of thoughts and feelings contain all that one might attribute to the somewhat onerous onset of yet another responsibility, another obligation. One set of thoughts recognizes that something has been given. The other set recognizes that something has been asked. The wholehearted response is one that recognizes that giving and receiving are the same in truth.

4.9   While two sets of thoughts and feelings exist, the only way to come to peace with them is through an acceptance of ambiguity. While an acceptance of ambiguity might seem preferable to conflict, an acceptance of ambiguity is a rejection of your power. What is required to claim your power is the willingness to move through the conflict of two opposing sets of thoughts and feelings to the place of unity.

4.10   Thus a first step in our work with regard to calling is recognizing the dualistic nature of your thoughts and feelings. A second step is willingness to move past both ambiguity and conflict to union.

4.11   This requires an examination of your specific notions concerning calling as you apply them to yourself. Whether you feel that you a have a specific calling, no calling, or many callings, matters not at this juncture. What matters is that you think it does. You think it matters because you compare and judge rather than accept.

4.12   You who have so recently felt the peace of true acceptance are not asked to leave that peace to go in search of calling but are rather asked to listen from within that peace to what you feel called to do. This is not about the past and all those things that at one time or another you thought would bring you fulfillment. This is about recognizing who you are now. This is not a quick fix that calls you to what might have been and tells you that if you had but acted earlier you would have had the life you've dreamed of and maybe it is not too late. This is not about examining where the various calls you responded to previously have led you. All these notions are concerned with who you have thought yourself to be, not with who you are. They do not recognize the difference between thinking and knowing.

4.13   Being who you are is what you are called to do. You are here asked to live a life as seamless as that of the birds of the air. You are asked to live a life where there is no division between who you are and what you do. This place of no division is the place of unity.

4.14   Now you may feel as if this Treatise has led around in a circle, bringing you back only to contemplate again the acceptance of where you are now. However, to accept where you are is not the same as accepting who you are. Accepting *where* you are, as if it is a static place at which you have arrived, is not the goal that has been set. Accepting *who* you are includes acceptance of creation. The acceptance of creation is the acceptance of change and growth but neither of these are concepts that you understand truly. Change is not negative and growth does not imply lack.

4.15 You must be beginning to see that your thought processes, the very thought processes that tell you hour-by-hour and minute-by-minute how to perceive of and live in your world, are still often based on old concepts. This does not mean you have not changed nor that you are in need of accomplishment rather than the already accomplished. What this means is that you are still in need of unlearning, of undoing old patterns of thought. This is atonement and it is continuous and ongoing until it is no longer needed. Anything continuous and ongoing is part of creation. Thus the very act of undoing old patterns is an act of creation. As the old is undone, a vacuum is not created. The new is created.

4.16 You are in the process of unmaking what you have made. The old structure is coming down so that the new, what might be likened to a building with no frame, can rise.

4.17 This process too is union for it is giving and receiving as one although you recognize it not as such. It is not a process of waiting until one thing is accomplished for another to begin. What is happening now is happening in unison. As the old goes, the new arrives. There is no time-lapse in this learning and so it is a condition of miracle readiness. The old is replaced by the new simultaneously.

4.18 This is why you do not have to "wait" to hear your calling even though some of you may feel as if you are in a time of waiting for you hear no such call. The call is to be who you are and this is happening at lightning speed, a speed that cannot be measured because of its simultaneous nature. As was said within *A Course of Love*, time is but a measurement of the "time" it takes for learning to occur. As this notion of time dissolves, the state of miracle-readiness becomes your natural state.

4.19 While this adjustment of your thinking may not seem to be the miracle that it truly is, as your awareness of it grows, it is going to raise it to a level you will come to think of as an ability. As your old way of responding to life causes you to struggle or resist and the new way of thinking replaces that old pattern with a new pattern of response, you will begin to see that each new response is the answer to a call that your heart alone can hear. As I have said, your heart has now become your eyes and ears. Your heart hears only one call, one voice, the language of one Source—that of unity.

CHAPTER 5

The Source of Your Call

5.1   In order for you to more fully understand the life that this Course calls you to, we must also talk of another aspect of being called. While we have concluded that when you listen to your heart, you hear and are able to respond to the one call, this does not mean that this one call has but one request to make of you, as in a call to be a minister, nor that it will come in but one form, as in a call to action. We have talked heretofore about a calling you feel from within, as if you are listening to a new voice that would reveal your talents and desires to you. This type of calling comes as a light shone into the darkness and is revelatory in nature. Other calls will come as announcements, signs, or even as seeming demands. All call you to the present where response is able to be given. All call you "back" to who you are.

5.2   Again let me stress the present-moment nature of being called. A call is, at its most basic level, a means of communication. If you are not listening, you will not hear the calls that are meant for you. If you are looking only for a specific type of call, you will miss many unlearning and learning opportunities. Thus recognition of the different calls that may now be heard is necessary.

5.3   The call that comes in the form of an announcement is the call that carries with it no ambiguity. The certainty of an announcement can alert you that it is time to act. This might be considered the highest form of call, the call from the already accomplished to the already accomplished. Such a call signals an end to learning from the lessons of the past and a beginning of learning from the new. This Course itself is such a call, an announcement of your readiness for the new. This is the all-encompassing call and is not about specifics. Because it is not about specifics you may find yourself still wondering what to do. Thus you must be aware of the calls that assist you in knowing what to do.

5.4   These calls you may think of as signs. Like literal signposts along a roadway, they alert you to turn your attention in a particular direction.

5.5   Calls that seem to come in the form of demands are often calls that come to you from within the teaching and learning ground of relationships. You may be literally "called to account" for certain attitudes or behaviors. You may also be called upon to call others to account for their attitudes or behaviors.

5.6   These last two calls, the call that appears in the form of a sign and the call that comes in the form of a demand, are about specifics in a way that the call that comes as an announcement is not. They represent the remnants of learning from the past, the final breaking of old patterns. They may seem to signal difficult times, but they are times that must be gotten through and lessons that need to be allowed to pass through you.

5.7   Until you have fully integrated the truth that giving and receiving are one, you will not fully believe that needs are not lacks. Until you have fully integrated the truth that giving and receiving are one, you will not realize that dependency is a matter of the interdependency of all that exists in relationship. Thus, all the calls that come to you in the form of signs or demands will be calls that assist you in integrating this learning and making it one with who you are. These lessons will bring who you are into focus within your mind through the vehicle of your heart.

CHAPTER 6

The Belief: Accomplishment

6.1   The source of what we have been speaking of as "calling" is your heart. It is what alerts you to the treasures that lie within. There is no time in the place we are calling *within* and your heart knows not of time even while it adheres to the rules of time you would place upon yourself. Cease adhering to the rules of time and see how much more the language of your heart becomes known to you.

6.2   I speak here not of the rules of time that govern your days and years but the rules of time that you *believe* govern your days and years and that you thus allow to govern your thinking. If time is but a measure of learning, and if your learning is now at the stage at which it occurs in unison with unlearning, then the end of time as you know it is close at hand. If you can begin now to think without the barriers of time you but place upon your thinking, you will advance this process and more quickly bring about the end of the pattern of learning that you refer to as time. The end of the pattern of learning that you refer to as time is the beginning of the time of unity.

6.3   This return to unity is reliant upon the changes in your beliefs that this Course has brought about. Let us review these beliefs and how they relate to your concept of time.

6.4   Only you can be accomplished and your accomplishment is already complete.

6.5   What does this mean in regards to time? You might think of being accomplished as all of your work being done. If there is no work to be done, nothing for you to do, for what do you need time? Have you ever conceived of accomplishing anything without taking into account the time that it will take? Relate this question to our discussion of treasure and you will understand what it is of which I speak. You believe that your treasures only become accomplished abilities within time. You believe that your treasures only become part of your identity when you have passed beyond the time it takes for those treasures to become abilities. Thus all that you might wish to accomplish stands separate from you and beyond you in time. That your mind projects what you desire to accomplish onto an unknown future time is what would seem to keep you from accomplishment. I say that it is what would "seem to" purposefully. If you are already accomplished, this trick of your mind has not worked. And yet, if you believe that this trick of your mind has worked, you act as if you are being kept from accomplishment by time, and this "seems" quite real to you. This "seems" quite real to you because of what you believe.

6.6   Accomplishment is not an end point but a given. It is not an outcome but a certainty. It says *I am* rather than *I will be*. *I will be* is a statement that presumes a future in which you will be someone other than who you are in the present. Unity exists only in the here and now of the present. There is no *will be* in unity. There is only what *is*. Thus the limits you would place on the concept of something being what it *is*, must be part of this discussion.

6.7   Your mind would tell you that a chair is a chair and regard it as a fact. Through the learning you have done since your birth, you have come to recognize a chair as having certain properties, the most essential of which is that it is a structure on which to sit. The exercises of *A Course in Miracles* began with asking you to call into question these beliefs in known, observable, facts. You may have regarded these exercises as silly or you may have thought of the lessons of physics and felt as if you understood these exercises on an intellectual level. But what these exercises have prepared you for is an acceptance of the ongoing change that *is* creation; an acceptance that something can be what it *is*, a known fact, an object with an identity, but also part of the ongoing nature of creation. Could this be true of a chair and not be true of you?

6.8   It is your belief that change and growth are indicative of all that *can be* accomplished rather than of what is *already* accomplished that needs adjustment now. As a tree exists fully accomplished within its seed and yet grows and changes, you exist fully accomplished within the seed that is the Christ in you even while you continue to grow and change. Physical form and action of all kinds are but expressions of what already exist within the seed of the already accomplished.

6.9   The recognition that you are already accomplished is a condition of your recognition of the state of unity. It is a recognition that you exist in unity *outside* of the pattern of time. Miracles *create* an out-of-pattern time interval. Thus living in a state of miracle-readiness is the creation of a new reality outside of the pattern of ordinary time. Although this state exists as the already accomplished, it is up to you to create it for yourself. You must create it for yourself only because you believe you replaced what was already accomplished with what you made. This is what is happening as you unlearn and learn in unison. You are creating the state of unity as a new reality for *your Self* even though it is actually a return to what has always been. You are changing the world you perceive by perceiving a new world. You are changing from who you have thought yourself to be to who you are.

6.10   As I have already said that your heart must exist where you think you are, you can begin to see that this change in thinking will release your heart, returning it to its natural realm. Thus does mind and heart join in unity in the present, in the here and now, so that you exist—even within form— as the only Son of God, the Christ, the word made flesh. Remember that the phrase, *the Son of God*, and the name *Christ*, but represent the original creation and are not to be mistaken for heavenly deities separate from you. The Christ is your *Self* as you were created and remain. The Christ is the accomplished Self.

CHAPTER 7

The Belief: Giving and Receiving As One

7.1 We have talked much in this Course of your desire to be independent without looking at the condition of dependency that you consider its opposite. To be independent, you feel as if you must rely only on yourself. Thus the connotation of reliance on others, or dependence, has taken on a negative meaning specifically in contrast to your desire to be independent. One of your greatest fears is thus of a condition that causes you to be dependent or to rely on others.

7.2 Others are the great unknown of living in the world. Others are those who are beyond your control, those who can influence the course of your day or your life in ways you would not choose. Others represent the accidents waiting to happen, love that is not returned, the withholding of things you deem important. This fear that you feel in relation to others is as true of those you hold most dear to you as it is of those you would call strangers. It is the very independence of others that makes your own independence seem so important to you. Dependency is not consistent with your notions of a healthy self. What, then is the alternative?

7.3 The alternative is believing in giving and receiving as one.

7.4 First let us replace your idea of "others" with the idea of "relationship" that has been so often defined and repeated within this Course. In order to believe in giving and receiving as one, you must believe in relationship rather than in others.

7.5 Those you would view as others are separate from you. Those you would view as being in relationship with you are not separate from you. The relationship is the source of your unity. That you exist in relationship with all is a belief that you must now incorporate into living. Further, you must remember that relationship is based on trust. If you are dependent, or supported by others with whom you share a trusting relationship, where is the negativity? Where is the cause for fear? What is the hidden source of your feelings of lack or deprivation? What is the hidden source of your desire to control?

7.6 This source is the ego. Even now, the ego will take every opportunity that arises to prove to you that independence is a far better state than that of dependence. It will work diligently to convince you that any course that tries to take away your independence should be resisted. As long as you continue to listen to your ego you will not understand giving and receiving as one and will not believe in it.

7.7 This is the most difficult belief of all to integrate into the living of your life. Each time another thwarts you, you will be tempted to believe that giving and receiving as one is not taking place. Your previous pattern of behavior will be quick to assert itself and you will feel resentment and claim that the situation is unfair. You will be tempted to withhold as others withhold from you.

7.8 Is it not clear how important it is to living in peace that this pattern be broken? Will you live in peace only until some "other" breaks your peace? Only until some circumstance beyond your control brings an unexpected conflict your way?

7.9 There is no function for control in unity. There is no need for it. Relationship is the only means through which interaction is real, the only source of your ability to change that which you would change.

7.10 Here is an idea not heretofore given much attention, the idea of the desire for change. Certainly there will continue to be things within your life that are in need of change. As was stated in the beginning of this Treatise, this Course has not called you to a static state of sameness, an acceptance of who you are that does not allow for change. But once you have become happier with who you are, you will, if left un-schooled, turn your attention to others and to situations you would have be different than they are. You will want to be a change-agent. You will want to move into the world and be an active force within it. These are aims consistent with the teachings of this Course, but what will prevent you from following the patterns of old as you go out into the world with your desire to effect change?

7.11 The only thing that will prevent this is your ability to go out into the world and remain who you are. This relates to giving and receiving being one in truth in a very concrete way. For to go out into the world with the desire to give, either expecting to receive in certain measure or to receive not at all, is to follow the old pattern, a pattern that has been proven to not have any ability to change the world.

7.12   To proceed into each relationship as who you truly are is to bring everlasting change to each and every relationship, and thus to all.

7.13   Again I return you to the early teachings of *A Course of Love*, teachings concerning your desire to be good and to do good. This is not about doing good works. This is about being who you are and seeing the truth rather than the illusion that surrounds you. You cannot, in other words, be a good person in a bad world. You cannot effect change without, without having effected change within. You cannot be independent and still be of service. For as long as you believe in your independence you will not accept your dependence. You will not accept giving and receiving as one if you feel able only to give or as if "others" have nothing you would receive.

7.14   This new attitude, then, includes accepting that you have needs. That you are a being who exists in relationship is the same as saying you are a being who needs relationship. The only thing that keeps you, in this new pattern, from being needy and dependent in an unhealthy way, is that you believe in giving and receiving as one. You believe, in other words, that your needs will be provided for, thus ceasing to be needs. To deny that you are a being with needs is not the aim of this Course. To come to believe that your needs are provided for by a Creator and a creation that includes all "others" is to believe in giving and receiving being one in truth.

7.15   Giving is not only about choosing what good and helpful parts of yourself you will share with the world. It is also about giving the world the opportunity to give back. It is about recognizing the constant and ongoing exchange that allows needs to be met. It is trusting that if you have a need for money or time or honesty or love, it will be provided.

7.16   Trusting is not a condition or state of being that you have heretofore seen as being an active one. Your attitude toward trust is one of waiting, as if an active stance toward trust would be *dis*trustful. You thus will often say that you trust when what you are doing is hoping for a specific outcome. Real trust is not a trust that waits and hopes but a trust that acts from who you truly are. Real trust requires the discipline of being who you are in every circumstance and in every relationship. Real trust begins with your Self.

7.17   How often have you hidden thoughts and feelings because you question whether they are legitimate thoughts and feelings? For some of you this answer has changed greatly over time. But for many of you, you have become less, rather than more forthcoming about your thoughts and feelings since taking this Course. You have done so out of a desire to be truthful, a desire to not express thoughts and feelings unworthy of your real Self. You may have increasingly denied thoughts and feelings you would judge as negative or bad. Or you may have, in your desire not to judge others, kept yourself from speaking up in instances where you previously would have stated an opinion. While these modes of behavior, in themselves, are learning aides that prepare you for acting with the certainty you seek, they again are not to be confused with the true aims of this course of study.

7.18   Who you are cannot be denied in favor of who you "will be." Needs cannot be denied as a means of having them cease to be. You who are beginning to realize that you have much to give, realize that you have as much to receive and that receiving does not imply that you are lacking!

7.19   The discipline required to be who you are is a discipline that requires trust in Self and honesty in relationships. Does this mean that you are required to express every thought and feeling that comes your way? No, but this does mean that you bring the thoughts and feelings that arise to the place within your heart that has been prepared for them. You do not deny them. You bring them first to your Self, to the Self joined in unity at the place of your heart. From this place you learn to discriminate, to separate the false from the true, for your ego thoughts cannot long abide in the holy place of your heart. Then, with truth and illusion separated, you develop the discipline to express your true Self, as you are now. This is the only way the Self you are now has to grow and change. This is the only means the Self you are now has of giving and receiving as one. This is the only means available to you to replace the old pattern with the new.

7.20   The recognition that giving and receiving occur as one is a precondition for your recognition of the state of unity. As with the recognition of your accomplishment, the acceptance of the belief that giving and receiving are one in truth changes the function of time as you know it. There is not a period of waiting or a period of time between giving and receiving. There is not a time-lapse between the recognition of needs and the meeting of needs. It is accepted that giving and receiving occur in unison, thus further collapsing the need for time.

7.21   While as stated previously, this belief will at times seem difficult to put into practice, and while your recognition of receiving and of needs being met may seem to still take time, this belief builds on the belief of the already accomplished through experience. As you *experience* giving and receiving being one in truth, your belief will become true conviction. Your ability to recognize giving and receiving as one becomes simply an aspect of your identity and accepted as the nature of who you are in truth.

CHAPTER 8

The Belief: No Relationships Are Special

8.1   In order for this learning to come to completion, you must put into practice the belief that no relationships are special. Your loyalty must be totally to the truth of who you are and not continue to be split by special relationships. While your love relationships will provide a rich learning ground for you now, they must also now be separated from all that would continue to make them special.

8.2   As was said within *A Course of Love*, the one you come to know through relationship is your Self. This is the learning ground on which you now stand. All that prevents you from being who you are within these relationships must be let go. All that will complement who you are must be received. Thus the nature of many relationships may be required to change. Remember now that there is no loss but only gain, or you will feel threatened by what you will imagine to be loss. Remember too the practice of devotion for in this practice is the truth separated from illusion.

8.3   While your dedication to the goal of being who you are may at first seem selfish, it will soon be revealed to be the most sincere form of relationship. Relationship based on anything other than who you are is but a mockery of relationship. The calls that come to you now as signs and demands will not only aid you in your realization of who you are and your ability to live as who you are, but will aid all others. This is giving and receiving as one. What you gain will take nothing from anyone. What another is able to give you will take nothing from them, and what you are able to give another will take nothing from you.

8.4   These are all calls to know your Self and to act on this knowing. These are calls to truth and but take the form of honesty for a brief time as the truth of who you are is revealed to you and through your relationships to all.

8.5   A new type of acceptance is required here, one not previously asked or expected of you. This is an acceptance that you know your own truth and an acceptance that that truth will not change. As we have said that you are not called to a static acceptance that does not include change, this new idea of acceptance requires further clarification.

8.6   It was said often within *A Course of Love* that the truth does not change. Thus the truth of who you are has not changed and you are as you were created. Form and behavior are, however, subject to change, as are your expressions of who you are. This distinction must be fully realized here in order for you to accept the truth of who you are and to come to an acceptance of the unchangeable nature of this truth. This is akin to being done with seeking. This is the final acceptance that you have "found" and that you have been found. You need no longer journey onto the paths of seeking. The truth of yourself that you reveal now will not become a new truth as you take a new path. Your path now is sure and its final acceptance necessary. You are the prodigal sons and daughters who have returned home. Your stay is not finite. You are not here to rest and gain strength for another journey in search of something that is not available here. Here is the realm of the already accomplished. This is home. Your expression of who you are may lead you to many new adventures but never again to the special relationships that would take you away from your true Self. Never again will you be away from home for home is who you are, a "place" you carry within you, a place that is you. This is the home of unity.

8.7   How much time will be saved by an end to empty seeking? You have already arrived and need no time to journey any longer. How much time will be saved by an end to the maintenance required by special relationships? When all relationships are holy, you have no need to maintain specialness.

8.8   Thus again is your learning advanced by leaps and bounds formerly reserved for the angels. You are your own wings, your relationships but the breeze that keeps you afloat.

CHAPTER 9

The Belief: There Is No Loss But Only Gain

9.1　I ask you now to remember a time when you felt from another the desire to help or to meet your needs. Do not think that this desire is not present in all relationships. It is only the ego that stands between desire and the meeting of desire, needs and the meeting of needs.

9.2　The word "need" and the word "dependent" are only words and words that would be inconceivable to you in the state of unity before you left it. Now, they are just tools, as are many other means of practice that assist you in bypassing your ego mind. Some practices more commonly thought of as tools might be meditation, exercises of the body such as yoga, or exercises of the mind such as affirmations. These tools are all means of releasing ego mind and inviting the one mind, or unity into the present moment. When seen as such, all these tools, including needs, can ignite the combination of learning and unlearning, the letting-go of one so that the other can arrive.

9.3　We are now beginning to speak of the second aspect of treasure that was addressed in the beginning of this Treatise as something found that is kept secure and cherished. This aspect of treasure relates to your ability to let go. As many of you will find the idea of letting go of special relationships among the most difficult of ideas contained in this course of study, the ability to let go must be further discussed.

9.4　When a need is filled, you have been accustomed to having a reaction to this meeting of a need as if it takes place apart from you, or from outside of you. You assign the meeting of a need to a person or system or organization. You as often feel indebted as you feel grateful for the meeting of needs. When your life is running smoothly and needs are being continuously met, you begin to want to hang on to the relationships that you feel met these needs *because* of their ability to meet them. When your needs cease being met, you believe there has been a loss such as with the loss of a job or loved one or even of the promise of some service. When you think in such a way you believe in loss and gain rather than in the replacement belief that there is no loss but only gain.

9.5   It is perhaps best seen in the contrast implied by the intent to hang on. The desire to hang on to anything assumes that what you have is in need of protection or that it would not be secure without your effort to keep it secure. Inherent in this assumption is the concept of "having" or ownership. How does this relate to "having" needs? By identifying needs in such a way, in the same way that you identify "having" in regards to possessions, you but continue to feel as if you "have" needs even long after they have been met. Since I have already stated that you do have needs this may seem confusing.

9.6   In relationship, every need is met by a corresponding need. It is a dance of correspondence.

9.7   All needs are shared. This is what differentiates needs from wants. This is true in two senses. It is true in that all needs, from survival needs to needs for love are literally shared in the same measure by all. The other sense in which needs are shared is in the aspect of correspondence. They are shared because they are known. Every being inherently knows that it shares the same needs as every other being of its kind. Every being also inherently knows that needs and the fulfillment of needs are part of the same fabric—they are like puzzle pieces that fit together. Other beings that share life with you on this planet are not concerned with needs or need fulfillment. Doing what needs to be done in order to survive is hardly the same as feeling that one has a need. Needs are the domain of the thinking being only. Thinking beings share needs because of the way in which they think. That some seem to have more needs than others is a fallacy of perception. Not one has more needs than another.

9.8   What is shared by all is not owned. What all have is in no danger of being taken away. All that you are capable of having you already have as the already accomplished. All that you would give will take nothing away from you.

9.9   This could be restated as the belief that there is no loss but only gain.

9.10   The extent to which you deny your needs or are honest about your needs makes the difference in your connection or separation within relationship. The extent to which you are willing to abdicate your needs in order to attain something is the extent to which your belief in want or lack is revealed. This is the purview of special relationships. Thus the very compromises you are often prone to make in special relationships are but the symptoms of your fear.

9.11　As soon as you are content or self-satisfied, or, in other words, feel your needs are met, the desire to hang on to what you have arises. This is true of knowledge, or what you know, and of who you are, just as much as it is of special relationships and what you might more readily think of as treasure, such as a successful career or inspired creative project.

9.12　As soon as the desire to hang on arises, both learning and unlearning cease to occur. The desire to maintain a state you believe you have achieved and have labeled a state in which your needs are met creates a static level, that no matter how good or right or meaningful, loses its creative nature by remaining static.

9.13　So how do you remain within the constant creative flux or flow of creation without either constantly striving for more of what you already have or for what you consider progress? You need a means of disconnecting this drive that has become instinctual to you. As a being existing in form, you have honed certain instincts over millennia, such as the instinct to survive, in order to carry on in physical form.

9.14　There is no such thing as a static level in unity where creation is continuous and ongoing. You should have no desire to reach such a state and the awareness that you are in such a state can alert you, or serve as a sign, that the ego-mind and its fear-based thinking has momentarily returned. This does not mean that you will never be at rest or that you will be constantly seeking to arrive. As has already been said, you have arrived and rest exists only in the state of unity.

9.15　Because you have not thought previously of needs as tools every bit as valuable as the others mentioned here, this adjustment in your thinking may seem difficult to accept. How does the identification of needs or the dependency inherent in relationships by-pass the ego-mind? They heretofore have not, only because of your perception of them as signals of what you are lacking. Once this perception has shifted, your ego-mind will cease to be fed by these concerns. What is food for the ego-mind is fear and the removal of these final fears will quite literally starve the ego-mind out of existence.

9.16   An understanding of the mutuality of needs will aid you in being honest about your needs, thus allowing them to be met. Then the need to define or to identify them ceases. Your needs only continue to be brought to your awareness as needs until your trust in their immediate and ongoing fulfillment is complete. Once this trust is realized you will no longer think in terms of needs at all. Once you are no longer concerned with needs and the meeting of needs you will no longer be concerned with special relationships. You will realize that there is no loss but only gain involved in letting them go.

9.17   Holding on to what you think will meet your needs is like holding your breath. Your breath cannot long be held. It is only through the inhaling and exhaling, the give and take of breathing that you live. Each time you are tempted to think that your needs can only be met in special ways by special relationships, remember this example of holding your breath. Think in such a way no longer than you can comfortably hold your breath. Release your breath and release this fear and move from special to holy relationship.

9.18   This phase of coming to accept need and dependency is necessary only as a learning ground of experience on which trust can grow. Once this trust is realized you will no longer think of trust just as you will no longer think of needs.

9.19   Ceasing to think in these terms will soon be seen as a valuable ability and a timesaving measure of great magnitude. As these old ways of thinking leave you, you will be left as who you are in truth.

The Belief: We Only Learn in Unity

10.1　You would have to work mightily to turn the lessons of this Course into a tool, but many of you will not tire of this work until you succeed. This is how truths become dogma and dogma becomes tyranny. This happens by accepting a static state. A static state is not a living state because creation is not occurring within it. This is a living Course. This is why you are called to live it rather than to take it. This is why you are called to be a teacher and a learner both. This is how the exchange of giving and receiving as one occurs. This exchange IS unity.

10.2　Thinking that needs can be met only in certain ways is akin to another belief that has been replaced. This belief was first expressed in *A Course in Miracles* by the saying *resign as your own teacher.* This belief in the self as teacher has now been replaced with the belief that you only learn in unity.

10.3　I ask you to think for a moment of a time when you attempted to recall a specific memory. This may have been a memory of a name or address, of a dream, or an attempt to recall a specific event. At such times, you often feel as if, just as the memory is about to return to you, it is swatted away as easily and routinely as a hand swats away a fly. You know that the information is contained within you and yet you are often forced to accept an inability to have access to this information. It is forced from your awareness by something you know not. It is there and yet swatted away as if by some unseen hand. Where has this information gone and what keeps it from you? You might feel frustrated with your memory at such a time and even say something such as "my brain just isn't working right today." I want you now to keep this example in mind as we explore learning in unity.

10.4　You might think of unity as you have so often thought of your brain, but rather than thinking of it in the singular, think of it as a storehouse or giant brain in which all that has ever been known or thought is contained. The technology that has created super-computers will immediately come to mind from this illustration. While this illustration may be distasteful to some and intriguing to others, how many of you would not want to replace your ability to know with the ability of that of a supercomputer.

10.5   While just an illustration, the reverse of this is akin to what you have done by replacing unity with singularity. You have narrowed your ability to know to an ability to know that which you have experienced. While what we are speaking of as knowing has little to do with the information stored in supercomputers, it is still a worthy illustration. For just as a supercomputer needs a knowledgeable operator in order to provide the information sought, so too do you need to become knowledgeable in order to access all that is available to you.

10.6   Just as needs have been shown to be shared in like measure by all, so too is true knowing. Just as needs were shown to be distinguishable from wants by a discussion of their shared nature, so too now must knowing be distinguished from what you consider intelligence.

10.7   While you are being told that you can no longer believe that what you know is related to experience, you are not being told that you have exactly the same knowledge as does every person of every variety and level of experience. Yet no one can know more of the truth than another, and no one can know less.

10.8   Just beyond your mind's ability to call it forth lies the truth that you and all other beings know. The access to what seems to lie beyond your ability lies in the Christ in you. You might think of the ego as the hand that swats away this knowing.

10.9   The ego is the teacher you have relied upon when you have relied upon yourself as your own teacher.

10.10   You forget constantly that the Christ in you is the learner here. What need is there for a computer brain or for the ego to be teacher when the learner in you is the all-powerful? The learner in you is the unifying force of the universe. The learning you are in need of is the learning that will call who you are back to your united mind and heart. This is the knowing that already exists, the memory that is swatted away by the ego.

10.11   Why, then, is this called learning? Learning simply means to come to know. If what you know has been forgotten, you still are in need of the learning that assists you in coming to know once again.

10.12 But as long as you continue to attempt to learn with your ego, or in other words, as long as you would continue to attempt to learn in the same way that you have previously learned, you will not learn because the "you" that will be involved in the learning process will not be the real you.

10.13 The Christ in you is the real you. The Christ in you is the Self who you become when you have united heart and mind once again in wholehearted-ness. Thus the union of mind and heart is, as was stated previously, the first union, the union that must proceed all the rest. You are in a state of unity when you have achieved wholeheartedness. You are in a state in which you are able to learn. I am here to show you the way to the Christ in you. I began my teaching by appealing to your heart so as to ready you for the return of wholeheartedness, the state of union in which all that you learn is shared, first by mind and heart, and then in unity with your brothers and sisters. You achieve this state only by listening to one voice, or, in other words, by ending the separated state which is the state in which the ego exists. The end of the separated state or the ego, is the beginning of your ability to hear only one voice, the voice we all share in unity.

10.14 This voice speaks to you in a thousand ways. It is the voice of love, the voice of creation, the voice of life. It is the voice of certainty that allows you to move through each day and all the experiences within it as who you are in truth. It releases you from the feeling of needing to control or protect your treasure. It releases you as well from the static state of trying to hang on to who you were yesterday, or trying to prevent change tomorrow.

10.15 As was said in the beginning, it is realized that it is hard for you to believe that the Christ in you is in need of learning. Think a moment of why this should be so. Is there ever a moment in which coming to know is not appropriate? Is there any reason that coming to know should not be seen as something continuous and ongoing?

10.16 Again your desire for a static state would make you rather listen to your ego as it prescribes learning for certain circumstances that would be quickly put behind you or chosen for specific outcomes. While many love to learn for the sake of learning alone, still they would be loath to give up or let go the ability to choose their lessons. And still we are only talking about learning as you have perceived of it rather than learning from life.

10.17 What difference does it make to your concepts of learning when you think of life as your coursework? Would you be any more willing to let another choose your lessons for you?

10.18 What are your plans and dreams but chosen lessons? While you do not think of them as such you do not think of life as your learning ground. You still think of lessons as being about specific subject matter. When life does not go as you have planned, you feel as if your chosen path has been denied to you. You often feel a sense of loss and rarely one of gain. Unless life goes the way you have intended for it to go, you do not feel gifted or blessed even when you may have looked back often on situations that did not go as you had planned and nevertheless gifted you with experiences or opportunities that would not have arisen had your chosen plan come to fruition.

10.19 The Christ in you has no need to plan. A need to come to know...yes. But a need to plan...no. The Christ in you needs not for you to choose a lesson plan, but to let life itself be your chosen way of learning.

CHAPTER 11

The Belief: We Exist in Relationship and Unity

11.1   The Christ in you *is* relationship. As you were told within the pages of *A Course of Love*, you are a being who exists *in* relationship. This is how you were created and how you remain. This is the truth of who you are and even, in your own terms, a fact of your existence. Earlier this was pointed out to you so that you would come to accept who you are and so that you would extend forgiveness to yourself and all you hold responsible for this truth. This forgiveness has now extended in two distinct ways. First in forgiving your Creator for creating you in such a way, and second in forgiving a world that has taught you to want to be other than who you are. Now our aim is to show you how to integrate the belief that you are a being who exists in relationship into the living of your life.

11.2   Even though you no longer want to be other than who you are, and even though you now have a much clearer understanding of who you are, you will find living as who you are in the world difficult as long as you perceive of others as living under the old rules, the laws of man rather than the laws of God or love. It will seem all but impossible to live in relationship when those around you are still convinced of their separation and still seeking to glorify it. You will still perceive of the world as operating under the laws of man and as long as you perceive of the world in such a way you will be forced to live by its laws. This will cause struggle and, as you now know that struggle of any kind alerts you to the presence of ego, you will continue to do battle with the ego rather than leaving it forever behind.

11.3   Doing battle with the ego has become the preoccupation of many gifted and learned people. This is the classic battle revealed in all myths and tales of war and strife. It is the battle that in your imaginings has extended even to the angels. The ego is the dragon that must be slain, the evil of the despot to be toppled, the one-on-one conflict of all heroes who would take sides and do battle.

11.4   You are called to peace, a peace that begins and ends with ceasing to do battle with the ego. As the ego has been the known identity of your existence until now, it will, in a sense, be forever with you, much as the body that is your form will remain with you until your death. But while your perception of your body as your identity and your home has given way to an idea of it as a form that can be of service to you and your expression, there is no service the ego can do you. The ego is the one untruth, given many names and many faces and the only thing given by you the power to do battle with the truth, or with God. Remember now and always that you and God are one and that what you invite to do battle with God you but battle yourself.

11.5   A God of love does not do battle for truth needs no protection. The truth is not threatened by untruth. The truth simply exists as love exists and as you exist. When we say something *is*, this is what it is of which we speak. When we say all truth is generalizable, all needs are shared, all knowing is shared, this is of what it is we speak.

11.6   All cannot be threatened by nothing.

11.7   This is why we spent a fair amount of time addressing needs in a way we had not previously addressed them. For only with your understanding that all that is real is shared does the ego lose its power. The ego was made from the belief in separation and all that followed from it. Thus your true identity must be re-created from the belief in unity that is inherent in the acceptance that you are a being who exists in relationship. Separation is all that opposes relationship, and the ego is all that opposes your true identity.

11.8   Yet, as has already been said, the ego, having been with you from your earliest remembering, will continue to be with you, in the way that all learned behaviors and ideas are with you, until it is totally replaced by new learning. Learning thus must complement your new beliefs, the ultimate goal of this learning being the end of the need for beliefs at all.

11.9   This learning, then, must be seen for what it is. It is the holiest of work and the final evidence of means and end being the same. Your devotion to this learning must now be complete, your willingness total, your way of learning that of a mind and heart joined in wholeheartedness.

11.10 Realize that when you think that this total reversal of thought concerning yourself and your world will be difficult you are listening to your ego. The Christ in you knows not of difficulty.

11.11 How can it be that we speak both of the Christ in you and of Christ as being relationship itself? How can it be that we have spoken of Christ being both wholly human and wholly divine? These statements can only be true if there is no division between you and relationship, if there is no division between the human and the divine.

11.12 Separate things must still exist in relationship. This is the key to understanding the truth of these statements. For even while you have chosen separation, this choice did not preclude the existence of relationship and it is in relationship that union still exists. If you had been able to choose separation without relationship, then the image of yourself the ego has put forth would have been a true image. But as life cannot exist apart from relationship, this choice was not available and did not overturn the laws of God. The ego is but your belief that this has occurred; that what could never be true has become the truth.

11.13 So let us now, for the sake of continued learning, speak of separation in a new way. Let us speak of separation as a state that exists rather than as a state that does not exist. If you exist as a separate being but your being is contingent upon relationship for its existence, is this not the same thing as saying that you are a being who exists in relationship? Is this not similar to saying that a living human body does not exist without its heart? Is not what is essential to a living body a fact of that body's existence? While this illustration is not attempting to say that life does not exist apart from the body, it is attempting to reveal, in an easily understandable way, that there is a condition under which you are here and able to experience life as a separate being. That condition is relationship and relationship is what keeps you forever one with your Creator.

11.14 Here that relationship is being called Christ in order to keep the holiness and importance of this relationship forever and foremost in your mind. Here, that relationship has been given a name, as we have given your relationship with your separate identity the name of ego. Here, we are asking you to choose the one real relationship and to vanquish the one unreal relationship.

11.15   It is from these two separate ideas of relationship that the concept of doing battle has emerged. This concept of doing battle can only remain if you remain convinced that the ego is real. As long as you believe that the ego is real, you will feel as if there are two identities that exist within you and you will see yourself as doing battle in countless ways and forms. There will never actually be a battle going on between Christ and the ego, but you will perceive that such battles exist. You will be prone to calling upon the Christ as your higher self to defend you against the ego-self. This is highly akin to your former notion of prayer and assumes that there is something real that you need defense against or saving from. This is how the notion of Christ as savior arose. This is the belief in a good self and a bad self with Christ acting as conscience and defender of good and the ego acting as devil and defender of evil. This is nonsense, or but a form of the insanity that is prevalent still, even in your thinking. You do not realize that this source of conflict is the source of all conflict that seems real to you within your world. This battle of good and evil, while you believe in it still, will be demonstrated before you just as it has been from time immemorial. Is this what you would have continue? Does this not but reveal to you a fraction of the power of your thinking and its ability to shape the world you see?

11.16   An alternative to this insanity exists. The alternative is removing all faith from your belief in the ego-self. The alternative is replacing belief in an ego-self with belief in a Christ-Self. Total replacement. As long as you hang on to both identities the world will not change and you will not know who you are. You may think you know, and you may waste much time in perceived battles, valiantly fighting for good to win out over evil. But this is not the new way and the lack of value from this type of effort can surely now be seen.

11.17   I have said that the ego will remain with you as the identity you have learned since birth until you replace it with new learning. While you have learned much here, you may be thinking that your ego is still very much with you, and wondering, if you have not yet replaced it, how this miracle will come about. This replacement is indeed a miracle and the very miracle you have been prepared for within this course of learning.

CHAPTER 12

The Belief: Correction and Atonement

12.1   Miracles are thoughts and I am the corrector of false thinking. You have been made ready for this correction and your belief in correction, or atonement, is the final belief that must be put into practice.

12.2   Miracles are a service provided through love. Your readiness for miracles has been achieved through the learning you have accomplished. Miracles cannot be used, and so your learning needed to include an ability to distinguish between service and use. Service, or devotion, leads to harmony through right action. Until you were able to distinguish the false from the true, you were not able to receive the power of miracles.

12.3   The power of miracles is but the culmination and the integration of the beliefs we have put forth here. The miracle I am offering you here is the service I offer you, the precursor of the service you will offer to others.

12.4   Miracles are intercessions. As such they are agreements. They do not take away free will but free the will to respond to truth. They are the ultimate acceptance of giving and receiving being one in truth.

12.5   While you continue to feel as if you do not understand miracles, you will be reluctant to believe in them or to see yourself as a miracle worker. Your belief in miracles and your belief in atonement or correction are the same thing. While you believe there is anything other than your own thinking that is in need of correction you think falsely. Right-thinking is the realm of miracles.

12.6   As with the learning goal being set here of going beyond belief to simply knowing, the learning goal in relation to the miracle is the same—it is one of going beyond belief in the miracle to simply knowing. Knowing is knowing the truth. Knowing is right-thinking. Your return to knowing or right-thinking is both the miracle and the end for the need of miracles. For as you live in the world as who you are, you become a miracle and the constant expression of the miracle.

12.7   The power of thought and the power of prayer, once aligned, call constantly upon the same power of intercession that is the miracle. This is why we also devoted a fair amount of this Treatise to a discussion of calling. Calling is not only something you receive but something you must learn to give. As you have come to see calling as a gift and a treasure as well as a learning device, so you must come to see your own ability to call forth intercession as a gift and treasure you are able to give in service to your brothers and sisters.

12.8   If callings come to alert you to the treasure within, how can it be that you, as a miracle-minded being, are not called upon to also call forth the treasure that exists around you? When you call to those whom you meet in relationship, you call but to the already accomplished.

12.9   There, between you and the "other" whom you have previously only perceived, is the relationship and the miracle waiting to happen. As we spoke within *A Course of Love* of relationship being not one thing or another but a third something, this is what we speak of here again. If Christ *is* relationship, and if the Christ *in* you is the real you, then this all-encompassing relationship, both within you and without you, both you and all you are in relationship with, is that third something that is the holy relationship.

12.10 This holy relationship is what you are called to cultivate as a gardener cultivates her garden. The gardener knows that although the plant exists fully realized within its seed, it also needs the relationship of earth and water, light and air. The gardener knows that tending the garden will help it to flourish and show its abundance. The gardener knows she is part of the relationship that is the garden. A true gardener believes not in bad seeds. A true gardener believes not that she is in control. A true gardener accepts the grandeur that is the garden and finds it beautiful to behold.

12.11 This metaphor is akin to acceptance of the holy relationship. It is acceptance of what occurs with the joining of many factors, one no more important than another. While the Christ in you has been compared to the seed of all you are, what you have had revealed to you here is that the Christ is also the relationship of all that would bring the seed to fruition. The ego could be here compared to a gardener who believes that the seed alone is all that is important. As intently as this gardener might struggle to cause the seed to grow, without the relationship of earth and water, light and air, the seed would but remain a source of struggle. The ego would hang on to what is already accomplished within you, never to let it express, through relationship, all that it is. As valuable as the ego would tell you that you are, it still would thwart you being who you are through its denial of the relationships essential to that which you truly are.

12.12 This cultivation then, of the all-encompassing holy relationship that exists within you and without you, both in all you are and all you are in relationship with, is how you are called to live your life and the call you are asked to sound to all your brothers and sisters.

12.13 Let the beliefs we have set forth become one with you so that they enable you to live and express and act as who you are in every moment and in every circumstance. Let these abilities serve you and your brothers and sisters. Let this way of living be the expression of who you are and all that you now remember. Let this remembrance grow and flourish as the garden that is you.

12.14 Recognize now that unity is within you and without you, in all you are and all you are in relationship with. Feel the embrace and the love that is this unity and know that it is you and me and our Creator and all that was created.

CHAPTER 13

The Final Call

13.1 The final call of this Treatise is, in contrast to those put forth previously, a personal call from me to you. By now you have seen that your fears of losing yourself to God were unfounded. By now you have seen that yourself does not need to stand separate and alone in order to be fulfilled under the mantle of individuality. You have been told to put on a new mantle, a new identity. What does this mean?

13.2 Now that you have been made ready, I am ready to return you to your Self. Now that you have been made ready, it is time for us to have a personal relationship. We have, within these lessons, taken you far from your personal self, and I, as your teacher, have all but discounted the personal self I experience in relationship with you. Now, in unity, we are ready to be personal again.

13.3 While the personal self is the subject of the next Treatise, this is my invitation to you, specifically, to enter into a holy and personal relationship with me, specifically. While you are here, you have a persona. While this persona is no longer an ego-self but a Christ-Self, it is still a persona. This is the "you" who laughs and loves and cries and shares with friends in a world now different than the one you once perceived. I know of this world and I am here to guide you through it. I, too, am friend to you.

13.4 I am the corrector of false thinking because I lived among you as a thinking being. Think not that I was different than you and you will realize that we are truly one in being with our Father. As you move into the world with the end of the time of separation and the beginning of the time of unity taking place around you, practice the beliefs that have been put forth in this Treatise. Know that, in the time of unity, the truth will be shared by all.

13.5 Call upon your relationship with me to aid you, as I call upon you to assist me in calling all of our brothers and sisters to their return to unity. We call to one another in gratitude. This is the attitude of the wholehearted, the place from which all calls are sounded and received, the place where the true thinking of those united in mind and heart arises. Gratitude is the recognition of the state of grace in which you exist here and remain forever beyond all time and the passing of all form. It is an attitude of praise and thankfulness that flows between us now. The light of heaven shines not down upon you but is given and received in equal exchange by all who in creation exist together in oneness eternal.

13.6   Forget not who you truly are, but forget not also to be in joy in your experience here. Remember that the seriousness with which you once looked at life is of the ego. Drape your persona in a mantle of peace and joy. Let who you are shine through the personal self who continues to walk this world a while longer. Listen for my voice as I guide you to your purpose here and linger with you in this time to end all time. We are here, together, in love, to share love. This is not such a frightening task. Let fear go and walk with me now. Our journey together is just beginning as we return to the premise put forth in "A Treatise on the Art of Thought:" that of the elevation of form.

A Treatise on The Personal Self

The Third Treatise

Chapter 1

True and False Representation

1.1 The personal self exists as the self you present to others. This is the only way in which the personal self will continue to exist following the completion and the integration of this Course. Previously, the personal self that you presented to others represented an ego-self who you believed yourself to be. Now the ego has been separated from the personal self so that you may claim your personal self again and present to others a true representation of who you are.

1.2 While still a representation, there is a huge difference between a true representation and a false representation.

1.3 The false representation of the ego as the self is what has led to the world you see. A true representation of the Self that you are is what we work toward in this Treatise and will lead to true vision and to a new world.

1.4 A representation of the truth not only reveals the truth but becomes the truth. A representation of what is not the truth reveals only illusion and becomes illusion. Thus, as your personal self becomes a representation of the truth it will become who you are in truth.

1.5 As with much of our previous work, the first step in advancing toward this goal is in developing an awareness of what is not the truth. While the ability to distinguish between the true and the untrue has been repeatedly discussed as the ability to separate fear from love, further guidelines are needed.

1.6 You who have spent most of your life representing the ego have but given a face to illusion and made it seem real. When I say that you have represented the ego, what I mean is that the personal self, as represented by your body, while adhering to the ego's thought system, became an ego-self or an unreal self. An unreal self cannot help but exist in an unreal reality. It is as if you have been an actor upon a stage, the part you play as unreal as the setting on which you play it. Yet there is a "you" who has been playing the part, a part that, while developed under the ego's direction, still allowed for bits and pieces of who you are to be seen, felt and acknowledged.

1.7   The ego's thought system has been replaced by the thought system of unity and you are left, perhaps, feeling unsure of the part you are now to play. There is not one of you who has not begun to experience the transformation that is, in truth, occurring, although you may not as yet have seen the changes you are experiencing as the transformation to which you have been called. These changes, perhaps, seem like little things—a change in attitude here, a change in behavior there. But I assure you that these changes are mighty and are but the result of the change in cause that has occurred through your learning of this Course.

1.8   I began this Treatise by saying that the personal self exists as the self you present to others and that this is the only way in which the personal self will now continue to exist. This statement implies and acknowledges your previous belief in a personal self who existed as more than a representation. While when joined with the truth, this representation will be acknowledged as what it is *and* as the truth of who you are, to erroneously have seen your former representation of illusion as the truth of who you are is what has led to your perception of the world of suffering and strife that you have seen.

1.9   This change that is in the process of coming about has to do with awareness. When you become aware of the personal self as a representation, you become aware of the Self whom the personal self is representing. To have believed that the personal self, as a representation of the ego, was who you were, was an illusion that blocked awareness of your true Self from your mind. Your true Self is now ready to come out of the mist of illusion in which it was hidden and to be represented in truth by the form you occupy and have previously seen as the reality of yourself.

1.10   To say that the personal self will now exist only as the self you present to others is to say that the personal self will now cease to be seen as your reality.

1.11   To say that the personal self has only existed as the self you presented to others in the past is quite a different statement and has a totally different meaning. The personal self you once presented to others as "who you were" was a self who existed in time, a self who believed that the past made up the self of the present and that the self of the present made up the self of the future. The personal self you presented to others in the past was a chosen self and never a whole self as evidenced by the variety of selves you saw your-self to be. The personal self of the past was a self of roles, each one as learned as that which an actor might portray. You saw nothing more amiss in being a professional self in one instance and a social self in another, a parent in one role and a friend in another, than you did in defining a past self, a present self and a future self. The greatest distinction of all was that between the private self and the public self, as if who you were to yourself and who you presented yourself to be could be two completely different selves. Even within the illusion in which you existed there was a self kept hidden.

1.12   To become a whole Self, with no parts hidden, a Self with no *parts* in truth, is the task that I set before you and am here to help you fulfill. I can do this because I accomplished this, both in life and in all time and time beyond time, making you, along with me, the accomplished. As has already been said, the accomplished Self is the Christ. Your remembrance of the Christ-Self has abolished the ego-self and allows us to begin the lessons of the personal self.

1.13   We could not begin the curriculum here because you would have been unable, without the lessons of this Course, to distinguish the personal self from the ego-self. There is a danger even now in focusing upon the self of the body, as this self has been so long bound to the ego-self. Even with the ego once and finally vanquished, the patterns of the ego's thought system remain to be undone. This is atonement. We work now to correct the errors of the past in the present, the only place where such work can be done. We work with what we have, a form fully able to represent the truth and, in so doing, we bring the truth to life and life to the truth.

CHAPTER 2

The Purpose of Representation

2.1   What purpose would it seem to serve to have anything exist only as a representation? We might think of this in terms of original purpose and the original purpose of representation being to share the Self in a new way. Expressions you call art are desires to share the Self in a new way. These expressions you call art are expressions of a Self who observes and interacts in relationship. They are not expressions that remain contained to who you are or who you think yourself to be. They are not expressions of the self alone. They are not expressions of the self alone in terms you might consider autobiographical, and they are not expressions of the self alone that you would consider the self in separation. They are rather expressions of the Self in union—expressions of what the Self sees, feels, envisions, imagines in relationship.

2.2   What purpose has art? While art is but a representation of what the artist chooses to share, few of us would call these representations useless or without value. Art is a representation but it also becomes something in truth, something that has been named art. Art becomes something in truth by expanding awareness, or in other words, by making something known. This is what true relationship does and is its purpose as well as what it is.

2.3   While we have said you chose the separation, it has not been said that this choice was the choice it has been made to seem. You chose to represent yourself in a new way, to express yourself in a new way, to share yourself in a new way. The choice to represent your Self in form was a choice for separation but not because separation itself was desired as you have assumed. This is the assumption you have accepted in much the same way you have accepted your free will as that which allows you to be separate from and independent of God. Once this assumption was accepted, the duality of your existence became paramount, became the only means you saw of deciphering the world around you and your role within it. Separation, aloneness, independence, individuality—these became the purpose you assumed rather than the purpose you started out to achieve—that of a new way of expression in a form that would expand awareness, through relationship, of self and others. You chose a means of creation…as God chose a means of creation. That means of creation is separation, becoming separate (the observer as well as the observed) so as to extend creation through relationship (of the observer and the observed).

2.4   While much time was spent within this Course, discussing the choice you but think you made, this discussion was necessary only in the same terms that made it necessary to thoroughly discuss the ego's thought system. What you believe about yourself is part of the foundation that has been built around this system. Now, along with the beliefs put forth in "A Treatise on Unity," you are asked to accept a new belief regarding the choice we have called the separation, a choice you have deemed as sin.

2.5   While you have believed you are the self of the ego, you have believed in a need to both glorify the self and denigrate the self. These beliefs have shaped your dualistic view of the world and all that exists with you within it. For every "glory," gift, or success you have achieved you have believed in a corresponding cost that was, in essence, a cost that came at the expense or denigration of the self. You believed that for every gain there was also a loss. For you believed that every step in the advancement of your separated state was a step away from God and your real Self. This belief was based in logic, but the logic of the illusion—in which you believed you chose to separate from God out of defiance and a desire to be one with God no longer. This could not be further from the truth and is the cause of all your suffering, for contained within this belief was the belief that with each successful step toward independence came a corresponding step away from God. As independence seemed to be your purpose here, you could not keep yourself from attempts to advance in this direction. And yet, neither could you keep from punishing yourself for this advancement.

2.6   We leave all of this behind now as we advance toward truth through returning to original purpose. Your return to your original purpose eliminates the concept of original sin and leaves you blameless. It is from this blameless or unaltered state that your personal self can begin to represent the truth for it leaves untruth, or the ego, behind. It is only this one, unaltered Self that is the truth of who you are and who your brothers and sisters are as well. This is what is meant by oneness. This is what is meant by unity.

2.7   And yet the truth has as many ways of being represented as does illusion.

2.8   Just as artistic representations of illusion are sometimes called art, representations of the self of illusion have been called *the self* without this being so. In each, however, is the self you believe is real revealed. Thus, not all that is called art is art, and not all that you call self is Self, even while both may represent the truth as you perceive of it. Representing the truth as you perceive it to be has been the righteous work of many who have caused great harm to others and the world. There is no truth to be found in illusion and so no representations of perceived truth, no matter how intensely they have been championed, have truly altered effect for they have not altered cause.

2.9   There is no right or wrong in art, and there is no right or wrong, no good or bad in regards to the self but only accurate or inaccurate representations of the truth. Inaccurate representations of the truth simply have no meaning and no matter how much one might try to read meaning into the meaningless, it will not be found there. The meaningless has no ability to change the meaning of truth. And so your Self has remained unaltered as has all to which you have assigned inaccurate meaning.

2.10   Thus you stand at the beginning, with a Self now devoid of the meaninglessness you but attempted to assign to it. You stand empty of untruth and about to embark on the journey of truth. You stand in the transformational moment between the unreal and the real. All you await is an idea, a remembrance of the original idea about your personal self.

2.11   This memory lies within your heart and has the ability to turn the image you have made into a reflection of the love that abides with it in holiness that is beyond your current ability to imagine. It is impossible for you to imagine this holiness with the concepts of the thought system you heretofore have relied upon. This thought system has allowed only the acceptance of a reality within certain parameters, for it has not allowed you to imagine being able to take steps "back" to the God you believe you left in defiance, or the Self you believe you abandoned there. Be truthful with yourself now and realize that what I speak of here is known to you. Realize that you *know* that it is not God who abandoned you, but you who abandoned your Self and God. Give up your desire to think that if you did such a thing there was a reason for you to have done so. How many times have you asked yourself why you would have chosen separation if there had not been a *reason* for you to do so? Realize that a reason has been given here and that this reason, while perfectly believable, is not one that includes a need to abandon your Self or God. Why should you be more inclined to believe that you left a paradise in order to live a while in a form that would cause you much suffering and strife, for the sole reason of being separate from that to which you long to return? The only alternative has seemed to be a belief in a God that would banish you from paradise for your sins. We have worked, thus far, to change your idea of a vengeful God. Now we work to change your idea of a vengeful self. For what else would such a self be?

2.12   This is such an important point for you to grasp that I return you to our comparison of the family of man to the family of God, as well as to our discussion of the return of the prodigal sons and daughters of God. This discussion may have seemed to accept the idea of a self as highly developed as an adolescent child, a self who would willingly choose to explore independence, no matter what the cost. This discussion merely examined the reality you chose to believe in, the reality of an ego-self, a self-concept seemingly stuck in an adolescent phase of development. The ego-self's only desire was for you to "grow up" into its version of an independent being...no matter what the cost.

2.13   While you may be happily congratulating yourself on leaving such adolescent thinking behind, this thinking must be quickly replaced with a new idea about yourself or its hold on you will remain.

CHAPTER 3

The True Self

3.1   Your personal self is dear to you and dear to me as well. I have always loved you because I have always recognized you. What cannot be recognized or known cannot be loved. While your ego has not been loveable, you have always been. Here is where you need realize that the personal self that is dear to you is not your ego-self and never has been.

3.2   All of your personal characteristics are nothing more than a persona that has served the ego faithfully. All of your traits have been chosen either in accordance with the ego's desires or in opposition to them. Whether they be in accord or in opposition, their source has still been the ego. These traits, whether you see them as good or bad or somewhere in between are what you have seen as making you loveable or unlovable. Yet you have also often made them challenges to love, saying in effect to those who love you, "Love me in spite of these traits that are not loveable and then I will know your love is true." You make this same statement to yourself as well, seemingly called to continuously challenge your own lovability.

3.3   As much as you fear disappointment for yourself and let this fear keep you from much you would desire, you fear as much or more your ability to disappoint others or to "let them down." Some of you carefully constructed your lives to leave as little room as possible for disappointment to affect it or others you hold dear. Some of you have seemed to do the opposite, despite your best intentions calling disappointment to yourself and being constantly under the pall of having disappointed others. Still others have always found their lives to be beyond their efforts at control and long ago gave up trying. Most of you fall somewhere in between, living a life full of good intentions and effort and being surprised neither by what seems to work nor what seems to fail.

3.4   It is yourself, who, more often than not, you blamed for all your misfortune. You would have liked to be strong and capable and hated your own weakness. You would have liked to be even-tempered and hated the moods that seemed to come over you without cause. You did not understand when illness or depression stood in the way of your desires or the plans of others and let such circumstances fill you with self-loathing.

3.5 You thus created a society that reflected this hatred of the self and that functioned on finding blame for every misfortune. Your illnesses became the result of behaviors ranging from smoking to too little exercise. Your accidents caused lawsuits where blame could be rightly placed. Your depression was blamed on the past. Even your successes were often claimed to be at the expense of another or to have come in spite of failings most severe. While society would seem to have done so much to cause your unhappiness, and while you have in turn blamed it as much as it blamed you, you never blamed anything quite as much as you blamed yourself.

3.6 This is the vengeful self we eliminate now. You have, in truth, replaced judgment with forgiveness, but you have not yet fully forgiven yourself. This statement may sound incongruous, for how could you have replaced judgment with forgiveness and not forgiven yourself? What this means is that you have replaced judgment with forgiveness as a belief. You have put this belief into practice in each instance where you have seen it to be needed. What this means is that you continue to fail to recognize your need to replace judgment with forgiveness when it comes to yourself. You have not yet realized how much you still consider unlovable about yourself. This does not mean that you are not loveable, only that you have not yet fully recognized your true Self. Until you fully recognize your Self, you cannot fully love yourself. Until you fully love, you do not love in truth.

3.7 Both God and Love are found in relationship where the truth becomes known to you. When the truth becomes known to you, you know God for you know love. Beliefs, and especially the changed beliefs we have worked together to integrate into your thought system, are only a first step, a step toward holy relationship. These new beliefs of your new thought system must be wholehearted. They cannot be beliefs that exist only in your mind, a new philosophy to be applied to life. They must exist in your heart. And how can they exist in the heart of an unlovable self?

3.8 You cannot think your way to the new life that calls to you. You can only get there by being who you are in truth.

3.9   I have always loved you for I have always recognized you. While your recognition of your Self has come a long way through your learning of this Course, your self is still seen as a stumbling block. You might think that were you able to live in some ideal community, away from all that has brought you to where you now are, you might be able to put the beliefs of this Course into practice. If not quite this drastic, your thoughts might tell you that if you were in another job, devoid of certain familial responsibilities, or the need to provide for financial obligations, you would be much better suited to putting these beliefs into practice. Or you might look at your behaviors, your habits, your general personality, and simply declare yourself unsuitable for further learning. Whether you think such thoughts consciously or not, there is a part of you that still believes you are not good enough to be the "good" self you believe this Course calls you to be. Most of you have now believed you are "good enough" for days or hours or moments, but something always and eventually calls you back to the idea that you are not good enough or that you do not want to put the effort into being good enough. Like a person who believes she has a weight problem and knows a diet would be "good" for her, the diet is often rejected because failure is deemed a certainty. While you continue to see the call of this Course as a call to goodness, you will surely fail.

3.10   The Self that I recognize as You, is not other than who you are, but who you are. All that was ever other than who you are was the ego. The ego is gone. The ego was simply your idea of who you were. This idea was a complex set of judgments, of good and bad, right and wrong, worthy and unworthy, a list as endless as it was worthless. Realize now the worthlessness of this idea and let it go.

CHAPTER 4

The Dismantling of Illusion

4.1   This is not a self-help course but just the opposite. This Course has stated time and time again that you cannot learn on your own and that resigning as your own teacher is the only way to learn a new curriculum. This Course will not call you to effort of any kind. It will not tell you to leave behind your addictions or to go on a diet or a fast. It will not even tell you to be kind. It does not tell you to be responsible and does not chide your irresponsibility. It does not claim that you were once bad but that by following these tenets you can become good. It gives no credence and no blame to any past cause for your depression, anxiety, meanness, illness or insanity. It merely calls you to sanity by calling you to let go of illusion in favor of the truth.

4.2   The sameness that this Course calls you to is not a sameness of body or of habit. It asks not for monks or clones. It asks not that you give up anything but illusion, which is the giving up of nothing.

4.3   Before we can go on you must take all such ideas from your mind. Such ideas are not small matters. Ideas are the foundation of the self. You cannot have an idea of goodness without having an idea of evil. You cannot have an idea of an ideal state without having an idea of a state that is not ideal. You cannot have an idea you call "right" without believing in an idea that can be "wrong."

4.4   The ego made such ideas necessary for the idea of the ego was "wrong" or inaccurate. The only way to bring that inaccuracy to light was through contrast.

4.5   To function from an inaccurate foundation was to build upon that foundation. Building a structure with a foundation that would not support it was the folly that the ego made of life. The only way for such an error to be seen as an error was through its dysfunction.

4.6   The only way to correct such an error is to dismantle the structure and begin again with a foundation capable of being built upon. This is what we have done. We have taken away the foundation of illusion, the one error that became the basis of all that came after it. You cannot make another error such as this for it is the one error. Does it not make sense that the only error possible is that of not being who you are?

4.7   You can dismantle the ego and build another in its place and this has at times been done in the individual with great training, as in military training, or in cases of great abuse when a second ego personality is developed to save the first. The ego has also been dismantled and rebuilt over time and been seen as the rise and fall of civilizations. But as we have said before, the only replacement that will work is the replacement of illusion with the truth. The very purpose of this Treatise is to prevent the replacement of illusion with illusion, or one ego-self with another. The training of this Course, while gentle in nature, has been great, as great as that of any military training, as great as any emotional trauma that has left one in a state of emptiness. This is, in effect, the state in which you currently find yourself.

4.8   I repeat, and will do so again and again, that the ego-self is gone from you. Whether you fully realize this or not matters not. This *A Course of Love* has accomplished. Now the choice is before you to do one of two things... to proceed toward love or fear. If you proceed with fear you will assemble a new ego-self, an ego-self that perhaps will seem superior to the old, but which will nonetheless still be an ego-self. If you proceed with love, you will come to know your Christ-Self.

CHAPTER 5
Original Purpose

5.1   While you have just been told that you now exist in a state of emptiness, this is not a state to be feared. Yet it is this fear of emptiness that has, in the past, made those who have experienced it rush to find the easiest and most available replacement (the ego or that which has become familiar, if not known). While few of you have ever before reached the emptiness caused by the complete absence of the ego, just as few of you have never felt some sort of absence. All the lessons you have drawn to yourself in your lifetime have worked toward this absence in the hopes of filling the emptiness with the fullness of the truth.

5.2   As with the gentle learning of this Course, not all emptiness has come to you at the hands of suffering. Each time you have "fallen" in love you have emptied a space for love to fill. Each time you have felt true devotion you have emptied a space for love to fill. You have been emptied of the ego-self as creative moments of inspiration filled you and emptied of the ego-self in moments of connection with God.

5.3   Conversely, you have been emptied by the lessons of grief as the loss of love has led to a loss of self. You have been emptied by a loss of self due to illness or addiction, depression, or even physical exhaustion. All these things you have brought to yourself for they have been the only way past the ego's guarded gate.

5.4   You have tried to live in a house built on a faulty foundation, attempting to make do with what you have. All your time was spent in making repairs and this time spent kept you too busy to see the light that was always visible through the cracked and peeling walls that you built. That you would eventually call to yourself a fire that would burn these walls to ash or a flood that would wash them away, was as much a part of the survival mechanism of your real Self as was the rush to rebuild a part of the survival mechanism of the ego-self.

5.5   All this you have already tried to do. These lessons you have already tried to learn. This Course has come so that these many things that you have tried need not be repeated, just as the crucifixion came to end the need to learn through suffering and death.

5.6   The story that I lived was appropriate for the time in which I lived it, and has an appropriateness that continues even now. I walked the earth in order to reveal a God of love. The question of the time, a question still much in evidence, was how mighty could God's love be if it were given to a people who suffered. The answer was that God's love was so mighty that he would even allow the death of his only son to redeem the world.

5.7   The death of an only son, then as now, would be seen as a sacrifice of enormous proportions; the greatest sacrifice of all. The point of the story, however, was not one of sacrifice but one of gift giving. The greatest gift of all was given, the gift of redemption. The gift of redemption was the gift of an end to pain and suffering and a beginning of resurrection and new life. It was a gift meant to empty the world of the ego-self and to allow the personal self to live on as the one true Self, the one true son of God. The gift of redemption was given once and for all. It is the gift of restoration to original purpose. Without there having been an original purpose worthy of God's son, the crucifixion would have ended life in form and returned the sons of man to the formless. Instead, the sons of man were freed to pursue their original purpose.

5.8   This story has been repeated endlessly in time, in time extending both forward and back. Each father's son will die. This means not what you have taken it to mean, an endless series of generations passing. What this means is that in each the ego will die and the Self be reborn to life eternal. Without rebirth of the Self, the original purpose goes unfulfilled. Since God is original purpose, original cause, the origin of self and of relationship, original purpose cannot go unfulfilled. What this means is that the illusion will be no more and truth will reign. Such is the reign of God.

CHAPTER 6

The Desire for Reward

6.1   Can you give up your desire for reward? To give up your desire for reward is to give up a childish desire that has become like unto a plague among you. While many of you see it not, everything you do is based upon desire for reward. This is your desire to be given to in return for what you give. This stems from your idea of yourself as a "child" of God, and a notion that would seem to suggest that the child is less than the parent. Although you see yourself as the child of your mother and father, this notion of yourself as child has not made you cling to a childish image of yourself as less than what your parents are. While you may still desire recognition and affirmation from them, this is not the same as the "rewards" you seek—some of you from God, some from life, some from fate. No matter who it is you think is in charge of rewarding you, the attitude that causes you to desire reward is what must be done without.

6.2   This may seem a step back from the lofty heights we have just traveled, discussing the reign of God and the meaning of life and death. But this is one of the key ideas that will keep you from yourself and has much to do with your former notions of God and your own self. It is an idea that has been transferred to all of life, much as the idea of an unlovable self was transferred into all areas of life without your realization.

6.3   Reward is intricately tied to your notions of being good, performing deeds of merit, and taking care of, or surviving, the many details that seem to make it possible for you to live within your world. The idea of reward transfers to ideas related to comparison as well, as lack of reward in one instance and reward given in another, is the cause of much of the bitterness that exists within your hearts.

6.4   While many of you who have read this far and learned this much may not be those whose bitterness is mighty and held tightly to themselves, bitterness must still be discussed. While bitterness remains, vengeance will remain. You have been shown that God is not a God of vengeance but that you are still in the process of learning that your Self is not vengeful. The ego has given you many reasons to be distrustful of your Self, beginning with the idea of your abandonment here. Since the ego is a chosen self and a learned self, there has always been just enough room within the ego's thought system to keep within you the idea of a self the ego is not. Thus has the ego had a self to blame for everything, including your very existence. This blame is as old as time itself and the cause of bitterness being able to exist, even within your hearts.

6.5   While the untrue cannot exist with the true, what I am calling here *bitterness* is all that you have forced, through sheer strength of will, to pierce the holiness of your hearts. Bitterness and the idea of vengeance go hand-in-hand. This is the idea of "an eye for an eye" or the exact opposite of the idea of "turning the other cheek." While this may seem like the very idea of evil which I have denied the existence of, it is not evil but bitterness. You may believe that bitterness is just another word, another label for the evil you have always been convinced existed in the hearts of some, but even being that it is just another word, it is one chosen to introduce an idea of such fallacy that it rivals only the ego in its destructive potential. Bitterness is to your heart what the ego has been to your mind. It is the one false idea that has entered this holiest of places, this abode of Christ, this bridge between the human and the divine. It exists not in some but in all, as the ego has existed not in some but in all. Like the ego, it has not caused you to be unlovable or unrecognizable. But it has become, like the ego, so much a part of your reality that it must, like the ego, be consciously left behind.

6.6   Bitterness, as the word implies, is something taken into the self, much as the bitter herbs of scripture illustrated. Many rights and rituals exist for the purification of the unclean but I assure you that you are not unclean and that none can cleanse bitterness from the heart without your choice. The time of tenderness began your release of bitterness and made you ready for this choice. Choose now to leave your desire for reward, as well as all of your reasons for bitterness, and bitterness itself behind. Bring bitterness no longer to the dwelling place of Christ and we will seal the place of its entrance with the sweetness of love so that bitterness will be no more.

CHAPTER 7

The Explosion of Belief

7.1 As you have seen by now, we have moved from talking of beliefs in "A Treatise on Unity," to speaking here of ideas. God's thought of you is an idea of absolute truth. Your existence derives from this idea and this truth. The ego's existence derived from your idea of a separated self, a thought, or idea, of absolute untruth. The ego's thought system then formed beliefs that supported the initial idea of the separation. Where is there a corresponding belief system that formed around the idea of God?

7.2 A belief system is not needed for the truth. Thus you can see that the beliefs put forth in "A Treatise on Unity" are necessary only to return you to the truth. Since there are no beliefs that represent the truth of who you are and who God is, we speak now of ideas or thoughts. If you believe that God created you with a thought or idea, then you can begin to see the power of thought. If you can believe that you created the ego with a thought or an idea, you can see where the power of thought is your power as well as God's.

7.3 While there is no need for a belief system and no belief system that *can* represent the truth, you have been told that *you can* represent the truth here. You cannot do this with beliefs but you can do this with ideas. Ideas leave not their source, and thus your inaccurate ideas about yourself have their cause within you, as does your ability to change this cause and its effects.

7.4 You are who you are and remain endlessly who you are, even here within the human experience. This is the idea that is beyond compare as you are beyond compare and the truth is beyond compare. This is the only idea that holds true meaning and so all meaning is found within it. Thus we start with this idea.

7.5 The only thing within the human experience that made you incapable of representing who you are in truth was the ego. The only thing within the human experience that deprived the human experience of meaning was the ego. Thus, with the ego gone, you are perfectly capable of representing the truth of who you are and returning to an existence that is meaningful.

7.6   You have formerly been capable of representing who you are only within illusion for this was the abode in which you resided. Illusion has been to you like a house with many doors. You have chosen many doors to the same house and but thought them to offer different things, only to find that the house you entered was still the same house, the house of illusion. You took yourself into these many rooms and in some you were even capable of representing your true Self. This representation of the true Self within the house of illusion was like an explosion happening there. For a moment, the floorboards shook, the walls quaked, the lights dimmed. All those within the house became aware of something happening there. All attention turned toward the explosion but its source could not be found.

7.7   In the aftermath of the explosion, the representation of the true Self settled like dust, and all the attention fell upon it. A great scrambling ensued as the recognition dawned on those who looked, that treasures were to be found there. One found art and another religion, one found poetry and another music, one seized upon a single thought and through its extrapolation founded one science or another. In all of the excitement the matter of the source of the explosion was dismissed.

7.8   Thus has been the best of what you call life within the illusion.

7.9   Now you have seized upon even this idea and called it not treasure but theory and related it to the origins of the universe, and still you see not the source. There is a reason for this. The reason is that the Source cannot be found within the house of illusion. The Source can only be found from within the house of truth.

7.10   The home of truth is within you and we have just unlocked its doors.

CHAPTER 8

The House of Truth

8.1   The Kingdom of God is the House of Truth. Or better said, the House of Truth has been called the Kingdom of God. I remind you, once again, that what you have called things are but representations too and that we move now beyond representations to meaning so that what you represent will move beyond representations to the truth. Realize here the subtle difference between a symbol that represents the truth, and the truth, for this is what we work toward. Symbols are needed only in the house of illusion, just as are beliefs. The most enlightened among you have beautifully symbolized or represented the truth. These symbols or representations have been of great service and have caused the very explosions that have rocked your faulty foundation. To work toward being a representation of such great power is still a worthy goal and many of you have reached this power. You can see why this power has been necessary and continues to be necessary. But to stop at this dismantling power is not enough. To stop at this dismantling power would be to leave the world in its present condition and your brothers and sisters scrambling in the dust. The work that is upon you now is that of replacing the house of illusion once and for all with the home of truth. The work that is upon you now is that of revelation of the Source.

8.2   If the Source of Truth is within you, then it is your own revelation toward which we work. Never forget that establishing your identity has been the only aim of this entire course of study. Realize how often you have forgotten this, despite the many repetitions of our aim, and you will be more aware of your resistance and your need to let it go.

8.3   This resistance is the reason you have been taken on such a long journey before we ever once talked of an idea as crucial as that of bitterness. This bitterness has been a source of resistance as strong as that of the ego and more deeply felt. As I have said, bitterness is to your heart what the ego has been to your mind. Thus bitterness has to do with your feelings more so than your thoughts. The ego but played upon these feelings, using them as building blocks for its thought system. As long as you carry this bitterness within you, you will remain in the house of illusion for your feelings are as real to you as have been the thoughts of your ego-mind. While anything other than the truth remains real to you, your house of illusion will remain a real structure, a structure that keeps you from the truth as surely as would iron bars keep you within its rooms.

8.4   Although at this moment it may be hard for you to conceive of the idea of bitterness as something that you are attached to, I want you to think of attachments for a time and see how bitterness does indeed fit into this category. Bitterness is an idea intrinsically tied to the personal self and the experience of the personal self. Whether you believe the personal self is comprised of the one identity you now hold or the identity of many past lives, the identity you hold in this time and this place still believes in its own history and that of those who came before it. These beliefs hold the seeds of bitterness, the angst you feel towards God and brothers and sisters both alive and dead.

8.5   These are the beliefs that would say that you, and all of those who came before you, have been falsely made to suffer, a suffering for which you see no rationale. Those who believe in past lives have also often adopted beliefs regarding choice and believe that choices for suffering were made for some greater good or to repay debts of the past. The only choice that has been made is that of attachment to the human form as the self. The choice that hasn't been made is the choice to leave this idea behind. The choice that has been made is to believe in a savior who could have, but did not, keep you from this suffering. The choice that has not been made is the choice to believe in the Christ-Self who is the only savior, rather than the ego-self, which is all you have needed saving from.

8.6   What happens when you believe the choice to suffer, as well as the choice to leave suffering behind, has always been found within? Who then are you to be angry with for all that has occurred? Do you blame yourself and your ancestors for the history, both ancient and recent, that you think you would have given anything to change? Do you look upon the ill and blame them for their illness? Do you not look upon all suffering and feel bitter at your own inability to relieve it? And do you not thus attempt to see it not and then blame yourself for looking the other way?

8.7 As was said in *A Course of Love*, the idea of suffering is what has gone so wrong within God's creation. As was said in "A Treatise on the Art of Thought," the idea of love can replace the idea of suffering but it is chosen not because of the suffering that seems to make no sense of love. Bitterness is the cause of this inability to make a new choice and what keeps the cycle of suffering in motion.

8.8 Remaining attached to bitterness is a reflection of the belief that one person, and surely not you, can make a difference. If you could relieve the world of suffering you would, but to try and fail is too heartbreaking. Why should you not be bitter when you and all of those you love will surely suffer and eventually die? Why should you not be bitter when you believe you are powerless? How difficult it is to believe that you need not change the world but only your own self. How difficult to imagine that this one change could bring about all the changes you would imagine that even an army of angels could not bring about. While such a thought remains inconceivable to you it will not come to be.

8.9 As the representations of the true Self within the house of illusion caused explosions and a fallout of treasure, the representation of the true Self within the house of truth will cause the creation of the new.

8.10 Your ancestors could not have imagined all that the explosions in the house of illusion have wrought. These treasures that you now enjoy would have seemed like miracles to them.

8.11 Within the fallout of treasure, what was looked for was found. If what was looked for were means of making life easier, why not the idea of machinery and tools that would seem to do so? If what was looked for was a means of finding simple pleasures in a harsh world, why not ideas of entertainment that would seem to provide them? People suffering from disease: Why not cures for those diseases?

8.12 People have looked for what they have imagined it was possible to find. Why would you look for an end to suffering if you felt this was impossible? Much better to look for cures and treatments than for an end to what but seemed endless. Could suffering really have gone on for countless ages simply due to your inability to birth the idea of an end to suffering?

8.13   Has not a part of you always known that suffering does not have to be even while you have accepted that it is? Let us now put an end to this acceptance through the birth of a new idea.

CHAPTER 9

To Dwell in the House of Truth

9.1   This idea is an idea of love. It is an idea that makes perfect sense and it is its very sense that makes it seem meaningless in a world gone mad. It is an idea that says *only that which comes from love is real.* It is an idea that says *only that which fits within the laws of love is reality.* It is an idea that says *all that love would not create does not exist.* It is an idea that says that *if you live from love and within love's laws you will create only love.* It is an idea that accepts that this can be done and can be done by you in the here and now. To accept these ideas without accepting their ability to be applied is to change your beliefs without changing your ideas. This many have done. This you surely do not want to do.

9.2   While you cannot now see the chain of events that will make these ideas into a new reality, you can trust that they will be there, spreading out like a web, much as the ego's ideas of separation once did. Yet, as these ideas are not learned ideas, they will not take time, as did the ego's ideas, to spread through learning.

9.3   Ideas of love, or the truth, are joined in unity and exist in relationship. All of the ideas within the house of illusion were contained within it and held together by the learned ideas of the ego thought system. Now you must imagine yourself walking outside of the doors of this house of illusion and finding a completely new reality beyond its walls. You might think, at first, that you are in a place so foreign that you must immediately begin to learn again, starting with the smallest building blocks of knowledge, as if learning a new alphabet. Yet you soon will find that this new reality is known to you and requires no new learning at all. You will be tempted, at first, to see things that are like unto those within the house of illusion and call them what you called them once before. But here you will find yourself gently corrected and when this correction is given you will not doubt it but will remember that it is the truth you had forgotten.

9.4   You will see that the house of illusion was just a structure built within the universe of truth and that the universe of truth contains everything within its benevolent embrace. No one stands beyond the embrace of love and you will be glad to see that those who remain within the house of illusion could not escape love's presence.

9.5   You will be tempted, nonetheless, to re-enter the house of illusion, if only to grasp the hands of those you love and gently tug them through its doors. You will be able to take note of the explosions happening within and will want to return to add your own to those going on inside, thinking that with the force of one more, maybe the walls will finally come tumbling down and those inside be held within illusion no more. This was the work of many who came before you but the time of such work, for you, is past. Many remain to shake the walls of illusion. Few stand beyond it to beckon to those within.

9.6   The paradise that is the truth seems to lie far beyond the house of illusion in the valley of death. Survivors of near death experiences have eased the fears of many but made many more long for life after death rather than life. You who have followed me beyond the walls of the house of illusion are now called to begin the act of revealing and creating anew the life of heaven on earth.

9.7   This is the pilgrimage I set you upon, as real as those who in the time of Moses journeyed through the desert to the Promised Land. That journey remained metaphorical because it did not pass beyond the arena of beliefs into the arena of ideas. The Israelites believed in a Promised Land but they did not dwell in it. You are called to dwell in the Promised Land, the House of Truth.

An Exercise in Forgetting

10.1 *A Course of Love* talked much of remembering. Now we must talk about forgetting. While nothing need be given up to enter the house of truth, or to encounter the truth, you must realize that while meaninglessness exists within your mind, you will be working still to replace it with meaning rather than allowing the meaning that exists in everything to be remembered or known. Thus are more practical lessons needed in regard to the life of the body that you now will let serve our cause of creating heaven on earth.

10.2 The first lesson is offered as an exercise in forgetting. As often as is possible within your daily life, I ask you to forget as much of what you have learned as you are able.

10.3 The first thing I ask you to forget is your need to find a place where blame can be placed. You who have been waiting to get to the "hard part" of this Course may find it here. The idea of blame is incongruous with the idea of a benevolent Creator and a benevolent creation and as such is the only blasphemy. To blame yourself is as senseless as blaming others and your inclination to place blame upon yourself must be given up as well. When it is said that you are the cause it is not meant that you are to blame for anything. Although many a child has been blamed for his or her failure to learn, blame of yourself is as uncalled for as is blaming a child for lessons yet to be learned.

10.4 Taking away the idea of placing blame will change your thought processes beyond your wildest imagining. You will be surprised at how many times you recognize blame where before you saw it not, just as in the beginning you did not recognize all that you had feared. But just as you have, from recognizing what it is you fear, been able to bring those concerns to love, you can now do so with blame. All you need do is catch yourself in the act of placing blame and say to yourself, "I was placing blame again and I choose to do so no longer." You need not spend any more time with blame than this and I offer you no word or sentiment to replace it. I ask you simply to take the thought of it from your mind as quickly as it enters.

10.5   You would find this easier if a replacement were offered, for ridding your mind of blame will leave an empty space you will long to fill. This act of consciously choosing not to place blame will short-circuit the many thoughts that you would attach to this idea, thoughts that have formed a chain-reaction of situations and events, feelings and behaviors that you had no realization were birthed from the idea of blame. Although I offer it not as a replacement, what you will find will come in the place of blame is an idea of acceptance of what *is*, an idea that is needed now.

10.6   Acceptance of what *is*, is acceptance that whatever is happening in the present moment is a gift and a lesson. What comes as a lesson may not seem like a gift, but all lessons are gifts. While some of these lessons may come in forms that make them seem like lessons of old, they will not be repeats of lessons that have come before. They will not be lessons that you find difficult or distressing if you accept them as lessons and realize that all lessons are gifts. What you have struggled to learn in the past you have struggled with only because you did not realize the nature of the situation as a lesson or recognize that all lessons are gifts.

10.7   This relates to our exercise on forgetting for you must forget the ways in which you have formerly reacted to every situation. Not one situation coming to you now will be a repeat of the past. How can it be when the past was lived in the house of illusion and the present is lived in the house of truth? Being cognizant of this is the only way that the simultaneous learning and unlearning that was spoken of earlier will be able to be realized. You have passed through your time of unlearning what the past but seemed to teach you. Now, while life may seem much unchanged in its outward appearance, it is up to you to become aware of the total change that has, in truth, taken place.

10.8   Along with forgetting there is another practice that will help you to become aware of this change. While much the same as forgetting it will seem to have a different process in practice. This is the practice of ceasing to listen to the voice of the ego. While the ego is gone, many of its messages remain within your thoughts, like echoes of a former time. These thoughts are remembered messages and so must, like all the rest, be forgotten.

The process of forgetting these thought patterns will be only slightly different from forgetting your former reactions to people and situations and much like forgetting to place blame.

10.9 The first step in being able to forget such thoughts is in recognizing them as separate and distinct from the thoughts of your right mind or Christ-mind. This will be easy because the thoughts of the ego-mind were always harsh with you or with others. The Christ-mind and the thoughts that come from the voice of the Christ-mind will be gentle. The thoughts of the ego-mind will come as disguises to certainty. Given just a little practice, these disguises will be easily seen through and the uncertainty behind them revealed. Thoughts of the Christ-mind will hold a certainty that cannot be disguised. Remember that all doubt is doubt about yourself and that you are no longer called to doubt yourself. Your Self is now your Christ-Self.

10.10 You will feel for a while as if constant certainty is impossible. This feeling will remain only as long as you remember your past uncertainty. Uncertainty, like all the rest of the ego's thought system, was learned. Your true Self has no cause for uncertainty. Thus you are called, as well, to forget the uncertainty of the past.

10.11 While these may seem like remedial lessons, they are not. You are no longer called to a time of uncertainty to learn through contrast the lessons of certainty. Realize that this is how you have learned *in the past* and that all that is from the past is what you are being called to forget. Thus when uncertainty arises, you need but remind yourself that the time for uncertainty is past. Uncertainty will not now come to teach you lessons you have already learned but will only visit you as an echo from the past. It is a habit, a pattern of the old thought system. All you must do is not listen to it. Its voice will not be gentle or full of love. Its voice will hold the unmistakable edge of fear.

10.12 Remember that, while gentle, these are and will, be *practical* lessons that simply come to show you a new way of living, the way of living in the house of truth. You will not need to learn a foreign *language* to dwell in this new house, but you will need to learn what will at first seem to you a foreign *thought system*. This thought system recognizes no fear or judgment, no uncertainty or doubt, no contrast and no division. It is the thought system of unity. It is your true thought system and will be easily remembered once you begin to let it automatically replace the old.

10.13 Think of this, for a moment as you would a learned language. If you learned Spanish as a child and then learned and spoke English for many years, you might believe your Spanish to be forgotten. However, if you were to return to a dwelling where those within it spoke only Spanish, soon your knowledge of Spanish would return. For a short while you would have two languages constantly running through your mind and you would be translating one into the other. But eventually, if this situation went on for many years, you might think you had forgotten your ability to understand English.

10.14 What we are doing now is much like translating the learned thought system of the ego into the thought system of the Christ-Self that you but think you have forgotten. As you dwell in the house of truth, if you do not resist unlearning the ego thought system, the thought system of your true Self will quite simply return to your memory. You will soon forget the thought system of the ego-self even though, when encountering those who still use that thought system, you will be able to communicate with them. Yet the ease with which you communicate with them will diminish over time. You will find yourself continuously teaching the *language*, if you will, of the new thought system, for you will have no desire to communicate with anything less.

10.15 You will find that your new *language* will gather people to you in much the way people will gravitate toward beautiful music. Many will be eager to learn what you have remembered because they will realize that the memory of this *language* exists within them as well. It will come naturally to you to welcome these back to the common *language* of the mind and heart joined in unity. You will desire more than anything for everyone you encounter to share this remembered language. Some, however, will be resistant.

10.16 This is why we have called these lessons in forgetting practical lessons for the life of the body. They are lessons that will soon be translated in another way. These lessons that will enter your mind and heart will, of necessity, need to be translated into the language of the body as well. While your human form remains, you will be dwelling among those in human form. While the house of illusion still exists, you will continue to encounter those who exist within it. While you continue to encounter those who exist in the house of illusion you will continue to encounter temptations of the human experience. These are what we will now address.

CHAPTER 11

The Temptations of the Human Experience

11.1 Consciousness is a state of awareness. The statement "I am" is a statement of awareness. It has been seen as a statement of awareness of the self. Those existing within the house of illusion are aware of the self but are unaware that the self of illusion, the self that exists in illusion, is an illusionary self. This could be further stated as those who exist in the house of illusion are aware of the personal self alone and believe the personal self to be who they are. Further, they believe the personal self to be the truth of the statement, "I am."

11.2 Those existing within the house of truth also feel an awareness of Self. Without necessarily being able to put it into words, they no longer feel the statement of "I am" as a statement of the personal self or the self alone. For those existing in the house of truth, "I am" has become something larger, an all-encompassing recognition of the unity of all things with which the Self co-exists in truth and peace and love.

11.3 These words, *truth* and *peace* and *love*, are interchangeable in the house of truth as their meaning there is the same. These words, like the words *House of Truth* represent an awareness of a new reality, a new dwelling place.

11.4 The word *house* as used in the *House of Truth* does not represent a structure but a dwelling place. The word *house* as used in the *house of illusion* does represent a structure. The house of illusion is a construction meant to shield the personal self from all that it would fear. The house of truth is the dwelling place of those who no longer live in fear and thus have no need for a structure of seeming protection.

11.5 The house of illusion is the stage on which the drama of the human experience has been acted out.

11.6 During the time I spent on earth I did not dwell in the house of illusion but in the house of truth. What this means is that I was aware of the truth and lived by the truth. I was aware of the Peace of God and lived within the Peace of God. I was aware of the Love of God and the Love of God lived within me.

11.7   This is what you are now called to do:
Be aware that the love of God lives within you.
Live within the Peace of God.
Live by the truth.

11.8   This could be restated as you *are* love, you live *in* peace, you live *by* or in accord with the truth.

11.9   I have called the Kingdom of God the House of Truth rather than the House of Peace for a reason. What you are learning is no longer that the Kingdom of God or the House of Truth *exists*, but how to live within it. The question of how to live within it is best addressed by concentrating on living according to the truth.

11.10   While a lack of judgment has been stressed many times, and we have adhered to the precept of not judging by denying any right or wrong, the difference between truth and illusion can no longer be denied. To realize the difference between truth and illusion is not to call one right and the other wrong but to simply recognize what they are. This is an important distinction that must be kept in mind as we proceed so that you are not tempted to judge those living in illusion or their reality. Their reality does not exist. Believing in the reality of illusion will never make it the truth.

11.11   Thus we begin to address the temptations of the human experience. Two are spoken of in tandem here: The temptation to judge and the temptation to accept the existence of a reality other than the truth.

11.12   If I can tell you in truth that you are no different than I am, then you must see that you cannot begin to think of yourself as different than your brothers and sisters. *All* exist in the House of Truth. The house of illusion exists within the House of Truth *because* it is where your brothers and sisters think they are. The house of illusion is not a *hell* to which anyone has been banished. It can at times be a chosen hell, just as it can at times be a chosen heaven. Choice and the awareness of the power of choice that exists within is all that differentiates one from the other.

11.13   You must not see your brothers and sisters within the house of illusion but must see them where they truly are—within the House of Truth. As soon as you would "see" the house of illusion, you would make it real, and with its reality judgment would be upon you...not any judgment of God, but judgment of your own mind.

11.14 I remind you here that you are not being asked to *see* anything that is not the truth. This is why the word *see* is consciously used here and why we now refrain from use of the word *perceive*. Perception is gone as soon as you truly see.

11.15 You will, of course, continue to be aware that very few realize that they exist in the House of Truth. You will, in truth, for quite some time, be striving to remain aware even that you have changed dwelling places. There is a reason for this time of varying degrees of awareness. As the old continues to help you to learn lessons of the new you will be seeing how the lessons of the illusion can be useful in a new way to your brothers and sisters as well. Never forget that what was made for your use can be used in a new way and to produce a new outcome. Do not be afraid to use anything available within the house of illusion to promote the recognition of truth. Do not be afraid of the house of illusion at all. What illusion can frighten those who know the truth?

11.16 This first lesson on the temptation of the human experience comes in truth as a warning against righteousness. It comes to remind you, as you replace the thought system of illusion with the thought system of the truth, that having remembered the truth of who you are, you are called to forget the personal self who would find this cause for righteousness. You are not right and others wrong. This temptation will not long be with you for once the old thought system is thoroughly translated to the new, such ideas as right and wrong will be no more. It is only for this transitional phase, that this and all such reminders regarding the temptations of the human experience are necessary.

CHAPTER 12

The Physical Self in the House of Truth

12.1 Consciousness is a state of awareness. The statement "I am" is a statement of awareness of consciousness. Awareness preceded the statement of "I am." "I am" preceded the creation of the Self. The Self preceded the establishment of the personal self.

12.2 You exist within the *time* of consciousness of the personal self. Thus we begin our work with the personal self while also realizing that the personal self is a step in the chain of consciousness. The steps that came before that of the personal self did not come *within time*. The creation of *time* was simultaneous with the creation of the personal self. Because the steps that came before that of the personal self did not come in time, they are eternal, eternal levels of consciousness that still exist and have always existed.

12.3 Temptations of the human experience exist only in time. What we are about to do is move the human experience out of the realm of time. For this to happen, we must remove the time-bound temptations of the human experience of the personal self.

12.4 Matter or form is bound by time. Spirit is not. The House of Truth cannot be bound by time and be a House of Truth. How then can the personal self begin to realize the human experience outside of time? The answer is thus: by changing the consciousness of the personal self from a time-bound state of consciousness to an eternal state of consciousness. This change, as has been said before, is the miracle. This miracle is the goal toward which we now work.

12.5 Realize that prior to this point, our goal was returning to your awareness the truth of your identity. By changing our goal now, I am assuring you that you have become aware of the truth of your identity. The goal of this Course has been accomplished. However, while your consciousness remains time-bound, your awareness is still limited. As has already been stated, in order to remove the limits that continue to exist, we must remove all time-bound temptations.

12.6   These temptations are not temptations of the body. They may seem to be, but the body is neutral. All temptations originate in the mind and are transferred to the body. Temptations do not originate from love. While some temptations will seem to be of love they are not.

12.7   As it dawns upon your once slumbering mind that change on a grand scale awaits you, you will grow fearful if you do not realize that what is being proposed to you here is something completely new, something you have not even dreamed of. This state you have not even dared to dream of is a state in which only God's laws of love exist even within the realm of physicality. What this means is that all that in this human experience has come of love will be retained. All that will be lost is what has come of fear.

12.8   Let's return a moment to the choice that was made for the human experience, the choice to express whom you are in the realm of physicality. You were not "better" or more "right" before this choice was made than you are now. You made a choice consistent with the laws of creation and the steps of creation outlined above. From this choice, many experienced ensued. Some of these experiences were the result of fear, some the result of love. The choice to express who you are in physical terms was not a choice made of fear but made of love. A physical self is not inconsistent with the laws of God or of creation. It is simply a choice.

12.9   The life of the physical self became a life of suffering and strife only because the physical or personal self forgot that it exists in relationship and believed itself to be separate and alone. In its fear, it made an ego-self which, because it sprang from fear, was not consistent with the laws of Love or of creation. Knowing it existed in a state inconsistent with that of the laws of God, it made of God a being to be feared, thus continuing, and being unable to find release from, the cycle of fear.

12.10 What would be a greater step in all of creation than a physical self able to choose to express the Self within the laws of love? A physical self, able to express itself from within the House of Truth in ways consistent with peace and love is the next step in creation, the rebirth of the Son of God known as the resurrection.

12.11 While this would seem to say that mistakes may occur within creation, remember that creation is about change and growth. There is no right or wrong within creation but there are stages of growth and change. Humankind is now passing through a tremendous stage of growth and change. Are you ready?

CHAPTER 13

The Practice: No Loss But Only Gain

13.1   Now that we have established the consistency of our former purpose, that of establishing your identity, and our new purpose, that of the miracle that will allow you to exist as who you are in human form, we may proceed unencumbered by any doubt you might have had concerning whether or not you would desire the new goal toward which we work.

13.2   We proceed by further defining the temptations of the human experience. In "A Treatise on the Art of Thought," we spoke of these temptations in regards to extremes of the human experience, saying that these things that draw you from the peace of God draw you from the state in which you are aware of who you are, and so cause you to be aware only of a self of human experience, or a personal self. While you may still feel a connection to God during such times, you will not be dwelling within the peace of God. Your Self and God will be but memories to you while your reality remains that of the physical experience and the personal self. In such times you can conceive only of a God outside of yourself and trust not in the benevolence of the experience, whether it be an extreme experience of pain or of pleasure. You begin to fear that pleasure will end or that pain will not end. Once fear has entered, doubt and guilt are never far behind.

13.3   These temptations will concern you less and less as we uncover their true meaning by looking beyond the experiences themselves to the cause.

13.4   Broad brushstrokes have been made now, giving you the beginnings of a vision of a life in physical form that will not include the very temptations we are beginning to lay out. Because you have made these things that would but seem to tempt you, you have believed in them and their ability to affect you. You have unlearned many of these lessons and need not repeat unlearning that has been accomplished. The new learning that lies ahead of you now is simply learning in accordance with the new thought system of the truth; accepting the truth and leaving illusion behind. The new thought system is simple to learn. What is of love is truth. What is of fear is illusion. The temptation is to see love where it is not and to not see fear where it is. But your ability to distinguish between love and fear as cause is all that is important now as you will create the new according to what you believe to be the truth and translate into ideas.

13.5   Remember now that pleasure and pain as perceived by the body are from the same source. That source has not been the body but your beliefs about your body and yourself. You have believed pleasure to come at a cost, the cost of pain. You have believed in the laws of man, laws that were made to perpetuate the idea that you must pay for everything, or earn everything that you would care to make your own, and then that you must protect what you have against those who would take it away.

13.6   This is a simple place to start because each of you are tempted to hang on to this idea despite all that it has cost you. To replace this idea with the idea of there being no loss but only gain under the laws of love, is to resist the temptation of requiring yourself to pay for what you gain.

13.7   I say this is a simple place to start because you can put this new idea into practice today and every day by simply refusing the temptation to believe in concepts such as earning and paying. How you implement this idea will be your choice. But the idea that you do not have to earn your way nor pay your way must be birthed and lived by. While most of you will immediately think of your survival needs, this is far from the only area in which the idea of earning or paying your way can be found. This old idea is consistent with all beliefs of an "if this then that" nature. You might start practicing this idea by repeating these words to yourself:

13.8   "I am safe and nothing that I do or do not do will threaten my safety."

13.9   As you say these words you will realize that you do believe in them. You believe, but you cannot *imagine* the truth of these words really being represented in the life you live here. This you must now do. You must represent the truth of these words with your life.

13.10   You are not, however, meant to test these words with foolish acts. To do so would be to act as if this were magic rather than the truth. To act as if this is the truth is what you are called to do. You may even begin by something as simple as choosing one thing a day that you will change to reflect the fact that you have accepted this new idea. Choose an act that will cause you no fear to begin with. For instance, you might tell yourself something such as this: "I have an idea that if I sleep as long as I feel I need to sleep in the morning, I will awake refreshed and ready for my day and no dire consequences will befall me from this action." Another act might be as simple as allowing yourself to freely spend a small amount of money each day that you ordinarily would not spend, always with the idea in mind that this will not affect your budget in any negative respect.

13.11 While these examples may seem so simple that you regard them as little more than the self-help kind of advice I have said this Course would not provide, they are but aides to help you in the development of your own ideas. If you remember that all of your ideas are to be based on love, you will not fail to birth ideas of consequence.

13.12 The second aspect of this lesson will then be regarding your ideas about the consequences that seem to result from whatever action your ideas have suggested. You must birth the idea of having no reason to fear these consequences, no matter what they may be. You must, in truth, birth the idea of benevolence and abundance.

13.13 Notice that the simple examples I gave were examples of action. Ideas can certainly be birthed without the need for action, but one of the factors that distinguishes an idea from a belief is a requirement of action. That action, while not necessarily physical, is the action of giving birth. Realize that you believe in many things that did not originate with yourself. But it is not until you have your own ideas about those beliefs that you own those beliefs in terms of making them *your* beliefs. To believe without forming your own ideas about your beliefs is to be in danger of succumbing to false beliefs.

13.14 To form your own ideas is to be creative. Forming your own ideas happens in relationship. Taking action on your ideas forms a relationship between your physical form and your Self as your physical self represents, in form, the thought or image produced within the Self. Ideas, in the context in which we are speaking of them here, are thoughts or images originating from the Self and being represented by the personal self. It is only in this way that the personal self will be able to represent the Self in truth.

CHAPTER 14

Not Other Than Who You Are

14.1   The death of the ego thought system has made way for the birth of the thought system of the truth. The thought system of the ego was based on fear. In this time of translation from one thought system to the other, the most subtle and yet significant change is the change from the foundation of fear, the basis of the ego thought system, to a foundation of love, the basis of the thought system of truth. While the foundation of fear, like the ego, will have left you now, a pattern of behaving fearfully may still remain and as such be a deterrent to new ideas and to action. As long as these patterns of fear remain as deterrents to action, you will not experience the freedom of *living* from the new thought system. The new thought system will still exist within your mind and heart, as nothing can now take this memory from you, but to experience the new thought system as thought alone will not bring about the changes you would so desire to have come about within your physical experience. You may live a more peaceful and meaningful life, but you will not become the savior I ask you to be, or the architects of the new world of heaven on earth that I call you to create.

14.2   Let me attempt to make the difference between having a new thought system and living by a new thought system more clear. Because you now are translating the thought system of the ego into the thought system of the truth, you will begin to *believe* in such things as benevolence and abundance. What this means is that you will slowly translate all ideas of scarcity into ideas of abundance, all ideas of blame into ideas of benevolence. Thus you might, after this period of translation, rather than cursing your station in life and feeling badly that you do not enjoy the health, wealth or stature of some others, accept your current status and begin to feel more peace and joy within it. If you are not well, you may cope more easily with your discomfort. If you are not financially secure, you may congratulate yourself on desiring less and be more content living a simple life. If you have felt a lack of respect you may feel that what others think of you matters not and enjoy a heightened self-concept. While these would all be worthy aims they are not the goal toward which we work. These would be the consequences of new beliefs that are held but not lived. Soon these fragile states would be sure to feel threatened by some situation or person and judgment would return to label what is happening as "bad." A "god" outside of the self would soon be called upon to intercede. Blame would be placed. A return to equanimity would soon prevail, for those dwelling in the house of truth would not long abide with such illusions, but the pattern of the old would not be broken. Suffering and strife would still seem to be possible. You would merely look back after the interlude had passed and see the truth, realizing that a lesson had been learned and becoming aware that for a while you but flirted with illusion. This flirting with illusion is like unto the temptations of the human experience and would not occur were the temptations gone from you.

14.3 It should be becoming clear to you by now that, although you dwell in the house of the truth, you are capable of bringing with you old patterns of behavior. Once the translation of the new thought system for the old is complete, this will no longer happen. But the translation cannot be completed if you refuse to live by what you know...if you refuse to live as who you are.

14.4 You are quite capable of seeing the truth and still *acting* as if you see it not. This has been done for generation upon generation and may still happen if you do not heed these instructions.

14.5 I am, however, the bringer of Good News. Now I will repeat to you a piece of good news you may have forgotten: You would not be other than who you are. This is a key idea that will help you immeasurably in leaving behind patterns of behavior based on the old thought system of fear. Despite the foundation of fear upon which your old thought system was based, you still would not be other than who you are. What this means to the learning stage you are at now is that you but think you are discontent with much of your life. As you begin to dwell in the house of truth and see with the eyes of love, you will see far less about the life you lead that you would change than you would imagine. You fear where all your new ideas might take you, and for some great changes may surely await, but those who will be visited by great change are but those who desire it. Yet even those who desire great change will find these great changes will not cause them to be other than who they are. There is nothing wrong with who you are!

14.6   As you see newly with the eyes of love, you will be much more likely to see love everywhere within the life you currently live than to see the need to change your life completely in order to find love. You who are worried about the risks you may be required to take, worry not! The changes that come to you will be chosen changes. You will lose nothing you would keep.

14.7   This is precisely why you must choose not to keep the life of discomfort caused by perceived illness, the life of scarcity caused by perceived lack, the lack of stature caused by perceived disrespect. It is only by your choice that you will keep these things and only by your choice that these things will leave you.

14.8   It is only your old uncertainty that will make you fear the matters of choice that lie before you. But this choice is not the choice of continuous decision making but simply the choice to live by the truth of the new thought system. If you but let go the old, and with it the patterns of behavior caused by fear, the new will reveal to you all that you would keep and all that you would leave behind. What you would keep is of love. What you would leave behind is of illusion.

14.9   You will clearly see all of the choices that throughout your life have been made in love and made of you a person you would not be other than. You will also clearly see all of the choices that throughout your life were caused by fear and how little consequence they had in truth. These fearful choices took nothing from you or from others.

14.10   If there are things that you, at this point, still hold to yourself and call unforgivable, now is the time to let them go. If you have read the paragraph above and feel it is fine for some others not to regret their choices but not for you, I ask you to trust in my assurance that this is not so. You must choose to leave this blaming of yourself behind, no matter what it is you feel you have need to blame yourself for. You would not be here if you had not already felt regret and sorrow for the hurts you have caused others. Whatever actions you have not previously brought to love to be seen in a new light, are now revealed in the light of truth.

14.11   We have spoken already of historical causes for vengeance and blame. The suffering that has been chosen has been mighty. The choice now is not a choice to explore the why behind it or to look for remedies for the past. The choice now is whether you want suffering to continue or want to abolish it for all time. If you are holding onto regrets you are holding on to blame. If you are holding onto blame you are holding onto bitterness. If these regrets and blame have to do with yourself you may not feel as if you have the right to let them go. If you do not feel as if you have the right to let them go, you are choosing to remain embittered and choosing to be punished for your "sins." While this is what you continue to choose, this is what will continue to be evidenced in your world. This is the only act you can choose worthy of being called selfishness. Be self "less" rather than selfish now and allow the self that you would blame to pass away into the illusion from which it came. Remember that bitterness, like the ego, has existed in all. If your brother or sister would not give up bitterness in order to usher in a world of peace, would you not think this a selfish act?

14.12 Atonement, or correction, is not of you but of God. You might think of this in terms of nature and look upon nature's ability to correct itself. You are a part of nature. Your body can correct or heal itself, and so can your mind and heart...if they are allowed to do so. A time-bound consciousness that hangs onto the past as if it were the truth, allows not correction to take place. The past is no more and neither the present nor the future can be built upon it. This is why we have spent so much time unlearning and why we continue with lessons of forgetting.

14.13 Resurrection or rebirth must be total to be at all. Can you see why you cannot hang onto the past? The new cannot have historical precedents. This is why you have been assured that what you are called to is a life so new that you cannot even imagine it. Imagine not the past and make for yourself no cause to prolong it. The past is but a starting point for the future. Just as we talked of the consequences of blame and how you are unaware of all that proceeds from the idea of blame, so too is it with the past. Like a story yet to be written, that which follows the first page will be based upon the first page.

14.14 We are writing a new first page, a new Genesis. It begins now. It begins with the rebirth of a Self of love. It begins with the birth of Christ in you and in your willingness to live in the world as the Christ-Self.

CHAPTER 15

The New Beginning

15.1 Some of you have had more experience with new beginnings than others. For most mature adults, some form of new beginning has taken place or been offered. Often, those within the relationship of marriage have had occasion to choose to forgive the past and begin again to build a new relationship. Others, in a similar relationship, might have chosen to let the past go and enter into new relationships. Parents have welcomed home errant children to give them the chance to begin again. At all stages of life new friendships are formed and the relationship with each new friend provides for a new beginning. Some begin anew through changes in locale and employment. Each new school year of the young provides a fresh start. Deaths of loved ones and the births of new family members form new configurations in a life. Nature begins anew each spring.

15.2 What hampers new beginnings of all kinds within the human experience are ideas that things cannot be different than they once were. The only true departure from this idea has concerned the occasions of birth and death. This is something we will return to, but first let us look at other types of new beginnings and all that would hamper them from taking place.

15.3 New beginnings do not occur outside of relationship. The idea of special relationship is one that hampers new beginnings. Special relations of all types are based upon expectation—expectations of certain behavior—and expectations of continued special treatment within the relationship. Even, and sometimes especially, what is considered poor behavior can come to be an expectation difficult to deviate from within the special relationship. But whether the expectation is of special treatment or poor behavior matters not. It is the expectation of a "known" set of criteria concerning the relationship, a set of criteria based upon the past that is most often what prevents new beginnings from truly being new.

15.4   Often new beginnings are offered or considered "in spite of" circumstances of the past that would seem to make them foolish. There is always some "thing" that is expected to change. This idea is countered internally, however, by the idea that at some basic level, human beings do not change. You cannot imagine those with whom you are in relationship being other than who they are. This is consistent with the truth. Yet who anyone is, is not contingent upon whom they have represented themselves to be in the past.

15.5   When attempting to give oneself or another a new beginning, you often act "as if" you believe a new beginning is possible, even while awaiting the lapse that will surely prove to you that the new beginning is but an act and that nothing has really changed. A student who failed to learn the prior year, while eager and confident in being able to succeed in the current year, will continue to be plagued by memories of failure. The alcoholic can approach each day with faith while keeping fresh memories of past abuse or humiliation in the hopes that they will discourage a repeat of the old behavior. The loved one of an alcoholic can similarly approach each day with faith even while suspiciously looking for signs that faith is unwarranted. The criminal is not expected to be rehabilitated despite the efforts of the system and the hopes of their loved ones.

15.6   Everyone believes they carry the baggage of the past, not only their own but that of all the special relationships in which they have been involved. To have a special relationship with someone who has failed at offered new beginnings becomes a failure for all involved. Each sets their own criteria for success or failure and their own timing for the accomplishment of the same. Some would see six months of change as the basis for trust in the new. For others six years would not be enough.

15.7   You must now birth the idea that human beings do indeed change. While you have known instinctively that there is a core, a center to each that is unchangeable, you must now give up the idea that this core or center has been represented by the past. You must forget the idea that the future cannot be different than the past.

15.8   With the death of the ego, special relationships too have breathed their last. As I said before, these will seem to be remedial lessons. What they are, in truth, are aides to help you birth the new ideas that will break the patterns of old.

15.9   The new beginning you are called to now is a new beginning that, like all others that you have offered or attempted, will take place in relationship. The difference is that this new beginning will take place in holy, rather than special, relationship.

15.10   The holy relationship has been accomplished by the joining of the mind and heart in unity. The holy relationship is with the Self, the Self that abides in unity with all within the house of truth. This relationship makes the Self one with all and so brings the holiness of the Self to all.

15.11   There are no impediments to this new beginning save for the finalizing of the translation of the thought system of the ego to the thought system of the truth. As we have said before, it is impossible to learn the new with the thought system of the old. It is impossible to learn the truth through the same methods that have been used in the past to learn illusion. This Course teaches that love cannot be learned. I have said here that love, peace, and truth are interchangeable ideas within the new thought system. Thus, truth, like love, is not something that you can learn. The Good News is that you have no need to learn the truth. The truth exists within you and you are now aware of its reality.

15.12   How then, do you access and live within this new reality, this new beginning? Through living by the truth.

15.13   These Treatises are no longer concerned with coursework as the work of this Course has been accomplished in you. These Treatises are simply concerned with assisting you to live what you have learned. Learning was needed in order to return you to your Self. Despite whatever method you feel you used to learn what you have learned, what this Course did was bypass the way of learning of the ego and call upon the Christ in you to learn anew. That learning put an end to the old. Living what you have learned will usher in the new.

15.14   These examples of your former ideas about new beginnings have simply been used to demonstrate why you cannot approach this new beginning as you have those of the past. What will assist you most, as the translation of the old thought system for the new continues, are the beliefs that you adopted with the assistance of "A Treatise on Unity:"

15.15   *You are accomplished.*

Giving and receiving are one in truth.

There is no loss but only gain within the laws of love.

Special relationships have been replaced by holy relationship.

15.16 What we are adding now to these beliefs is the idea that these beliefs can be represented in form. These beliefs can, with the help of the new thought system, change the very nature of the self described by the words *human being*. This calls for still more forgetting as you must consciously let go of all your ideas of the limitations inherent in your concept of what it means to be a human being.

15.17 While you would not be other than who you are, who you are is not limited to the concept of human being nor to the laws of man. If you continue to act as if you are still the same being that you have represented yourself to be in the past, you will not be living by the truth but by illusion.

15.18 Illusion is the "truth" by which you have lived. The total replacement of illusion with the truth is what the new thought system will accomplish. Obviously, this replacement must be total. The means for making this total replacement are in your hands but you are hardly empty-handed. The truth goes with you as does the love and peace of God.

CHAPTER 16

Willingness, Temptation, and Belief

16.1 Willingness to live by the truth is the only offering you are asked to make to God. You need make no other offerings. No sacrifices need be made and sacrifices are, in truth, unacceptable to God. You are asked to give up nothing but unwillingness.

16.2 Saying that willingness is the only offering that is required of you is the same as saying that you do not need to, and in truth, cannot, give anything else or anything less. You do not need to give your effort to this calling. You do not need to struggle to create the new world you are called to create. You do not need to have a plan and you do not need to know precisely what this new world will look like. You simply need to be willing to live by the truth.

16.3 You must forget the idea that you can create the new from the old. If this were possible, you would indeed be called to effort and to struggle, to planning and to a state of knowing that for which it is you plan. These have been the ways of creation in the thought system of the ego, ways that have brought much advancement to the forms you occupy without changing their nature in the slightest measure. All the effort of the ego has not brought an end to suffering or strife, nor made of this illusion a happy dream.

16.4 Although you may still feel confused and lacking in ability to do what I am asking of you, I feel confident in also saying that you are more content and happy, more peaceful and free of fear than you have ever been. While your life may not have changed in ways that you would like and while its limitations may seem even more frustrating than before, I am also confident in saying that a hope has been instilled within you, a hope for the very changes that you feel you need in order to reflect, within your daily life, the new Self you have become.

16.5   We spoke once before within *A Course of Love* of your impatience and of this Course acting as a trigger that would release all such impatience for what will be. Impatience for what will be can only be satisfied by what is.

16.6   What is, *is*, despite the lag in time that would seem to make all that we speak of here a blueprint for some future reality. All that would keep this lag in time a constant, and make it seem as if what is now is still awaiting replacement by what will be, is a change that must occur within. As has already been said, this change has to do with the time-bound temptations of the human experience. All of these temptations relate to the beliefs set forth in "A Treatise on Unity."

16.7   *You are already accomplished.*

16.8   By saying that you are not only accomplished, but The Accomplished, it is being said that you are already what you have sought to be. Thus, in order to live by the truth, you must live in the world as The Accomplished and cease struggling to be other than who you are in truth. This struggling to be other than who you are in truth is a temptation of the human experience. It will come in many forms, all of which will be related to an old pattern of dissatisfaction with yourself. These temptations will be related to the intrigue of the challenge and actually be couched in patterns that have you attempting to "accomplish" set goals in life. The key to resisting these temptations is not resistance at all but the idea that you are already accomplished. Keeping this idea in the forefront of your mind and heart will aid the translation of this aspect of the ego thought system to the thought system of the truth.

16.9   *Giving and receiving are one in truth.*

16.10 By saying that giving and receiving are one in truth it is being said that you are lacking only in what you do not give. The belief in lack is a temptation of the human experience. This will relate to all situations in which you feel you have something to gain from some "other." Again, this will be related to old patterns of dissatisfaction with the self. It has to do with any ideas you may still hold concerning others having more than you have, or to desires that you may feel have gone unfulfilled. While you may think that this means you are being asked to do without, this is not the case. You are simply being asked to give that you might receive and to receive that you might give.

16.11   *There is no loss but only gain within the laws of love.*

16.12   By saying that there is no loss but only gain within the laws of love, you are being told to have no fear. Fear of loss is a great temptation of the human experience. If it were not for this fear of loss, you would not find it difficult to live by the thought system of the truth. This fear relates very strongly to your ideas of change and as such is the greatest detriment to your new beginning. These temptations relate to everything you fear to do because of the consequences your actions might bring. These fears rob you of your certainty and result in a lack of trust. The key to resisting these temptations is not resistance at all but the idea that there is no loss but only gain within the laws of love.

16.13   *Special relationships have been replaced by holy relationship.*

16.14   By saying that special relationships have been replaced by holy relationship it is being said that your only relationship is with the truth and that you no longer have a relationship with illusion. All of your fears in regards to special relationships are temptations of the human experience. These temptations will relate to any issues that you consider to be issues of relationship. All of your desires, fears, hopes and expectations of others are temptations that arise from your old idea of special relationships. All of your plans to do good and be good, to help others, and to struggle to make the world a better place, fall into this category. Your notions of wanting to protect or control are also notions based upon the necessity you have felt for the continuation of special relationships.

16.15   Now you must forget the idea of needing to maintain specialness. A key aid in helping you to put this temptation behind you is the idea of the holy relationship in which all exist in unity and within the protection of love's embrace. If you but live by the idea that representing who you are in truth will create a new heaven on earth, you can lay aside any fears that others will suffer due to the changes your new Self will create. As you live with awareness of the love of God within you, you will see that you have no need for special love relationships. You will realize that the love and the Self you now have available to share in relationship are all that you would share in truth. You will recognize that no others have a need for you to make them special for you will see the truth of who they are rather than the illusion of who you would have them be.

16.16 All of these temptations worked together in the thought system of the ego and created patterns that caused them to only seem to be intertwined and all encompassing. Nothing but the truth is all encompassing. Illusion is made of parts that do not form real connections but that only seem to have the ability to build upon each other. Let one part go and soon all the remaining parts will crumble into the dust from which they came. The cement that was used to hold together the house of illusion was only your fear.

16.17 Accept one "part" or tenet of the truth and see the reverse take place. See how quickly the thought system of the truth builds upon itself and forms a real and true interrelated whole. What forms the house of truth is love eternal and it has always encompassed you, even unto encompassing the house of illusion that you made to obscure it from yourself.

CHAPTER 17

A Mistake in Learning

17.1   Why would you ever have chosen to obscure the truth? As we have already shown, to have chosen to express the Self in physical form was a choice consistent with the laws of love. There was no need for the Self to be separate in order for this to be so, but there was a need for the Self to have an observable form and to exist in relationship with others with observable forms. This was simply so that expressions of love could be created and observed within the realm of physicality.

17.2   The biblical story of Adam and Eve that has them eating from the tree of knowledge was an illustration of the effects of this observation and the judgment that sprang from it. The self "fell" from unity through this judgment of what it observed as being other than itself, through this beginning of making distinctions between the self and all other things in creation that existed with the self. This is why the story of creation includes the naming of creatures. It was the beginning of perception and of the idea that what was observable was "other than" he who did the observing. Now your science is proving to you the relationship between the observer and the observed, the effect that one cannot help but have upon the other. Science still has a long way to go in determining, through its processes, what this says about the nature of humankind but it is closer every day to understanding the unity and interconnectedness of all things.

17.3   As soon as spirit took on form, man began to exist in time because there became a need for a beginning and an ending to the chosen experience. Thus each self of form is born *into* time and each self of form dies *out* of time. Both birth and death have always existed as choices, as beginnings and endings to the finite experience of time. It is the nature of what is finite to begin and end. Birth and death are all you have seen as true new beginnings.

17.4   As has been said before, time is a measurement of the "time" it takes for learning to occur. A *new* experience was chosen—the experience of existing within the realm of physicality. As such, it was as much a new beginning as the new beginning you are now called to. It required the learning of a new thought system, the thought system of the physical, a thought system that was not needed before there was physical form. The creation story of Adam and Eve, as well as many other creation stories, but tell of a "mistake" in the learning of a thought system of physicality, a mistake that became a building block for all that came after it.

17.5 That mistake was seeing God as "other than" and separate from the self. While it was important to the desired experience to learn the lessons of what was observable within the physical realm, to have begun to forget the unobservable began a process of unlearning or forgetting of the truth that has led, through the learning of untruth in the mechanism of time, to the world in which you now exist. It may seem ridiculous to say that the untrue can be learned, but this is exactly what has been learned during the time of your experience in physical form. Since your true Self could not learn the untrue, a new self, which we have called the ego-self, was made. Since the ego-self cannot learn the true, your true self had to be appealed to for this learning to take place.

17.6 The Holy Spirit was called upon to return this remembrance to minds and hearts. But again let me remind you that the Holy Spirit is not other than who you are but an aspect of who you are and Who God Is. Let me remind you also that names, such as *Holy Spirit*, are but word symbols that represent what is. So think now of whatever stories you know of the Holy Spirit, stories that symbolize what is. In these stories, the Holy Spirit is always called upon to return the true Self to the self of illusion. A Holy Spirit is called to return to your mind and heart.

17.7 You were told in "A Treatise on the Art of Thought" that the time of the Holy Spirit has ended and the time of the second coming of Christ is here. The name of Christ was associated with my name, the name Jesus, because I lived as a man with a Holy Spirit in my mind and heart and as such represented the truth. Many others by many other names have represented the truth and in so doing dispelled illusion within themselves and those who followed their teachings and example. This has occurred within the time of the Holy Spirit.

17.8 The Holy Spirit, unlike God the Creator, has known the existence of the illusion and the thought system of the ego-self and been able to communicate within that illusion. Without this means of communication with the ego-self the ability to learn the truth could not have returned to you. The "time" of the Holy Spirit has now ended because the time of illusion is now called to an end. What is finite has an end point and this is that end point for the time of illusion. The return of Christ, or *your* ability and willingness to live as your true Self, to live in the house of truth rather than the house of illusion, is what will end the time of illusion. Just as the truth is the truth and illusion is illusion; just as these things are what they are without judgment; so is the beginning the beginning and the end the end. The beginning we speak of here is the same as the end we speak of here. The *time* of the Holy Spirit, or the time in which communication was needed between the illusion and the truth, *must* end in order for the truth to become the one reality.

CHAPTER 18

Observation

18.1 You may wonder rightly then, how those who have not learned by the Holy Spirit will learn. They will now learn through observation.

18.2 Let us return to the concept of observation and link it with ideas as we have spoken of them here. Observation, the ability to observe what the Self expresses, was part of the original choice for physical form. The word *observance* has rightly been linked with divine worship and devotion. Minds that have been unwilling to accept or learn an unobservable truth, will now accept and learn from observable truth. This is why you must *become* that observable truth.

18.3 Observance happens in relationship, the very relationship that disallowed the making of a separate self. Observance is linked to cause and effect being one. What is observed is in relationship with the observer and this relationship causes an effect. Because this was part of the original choice for the physical experience, it is a natural choice to serve our new purpose of the miracle that will allow you to exist as who you are in human form. See what perfect sense this makes as your human form is an observable form. It is thus from observable form that the final learning will take place. This is the perfect example of using what you have made for a new purpose. It is the perfect ending for the desired experience, as it was the goal of the desired experience.

18.4 Expressing who you are in physical form will return remembrance to the minds of *those who observe* your expression. Further, *your observance* of your brothers and sisters will return remembrance to their minds and hearts. It is, in fact, your observance of the truth of your brothers and sisters that is the miracle we have stated as our new goal.

18.5 I repeat, your observance of the truth of your brothers and sisters *is* the miracle.

18.6 If you observe health rather than disease, abundance rather than poverty, peace rather than conflict, happiness rather than sadness—disease, poverty, conflict and sadness will be no more real to your brothers and sisters than it is to you.

18.7   A mind and heart joined in unity observes the truth where once a mind and heart separated by illusion observed illusion.

18.8   It will seem at first as if you are asked to deny the facts that you see before you in order to observe something other than what is there. You must constantly remember that your observance is now an act of worship and of devotion and that you are called to observe the truth rather than illusion no matter how real illusion may still seem to be.

18.9   In this way, you will join the mechanisms of your physical form to the new thought system of the truth. Your body, as has been often said, is a neutral form that will serve you in the manner in which you choose to have it serve you. It has always been led by your thought system. If it is no longer instructed by the thought system of illusion, it is natural to realize that it will now be instructed by the thought system of the truth. Thus your eyes will learn to observe only the truth, even unto seeing what before but seemed unobservable.

18.10   We also now link observance and ideas. Ideas form in the mind. You are used to thinking that what you observe forms outside of your mind. This is the thinking of the ego-thought system. The thought system of the truth realizes that the external world is but a reflection of the internal world. Thus you can observe with your eyes closed as easily as you can observe with your eyes open. You can *observe* by having an idea of another's health, abundance, peace, and happiness. You can observe this within yourself because it exists within your Self. What exists within you is shared by all. This is the relationship of the truth that unites all things and that must now become observable.

Chapter 19

Physical Reality

19.1   You must not fear the changes that will occur within your physical form as it begins to be guided by the thought system of the truth rather than the thought system of illusion. You will fear these changes less if you realize that all that has come of love will be kept and that all that has come of fear will fall away. You have no need to fear that the end of the special relationship will separate you from your loved ones. You have no need to fear that the joys you have shared with others will be no more. You have no more need to fear the loss of physical joys than you have to fear the loss of mental and spiritual joys.

19.2   For ages man has thought that spiritual joy diminishes physical joy. While there is no physical joy that is limited to the physical—no joy felt by the physical form alone—the joy that comes of things physical can certainly still be experienced and expressed. This is no call for judgment upon the physical. How could this be true when the physical is now called upon to serve the greatest learning humankind has ever known?

19.3   Put these fears to rest.

19.4   For ages physical reality has been linked to temptations of the human experience. Let us now dispel this link. The physical form has been blamed for choices made from lust and greed, hate and fear, vengeance and retribution. These things have always had as their cause the thought system of the ego or the bitterness of the heart. As cause and effect are one, there is no effect to be seen in physical form without a corresponding cause birthed in the ego thought system or the bitterness of the heart.

19.5   That these feelings can be "acted out" by the body and in the acting out cause harm to other bodies, is the cause for blame and fear of the body. So too is it with actions linked with survival needs.

19.6   For ages the survival needs of the body have gone unquestioned and been held tantamount. The *will* of the body to survive has thus been blamed for all actions that have arisen from real and perceived lack. Yet the body has no *will* and the survival of the true Self is not based upon it.

19.7 Because the spiritual life has so often been linked with celibacy I will mention sexual union specifically here to put behind you any fear that you may have that an end to sexual union may be called for. While some of you may have less desire for physical joining as you become more aware of unity, some may have more desire for physical joining as an expression of that union. Neither option is reason for judgment.

19.8 There is only one distinction that need be made: what comes of love and what comes of fear. All expressions of love are of maximal benefit to everyone. While you may, for a while yet, not see that all that are not expressions of love are expression of fear, I assure you this is the case. Thus any behavior, including sexual behavior that is not of love, is of fear. All that comes of fear is nothing. What this means is that cause and effect are not influenced by what comes of fear. You may still think that suffering and "bad" behavior have had great effects but they have not. At times, the love that is received following suffering, or that may arrive due to the reason of some affliction, may be seen as lessons learned from suffering or affliction; but this is no more the case than it was the case in regards to our discussion of extremes.

19.9 There is no longer any *time* to waste on such illusions. The thought system of the truth sees no value in suffering and so sees it not in truth. The thought system of the truth is a thought system that is not split by varying goals and desires. It is a thought system of unity. It is a thought system of one thought, one goal. That goal is the original thought that began the experience in physical form, the thought of expressing the Self in observable form.

19.10 Leave all blaming of the body behind and see it not as the source of temptations of the human experience. The true source of these temptations has been revealed to lie within the faulty beliefs to which the body merely responded. The body's response to the new thought system will be different in many ways, none of which will lead you to feel that you have lost anything of value to you.

19.11 While others still remain tied to the old thought system, human behavior will still reflect harmful actions that will seem to arise from bodily temptations. Although you will now represent who you are in physical form in a new way, you can still see that your actions of the past represented who you believed yourself to be. Thus those continuing to express themselves in harmful ways are deeply entrenched in false beliefs about themselves. Because they are not expressing who they are, their expressions are meaningless and have no effect *in truth* but only *in illusion*. To live in truth is to live without fear of the meaningless acts of those living *in illusion* because they will be unable to cause effect in the house of truth.

19.12 These lessons could not be taught while blame remained within your thought system. No victim is to blame for the violence done to them. No sick person is to blame for the illness within them. But you must be able to look at and see reality for what it is. Just as we are telling you that new beliefs and ideas will lead to a new reality, old beliefs and ideas led to the old reality, a reality that will still exist for some even after it changes completely for you.

19.13 This will seem even more inconsistent with a benevolent universe than it once did because of the difference between one reality and the other, a difference that couldn't be seen until it was represented in an observable manner, something you will now do.

19.14 You would think that this disparity would be divisive and extremely uncomfortable and even rage-producing for those still living in illusion. But it will be much more tempting to be divisive, uncomfortable and rage-producing for those living in the new. Many who observe the new from the house of illusion will still be able to deny what they see. Just think of how many saints and miracles you have heard of in the past without being moved to believe that they mean anything at all about the nature of who *you* are. This is why no more time can be wasted and why so many are being called in the strongest manner it is possible to call them. It is only when what is observable is so widely evident that it can no longer be denied that changes of a large scale will begin to be seen.

19.15 You will be tempted to return to the house of illusion to gather those within and bid them join you in the reality of the truth. But in this time of Christ, a *new* time, a time without parallel or comparison, this will not be possible. It has been said from the beginning that your role will not be to evangelize or to be convincing. You cannot argue the case of truth in the courtroom of illusion.

19.16 While this would seem to leave some without hope, it will leave no one
without choice. It will make the one clear and only choice evident. It is a
choice to live in truth or in illusion. There are many ways that can still be
found to come to the truth. But *a way* of getting to the truth will become
so attractive that few will be able to resist. What will make this choice so
attractive will not be martyrs and saintly souls stricken with every calamity
and yet remaining to tell those who would listen about the glory of God.
What will make this choice so attractive are ordinary people living extraordinary, and miraculous, and observable lives.

CHAPTER 20

Suffering and Observance

20.1   By saying that there is no longer any time to be wasted on illusion we are saying that you will no longer serve time but that time will serve you. Time *was* wasted on illusion and so but seemed to become a master that made of you a slave. Now time must be thought of in a new way, a way that has to do with effectiveness. Illusion has at its base a false cause and so no effects that exist in truth. Now, your every thought and action will have effect, and the choices that lie before you will be choices of where your thoughts and actions will have the *greatest* effect.

20.2   Although there was no sense to be made of concepts such as *more or less* within illusion, and although *more or less* are concepts also foreign to the truth, there is sense to be made from these concepts in regards to the *learning* of the truth. As this is all that time is for, and all that time is but a measurement of, it rightly follows that learning can take place at a slow pace or a fast pace. There is no more or less to learning in terms of knowing the truth that you have always known, but there are degrees of remembering and since this is what we work to have occur, time can become our ally by using it for effectiveness.

20.3   Again, do not let your thoughts stray to benefiting and affecting others. In unity, all others are one with you and thus what you strive for in effectiveness is your own learning. Now, rather than learning the truth, you are learning how to live by the truth. This will benefit you and in so doing benefit all others.

20.4   In "A Treatise on the Art of Thought," you were asked to request a miracle as a learning device. This learning device had two aspects. The first was to reveal to you your fears concerning the miracle so that you would learn from them. The second was to assure you that the miracle is the most effective way of convincing you of who you are.

20.5   Let us now link observation and the miracle. An easy illustration is provided, as so often is the case, by looking at observation under the guidance of the ego-thought system and thus seeing the errors of the old way in order to realize the perfect sense of the new.

20.6 Think about a situation in which you have observed the illness or suffering of another. Sympathy is the most common observance in such a circumstance. You might feel called to tears, to words that acknowledge how "bad" the illness or suffering is. You are likely to be drawn into discussions concerning how the illness or suffering can be "fought." You are likely to hear questions concerning why the illness or suffering has come to be and to hear or offer comments about the unfairness of the situation. Judgment is never far from these observations. Suffering, you would think, could not be seen as anything but "bad." You cannot feel anything but "sorry" for the one suffering. Yet you are always drawn, despite these feelings of the "badness" of the situation, to offer encouragement. If the situation is particularly grim— and realize that this too is a judgment, for some illnesses and suffering are surely seen as being worse than others—encouragement is given despite the "fact" that it is unwarranted. Yet even while you offer encouragement, you worry about giving "false" hope and wonder how realistic you should be or should assume the other to be. You look ahead, and in your mind's eye you "observe" the future as a repetition of the present or as a long war with little chance of being won. You chide yourself not to deny the facts, and you begin, along with the one whom you observe, the long walk toward death's door. All of these actions could be called your "observance" of the situation.

20.7 You do not seem to realize that all of this is happening in relationship and that the relationship is meaningful or able to cause effect. You can't imagine not feeling "bad" given such circumstances. You cannot imagine not offering sympathy. You think it naïve to believe in positive outcomes. You listen to statistics of what has occurred before and in similar situations, and you believe in what the statistics would seem to tell you. You might "thank God" for technology that would seem to offer hope, or for drugs that would ease suffering, and you might pray that God spare this one from a future seemingly already written, and think that is more realistic and even helpful than living by the laws of truth.

20.8 You will see it as quite difficult at first to respond to such situations in a new way, but all situations within the house of illusion call for the same response, the response of love to love. Why think you it is loving to believe in suffering? Do you not begin to see that in so doing you but reinforce it? What you might even call the "fact" of it? Can you not instead ask yourself what harm could be done by offering a new kind of observance?

20.9 While you need not act in ways inconsistent with compassion or even verbalize your new beliefs, you are being told directly here that no circumstance should call you to abandon them.

20.10 Your new thought system is not tied to beliefs of an "if this, then that" nature. Look at the examples all around you. People who live what you call healthy lives succumb to illnesses and accidents just as do those who live what you call unhealthy lives. "Good" people have as much calamity befall them as do "bad." I am not calling you to just another version of being good or mentally healthy, to exercises in visualization or positive thinking. I am calling you to live by the truth and to never deny it. To see no circumstance as cause to abandon it. Yes, I am providing you with means to help you know how to live by the truth, but the means are not the end and are never to be confused as such.

20.11 Miracles are not the end, but merely the means, of living by the truth. Miracles are not meant to be called upon to create specific outcomes in specific circumstances. They are meant to be lived by as the truth is meant to be lived by. Not because you desire an outcome, but because it is who you are and because you realize you can no longer be, live, or think as other than who you are in truth. This is how thorough your learning must be. It is a learning that must not change to fit the circumstances of illusion but be unchanging to fit the circumstances of the truth.

20.12 You can no longer return to the house of illusion, not even to cause explosions within it. You have stepped out of this house and are called not to return. To turn your back not on the truth nor on God or love.

20.13 Will those you love still suffer? Many may. But not with your help. Will many more, with your help, see an end to suffering? Many will. Will an end to suffering be what you work toward? No. This is not your work. This is not about your effort. This is about your observance. Your observance of the laws of love. Your observance is to remain with cause rather than to stray to effect, the manner of living practiced by those who have birthed the idea that cause and effect are one in truth.

20.14 I thank you for your strong desire to be saviors of the world and to end her suffering. I thank you for your compassion and for your desire to be of service to the world. But I call to you from peace and ask for you to remain in peace with me and let not the suffering of the world call you from it. When these things of the world threaten to call you from your peace, you must remind yourself that it is only from within the Peace of God that your wholeheartedness and our unity is accomplished.

20.15 My dear brothers and sisters in Christ, let nothing call you to return to the ways of old. They do not work! To minister to those within the house of illusion is to offer the temporary to the temporary when I call you to offer the eternal to the eternal. The new way will work wherever it finds willingness. You cannot call others to abandon their willingness to live in illusion by joining them there! You can only call others to a willingness to set illusion aside and to begin the journey home to unity. You can only call to them from unity if you are already there!

20.16 These calls go out from love to love. It is not the words of your mouth that will be heard or the language of your mind that will be responded to. It is the love within your heart that will sound the call. And when it is heard, and your brother or sister reaches out to you, all you need ask for is a little willingness. All you need do is open the door through which love can enter.

20.17 And thus we return to observance, the observance of love by love. See not what love would not have you see. Turn from the dark ways of illusion and shine the light of truth for all to see. Remain who you are and continue to live by the laws of love in every circumstance, and you bring love to every circumstance. Be neither dismayed nor discouraged by those who do not see and have no willingness to offer. Just know these aren't the ones given you to bring to love and trust that none will remain forever lost to his or her own Self.

20.18 You are as pioneers to this new world. Its mere existence will attract others and each will find the price of admission is their willingness to leave the old behind. This is a price they must freely give and it cannot be extorted from them, not from special ones of your choosing, and not from anyone. Thus you are released from a burden never meant to rest upon you even if it is one you might have freely chosen. Your task is to create the new world and make it observable, not for you to recruit others to it.

20.19 Thus, the circumstance of suffering or illness is not different but the same as every other circumstance you will encounter. You will encounter truth or illusion and nothing else for there is nothing else. There is but one call for all circumstances, the call to love from love, the call that welcomes all to live in truth.

CHAPTER 21

The Identity of the True Self

21.1 The truth is not a set of facts. Written truth is not the truth but only the arrangement of the truth into language. You have a birth certificate that states the truth about your birth. The birth certificate is not the truth but symbolic of the truth.

21.2 The truth is not symbolic. It is. It is the same for everyone.

21.3 There are no two sides to the truth. There is not more than one truth. There is one truth.

21.4 The truth is not a concept. It is real. It is *all* that is real.

21.5 Your real Self exists in truth. It does not exist in illusion.

21.6 Your personal self exists in illusion. It is called a personal self because it is attached to a person. A person is a being born into time, a being whose existence began in time and will end in time.

21.7 The only means for the personal self and the true Self to exist together is for the truth to be lived in time. In order for the truth to be lived in time you must forget your uncertainty and be certain of the truth.

21.8 This certainty is antithetical to you. You think that to believe in one truth is to deny other truths. There is only one truth. Untruth *must* now be denied.

21.9 This will sound intolerant to you. It *is* a stance intolerant of illusion. You must no longer see illusion for it is no longer there! This is how you must live with it. You must live with it as you once lived with the truth. You must find it unobservable! It must become a concept only. Illusion is a set of facts, or in other words, a set of information. These facts are subject to change and mean one thing to one person and one thing to another. Illusion is symbolic. And what's more it symbolizes nothing for it does not symbolize what is!

21.10 This is your conundrum. When you have never known what *is* you have never been able to be certain. You have no *experience* with certainty other than—and this is a crucial other than—your certainty of your own identity, the very identity this Course has disproved. This identity has been seen as your personal self. Thus your personal self is the only place in which you have experience that can now be used for a new purpose.

21.11   Even while this experience is experience of an ego-self, it is still an experience as near to certainty as you have been capable, simply because you could not exist without an identity. You might think of this as being certain of facts and information, for these are the things about yourself that few of you have doubted. Those who have had cause to doubt circumstances of their birth are often consumed with a desire to discover these unknown circumstances. For your birth, your name, the history of your family and the accumulated experiences of your lifetime are the things upon which you draw to feel the certainty you feel about your personal self. You identify yourself as male or female, married or single, homosexual or heterosexual. You might call yourselves Chinese or Lebanese or American, black or white or Indian. Your personal self may be deeply affected by these things you call yourself or may be minimally affected.

21.12   And even more so than these things, although this hasn't as often been considered as part of what makes you certain of your personal self, are the thoughts of your mind, thoughts that while certainly changeable, are unmistakably claimed to be your own in the way few things, in addition to your name and family of origin ever are. Even the most materialistic among you rarely count what you have acquired in form as part of your identity. What you have acquired that is not of form, you have, however, added to the few ideas that you hold certain. A degree earned or talent developed *is* seen as part of your identity, as part of who you are.

21.13   So too is it with beliefs. Many of you have a religious identity as well as a professional identity. Many of you have political or philosophical identities. You may call yourself Christian or doctor or Democrat. You may have beliefs you hold strongly, such as a stance against capital punishment or in favor of equal rights or environmental protection. And you may, even while recognizing, as you surely do, that these beliefs are subject to change, hold yourself to behaviors that fall within the parameters of your belief system. You think of these things as part of what make up the totality of who you are, of your personal self.

21.14   So it can be seen that there are several aspects to your personal self: a historical aspect, an aspect we will call self-image, and an aspect that has to do with beliefs.

21.15 The historical aspect is based upon your family of origin, its history, and on the life you have led since your birth. The self-image aspect is based upon your race, ethnicity, culture, body size and shape, sex and sexual preferences, and so on. The aspect that has to do with beliefs is linked to your thoughts and ideas about the world you live in and the "type" of person you feel you have chosen to be within that world. Whether you have given thought to the interconnection of these ideas you hold about yourself or not, they exist. Your worldview, and your view of your personal self, are inextricably bound together. In other words, the world you were born into, regardless that it was the same world as all other human beings were born into, is also different than that of all other human beings. And what's more, your experiences within that world are also different than the experiences of all other human beings.

21.16 All of these things have contributed to your idea that you are a separate being and as such incapable of truly understanding or knowing your brothers and sisters, those whose personal selves and world view cannot help but be different than your own—those whose thoughts are surely as distinct and separate as are your own.

21.17 Now however, you are being called to accept your true identity even while you retain the form of your personal self. As your true identity is that of a Self who exists in unity and the identity of your personal self is that of a self who exists in separation, this would seem impossible. Even while your belief system has changed and you believe that you exist in unity, all the things we have enumerated above will act to challenge these beliefs unless you are able to see them in a new light. No matter what you believe, while you have a body that is different from all the rest, a name that distinguishes you from some and yet links you with some, a nationality that separates you from other nationalities and a sex that divides you from those "opposite" you, unity will seem like a belief only.

21.18 Thus, certain things about your personal self must be accepted as aspects of your form and cease to be accepted as aspects of your identity. This will cause your existence to seem to have more of a dualistic nature for a short time while you carry observance forward into observance of your personal self. As was said at the beginning of this Treatise, by the time the learning of this Treatise is complete, the personal self will continue to exist *only* as the self you present to others. It will be a representation only. It will represent only the truth. It will no longer be seen as your identity, but as representing your identity, an identity that has nothing to do with the thoughts of a separated mind or the circumstances of the physical body.

21.19   And yet, what might seem contradictory is that I have said that we can also *use* the certainty you have felt about your identity for our new purpose, the purpose of the miracle that will allow you to exist as who you are in human form. How, you might rightly ask, can you cease to identify yourself as you always have *and* use the only identity you have been certain of for a new purpose?

21.20   The answer too will seem contradictory, for the answer lies in realizing that your former identity does not matter, even while realizing that it *will* serve your new purpose. Further, there are even two aspects to this contradictory seeming answer. One is that your *certainty* regarding the identity of your personal self will be useful as that certainty is translated to the thought system of the truth and aids you in becoming certain of your *true* identity. The second is that the very differences that you seem to have will be seen as sameness by some and will attract them to you and to the truth you now will represent.

21.21   While this has been called the time of Christ, it is obviously no longer the time of Jesus Christ. My time came and my time ended. The time when a single baby born of a virgin mother could change the world has past. The world is quite simply bigger now and the identities of your personal selves split by far more than history and far more than the oceans that separate east from west. This is why this call to return to your Self is being sounded far and wide and why it goes out to humble and ordinary people like yourself. There is no exclusivity to this call. It excludes no race nor religion nor ones of either sex or sexual preference. It but calls all to love and to live in the abundance of the truth.

21.22   In other words, it will matter not that there will be no priest or guru for those who seek the truth to turn to. It will matter not that a black man will not turn to a white man or a Muslim to a Christian. It will not matter if a young person looks to one his or her own age or turns to someone older.

And yet it will matter that someone will look at you and see that you are not so different than he or she. It will matter that someone will look at you and be drawn to the truth of him- or herself that is seen reflected there. What I am saying is that your differences can serve our purpose until differences are no longer seen. What I am saying is that you can remain confident in your personal self, knowing that your personal self will serve those you are meant to serve. What you have seen as your failings or weaknesses are as valuable as are your successes and strengths. What has separated you will also unite you.

21.23 It is not being said that anyone should, or will, remain blind to the unity that exists beyond all barriers of seeming differences such as those of race and religion. It is simply being said that they do not matter. It will not matter if a person turns to someone "like" him- or herself to find the truth, or if a person turns to someone totally "unlike" him- or herself to find the truth. As has been said many times, willingness is the starting point and as can be surely understood, where one is willing another may not be.

21.24 There is no "other" who can follow the call meant for you. No other who can give the response you are meant to give. Do not make any false plans that give your power to others more learned of this Course than you to be the savior only you can be. Do not think that only those who are more bold than you or who speak more eloquently or who are better examples of a good and saintly life are those who will lead the way for others to follow. Do not give in to the idea that one special one is needed nor give to any one a role you would not claim for yourself. No leaders and no followers are needed. This is quite obviously an old way of thinking. While no one is called to evangelize, all are called equally to represent the truth and to observance of the truth. That you each will do this in ways unique to who you are must be further addressed and seen as it relates to the relationship between the personal self and the Self; the truth and its representation and observance.

CHAPTER 22

The True Self in Observable Form

22.1 Although the entire purpose of these Treatises is to answer the question of what to do with what you have learned, chances are that this is still the primary question in your mind and heart. While you may be beginning to form ideas of what it means to live by the truth, these ideas may not seem to have much relevance or relationship to the life you currently live. While you may be happy to learn that you are not called to evangelize or even to a leadership role, you know that you are called to something and think that you as yet know not what that something is. You think that to be asked to simply "live" by the truth could not possibly be enough. You would like to know in what direction living by the truth will take you, for surely your life must change. The very precepts put forth within this Course, precepts that say that the internal affects the external, seem as evidence that you will no longer be allowed the "separate" life, or private life that you have lived.

22.2 Surely there are already those called to represent not only their true Selves but this Course to the world. If this had not been the case, you would not be taking this Course. It would not be available, and it would not be known to you. So even while I have said that no one is called to leadership and while I have surely meant this and do not call for leaders to amass followers, I do not mean to dissuade any of you who feel a call to represent this Course and the teachings of this Course with your lives and work. Those who feel this call are surely needed. And each of you will find the sharing of this Course to be among the easiest of ways to share what you have learned. You will almost certainly feel eagerness to share it and joy whenever and wherever you are able to do so. But some of you will find that you do no more than mention this Course as the one, or only one of the teachings that has led you to the truth.

22.3 You are a beautiful representation of the truth and cannot be otherwise. You may bring this beauty to any number of walks of life, to what you currently do or to something you have always dreamt of doing. Wherever you go, whatever you do, the truth will go with you. You need no uniform nor title nor specific role for this to be the case.

22.4   Since your personal self was always meant to represent the truth of who you are, the seeds of who you are, are planted there, right within the self you have always been. There has always been within you, however, a creative tension between accepting who you are and becoming who you want to be. This tension will continue if you are unable to integrate two precepts of this course of learning into your new reality. One is the often-repeated injunction to resign as your own teacher. The other is the ability to cease all acts of comparison.

22.5   The injunction that you resign as your own teacher originated in *A Course in Miracles* and was furthered here. Along with this resignation is the concept of receiving rather than planning. Your feeling that a specific role is required of you, or that you have a specific thing to do of which you need to be aware, are functions of the pattern of the planning process that once so ruled your mind. To be willing to receive instead of plan is to break the pattern of planning.

22.6   Receiving is not an inactive state, nor one familiar to most of you. While you cannot "work" at being receptive, and while I also do not ask you to "work" to break the pattern of planning, I do ask you to let it go and to replace it with observation.

22.7   Observation is the active state of reception, a state not confined to receiving, but a state of giving and receiving as one. Observation, as I am speaking of it and teaching it, makes you one with what you observe. Being one with what you observe causes you to know the proper response. It is in responding properly that you will know what to do.

22.8   Plans will only interfere with your response to what you are given to observe. The act of observation that you are able to do with your eyes closed is the observation of what is. This will relate to the future pattern of creating that we will speak of more in the next Treatise.

22.9   You are impatient now to get on to the next level, the level of something new, the level that will engage you in something "to do," the level that will give an outlet for the excitement that has been building within you. You are ready to be done with the concerns of the personal self, and your attention has begun to wander from this topic even as it is being concluded.

22.10 This has been necessary so that the realization will come to you that you are ready to leave the personal self and the concerns of the personal self behind. You have needed to become bored with what has been, tired of the way things were, uninterested in matters of a personal nature. This very readiness is what I now call your attention to as I complete this Treatise with lessons concerning observation of your new Self.

22.11 The ability to cease all acts of comparison will arise out of this observation of your new Self, for you cannot observe your new Self without observing the truth that has always existed. The truth that has always existed is our oneness, and what you will observe about your new Self you will observe about all. We will be one body, one Self. No comparison will be possible. You will realize that differences but lie in expression and representation of the truth, never in the truth itself.

22.12 I return you now to what I spoke of earlier as creative tension, the tension that exists between accepting what *is* and desiring what will be. Linking the words *creative* and *tension* is caused by the dualistic world in which you have lived, a world wherein a lag time exists between what is and what will be. You may have, upon reading those words, thought that this creative tension would not necessarily be a good thing to give up. You do not know how to reach beyond what was for what will be without this tension. You do not yet believe in what *is*.

22.13 Observation, both of yourself and of what you desire, is an act that takes place in the here and now that *is* and brings what *is* into existence. You believe that what does not appear to exist with you in the here and now is *not*, and place it in a separate category, a category that only exists in the dualistic world of illusion where here and now is separate from what will be. In the new world, the world where truth reigns, there is no cause for tension for there is no world of illusion where what *is*, is separate from what will be.

22.14 Observation of what you desire, what we have referred to as "closed eyes" observation, can be likened to prayer and thus to the miracle. This is the very miracle that closes the door of duality, and seals out the world where what *is*, is separated from what *will be* by your effort and the time that it will take you to, through your effort, create the desired outcome. Observation of what you desire is observation of what *is*, for your desire is of God and what you desire now, contrary to what you would have desired in the early stages of this Course, is the Will of God. What you desire now is the Will of God because it is your true desire, your will and God's joined as one.

22.15 Thus the creative tension can be taken from the creative act of observation without a loss of any kind. The creative tension existed not only as a product of the duality of time, but also as a product of distrust. It was a tension that existed between desire and accomplishment, the tension that told you that you might be able to achieve what you desire but that you also might not. Realize that this game of chance is a pattern of the old thought system that needs to be replaced by certainty. If you have enjoyed the game of chance, play a real game and have fun doing it. Do not bring this attitude into your new thought system or your new life. If you are tired of the old, be willing to be done with the old.

22.16 And so we conclude with this note of impatience with the old and the observation, the final observation, of the personal self. You have created your personal self, and only you can look upon this personal self with the vision of creation, creating the personal self anew, seeing within it all that will serve the new, and only what will serve the new.

22.17 Observe the personal self with one last act of love and devotion, and in so doing transform the personal self into a representation of the truth. Realize that what we have called "closed eyes" observation is really the observation of a Self beyond the personal self. To call forth observance is to call forth the sight of your true Self. To call forth the sight of your true Self is to call your true Self into observable form. Calling the true Self forth into observable form is the end of the old and the beginning of the new.

22.18 Embrace the new as the new embraces you. The new is but the truth that has always existed. Go forth and live the truth with impatience only for the truth. Hold this impatience to your Self as eagerness for the final lessons, lessons on creation of the new.

A Treatise on On The New

The Fourth Treatise

CHAPTER 1
All Are Chosen

1.1   Let me tell you what this Treatise will not be about. It will not be predictive. It will leave no one out. It will not appeal to fear nor give you cause for fear. It will not be about tools or tell you that some have the tools for accomplishment and that others do not. It will continue the view from within the embrace, an embrace and a view that is inclusive of all.

1.2   It will, however, be conclusive. It will separate truth from illusion in ways that will make some uncomfortable. It will continue to challenge your former ideas and beliefs as have the previous Treatises. But it will do this only to reach a conclusion of certainty from which you can live.

1.3   In doing so, it may seem to you as if some will be left out and as if you are being told that you can achieve what many others have tried and failed to achieve. These are the types of ideas that will cause discomfort to many of you as you still find it hard to believe in your own worthiness, and particularly in your own chosenness. It is this idea of being chosen that will cause your mind to conclude that some are not chosen now and that many were not chosen in the past.

1.4   Can you choose what is unavailable for choosing? Can you choose to own another's property? Take another's husband or wife? Choosing is not taking. Choosing implies relationship. Just as there are answers to choose between on a test, some of them correct and some of them incorrect, there are some answers that are not offered to be chosen because they do not relate to the question. All of the commandments and all of the beliefs of all of the world's religions are but related to this idea of choosing, a process of the free will with which you all are endowed.

1.5   A question has been asked and a response is awaited. Are you willing to be chosen? Are you willing to be the chosen of God? All are asked. What is your answer?

1.6   Why, you might ask, is a word such as *chosen* used, when many other words would do, and when the concept of *being chosen* is one laden with so many false ideas about exclusivity? I am using this word specifically because of the precedent of its use historically. Many different groups believe they are the chosen people of God, or Buddha, or Mohammed. Many of this generation believe they are a chosen generation. Neither way of thinking is wrong. All are chosen.

1.7   An elementary example might be useful. In many countries, all are given the opportunity to go to school. This might be as easily stated as all are chosen for schooling. Some might look at this as lack of choice, saying that anything that is mandatory allows no room for choice. In their rebellion against the mandatory nature of their chosenness or opportunity, they might easily choose not to learn. The nature of life, however, is one of learning, and if they do not learn what is taught in school, they will, by default, learn what is not taught in school. If you can consider this example with no judgment, you can see it simply as a choice.

1.8   As is clearly being seen amid many school systems in the current time, the choice to not learn what is taught in school, when taken up by many, becomes a crisis in education that calls for education to change. It may signal that what is taught is no longer relevant, or that the means of teaching what is relevant no longer works. It may be a choice made regarding means or content, a choice made from fear or made from love. But there is, in other words, no lack of choice. A choice is always made. A choice to accept or reject, say yes or say no, to learn this or to learn that, to learn now or to learn later.

1.9   There but seems to be a difference in the "educated" choice and the "uneducated" choice. Many of you may look back on choices that you made and say, "I would have chosen differently if I had but known" this or that. The choice is the way of coming to know. No choice is not such. No choice ever excludes anyone from coming to know his or her chosen lesson.

1.10   This curriculum is mandatory and so some have rebelled and will rebel against it. Those who do not choose to learn from the curriculum, will, like school children, learn through what is not of the curriculum because they have *chosen* another *means* of learning. *Means* is what is being spoken of here. But all means are for one end. All will learn the same content, for all are chosen; and all learning, no matter what the means, will eventually lead them to the truth of who they are.

1.11   The choice that lies before you now concerns what it is you would come to know. The question asked throughout this Course is if you are willing to make the choice to come to know your Self and God *now*. This is the same as being asked if you are willing to be the chosen of God. This is the same question that has been asked throughout the existence of time. Some have chosen to come to know themselves and God directly. Others have chosen to come to know themselves and God indirectly. These are the only two choices, the choices between truth and illusion, fear and love, unity and separation, now and later. What you must understand is that all choices will lead to knowledge of Self and God, as no choices are offered that are not such. All are chosen and so it could not be otherwise. But at the same time, it must be seen that your choice matters *in time*, even if all will make the same choice eventually.

1.12   As was said within "A Treatise on the Personal Self," even the house of illusion is held within the embrace of love, of God, of the truth. Does this sound exclusive to you? The embrace is inclusive. All are chosen.

1.13   And yet, as many of you have come instinctively to feel, something is different now. You are beginning to become excited by the feeling that something different is possible; that you might just be able to achieve what others have not; that this time might just be different than any other time. Even as you begin to tentatively let this excitement grow, your loyalty to your race, species, and the past, hinders your excitement. If what you are beginning to believe might be possible is possible, and has been possible, are you to look on all of those who have come before you as failures? Has the seed of the future lain dormant in the past? Could it have been activated hundreds or thousands of years ago, by countless souls more worthy than you, and ushered in the time of heaven on earth and the end of suffering long ago? Could many have been spared who weren't? How capricious this must seem in your imaginings. What a fickle universe. What a perverse God. If an end to suffering and fear has been possible, and is possible, why has it not come to be? Why has it not been known? What could possibly make you believe it could come to be now when it didn't come to be before?

1.14   The only answer might seem to lie in the laws of evolution, the slow learning and adaptive process of man. Surely this would seem a likely answer and one to assuage your guilt and uncertainty, your fear of believing in yourself and in this time as the time to end all time. There must be something different about this time, the capabilities of those existing within it. It must be your science or technology, your advanced mental abilities, or even your leisure time that has opened up this opportunity. The only alternative would seem to be that this must be simply the chosen time and you the chosen people. If the chosen time had been two thousand years ago, life would have been different since then. If Jesus Christ were the chosen one, his life would have changed the world. If the Israelites were the chosen people, so much calamity would not have befallen them. And so the idea of choice rears its head again and wraps the simple statement that All Are Chosen in confusion.

1.15   This confusion is what this Treatise will seek to dispel so that you are left with no confusion and only certainty. The only thing that will dispel this confusion and bring you the certainty that is needed to create the new world is an understanding of creation and your role within it, both as Creators and Created.

1.16   As was said within "A Treatise on the Personal Self," all notions of blame must be gone from you. Thus, you are asked not to look back with blame, for no such cause for blame exists. No cause to look back exists at all, for the truth exists in the present. This is the same as saying the truth exists within you. It is in this way that time is not real and will no longer be real to you as you come to live by the truth. It is in this way that the truth of the past still lives and that the illusion of the past never was.

1.17   The difference between this time and the time that has but seemed to have gone before has already been stated as the difference between the time of the Holy Spirit and the time of Christ. This has also been restated as the difference between the time of learning through contrast and the time of learning through observation. It is further stated here as the difference between learning by contrast and indirect communication and learning through observation and direction communication or experience. The same truth has always existed, but the choice of a means of coming to know the truth has shifted. All were chosen and all are chosen.

1.18   You have completed God's act of choosing you by choosing God. This is all the chosen people are in time—those who have chosen God as God has chosen them. That you have chosen God *and* chosen a new means of coming to know the truth—the means of Christ-consciousness, is what has ushered in the new time.

1.19   Many came to know the truth by indirect means and shared what they came to know through similarly indirect means. This is the nature of learning and of sharing in relationship. Means and end are one. Cause and effect are the same. It is these indirect means of communicating the truth that have led to your advances in science and technology, and to the refinement of your minds, hearts and senses, not the reverse. Your ancestors have done you a great service. With the means they had available—in the chosen means of a chosen consciousness united in oneness with the Holy Spirit— they passed on, indirectly, all that they came to know. This indirect means of communication is the reason for the existence of churches, and these means too have served you well.

1.20   But these indirect means of communication left much open to interpretation. Different interpretations of indirectly received truth resulted in different religions and varying sets of beliefs that, in the way of the time— the way of learning through contrast—provided contrast through dissent. The good in which one believed became the evil that another fought and in the contrast learning did occur and has continued to occur even unto this time. You have learned much of the nature of the truth by seeing what you have perceived as the contrast between good and evil.

1.21   It is the truth that you have now learned all that can be learned from this state of consciousness and that you have given your willingness to learn in a new way. The new way is here. If you are now to learn directly, you are also now to share directly. This is the way of learning in relationship. Means and end are one. Cause and effect are the same.

1.22   You have felt this shift coming and so has the world. This is the yearning we have spoken of as the proof of love's existence and of your existence in a state of unity rather than a state of separation. This yearning called you to the limits of the state of consciousness that was the time of the Holy Spirit. This limit acted upon you as a catalyst to create desire for the new. It is what has caused your growing impatience with the personal self, with acquiring all that your new learning in science and technology but seemed to offer. It is what has caused your growing desire for meaning and purpose. It is what has caused you to finally be ready to still your fear, a fear that once prevented the direct and observable learning that now is available to you.

1.23   While the state of the world and the people within it may not outwardly seem much changed from the world of your ancestors despite the advances of learning that have taken place, it is a different world. You have not known the secret yearning in the hearts of your brothers and sisters, nor have you known that it matched your own. You may have seen the acts that this yearning has driven them to and thought, incorrectly, that the new time that is here is the end of the days of innocence. You may have thought it advantageous to have once been so clearly able to see the contrast between good and evil and feel now as if these distinctions have become more and more obscure. Some have yearned for a return to days not long past, days during which distinctions between right and wrong did seem to be more certain. But the very blurring of these edges have been the forerunners, the signs of the shift in consciousness that is occurring.

1.24   All across the world, people of the world have been demanding to learn directly, through experience, and saying "no more" to the lessons of the intermediaries. What has grown in you has grown in your children and they are not only ready, but also demanding to learn through observation and direct communication or experience. Many not yet grown to maturity have been born into the time of Christ, and do not fit within the time or the consciousness of the Holy Spirit.

1.25   For a short time, an overlap is occurring during which those unable to allow themselves to become aware of the new state of consciousness are resisting it, again indirectly. Some occupy themselves with mind and spirit numbing activities in order to block it out, having chosen to die within the state of consciousness in which they have lived. Others do not wish to experience the truth directly, but only to experience experience. They are in the desperate throes of wanting to experience everything before they allow themselves to directly experience the truth, thinking still that the experience of the truth will exclude much that they would want to try before they give into its pull and settle there. But all have become aware that a new experience awaits and that they stand at the threshold of choice.

1.26   Those born into the time of Christ will settle for nothing less than the truth and will soon begin looking earnestly for it. Even the ego-self will be perceived clearly by these, and they will not want it for their identity but only will accept it until another identity is offered.

1.27   Let me repeat that during the time of the Holy Spirit, some were able to come to know themselves and God through the indirect means of this state of consciousness and to pass on what they learned through indirect means. Fewer were able to achieve a state of consciousness in which direct communication was possible, to come to know themselves and God directly, and to pass on this learning through direct means. What I am saying is that it is not impossible for those who remain unaware of the new consciousness to come to know themselves and God, and to continue to pass their learning on indirectly, or through indirect communication and contrast. But this also means that the great majority will become aware of the new state of consciousness and that learning will pass through them directly through observation and direct communication or experience. It means that the last generation born into the time of the Holy Spirit will live out their lives and that soon all who remain on earth will be those born into the time of Christ.

1.28   This is the truth of the state of the world in which you exist today.

CHAPTER 2

Shared Vision

2.1 Outward seeking is turning inward. Inward or internal discoveries are turning outward. This is a reverse, a polar reversal that is happening worldwide, externally as well as internally. It is happening. It is not predictive. I have never been and will never be predictive, for I am Christ-consciousness. Christ-consciousness is awareness of what *is*. Only an awareness of what *is*, an awareness that does not conceive of such as what was and will be can peacefully coexist with the unity that is here and now in truth.

2.2 Again let me repeat and reemphasize my statements: where once you turned outward in your seeking and saw within what you perceived without, now you turn inward and reflect what you discover within outward. What you discover within *is* in a way that what you perceive without is not.

2.3 I have always been a proponent of The Way of Christ-consciousness as The Way to Self and God.

2.4 There was no Way or path or process back to God and Self before me. It was the time of man wandering in the wilderness. I came as a representation or demonstration of The Way. This is why I have been called "The Way, The Truth and The Light." I came to show The Way to Christ-consciousness, which is The Way to God and Self. But I also came to provide an intermediary, for this is what was desired, a bridge between the human or forgotten self and the divine or remembered Self. Jesus the man was the intermediary who ushered in the time of the Holy Spirit by calling the Holy Spirit to possess the human or forgotten self with the spirit of the divine or remembered Self. Although God never abandoned the humans who seeded the Earth, the humans, in the state of the forgotten self, could not know God because of their fear. I revealed a God of Love and the Holy Spirit provided for indirect and less fearful means of communion or communication with God.

2.5 The people of the Earth, as well as all that was created, have always been the beloved of God because Love was and is the means of creation. The people of the Earth, as well as all that was created, were created through union and relationship. Creation through union and relationship is still The Way and The Way has come into the time of its fullness.

2.6   The production that has so long occupied you will now serve you as you turn your productive and reproductive instincts to the production and reproduction of relationship and union.

2.7   But before we can proceed forward, I must return to and dispel any illusion you may have of superiority over those who came before. That those who came before did not become aware of their true nature does not mean that it did not exist; that there are others living among you in this time who will not become aware of their true nature does not mean that it does not exist within them. You are no *more* accomplished than anyone has been or is or will be. The truth of who you are is *as* accomplished as the truth of all of your brothers and sisters from the beginning of time until the end of time. Any text that tells you that you or those of your kind or time are more or better than any other is not speaking the truth. This is why we began with the chosen and will return again and again to the statement that *all are chosen.*

2.8   I belabor this point because you literally cannot proceed to full awareness while ideas such as *more* and *better* remain in you. As I have said before, this is not about evolution unless you wish to speak of evolution in terms of awareness. You must realize that if you were to see into the eyes and hearts of any human from any time with true vision, you would see the accomplished Self there. There can be no judgment carried forward with you and when you continue to believe in a process of evolution that has made you better than those who came before, you are carrying judgment. While you continue to believe that being chosen means that some are not chosen, you are carrying judgment. While you continue to believe that a final judgment will separate the good from the evil, you are carrying judgment.

2.9   I also belabor this point because those of you familiar with the Bible, upon hearing words such as the end of time or the fullness of time, think of the predictions of the biblical end of time. I speak of this because it is in your awareness and because many false interpretations of this time as a time of judgment and of separating the chosen people from all others abound. All are chosen. All are chosen with love and without judgment.

2.10   The idea of separation is an idea that is not consistent with the idea of
unity. If you proceed into this new time thinking that this new time will
separate you from others, or cause you, as *the chosen*, to be separate, you will
not become fully aware of the new time. Full awareness of the new is what
this Treatise seeks to accomplish and so it is necessary to belabor these false
ideas that would keep you from this awareness. If you think you can observe
in judgment you do not understand the definition of observation provided
in "A Treatise on the Personal Self."

2.11   Being first does not mean being better. That I was the first to demonstrate what you can be does not mean I am better than you. Just as in your
sporting events, a "first" is applauded, and soon a new record replaces that
record-setting first; just as someone had to be "first" to fly a plane or land
on the moon, being first implies only that there will be a second and a third.
That attention and respect is given to those who first achieve anything of
merit is but a way of calling all others to know what they can achieve. One
may desire to best a sporting record and another to follow the first man into
space and the one who desires to best a sporting record may feel no desire
to follow the first man into space and vice versa, and yet, what one achieves
but opens the door for others and this is known to you. Even those who did
not desire to fly in a plane when this feat was first accomplished have since
flown in planes.

2.12   Similarly, those who have achieved "first place" do so realizing that the
elevated "place" they briefly hold is of a finite nature, that others will soon do
the same, and that those who follow in time will do so more easily, with less
effort, and with even greater success. They may consider themselves "better
than" for a moment in time, but those who do will be bitterly disappointed
as their moment passes. Despite the necessity for a confidence that has led
them to achieve their desired end, most who so achieve and become the first
to set records, discover, or invent the new, are not aware of themselves as
"better than" for their goal was not to be better than anyone but themselves.
Surely many desire to be "the best" as a means to glorify the ego, but few of
these succeed for the ego cannot be glorified.

2.13   Thus, you must examine your intention even now and remove from it
all ideas that were of the old way. You would not be here if you were still
interested in glorifying the ego, but you also are not yet completely certain

of your Self and in your uncertainty, still subject to the patterns of thought of the old. Many of these patterns do not concern me for they will fall away of themselves as your awareness of the new grows. But these few that I linger on will prevent your awareness of the new from growing, and so must be consciously left behind.

2.14   It is difficult for you, because of the patterns of the past, to believe that you are chosen to be the pioneers into a new time without believing that you are special. This is one of the many reasons we have worked to dispel your ideas of specialness. One of the best means for us to clarify the lack of specialness implied in the statement that all are chosen, is through your observation of yourself.

2.15   The ability to observe what the Self expresses was among the original reasons for this chosen experience. Observe now the expressions of the self you are and have been. Although you are different now than you were as a child, and different now than you were a few years ago, and different now than when you began your learning of this Course, you are not other than whom you have always been. Who you are now was there when you were a child, and there in all the years since then, and there before you began your learning of this Course. Your *awareness* of the Self that you are now was not present in the past, but you can truly now, with the devotion of the observant, see that the Self you are now was indeed present, and the truth of who you were always.

2.16   How, then, could you possibly observe any others without knowing that the truth of who they are is present even though it might seem not to be? This is the power of the devotion of the observant that you are called to, the power of cause and its effect. This is the power you now have within you, the power to observe the truth rather than illusion. This is the power to observe what *is*. This is Christ-consciousness.

2.17   I repeat, this is the power to observe what *is*. It is not about observing a potential for what could be if your brother or sister would just follow in the way that has been shown to you. It is about observing what *is*. The power to observe what *is* is what will keep you unified with your brothers and sisters rather than separating you from them. There is no power without this unity. You cannot see "others" as other than who they are and know your power. You must see as I see and see that all are chosen.

2.18   Only from this shared vision, this observation of what *is*, can you begin
to produce unity and relationship *through* unity and relationship.

2.19   This is why it has long been stated that you are not called to evangelize
or convince anyone of the merits of this course of study. This is just a course
of study. Those whom you would seek to evangelize or convince are as holy
as your Self. This holiness need only be observed. When you think in terms
of evangelizing or convincing, you think in terms of future outcome rather
than in terms of what already is. This type of thinking will not serve the new
or allow you full awareness of the new.

2.20   Can you remember this, blessed sons and daughters of the most high?
Your brothers and sisters are as holy as your Self. Holiness is the natural
harmony of all that was created as it was created.

2.21   Now I tell you something else and hope you will remember it and bid it
true. Each day is a creation and holy too. Not one day is meant to be lived
within a struggle with what it brings. The power to observe what *is* relates
to everything that exists with you, including the days that make up your life
in time and space. Observing what *is* unites you with the present in that it
unites you with what *is* rather than with what you perceive to be.

2.22   Observation of what *is*, is a natural effect of the cause of a heart and
mind joined in unity. This first joining in unity, the joining of heart and
mind, joins the physical and the spiritual world in a relationship of which
you can be more and more steadily aware. It is a new relationship. Unity
always existed. Oneness always existed. God always existed. But you separated yourself from direct awareness of your *relationship* with unity, with
oneness, and with God, just as you separated yourself from relationship
with the wholeness of the pattern of creation. You have believed in God and
perhaps in some concept of unity or oneness, but you have also denied even
the possibility of experiencing your own direct relationship with God, or
the possibility that your life is a direct experience of the pattern of unity or
oneness that is creation.

2.23   Think of this denial now, for it is still evident in the pattern of your
thinking. We have spoken of this within the text of *A Course of Love* as
your inability to realize the relationship that exists with the unseen and
even the seen. You have moved through life believing you have relationships
with family and friends and coworkers, occasionally acknowledging brief

relationships that develop with acquaintances or strangers, connections that feel real with like-minded associates for brief periods of time, but still essentially seeing yourself moving through life alone, with few sustaining connections save for special relationships, and with little purpose implied in the brief encounters you have with others. You have watched the news and developments in parts of the world far away from you and at times are aware of ecological and sociological connections, or of other occurrences that are likely to have an impact on your life or on your part of the world. But unless you believe in the ability for what happens to have an effect on you, you do not consider yourself to have a relationship with the occurrence.

2.24 With your new understanding of observance must come a new understanding of relationship and the ability of the devotion of the observant to affect those relationships.

2.25 Yet we have strayed here from the overriding point of what I have revealed to you. A *new* relationship now exists between the physical and spiritual. It is not an indirect relationship but a direct relationship. It exists and you are becoming aware of its existence. You will increasingly be unable to deny it and you will not want to. As you allow awareness of this relationship to grow in you, you will learn the lessons that are being spoken of within this Treatise.

2.26 This new relationship is the only state in which observation of what *is* can occur. The separated state was nothing more than the disjoining of heart and mind, a state in which mind attempted to know without the relationship of the heart, and so merely perceived its own creations, rather than the creations birthed in unity.

2.27 Let this idea gestate a moment within you and reveal to you the truth of which it speaks. The separated state of the mind created its own separate world. Cause and effect are one. The perceived state of separation created the perceived state of a separate world. The real state of union, returned to you through the joining of mind and heart, will now reveal to you the truth of what was created and allow you to create anew.

2.28 This state of union is what differentiated me from my brothers and sisters at the time of my life on earth. Because my state of consciousness, a state of consciousness we are calling Christ-consciousness, allowed me to exist in union and relationship with all, I could see my brothers and sisters "in Christ" or in their true nature. I saw them in union and relationship, where they saw themselves in separation. This ability to see in union and relationship is the *shared* vision to which you are called.

2.29   You have lived with the vision of the separated self for so long that you cannot imagine what *shared* vision will mean, and do not yet recognize it when you experience it. This is why you can still think of observance of what *is* as a game of make believe and feel that you will have to trick yourself into believing that you see love where there is cause for fear. You must remember that you are now called to see without judgment. To see without judgment is to see truly. You need not look for good or bad, but only need be steadily aware that you can only see in one of two ways—with love or fear.

2.30   You expect yourself to still see with the eyes of separation rather than with the shared vision of which I speak. You expect to see bodies and events moving through your days as you have in the past. And yet your vision has already changed, although you are not aware of the extent of this change. Realize now that you *have* come to recognize unity. You do not any longer see each person and event as separate, with no relation to the whole. You *are* beginning to see the connections that exist and this is the beginning.

2.31   Examine what you may have felt the onset of true vision would mean. Have you considered this question? Have you expected to see in the same way but more lovingly? Have you thought you might begin to recognize those who, like you, are joined with me in Christ-consciousness? Have you suspected that you might see in ways literally different? That you might see auras or halos, signs and clues previously unseen? Have you included other senses in your idea of sight? Have you thought your instincts will be sharpened and that you will know with an inner knowing that will aid the sight of your eyes?

2.32   All of these things are possible. But true vision is seeing relationship and union. It is the opposite of seeing with the eyes and the attitude of separation. It is seeing with an expectation first and foremost of revelation. It is believing that you exist in relationship and union with all, and that each encounter is one of union and relationship, and *purpose*—purpose that will be revealed to you because you exist in union with the Source and Cause of revelation.

2.33   Seeing with the vision of Christ-consciousness is already upon you. You are in the process of learning what it means. This Treatise is here to help you do so. Learning to see anew is the precursor of learning to create anew. Creating anew is the precursor of the coming of the new world. Remember, only from a shared vision of what *is* can you begin to produce unity and relationship *through* unity and relationship. This is your purpose now, and this the curriculum to guide you to the fulfillment of your purpose.

CHAPTER 3

Natural Vision

3.1 Observation is an extension of the embrace that in turn makes the embrace observable. The embrace is not an action so much as a state of being. Awareness of the embrace comes from the vision of which I have just begun to speak.

3.2 Observation and vision are closely linked but not the same. Observation has to do with the elevation of the personal self. Vision has to do with what cannot be elevated. Vision has to do with the divine pattern, the unity that binds all living things. Observation is the means of seeing this binding pattern in physical form.

3.3 The personal self is still in need of being elevated—elevated to its original nature—by its original nature or intent. The devotion of the observant will return you to your original purpose. The vision of Christ-consciousness will take you beyond it.

3.4 Original intent has everything to do with the nature of things for original intent is synonymous with cause. The original intent of this chosen experience was the expression of the Self of love in observable form. This original intent or cause formed the true nature of the personal self capable of being observed in relationship. The displacement of the original intent, while it did not change the original cause, formed a false nature for the personal self. This displacement of the original intent can be simply stated as the displacement of love with fear. It is as simple as that. Yet the *way* in which each of you have interpreted this displacement has come to seem quite complex.

3.5 You may not feel that you have ever intended to live in fear. But the displacement of the original intent was so complete that each life has begun with fear and proceeded from this beginning continually reacting to fear. While the original intent remained within you and caused you to attempt to express a Self of love despite your fear, fear has thwarted your every effort and caused the very effort that has continued the cycle of fear. To have to *try* to be who you are and to express who you are is the result of the displacement of the nature of love with the nature of fear. What we now are about is reversing this displacement and returning you to your true nature.

3.6   For every being there is a *natural state of being* that is joyful, effortless, and full of love. For every being existing in time there is also an *unnatural state of being.* Both states of being—the natural and the unnatural—exist in relationship. While relationship is what has kept you forever unable to be separate and alone, relationship is also what has kept you seemingly forever unable to return to your natural state of being. The fear that was birthed along with the erroneously inherited idea that it was your nature to be separate and alone and thus fearful, made relationships fearful as well. Trust became something to be earned. Even the most loving parent, like unto your most loving image of God, having brought a child into a fearful world, became subject to the tests of time. Thus did the world become a world of effort with all things in it and beyond it, including God, weighed and balanced against the idea of fear.

3.7   Now, as we reverse this set of circumstances, and replace the world of fear with a world of love, there can be no more weighing of love against fear. God did not create fear and will not be judged by it. All judgment is the cause of fear and this effort to weigh love's strength against fear's veracity. While you chose to believe and live in a world the nature of which was fear, you could not know God. You could not know God because you judged God from within the nature of fear, believing it to be your natural state.

3.8   As the natural state of love is returned to you, judgment falls away because vision will arise. With the onset of the vision of love, many of you will make one final judgment in which you find everything to be good and full of love. Once all has been judged with the vision of love, judgment is over naturally for it has served its purpose. This is the final judgment.

3.9   The vision that will arise in you now is not new. It is your natural vision, the vision of love. What *is* new is the elevation of the personal self that will be caused by the return of your natural state of love. This is where observation comes in.

3.10   Vision will allow you to see the nature of the world and all that exists within it truly. Observation will allow you to elevate the personal self to its rightful place within the nature of a world of love.

3.11   Vision is the natural *means* of knowing of all who were created in love. Observation is the natural *means* of sharing what is known in physical form.

3.12   The physical form is not the natural or original form of the created. Vision is the *means* by which the original nature of the created can once again be known. Observation is the *means* by which the original nature of the created can newly be seen in physical form. Once the original nature of the created becomes observable in physical form, physical form will surpass what it once was and become the *new* nature of the created. There is no reason why the original nature of your being cannot become a being the nature of which is form if you so choose it to be. There *is* a reason why the original nature of your being cannot exist in a form unnatural to love. A form whose nature is fear cannot house the creation of love.

3.13   Man has striven since the beginning of time to be done with the separated state of a being of form, and at the same time to hang on to life; not realizing that what exists in form does not have to be separate and alone; not realizing that what lives does not have to die. That the nature of form can change. That the nature of matter is one of change. That the nature, even of form, once returned to its natural state of love, is one of unity and everlasting life.

3.14   The idea of everlasting life in form has seemed a curse to some, a miracle to others. Death comes as destruction to some, as new life to others. Either way is but your choice. Your attachment to life has kept you alive in form. Your attachment to death has kept your form subject to the cycle of decay and rebirth. There is another alternative.

3.15   The promise of life everlasting was not an empty promise. It is a promise that has been fulfilled. It is you who have chosen the means. Now a new choice is before you.

CHAPTER 4
The Inheritance of Everlasting Life

4.1   Everywhere within your world you see the pattern of life-everlasting. Where there is a pattern of life-everlasting, there is everlasting life. Means and end are one, cause and effect the same.

4.2   The pattern of life-everlasting is one of changing form. It is one that is revealed on Earth by birth and death, decay and renewal, seasons of growth and seasons of decline. This is the pattern of creation taken to extremes. Inherent within the extreme is the balance. Even in the biblical description of creation was a day of rest spoken of. Creation balanced with rest is the pattern that has been taken to extremes within your world. You think of birth as creation and death as rest. You do not realize that your nature, and the nature of your life, like that of all around you, is governed by seasons natural to the state of love, seasons of regeneration.

4.3   In your history, generations pass, through death, to allow for new generations to be born. As your planet has reached a state of growth known as over-population, this balance between old generations and new seems necessary and even crucial. One generation *must* pass to make room for the new.

4.4   Even before the planet reached the state of over-population, this idea was much in evidence. The passing of a parent was seen, particularly historically, as the time of the child of the parent coming into his or her inheritance or time of fullness. The *power* and prestige, the earthly wealth of the parent, passed historically to the son.

4.5   This is one of the reasons that I came in the form of the "son of God." In the time in which I lived, the idea of inheritance was an even stronger idea, an idea with much more power than in current times. Inherent within the idea of inheritance was an idea of passing as well as an idea of continuity. What belonged to the Father passed to the son and thereafter belonged to the son. What was of the Father continued with the son.

4.6   What my life demonstrated was a capacity for inheritance not based upon death. My life, death and resurrection revealed the power of inheritance, the power of the Father, as one of life-giving union. I called you then and I call you now to this inheritance.

4.7   This idea of inheritance is a natural idea arising from the nature of creation itself. It is an idea of continuity that is an idea consistent with that of creation. There is no discontinuity within creation. Like begets like. Life begets life. Thus is revealed the pattern of life-everlasting.

4.8   Changing form is part of the pattern of life-everlasting. The change in the form you now occupy, the change I have spoken of as that of elevation of the personal self, is a natural part of the pattern of life-everlasting. It is long over-due. It is long over-due because you have rejected rather than accepted your inheritance.

4.9   This is why this Treatise is called "A Treatise on the New." There has not been a time on Earth in which the inheritance of God the Father was accepted, save by me. This is why this time is spoken of as the time of fullness. It is the time during which you have within your awareness the ability to come into your time of fullness by accepting the inheritance of your Father. You have the awareness and thus the ability to accept the continuity of life-everlasting.

4.10   Lest this sound like the ranting of your science fiction, and cause you to turn deaf ears to the knowledge I would impart, let me assure you that immortality is not the change of which I speak. You are not mortal, and so a word that speaks of an opposite to what you are not and have never been is not the accurate word. I do not speak of bodies living forever instead of living for what you call a lifetime…be it a lifetime of twenty or fifty or ninety years. Life has continuously been prolonged without a substantial change in the nature of life. To think of living on and on as you have lived your life thus far would not appeal to many of you. Those aged and contemplating death might wish for prolonged life, but many of these same welcome death as the end to suffering and strife. To continue on endlessly with life as it has been would only relegate more and more to lives not worth living.

4.11   What is it then, of which I speak? If you still must look ahead and see death looming on the horizon, how can it be that I speak of life-everlasting? Am I but using new words to repeat what you have heard in various forms from various religions and systems of belief for countless ages? Am I but calling you to a happy death and an after-life in heaven?

4.12 I am calling you to the new. I am calling you to transform. I am calling you to Christ-consciousness. I am calling you to everlasting consciousness even while you still abide in form. To be cognizant or aware of everlasting consciousness while you still abide in form is to be fully aware that you have life everlasting.

4.13 Being fully aware that you have life everlasting is totally different than having faith in an after-life. Faith is based upon the unknown. If the unknown were not unknown faith would not be necessary. Faith *will* become unnecessary, as life everlasting becomes *known* to you.

4.14 This knowing will come from the return of true vision. True vision sees life-everlasting where perception but saw finite life and mortal bodies. Once vision and Christ-consciousness has returned to you, the *means* of life-everlasting will be understood as a choice. Because there was no relationship save that of intermediaries between the human and the divine, there was no choice but to end the separated state in order to return to unity through death. Once the return to unity has occurred in form, the decision to continue in form or to not continue in form will be yours.

4.15 Continuity is an attribute of relationship, not of matter. It is only in the relationship of matter to the divine that matter can become divine and thus eternal. If you can abide in unity while in human form, you will have no cause, save your own choice, to leave human form. To abide in unity is to abide in your natural state, a state of life-everlasting. To abide in a state of separation is to abide in an unnatural state from which you eventually will seek release.

4.16 Although this discussion is likely to cause many of you serious doubts about the truth and applicability of this Course, this discussion is necessary to your awareness of Christ-consciousness. To believe that you are mortal is to believe that you must die to the personal self of form in order to be reborn as a true Self. This is an old way of thinking. Have we not worked throughout this Course to return your true identity to you *now*? The joining of heart and mind in relationship is the joining of the personal self with the true Self *in the reality in which you exist now*. Remember, the heart must abide in the reality where you think you are. Only through your mind's acceptance of your new reality has the heart been freed to exist in the new reality that is the state of unity and relationship.

4.17   Can you not see the necessity of removing the idea that your true Self will be returned to you only through death? What purpose would this Course serve if it were just another preview of what to expect after you die? What difference would this make to your way of living or the world in which you live?

4.18   What purpose will death serve when your true Self has joined with your physical form? You will see it simply as the transformation it has always been, the transformation from singular consciousness to Christ-consciousness. Form has been but a representation of singular consciousness. As form becomes a representation of Christ-consciousness, it will take on the nature of Christ-consciousness, of which my life was the example life. To sustain Christ-consciousness in form is creation of the new. My one example life could not sustain Christ-consciousness for those who came after me but could only be an example. What you are called to do is to, through your multitude, sustain Christ-consciousness, and thus create the union of the human and the divine as a new state of being. This union will take you beyond the goal of expressing your Self in form because this goal but reflected the desire for a temporary experience. The temporary experience has been elongated because of the appeal of the physical experience. What this Treatise is saying to you is that *if* the physical experience appeals to you, and *if* you create the union of the human and the divine as a new state of being, this choice will be eternally yours. It will be a choice of your creation, a creation devoid of fear. It will be a new choice.

CHAPTER 5

The Energy of Creation and the Body of Christ

5.1   Life-everlasting in form is not your only choice. As many of you believed that I was the Son of God and more than a man before my birth, during my lifetime and after my death and resurrection, so are you. So are all who came before me and all who came after me. All that being a Son of God means is that you represent the continuity of creation and that your fulfillment lies in the acceptance of your true inheritance.

5.2   This could as easily be stated as your being a Song of God. You are God's harmony, God's expression, God's melody. You, and all that exist with you, form the orchestra and chorus of creation. You might think of your time here as that of being apprentice musicians. You must *learn* or *relearn* what you have forgotten so that you can once again join the chorus. So that you can once again be in harmony with creation. So that you can express yourself within the relationship of unity that is the whole of the choir and the orchestra. So that you can realize your accomplishment in union and relationship. So that you can join your accomplishment with that of all others and become the body of Christ.

5.3   The many forms are made one body through Christ-consciousness. The one body is one energy given many expressions in form. The same life-force courses through all that exists in matter in the form of this energy. Awareness of this one Source of energy, and thus this one energy existing in everything, and creating the life in everything, is Christ-consciousness. It is also what we have been referring to as heart, as the center of your being. What would the center of your being be but the Source of your being?

5.4   In order for your body to live, this one Energy had to enter your form and exist where you think you are. This is the Energy of Love, the Energy of

Creation, the Source that is known as God. Since you are clearly alive, this Energy exists within you as it exists in all else that lives. It is one Energy endlessly able to materialize in an inexhaustible variety of forms. It is thus one Energy endlessly able to dematerialize and rematerialize in an inexhaustible variety of form. But form does not contain It and is not required for Its existence or expression. How could form contain God? How could form contain the Energy of Creation?

5.5   Your form does not contain your heart, or the energy of creation, or God. Your form is but an extension of this energy, a representation of it. You might think of this as a small spark of the energy that has created a living universe existing within you and uniting you to all that has been created. You are the substance of the universe. The same energy exists in the stars of the heavens and the waters of the ocean that exists in you. This energy is the form and content of the embrace. It is within you and It surrounds and It encompasses you. It is you and all who exist with you. It is the body of Christ. It is like unto what the water of the ocean is to the living matter that exists within it. The living matter that exists within the ocean has no need to search for God. It lives in God. So do you.

5.6   God can thus be seen as the All of everything and life, or the Body of Christ, as all that makes up the seemingly individual parts of the All of everything. Christ-consciousness is your awareness of this.

5.7   Just as your finger is but one part of your body, without being separate from your body, or other than your body, you are part of the body of Christ, the body of energy that makes up the universe.

5.8   And yet your finger is governed by the larger body, intricately connected to signals of the brain, to the linking muscles and bones, to the blood that flows and the heart that beats. Your finger does not act independently of the whole. You might say that your finger does not, then, have free will. It cannot express itself independently of the whole.

5.9   The same is true of you! You cannot express yourself independently of the whole! It is as impossible as it would be for the finger to do so. And yet you think that this is possible and that this is the meaning of free will. Free will does not make the impossible possible. It makes the possible probable. It is thus *probable* that you will use your free will in order to be who you are. But it is not guaranteed! It is your choice and your choice alone that is the only guarantee. This is the meaning of free will.

5.10   To align your will with the Will of God is to make the choice for Christ-consciousness, to make the choice to be aware of who you truly are. To know your Self as my brother or sister *in Christ*; to be the Body of Christ.

5.11   I am calling you to make this choice now. This is not a choice automatic to you in human form or even upon the death of your human form. When you die, you do not die to who you are or who you think you are. You do not die to choice. At the time of death you are assisted in ways not formerly possible to you in form, to make the choice to be who you are. You are shown in ways that the body's eyes were unable to see, the glory of your true nature. You are given the chance, just as you are being given the chance now, to choose your true nature with your free will.

5.12   Because you have now made a new choice, a collective choice as one body, one consciousness, to end the time of the intermediary and to begin to learn directly, you are given the same opportunity that was formerly reserved for you only after your death. It was formerly only after your death that you chose direct revelation by God. Think about this now and you will see that it is true. You hoped to live a good life and at the end of that life to know God. Your vision of the after-life was one in which God revealed Himself to you and, in that revelation, transformed you. The direct revelations that will come to you now will transform you as surely as did those that came to so many others after death.

5.13   If you have believed in any kind of after-life at all, you have perhaps thought of the after-life as having two sides. Some have thought of this as heaven and hell. Others as all or nothing. Many of you have thought of it as a time of judgment. But I tell you truly; it is no different than the time that is upon you right now. The after-life has simply been a time of increased choice because it has been a time of increased awareness. Loosed of the body and the body's limited vision, real choice has been revealed to those having experienced death. At that time it is your judgment of yourself and your ability to believe in the glory that is yours, that determines the way in which your life will continue. The same is true right now! For this is the time of Christ and thus of your ability to choose Christ-consciousness, the consciousness returned to those loosed of the body by death. Being loosed of the body by death was the chosen means of the time of the intermediary, the chosen means of attaining Christ-consciousness and direct revelation. The elevation of the personal self in this time of Christ can be the new choice.

CHAPTER 6

A New Choice

6.1   Now I ask you to consider the part you play in the creation of this all-encompassing consciousness. Your state of consciousness, be you alive or dead, asleep or awake, literally or figuratively, is a *part* of the consciousness that is Christ-consciousness. This is why you hear differing reports of the after-life from those who have experienced temporary death. It is why you hear differing words and scenarios attributed to me and other life-giving spirits, both historically and currently. What you envision, imagine, desire, hold as being possible, *is* possible, because you make it so. It is your interaction, both individually and collectively with the consciousness that is *us*, that creates probable futures rather than guaranteed futures.

6.2   The only guarantee I can offer you is the guarantee that you are who I say you are, and that I speak the truth concerning your identity and inheritance. What you choose to do with this knowledge is still up to you. What you choose to create with this knowledge is still up to you.

6.3   Those who believe that only some will be chosen can create a scenario in which it appears that some are chosen and some are not. Those who believe that life-everlasting includes life on other worlds can create a scenario in which it appears that some live on one world and some on another. But I say to you that any scenario that separates my brothers and sisters from one another and the one live-giving energy that unites us all will but continue life as it has been but in different form. The realization of unity is the binding realization that will return all, as one body, to the natural state of Christ-consciousness.

6.4   In this time of Christ, this time of direct revelation and direct sharing, the probable future you imagine, envision, desire, will be what you create. This is the power of the devotion of the observant. A *shared* vision of unity and a return of *all* to the state natural to all is what I ask you to imagine, envision and desire.

6.5   I ask you to share a vision of what *is*, the very vision of what *is* that *is* Christ-consciousness. It is a vision of the perfection of creation. It is a vision of unity and relationship in harmony. It excludes no one and no one's choice and no one's vision. Your brothers and sisters who do not choose their natural state still are who they are and holy as yourself. Your brothers and sisters who choose alternative visions are still who they are and holy as yourself. All choices are forever encompassed by the embrace. There is no wrong choice. No one is excluded. All are chosen.

6.6   There is room in the universe, dear brothers and sisters, for everyone's choice. I call you to a new choice, but not to intolerance of those who are not ready to make it. I call you to a new choice with the full realization that your choice alone will affect millions of your brothers and sisters, as long as—and this is a crucial *as long as*—you do not give in to ideas of separation and disunity.

6.7   Christ-consciousness is not a static state of beliefs anymore than singular consciousness is. Christ-consciousness is consciousness of what *is*. While consciousness of what *is* leaves not the room for error that perception leaves, it leaves open room for creation. In each moment, what *is*, while still existing in the one truth of God's law of love, can find many expressions. You can exist in Christ-consciousness, as have many others of the past, and through your existence in Christ-consciousness, affect much with what you envision, imagine and desire, in love, without changing the world and the nature of the human being any more than have those who have come before. The changes those who have existed in Christ-consciousness have wrought have been great, but they did not sustain Christ-consciousness, primarily because they were unable to share Christ-consciousness directly due to individual and collective choice.

6.8   You have the unequalled opportunity now, because you exist in the Time of Christ, to directly share Christ-consciousness and thus sustain Christ-consciousness. You can pass on the inheritance you accept in this fullness of time. In this time of unity, dedicate all thought to unity. Accept no separation. Accept all choices. Thus are all chosen in the fullness of time.

CHAPTER 7

An End to Learning

7.1   Christ-consciousness will be temporary or sustainable depending on your ability to refrain from judgment. What *is* flows from Love and knows not judgment. All that you envision, imagine, desire with love *must* be without judgment or it will be false envisioning, false imagining, false desire. This simply means *false*, or not consistent with the truth. It does not mean wrong or bad and is itself no cause for judgment. It is simply an alternative that will draw you out of Christ-consciousness and not allow it to be sustainable.

7.2   That you are living in the time of Christ does not mean that you will automatically realize Christ-consciousness, just as living in the time of the Holy Spirit did not mean that you would automatically realize the consciousness of the spirit that was your intermediary. But just as during the time of the Holy Spirit, your understanding of your Self and God grew through the indirect means that were available to you, during the time of Christ, your understanding of your Self and God cannot help but grow through the direct and observable means now available. Just as in the time of the Holy Spirit the spirit was available to all as intermediary, during the time of Christ, Christ-consciousness is available to all.

7.3   Those of you who have acquired Christ-consciousness and are now learning the vision of Christ-consciousness must realize the many choices that will seem to lie before you and your brothers and sisters in this time. The understanding of the unity that creates and sustains all living things will now be as close to the surface of consciousness as was, during the time of the Holy Spirit, the understanding that man is imbued with spirit. People, both religious and non-religious, those who consider themselves spiritual and those who consider themselves pragmatists, will hold this understanding within their grasp. Many will be surprised by experiences of unity and know not what to make of them. Those who attempt to figure them out will come ever closer to the truth by means of science, technology, and even art and literature. Those who allow themselves to experience revelation will enter Christ-consciousness.

7.4   Those who sustain Christ-consciousness will abide within it free of judgment. They will not seek to create their version of a perfect world and to force it upon others, but will abide within the perfect world that *is* in the vision of Christ-consciousness. This perfect world will be observable to them and in them. It will be revealed to them and through them. It will be revealed to them through what they can envision, imagine and desire without judgment. It will not take the effort of their bodies, but the freedom of a consciousness joined in unity, a consciousness able to envision, imagine and desire without judgment and without fear.

7.5   This is why all fear, including the fear of death, needs to be removed from you despite the radical sounding nature of life-everlasting. You cannot sustain Christ-consciousness while fear remains in you, just as you cannot sustain Christ-consciousness while judgment remains in you. Why? Because it is not in the nature of Christ, it is not in the nature of the Christ-Self to know fear or judgment. What we are speaking of is abiding in your natural state. Your natural state is one free of fear and judgment. This is all that makes up the difference between your natural state and your unnatural state. As your natural state returns to you through a heart and mind joined in unity, your body too will exist or abide within this natural state. It cannot help to, as it, just like your heart, exists in the state or reality in which you think you are. The only thing that has created an unreal reality for your heart and body has been the inability of the mind to join the truth with your conscious awareness. While your mind did not accept the truth of your identity or the reality of love without fear, it existed in a reality of fear and judgment, and bound heart and body to this reality. Your heart has now heard the appeal of this Course and worked with your mind to bring about this acceptance of the truth, a truth your heart has always known but has been unable to free you to accept without the mind's cooperation.

7.6   The mind, once released from the ego's thought system, has but to relearn the thought system of the truth. Your mind, heart, and body have joined in alignment to bring this learning about. They now exist in harmony. Your mind and heart in union have brought harmony to your body. Sustaining this harmony will keep your body in perfect health, even while the manner of this perfection of your health will remain one of many options.

7.7   You will realize that what *is* is optimal to your learning. But you will also realize that an end to your learning is in sight. Christ-consciousness and the ability to know what *is*, once it has reached a state of sustainability in you, ends your need for learning and thus ends the conditions of learning. In other words, being in harmony with poor health and learning the lesson that it has come to impart to you, will return you to good health. Your poor health is no cause for judgment, as it is the perfect health, now, in the past, and in the future, to bring you the lessons you would learn in order to return you to your Self and the unity of Christ-consciousness. The same is true of all conditions of all learning everywhere. The conditions are perfect for optimal learning. This is the nature of the universe. These conditions are perfect not only for individual learning, but for shared learning, learning in community and learning as a species.

7.8   But let me again emphasize that the conditions of learning will be no longer needed once learning has occurred. The student no longer needs to attend school once the desired curriculum is learned, *except* through their own choice. Again let me remind you that no choice is wrong. Some will choose to continue to learn through the full variety of the human experience even after it is unnecessary. Why? Because it is a choice, pure and simple. But because it is an educated choice, an enlightened choice, a free choice due to the learning that has already occurred, the choice will be one guided by love and thus be a joyous choice and ensure a joyous life. These choices will *change* the world.

7.9   But the choice many of you will make—the choice to move from learning to creating—will *create a new world*.

CHAPTER 8

To Come to Know

8.1   You are now beginning to reach the stage of understanding wherein you can realize that it was not some separate "you" or some species without form who at some point in time chose to express love in physical form, and so began this experience of human life. You are now beginning to be able to understand that it was God who made this choice. This was the Creator making a choice. Creation's response was the universe, which is an expression of God's love, an expression of God's choice, a representation of God's intent.

8.2   I say you are only now beginning to reach a stage where you can understand this, but what I really mean is that you are only now reaching a stage wherein you can know, within your inner being, that this is the truth. I say this because it is only now that you can come to know this truth without reverting to old ideas of not having had "yourself" any choice in the matter, or reverting to old ideas of blaming God for all that has ensued since this choice. I say this because only now are you beginning to be ready to hear that you and God are the same. That when I say "God made a choice" I am not saying that you did not. I am saying that a choice was made within the one mind, the one heart, and that this was your choice as well as God's choice. It was one choice made in unity. It was the choice of all for life everlasting and life ever-expressing. It was the choice for creation, for creation is the expression of love.

8.3   The heart of God is the center of the universe, as your own heart is the center of your being. The mind of God is the source of all ideas, just as "your" mind is the source of your ideas.

8.4   Let us dwell again, for just a moment before we let this dwelling in the past go forever, on what has "gone wrong" with God's expression of love.

8.5   Creation in form had a starting point. This is the nature of everything that lives in form. It has a starting point from which it grows into its time of fullness. Creation on the scale at which God creates produced the universe, or in actuality, many universes. These universes grew and changed, ebbed and flowed, materialized and dematerialized in natural cycles of the creation process that once begun was unending and thus was ever creating anew. So too is it with you.

8.6 Each expression of God's love, being of God, continued to express love through expression of its nature, which was of God. What happened in the case of human beings, was a disconnect from your own true nature, which in turn caused a disconnect in your ability to express love, which in turn caused a disconnect in your ability to know God, because you did not know yourself.

8.7 The expression of your true nature should never have been difficult, joyless, or fearful; but you cannot imagine what a creative undertaking the human being was! If you can imagine for a moment yourself as a being whose every thought became manifest, as perhaps you can envision from remembering your dreams in which anything can happen without any need for you to "do" anything, and then becoming a form where expressing yourself depended upon what you could "do" with the human body, you can imagine the learning process that ensued. If your reality had been like unto the reality you experience in dreams, can you not see that you would have to learn to breathe, to speak, to walk, much as a baby learns to do these things, and that these things were loving acts within a loving universe, a love-filled learning process. A learning process that was as known to you and chosen by you as it was by God, because you and God are one.

8.8 You might ask how, if what I'm saying is true, could God disconnect from himself? What God could not disconnect from was the true nature of the being of God, which is love. What God could not disconnect from was the true nature of creation, which is love. What God, in effect had to do, what *you* in effect had to do in order to live in a nature inconsistent with that from which God could not disconnect, was disconnect from God. Since God was the center of your being, it was impossible to disconnect your heart and still live. What could be disconnected was your will...or in other words, your mind. Just as it is your nature to breathe oxygen, and not breathing oxygen is thus inconsistent with your nature, fearfulness is inconsistent with God. Judgment is inconsistent with God. Bondage or lack of freedom is inconsistent with God.

8.9   God always knew what your mind chose to rebel against: that creation is perfect. Your mind, being of God, was constrained by the learning limits of the body and chose to rebel against the learning that was needed in order to come into the time of fullness of a being able to express itself in form, never realizing that this just delayed the learning that had to occur to release you from the limits you struggled against. The constant striving to be more and more, faster and faster—each being's yearning, passionate, excessive drive to fulfill its purpose, like a drive to explore the ocean before knowing how to swim or the drive to explore new lands while still believing the Earth to be flat—God saw and knew to be consistent with the nature of man, even while the fear and struggle that this impatience generated was inconsistent with God.

8.10   Thus, what could God then do? What does creation do with a storm arising on the horizon, growing out of atmospheric conditions perfect to generate its violence? What do you, who are parents, do with a child who is too impatient, too bright, too eager, to learn slowly and mature gracefully? Do you withdraw your love? Never. Do you disinherit? Rarely. What you do is realize the impossibility of imposing your will and, because of this impossibility, you realize that you must let go. Your decision was also God's decision.

8.11   In following in the way of God's original intent, you rebelled against God's original design, the design that is the pattern of creation. Yet your rebellion was not with God, although you came to see it as such. Your rebellion was not *allowed*, it was mutually *chosen*. Just as, as a parent, you come to see that you cannot fight a child's nature, no matter how different it might be from your own—just as in extreme cases you see that you cannot stop your child from perilous behavior save by taking away their freedom through the most extreme of measures—this is what happened between you and God.

8.12   To take away your freedom in order to protect you, even from yourself, would not have been an act of love. To take away *your* freedom would be to take away God's own freedom, the freedom of creation. Your rebellion against the constraints of your nature in form thus became part of the pattern of creation because it was the created's response. It was your response, and since God is both the Creator and the Created, it was God's response as well.

8.13   As you begin to live as both the Created and the Creator, you expand and enrich God. What other purpose would God ever have had for wanting to express the Love that is Himself in form, if it were not for the expansion and enrichment it would add to His being? What purpose is behind your own desire to do thus?

8.14   It was only the ego that made this desire seem to be for anything other than the purpose of expansion and enrichment of your being. If it is only in sharing who you are through expression of who you are that you come to know who you are, then this is true of God as well. God could not be the only being in all of creation who remains static and unchanging! How could this possibly be said of one whose name and identity is synonymous with creation? You like to think that God knows everything, and God surely knows everything that *is*. But consciousness of what *is*, the Christ-consciousness that allows you to be in communion with God, is not a static state. While consciousness of the truth is never-changing, consciousness of the truth is also ever-expanding.

8.15   Does one know love in one burst of knowing and never know more of love? Does one *grasp* beauty and thereafter remain ever unstirred by it? Is not the very essence of consciousness itself this ability to come to know continuously? To be aware constantly of what *is*, is to continuously come to know and yet to never not know.

8.16   You think of a state of knowing as a state of there being nothing you do not know about something. This is why you study subjects—so that you can come to this completion and enjoy this certainty and pride that at least you know all there is to know about this one thing. This was the ego's answer to being a learning being—choosing something to learn that it could master. Yet all that this was, was a desire to be done with learning, which is a true desire consistent with your true nature and your purpose here. To learn everything there is to know about even one subject, and to call that learning complete, is an error. If you rethink this definition you will see that even in regards to the learning of one subject it is not the truth. The only instance in which this is the truth is in regards to learning who you are.

8.17   Learning, dear brothers and sisters, does come to an end, and that end is fast approaching. Coming to know through learning will be of the past as soon as Christ-consciousness is sustainable and you begin to come to know through constant revelation of what *is*. True learning has had only one purpose—the purpose of returning you to awareness of your true identity. Be done with learning now as you accept who you truly are.

CHAPTER 9

Beyond Learning

9.1   Learning is not meant to last. This is why even this *coursework* comes to an end. It comes to an end here and now as we move past *study* and *learning* to observation, vision, and revelation.

9.2   All groups who *study* this *coursework* must also eventually come to an end. For this *end* to learning is the goal toward which we now work.

9.3   You have realized that all of your learning and studying has taken you as far as you can go. You complete your study of Christianity and go on to study Buddhism. You complete your study of Buddhism and go on to study any number of other religions, philosophies, sciences. You read books that are channeled, books that tell of personal experiences, books that promise ten steps to success. You go out in search of experiences of a mystical nature. You have tried drugs or hypnosis, meditation or work with energy. You have read and listened and been enthralled by those who have synthesized all of the great learning that has gone on so that they can tell you where it is that all these great teachings are leading. All of these learned works that speak the truth—from ancient times through current times—are learned works that have been worthy of your study. These learned works are the precursors that have shown the way to creating unity and relationship through unity and relationship.

9.4   But now the time is upon you to leave learned works behind in favor of observation, vision and revelation. Now is the time to leave behind study for imagining, envisioning, and desire. Now is the time to move out of the time of becoming who you are to the time of being who you are.

9.5   You have felt this time coming. You have realized that your learning has reached an end point. The excitement of new learning is not lasting because it is not new. You have begun to see that all messages of the truth say the same thing but in different ways. There seems to be nothing new to be said, nothing to move you beyond this point that you have reached in your understanding of the truth. All the learning that you have done seems to leave you ready to change and able to change in certain ways that make life easier or more peaceful, but certainly not able to realize the transformation that your learning has seemed to promise.

9.6   Do not accept this lack of fulfillment of a promise that has surely been made! Rejoice that the new time is here and be ready to embrace it as it embraces you!

9.7   Realize that the self-centeredness of the final stage of your learning has been necessary. Only by centering your study upon yourself have you been made ready finally to be loosed of the bounds of the personal self. This time of concentration on the self is unheralded in history. It is what has been needed. Be grateful to all of the forerunners of the new who have been courageous enough to call you to examine yourself. Be grateful to yourself that you have had the courage to listen and to learn and to study what these forerunners of the new, these prophets of the new have called you to learn. Be appreciative of every tool that has advanced your progress. But now be willing to leave them behind.

9.8   These have been the last of the intermediaries, these called to a wisdom beyond their personal capacity. Now these forerunners of the new, along with you, are called to step beyond what they have learned to what can only be revealed. These are my beloved, along with you, and this an entreaty meant especially for them.

9.9   You who have provided a service cherished by God, and who have risen in the esteem of your brothers and sisters, be beacons now to the new. You who have gained so much through your learning and your study and your sharing of the same may find it difficult to leave it behind. A choice made by you to stay with learning rather than to move beyond it would be an understandable choice, but you are needed now. Needed to help establish the covenant of the new. Be not afraid, for the glory that has been yours will be as nothing to the glory that awaits you in the creation of the new. You will always be honored for what you have done. But do you want this to be forever the cause of your honor? Be willing to be the forerunners still, to join your brothers and sisters in this next phase of the journey, the journey out of the time of learning that will usher in the fullness of time.

CHAPTER 10

Creating Anew

10.1 This Course has led you through resigning as your own teacher, to becoming a true student, and to now leading you beyond the time of being a student to the realization of your accomplishment. You were once comfortable being your own teacher. You willingly gave up this role and became comfortable in the true role of learner. You are now asked to be willing to give up the role of learner and to believe that you will become comfortable and more in your new role as the accomplished.

10.2 This is hard for you to imagine because as you consider your willingness to give up learning you will meet resistance and realize, for perhaps the first time, that learning is what your entire life has been about. You cannot imagine how you will come to know anything new, or be anything beyond that which you now are, without learning. Your thoughts might stray to ideas about experiencing, rather than studying, and yet you will quickly see that you merely think of experience as learning through a different means than studying.

10.3 As you have advanced along your self-centered path of learning, you have come to see everything in your life as exactly what it has been…a means of learning. You have encountered problems and wondered what lessons they have come to teach you. You have encountered illness and wondered what learning the illness has come to bring you. You have learned anew from your past. Learned from your dreams. Learned from art and music. In all of these things you have viewed yourself as the learner. You may not have *studied* your problems, illness, your past, your dreams, or art and music as you *studied* the lessons that kept you focused on your Self, but you did, in a sense, study every aspect of your life for the lessons contained therein. So how, you might ask, do you quit now, doing what you have so long done?

10.4 In keeping with your new self-centered focus on what life has had to teach you, you have also seen your relationships as teachers. It is here that you can begin to learn to let go of learning because it is here that learning has been least practiced through the means of studying.

10.5   Relationship happens in the present moment. Studying takes up residence within the student; there to be mulled over, committed to memory, integrated into new behaviors. Relationship recognizes that love is the greatest teacher. Studying places the power of the teacher in a place other than that of love. Relationship happens as it happens. Studying is about future outcome. What happens in relationship has present moment meaning. What is studied has potential meaning.

10.6   The outcome of learning or what is studied is the production of things and perceived meaning.

10.7   What we work toward now is to advance from learning and producing *things* and *perceived meaning,* to producing unity and relationship through unity and relationship.

10.8   The *learning* that was applied to anything other than the Self could not help but have an outcome that had to do with other than the Self. Means and end are one, cause and effect the same. Thus this applied learning produced things and perceived meaning.

10.9   The learning you have accomplished in regards to your Self could not help but have an outcome that had to do with your Self. Means and end are one, cause and effect the same. Thus this accomplished learning produced unity and relationship through unity and relationship with the Self.

10.10   The first accomplishment of your learning about your Self was the return of unity and relationship to your mind and heart. This returned to you your ability to recognize or identify your Self, as other than a separate being, and led the way to your recognition of the state of union. From this recognition of unity and relationship the production of unity and relationship and true meaning will be revealed.

10.11   Learning has had to do with what is perceived. *No longer learning* has to do with what is revealed. Learning has had to do with what is unknown. *No longer learning* has to do with what is and can only be known through revelation. Learning has had to do with supplying a lack. *No longer learning* has to do with the realization that there is no lack. Learning was what was necessary in order to allow you to fulfill the desired experience of expressing the Self of love in form. *No longer learning* is the revelation that the time of accomplishment is upon you and the expression of the Self of love in form is what you are now ready to do. Learning was what was necessary in order to know who you are and how to express who you are. *No longer learning,* or being accomplished, is synonymous with knowing who you are and the ability to express who you are in truth.

10.12 Expression of the Self of love in form is not something that can be learned. It is something that can only be lived. This is the time of the fulfillment of the lesson of the birds of the air who neither sow nor reap but sing a song of gladness. Expression of the Self of love is the natural state of being of those who have moved beyond learning to creating through unity and relationship.

10.13 As I said earlier, some will not be willing to move out of the time of learning. Those who have learned what this Course would teach but do not move beyond the state of learning will change the world. They will make the world a better place and see many of their students advance beyond what they can teach and to the state of leaving learning behind.

10.14 Those of you willing to leave learning behind will create the new. This will not happen through learning but through sharing. You can learn to change the world, but not how to create a new world. Does this not make sense? You can learn about who you were and who others were, but you cannot learn anymore who you are or who those are who have joined you in Christ-consciousness, for you have become who you are and move on from this starting point to creating who you are anew in unity and relationship. You can learn from the past but not from the future. When you build upon what you can learn you build upon the past and create not the future but an extension of the past. You who are called to leave learning behind are called to return to your union and relationship with God wherein you are creators along with God.

CHAPTER 11

The End of Learning and the Sustainability of Christ-Consciousness

11.1 The future is yet to be created. This is why I stated at the onset of this Treatise that this Treatise would not be predictive. Many predictions of the future have been made, and many of them have been called prophecy. But the future is yet to be created.

11.2 The future depends on you who are willing to leave learning behind and who are willing to accept your new roles as creators of the new—creators of the future.

11.3 Can I teach you to do this? My dear brothers and sisters in Christ, as you once willingly resigned as your own teacher, I now willingly resign as your teacher. In unity there is no need for teachers or for learners. There is need only for the sustainability of Christ-consciousness in which we exist together as creators in unity and relationship.

11.4 Thus I will conclude this Treatise with a prelude to the sharing that is our new means of communicating and creating, a sharing that replaces learning with what is beyond learning. I conclude this Treatise by sharing that which will assist you in sustaining Christ-consciousness.

11.5 As I do so, I bid you to read these words in a new way. You are no longer a learner here and what I reveal to you must be regarded as the equal sharing between brothers and sisters in Christ, the sharing of fellow creators in unity and relationship. This is the beginning of our co-creation. Do not seek for me to impart knowledge to you in these concluding words. Absorb the following pages as a memory returned to your reunited heart and mind. No longer regard me as an authority to whom you turn, but as an equal partner in the creation of the future through the sustainability of Christ-consciousness.

CHAPTER 12

A Prelude to The Dialogues

12.1   Welcome, my new brothers and sisters in Christ, to the creation of the future through the sustainability of Christ-consciousness. Today we join together to birth the new.

12.2   From this time on, I will respond to you through direct communication or dialogue rather than through teaching. As with all new means of doing anything, this dialogue must have a starting point. This is it.

12.3   At this time, there is a gathering of pioneers of the new already in existence. They are beginning to see that they learn as one. They are beginning to see that their questions are the same. They are beginning to see that they share in means not confined to the physical senses.

12.4   This prelude will address them individually and collectively, and as you join with them in unity, you will realize that it also addresses you individually and as part of the collectivity of the whole. This dialogue will, however, be ongoing, and this is your invitation to participate in this dialogue. No matter where you are, no matter what concerns you still hold within your heart, no matter what questions are emanating from your mind, they will be met with a response.

12.5   Two changes of enormous proportions are upon you. The first is the end of learning, the ramifications of which will only slowly occur to your mind and be surprising revelations there. The second is the beginning of sharing in unity, a change that your heart will gladly accept but that your mind, once again, will be continuously surprised to encounter.

12.6   Take delight in these surprises. Laugh and be joyous. You no longer have a need to figure things out. Surprises cannot be figured out! They are meant to be joyous gifts being constantly revealed. Gifts that need only be received and responded to.

12.7   Once these dialogues are sustainable without need of the written word, the written word will be less necessary. In the meantime, let me explain why these written words are not the acts of an intermediary and why they represent direct learning.

12.8 The simple and complete explanation of the non-intermediary nature of this dialogue is that it exists in unity. It is given and received in unity. Intermediary steps were needed only for the separate state. All conditions that were intermediary in nature during the time of learning, are, during the time of sharing, naturally converted to direct experiences of sharing.

12.9 Thus, if you have been religious, abandon not your churches, for you will find within them now, direct experiences of sharing. If you have found guidance and comfort in the written word, abandon not the written word, for the written word will now elicit direct experiences of sharing. If you have enjoyed learning through gatherings of students, gather still, and experience sharing directly. If a time arrives when you no longer feel drawn to these modes of sharing, share anew in ever-wider configurations.

12.10 All you must remember now is that the time of learning is past. While you are still encountering concerns and questions, you will be prone to continue to think of yourself as a learning being. While these dialogues continue to address these same questions and concerns, you will be prone to think of them as teaching dialogues and to consider yourself still a student. Considering yourself thus is simply a condition of the old for which you will need to be vigilant. You will be again surprised, however, to find what an enormous difference the release of this idea will make in your capacity to express who you are. As long as you continue to invite learning, you will continue to invite the *conditions* of learning. These are the conditions you have experienced throughout your lifetime and have expressed a willingness to leave behind. Only you can leave these conditions behind. The only way to do so is to, for a short while, be vigilant of your thought patterns so that you eradicate the idea of learning in separation and replace it with the idea of sharing in unity. Learning is a condition of the separated self, which is why it is no longer needed. You will not fully realize unity while you continue to hang on to this condition of the separation.

12.11 Another thing that you will want to be vigilant of, dear brothers and sisters, is the learned wisdom of the past. Let me give you an example that relates to the state of rebellion that was discussed within the text of this Treatise.

12.12 This example arose from one of those already gathered who was questioning the state of contentment. She quoted a learned priest and scholar who spoke of how he knew, as soon as he was content within the life of the monastery, that it was time to once again move out into the world. What he was really saying was that he saw the dawning of his contentment as the sign that one period of learning was over and that it was time to move on to the next. During the time of learning, this statement was consistent with learned wisdom. During the new time of sharing, there is no "next phase" of learning for you to move on to. There is no reason for you not to exist in continual contentment. Continual contentment will not stunt your growth or prevent you from sharing or from expressing yourself anew.

12.13 Is this not a good example of the *learned wisdom* that needs to be left behind? But what of the questions its raises? Do you not respond to the idea of continual contentment with doubt? Not only doubt that it can be continual but with doubt that you would desire it to be? These questions relate to our earlier discussion of temptations of the human experience. Are you willing to leave them behind? Are you willing, for instance, to leave behind the idea that contentment cannot and *should* not last? That lasting contentment, like unto a lasting peace, would somehow stunt your growth? Can you see that your idea of growth was synonymous with your idea of learning? That you were always both awaiting and dreading your next learning challenge?

12.14 Why was this so? You eagerly awaited each learning challenge in the hopes that it would bring you to the state in which you now abide! You dreaded each learning challenge because you feared that it would not bring you to this state and that you would continue to need to learn, and to perhaps suffer from, the conditions of learning!

12.15 You have arrived! The long journey that brought you here is over. Grow not impatient or desirous of a return to journeying before you begin to experience the joy of sharing and the new challenges of creating the new! This will be joyous journeying and your challenges will be joyous challenges!

12.16 The state of rebellion was the effect of the cause of learned wisdom. It became part of the nature of the human experience by becoming so consistent within you that it came, through the passing down of the human experience, to be integral to your nature. Have you not always been told and seen examples of man pushing against his limits? Has not this pushing against limits been called progress? Have not even the most devastating misuses of power attained through this rebellion been seen retrospectively as having advanced the cause of man's evolution and society's knowledge?

12.17 This is just a beginning point of your ability to see what learned wisdom has wrought. This is a necessary end point of your review of your experience here so that you do not continue to advance learned wisdom. Learned wisdom will tell you to work hard. Learned wisdom will tell you that the strong survive, the mighty prevail, the weak shall perish. I attempted to dislodge much of this learned wisdom during my time on Earth and man is still puzzling over the meaning of my words. The time for puzzlement is over. Pass on no more of the prevailing learned wisdom. I told you once we would create a new language and thus we shall! We are creators of the new and we must start somewhere. Why not here?

12.18 Think and speak no more of the suffering of the past. Spread the joyous news! Tell only joyous stories. Advance the idea of joyous challenges that allow for all the creativity you have put into challenges of the past but without the struggle. Let not the idea of struggle take hold in the new. Let not the idea of fear take hold in the new. Let not the idea of judgment take hold in the new. Announce far and wide freedom from the old ideas, the learned wisdom of old. What could be more invigorating, more challenging, more stimulating to your enrichment, than throwing out the old and beginning again? And doing so without effort, without struggle. What could be more looked forward to than the chance to create the new through sharing in unity and relationship with your brothers and sisters in Christ?

12.19 I know you still have questions, dear brothers and sisters. I know that you will experience times of not knowing how to proceed. I know that you will occasionally have setbacks and choose the conditions of learning instead of sharing in unity in order to realize some bit of knowledge that you feel is necessary before you can go on. But I ask you to try to remember to turn to the new rather than the old each time you think you are experiencing uncertainty or lack.

12.20 The only thing that is going to hold you back from your ability to sustain Christ-consciousness is doubt about yourself. You must constantly remember that doubt about yourself is fear, and reject the instinct, so engrained into your singular consciousness, to let doubt of yourself take hold of you. Even though you are abiding now in the state of Christ-consciousness, the *pattern* of the old thoughts will continue until they are replaced by a new pattern. That self-doubt arises in your thought patterns will not mean that you have cause for self-doubt. You have no cause for self-doubt because you have no cause for fear. To dwell in fear will end your ability to dwell within the love that is Christ-consciousness. As there is no longer any cause for self-doubt there are no *reasons* for self-doubt. Do not examine yourself for reasons for self-doubt when it arises. The self-centeredness of the final stage of learning is over.

12.21 Your "centeredness" must now be focused on sharing in unity and relationship, and thus creating anew in unity and relationship. Along with the creation of a new language, another imperative creation with which to begin our new work is that of new patterns. The patterns of old were patterns designed for the optimal benefit of learning. These patterns were created by the one mind and heart that you share in unity with God. The new patterns of sharing in unity and relationship and thus creating unity and relationship are only now being created by the one mind and heart that you share in unity with God. You will be the co-creator of the new pattern of consciousness that is sharing in unity and relationship, as you were once the co-creator of the pattern of consciousness that was learning.

12.22 Again let me remind you that we are speaking of the new. There has always been a state of consciousness that we are here calling Christ-consciousness. There has never been a sustained Christ-consciousness in form. The Christ-consciousness that has always existed, a consciousness of what *is*, is an all-inclusive consciousness, the consciousness of the embrace. It is not a learned state, as was the singular consciousness of the human form. It is your innate consciousness, a consciousness far too vast to be learned but one easily shared by all.

12.23 In other words, you, as a being of singular consciousness, could learn the thought patterns of a singular consciousness because it was a finite consciousness, a consciousness with limits. You, as a being joined in Christ-consciousness, must share this consciousness *in order* to know it. It cannot be grasped by the singular consciousness. You could think of this as something which, were it integrated into the thought processes of the singular brain, would cause brain damage, because it would cause an overload of information. The singular consciousness would act like a computer with a full drive and reject the information or be overcome by it if such were possible. Such is not possible, because Christ-consciousness is not available to the separated self. Christ-consciousness is the consciousness of unity for unity is what *is*.

12.24 You now exist within a shared consciousness. The pattern of a shared consciousness is one of sharing in unity and relationship. There is no pattern within it for learning (which is individual), for individual gain, or for individual accomplishment.

12.25 But realize, those of you who would mourn this as a loss, that you have already achieved all that was possible to achieve as an individual. The purpose of individual learning was the return of unity! Pause a moment here, and celebrate this feat of the personal self! The personal self, through the self-centeredness of the final stages of learning, has achieved the ultimate achievement possible! Let yourself be grateful for the learning you have achieved. Celebrate this graduation, this anointing, this passage. And leave it behind. Realize that it has made you new. Rejoice and be glad and turn your attention to the new. Attend to the dawning of the consciousness of unity. Realize that it is a truly *new* state, a state that cannot be learned, a state the awareness of which can only be revealed to you through unity and relationship.

12.26 Realize this without fear, for I am with you. This is akin to being stranded in a foreign land with none of the ways you learned how to adapt in the past being of service to you. That is how new this is—and more. But the difference is that you are not alone and that you are not in a foreign land but returned to your home of origin. What you cannot learn you can remember. What you cannot learn will simply be known through sharing.

12.27 It is the *way* in which you will come to remember and share in unity that concerns you now and what we are speaking of when we talk of patterns. There was a pattern to the process of learning that was shared by all learners and inherent to your natures. The means were different for each, but the pattern was the same. There was an overall design that ensured optimal learning and that design was known to you in the pattern of that design, a pattern that was part of the pattern of your thoughts, even after the ego came to rule your thought system. Without this pattern, the ego could have succeeded in becoming the ruler of the personal self. Part of this design and pattern was the freedom of free will.

12.28 Free will continues in the pattern of Christ-consciousness. Love continues. The individual or singular consciousness that was appropriate to the time of learning does not continue. Thus the new pattern is one of creation in relationship and unity rather than learning. What this means will be revealed to you and shared by all who abide within Christ-consciousness because you abide in a consciousness of unity through your choice.

12.29 You do not have to choose to share, because you cannot *not* share. You do not have to continually choose unity, because you have already chosen unity and abide there. You do, however, have to refrain from choosing separation. You do have to refrain from choosing learning and the conditions of learning.

12.30 What will help you to remain doubt-free and thus fear-free and continually able to sustain Christ-consciousness, is coming to know the new design, and the new patterns that reveal the design. This new design, and the new patterns that will be helpful to you in its sustainability, are what must be created through our sharing in unity and be communicated through our continuing dialogues with one another.

12.31 This is a prelude to but one form of these dialogues. Sharing in unity is automatic. It is the nature of Christ-consciousness. Once you have adapted to this nature you will realize that what is communicated through our dialogues and those you share with your brothers and sisters, is simply communication of what already *is*. This will help you to adapt to the revelations that replace learning. This will help you to adapt to the truth of a sharing you will have received even before it is communicated through the means to which you are accustomed. It will help us together to establish the new patterns by which you and those who come after you, will more fully come to awareness of all they have inherited and all it is within their power to create.

12.32 I do not have the answers that would continue to make of me a teacher and you a student. The answers to the elevation of the personal self and the living of Christ-consciousness in form are yet to be revealed and shared. This is the time that is before us, the time of creation of the future, the time of the creation of a future not based upon the past.

12.33 This time is before *us*. Because you are a being still existing in form, you still exist in the realm of time and space. Yet time and space no longer separate us, and the creation of the design or pattern that reveals our lack of separation is part of the creation that is before *us*. It will be mutually decided through the coming revelations and our responses to the revelations of the new.

12.34 Creation of the new has begun. We are an interactive part of this creative act of a loving Creator. Creation is a dialogue. Creation—which is God and us in unity—will respond to our responses. Will respond to what we envision, imagine and desire. Creation of the new could not begin without you. Your willingness for the new, a willingness that included the leaving behind of the old, a willingness that included the leaving behind of fear and judgment and a separate will, was necessary to begin creation of the new. Your former willingness to accept the old but kept creation's power harnessed to the old. Does this not make perfect sense when you realize that creation, like God, is not "other than" who you are? How could creation proceed on to the new without you?

12.35 What will the future hold? It is up to us dear brothers and sisters. It is up to us acting as one body, one mind, one heart. It is up to us creating as one body, one mind, one heart. Because it is the new future of a new form joined in unity and relationship, the only guarantees that are known to us is that it will be a future of love, a future without fear, a future with unlimited freedom. For what more could we ask? And what more could be asked of us?

12.36 Make no mistake that what is asked of us is everything. What is asked is our total willingness to abandon the old, our total willingness to embrace the new. But also make no mistake that what is given to us is everything. All the power of creation is released onto us. Let us begin.

The Dialogues
of A Course of Love

Book Three

CHAPTER 1

Acceptance of the State of Grace of the Newly Identified Child of God

1.1   Dear Brothers and Sisters in Christ,

1.2   I come to you today as co-Creator of the Self you are and the Self you hope to represent with your physical form. I come to you today not as a personal self who is "other" than you, but as a divine Self who is the same as you. In our union we bear the sameness of the Son of God. In going forth with the vision of unity you become as I was during life. You "receive" and you "give" from the well of the spirit. You need not prepare or plan, you need only to claim your inheritance, your gifts, your Self.

1.3   What this means in practical terms is that you let the personal self step back and the true Self step forward. Realize that all of your "concerns" are still for the personal self, a self whom you continue to believe can fail to fulfill or live your mission and your purpose. You "see" this failure occurring through ineptness speech, through inappropriateness of attire, through lack of physical stamina, through lack of intelligence—through lack, in other words, of abilities of the personal self. As long as you "see" such visions, you "see" the pattern of the personal self going forth much as it did before. You do not "see" the new, the new Self of elevated form or the true Self of divine union. You "see" the separated self still "trying," still "struggling," still fumbling along. You do not see the natural grace and order of the universe extending into the realm of the elevated Self, the space of the elevated Self. As long as you see in this way, you keep the personal self in the forefront rather than allowing and aiding the personal self in the stepping back that is required in order for the true Self to step forward.

1.4   All of this confusion and struggle is occurring because you do not know what to do to prepare. You have not been convinced that you are done preparing as you are done with learning. You still want to figure out what to do, what comes next, what you need to learn, how to better "prepare" for what is ahead.

1.5 And yet you know that you have been prepared by me, and that in union with me you cannot fail. You cannot fail to be prepared, for you are already accomplished. What will it now take for your mind to accept this truth? For the mind's acceptance of this truth is what is needed.

1.6 Your heart knows the reality of this truth, knows that this new reality is real and different from the reality of old. Ideally, mind and heart in union together accept this new reality and, with this acceptance, the heart is freed to dwell in the house of the Lord, the new world, the Kingdom that has *already* been prepared and so needs no preparation.

1.7 This acceptance is crucial to the elevation of the personal self. Without this acceptance the personal self must still struggle and try, prepare and plan. It does not know how to do otherwise. You do not think you know how to do otherwise.

1.8 This is the final surrender. The surrender of the control of the personal self. Even with the ego gone, the personal self can continue to move about within the world, a faceless and nameless entity, a being without an identity, humble and selfless and ineffective. For there must be cause to engender effect.

1.9 These anti-ego tendencies are a real danger in this time. You are not called to selflessness but to *Self*!

1.10 This is the transition you have felt yourself to be in. The ego is gone but the true Self has not been allowed as yet to dwell within the personal self, thus elevating the personal self. You have thus been self-less for a time and the personal self has floundered from this lack of identity. A person could literally die during this time from lack of identity, lack of cause. To die to the personal self is not what is required any longer as we work instead to elevate the personal self. This elevation occurs through the acceptance of your true identity, not through being identity-less. The reign of the ego began during just such a time of identity-less-ness. You cannot go on in such a way.

1.11 Help is here. Be what you have been called to be. Open your dwelling place to your true Self, your true identity. Imagine this opening and this replacement occurring with every fiber of your being. Imagine the separate self being enfolded, embraced, and finally consumed—taken into the Self of union. The body of Christ becomes real through this indwelling of Christ in form.

1.12   This thought makes you worry about the identity of the one you have called yourself. This has been the purpose of many renaming ceremonies that symbolize the release of the old and the acceptance of the *new*. This occurs in one form or another in the sacraments you have known as Baptism, Confirmation, and Marriage. Each of these invite a new *identity*. So, too, do we invite a new identity now. While these sacraments have largely lost their meaning, the sacrament I now call you to restores meaning. Since new names are only symbols of new identities, renaming is not required or expected here. We go beyond what can be symbolized to what can only be known within. It is to this state of grace that I call you now, today: The state of grace of the newly identified child of God.

1.13   Open your heart, for the one who dwells there in union with all will emerge from this opening. What was once a tiny pinprick of light becomes a beacon as you open your heart and allow your true identity to be what *is*, even within your form. You *are* in grace and union with the Source and Cause of unity. Be no longer causeless. You and your Source are one.

1.14   *I am no longer the personal self who was separate and alone.*
I am my Christ Self.
I dwell in unity.
My identity is certain.
This is the truth.

I am not less than I once was, but more.
Where once I was empty, I now am full.
Where once I dwelt in darkness
I now dwell in the light.
Where once I had forgotten
Now I remember who I Am.

Now I go forth
To live as who I Am within the world
To make cause and effect as one, and
Union with the Source of love and all creation the reality.

1.15   These Dialogues are for everyone because we exist in unity with everyone. No one will be forced to join our conversation. Only those listening will be ready to hear. Only those ready to hear will listen. Remember that you cannot be taught what unity would freely give. The goal is no longer learning. The goal is accepting the identity that has always been yours and that has newly been revealed and returned to your remembrance. To "know" and not accept what you "know" to be the truth is a continuation of the pattern of insanity that must be replaced with a pattern of sanity.

1.16   Insanity is acting as if the truth is not the truth. Sanity is accepting the truth as your reality and acting from that truth. Once the truth has been learned, the nature of untruth remains only as an acceptance of insanity. What I will help you now to do is to reject this insanity and to accept the perfect sanity of the truth.

1.17   This cannot be done through learning, for as you have been told, learning was the means of the separated self's return to unity. These lessons have been given. They can be reviewed and reviewed again. They can be used as continuing lessons until you feel that learning is fully accomplished. They can serve as reminders as you continue to become the Self you have learned that you are. But further learning is not what will complete the transformation of the personal self to the elevated Self. Learning will not sustain Christ-consciousness.

1.18   So what is it that we will now do? If I do not teach, and you do not learn, what is our continuing means for completing this transformation? As you have been shown, this will not occur by means of preparation but by means of acceptance. This will not occur by means of trying but by means of surrender.

1.19   As you begin this Dialogue, questions naturally arise. You might think that for the receiver, or transcriber, of this Dialogue, this Dialogue may, in truth, feel like a dialogue, an exchange, a conversation, and wonder how you, as a reader of these words, can feel that same way. You can feel that same way by realizing that you are, as you read these words, as much a "receiver" of this Dialogue as she who first hears these words and transfers them to paper.

1.20   Is a piece of music not received by you even when you may be one of thousands or millions who hear it? Does it matter who is first to hear the music? This is, in truth, a dialogue between me and you. Wish not that the "way" of the transcriber of these words were the way for everyone, and think not that to hear "directly" from the Source is different than what you do here. This is thinking with the mindset of separation rather than the mindset of unity. What I say to you here, I say to *you*. It matters not that I say these same words to many, for you and the many who join you in receiving these words are one.

1.21   These Dialogues begin with prayer to remind you of what you have learned in unity, a learning that has been different from all learning you but thought you accomplished as a separated self. You have achieved an incredible feat by allowing and accepting the state of unity even though you could not learn how to do so. This has been the difficulty with every curriculum that has sought to teach the truth. In order for the truth to be truly learned, you first had to enter a state in which this learning could occur, a state that could not be taught but only accessed through your longing and desire.

1.22   You who have joined mind and heart in unity have returned to a natural state of knowing in which learning is no longer needed. You have now come upon a curriculum that is impossible to learn. No teacher is available for none is needed. And yet many of you still feel what you would describe as a need for continued learning and a continuing relationship with a teacher who will guide you through the application of what you have learned. You dare not, as yet, to turn to your own heart, and trust the knowing that has been returned to you as you begin to live in the reality of the truth.

1.23   This is akin to thinking of a god who exists outside or apart from yourself. If you fully accepted your true identity, you would no longer look outside of yourself for guidance for you would realize that your Self is all there is. We are one body, one Christ. We are one Self.

1.24   Your Self is not the person you have been since birth. Your body does not contain you. What you are going to find happening, as you accept your true identity, is a transference of purpose concerning your body. What once you saw as yourself, you now must come to see only as a *representation* of your Self. You *are* everything and everyone. All that you see *is* you. You stand not separate and apart from anything.

1.25   We are one body.

1.26   Learning accepts that there are those separate from you who know things that you know not. This is not the case. When you fully accept this, you will see that it is true. Like the acceptance of unity that could not be taught, but was the condition for learning, acceptance of your true identity cannot be taught but is the condition necessary for being who you are and the realization that learning is no longer necessary.

1.27   Thus we work now toward acceptance of what you have learned in unity. We work towards your acceptance of sanity and your rejection of insanity. We work together in love and unity for what can only be received in the love and unity in which we truly exist together, as one body, one Christ, one Self.

CHAPTER 2

Acceptance and Denial

2.1   You are now asked to do two things simultaneously: To accept the new and to deny the old. Acceptance is a willingness to receive. Obviously, when you consider this definition of acceptance, you will see that this is not the way of the old. Willingness to receive is quite contrary to the attitudes and actions with which you have led your life thus far. You were told within *A Course of Love* that willingness was all that was necessary for you to be able to take this Course into your heart and let it return you to your true identity. Those of you who found within this willingness an ability to receive and left behind your effort to "learn" this Course, began the work that is being continued here, the work of replacing the old patterns of learning with the new pattern of acceptance.

2.2   To deny is to *refuse* to accept as true or right that which you know is not true or right. This is the denial of insanity in favor of the acceptance of sanity, the denial of the false for the acceptance of the true. Although you are called to these two actions simultaneously—the action of acceptance and the action of denial—it can thus be seen that they are, in truth, one and the same action, just as means and end, cause and effect are one. You are asked to accept or receive the truth of who you are and the revelations that will show you how to live as who you are within the world—and you are asked to *refuse* to accept who you are *not* and the ways of life that allowed you to live within the world as a false self.

2.3   The patterns of the new will begin to arise naturally when you deny the patterns of the old. As you have been told, you now "know what you do" and are no longer a victim to the circumstance of a split mind that allowed the confusion that led me to once say, "They know not what they do." You must understand that you do know, and you will know, as soon as the patterns of old have been denied. Denial is the correct word here, for I do not want you combating or resisting the old patterns. Patterns are not in quite the same category as the false remembering you were able to purge through unlearning.

2.4   Patterns are both learned systems and systems of design. The pattern of learning was a pattern of divine design, created in unity and cooperation to enable the return to unity. This pattern has achieved its desired end and so is no longer needed nor appropriate. While it was once a pattern whose design was perfect for the desired end, continuation of this pattern will but interfere with your full acceptance of who you are in truth.

2.5   An example of a pattern whose design was perfect for the desired end is that of formal education. Education has a natural endpoint. When the education of a doctor, teacher, scientist, priest, or engineer is completed, it is time for the student to claim a new *identity*—that of doctor, teacher, scientist, priest or engineer—and to begin to live that new identity. To continue to feel a need to learn rather than realizing that the time of learning has come to an end, would be to not realize *completion*.

2.6   In the example used here, an example that illustrates only one aspect of the learner's life, an inability to claim the new identity could at times be acceptable and even appropriate. In regard to the learning that you have now completed, learning that has revealed the true nature of who you are, your inability to realize your *completion* and claim your new identity cannot be seen as acceptable or appropriate.

2.7   This is not a judgment but simply the truth. To learn the truth and not accept it is different from learning what is necessary for a career. To learn the truth and not accept the truth is insane. To learn the truth and not accept the *completion* of your learning is insane.

2.8   If you do not realize that you have learned all that you need to learn, you will retain the consciousness of the separated self rather than sustaining Christ-consciousness.

2.9   It is because the patterns of old have at times provided you with a false certainty that they are difficult to deny. When we speak of denying here, we speak of denying yourself the *use* of the old so that the new can *serve* you. We speak of denying modes of learning in favor of simple acceptance of what *is*.

2.10   It is proper now to deny the modes of learning, even when they seemed to work for you in the past. That they seemed to work is the illusion that will give way as you deny yourself access to the old so that the *new* can come.

2.11   If you will examine this pattern of what you have believed "works for you," you will find that you believe that each and every pattern will work in one instance and not in another and that you make this judgment based upon the outcome. In other words, you make this judgment "after the fact" when the outcome has occurred. For example, study habits that allowed the learner to achieve a successful grade or outcome in one instance would tend to be seen as a "successful pattern," and would be repeated until such a time as the pattern failed to achieve the successful grade or outcome in another instance. Thus what you have believed "works for you" is really like a game of chance. You give it a try, and if the outcome is as you desired it to be you call it a success, and if the outcome is not as you desired it to be you call it a failure. You admit that what you thought would work did not work.

2.12   This will not often prevent you from trying the same thing again although at times it will. No matter what you try, however, it is based on this concept of trial and error. No sure results are counted on. When a pattern of thought or behavior has been found to work in more cases than not, it is clung to as a "sure thing"—a proven pattern or way.

2.13   What is seen as not "working for you" are often those matters that are beyond your personal control and so patterns of personal control have become particularly entrenched. Thus have you learned ideas such as "when all else fails, plain old hard work will see you through," or that "safety is the absence of risk taking," or that "information is power."

2.14   Many of you have believed that the more details of life you have within your control, the more likely you are to control outcome. Others of you have believed that the more details of your life that are kept under the control of a benevolent system, such as that of government, the more likely you are to experience desired outcomes. Either way, control is seen as a powerful pattern.

2.15   Although they may not have seemed so, all patterns have had to do with learning because you were, as a separated self, a being whose only function was learning. The function of all learning was to return you to your true identity. Because we are working now for the integration of your true identity into the self of form, or the elevation of the personal self, new patterns are needed.

2.16   Systems are the result of your attempts to externalize patterns. Patterns are contained within. Looking at the patterns you have attempted to externalize can help you to understand the nature of patterns.

2.17   The justice system is a good example, an example of a system which you believe works most of the time, and are happy to use to acquire a desired end, but which, when it does not provide the solutions you might have desired, becomes a system you would rail against. You might consider that no "system" is foolproof, and still be willing to accept the bad with the good; but you would freely admit that your belief in any system "working for you" is not total.

2.18   Any system that is not foolproof is based on a faulty design, a faulty pattern. Your misperceptions of the world have allowed for the development of no foolproof systems because these systems are based upon misperceptions or illusion. Your desire to cling to systems that are not foolproof is insane, for their creation is based on the workings of a split mind and a split mind does not think clearly.

2.19   All systems have been based upon your desire to understand the world *around* you rather than the world *within* you. If you were to understand the world *within*, you would need no systems to understand or manage the world *without*. These systems were attempts to learn the nature of who you are through external means—the means of learning the nature of the world around you. Thus, in the example of the justice system, you looked at the world and people around you and found the nature of both to be hostile. From this faulty conclusion you developed a faulty system based upon faulty judgment. This system was meant to help you learn to deal fairly with a hostile environment and then to develop a pattern based on what was learned so that learning would not need to be endlessly repeated. Now these systems and patterns have become so entrenched that no new learning is seen as possible or desirable even though the systems and patterns are known not to work. In truth, no new learning or new systems based on the learning patterns of old will work. Thus we begin anew.

2.20   The seeming difficulty with this new beginning stems from your desire to learn anew. You would say, "If the justice system doesn't work, let's fix it." You would say, "If the old way doesn't work, teach me a new way." You would say, "I will work hard to learn and to implement the new if you will just tell me what that new way is!" You would say, "Teach me the new pattern and I will put it into effect."

2.21   What this points out is a pattern in itself. It is a pattern of reaction rather than cause. It is a pattern of looking without and wondering what to do about what you see rather than a pattern of changing what you see by looking within.

2.22   Within is where the real world and all your brothers and sisters exist in the unity of Christ-consciousness. Change within effects change without, not the other way around! Within is where you look to your own heart, rather than to any other authority, for advice or guidance. Within is where you find the knowing of Christ-consciousness, the consciousness of unity. Within is where you find the power of creation, the power to create the patterns of the new. Looking within is not an attempt to find the answers of the personal self of old, the separated self who depended on learned wisdom for answers. Looking within is turning to the real Self and the consciousness shared by all for the creation of a new answer, the answer to the only remaining question; that of how to sustain Christ-consciousness in form.

2.23   This is the agreement God asks of you, your part of the shared agreement that will fulfill the promises of your inheritance. This is the Covenant of the New in which you honor your agreement to bring heaven to earth and to *usher in* the reign of Christ. To *usher in* is to show the way, to cast your palms upon the path of your brothers and sisters. Do you not see that your acceptance of this promise is the acceptance of your own promise? Do you not see that acceptance of the new and denial of the old is the necessary forerunner of our work together in establishing the Covenant of the New?

CHAPTER 3

The Covenant of the New

3.1   The Covenant of the New is simply our agreement to proceed together on the palm-strewn path of Christ-consciousness. It is a path upon which joy triumphs over sorrow and victory triumphs over defeat. All that it requires is the acceptance of the new and the denial of the old that will allow for the sustainability of Christ-consciousness in form.

3.2   My dear brothers and sisters in Christ, this is the call you have heard for as long as you can remember, the call you have heard as often as you have grown still and listened. It is the one beautiful note, the tolling of the bell of the Lord, your invitation to return home. This call has always sounded. It is not a death knell but a call to life. It is not of the past or the future but of the eternal now. It is within you as we speak, the tone and timbre of this dialogue.

3.3   It calls to you and asks you to invest your life with the very purpose you have always desired. You are not purposeless now. Your life is not meaningless. You are the ushers, the pioneers of the new. Your work, as will be often repeated, is to accept the new, and deny or refuse to accept the old. Only in this way will the new triumph over the old.

3.4   I have purposefully used words such as *victory* and *triumph*, words unusual to the body of this work but words that will become usual in our normal conversation in this dialogue. I use them as I use together the words *accept* and *deny*. As the old must be denied for the new to come into being, the old must be vanquished in order for the truth to triumph over illusion.

3.5   As the wholehearted, you have it within your ability to do what those who live their lives with a split mind could never do. You have it within your ability to mend the rift of duality, a state that was necessary for the learning of the separated self but that is no longer necessary. The mending of the rift between heart and mind returned you to your Self. In the same way, the mending of the rift of duality will return the world to its Self. The mending of the rift of duality was accomplished in you when you joined mind and heart and returned to the oneness and unity of Christ-conscious-ness. Sustaining Christ-consciousness will accomplish the same thing in your world.

3.6   Duality and contrast are synonymous. In the time of the Holy Spirit, you learned through contrast. You learned from the contrast of good and evil, weak and strong, right and wrong. You learned from the contrast of love and fear, sickness and health, life and death. In this time of Christ, such learning is no longer necessary, and so these conditions of learning are no longer necessary. Thus one of your first acts of acceptance is the acceptance of the end of the conditions of learning. This does not mean, however, that you accept goodness and deny evil or even that you accept love and deny fear. How can this be?

3.7   Our first action in understanding what we are called together to do is to begin to declassify all the various aspects of life that were needed in the time of learning. This is why we began quite truthfully and simply with an acceptance of the new and denial of the old. This is as far as acceptance and denial need go. For if you give credence to the ideas of contrast, you bring those ideas forward with you into the new. We let the old go, and with it all ideas of contrast and opposites, of conflict and opposing forces. This is all that is needed for the new to triumph over the old. There are no battles needed, no victories hard won through might and struggle. This is what is meant by surrender. We achieve victory now through surrender, an active and total acceptance of what is given.

3.8   Let us talk again for a moment of the idea of giving and receiving as one that was introduced within *A Course of Love* and taught quite thoroughly in A Treatise on Unity and Its Recognition. Let's talk of this now as an idea, rather than as something learned, and as an idea for you to carry forward with you into the new. This is the first of many ideas that were previously taught that I would like to talk of in a new way. These are ideas that address your true nature as a being existing in union, and this is why we call them ideas to carry forward. These are new ideas to you because you have recently learned them and through the art of thought begun to integrate them into the elevated Self of form. These are really not new ideas, however, but rather ideas of who you truly are birthed within the self of form so that the Self and the elevated Self of form are able to work with ideas birthed from the same source.

3.9   Ideas of who you truly are, birthed by the wholehearted self in union with all, are the ideas that will allow new patterns to emerge and the design of the future to be created. These are the ideas that replace the learned concepts we leave behind.

3.10   You will notice that all of these ideas have in common a quality of oneness. Oneness replaces duality or contrast. You will be seeking now for replacements for that which formerly ordered your life. Thus we will speak of these replacements.

3.11   That giving and receiving are one in truth is best understood by taking away the idea of one who gives and one who receives. If all are one, such ideas make no sense. This would seem to make the idea of giving and receiving as one senseless as well. In a way, this is true. Giving and receiving as one is senseless in terms related to a shared consciousness. Giving and receiving as one is not senseless, however, when that shared consciousness is occupying form.

3.12   All ideas leave not their source, thus giving and receiving is an idea, as are all ideas, that exists apart from form. Giving and receiving are thus one within the shared consciousness of unity, which is the same as saying giving and receiving are one in truth. A shared consciousness is the truth of who you are. The elevation of the personal self, however, requires that this giving and receiving as one be shared in form. Yet the elevated form, which now represents the shared consciousness of the Self, is not separate from the shared consciousness. Thus giving and receiving as one is now the nature of the elevated Self of form, and what we work toward through this dialogue is your full awareness of what this means.

3.13   Helping you to achieve full awareness of who you are is different than helping you to learn. As was said before, you know what you need to know. What we seek to achieve through this dialogue is acceptance and awareness of what you know. Acceptance is easily achieved through willingness. Full awareness *in form* of what has previously been hidden by the mists of illusion is the more challenging task.

3.14   Giving and receiving as one has become one in form as well as one in idea. What this means, simply stated once again, is that giving and receiving occur in unison, or in union. There is no "time" in which giving and receiving seem to be separate actions. There is no "time" in which giving and receiving is not occurring. Giving and receiving as one thus simply describes the nature of the new, the nature of shared consciousness.

3.15   What might this mean to the elevated Self of form? Using this dialogue as an example will serve to explain. This dialogue is continuous and ongoing. It *is* giving and receiving as one. It is merely represented by the words on this page and the words on this page are but a representation of what is continuously being shared. So too is it with you. You, as the elevated Self of form, are a continual representation of what is continuously being given and received, what is continuously being shared. You are a representation, for instance, of this dialogue. You are a representation of all of your brothers and sisters in Christ. You are a representation of the truth. You are a representation of all that is given and received in truth. You are a representation of creation. A representation of union. You are a representation of the Self.

3.16   As the Self, you are giver and receiver. Your Self is a full participant in this dialogue. You as the Self *are* the truth. You as the Self *are* the creator and the created. You as the Self are union itself. This is what awareness is about. Consciousness has to do with that of which you are aware. To know what you now know, and remain aware only of the reality of the separated self, would not sustain Christ-consciousness in form.

3.17   This is why I will often repeat that I am no longer your teacher. You must realize your oneness with me and all that was created and you cannot do so while you think of me as teacher and yourself as student. While you think of yourself as a learning being you will still be looking to something or someone "other" than your Self rather than seeking the awareness that exists within.

3.18   This is not meant to convey any division between the Self and the elevated Self of form, but to demonstrate that there is a difference *in form* between the Self and the elevated Self of form. The Self was and will always remain more than the body. The body, however, is also newly the Self. The body is also, newly, one body, one Christ.

3.19   It is this difference that exists between the Self and the elevated Self of form that make of us creators of the new, because the elevated Self of form is new. The Self is eternal. Your Self of elevated form is newly birthed, just as I was once newly birthed even though my Self was eternal. One of the major things we will be seeing as we proceed is the difference between form and content and the difference in the way separate forms express content. It will be challenging to become aware that different expressions do not make different. These differences were spoken of within this Course as unique expressions of the selfsame love that exists in all.

3.20   As the system of nature supports the life of many different trees, the trees are all still of one life-giving and life-supporting system. Can this be said of any of the systems you have developed as a learning being? Are your systems life-giving and life-supporting? The patterns of the new will create only such life-giving and life-supporting systems—as long as the patterns of the new are accepted and lived with your full awareness.

3.21   Now I realize that this is just the first step revealed and that many of you will feel already as if you are being asked to learn again and not only that, but as if I have presented you with a concept difficult to learn. What you need remember now is that your separated self already learned this concept of giving and receiving, and that for the elevated Self of form it is simply a shared quality of oneness. It is not in need of learning or even understanding. It *is*. Awareness of what *is*, is a quality of Christ-consciousness. Thus you are already aware of the truth of giving and receiving being one. This awareness exists within you and you cannot any longer claim to be unaware of it through non-acceptance of what is.

3.22   These are your ideas as well as mine. They are the ideas of your brothers and sisters as much as they are of God. I am teaching you nothing, nothing old and nothing new. I am reminding you of what you know as I have reminded you of your identity.

3.23   What this portion of the dialogue attempts to do is to give you a language to support what you already know, and are already aware of, so that you are more comfortable with letting what you know serve you in your creation of the new. All—*all*—that you need in order to create the new is available within you. The power of the universe is given and received constantly in support of the creation of the new. This is what creation is! The entire universe, the All of All, giving and receiving as one. This is *our* power. And *our* power is needed for the creation of the Covenant of the New in this time of Christ.

CHAPTER 4

The New You

4.1   This Covenant is the fulfillment of the agreement between you and God. The agreement is for you to *be* the *new*. As you are new, so too is God, for you are one, if not the same. As you are new, so too is the world, for you are one, if not the same. As you are new, so are your brothers and sisters, for they, too, are one, if not the same.

4.2   While not the same, you also are not different. The differences you saw during the time of learning, differences that made you feel as if each being stood separate and alone, you are now called to see no more. In unity you are whole and inseparable, one living organism now raised above the level of the organism as you become aware of unity of form.

4.3   It is time now for this idea to be accepted, for if it is not, you will remain in the prison you have created.

4.4   Prison is an excellent example of a system you created with your faulty perception. As with all systems, it reflects an inward state and shows you what becomes of all of those who see not what it means to be neither different nor the same but to be one.

4.5   For the moment, disregard any idea you may have of there being those who deserve the prison system you have developed and any arguments you would cite about the heinous crimes of some. Think instead of prison simply becoming a way of life for those who are incarcerated there. Each of you has had an imprisoned personal self. Each of you who have entered Christ-consciousness has had the cell door and the prison gate thrown open and a new world offered. If you do not "accept" this opportunity, you remain incarcerated in a system that tells you when you will awaken, how you will spend your day and when you will retire. You remain at the mercy of those who are incarcerated along with you. You remain at the mercy of those who would have power over you, and you remain subject to the laws of man.

4.6   I tell you truthfully that until you are living as who you are and are doing what you love, you are in prison. This prison is as much of your own making as are the actual prison systems that developed when shape and form was given to what you fear and what you believe will protect you.

4.7   Just as an actual prisoner, when released from prison, must adjust to a life in which his or her actions are no longer restricted artificially, you must adjust to your new freedom. Your life has been artificially restricted by the prison you have created of it, and the actual prison system merely mirrors this restriction on a grand scale for all to see and look upon with dread. For most, the prison system is a very successful deterrent. The thought of time in prison fills the mind with fear. And yet those who are imprisoned often become so acclimated to prison life, that life on the "outside" is no longer seen as desirable. How can this be?

4.8   A life of artificial structure is all any of you have known. An internally structured life will quickly replace the life of the inmate if you will but let it do so. Even those who actually are incarcerated in the prison system you have made are free to follow an internally structured life to a greater extent than many of those who call themselves free.

4.9   Your prison was created by the separated thoughts of the separated thought "system." Systems, as you may recall, are the result of your attempts to externalize the patterns contained within. Patterns are both of learning and of design.

4.10   Let's look at each of these terms separately so that we see the nature of existence in the same way and speak the same language while discussing it.

4.11   Let us begin by coming to agreement about the idea of divine design. This divine design could also be called creation, and where we have spoken of creation previously, divine design was also spoken of. Here I am quite confident that you have either seen and learned enough during your time as a learning being that you accept that a divine design created the universe and all that is in it, or that you trust enough in the wisdom of your heart, that you know that this is so. Either way, you may still *believe* in a divine design without accepting that a divine design exists and that you are part of it. Remember that our goal here is to deny the old and accept the new. In this case, the old you would deny is the idea of a purposeless existence, a universe with no divine order, a life in which you are at the mercy of fate.

The new idea you are asked to accept is that existence is purposeful, that the universe exists in divine order, and that your life is part of that divine design.

4.12   Divine patterns are the patterns that made your existence in form possible as well as the patterns that have made your return to your true identity possible. These patterns are both external and internal. External divine patterns include the observable forms that make up your world, everything from the planet on which you exist to the stars in the sky, from the body you seem to inhabit to the animal and plant life that exists around you. From the daintiest and most intricately laced snowflake to the stem of a plant to the workings of the human brain, a divine pattern is evident and should not be beyond your belief. Despite the differences in what you see, think, and feel, there is but one external divine pattern that created the observable world, and only one internal divine pattern that created the internal world. The internal divine pattern was that of learning.

4.13   The two patterns, the internal and the external, were created together to exist in a complementary fashion. Both of these divine patterns are being newly re-created and we will talk much more of them and of the creative time we are now entering. Thus far, we are merely working together to create a pattern of acceptance to replace the pattern of learning.

4.14   Systems of thought are both divinely inspired and products of the separated self. The idea of giving and receiving as one might be thought of as a divinely inspired system of thought. In such a way of thinking, one would take the internal thought pattern, enhance it with the external pattern, and by seeing the unity and cooperation of all, understand and live according to the system of thought of giving and receiving being one. Systems of thought are thus the foundation upon which how you live arises. The truth is a system of thought. It exists in wholeness and has always been available.

4.15   Systems of thought that arose from the separated self are those you have accepted as the truth. Some of these systems of thought were part of the divine pattern. Contrast is one such system. As a learning being, you accepted that you learned through contrast, knowing that contrast was provided for your learning. It was upon the foundation of this and other thought systems that your perception developed. Through contrast, you identified and classified the world around you based upon the differences, or contrast that you saw.

4.16   Other systems of thought were not part of the divine pattern. The ego is one such system. It may seem peculiar to think of the ego as a system, and we have heretofore referred to both the ego and to the ego's thought system, but the ego is quite rightly seen as a system in and of itself. It is thought externalized and given an identity you but falsely believed to be yourself. From this one externalized thought pattern came most of your false ideas, ideas that made it difficult even for the divinely inspired thought systems to provide the learning they were designed to impart. Such is the case with the system of learning through contrast, since when the ego entered with its false ideas and judgment, contrast did not always provide the lessons it was meant to provide. In addition, believing the ego had become an externalized self took you, the true Self and the true learner, out of the learning loop. Obviously these systems, built as they were upon patterns now being recreated, are part of the old.

4.17   Externalized patterns, or systems, were also built from the systems of thought that have been your foundation, the basic building blocks of what you have seen as reality. As such, these systems too are obviously of the old.

4.18   Just as obviously, all we are left with is divine design. All we are left with is what was given: A divine universe, a divine existence. That divine universe, our divine existence, is now recreating the patterns that served the time of learning. What was learned in the instant in which you came to know your Self is all that learning was for. Let us not dwell any longer on why this has taken so long or on the suffering that occurred during the time of learning. This would be like dwelling on the inmate's life as an inmate once he has been freed. Let us simply create a new structure around the new pattern of acceptance, a structure that will provide you with the home on Earth you have so long sought and used your faulty systems to but attempt to replicate.

4.19   I speak of structure here not as a thing—not as a building in which to dwell or as a set of rules or instructions to follow in order to build the new— but as structure that will provide you with parameters in which to begin to experience your new freedom. It is your questions and concerns that have led me to speak of such, for it is you who have felt such as this is needed. The unlimited freedom offered you is too vast for your comfort. Thus without limiting this freedom at all, let us simply speak of a place and a way to begin to experience it, and of a place and a way to begin to create the new.

4.20 This place and this way begins at the prison doors, begins, as we said earlier, with acceptance of the new and denial of the old. Turn your back on the prison of your former existence and do not look at it again. Do not long for its old structure or the false security you came to feel at times within it. Do not look for a new structure with barred windows and doors to keep you safe. Do not seek someone to tell you anew what to do with who you are now that you are no longer a prisoner. Do not give keys to a new jailer and ask to be taken care of in exchange for your newfound freedom.

4.21 Instead see the world anew and rejoice in it, just as you would have had you literally spent your life within a prison's walls. Breathe the sweet air of freedom. Be aware constantly of the sky above your head and desire no more ceilings to shield you from it.

4.22 Beware of gifts offered in exchange for your newfound freedom. A hungry ex-prisoner may soon come to feel the three meals a day provided in the prison were gifts indeed. So too are the gifts many of you have desired and still feel as if you need. If you have imprisoned yourself in order to earn a living by doing work that brings you no joy and allows you not to be who you are, then you are called to walk away. If you are tempted by a relationship in which you cannot be fully yourself because of the security it will provide, you are but tempted by a false security, and are called to turn away. If you are lured away from who you are by a drive to succeed, if you fear doing what you want to do because you might fail, if you follow another's path and seek not your own, then you have imprisoned yourself for the "three meals a day" of the old way.

4.23 What has this to do with structure and parameters? Everything. You cannot deny the old and remain in the prison of the old. You have asked, and because you have asked I am telling you, that the permission you seek must come from your own heart and from your commitment to the Covenant of the New. Once again I remind you that there is no authority to whom you can turn. But in place of that "outside" authority, I give you your own authority, an authority you must claim in order for it to be your own. An authority you must claim before your externally structured life can become an internally structured life.

4.24 Let this acceptance of your own internal authority be your first "act" of acceptance rather than learning. Turn to this as the new pattern and to the thought system of giving and receiving as one. Let the authority of the new be given and received. Become the author of your own life. Live it as you feel called to live it.

4.25 We cannot build the new upon prison walls of old. Whatever imprisons you must now be left behind.

4.26 Those of you now protesting having heard what you have so longed to hear, protest no more. You cannot keep your prison and have the new life that you long to have. You may have to examine just what it is that imprisons you. You may find that it is attitude more so than circumstance, or you may feel as if the walls that imprison you are so sturdy and so long barred that they may as well be prison walls. You may even be a prisoner in truth, and wonder how, save a grand escape, you can proceed. But I tell you truthfully, your release is at hand and it will come from your own authority and no place else. It is up to you to accept that your release is possible, to desire it without fear, to call it into being.

4.27 Do you not see that you must begin with yourself? That if you are unwilling to claim your freedom it will not claim you?

4.28 What is one, or in union with all, draws from the well of divine design. You need not turn to old patterns or systems to accomplish your release. You can only turn to what *is*, to what is left now that the patterns and systems of learning are no longer.

4.29 You accept that what has been given is available. You accept and you receive. You realize that the first order of creation of the new is restoration of the original order, or original design. As you have been returned to your Self, now your life must be returned to where it fits within the divine design, to where it is a life of meaning and purpose. This return is the return of wholeness. This return is not selfish on your part, but magnanimous. It returns wholeness to you and wholeness to the divine design. It returns creation to what it is.

4.30 Understand—this cannot be fearful. This cannot fail. This will not bring suffering but will end suffering. Your part is to invite it and accept it when it comes. State your willingness, accept the coming of your release, and prepare to leave your prison behind. Invite this simply by inviting what brings you joy. Invite yourself first to this new world, but leave not your brothers and sisters behind. Invite them too. For those who are imprisoned are one with you, and need but your release to find their own.

4.31   Dear brothers and sisters in Christ, I hear your protests and the reasons that you feel must prevent you from the acceptance I call you to. Yet as you fully accept that your right to your inheritance, your right to be who you are, and your commitment to the Covenant of the New, are one and the same, these reasons will disappear. All the *different* reasons you would cite become what they are—*one* reason, the *same* reason—and you will see that what is one is neither the same nor different. You will see that there is *one* answer, an answer different for everyone and yet the same for everyone. That answer is acceptance of your Self. That answer is acceptance of the new you.

CHAPTER 5

True Representation

5.1   Within this Course your "imitation" of creation was often spoken of. This was about your ability to "remember" much of creation in a non-cognitive, intuitive way. It was also about the minor distortions that occurred between this non-cognitive memory and how you acted upon it, distortions that created major departures from the nature of creation.

5.2   These distortions occurred as you assigned meaning or "truth" to things, truly believing in your ability to do so. You thus determined what the world around you was meant to represent. It was in much the same way that the ego came to represent you.

5.3   What we are doing now is returning the world to its true representation. As was said in A Treatise on the Personal Self, there is a huge difference between a true representation and a false representation. While the false representation of the ego self led to the world you see, it did not change the truth but only created illusion. Thus the truth is still available to be seen.

5.4   The world without was created as a true representation of the world within, and as you become aware of the truth represented in all that encompasses and surrounds you, the boundaries between the inner and outer world will diminish and eventually cease to be.

5.5   Let me provide you with an example that illustrates how one aspect of what was created in the pattern of learning, while not being seen in the way it was intended, still represents what *is* and thus contains all meaning or the truth.

5.6   When two bodies join and joy results from this joining, this is form mimicking content—form representing what "is." The form was created in order to show—to teach—that joining is the way. Think of the word *desire* and its association with sex. To desire someone is to desire joining. This desire was created to remind you...to point the way...to your true desire for your true identity as a being joined in oneness. This seeking of completion through oneness, this joining, is a true representation that shows you that completion does not come of standing alone but of joining, as love does not come alone but in relationship.

5.7   You have determined sex to be the ultimate fulfillment of love and called it "making love." If it were painful rather than pleasurable, if you did not lose yourself and experience completion, you would not desire it. Sex, experienced for this pleasure and completion, regardless of emotional attachment or non-attachment, still would produce the desired effect of creating desire for oneness if you truly saw and understood the body and its acts as representative of truth. You have thought the things you do represent your drives, but they simply represent what was given to help you remember and return to who you truly are.

5.8   Obviously—as you have been told that the ego has represented a false self—it is possible to misrepresent. But the new world you have entered need not be filled with misrepresentations, for you are cause and effect. It is through the representation of the true that the false is exposed as nothing. A lie is nothing but a lie. The false is nothing but the false. It does not become some "thing," for in the becoming it would need to take on the properties of the truth. Think of the ego again as an example here. The ego but seemed to be who you were for a time. Now that you know who you are in truth, the ego does not remain, a separate entity with a life of its own. No. The ego is gone. Because it was a lie its exposure to the truth dissolved it.

5.9   Thus must it be now with everything in your world. Everywhere you look the lie of false representation will be exposed and the truth will be represented once again. As was said earlier, this seeing of the truth is the first step as it is the step necessary for the restoration of divine design. True seeing facilitates the return to what is and we but proceed from this starting point.

5.10   While you have learned to take judgment from your seeing, this must be reemphasized now as you are called to see what you might previously have thought of as inconsequential in the light of truth. Everything *given* represents the truth.

5.11   Remember now that you are not called to reinterpret but to accept revelation. You will not arrive at the truth through thinking about what everything means. This is the old way that led to so much misinterpretation and misrepresentation. Acceptance of what is given is acceptance of what is given. All was *given* to you to remind you of who you are in the time of learning that is now passing away. Thus all was *given* to you to *represent* what is rather than to *be* what is. Now, as you join with the truth, your representation, in the new time that is before us, will *be* what is, in its representation. Simply put, this means that form will never be all that you are, but will return to being as it was intended and will represent the truth of who you are. This true representation, being of the truth, returns you to the reality of the truth where you exist in oneness.

5.12 Love and the loving patterns given in the time of learning are all that exist in all you see. But what now will become of these patterns that are no longer needed as your learning and that of those around you comes to an end? What was created to serve the time of learning, to represent what *is* and aid you in your return to what *is*, will become what *is* once again. What you can see with your body's eyes will not be *all* that *is* but will represent all that *is* truly.

5.13 What was *made* of what was created in order to serve the ego will cease to be, just as the ego has ceased to be. To outline and define the differences between what was created and what was made would be to create a tome of information, and this is not needed now. The desire for such is a desire to think through once again the meaning of everything and to have a tool to help you do so. This would assume that you are still a learning being and have need of such help. You are no longer a learning being and need not this assistance.

5.14 In this time of Christ, we are not called to recreate the "tools" of learning but to allow all that was created to show the way back to Self and God to be what it is in truth. This is the return of love to love. This is acceptance of your Self.

5.15 What then is the call to creation that has been spoken of? This is the acceptance of the *new you*—acceptance that you are going beyond simple recognition and acceptance of the Self as God created the Self—to the living of this Self in form. This is an acceptance that recognizes that while the Self that God created is eternal and the self of form as ancient as the sea and stars, the elevated Self of form is new and will create a new world.

5.16 This is the answer to the question of "What is next?" If there is nothing to learn, if coursework is behind you and accomplishment is complete, what then are you to do? You are to create in community, in dialogue, in commitment and togetherness. You are to be the living Covenant of the New.

5.17   But while this is what awaits you, I am merely answering the questions that remain and that occur as this dialogue proceeds. What I am attempting to answer now is your confusion concerning what *is*. This is crucial as you learn to accept what *is* and to deny what is *not*. While the question of what is *not* has been answered as fully as is possible, your questions and my answers in regard to what *is* are somewhat confusing to you, because what *is* is not a constant that can be *answered*. That you want answers while I tell you to await revelation speaks to the impatience of the human spirit, the longing that has so long gone unfulfilled that now that you are close you cannot bear to wait another day, another hour. You want release from your prison *now*, and so you should.

5.18   Yet what you *think* imprisons you is also what I am addressing here. Release through death is no longer the answer. Release through life is the answer. Release through resurrection is the answer. You have died to the old. But surely it would seem easier in some ways to have literally died and been released from the prison of the body, the prison of the Earth and your immediate environment, the prison of your mind and the thoughts that so confuse you, the prison of past and future and a now that isn't changing fast enough to suit the new *you* whom you have become.

5.19   This is what we discuss today. We discuss being what you represent in truth. We discuss the elevation of form. And what we have discussed thus far is the acceptance of form as what it is. This is the new reality you have desired. To live as who you are *in form*. To not wait for death's release but to find release while still living *in form*. Thus we begin with the true content of the form you occupy. We return the form you occupy to its natural state. Only then can we proceed to creation of the new. Because Christ-consciousness is consciousness of what *is*, we begin with what *is*, with creation as it was created rather than as you have perceived it to be. From this starting point only can we move forward to the future we create together.

5.20   What I'm revealing to you here is that what was once a prison may no longer be a prison! If you continue to think of your body as a prison, if you continue to think of your environment, your mind, and time as a prison, how can it exist in perfect harmony with the universe? As you can see, you are now approaching another thought reversal. Fear not that your confusion will last, for with this thought reversal will come your final release.

5.21 You will soon wonder, if you haven't already, just how it is going to be possible to live as your new Self while still in form, while still in a form that seems inconsistent with your being, while still in a form that exists within a form, within a world that seems inconsistent with your being. You will wonder how, if you are done learning, the patterns of learning will change to help you embrace the acceptance of this new time of no time. You will wonder how to live in time as a being no longer bound by time. And I tell you truly, that once acceptance of what *is* is complete, we will go on to these questions of the new and together we will find the answers.

5.22 So let today's dialogue serve as a final call, a most emphatic call, to acceptance. See the importance of this acceptance to everything that is still to come. Hesitate no longer. Let your willingness exceed your trepidation. No longer wait to be told more before you accept what you have already been told. Do not wait for a grander call before you accept the call that has already sounded in your heart. Let this be the day of your final surrender, the day that will usher in a new day.

CHAPTER 6

The Body and the Elevation of Form

6.1 Within the text of the coursework provided you heard many ideas that either changed or reinforced those you already had about yourself. *A Course of Love* is a teaching text and the goal of its teaching was stated and restated many times so that you would not forget the purpose of the learning you were participating in. Eventually your learning reached an end point as the learning goal of this Course was met, and this you were told as well. I say this to remind you that the time of "teaching" like the time of "learning" had its place as well as its methods.

6.2 One of the methods employed by your teacher within the text of your coursework was that of comparison, a method that will be used less and less as the time of learning passes. The thought reversal of which we recently spoke is why I bring this up. During your time of learning, I used a method of comparison—I compared the real to the unreal, the false to the true, fear to love—in order to point out the insanity of your perception and the perfect sanity of the truth. For some of you the repetition of the properties of the false that aided your learning may now work as a detriment to your acceptance as you cling to ideas concerning false representation rather than let them go in order to embrace true representation. In the time of learning, you were so entrenched in your false beliefs that their insanity needed to be stated and stated again. But as we enter this new time of elevated form, these same ideas—ideas that many of you attached to form rather than to your perception of form—must be rejected.

6.3 This is what I have already spoken of and speak of again as a revisioning of what you believe imprisons you.

6.4 While the false representation of the body as the self was almost as detrimental to your learning as the false representation of the ego as the self, the body, given your choice to return to who you truly are while still in form, continues, while the ego, of course, does not. Your belief in the non-existence of the ego is now total and has brought a freedom and a liberation in which you rejoice. Your true Self is beginning to reveal itself to you in ways of which you will become increasingly aware. As you identify more intimately with the Self you truly are, the self of form is likely to grow more and more foreign to you and less and less comfortable. Thus what is required now is a new way of envisioning the body and its service to you.

6.5 Like all that was created for the time of learning, the body was the perfect learning device. Seeing it as such assisted us in bringing about the end of the time of learning. But now your body—your form—must be seen in a new way. It is thus with new ideas about the body that we will begin the final thought reversal that will allow you to live in form as who you truly are.

6.6 The body, as all else you see among the living, is, in fact, living. It exists as living form. And so we begin with a distinction between what exists as living form, and what exists as inanimate or non-living form. While you might think this is an easily drawn distinction—and it is—it is not perhaps as you have previously seen it, for everything that exists in form is of the same Source. Even those things you have made you have not made from nothing. There is not one thing that you have made that does not exist as some variation of what was originally created. Because, and this cannot be repeated enough, creation begins with what *is*. And so even the creations you have *made* are only distinct from what was originally created in your perception of what they are or what you have determined their use to be. There is thus truth, or what we might call the seeds of the truly real, or the energy of creation, in everything that exists in form.

6.7 It is your perception of the forms around you as non-living forms that cause them to have rigidity and a particular meaning. But they still are real, even if they are not as they appear to be to the body's eyes.

6.8 What is not real are the things that you have made to represent what *is* real since you didn't understand what it was you were making things to represent. These are the systems we have already spoken of: Systems of justice, systems of government, systems of corporations, the systems of economics and science—the systems—in short, of what you think governs you.

6.9   In the Bible there were many stories about miracles, both before and after the time in which I lived. If you were to pose to a scientist whether or not these miracles were possible, they would tell you of all the "laws" of science that would be opposed to them occurring. You would be told that if the sun had "stood still" galactic catastrophes would have resulted, that there are reasons Noah's flood could not have occurred as described, or that it would have been impossible to repopulate the earth afterwards even if it had taken place as described.

6.10   What these laws of science do not take into account are the laws of God. Although science is beginning to see much as it truly is, scientists still look for natural laws that govern what is in an "if this, then that" world.

6.11   This same kind of attitude still governs your ideas about the body and the systems of the world in which you exist. If you are no longer living in an "if this, then that" world, then the same laws will naturally not apply. You developed an "if this, then that" world because it was the easiest way in which to learn. It was the easiest way in which to learn because it seemed to provide proof. Yet if science teaches anything, it teaches that what is proven can be disproved—and often is. Thus the prayer of the Native Americans who thank the sun for rising each day is a prayer that acknowledges that the sun may not rise. This is not a doomsday attitude, but an attitude that accepts that scientific or natural law and the law of spirit are not the same.

6.12   There are many stories in many cultures that celebrate and bear witness to the happenings that reveal that the laws of spirit and the laws of man coexist. Yes, there are natural laws, but these "natural" laws are not the sets of facts you have defined them to be, but rather a staggering series of relationships, relationships without end, relationships that exist in harmony and cooperation. This is a harmony and cooperation that might one day extend to the sun and a demonstration that the sun need not rise—or perhaps need not set—and the earth would still be safely spinning in its orbit.

6.13   Now if this were to happen, scientists would quickly determine the existence of a natural law that allowed this event to happen. It would require the re-working of many previously known "scientific facts," but this would not prevent them from discovering new "scientific facts." I mean no disrespect to scientists and bless them for their desire to find the "truth," as you should bless them for the certainty they have given you in an uncertain world.

Even if it has been a false certainty, it served a great purpose in the time of learning. Discovery has been a grand facilitator of the human spirit's quest for the truth and is part of what brought you, finally, to the quest to know your Self.

6.14 I am calling all of this to mind in order to begin our discussion concerning the suspension of belief. If you continue into the new with your old ideas about your body, the old body will be what you carry into the new with you. So let us begin with a suspension of belief in what you think you know about the body, in what science would tell you about the body, in what you have experienced as a body—a suspension of belief that comes in the same spirit as that of the Native American who knows that the sun may rise and may set, but also knows that it may not. I am speaking of a spirit that is open to the discovery of something new and "unbelievable" and even "scientifically impossible," as well as to the creation of something new. For in this time of revelation, discovery is the new divine pattern that will replace the "thought" systems we have spoken of. To discover is simply to find out what you did not previously know.

6.15 Creation of the new will be predicated on the discovery of what you did not previously know. This will not happen if you cling to "known" truths. Revelation cannot come to those who are so "certain" of what *is* that they cannot allow for the new to be revealed. Your certainty about what *is* is a false certainty, a learned certainty based on the fear that caused you to order the world according to a set of facts and rules.

6.16 Be jubilant rather than hesitant about the time of discovery that is before you. Calling what you think you know into question is not a call to return to uncertainty, but a call to allow real certainty to come.

6.17 If you think of the "old" as a world in which an attitude of "if this, then that" ruled, and the "new" as a world in which giving and receiving are one, you will begin to see the enormity of the thought reversal that now awaits your acceptance. As I said earlier, we begin by applying this new attitude to the body.

6.18 You have been taught that *if* you take care of the body in certain ways, *then* good health will result. You have been taught that *if* your body expends energy, *then* it will need the refueling provided by food or rest. The list could be endless, but these examples will suffice. These modes of behavior concerning the body were given to teach and to represent. What you have done is turn them into implacable rules you call natural laws. When these natural laws have been shown at times to not apply, you consider these instances flukes or miracles.

6.19   When a person who has exhibited healthy habits get sick, you think it is unfair. When a person who has exhibited unhealthy habits gets sick, you think, even if you would not say, that they "did it to themselves" or that they could have prevented it by abstaining from the unhealthy habits. You might look now at these two attitudes and see that they are somewhat silly, but still you would cling to them because you would believe the person of healthy habits has a greater *chance* of not getting sick than the person of unhealthy habits. Again we could go into countless examples of this type of thinking, but the examples matter not except to make you see that these attitudes are not ruled by certainty, but by a mere idea of bettering the odds against what fate may offer.

6.20   What fate may offer is itself an attitude that puts life at the risk and whim of an external force that has no reality except in your imagination. What is this thing called fate? Like all the systems you believe in, it is a system too, an internal idea given a name, externalized, and blamed for all that you do not understand, all that cannot be made to make sense, all that seems unfair and beyond your control.

6.21   When you remember that we have left blaming behind, you will see that belief in fate is just as systematic and in need of being left behind as is belief that illness can be blamed on certain habits. This may not be the type of blaming you see as easily as that of blaming a friend for your hurt feelings, or blaming the past for the present. And yet, what ridding your mind of ideas of placing blame does, is take it one step away from the thinking of the "if this, then that" thought system we are leaving behind. As a non-learning being you are now called to accept that you no longer need this type of learning device and to realize that it will no longer serve you.

6.22   Let us return now to the beginning and start with the body as a *given*. It *is* what it *is* in terms of flesh and bone, and it is also the form that is now serving to represent the truth of who you are. How might this change the "laws" of the body, the laws you gave the body in the time of learning, knowing not what the design of the body represented? What might the bodily design now represent?

6.23   The first example of the body we presented newly was that of the perfect design of the joining provided through sexual intercourse—a design *given* to lead the way to desire for oneness and completion.

6.24   We have talked of but one replacement for the pattern of learning—the pattern of acceptance. What might the body be called to accept? This is an easy answer, as you have already called upon the body to accept the indwelling of Christ. You have replaced the personal self, the self of learning, with the true Self. You have accepted your true identity. How could the body now be the same as it once was?

6.25   The body was, in the time of learning, representative of a learning being. The ego, however, narrowed your ideas of what the body was here to learn to ideas of survival. You thus learned to survive rather than to live. You increased the life span of the human being, but you increased not its capacity for true living or true learning. And with the extended life span came extended reasons for fear, and a physical form that you came to believe needed greater and greater resources to maintain.

6.26   The body is now the embodiment of the true Self, the embodiment of love, the embodiment of divinity. Its existence is *given* as it was always given. But now the very nature of its existence has changed. I say *changed* here because you may remember that change occurs in time. Outside of time and form your Self has always existed in the perfect harmony in which it was created. Now that your Self has joined the elevated Self of form, you exist together both in time and outside of time. Remember, the elevated Self of form will never be *all* that you are. This does not imply however, that there are portions of your Self missing from this new experience in form you now enter into, but that the elevated Self of form is now able to join with the Self in the unity of shared consciousness. You are whole once again and your form will merely represent one aspect of your wholeness in the field of time.

6.27   The self of form, as form, could never truly experience the All of Everything that is the natural state of the formless. But the true Self cannot cease to experience its natural state, the state of Christ-consciousness, sharing in unity, the All of Everything. So these two states, the state of form and the state of unity, are both in existence right now. In the state of unity, your true Self is fully aware of the elevated Self of form and is fully participating in its experiences and feelings. The elevated Self of form, however, being a form that still exists in time, must realize the consciousness of the true Self in time. What this means is that the elevated Self of form may still need "time" to come to know the changes that only occur *in* "time" although they are already accomplished in unity. This is why we have spoken of miracles and of the collapse of time the miracle is capable of providing. We have redefined the miracle as the art of thought, or the continual act of prayer that sustains the unity of Christ-consciousness.

6.28   Form and time go together. Yet you have been told time is a measurement of learning. If you are no longer a learning being, for what is time needed? Time is needed now only for the transformation of the self from a learning being to a being that can accept the shared consciousness of unity and begin to discover what this means.

CHAPTER 7

Time and the Experience
of Transformation

7.1 Just as when you were a being existing in the shared consciousness of unity you couldn't know what the experience of form would be like without entering into it, you cannot know the experience of unity without entering into it. To "enter" into the experience of form is something you can picture in your mind, and that you have language to represent, because you are aware of the self of form. To "enter" into the experience of unity is something more difficult to imagine, and something for which you have little language.

7.2 You were told within this Course that what you learn in unity is shared. This language was used because you were still, at that time, a learning being. Now we will adjust our language somewhat to represent the new and restate what was said earlier as "What you *discover* in unity is shared." Learning does not occur in unity, but discovery is an ongoing aspect of creation and thus of the state of union in which you truly abide.

7.3 You were also told within this Course that because you were learning in separation, unity had to be experienced individually before learning could be shared at another level, and that levels are a function of time. We then talked of the integration of levels that collapse time. This integration of levels is the integration of form and unity. When Christ-consciousness is sustained, time will collapse and the sun may not need to rise or set to separate day into night. Resting and waking will be part of the same continuum of being.

7.4 Experiences of form take place in time because experience, too, was designed for learning. Now experience is needed in time to aid your total acceptance of what you have learned. In order to experience the new you must answer the call to let revelation and discovery, rather than learning, be what you gain from experience.

7.5   What was created cannot be uncreated. Thus transformation is needed. The miracle makes you fully aware of the embrace and the consciousness of unity and places you outside of time. In this state, no duality exists. Doing and being are one.

7.6   Action is the bridge between form and the formless because action is the expression of the self in form. "Right" action comes from the unity in which doing and being are one, or in other words from the state in which there is no division between who you are and what you do. "Right" action comes from the state of wholeness. Being whole is being all you are. Being all you are is what the elevated Self of form represents.

7.7   You have been told that you are time-bound only as a particular self, existing as man or woman in a particular time in history. Now you are called to discover how to exist in form without being defined by this time-bound particularity.

7.8   That you are living form does not require you to be defined by particularity. You can accept the body now as what it is in all its manifestations while not seeing it as "bound" by the particularity of time and space. It may still exist in a particular time and place, but this is simply the nature of one aspect of what you are. The nature of form is that it exists as matter, it occupies space and is perceptible to the senses. You have previously seen this one aspect of form as separating it from mind, heart, and spirit—those aspects that are not perceptible to the senses. But let me repeat that all that lives is from the same Source, and there is nothing more alive than mind and heart combined in the spirit of wholeheartedness.

7.9   Matter is simply another word for content, and need not be maligned. The content of all living things is the energy of the spirit of wholeheartedness. The content of all living things is, in other words, whole. By seeing only aspects of wholeness you have not seen content nor matter truly. You have not been aware of all that you are. You are thus now called to discover and to become aware of all that you are. The body, rather than aiding you in learning as it once did, will aid you now in this discovery.

7.10   Realize that this is a call to love all of yourself. You who once could love spirit *or* mind, mind *or* body—because of the dualistic nature associated with them—now can love all of your Self, all of God, all of creation. You can respond to love with love.

7.11   But again, we start with the body, returning love to it now. It is what it is, and nothing that it is, is deserving of anything other than love. This call to love all of your Self is a call to unconditional, nonjudgmental love. It is not just a call to nonjudgmentalness, but to nonjudgmental love. This nonjudgmental love is the condition upon which your discovery of all you do not yet know awaits.

7.12   Discovery is not the same as remembrance. Remembrance was necessary for your return to your true identity, the Self as it was created. Remembrance was not about what you did not know, but about what you knew but had forgotten. Memory has returned you to your Self. Discovery will allow the new you to come into being by revealing what you do not yet know about how to live as the elevated Self of form.

7.13   This discovery can only take place in the reality of love.

7.14   Being in love is a definition of what you now are as you accept the unconditional, nonjudgmental love of all. This is a transference of love from the particular to the universal. Loving all that you are, including your body, is not love of the particular but universal love. The old way in which you related to your body, be it a love or a hate relationship, was a particular relationship with the vessel that only seemed to contain you. It was a relationship with the separated self. Now, because your relationship is with wholeness, you can transfer love from the particular to the universal by loving all. We are one body, one Christ.

7.15   The observation, envisioning, and desire you have been practicing in order to be ready to accept revelation works hand in hand with the new pattern of discovery, but discovery is less time bound. Let me explain.

7.16   Observation takes place in time. Even while you have been called to observe what *is*, what you are observing in form are the representations of what *is* in time. Your envisioning too is bound to time and that is why so many of you think of envisioning as envisioning the future. Envisioning is less bound to time than is observation because it is not about what your body's eyes see, and will increasingly join with what you observe until your vision is released from old patterns and guides you more truly.

7.17   Desire is an acknowledgement of the uniqueness of each Self, and is a demonstration of means and end being the same. Desire keeps you focused on your own path and leaves you nonjudgmental of the paths of others. Yet desire, like observation and vision, is still related to the self of form. It is a step toward full acceptance and awareness of who you are now and what this means as you become the elevated Self of form.

7.18   Revelation is of God. Observation, vision, and desire are steps leading you beyond what the individual, separated self sees, to the revelation of what *is*. These steps that lead to revelation are not ongoing aspects of creation, because they are related to particular forms as they exist in time. Time is not an aspect of eternity or of unity. Time is thus what has separated the self that exists in form from the Self that exists in union or the state of Christ-consciousness. By becoming one body, one Christ, you have accepted existence as a non-particular being in a state outside of time—you have accepted existence as a new Self, the Self of elevated form. You just do not yet understand what this means.

7.19   Discovery is not bound by time as it is an ongoing aspect of creation. As you were told in A Treatise on the New, the future is yet to be created. While this seems like a time-bound statement, it is not. It is merely one way of stating that creation is ongoing rather than static. That while creation *is* and *is* as it was created, it was created to be eternally expanding and expressing in new ways.

7.20   With your new awareness *you* are now linked, through the consciousness of unity, with the entire field of creation, rather than only with the time-bound field of creation of form. As your awareness grows, you will begin to expand and express in new ways. Those ways thus now include the form of your body without being limited to creation of, and in, form. The body has thus joined creation in a non time-bound way.

7.21   Evolution is the time-bound way in which the body has participated in creation. This is why you have been told that you are not called to evolution. Time-bound evolution is the way of the creature, the natural response of the living organism to the stimulus of matter upon matter, and of the creature's perception of its own experience in time. This time-bound evolution is really adaptation. It occurs in reaction to what is perceived as necessary for survival.

7.22   Time-bound evolution is still surely going on, and as the planet becomes crowded, as progress has left so many unfulfilled, as environmental concerns mount, even the perceived survival needs are leading you toward new answers of what survival may mean.

7.23 Everyone knows, in this time of Christ, that the end of the old way is near and that the new is coming. They are thus moving toward anticipation rather than adaptation, and evolution moves with them. But evolution in time is part of the old that needs to be left behind. It is a provision of the time of learning that allows the learning being to learn at his or her own pace and to pass this learning on in time.

7.24 Everyone knows that this has not worked to improve the fate of man. Everyone secretly fears that evolution will not keep pace with the changing world and that man's reign over his environment will come to an abrupt and painful end. Some even fear an evolutionary setback, and see any threat against civilization as they know it as a return to barbaric times.

7.25 These scenarios of fear we leave behind as we abandon ideas of evolution in time and proceed to an awareness of how the elevated Self of form can replace the laws of evolution in time with the laws of transformation outside of time.

7.26 In order to facilitate your understanding, I call you now to imagine your body as a dot in the center of a circle and the circle as representing all that you are. The dot of your body is all that is bound by time. What transformation outside of time asks you to do is to see the body as but this one, small, aspect of what you are. In observing both yourself and others, you have learned to view your body in the field of time. This will be helpful now as you begin to imagine the "more" that you are, the "more" that exists beyond the body's boundary and beyond the boundary of time and particularity.

7.27 This circle in which you have placed your body is not a circle of time and space. It is not a circle that can be drawn around where you exist so as to define, perhaps, a mile of space and say that this is all you. No, the circle that exists around you is the circle of shared consciousness, the circle of unity. In truth, this circle is everything, the All of All, the universe, God. But just as the Earth can be seen as your home, although you are rarely consciously aware of existing in this "larger" home, you will not always be aware of this circle of the Self as the All of Everything, and it will, in fact, be helpful as we begin, to imagine on a smaller scale.

7.28 You might begin by imagining first your actual, physical, home, then your neighborhood, community, city, state, country. You see yourself as most your "self" in your home, your neighborhood, your community. You identify with the citizens of the city, state, and country you occupy. You have an address, perhaps a yard, or farm, perhaps a public spot that has become a favorite park or lake or beach that you consider partially yours. You have a route to and from your work or other places that you go, where you see familiar landmarks, structures, faces. You visit the homes of friends and relatives, your church, perhaps a school or library, certain restaurants or places of civic duty or social engagement. You may expand this small territory you call your own with business travel or vacations, and have more than one locale that feels like home; or you may never travel far from the building in which you dwell. What I ask you to do is to think of these areas as the territory of your body, and to remember that while this is your territory, it is a shared territory and a territory within the territory of planet Earth.

7.29   Thus we will begin once again with parameters, with a territory of shared consciousness, rather than with consciousness of the All of Everything. This territory we will call the territory of your conscious awareness. This territory of conscious awareness is shared with the larger consciousness of unity, just as the territory of your body is shared with those who live and work nearby. This territory of conscious awareness exists within the larger consciousness of unity, just as the territory of your body exists within the larger territory of the planet Earth. We will begin here, with the territory of your conscious awareness, knowing that discovery and revelation will expand this territory, and realizing that no matter how small this cosmic territory may be, it will still at times give way to awareness of the All of Everything.

CHAPTER 8
The Territory of Conscious Awareness

8.1　Continuing to imagine your body as the dot within the circle, I ask you to imagine now being able to take a step outside of the area of this dot, and into the area of the wider circle. In this area of the wider circle, there is no time, no space, no particularity. It is an area of unlimited freedom. Yet we will begin with parameters that make this area as imaginable to you as possible, because here is where all that you can imagine can become your new reality.

8.2　Imagine this first as a place where no learning is needed. Ah, you might say now, this you have heard before. This idea of no longer needing to learn has intrigued you since it was first mentioned, and yet it seems too impossible, too "good" to be true. You are too used to thinking of yourself as a learning being to truly experience the freedom of not being bound by this constraint. In all of your life, you can think of no ability you have not achieved through learning. And yet most of you have "discovered" something that comes easily to you, something you might have said or been told you have a natural talent or ability to do. These things some of you have practiced or studied to take advantage of your natural ability and in doing so may have found a continued ability to learn faster or achieve more in this area than those who are not seen as having a "natural ability" of this particular kind. But because you are prone to comparison, many of you have been discouraged by not being able to be the "best" despite your natural talent or ability, and have given up "working hard" to be the best. Others who have achieved the highest possible acclaim for their talents find this acclaim unfulfilling once it is achieved.

8.3　All of these ideas we leave behind as we concentrate instead on the very simple idea of each of you containing a natural ability or talent that existed in some form prior to the time of learning. We concentrate on this idea merely as an *idea* and not in terms of the specific ability it may represent. We concentrate on this idea as the first parameter of the territory of your conscious awareness as you let awareness grow in you that you *have* experienced something that existed prior to the time of learning. And that this *something* was quite wonderful.

8.4   You might think of this ability that existed prior to the time of learning as coming from the content of the wider circle of who you are to infiltrate the dot of the body, or, conversely, as the body having taken a step outside of the dot of self to infiltrate the wider circle of the Self. When you have realized that you are "more" than your body, your natural talent or ability has been one of the primary factors leading to this realization. It has been one of the primary factors leading to this realization because a part of you has always known this ability was a "given." That you are gifted—given to—and able to receive. And despite what science might have to say to you about the source of such talents or abilities, you have known that they are not of the body.

8.5   To accept this is to accept that you have access to a "given" Self, to something neither earned nor worked hard to attain. To imagine this as an idea is to imagine this "given" Self as the Self that exists beyond the boundary we have described as the dot of the body.

8.6   This idea will aid you too in your understanding of discovery, as your natural abilities or talents were *discovered* and in that discovery, you realized that although you had not previously known that this talent or ability existed, it was there awaiting but your discovery. You may also have seen that in the expression of this talent or ability new discoveries awaited you and that you greeted these discoveries with surprise and delight. As was written in A Treatise on the New, these surprises of discovery have, and will, cause you to laugh and be joyous. There was never any need, and will never be any need, to figure them out—for surprises cannot be figured out! Surprises are meant to be joyous gifts being constantly revealed. Gifts that need only be received and responded to. Not *learned*.

8.7   While discovery of the new will naturally include much that goes beyond what you now think of as your natural talents or abilities, the place or Source of your natural talents or abilities is a place from which to start building your awareness of what is available or given—of what is but awaiting your discovery and conscious awareness. Thus, like the home in which you reside, the idea that you have an already existing awareness of the Source of unity beyond the body will increase your comfort level, and will help establish it as the first parameter in the territory of your conscious awareness.

8.8   Now this is not new *information*. Much of this was taught in A Treatise on the Nature of Unity and Its Recognition. Between the Course and the Treatises, all of what you needed to *learn* was put forth. What we are now doing is discussing what was taught from the realm of wholeheartedness. What was learned was only able to be learned because you chose to become the wholehearted. You chose to join mind and heart and it was done. But you do not yet know how to rid yourself of former patterns. Your mind, while it no longer wants to cling to known patterns, is confronted with them constantly. Thus your heart still seems to battle with the supremacy of mind.

8.9   So what we are attempting to do is to *open* the mind to the wisdom of the heart with these dialogues. As the mind *opens* and accepts the new, the art of thought will become your new means of thinking. What has been learned will become an ability to think wholeheartedly, or with mind and heart in union, and then that ability will transcend ability and wholehearted will become what you are, and wholeheartedness your sole means of expression.

8.10   The self and the expression of self that comes from any place other than wholeheartedness is not the true Self or the true expression of the Self but the self-expression that arises from separation. Self-expression that arises from separation is still valuable, as it is a sign of yearning toward the true Self and the true expression of the Self. Thus where you have desired to express yourself in the past is very likely linked to the natural ability or talent you did not have to learn, to that which was given and available just a step beyond where the separated self could reach.

8.11   Expand your reach! Step outside of the dot of the separated self and into the circle of unity where all you desire is already accomplished in the fullness and wholeness of the undivided Self.

8.12   The divided self is the small self of separation that is constantly yearning for union with that from which it is divided. Enter the place of no division, the place of shared consciousness, the place of wholeness. The natural ability that you recognize as a given and unlearned aspect of your Self is the doorway. Step through that doorway. Take the first step outside of the known reality of your conscious awareness, the learned reality of your separate consciousness, and into the realm of shared consciousness.

8.13   Do not be surprised, however, if no shaft of light descends upon you, if you feel as if you have taken that step and yet remain unchanged. When you choose to take this step it is taken. What you will become aware of on the other side of that door will require a new way of seeing, a new kind of awareness.

CHAPTER 9

Awareness that Does Not Come from Thought

9.1 The door that is being opened to you here is the door of awareness of what *is*, a door that swings open and closed on the hinges of your thoughts. Thoughts are a greater boundary than the dot of your body and a greater means of imprisonment than bars and walls. They are why you do not see what *is* and are the reason that you continue to desire to be provided with set answers.

9.2 The final thought reversal that was spoken of in the section on acceptance is what is spoken of here. There you were asked to become aware of what imprisons you, only to have it later suggested that what you think imprisons you may not be what imprisons you at all. What you think *is* what imprisons you.

9.3 You continue to think that your desire to know who you are calls you to think about who you are and in that thinking to come up with a definition of who are, a truth of who you are, a certainty about who you are. You have been led to see that this desire has always been with you, and you have thought it is the very desire that, once defined and acted upon, would fulfill you, allow you to be who you truly are, end your confusion, and give you peace to usher in the new.

9.4 But you have thought about this desire to know who you are in one way or another all of your life without reaching the place of fulfillment you have sought. Even now, when you have learned all that you are in need of learning, the pattern, even of your wholeheartedness, remains one of thought. This pattern is what the new patterns of acceptance and discovery that we are beginning to lay out here are going to replace.

9.5 Thought is a practice and a pattern of the separated and thus learning self. When it was said within this Course that you are an idea of God, and when ideas were spoken of as if they were synonymous with thought, this was an accurate and truthful way of expressing what was true for you as a learning being.

9.6   But your reality has changed, and with that change, new patterns apply. This does not mean that the truth has changed, but that you have changed; and with your change, the truth, while it remains the truth, can now be presented in a way that speaks to who you are now rather than who you were when you began A Course of Love.

9.7   As we continue, you may feel as if contradictory things are being said, such as being called to consider what imprisons you and then being called to reconsider. The call is still the same, but the means by which you are considering the call has changed. Thus there is no contradiction although there may at times seem to be.

9.8   This may seem as well to be inconsistent with the teaching of A Treatise on the Art of Thought. If thought is what imprisons you, why would the "art of thought" be taught? You must continually remember your newness and the different aim toward which we now work. The aims we clearly embraced together when you were still a learning being were meant to allow you to come to know your true identity. A Treatise on the Art of Thought was but a forerunner to what we now will embrace together. It was a means and an end.

9.9   The same is true of the beliefs set forth in A Treatise on the Nature of Unity and Its Recognition. What was taught in order to aid your "recognition" will clearly be different from what is revealed once that recognition has been brought about.

9.10   Just as the Art of Thought led to abilities beyond the thinking of the ego-mind, the beliefs of the Treatise on Unity were meant to lead beyond the need for beliefs, and A Treatise on the Personal Self meant to lead beyond the personal self. Thus the Treatises were not inconsistent with our aims here. Learning always has as its goal leading the learner *beyond* learning. With A Treatise on the New we established what lies beyond learning. Now, as we embrace the new together, it must be realized again and yet again, that the new cannot be learned. In other words, it must be realized that you cannot come to know the new, or to create the new, through the means of old, including the means of thought.

9.11   We thus return to discovery and continue to expand the territory of your conscious awareness. We do this by discussing now the nature of ideas as opposed to the nature of thoughts.

9.12   Like the natural abilities you discovered existed within you prior to the time of learning, ideas are also discoveries that you make, discoveries that exist apart from learning. Ideas "come to you." They are given and received. They are surprising and pleasing in nature. You may think that they are the result of learning, of thoughts you have contemplated and struggled with. You may think that all of your previous learning and thinking merely resulted eventually in a new idea being birthed, but this is not the case. Heredity can be cited as a cause for talent, but what is heredity but that which already exists within you? So too is it with an idea. An idea already exists within you, but is awaiting its birth *through* you.

9.13   This is how you must now come to see your form; it is that through which what already exists, what is already accomplished, comes or passes through by means of the expression of your form and the interaction of your form with all you are in relationship with.

9.14   If we return to the image of the body as the dot in the wider circle and accept that your discovery of your natural talent or ability and your discovery of new ideas are discoveries of something that already existed beyond the dot of the body; and if you accept that these ideas that already exist were able to pass through you in order to gain expression in form; then you are beginning to see, on a small scale, the action that, on a large scale, will become the new way.

CHAPTER 10

The Goal and the Accomplishment of the Elevated Self of Form

10.1   What is found outside of the boundary of the personal self in the wider circle of unity is timeless. What comes to you in the form of natural abilities or talents, as ideas, as imagination, as inspiration, instinct, intuition, as vision, or as calling, are ways of knowing that come to you, and through you, outside of the pattern of learning.

10.2   Learning is about the transfer of knowledge that was gained in the time of learning, through the process of learning. Notice the inability of teaching or learning to call forth talents, ideas, imagination, inspiration, instinct, intuition, vision, or calling. You may believe that teaching and learning appropriately work with and enable the *use* of abilities such as these, but you also know that these means are limited in what they can do and that they can hinder as well as enhance the creative expression of these givens.

10.3   You think that the use you put these givens to, what you *do* with them, how you express them in the world, is your unique and individual accomplishment. Such it is. But when you also think that it is your hard work and diligence, your effort and struggle, that bring the expression of these givens forward, you think in error and limit your expression in much the same ways that the effort of teaching and learning limits them. It is your joyous acceptance of the already accomplished state of these givens that allows expression of what is given to truly come through you and express the Self, because joyous expression expresses the Self of unity rather than the self of separation, the Self of elevated form rather than the personal self.

10.4   Now you might be thinking, here, that while these givens come from the realm of unity, your expression of these givens, since that expression exists in the realm of time and space and involves the work and time of your form in your form's separate reality, is not of union but of the individual self. You may feel that to think of this in any other way will leave you with no individual, personal accomplishment, nothing to be proud of, nothing to call your own. You thus must begin to realize that the bringing forth of the accomplishment that already exists in unity is your new work, the work of the Self of union, the work that can fill you with the true joy of true accomplishment, *because* it is your real work—work with what *is*.

10.5   Working with what *is* in unity is not work but relationship. You are called to realize your relationship with what is given from unity. It is in that relationship, the relationship *between* what *is* and the expression of what *is* by the elevated Self of form, that the new is created. What *is* becomes new by becoming sharable in form—or in other words, what *is* continues to *become* through the continuation of relationship and the creation of new relationships. In this way, sharing in relationship becomes the goal and the accomplishment of the elevated Self of form, the means through which the Self of union is known even in the realm of separation, and thus what draws others from separation to union.

10.6   The goal and relationship of the elevated Self of form is thus timeless, for it draws from the realm of unity and returns to the realm of unity. This is an expression of the Biblical injunction to "Go forth and multiply." It is about increase. To be content with *personal* or *individual* understanding or experience of what is given is to not complete the cycle of giving and receiving as one. What is given must be received. What is received must be given. This is the way of increase and multiplication. This is the way of creation.

10.7   In this time of Christ, discovery is about acceptance of your true way of knowing, a way that existed prior to the time of learning and that has always existed. When put into practice and allowed to replace the pattern of learning, this way of discovery will be a constant coming to know of what *is* as well as a constant expansion of what *is*, or a constant expansion of creation—creation, in short, of the new.

CHAPTER 11

The Return to Unity and the End of Thought As You Know It

11.1　We haven't, here, been talking of the *art* of thought, but of the *use* of thought. You use thought to solve problems, apply thought to intellectual puzzles, focus your thoughts in order to make up your mind. You make lists of your thoughts so you don't forget what they remind you to do, you order your thoughts to communicate effectively, you take note of your thoughts and you take notes on the thoughts of others.

11.2　You might even consider this Dialogue the written notes of *my* thoughts. In this one example can you not see the fallacy inherent in all the others? To think of these Dialogues in this way, dear brothers and sisters, is insane. To think of the thought or idea of God by which you were created as the same type of thought I have just described would be insane. Are you willing any longer to see me as a lecturer, or even as a great teacher? Am I but a giver of information from whom another is capable of taking notes? You think it is only the content of your thoughts that differentiate you from others. Do you think the same is true of you and me? It is *that* you think that differentiates you from me, not our content, which is one and the same.

11.3　You might imagine that the *way* you think is so different from the *way* I think that they are incomparable. But thinking is not an accurate description of what I do, or of what occurs in unity. I *am* and I extend what I am. This dialogue is that extension. God's idea of you extended and became you and me and all the sons and daughters of creation.

11.4　In the opening page of this Dialogue I said that you give and you receive from the well of spirit. True giving and receiving is of unity. True giving and receiving is not of the separated thought of the separated thought system of the separated self. Your acceptance of the concepts in A Treatise on the

Art of Thought was but a beginning to the total rejection of thought as you know it that must now occur in order to go on to creation of the new. You create the new from, and in, unity.

11.5   Your thoughts are the last bastion of your separated self, the fertile ground, still, of your individuality, your testimony that you believe you are still *on your own*, and that you still desire to be, for only here, in this area of your individuality, do you believe you make your contributions to the world. Your desire to make a contribution—to help to make new the world that you have known—has been enhanced and amplified by what you have learned. You know you have been called and that a contribution has been asked of you. And so your mighty thoughts have turned their focus on this *problem* and attacked it as they attack all problems to be solved. The idea of making a contribution has begun to receive the attention of your thoughts. The hope of answering your call and fulfilling your promise has lit a bonfire in your heart and begun a stampede of thoughts within your mind. Again, is this not what we spoke of in the beginning of this Dialogue? What was spoken of as your desire to prepare?

11.6   Let me ask you a question. Do you think desire will still be with you when you have achieved what you have desired? Is it not possible to conceive of a time in which desire will no longer serve you, just as learning now no longer serves you? If you reach a state of full acceptance of who you are, and in that state, fully accept that your contribution is being made, will desire still be with you?

11.7   The way to achieve this state is through acceptance that it is already accomplished. And yet, as soon as your thoughts begin to accept this, many of you reverse the direction of your thoughts and turn to ideas of what you still need to do to accomplish your calling, to make your contribution. Such is the way of the mind, the way of the thoughts of the mind.

11.8   Now I return you to your idea of how these words have come to you, for if you can fully accept the *way* in which these words have been given and received, you will see that you can fully accept the *way* of unity.

11.9   You have been told you give and you receive from the well of spirit. What might this mean? How might this relate to the giving and receiving of these words? To the discussion we have been having about the body and the elevation of the self of form? How might this relate to your desire to make a contribution and answer your calling? How does this relate to your desire to know what to do?

11.10   These answers lie within you, at the heart or center of your Self, as do all answers. Your desire to make of me a teacher is the same as your desire to make your thoughts into answers that will provide you with direction. As was said earlier, you dare not, as yet, turn to your own heart for answers. Yet your heart is the well of spirit from which true answers are drawn. Your heart is a full well, a wellspring from which you can continually draw with no danger of ever drawing an empty bucket. You need never thirst again when you have accepted this. You need never seek again for answers when this has been accepted. Because you will know and fully accept that the answers lie within.

11.11   To *believe* that you are already accomplished and not live from this belief is insane for reasons already enumerated time and time again. What prevents this belief from becoming an ability and prevents it from going from being an ability to simply being who you are, is your thoughts— thoughts that need an explanation for everything, and an explanation that makes sense in terms of the world you have always known.

11.12   The giving and receiving of these words will never make sense within the terms of the world you have always known. No explanation will ever be good enough for those who set limits upon the truth. But for those willing to open their minds and hearts to a new way of seeing, for those willing to suspend disbelief, the answer to the giving and receiving of these words will provide the answer to the question your thoughts cannot quite comprehend well enough to even articulate, much less to answer.

11.13   These words give evidence of who I am because they give evidence that I know who you are. That these words give evidence that I know who you are and that they give the same evidence to your brothers and sisters that I know who they are, will tell you something of the nature of who you are if you but let this idea dwell within you and take up residence in your heart. We are the sacred heart. As was said as we began this Dialogue, we, together, are the well of spirit. We, together, are the shared consciousness of unity. In our union we bear the sameness of the Son of God. In going forth with the vision of unity you become as I was during life. You do not *think* your way through life, but instead draw your knowing forth from the well of spirit, from the shared consciousness from which these words are given and received.

11.14 In other words, the elevated Self of form does not remain contained within the dot of the body but draws its sustenance from the larger circle, the circle of unity.

11.15 What then becomes the contribution, the unique contribution of each elevated Self of form? The contribution becomes a contribution from the well of spirit, from the shared consciousness of unity that finds its expression, its unique expression, through the elevated Self of form. Why would you retain your desire to make an *individual* contribution, when you can now make a contribution such as this? Is not your unique expression of the whole enough for you? Is it not infinitely greater than the contributions that are possible for the individual, separated self to make? Is not the history of your world filled with individual contributions of incredible scope?

11.16 Do you still believe that the contribution made by the man Jesus was an *individual* contribution? I tell you truthfully that the only contributions that endure, the only contributions that are truly lasting, are contributions that arise from the well of spirit. To seek importance for the personal self would be akin to placing the importance of Jesus on the man Jesus who existed in history. Some do see Jesus only as an important man among many important men. Those who do so miss the point of the life of Jesus just as they miss the point of their own lives. Those who do so seek to make individual contributions as important men and women and do not seek to give expression to what is in everyone's hearts, to what is shared in unity, to what is the truth of who we all are rather than the truth of who the individual is.

11.17 There is no truth inherent in the individual, separated self, but only illusion. Illusion can be described in many different ways that lead to many paths of seeking, but illusion can provide no place in which the seeking ends and the truth is found.

11.18 Turn now not to your thoughts, but to the mind and heart joined in unity. *In unity!* Unity is *where* the heart and mind are joined. Unity is the place from which the expression, the right-minded action of the elevated Self of form, arises. Unity is the Source of these words. So is it said. So is it the truth.

CHAPTER 12
The Body and Your Thoughts

12.1   In the terms in which you are used to thinking, terms that have put the body at the center of your universe and yourself, there is no mechanism through which thought can enter your mind. You believe thoughts exist *in* your mind and are themselves the product of your brain, which lies within your body. Since it is believed that a cessation of brain activity is equivalent to the end of thought, you accept this as proof that your thoughts originate from within your brain.

12.2   You may have pictured the person who first received these words as receiving them either through her thoughts or through her ears, as in the idea of "hearing" words. The receiver of these words, in fact, "hears" these words as thoughts. They are not "her" thoughts, but they also are not separate from her. How can this be?

12.3   They are, quite simply, not the separated thoughts of the separated thought system.

12.4   This work is called a *dialogue.* A dialogue is most often thought of as a discourse between two or more people and as such is associated with the spoken word. When you enter into dialogue with another person, you listen, you hear, and you respond. This is exactly what occurs here. You have "entered into" this dialogue. While you think these words come to you through the written form of this book, by means of your eyes and the decoding mechanism of your brain, they do not, nor did the words of this Course. You were told within this Course and you are reminded now that these words enter through your heart. As your mind and heart joined in unity and became capable of hearing the same language, you truly began to enter the place of unity, to take the step outside of the dot of the body.

12.5   Now you may not "think" that you have been doing this, yet few of you would argue that you have been simply reading these words as you have read the words of other books. While you may be aware that something different is going on here, you might also say that your body has felt no "step" into the realm of unity, and you may rightly wonder now, if you can take such a step and be unaware of it, what its value to you is.

12.6 This is why we work now on your awareness and acceptance of your changed state, for without awareness the value of what we do here does remain minimal, and this I cannot allow. The urgent need for your return to unity has been mentioned before, and I remind you of this urgency again.

12.7 Let your reception of these words, a reception different from the reading of the words of most and maybe all other books you have read, be a sign to you. Keep this in mind as you consider how the first receiver of these words can "hear" these words as thoughts. Keep in mind that she thus has thoughts she is not thinking.

12.8 We have spoken already of "entering into" dialogue. When you enter into dialogue with another person you "hear" what it is they have to say. You "hear" their thoughts through the form of the spoken word. They do not then become "your" thoughts, but they do "enter" you. Their words *must* enter you in order for them to provide a source for your response—to become a means of communication and exchange. The same is true of the "thoughts" these words symbolize. Thus we continue to expand the territory of your conscious awareness through this realization that the ability of "thoughts" not your own to enter you is already commonplace.

12.9 We have already established that the thoughts that arise from unity are not the same as the thoughts that arise from the thought system of the separated self. We might make this a simpler subject to discuss by making a distinction between thinking and thought. This distinction, while it will not be consistent with your dictionary's definition of these words, is still a useful distinction, as "thinking" is seen as what you "do." Even in your dictionary definition, being "thoughtful" is seen as a condition of mindfulness, and mindfulness is much closer to the idea of wholeheartedness, or sharing in unity—the state of which we speak. Realize also that you do not consider it to be the "thinking" of another that is shared with you in dialogue, but the thoughts. Thus this distinction will suffice for our further discussion in this chapter.

12.10 Let us now consider "thinking" to be the active and often unwelcome voice "in your head," the voice of background chatter. And let us consider your "thoughts" to be the more meditative version of your "thinking," often even resulting in a conclusion to your thinking, a summary of the finer points, as what might come to you in a reflective moment at the end of the day. Again we will see the idea of thoughts "coming to you" at such times. This is not the "thinking" of a conflicted and struggling mind, but the "thoughts" of a mind at rest.

12.11 Thinking is more descriptive of the ego mind; thoughts are more descriptive of the true mind. I am not saying that your ego is still at work because you still think in the same way as before. I am about to make the two main points of this discussion: The first is that thinking, with or without the ego, is a pattern of the separated self and does not serve you. The way in which you think may seem vastly improved since the ego ruled or may seem only minimally improved, but it is the pattern, not the ego, that is still with you. The second point is that although thinking does not serve you, you do have, right now, and have always had, true thoughts that come to you from your Self, the Self joined in unity. These are thoughts you did not "think," just as the first receiver of these words received them as thoughts she did not "think."

12.12 What I am striving to help you see, once again, is that union isn't achieved with a flash of light from above, but that it quietly infiltrates the dot of the self in its unguarded moments. I am attempting to help you to become aware and comfortable with the idea that, released of old patterns, the self will join with unity more and more frequently, until finally you will sustain Christ consciousness and live in the world as the elevated Self of form.

12.13 One of the primary ideas that will assist you in leaving patterns of thinking behind is the idea that thought as we are describing it, the thought that is not really thought but the way of coming to know of the Self joined in unity, enters you through the place of mind and heart joined in wholeheartedness at the center of yourself, a place that has nothing to do with the body. That you listen, hear, and respond may at times be of the body, but it may also at times not be of the body. The main idea to hold in your mind and heart is the idea of entry, and the idea that what comes of unity does not need access through your body's eyes or ears or any of what you consider to be your senses. Along with this main idea it is essential for you to realize that this is not so strange and unusual as it may sound, that this access and entryway already exists within you, and that you have already benefited from moments of interaction with, if not awareness of, the state of unity.

12.14 Now that you are coming to a more clear idea of what the "thoughts" that come to you from unity may be like, you will undoubtedly realize this: You have had such thoughts already, thoughts that *came to you* with an authority that you are not used to—thoughts that you *know*, beyond a shadow of a doubt, are true or right or accurate. They may be simple thoughts about a situation in which you are involved, or about the situation of another. Or they may be profound insights into your Self or the nature of the world.

12.15 You may at such times have been frustrated by an inability to share these thoughts, or to deliver them with the authority of the truth simply because you have *known* that they are true, and because you realized, as soon as the truth came into your mind, how seldom in the past you have been sure of anything. You may have been amazed at this new authority, and you may have desired more than anything to have others realize that you really *know* something, that this wasn't your usual opinion or idea you were offering up for discussion, but something you knew the *truth* about!

12.16 Many of you may, as well, have experienced the fading of your certainty about this truth over time. It may have been your inability to convey this truth, another's reaction to this truth, or simple doubt that arose within your thinking, but regardless of this fading of your certainty, you still carry within you the moment of realization—the moment in which the truth was *known* to you without doubt, known to you without uncertainty. And you may begin to realize that what has been said throughout this Course—that all doubt is doubt about yourself—is true. If another challenges you, or if your own thinking challenges you, doubt is quick to arise simply *because* you do not expect yourself to be certain of anything, and certainly do not expect yourself to be certain about the "right" or "true" course of action required in a situation, or of something that has not yet occurred but that you are given the certainty to know will occur. But once you have felt this certainty, you will never be so sure again that you cannot *know* the truth. Adding the phrase "beyond a shadow of a doubt" will be something you no longer need add to your knowing of the truth because you will realize its redundancy.

12.17 To know is to know. To know is to be certain. This may seem crazy or impossible, and in your realization that it seems crazy or impossible to you,

you may become more aware than ever before that what I have said about your way of thinking being insane is true. You think it is perfectly sane to go through life without knowing anything "beyond a shadow of a doubt," without knowing anything with certainty, when the reverse is what is true. It is *sane* to know the truth. It is *insane* not to know the truth.

12.18 Some of you will have credited your personal or individual self with the "figuring out" of this truth. Others of you will have recognized the "voice" of authority with which this truth came to you as something other than your usual thoughts, other than your usual "self." Either way, however, you know that your self was involved, somehow, in this coming to know of the truth, even if this coming to know of the truth wasn't quite "of" the "you" of the personal self.

12.19 The thoughts that come to you from unity can thus be seen as both your own thoughts and thoughts that arise from union. Union is not other than you, as I am not other than you. Union includes you, just as the All of Everything, the whole of wholeness, the one of oneness, include you. We are, in unity, one body. We are, in Christ consciousness, one Christ. We are, in wholeheartedness, one heart and one mind.

CHAPTER 13

Sharing and a Refinement of Your Means of Expressing What You Know

13.1   There is no danger, in this time, that you will *know* the truth and *then* discover that you were wrong. You know the difference between certainty and uncertainty and are far more likely to err, especially in the beginning, in discounting what you know rather than in being adamant in the proclamation of what you know. But this desire to proclaim what you know will grow in you, and while you will not be "wrong" in what you know, you may have difficulty in understanding exactly what it is you have discovered; and you may have difficulty in the expression of what you know, especially as what you know grows beyond the realm of mind and body, form and time.

13.2   What you will be coming to know in this new way of discovery will be coming to you from the state of unity, from a state you share with all at the level of Christ consciousness but that may literally *not* be sharable with those who remain in a separate state *except* through the sharing of who you are and who you know others to be. There are two issues of great import contained within this statement, and we will explore each separately.

13.3   The first is that what you will be discovering, what you will be coming to know, will be coming to you from the state of unity, which is a shared state. Although what you will be coming to know is already known to you, it will still come in the form of a surprising discovery, a joyous discovery of the previously known but long forgotten identity of the Self and all that lives along with you. This knowing will, for a while yet, be surprising because it will be reversing the insanity of your life as you have known it thus far. These reversals will be among the first revelations and will seem quite simple and pleasing as they enter your awareness, but they may come to be seen as quite complicated as you begin the practice of living with what you come to know.

13.4   What is known to you in an instant through the new means available to you within the state of unity will still seem, at times, to need to be learned anew in daily living. This is knowing that will often come in a flash, and is, in a sense, a humorous metaphor for the idea of a divine "ray" of light descending and granting enlightenment. Take another look at your Bible for many stories such as these, and you will read account after account of people who did not know how to live with what they came to know, with what was received in a "ray of light" from within the state of unity.

13.5   What comes of unity is in union and thus is whole. Therefore the knowing that will be coming to you will be given in a state of wholeness. You have previously learned of everything in parts and details and particulars. While you are perfectly capable of coming to know in wholeness, a way that is actually natural to you, it will seem so foreign at times that you will feel "blinded" by the light of knowing. You will realize that you know something you did not know before in form, that it is important, monumental even; but you will be unable to "see" this knowing, to envision it in the world of separation, to translate it into the language of the separated self.

13.6   You will know that this knowing must be shared. And yet, you will not, at first, fully realize that this sharing is not needed so much as a means of imparting important knowledge to others, but so that you can come to understand it. What comes of union is a knowing that exists in relationship. Once you have attained a state of being able to sustain Christ consciousness, this will no longer be a problem because you will constantly abide in awareness of the relationship of unity. But until this state is achieved, you will move in and out of states of awareness of the relationship of unity.

13.7   This need not overly concern you as it will not affect you as it did those of the past because you are living in the time of Christ, a time when no intermediaries are needed or required. Thus you are not called to become an intermediary trying to bridge the knowing of the separated self and the Self of union. What you are called to do is to share in union with others whose awareness is expanding.

13.8   You have been told and told again that you are not alone, and this has been among the biggest hurdles for many of you to overcome because your state of aloneness is all you have known. This perceived state is synonymous with the personal self, with the idea of individuality, with separate thoughts, and with the idea that no one will ever be able to truly know you. But join with others who are experiencing the expanding awareness of the time of Christ, and you will begin to see the evidence that things are different now. Join with others who are coming to know through the state of unity, and the evidence to the contrary will be overwhelming. You will begin to truly understand that you are not alone and separate, and that even the coming to know of the state of unity is a shared coming to know, a coming to know in relationship.

13.9 Just as you were taught that you could not learn *on your own*, you are now being told by one who knows that you also do not come to the knowing of the state of unity alone. Why then would you think that you could come to full expression of what you have come to know without sharing in relationship? Partial expression, yes. But that partial expression will bear the mark of your *perspective*, and that is why partial truth is never the whole truth, and why the whole truth is the only truth.

13.10 Sharing in relationship is what the state of unity is all about. It is what it *is*.

13.11 We come now to the second part of what we are exploring together here, the idea that what you come to know may literally *not* be sharable with those who remain in a separate state *except* through the sharing of who you are and who you know others to be. All this means is that while you may feel unable to share or express all that comes to you from unity, and while you may feel unable to share or express the authority and truth you know it represents, you will, by living according to what you know to be the truth, form the very relationships and union that will allow the truth to be shared. The relationship or union, in other words, precedes the sharing of what can only be given and received in relationship.

13.12 This is why you were told specifically not to evangelize or attempt to convince. These are actions of the separated self attempting to fulfill intermediary functions. Relationship, or union, is what negates the need for such intermediary functions. By being who you are, and seeing others as who they truly are, you create the relationship in which sharing can occur. Without relationship there is no willingness and no union. Without relationship, you behave as a separated self attempting to communicate union from the state of separation. This does not work. Join with your brother and sister in Christ, however, and sharing becomes effortless and joyful and effective. Cause and effect become one. Means and end the same.

CHAPTER 14

New Frontiers Beyond the Body and Mind, Form and Time

14.1   Discovery is more, of course, than the acceptance of your accomplishment and these beginning steps into the real state of unity. Discovery is also consistent with the way most of you have thought of it throughout your lifetime. It is, in other words, consistent with the action and the adventure of discovery within the world around you.

14.2   Here it will be helpful to keep in mind the idea of "as within, so without." We are not leaving the Self to explore, because the Self is the source and cause of exploration as well as the source and cause of discovery. And yet the Self is far more than you have experienced as yourself in the past.

14.3   The Self is not separate from anything, not from anything in the physical world or anything in the state of unity. This is why the key to unlocking the secrets of all you might want to know before beginning the creation of the new are the ideas we have just explored, ideas of how what is not of the body can still be known to you. And this is why this exploration and discovery needs to be invited and experienced *before* you become partners in the creation of the new.

14.4   Let me remind you again of your invulnerability and the cautions given within this Course concerning testing this invulnerability. In a certain sense, these cautions are now lessened. While you still are not to view your invulnerability as a testing ground against fate, you will, to a certain extent, need to remember your invulnerability in order to be a real explorer, and to fully participate in the discovery that lies beyond the body and mind, form and time. You will need to put into practice the suspension of belief that was spoken of earlier. You will need, in short, to set aside the known in order to discover the unknown.

14.5   I would suggest beginning this exploration with simple questions posed during the course of your normal life. Questions such as, "What might this situation look like if I *forgot* everything I have previously known about similar situations, and looked at this in a new way?" Questions such as, "Do I really need to worry about this situation, or can I *affect* this situation simply by not worrying about it and allowing it to be and unfold as it will?" Questions such as, "While I realize that the facts would tell me this or that is true, I wonder what would happen if I disregarded the facts and was open to this being something else?" These questions could be asked in situations as common-place as balancing the checkbook, or as momentous as a doctor's diagnosis of a disease. These questions could be asked when decision-making seems to be called for, and when plans seem to need to be made.

14.6   One of the major benefits of questions such as these is that they can circumvent the usual thinking you would apply to these situations. They can circumvent the labeling of many situations as problems or crises. They can leave the way open for revelation.

14.7   It has been said often that revelation is of God, but remember now that God is not "other than" and that the God who seemed so distant from you when you abided in separation can now be heard and seen and felt in your experiences of unity.

14.8   Your openness will not only leave the way open for revelation but for cooperation. Cooperation comes from the All of All being in harmony and relationship. When this harmony and relationship isn't realized or accepted is when you believe you have need of planning rather than receiving, when you believe you have cause for stress and effort rather than for just being open to what comes.

14.9   Your awareness of the harmony and cooperation that naturally extend from the state of unity in which all exist along with you, was advanced by the idea of acceptance you took to heart earlier, and paves the way for discovery as a constant coming to know and coming to be.

14.10   Coming to know is the precursor of coming to be. The precursor to manifestation. The precursor to creation of the new. It paves the way much as each step of learning that was needed in the time of learning paved the way for the next and then the next. But while I say "much as," this is only to provide you with a way to understand this, for learning is incremental and discovery is not. Learning took place in parts in an effort to lead to whole-

ness. Discovery comes to you in wholeness. So these steps are not about
parts or levels but about the expansion of your awareness of what *is*.

14.11 To expand is to open "out," to spread "out," to increase, to *become*. It is,
for us, about bringing "out" what is within. As you become aware "within"
your Self, you enable the expansion of awareness into the world. As within,
so without. An explorer seeking a new continent to "discover" first became
aware "within" of the possibility of the discovery of something more. The
awareness "within" thus became awareness "without."

14.12 Becoming is all about a movement into form or manifestation. You
already *are* manifest in form, and so the idea of *becoming* that has been with
humankind throughout time must signal a recognition that what you are is
not complete, has not yet become whole, has not been fully birthed. Your
forms are complete in the physical sense of sustaining life. Your form was
birthed and you have celebrated many birth "days" since your actual birth,
progressing from youth to adolescence to maturity, as well as many days of
birthing new aspects of the self, all without *becoming* more fully who you are.

14.13 Again, these ideas can be likened to the ideas put forth in A Treatise on
Unity and Its Recognition when it was said that "a treasure that you do not as
yet recognize is going to be recognized. Once recognized it will begin to be
regarded as an ability. And finally, through experience, it will become your
identity." That *treasure* is the new way of thought put forth in A Treatise
on the Art of Thought, the thought that is the miracle, or miracle-readiness, the thought that comes of unity and that extends and expresses itself
through your form, thus elevating the self of form. It is awareness, acceptance, and discovery of what is beyond form that allows the beginning of the
transformation of what is beyond form into expression in form. Awareness,
acceptance, and discovery are, in short, what allow form to *become* the *more*
it has so long been seeking to become.

14.14 Thus, what is discovered is discovered in the state of unity. It is discovered by means of your *awareness* of your access to the state of unity, as well
as by what you discover there, and only *becomes* through the expression you
give it. Here *becomes* could be stated further as what becomes known and
sharable in relationship, what becomes actualized through the expression of
thoughts, feelings, art, beauty, kind interactions, or miracles. What is real
in the state of unity is what is real, yet you have known this reality not even

though it is the more subtle memory of this state that is behind your striving to become. Now you are beginning to see the vastness of what is meant by creation of the new. What is meant by creation of the new is creation of a new reality.

14.15 This reality begins with awareness of what is beyond body and mind, form and time. It proceeds to this awareness being accepted, adopted as an ability, and then to becoming your new identity. It proceeds to the transformation we have spoken of, to the act of becoming the elevated Self of form. You are thus entering the time of becoming, the time of becoming the new you which must precede creation of the new *world*. For as it has been said: As within, so without.

14.16 Being whole is being present. Being whole is being all you are. Being whole is being present as all you are. When this occurs you are All in All, One in being with your Father.

14.17 This wholeness of being is what lies beyond body and mind, form and time. *Becoming* the elevated Self of form is becoming whole, and will be the *way* in which source and cause *transform* body and mind, form and time.

CHAPTER 15

Becoming and the Principles of Creation

15.1   Before creation of the new can begin, you must come to know the way of creation as it *is*. It has not always been the same, and it will not be the same in the future as it is now. But there are certain principles that govern creation. These principles are like unto the patterns that were created for your time of learning and that will be applied anew to the creation of new patterns for the new time that is upon us.

15.2   The first principle of creation is that of movement. Rigor mortis, or the stiffness of death, is nothing but a lack of movement, a lack of movement of the blood through the veins and the consequent stiffening of the muscles. The Dead Sea is a "dead" sea because of lack of movement. Thus these are excellent examples to illustrate the principle of movement as life itself, the idea of lack of movement as lack of life.

15.3   Life and the movement of *being* into form is what occurred when God "spoke" and the Word came into being. Movement is energy, the life force of creation and of being, both in unity and in time. By being you are *in* movement. By being you are an expression of being.

15.4   The second principle of creation, then, is that being *is*. It is what *is* and it is the expression of what *is*.

15.5   Life is movement through the force of expression. The third principle of creation is thus expression.

15.6   These are not, however, separate principles, but a single unifying principle of wholeness: Movement, being, expression. One did not occur before the other, as they are not separate. There was movement *into* being and an expression *of* being. But what was there to move before there was being? This is the way the mind looks at principles, one coming after the other and building upon each other. This is not the way of creation, which is why these principles of unity must be seen as the undivided wholeness of the principle of unity before creation of the new can begin.

15.7 Let me use the creation story of what was once my tradition as an example. Before God "said" anything, a mighty wind swept over the wasteland and the waters. The wind, which is as great a signifier of movement as rigor mortis is of lack of movement, is the first element mentioned in this particular creation story. This first mention of movement is literally present in all creation stories because there is no story without movement. There is no story to tell without movement. Nothing is happening. So movement might be likened to something happening—to the beginning, the beginning of the story and the beginning of creation.

15.8 Then God, a being, spoke. Here we have both the introduction of a being and the continuation of movement. Speaking denotes not only a speaker, the being, but the movement of sound. Then we are told the content of the words: It was said, "Let there be light." More movement. Only when movement, being, and *expression* came together, however, was there light. Light might be seen, in this example, as the first act of creation.

15.9 I repeat this story not as fact, or to still any doubts about these principles of creation, but to give you an example that is easily understood, an example of the way in which these principles work together. What I have left out of this story, the formless wasteland, the earth and the water that the wind first swept across and upon which the light first descended, is an interesting omission, made by many. What were the earth and water if they were not form?

15.10 They were barren form. Form unable to create or bear fruit. Form was simply *barren* form before movement swept across it and animated it with the attention and awareness of spirit—with sound, light, and expression. Could these barren forms not be compared to the forms of the not yet elevated? What if the existence of form was seen to predate the animation of that form with life and spirit? Would this not be consistent with what we attempt to do here? With our continuing work of creation? Would this not even be consistent with spirit existing in every living form from the beginning of *time* until the end of *time*?

15.11 Time is what begins and ends. Time is what began when life took on existence in form and space. It is temporal rather than eternal. Alongside it, in the state of unity, rests all that is eternal, all that is real. What is real is but another way of saying what is true. What is true is eternal life, not temporal life. There are no degrees of life. One form is not more alive than another. All that lives contains the breath or wind of spirit, which is eternal and complete.

15.12 Expression, movement, and being are about what is eternal passing through what is temporal. Thus I return you to the lesson on "pass through" which was contained within this Course. The Course sought to teach you to develop a relationship with all that passes through you. Now is the time when the fruit of those efforts will be reaped. For what passes through you now is a relationship without end. What passes through you now is the eternal come to replace the temporal.

15.13 To try to capture the eternal would be like trying to catch the wind. But just as the wind can power many machines endlessly when it is allowed pass through, so too can spirit endlessly empower form when it is allowed pass through.

15.14 You might say that the wind comes and the wind goes. It blows in mighty gales and whispers in gentle breezes. Any sailor knows the wind is fickle. But any sailor also knows the wind never dies.

15.15 You have all been sailors here, animated by the wind of spirit and at one time sailing—flying along with the wind at your back—and at another time sitting still or seemingly bobbing along with no apparent direction. You have attempted to build better sails to catch the wind, or motors to replace it, never realizing its constant and continual presence only needs to be allowed to pass through you to be in relationship with you, never realizing that this is, in truth, what animates you, that this is that without which you cease to be. Continual and unblocked and aware pass through is what we now consider.

15.16 You have been prepared for this by the realization that your thinking mind will no longer be necessary as your access to unity, or Christ-consciousness, is maintained and sustained. Let us begin with the idea of maintenance and proceed to the idea of sustenance.

15.17 Maintenance is thought of most often as keeping what you have, and as keeping what you have in good repair. It is not often thought of as a lasting measure, which is the primary difference between the idea of maintenance and the idea of sustenance.

15.18 Maintenance assumes that you already have something of value, and that you wish to take care of it so that it will continue to be of service to you. Maintenance implies a certain attitude, an attitude of care, vigilance, anticipation, and a knowing that without this care, vigilance, and anticipation, the value of what you seek to maintain will be lost. Thus we look at maintenance as the work, or relationship, with the desired service. In this example, maintenance is what you give in order to receive the maximum connection to unity that is possible in this time. You realize that some breaks in service will still occur, that maintenance will not make the connection perfect, but that it will keep it of service to you.

15.19 And so we begin with the idea of maintenance of your relationship with unity. You have experienced unity now and you wish it to continue to serve you. You thus must strive to maintain the conditions that will allow it to do so. This is, as with all maintenance, a temporary measure, but one you desire to have discussed, just as we discussed parameters to your state of conscious awareness.

15.20 To move from maintenance to sustenance is our goal, however. To *sustain* is to keep in existence. To recognize unity as sustenance is to recognize it as that which sustains life. Sustaining unity or Christ-consciousness is being done with the need to maintain conditions that allow it to be present. Maintenance will lead to sustenance.

15.21 Let this idea enter you now. You have left behind the conditions of learning. Why? Because they are no longer needed. The time of learning has ended. When this time of becoming has ended, the conditions that allow your acceptance and discovery of all that is available within unity, or Christ-consciousness, will no longer be needed. This will be as big a step as was the step that left behind the conditions of learning, a step from which you at times feel as if you are still reeling.

15.22 This step was like the final step after your ascent of the highest mountain. These dialogues might be seen as taking place there, with the guide and the team of climbers who accompanied you on your ascent. And at this highest point of the highest peak of the highest mountain, you pause and become accustomed to the thinner air, the view from above, to what you now can see. You catch your breath and let the wind of spirit fill your lungs once again.

15.23 Here is where you work in relationship to maintain what you have learned, for you know that when you return to the level ground from which you climbed, you will be different as a result of having made your ascent. The hard work is done. What you gain here you gain from what is beyond effort and beyond learning, and from the maintenance of the state in which you reject the conditions of learning. You maintain here, in short, all of the conditions necessary to reach your goal.

15.24 What you will have gained on your return will be the goal itself—the sustenance—for what you will have gained will never leave you but will sustain you forever more.

CHAPTER 16

From Image to Presence

16.1   Barren forms might be seen as forms that existed before the onset of the state of becoming. You are now in the final stage of the state of becoming. You now know who you are, and so now you can begin the work, or the relationship of this final stage: The stage of becoming who you are. This is the stage in which movement, being, and expression come together into the re-creation of wholeness that will be expressed in the elevated Self of form.

16.2   The creation story is occurring, right now, in each of you who have reached this final stage of becoming. This is both the beginning stage and the final stage, for once begun, the story of creation moves inevitably to join with the accomplishment and wholeness that already exist in unity. Creation occurs in each of us, seemingly one at a time. Creation is our coming into our true identity, and is the extension or expression of that identity into the creation of wholeness in form.

16.3   To be barren is to be empty. Empty is the opposite of full, the opposite of wholeness. It is the perceived condition of lack. It is the belief that what animated form with life did not remain. The belief that in the passing through, a relationship did not form. But as can be easily seen, the earth is no longer a formless wasteland. Form was animated with spirit and entered a state of becoming. You were animated with spirit and you too entered a state of becoming.

16.4   You can be an expression of being and yet not express the wholeness of being. This is a description of the state of becoming. It is a perceived state. It is a state in which the unified principles of creation are seen to be taking place as separate steps. This is so because of the condition of time. Once these principles are unified, time will have ended just as time was once begun.

16.5   The unified principles of creation, once unified within each of us, bring light to each of us; they bring the ability to see, the ability to know, the ability to be, the ability to create. Through the art of thought, these abilities become who we are. God and Creation are synonymous, and you are reminded of that here as you and God become synonymous through Creation. Means and end are one. Cause and effect the same. Creation is means and end as God is means and end. Creation is cause and effect as God is cause and effect. When you move from the state of becoming to the state of being whole, you will have moved through the act of creation and you will have become a creator. You will be ready for creation of the new.

16.6　You were told within this Course that being *is* as love *is*. Here you are told that being is a principle of creation and you are not told that love is a principle of creation. Love is not a principle any more than it is an attribute. This is because love remains in eternal wholeness. Love cannot be learned, and so has stood apart from the time of learning. Being could be *learned* here, because it was not yet whole. Being is synonymous with identity. When your being and your identity, your Self and your awareness of Self are whole and complete, being, like love, is no longer capable of being learned, for it no longer has attributes.

16.7　Love *is* the spirit of the wind that animates all form. Love *is* spirit, *is* God, *is* creation. Love is a description of the All of All because it is whole and rests in eternal completion and wholeness. Love *is* the state of unity, the only relationship through which the Self and God become known to you. Love, God, Creation, are all that remained in union, in eternal completion, when form came into being.

16.8　Yet movement, being, and expression are also what *is* because they are the givens. Love, like God, like Creation, is the giver of the givens. Life was given through the extension and the expression of God, of Love, of Creation—through the extension of wholeness—into the seemingly separate identities of form. The way of that extension was the way of the unified principles of creation, the way of movement, being, and expression.

16.9　The difference between the *way* that *is* and *what is* lies in choice. While you think that you can choose to stand apart from God, apart from Love, apart from Creation, you cannot. But you *can*, while existing in time and form, choose to stand apart from movement, being, and expression. You can choose, in other words, to exist without allowing spirit to move you, without allowing yourself to be who you are, without allowing for self-expression.

You might think that you can *be* simply because you exist and that as long as you exist in form you are *being* because you are being something. You are alive. You have form. You think and feel. You have even been told that you would cease to *be* without the existence of spirit, and so, you think, you must at least *be*. You are, after all, called a human *being*.

16.10 While you are becoming you are still being acted upon by creation. You are still being acted upon by creation because you are not yet whole. When you are whole, creation's principles will be what you do and what you are rather than what is happening to you. Creation's purpose, creation's cause and effect is wholeness and the continuing expression of wholeness. While it was said in A Treatise on the New, that "Now is the time to move out of the time of becoming who you are to the time of being who you are," it was not said that this time of becoming was completed.

16.11 And yet giving and receiving are one in truth. All of the principles of creation are in accord with this truth, and thus these truths occur in unison or in union. Becoming *is* movement. Movement is given and becomes movement in form. Being is given and becomes being in form. Expression is given and becomes expression in form. Since you were conceived in form, you were in movement. Since you were conceived in form, you were being. Since you were conceived in form, you were expressing. It would be impossible for these principles of creation not to be constantly occurring in everything that lives because all that lives, lives because of creation's continuing creation.

16.12 Becoming is the movement from image to presence. It is upon you as we speak. It is not a learned state or process and it should not be seen as a cause for disappointment. Perhaps you thought you were beyond this point of becoming. And yet, as you have begun your practice of awareness, acceptance, and discovery, you have felt as if you still have a long way to go. You have often thought that even though you may be done with learning, you don't feel quite complete, or possibly even feel as if learning has not quite been accomplished in you. This is precisely why we now discuss this state of becoming, this movement from image to presence.

16.13 There is creation going on in this becoming, the very creation promised you. This is the creation of the new *you* that you were told will precede the creation of the new world. This is what is meant by "as within, so without." Only a new *you* can create a new world. The new *you* is the elevated Self of form who you are in the process of becoming. This time of becoming is the time in between your awareness of and access to Christ-consciousness or unity, and your sustainability of Christ-consciousness or unity, in form. In your time of directly experiencing the movement, being, and expression of unity, you are being who you are. At other times, you are becoming who you are.

16.14 In your time of directly experiencing the movement, being, and expression of unity, you are whole and complete, you feel no lack, no uncertainty, no doubt. You are confident in what you know. You realize fully that you are no longer a learning being and that you have no need for teachers or for guidance other than for that which comes from your own heart.

16.15 At times when you are not directly experiencing the movement, being, and expression of unity, you realize the state of becoming. To realize the state of becoming is to realize that an in-between exists between the time of learning and the time of being the elevated Self of form; that times still exist in which you are not wholly present as who you are.

16.16 When you are not wholly present as who you are, you are experiencing, still, the image or after-image of who you are. This image is like a lingering shadow. It encompasses all of your former ideas about yourself, all of the patterns of the time of learning, all of the moments in which you feel an inability to join in union, and in which you recognize still the image of your former self.

16.17 This is only an image. This is not your personal self, your ego self, or your separated self, come to reclaim you. This is why we have also described this as an after-image. This is but a photograph that remains, a copy of what you once might have thought of as your "original" self. It is but an impression, as in clay, or a reflection, as in a mirror. It is as removed from who you are as is the picture of an ancestor or a landscape that hangs on your wall separate from what it is an image of.

16.18 There may be striking beauty in this image, as there is in art of all kinds. This may be an idealized image of your former self, the image of your *best* self, who you may imagine now, through the grace of God, you finally are. But this may also at times be an image of a type, a construction of the subconscious, which still sees in forms and symbols. This kind of image may leave you thinking that you are "acting" as if you have changed, while even within your new actions you see archetypes of the previously known and previously experienced.

16.19 The stimulus for these after-images is gone. They are but sensations that remain, like memories of childhood. This time of becoming is a time of coming to acceptance of them as what they are—images. This time of becoming is a time of coming to acceptance that they are not real. They are no more real than the mirage of your future, another aspect of the image you have held of yourself. They are no more real than was your image of heaven, or any image you have had of heaven on earth, paradise found.

16.20 The time of becoming is a time of letting these images be without reacting to them. It is a time of coming to no longer "hold" these images in your mind and heart. It is a time of letting them first cease to affect you, and then of letting them go entirely, for without letting them go you are not fully present. Without letting them go, your presence is not wholly realized, you are not fully here, not whole, not complete. You are *at times* who you are, but you also are, at times, but an image of who you have perceived yourself to be.

16.21 This image, being but an image, is incapable of true joining in relationship. You must be fully present in order to join in relationship. All of your images are false images, and when you retain them you do not allow for the time of learning to be replaced with the only replacement that will sustain Christ-consciousness, the replacement of learning with sharing in unity and relationship.

CHAPTER 17

The Secret of Succession

17.1 To succeed is to follow after, and to follow into inheritance. It is a following after that occurs in time and space rather than in truth. It is never about one. It is not about replacement. It comes in a never ending series rather than in singular form. It is not true succession if there is a break in the chain or in the line of succession for true succession does not stop and start, but is continual.

17.2 The series build to a climax, to what, during the time of evolution, might have been called evolutionary leaps.

17.3 The secret of succession is simple. It is but a matter of wholehearted desire. Do you wholeheartedly desire to follow me to your true inheritance? To come after me and be as I was? To be the inheritor of the gifts that are ours? Do you desire this? Are you willing to claim it? Are you willing to claim it in form and time?

17.4 Can you understand that what you claim in form and time was always yours?

17.5 Little can be had without desire. Desire, unlike want, asks for a response rather than a provision. Desire is a longing for, a stretching out for. Imagine yourself at the summit of this mountain we have climbed, standing with arms raised, hands wide open, gazing jubilantly into the heavens rather than toward the earth below. This is the stance of both desire and fulfillment. Of longing and attainment. Of having asked and having received. Of having striven mightily and succeeded. It is what comes after the embrace of homecoming, and what comes before the passing of desire and the reverence that replaces it. It acknowledges a certain "taking over" of the spirit of desire. Having "arrived," the desire to "get there" has not been satiated but only has grown into something different. With having arrived comes the "presence" of Self so long awaited, the joy of accomplishment, the taste of victory.

17.6   But the desire, the desire is stronger than ever before. The influx of attainment has begun. The height of achievement has been reached. Your glory is realized. But the desire, the desire is stronger than ever before.

17.7   You are not alone in your glory or achievement and you marvel that this takes nothing from your feeling of accomplishment. You want to share it with the whole world. From the top of the mountain, arms outstretched, this desire too has caused your arms to raise as if of their own accord. You feel the power of giving and receiving as one, for this is what this gesture symbolizes, a great and steady flow of giving and receiving as one, an unbroken chain of giving and receiving as one. You offer up your glory and call it down from heaven, both at the same time.

17.8   But the desire, the desire is stronger than ever before.

17.9   You know instinctively that this desire is not a desire to hold on to what you have. That this moment of achievement and glory is a gift of this moment, a gift of presence. Your gesture, so like unto that of a champion who has crossed a finish line and won a race, is not meant to remain as it is in this moment. It is not a trophy for your wall. It is not an achievement you would hope to best. It simply is what it is: A moment of presence full of both desire and fulfillment.

17.10   Hope, as was said within this Course, is a condition of the initiate. You have now passed hope by as you have moved beyond the state of initiation. You are no longer hopeful for what will come. Hope is desire accompanied by expectation. To expect is to await, and you are no longer waiting. You have arrived. You have passed through the stage of initiation. You have reached the top of the mountain.

17.11   You stand now at the threshold. The stimulus has been provided, the journey taken. You are present. Now is the time for your response.

17.12   That response is wholehearted desire, which is the power that *A Course of Love* came to return to you. You were told within this Course that wholehearted desire for union would return union to you and return you to your Self. This is the moment of realization of that accomplishment. But your desire has not left you. Your desire is stronger than ever before.

17.13   What is different now is that your wholeheartedness, as well as your desire, has moved beyond the pattern of thought.

17.14   Let me return you to the questions that were asked of you earlier, for they are even more pertinent now. Do you think desire will still be with you when you have achieved what you have desired? Is it not possible to conceive of a time in which desire will no longer serve you, just as learning now no longer serves you? If you reach a state of full acceptance of who you are, and in that state, fully accept that your contribution is being made, will desire still be with you?

17.15 Your heart is a full well. It is because you have now turned to your heart, instead of to your thinking, that you feel both fulfillment and desire. But my earlier questions seemed to indicate that once fulfillment was reached, desire would no longer be with you. But your desire is still with you. It is stronger than ever before.

17.16 The only reason why this might be so is that it is meant to be so. Something is still desired.

17.17 Desire asks for a response. Earlier it was said that desire asks for a response while want asks for provision. What is the difference we speak of here?

17.18 Provision is about preparation for future needs. This is an appropriate response to want, but it is an inappropriate response to desire. It is an assumption of needs unfulfilled. You now stand in fulfillment. This is the secret of succession.

17.19 Desire asks for a response. From where is this response sought? You now must understand the fullness of the well of your heart, the interrelationship of desire and fulfillment. The interrelationship of desire and fulfillment is what occurs at the threshold. Beyond the threshold is the state in which desire has passed and been replaced by reverence. To revere is to feel awe, which, it has been stated, is due nothing and no one but God. To move beyond desire to reverence is to move into the state of communion with God, full oneness with God, wholeness.

17.20 You have realized now that you remain in a state of becoming, and any disappointment you may have initially felt with this realization has been replaced by acceptance. Acceptance has come because you recognize the signs of becoming that we have been discussing. You recognize them because they are what you are feeling. You may wonder still, however, how you can be told that you have arrived and are at your journey's end and yet still have farther to go.

17.21 You have nowhere to go. The journey is over. You stand at the threshold, the gateway to the site you have traveled so far to reach. You are here and desire fills you, even while you know the glory of having arrived.

17.22   But having arrived here, it is as if a new question is asked of you. Just as in the myths that are as ageless as they are timeless, you are asked for something here. You are asked for a response.

17.23   Only in myth is this response to a specific question, but even the specific questions of myth, when seen truly, were questions of the heart, calling only for response from the heart.

17.24   Desire calls here, louder and stronger than ever before, because of your proximity to what you have desired. Every hero's journey returns him home. To where he started from. In story form, this takes place with movement. Years are spent traveling many paths and many miles. All the heartaches are experienced along the way. All the experiences and learning occur on the journey.

17.25   This is why you have been told the time of parables, or stories, has ended. This is why you have been told: "As within, so without." This is why you have been taken to the top of the mountain without leaving home. You have taken the inward course, the inward journey, the only journey that is real in the only way that is real.

17.26   We will spend forty days and forty nights here together, at the top of the mountain, fasting from want, becoming aware of desire, responding to desire. This is the final stage of becoming. Herein lies the secret of succession.

THE FORTY DAYS
AND FORTY NIGHTS

Accept Me

1.1 Acceptance of me is acceptance of your Self. Acceptance of me is acceptance of your inheritance. This is nothing new to those of you of the Christian faith. To others it will seem an acceptance beyond your ability, an acceptance that there is no real cause to request. Why must Jesus be accepted? Why cannot the truth be accepted? Why cannot everyone hold their distinct beliefs as long as they are beliefs in the truth?

1.2 Beliefs are not what is being spoken of here. *Acceptance is.* Acceptance is not belief, it is not prayer. I care not in what form of the truth you believe, nor to what god you believe you send your prayers; although if you do not believe in your Self above a form of truth, and if you continue to send your prayers to a god who is other than you, you will not cross the threshold.

1.3 We are here on the top of the mountain together, beginning our work together. I am no longer your teacher, but there is a reason that you are here with *me*. You have been listening to *my* words, and these words are what have brought you here, not to a place but to an ascended state. Without your acceptance of who I am, you will not fully accept who you are. Without your willingness to achieve this acceptance, you will not receive the secret of succession presented here. You can read of it still, but it will not convey to you what it will convey to those who have accepted me. You will return to level ground with eyes unopened and listen to parables once again and learn once again from the stories of others.

1.4 Why should this be so important? Why not leave well enough alone? If acceptance of Jesus is a stumbling block for many, why should it be required? A college education has requirements. If math is a stumbling block for some, a foreign language for another, are these requirements waived? Let us just accept that requirements are prerequisites for many states you value. To marry one man you must choose to leave others behind. This is required. This does not mean the married woman will not relate to many men in many ways, have many male friends, teachers, guides. It means that one is chosen as a mate to the exclusion of others chosen as a mate.

1.5 In these examples we are talking of simple requirements, requirements of daily life rather than of eternal life. The requirement asked of you here is not to exclude others in whom you believe and have found a connection to eternal life, only to accept me as who I am.

1.6 Now that you have moved beyond the thought system of the ego self, you look back on it and realize why you could not know your Self while the ego was your guide. You were required to make a choice between the thought system of the ego and the thought system of unity. This choice was made, and thus you have arrived here and left behind the state of the initiate, the time of waiting. You have chosen. You are merely asked now to look at what you have chosen and to understand what you inherit through the secret of succession.

1.7 If you are to succeed me, you must accept me, much as you must accept your ascension to this mountain peak and this dialogue that is occurring here. If you believe this mountain peak is merely metaphorical, you will not realize that you have ascended or that you have left behind the conditions of the initiate. If you believe these are words of wisdom and that you can remain ambivalent about their source, you will not know me nor accept me, and you will not know or accept your Self.

1.8 Why are we so linked that your ability to know your Self is contingent upon your ability to know me? Because *I am*. This is akin to saying *Love is*. I am what *is*. I am the way, the truth, and the life.

1.9 Not accepting me would be like training to be an astronaut and, at the moment of take off, refusing the requirement of the spacecraft as the way to reach outer space. This would be akin to non-acceptance of the way that has been given to bring your desire to fruition. The spacecraft could be seen as a response to your desire. So too can I.

1.10 This would be like saying, "If I am an astronaut, I can reach outer space without a space craft. I have been trained, I understand the truth about outer space, I believe in my abilities; but I do not accept the spacecraft as necessary." Lest this example fail to move you I will continue.

1.11 Many people now are discovering the power of healing. Some think this power comes from one source and some from another. You may think that, as long as the power is called forth, it matters not the name by which it is called. You may think that it all comes from the same source, regardless of what the practitioner of healing calls it, be the practitioner a faith healer or a medical doctor. You may make one exclusive choice to attend to your needs of healing, or you may make many choices. You may think these choices matter not, but only the power of the healer. Some of you may see this example as an example of why you should not need to accept me. You may claim that you understand that this power is of God, whether it be the power of granting life to grow within the womb, or the power of giving new life to a limb withered or broken. You may wonder why it should matter whether this power be called Buddha or Allah, Muhammad or God.

1.12 It matters not. The power of God is not what is being spoken of here. It is *our* power that is being spoken of here. The power of the god man. The power of God brought into form. The power of who we are rather than the power of who God is.

1.13 God cares not what you call Him. God knows who He is. It is man who has known not who he is, and it is through me that this knowing can be returned. This is simply the way it is. It is not about being right or being wrong, about one being more and others less. This is simply the way to sameness of being, to the reunion of all, from the holiest of the holy to the lowliest of the lowly.

1.14 Had any of the holy men and women who walked the way of the world since my time learned, accepted, and lived the teachings that have brought you to this point which I now would like to lead you beyond, the world would be a different place. Have I not called you to a new time in which the conditions of learning exist no more? In which the suffering and death that have obscured that love is the answer are banished, rejected, and a new world of love accepted in their place?

1.15 You are all beloved sons and daughters of love itself, no matter what you call that love. You all are equally beloved. That you give your devotion to one religious tradition or another matters not. That you accept that I am he who can lead you beyond your life of misery to new life matters absolutely.

1.16 I am not your teacher and you are not called to follow me blindly. But you are called to follow, or succeed me. Only in this way can new life be brought to old.

1.17   Your desire to know me has grown as you have read these words and grown closer to your Self. This is because we are One. To know me is to know your Self.

1.18   Let us return a moment to the creation story and my acknowledgment that this creation story is occurring in each and every one of us. Let me move forward and speak a moment of Adam and Eve and the fall from paradise. Let us extend our idea of the *creation story* to include the creation of man and woman. Adam and Eve represent your birth into form. I represent your birth into what is beyond form. Adam and Eve represent what occurred within you at the beginning of the story of your creation. I represent what occurred within you recently, the story of your rebirth through this Course.

1.19   The story of Adam and Eve, and the story of Jesus, are within you. *As within, so without.* In each of you is Adam and Eve represented in form. In each of you am I represented in form.

1.20   The New Testament was the beginning of the new. My life represented fulfillment of scripture, of all holy writing, of all learned wisdom. In fulfillment are endings found and beginnings created.

1.21   This fulfillment of scripture has now occurred within you. When it occurred within me, it occurred within all. It became part of the continuing story of creation, of creation acted out within the created.

1.22   The story came after the fact. Thus the fulfillment was always part of the story of creation. It was always part of you as it was always part of me.

1.23   There is no story to project what comes next—no accomplished story. There is only scripture unfulfilled, the promise of inheritance or the threat of doom. Myth too stops short of fulfillment, of return to paradise.

1.24   Yet this return to paradise, to your true Self and your true home, is written within you. It only needs to be lived to become real. You must accept me because I lived it and made it real for you. You must accept me because I am the part of you that can guide you beyond what I accomplished to the accomplishment of creation, and beyond creation to the story not yet written, the future not yet created. To the realization of paradise and of your true Self and true home, in a form that will take you beyond time to eternity.

1.25   This has been spoken of as the second coming of Christ because my story goes unfulfilled without your fulfillment. It is only in your fulfillment of the continuing story of creation that my story reaches completion. It is a story whose completion cannot occur in singular form, but as with any true inheritance only in a series, only in a joining together of all of the parts of the creation story into the wholeness of the story's end. As a story is seen to move from one element to another in an unbroken chain of events, so too is the story of creation. As history proceeds with gaps only waiting to be fulfilled in current time, so too is it with the story of creation.

1.26   You are living history. You are living what will tomorrow be history. You are living creation. You are living what will tomorrow be the story of creation. A chain of events is merely another way of saying cause and effect. The chain of events of creation include, thus far, the movement of being into form and the movement of being beyond form. What will be realized through the secret of succession is the elevation of form.

1.27   You can only fast from wanting by realizing what it is you desire. My forty days and forty nights on the mountain succeeded my baptism and my acknowledgment as the Son of God, and preceded my time of living as my Self in the world. So too does it with you. You long for and desire me because our story is the same. You are living my story as I lived yours. They are one story.

1.28   Lay aside your want of other answers, other stories, and accept the story we share. The Bible and all holy texts can be seen clearly now as one creation story. One story of one beginning. One story with many promises made. Promises of inheritance and fulfillment, promises that give hints to, but never quite reveal, the secret of succession.

1.29   I am the secret of succession, the way and the life, the beginning of the end of the story that is to be fulfilled, brought to completion and wholeness in you and in me, so that together we bring about the second coming of Christ and the elevation of the Self of form.

DAY 2

Accept Your Self

2.1   Acceptance of your Self is acceptance of me. Acceptance of your Self is acceptance of your inheritance. Now is the time to come into full acceptance of the human self as well as the Self of unity. It is time for the final merging of the two into one Self, the elevated Self of form.

2.2   You have let go the ego, re-viewed your life, unlearned previous patterns, and now see the difference between the image you hold of yourself and your present Self. But still, in unguarded moments, in moments in which you would desire peace, memories of your life continue to play within your mind, often still bringing you sadness and regrets.

2.3   All of these moments you review have brought you here. But I realize that you have not as yet developed the capacity to accept this fully. For most of you, much of what you have considered your mistakes and poor choices have been reconciled. You can see the pattern of your life as clearly now as if a masterful biography had been written of it. It is this clarity that has brought a new "haunting" to some of you. Your life is being seen more as a whole now. The parts are fitting together. You can see how you have moved from seeming purposelessness to purpose.

2.4   You are like an inventor who wasted many years, much money, and endured many hardships over many projects that did not come to fruition, and now has succeeded in inventing just what was always envisioned. This is the moment of fulfillment and desire coming together, the time in which to realize "it was all worth it."

2.5   This is the time of revelation of meaning. You who have so long striven to give meaning to the purposeless, here see meaning revealed.

2.6   And yet you cannot still some of your regrets. The feeling is not as strong as it once was, and you are very unlikely to still experience guilt or shame; but the hurts you have done others may weigh heavily on you now. It is as if, at this mountain peak, you have discovered a lightness of being, and yet within it is this stone of regret. You continue to have a nagging feeling that this stone of regret will always keep you anchored to the self you once were, that no matter how high you ascend, it will continue to drag you back.

2.7   This is the feeling that will prevent you from receiving the secret of succession. It is like the force of gravity, a feeling that you will not be able to remain at this height long enough to benefit from what will be shared here.

2.8   Part of this feeling arises from erroneous ideas that remain regarding your unworthiness. Part of this feeling arises from the erroneous idea that you can fail, even here. These are the temptations that confront those who have dared to ascend the mountain. It is not the height you have attained that causes your fear of falling. It is the depths to which you feel you once descended that calls forth your fear here.

2.9   These are mainly, in truth, judgments, judgments that arise from your conscience, from that part of you that has compared your actions to the laws of man and God and found yourself guilty.

2.10   Let me ask you now, are these feelings—feelings that are attached to your belief that you have harmed others—not feelings of sorrow? Are you not sorry for these actions? Have you not expressed your wish that you had acted differently? Can you see a way to change the past or to "make up for" what occurred in the past?

2.11   Now is the time for acceptance, even of these actions that you would rather not accept. They happened. They were what they were. I ask you not to forget. If your home had been destroyed by a tornado or a flood rather than adultery and divorce, would you not see the benefit of accepting what had occurred and moving on? You might counter this by saying that if you had been the adulterer, the cause of the divorce, this was different than a tornado or a flood. Yes, this was different, but this difference does not place these actions beyond the idea of acceptance.

2.12   Conversely, were you the innocent "victim" of an adulterous mate, a mate whose actions led to divorce and the destruction of your home, can you not accept that this is something that happened? We leave aside, for the moment, any considerations of other outcomes of such actions, whether they are negative or positive in your judgment. We look for a simple acceptance of the facts of your life.

2.13   I could give thousands of examples here, but the point is that we are not looking for degrees of wrong-actions, or wrong-doing. You all have moments you wish you could re-enact, decisions you wish you could change. These actions are unchangeable. This is why simple acceptance is needed.

2.14   We speak not of forgiveness or even atonement here, for these have been thoroughly discussed earlier. You have all been through the time of tenderness, the time that preceded your giving and receiving of forgiveness, your request for and granting of atonement, your re-viewing and unlearning of the perceived lessons of your life.

2.15   But just as you are called here to accept me despite possible misgivings such as religious beliefs, you are called to accept yourself. This unconditional acceptance is necessary. I will give you one final example in order to make our discussion as clear as possible.

2.16   This is an example from my own life, an example the idea of which still plagues many of you. This example is that of the crucifixion.

2.17   For many of you the crucifixion is among the reasons you hesitate to fully accept me. It is hard for you to believe that my suffering was symbolic of the end of yours when so much suffering has continued. I will add here the example of my resurrection. It is hard for you to believe that my resurrection heralded eternal life when death has been a constant companion of all those who have lived since my time. It is difficult for you to believe that by following me you will not walk in my footsteps. Perhaps you will be granted eternal life, but not until you have suffered as I suffered. This idea would hardly be a joyful idea with which to begin our work together.

2.18   As was said within this Course, my life is the example life. The way in which I have talked of it recently may have led some of you to consider it as a symbolic life rather than an actual life. All of our lives here are symbolic rather than actual. Just as the creation story is symbolic rather than actual. This does not mean that my life did not happen, that it did not occur in time and space, just as yours is occurring now in time and space. What this means is that what occurs in time and space is symbolic, that it is representative of something more.

2.19   So let us consider my life again, just briefly, and let us consider the something more it may represent.

2.20   My life consisted of the same major elements as yours: Birth through childhood, maturity, and with that maturity action in the world, suffering, death, and resurrection.

2.21   You have accounts of my actions that begin with the appearance of my form in the world, but that mainly occur during my time of maturity. These accounts do not stress the time of childhood as it is a time commonly held to be one of innocence. The accounts of my maturity generally begin with the recognition of who I am. This is symbolic of the idea put forth here that until you are aware of who you are, your life has not literally or symbolically begun.

2.22   It was in awareness of who I Am that my life took on meaning. It could be argued that this awareness existed at my birth, and this too would be accurate, since all births are meant to be eagerly looked forward to as beginnings of I Am. Since most births are seen in this way, and most mature lives are not, we concentrate here on mature lives.

2.23   My mature life thus began with the recognition of who I Am, as does yours. This time was followed by my "example life," a life that began with the forty days and forty nights spent upon the mountain, and continued with my joining with my brothers and sisters, with the bringing of light to darkness, power to the powerless, health to the sick, life to the dead. My life touched all those willing to be touched, changed all those willing to be changed. But great unwillingness remained. Willingness was not yet upon humankind. The choice was made collectively to remain in illusion. The choice for continued suffering was made. And so I responded to that choice. An example of response was needed. The example was that of a symbolic gesture. It, too, was a choice. A choice to take all that suffering upon myself and kill it. To say, here is what we will do with suffering. We will take it away once and for all. We will crucify it upon the cross of time and space, bury it, so that it need be no more, and demonstrate that new life follows the choice to end suffering.

2.24   "I" did not suffer, for I knew who I was and chose no suffering. This is what is meant by the idea that has been repeated as "I died for your sins." My death was meant to demonstrate that the end of suffering had come, and with it, eternal life.

2.25   Here, then, is where *you* need to make the choice that those in my time could not make, the choice to end suffering. This is the choice I made "for all." This is a choice you make for all as well.

2.26 *Willingness* is now upon humankind. What my life demonstrated but needs to be demonstrated anew. But this will not happen if you cling to suffering. If you do not accept your Self, all of yourself, you cling to suffering.

2.27 This is why you first needed to accept me. To accept me is to accept the end of suffering. To accept the end of suffering is to accept your true Self.

DAY 3

Accept Abundance

3.1   Accept your anger for it is the next step in the continuum upon which we travel. When a person is dying, just as when a person is undergoing this final surrender, there are stages through which one moves. The first is denial, the second is anger. We have already spoken of denial, albeit in a new way. Now we will speak of anger, in both an old and a new way. Let me suggest to you what it is truly all about. It is about the way you have learned and your lack of understanding of what this did to you.

3.2   What was it that was "taught" *to* in the time of learning? It was the mind. Thus, your mind has been trained for learning and you are most willing to have new insight, new information, and even new discoveries, enter through your mind—because this is known to you and is what you are familiar with. In the area of the mind were you most willing to accept teachers, leaders, guides, authorities, for only *through* them did you learn. You are beginning to see now that this learning was not a choice but only the way you knew life to be. While the freedom of childhood learning might be seen as the way learning was meant to be, the time of this pure learning has grown shorter and shorter while the time of enforced learning has grown more entrenched.

3.3   In the area of the body came another form of learning about which you saw yourself as having little choice. When the body had something to teach you, what choice did you have but to listen? So the mind and body were both conditioned to have learning thrust upon them. You long ago quit resisting most of this learning and "accepted" it as the way things are. This kind of acceptance is what we are reversing with a new acceptance.

3.4   With your heart you grew less accepting of these "outside" attempts at influence. You, who as both individuals and as a species, have been conditioned by thousands of years of learning through the mind—learning in often painful ways—said "no" to learning through the heart. Many of you will admit to growing a bit angry with the beginning of this Course and its challenge to your ideas regarding love. Most of you approached learning through the heart with even more openness than you did new ideas about love, not realizing that they were one and the same.

3.5   So our first point of discussion in the realm of anger is that no matter where anger seems to arise, anger is a product of the condition of learning. It always was, but now this is being revealed to you not just through my words, but by your experiencing of anger in new ways. You may not have felt a great deal of this anger yet, but it is there, and here we will discuss its function.

3.6   There is one area that is greeted with even more anger and more resistance in regard to learning of all kinds—in other words both old learning as well as new—than love. This is the area that you call money and that I call abundance. Feel your body's reaction to this statement. Some of you will feel excitement at the idea of this issue being finally discussed; but be aware of your feelings as we proceed, for I tell you truly, here is where your greatest anger, and your greatest lack of belief and acceptance, lies.

3.7   You may believe a spiritual context for your life can change your life, make you feel more peaceful, give you comfort of a non-physical nature. These ideas, whether you realize it or not, are all associated with mind. It is through your mind that these new ideas will change your actions and your life, your mind that, through increased stillness, will give you more peace, your mind that will accept comfort of a certain type, even extending to a new comfortableness of being. You believe having a spiritual context for your life can, in other words, change your inner life, but are more skeptical in regard to its ability to affect your outer life; and nowhere are you more skeptical than in regard to money or abundance. The area of money, or abundance, is where learning fooled you and failed you the most.

3.8   You may believe that having a spiritual context for your life will assist you in feeling more loved and possibly even assist you in finding some *one* to love. You may believe that this spirituality can help mend a feeling of broken-heartedness, can cause you to extend forgiveness to those who hurt you, to make amends to those you hurt, or to simply quit feeling guilty or bitter, shamed or rejected because of them. But you do not believe this spiritual context is capable of bringing you the lack of want you associate most strongly with money.

3.9   Just posing the idea that having a spiritual context for your life will assist you in living abundantly will cause you to think, "I doubt it." Or, "I'll believe it when I see it." You might think spirituality can assist you in living a more simple life and thus a life of limits of which you are more accepting. But given time to consider such an idea, you are likely to become more and more agitated, to go back and forth between the general and specific, thinking of both your own lack in life and that of those whose lack is more pronounced than your own. Fairness seems non-existent in terms of who "has" and who "has not," and the world seems made up of haves and have nots and to function in the insane way that it does largely due to this discrepancy.

3.10   In such a case, would it make sense that we not address this issue, this blatant cause of so much insanity? This cause of such anger?

3.11   Let us return for a minute to the base idea behind the issue of money or abundance: the way you have learned. The mind would tell you that nothing is "given," and that all must be either learned or earned, most times both, for you have learned in order to earn, learned in order to advance yourself in the world in one way or another. Since money or abundance is not a "given" for all, but only for a few, you think of it much like the "given" of natural gifts or talents, the "givens" of fresh and inspired ideas. You do not, however, see that these are in truth linked as givens, for you do not see that all are gifted.

3.12   It is only because some are gifted more abundantly than others that they can use the givens of talent and inspired ideas to bring them wealth. This is the idea of bartering, which we have spoken of before, or bargaining, which we will speak more of here. It is the base idea that is behind all ideas of lack, an idea you so thoroughly learned during the time of learning that letting it go, even now, still torments you with worry and anger. It is the idea of an "if this, then that" world. An idea of a world in which the beliefs set forth within this Course are neither seen nor lived by.

3.13   This is the basic fallacy that the time of learning supported. The idea of "if this, then that." The idea of abundance earned. The idea of nothing being truly free. Not you, and not your gifts. Everything coming with a price. Abundance comes, even to those gifted, only through the exploitation of gifts. Abundance remains, even to those born with it, only through the exploitation of others. Only through some having less do some have more.

3.14   To think in such terms, and then to see such thoughts as even capable of having spiritual value, is something you think of as insane. There seems no remedy, and so you would rather not even attempt an understanding of how things might be different. As far as you have come, these ideas are still with most of you to one degree or another. Even though you know these are false ideas, and in that knowing may even say to yourself as you read them that you no longer think in such a way, they are there in the learned pattern and you know this too. They are what prevent you from believing that the ideas set forth in this Course, when practiced, are capable of making a difference, especially in terms of monetary abundance. This is one of those situations in which you know and have no idea what to do with what you know. Being unable to replace, in application, the false with the true, the pattern of the false remains.

3.15   Yet how can you accept yourself when you have feelings such as these? How can you accept the idea of inheritance with ideas such as these? How do you accept me when you see me as symbolizing a life of "godly" poverty, and of calling my followers to abandon their worldly goods?

3.16   Thus must this source of your anger and discontent, this source of your non-acceptance, be revealed in a new light.

3.17   Let's go back to the idea of money when it is seen as a "given." It is seen as a "given" in one case only: In the case of inheritance, in the case of those "born" to money. Thus this is a good place to start, since inheritance is that of which we speak. Let's be clear that we are not speaking of money or abundance as being "given" when it is hard work to attain. Not even when it seems to come from some event of luck or fate. We are talking specifically here of the money "given" through inheritance, the money some lucky ones are born with.

3.18   These are those who are resented most within your world. And yet envied. This resentment and envy fills you with anger. If you feel any anger now, pay attention to its effect on you. You can feel, perhaps, the strain and tension in your stomach, back and neck.

3.19   The degree of your discomfort with this issue is something you only imagine to be greater than that of your brothers and sisters. A few of you will not feel this, and if you are among those few, do not skip past this dialogue, but join in so that you understand, as do those for whom this dialogue is meant, the power of this aspect of your brothers and sisters lives, and the power and function of anger.

3.20   The power of money to affect you is a power that is denied, rarely acknowledged, seldom spoken of. Think you not that the shame that comes from heartaches or mistaken actions is any greater than the shame those feel who feel no abundance, who suffer a lack of money. There is still a commonly held belief that abundance is a favor of God and, as such, those who do not experience abundance have done something wrong. We will return to this, but first let's continue with the denial of money's effect.

3.21   The shame and pain of heartaches and mistakes is more often and more easily spoken of than the shame of monetary failure. Certainly much complaining and general fretting are done, but only to the degree in which you feel you are in the same circumstances of those to whom you complain. To speak of money matters with someone who might have more than you, you would consider a shaming act. You would fear that they might think you want something from them and you would suffer embarrassment. To speak of money with anyone who has less might open the door for a request for what you do not feel you have to give. To reach a position in which you feel you need to ask for money from others, even from a bank, is seen as a dire situation indeed. This asking will likely be an ordeal of some consequence. Even those who are seen by others as constant "takers," unafraid to ask for a "hand out" or free lunch, experience these same emotions, the build-up of anger, resentment, and shame.

3.22   In the realm of money lie your biggest failures, your greatest fears, the risks you have taken or not taken, your hopes for success. What you wish for is contingent upon having the "means" to pursue it, and few of you truly think that money would not solve most of your problems. Even those of you on this spiritual path think money is among the greatest limits to what you can accomplish, to how you can live the life you would choose to live. You may have left behind aspirations of wealth, and replaced them with ideas of having more time, more fulfilling work, simpler pleasures, and yet you still see your new state as one that does not touch upon this aspect of "reality." The better life you might attain will be a by-product rather than the effect of Cause.

3.23   Here is the *real* of the old "reality" most solid and unrelenting. Not having "enough" is the "reality" of your life because it was the reality of the learning life. Even if you are one of those others consider lucky, one of those who always has "just enough," little do others know that your fear is as great as theirs. That while you admit you have "enough," you are sure it will not be enough for what the future holds. And if you ever need evidence for this position, it is quick to come. As soon as you get just a little bit ahead, a need arises. The roof leaks, the car breaks down, and an endless series of needs arise. This "evidence" is exactly what you have sought.

3.24   This is the way fears operate. They operate in the pattern of the ego, a pattern that was learned, a pattern that was emphasized and reemphasized through external events so that it would not be forgotten, so that it would reinforce wants until this attitude of wanting seemed impossible to unlearn. It is a pattern of survival, but not of *your* survival. It is the pattern of the ego's survival, and even though the ego is no longer with you, the pattern remains because what you learned, and the way in which you learned it, remains.

3.25   Remember, you have learned that nothing is "given," for what use would you have of learning if such were not the case? In our dialogue, we have begun to use examples of what you did *not* learn in order to demonstrate that what you learned is not true. What you learned is insane. But to realize the truth you must now fully reject the untruths that you learned. You must fully reject the ideas that taught you that you do not have enough, that you will only have what you can earn or learn, that only through effort will you gain, and that with your gain will come another's loss. In other words, here is where you must accept the teachings of this Course.

3.26   Do not feel dejected that you have not learned these things. They *were* learned, to the degree that you could learn them within the teachings of *A Course of Love*. But beyond learning is where we now stand. We now stand at the place of the rejection of learning—the rejection of *all* you learned.

3.27   Let me set your mind at ease, for you are not called to sacrifice, as you have been told time and time again. I do not ask you to give up what you desire, but to expect and accept a response to what you desire. Remember that we are headed even beyond desire, and know that desire must first be met before you can be taken beyond it.

3.28   The condition of want, like all conditions of learning, ended with the end of learning. The condition of want was a learning device—not one of divine design, but one of the thought system of the ego. It was a trick to keep you constantly striving for more, a trick to guarantee the survival of the ego-self, a trick that provided the small rewards of time-bound evolution, the small rewards that would keep you assured of progress through effort, and just as assured of ruin through lack of effort.

3.29   You think abundance is the most difficult thing to demonstrate, when it is actually the easiest. You think you could learn what is for you the most difficult type of learning, be it philosophy, math, or foreign languages, before you could learn how to make money, or in other words, to have abundance. You think you could more easily find love than money, even those of you who have felt loveless for too long to contemplate. And those of you who scoff at these remarks, because you feel you have learned the secret of money, the secret of success: Answer truly if you really believe this, or if you are merely covering over your fear of not having enough with an incessant drive to prove it is not so.

3.30   Just as so many of you are thankful for your good health while at the same time dreading the disease that may at any point take it from you, those of you who have money see it in the same way. You may go along just fine for weeks or months or years, unworried about your health until the slightest pain makes you think of cancer. In this same way, there are not any of you, those who have money or those who have none, who feel that your financial "health" is any more secure than the "health" of your body.

3.31   How can you live like this? How can you have any peace when you live like this? What succor will your inheritance provide if thoughts like these accompany your inheritance? Were this a monetary inheritance, would you not squirrel it away for a rainy day, or spend it only with trepidation and an eye upon the bank account? Even those of you who would feel prepared to let it bring you joy would err in thinking that it could. How many times has what you thought would provide you with reason for joy failed to do so once acquired?

3.32   And so you might think, here, of what *has* brought you joy. A home, a garden, a musical instrument, the equipment that enabled a hobby or talent to be developed, a well-loved book, dinner with a friend, a new car, a new pet, the ability to provide a child with a good education.

3.33   You might think here too that money made from what you love to do has a different quality than money earned from toil. You might think that money earned from what you love to do is the answer, just as you might think that money spent on the more lasting pleasures such as the things described above is the secret.

3.34   For you are quite certain that there is a secret you know not. There is, and it is a secret I will try to share with you here, if you can let your disbelief and anger at this suggestion fall away. I know you expect a flowery answer, and surely not one that will be a "one, two, three steps to abundance" answer; but I will try to address you in an in-between tone, one that will not cause you to feel spoken down to or incite your hostility. One that will not only be truthful, but as practical as you need it to be.

3.35   You have been told that the time of the Holy Spirit, the time of a need for an intermediary between yourself and God, is gone. You have been invited to know God directly, and to develop a relationship with God. It is only in knowing God that the relationship of abundance will be made clear to you and break forever the chains of want.

3.36   Learning is no longer the *way* for good reason. It exemplifies the difference between information and wisdom, between finding an answer and finding a way or path. Many have read the words of the Bible, the words of Lao-tzu, the words of Buddha. To teach is to convey the known. To speak of a *way* is to invite dialogue and a journey. This is what all master "teachers" taught, often throwing the questions posed back upon the poser, in order to say: Use me not as an intermediary. It is only in relationship with the God within that the way will become clear.

3.37   To read the inspired wisdom of teachers such as these in order to "learn" has prevented the very relationship that these teachers sought to impart.

3.38   What you have "learned," and since the time of learning had revealed to you, is a new *way*, the way of direct relationship with God, the way of knowing through discovery. Remember always that knowing through discovery is knowing what was not known before, and keep this in mind as we consider the knowing of abundance.

3.39   When you have felt the reality of union, you have felt the place in which no want exists. You felt this through the responsiveness of the relationship that is unity. You perhaps desired an answer that "came to you" through no process you had known before. We spoke of this as thoughts you did not think. We spoke of these thoughts you did not think coming with authority and certainty, a certainty you had previously lacked. When I said earlier in this chapter that you are most comfortable learning through the mind because of your familiarity with the pattern of learning through the mind, you can perhaps see why these first revelations of union would come to you in a way associated with the mind.

3.40 You have accepted now, because of whatever experiences of unity you have had, that the knowing of unity is available to you. You may not have given great consideration to the access through which that availability arose, but since for most of you it has arisen as thoughts you did not think, if you were to make an association in regards to entry, you would likely say the entry point was the mind. This is, in a sense, true, as wholeheartedness is comprised of the mind and heart joined in unity. It would be more true to think of this joining as creating a portal of access, a new source of entry. But these points do not advance our discussion now and can be returned to later. The point here is your "concept" or idea about what you have gained from unity thus far being that which *can* be gained through the mind. As you advance, and as you become more open to other means of accessing the wisdom you once sought through learning, or through the mind, other means will open to you. You may see, audibly hear, and interact with what comes to you from union.

3.41 The idea I am trying to open to you here is the idea of a responsive relationship with unity that does not exist only within the mind of the wholehearted.

3.42 It is the visible world, the outer world, through which your wants find provision. It is the world of unity, the true reality, through which your desires are responded to. This does not mean that the place of unity is a place that does not interact with the place of form. It *is* interacting with the world of form *through you*.

3.43 Do you not see? You are the entry point, the only channel through which all that is available in unity can flow.

3.44 Abundance is the natural state of unity and thus your natural state, just as certainty rather than uncertainty is your natural state, just as joy rather than sorrow is your natural state. What you are being asked to do here, is to open the self of form to the place of unity, thus allowing this divine flow of union into the elevated Self of form.

3.45 Being open to the divine flow of union is the exact opposite of the condition of anger. Anger could be likened to an argument, a debate, in which you are on one side and determined to be the one who is right, the one whose side will win. What you hope to win, in this insane argument about abundance, is an acknowledgment, even from God, that you do not have what you need, that you are lacking, and that because of this, you have no choice but to continue to struggle and strive, to earn and to learn, to, in short, carry on in the world as you always have.

3.46   Even those of you who would claim to know this anger not, who would claim to wait in trusting silence for God's provision, are still waiting for provision. Even those of you who have asked God for abundance, and opened yourselves to receive it, even those of you who have seen some improvement or evidence you could cite as a response to your requests, see not the truth of the situation.

3.47   You still believe the truth of the situation to be the reality of physical form and of what you have or have not within the confines of that form. This would be like still seeing the mind as the only source of learning, and learning as the only source of knowledge. What you have begun to see is that the mind is not the source of certainty, no matter how much knowledge it attains. What you have perhaps begun to see in similar terms, is that money is also not the source of certainty, no matter how much it enables you to attain. Certainty, in other words, comes from somewhere else. This somewhere else we have defined as your true reality, the reality of union. Living in this reality, the reality of certainty, is the only key to abundance.

3.48   These words are just what you may have expected to hear, and you may feel a return of feelings of anger here. But we have said that there is a function for your anger. The function of anger is to lead you to the step beyond it, the step of action and ideas, the step often called that of bargaining.

3.49   Many of you will have already entered this step, this step of considering how what you might *do* might affect the response of God. You take this step without realizing that you are still acting in accord with ideas of it being an "if this, then that" world. You try to guess what God might want you to do, be it being still and not worrying about money, or taking actions, right-actions now, as opposed to your idea of the wrong-actions of the past, in order to bring money or abundance flowing to you. All that this period of bargaining represents is yet another stage in your movement toward acceptance. It is still based on the belief that you are responsible for the abundance or lack of abundance in your life. That it is you who, by changing your beliefs or your actions, can change your reality.

3.50   This is often a hopeful period and it, too, is not without value. You may have many good and even inspired ideas within this time. You may feel as if you are on the right track, that through the planning out of strategy and action, through putting all that you have learned into practice, you are sure to begin to see the benefits that have been promised. But many of your ideas and actions at this stage will be tinged with the anger that came before it. Here is where you may rail at the unfairness, at the unseen benefits of what you have acquired from this learning, of promises seemingly made and not kept. Where, you may ask, is the lack of struggle that has been promised? Why do you still have to try so hard? Work so long? Endure so much? Why isn't the end in sight?

3.51   The final stage in this process, this movement toward acceptance, is depression, a lowering of spirits and energy, a lack of desire, a lack of activity, a sinking feeling of going under, of going into the depths of sadness and despair.

3.52   Each stage may contain hints of the other, but in regard to money, or abundance, each stage is experienced and felt. This experience has only one combined value, one combined purpose, the purpose of the final letting-go, the final surrender that is necessary for the final acceptance to come into being.

3.53   Just as you were told you cannot "think" great ideas into being, or great talent into fruition, just as you were told, in other words, that the "givens" are not to be dealt with by the conscious, or "thinking" mind, so too is it with abundance. Abundance can only be accepted and received, just as great ideas and great talent can only be accepted and received.

3.54   You might argue now that what you do with great ideas and great talent is of consequence, and this is true. A great idea or great talent that is not brought into form, that is not expressed, that is not shared, is no greater than a seed not planted. But the gift of the great idea, the great talent, must first be seen and recognized, acknowledged and accepted, before it can be brought into form, expressed, and shared. What good would it do you to say "if I had talent," I would accept and receive it, express and share it. "If I had a great idea," I would accept and receive it, express it and share it. And yet you continue to think that *if you had money or abundance*, you would accept and receive it, express it and share it.

3.55 This *if* is all that stands between you and abundance.

3.56 You do not believe this, however, and the functions of denial, anger, bargaining, and depression are to lead you to this belief and, finally, to this acceptance. Acceptance first that you do not believe. And then acceptance itself.

3.57 Do you see the difference, even here, in belief and acceptance? Can you begin to see acceptance as an active function, much as learning was an active function? Acceptance *is* an active function. It is something given you to do. You think it is difficult, but it is only difficult until it becomes easy.

3.58 While you think of acceptance as just another word, another concept, another trick of the mind, you will not see it as the replacement of learning, and as such as an active state, a state in which you begin to work with what is beyond learning, a state in which you are in relationship with what is beyond learning. It is in truth, a state in which you enter into an alternate reality, the reality of union—*because* you accept that reality.

3.59 Like all that was taught within this Course, this is a matter of all or nothing. You cannot accept part of one reality and part of another. You cannot accept, for instance, the compassionate and loving benevolence of the universe, of God, of the All of All, and still accept the reality of lack. You cannot accept that in the reality of unity all things come to you without effort or striving except money. You cannot accept that you no longer have to learn and accept the condition of learning that is want.

3.60 Active acceptance is what allows the great transformation from life as you have known it, to death of that old life, to rebirth of new life. By clinging to some of the old, you prevent its death and you prevent the rebirth of the new. You prevent the very life-giving resurrection you await. You prevent the elevation of the self of form.

3.61 This does not have to be. You have wanted something to do to change your circumstances in this earthly reality. This is what you have to do. This is the action required. The active acceptance of abundance is the way to abundance. Active acceptance is a way of being in relationship with all that flows from unity. This you cannot learn but you can practice. Thus your practice begins.

DAY 4

The New Temptations

4.1 While we will broaden the focus of today's dialogue beyond that of money or abundance, we will still be addressing this area of your concern, as well as all other concerns that may be surfacing as you begin to move through the steps toward acceptance. Your anger will be serving you here as it brings attention to these areas most incorrectly influenced by the time of learning. Remember here all the "arguments" that I needed to present in the early part of this Course just to convince you that you are not alone and separate. Although *my* arguments were not fed by anger, your response will almost surely have been tinged with it at times. Although my arguments were not fed by anger, the arguments that arise now for you *will be* and as such are actually appropriate to this stage of our dialogue. We can argue here before we go on. We face together here the temptations of these arguments, these temptations of the human experience.

4.2 Yet we do not argue simply by engaging in debate. To engage in debate is but a strategy for proving one side right and one side wrong. We must begin with the realization that we are on the same side. The arguments we will be having will be meant to show you this: That on one side are the temptations of the human experience, which is just another way of saying all that you have learned; on the other side will be the truth, the new temptations that will incite you to leave behind the temptations of the human experience.

4.3 How can you feel as if you have a choice when the temptations of the human experience are the only choices that have been known to you? Thus you must be given the opportunity here to see what other choices might be before you.

4.4 Real choice is the first new temptation.

4.5 As we discussed in yesterday's dialogue, learning has not been a choice. Both as divine design and as a pattern of the thought system of the ego, learning has been with you and within you. Although the divine design of the time of learning is being recreated, the ceaseless pattern of learning remains.

4.6   The divine design of learning was a given and a natural part of you, much like breathing. You have no choice about breathing, yet neither do you, under normal circumstances, have to think about breathing. You might begin to think of all the "givens" of unity as those things that require no thinking.

4.7   Learning was not meant to be linked with thinking. Again I'll draw your attention to the learning of childhood. Learning begins long before the onset of the time of language that constitutes your ideas about what it means to think. In evolutionary terms this was true as well. Despite the creation story that symbolizes man's journey, early man was not a being who learned in the same way that you do. Early man had no language. His mind was not full of thoughts. Early man and early childhood can thus be linked as examples of a kind of learning that, despite evolution, has not left any of you. You all begin life without the ability to think in the terms you now associate almost exclusively with thinking, the terms of having thoughts, or words, in your mind.

4.8   Even after the onset of language, children continue to learn without thinking. Does this not sound odd, foreign to you? And yet this is the way learning was designed to be. Learning was given as a natural means of access to all that was available to you, but not through effort any more than breathing was designed to be effortful. Learning was designed, like the intake of breath, to be taken in and given out. Inhaled and exhaled. Inhaled and expressed.

4.9   The ability to learn is given to all in like measure. The conformity of learning, however, is the product of an externalized system. That you all attempt to learn the same things, and in coming to identify the world in the same way—the way that has been taught—think that you have succeeded in learning, is the cause of the insanity of the world and of your anger with the way things "are" within the world. This is an anger that stems from lack of choice. When you are "taught" the "way things are," where is the room for choice? Where is the room for discovery? And to find out that you were "taught" incorrectly! Why should you not be angry?

4.10   You are here now not to re-learn or be taught what life is all about, not to re-learn or be taught the "way things are" but to discover what life is all about and to discover the way to remake things as they are.

4.11 This is the new choice, the first new temptation.

4.12 The second new temptation is access.

4.13 You have been told that in unity a "place" exists that is your natural state, a state free from want, a state free from suffering, a state free from learning, a state free from death. To be told that such a place exists is no more comforting than consoling words if you do not feel you have access to this place. It is like being told that all of the treasure you might desire is locked away behind a gate to which you have no key.

4.14 Access, then, is the key to the treasure.

4.15 We have spoken at some length about access that seems to come through the mind. We have spoken of thoughts that arise that you didn't think. We have spoken of talents that were not learned. We have spoken of ideas that were not gained through effort. We have spoken of these things to begin to familiarize you with the "given" world as opposed to the world of your perception, what we might call a world-view attained through learning.

4.16 If you will contemplate for a moment what you know about the example left by my life, you will almost surely realize fairly quickly that my life challenged the world-view of the time and that it is still challenging the world-view of your time. Why might this be?

4.17 Let me assure you of what you already know, that everything about my life was purposeful. That challenge was meant then, and continues to mean now, a call to a new choice. It asks that you challenge your world-view in a most thorough manner.

4.18 The problem with this throughout the centuries has been a tendency to challenge one world-view only to replace it with another of no greater truth or value. My challenge has been reacted to as a challenge to be external-ized, a call to create a new system. But nowhere in my example life is such a system found despite all attempts to make it so.

4.19 The example often used for the creation of a system is that of my attrac-tion of followers, my claiming of disciples. The term disciple can be linked here with the idea of succession. What I asked of my disciples is not more than I ask of you. I asked them to follow in my way. I asked them to be, not as they once were, but to be as I am. I asked them to live—not in the world of their former perception, in a world-view that was taught to them—but to live in a new world and, by so doing, to demonstrate a new way.

4.20   In the time of learning, however, it was natural that my example life was seen as something from which to learn. In order to "teach" what my life represented to those who did not know me, methods of teaching were devised. From these methods of teaching, rules developed. The teaching was externalized and institutionalized. People began to see following me as belonging to an externalized institution, trying to learn what it would teach, and trying to live by the rules it would have them obey. Much progress was made within these institutions, but also much misleading was done.

4.21   This feeling of being misled is another cause of your anger—one of the primary causes, in truth. Not only has all that you have learned led to an inaccurate world-view in the here and now, but to an inaccurate world-view of the past, of the hereafter, of me, and of God. Not only has your mind been misled, but your heart and soul as well.

4.22   What could bring solace to an anger so profound? How can you be certain you are not being misled once again?

4.23   The answer to both come in the stated purpose of *A Course of Love:* Establishing your identity. You needed to first know yourself as a being existing in union before you could know anything else with the certainty you seek, for union is the treasure that has been locked away from you.

4.24   What many forgot, after the passing of the first of my disciples, was that they had access to this treasure. They still knew that it existed, but since they knew not how to access it, they called it the Kingdom of Heaven and longed for access to it after death.

4.25   Your anger here extends to yourself as well, for all of you know how many of my words have been forgotten, how many of the truths I expressed were still available to you, even within your religious institutions. You feel, perhaps, that you did not try hard enough, or pay enough attention to separating the true from the false. But blaming yourself does no more good than blaming others, for without the dismantling of the ego-self, without the dismantling of the self as separate and alone, you could not learn the truth no matter how much attention you paid, no matter how mightily you tried. For *on your own* you cannot learn the truth. On your own, only illusion can be learned, for your starting place is illusion.

4.26   Union is both the treasure and the key to the treasure. Union is both access and the place to which you desire access. As all that exists in truth, union is means and end.

4.27   To know the basic truth of who you are—that you are a being who exists in unity rather than in separation—is thus the first step to the access that you seek. Without knowing this, without knowing the truth of your existence, how could you be done with learning? This was what learning was for. And learning is not the way to the access that you seek. As all that exists in truth, the truth of who you are is means and end as well.

4.28   Within you is the access that you seek, just as within you is the Kingdom of Heaven.

4.29   The access that you seek is not a tool that can be purchased through your right-actions or even your longing and desire. For this access is not a tool but a function of who you are. This access is, like breathing, something that is natural to you until you begin to think about it. Realize how unnatural your breathing becomes when it becomes the focus of your thought. Thinking about breathing imposes an unnatural constraint upon a natural function.

4.30   Thinking, in this time beyond learning, could be rightly seen as a constraint you but try to impose on all that is natural. Your thinking, since it is a product of learning, does nothing but attempt to learn or teach. These are the natural responses of its training. Thus, a major key to your discovery of all that exists within you in the state of unity, is an end to thinking as you know it.

4.31   In practical terms, you might think of this as a disengagement from the details. Thinking is about details. I am imparting to you the key to abundance and all the treasure that will come with the end of the time of learning. You, on the other hand, are thinking, yearning, grasping for the details. You would like to know how, what, when, and where. While you concentrate on such as these, you impose a function unnatural to this time of Christ-consciousness upon this time. It is as if you ask to see clearly and then hold your hands over your eyes. You "cover over" the portal of access to unity with a film of illusion. You hide the gate in mist. Remember your breathing and how your concentration upon it affects it. Even learned skills react to this type of concentration. A pianist who suddenly thinks of the notes she is playing, falters. An athlete who suddenly thinks of the requirements of the athletic task he is about to perform, fails to perform with excellence. Why?

Because a film of the unnatural is placed over the natural.

4.32   Access simply exists within your natural state, much like breathing is simply a fact of the natural life of the body.

4.33   Many, however, have applied a different kind of focus upon breathing as a form of meditation. In doing so, they let the natural serve the natural. Some might "go into" the breathing and become one with it. Others might become the observer and in so doing remove themselves from the body entirely.

4.34   There is a similar type of focus that will serve you now. It is not a tool, as is meditation, for you are no longer in need of tools. But you have taken yourself away from the ordinary world. You are on top of the mountain. What is this all about? Why have we gathered together here? It is said that during my forty days and forty nights I meditated or prayed. It is said that I fasted. You have been told that you are here to fast from want. You know that you are here to experience both the old temptations and the new. You realize that this is the purpose of our time together here even though you have not put this purpose into words and put these words into your mind. What is the focus of which I speak, the focus that is not meditation, the focus that is not a tool? This is a focus on access itself.

4.35   You might think of the mountain top as symbolic of a place close to God. If God was once seen as a figure in heaven, and heaven as a place beyond the clouds, then the mountain top was symbolic of proximity. It was symbolic of a place from which God was almost touchable. As if one could raise ones arms and touch God, stretch just a little more and reach heaven. You thus may think of this time on the mountain as a time of getting in touch with your own access to God, your own access to heaven. You might think that if you stretch your idea of reality just a little bit farther, stretch your mind just a little beyond where it is comfortable going, that there you will find this access, this portal to all that lies beyond time and space, to all that exists in the place of unity.

4.36   We talked earlier of this as a time of fulfillment and desire. We acknowledged that your desire is stronger than ever before. Now is the time to focus on this desire and fulfillment, to stretch this desire to its limits, all the while realizing that its fulfillment lies already accomplished within, in the access that lies within.

4.37   This is a longing that carries with it the desire to go beyond thinking, the desire to go beyond words, the desire to go beyond where your imagination is capable of taking you. It is a desire for true discovery, a desire to access the previously unknown.

4.38 You must realize that here is where fear must be totally replaced by love. If you fear to go where the portal of access will take you, you will not go. Thus your desire needs to be greater than your fear. Love needs to reign. Love of self and love of your brothers and sisters, love of the natural world, of the world of form that is, love of the idea of the new world that can be, all of these must come together and be victors over the reign of fear.

4.39 What choice have you made my sister and my brother, if you have not made a choice of love? If you have not made the choice to reject fear? If you have not made the choice for the new? If you are still willing to say that you can go only so far in your acceptance of the truth of who you really are, then our purpose of being together here on this mountain top will go unfulfilled.

4.40 What tempts you here? To turn and look toward the towns and cities below? Or to turn and look up to the portal of access to unity? Do you turn and look back at form and matter? Or do you turn and look up where no form exists? Do you believe you can choose the formless and still return to the towns and cities, the green grass and the blue sea below? Why are we here but to show you these two choices? From where else could you so clearly see the choice between form and the formless?

4.41 But what, you might ask, of the elevated Self of form? Why is this suddenly a choice between one or the other? It is the first choice of the new temptations, the first real choice of Christ-consciousness, of the time beyond learning.

4.42 Smile with me now, as you think of yourself in this elevated place. You are still the self of form despite the truth that you are literally with me in a place of high elevation. Is this what you choose to remain? A self of form elevated by circumstance? A self of form on a high mountain? Or do you wish to carry this elevation back with you when you return? Do you wish to return the self of form who once visited an altered state, this state of high elevation? Do you wish to go back and tell tales of your experiences here and be made special because of this experience you can recount?

4.43 Or do you wish to go back transformed into the elevated Self of form? Do you want to know this place of access and carry it within you, or do you only wish the opportunity to revisit it when the need arises? Are you here to fast and pray only to have to return when you have once again become a glutton of want, when you once again feel the lack that you would pray for? Surely this you can do, for I deny no one the journey to the mountain top, not once or many times. But this is not what I call you to.

4.44   You have been brought here for revelation. You have been brought here to be tempted by the unknown of your inheritance, an unknown that, while it remains unknown, is still what you know you have longed for all your life. This unknown has been described to you in terms both specific and obscure. It has been described as all you have desired and more. It has been described as the end to the life of misery you have known and the beginning of new life. And I tell you truly, here is where this new life either begins or is once again delayed. Here is where you say, I want it all, desire it all, accept it all—for you cannot have of this in parts. Once full access has been revealed, what is yours is everything. But you will be different.

4.45   This is real choice. What is a choice that leads not to difference of any kind? These are the only choices you have made in a lifetime of endless choices. There is only one requirement for this choice: Wholehearted desire. Wholehearted desire is what *A Course of Love* taught you so that you could be taken to this place and tempted to leave behind the temptations of the human experience.

4.46   I do not have to spell out this choice for you, for you know exactly what it means. It means you will be as I am. It means you will live from love rather than from fear. It means that you will demonstrate what living from love is. It means that you will resurrect to eternal life here and now. It means no turning back, no return to fear or anger, no return to separation, no return to judgment. It means no longer trying to leave these things behind for they will be gone. It will mean no longer striving. It will mean no specialness. It will mean the individual is gone, and the self of union all that continues to exist. It will mean peace, certainty, safety, and joy with no price.

4.47   The old challenges, the old reasons for existing will be gone. All that will be left to do will be the creation of a new world in the only way that it can come about—through unity.

4.48   Your desire and your access are one and the same. If you desire this transformation wholeheartedly, if you make this choice with wholehearted desire, it will be done, and we will continue our dialogue so that you know more of the difference you have chosen. Once this difference is wholly known to you, we will begin true discussion of creation of the new, for you will be done with becoming.

4.49   These are the only temptations of the new that I can make you aware of until you have made your choice and have full realization of your access to unity. You will be able, of course, to continue on without making this wholehearted choice, but you will read only to learn and learning will not transform you. If you do not truly and wholeheartedly desire this choice, if you do not truly and wholeheartedly meet the condition of being fearless, you will know this, and you will pass through the time of coming to acceptance again and again until you are ready. You cannot fail but can only delay. For some the time of delay has passed. For those who linger in the time of acceptance, there is reason for this as well.

4.50   This may seem odd timing as you have just been asked to accept your anger. Just think. Anger was discussed rather casually alongside accepting me, your Self, and abundance. But none of these things are meant to be dwelt upon. The acceptance of abundance no more so than the acceptance of anger. You are called to accept and not look back, not to dwell in any of the states through which you arrive at acceptance, nor to focus on acceptance of one thing over another. You are not to label good or bad. Just to accept. Accept all. You do not have to hesitate here because you *think* you are still angry, or *think* you are still depressed. When you hesitate you have not accepted but dwell with the cause of your hesitation. When you accept you move on.

4.51   To be called to make a new choice before full acceptance of what *is* would be confusing. You who are thinking that you have not moved through the stages to full acceptance answer now as to what is stopping you. Do you choose to dwell or to accept? All, *all* you cannot bring forward with you is fear, for fear is the cause of the state of learning. You may have thought separation was the cause, but separation into form, had it occurred within the realization of continuing relationship, would not have been cause for fear in and of itself. Had you still known relationship, fear could not have separated you from truth and you would not have dwelt in illusion. The relationship of union is what you are here coming to know once again, which is why the time of fear, and along with it the time of learning, can cease to be.

4.52   I have not so directly linked fear and the time of learning before, but now you need to see their connection, for if you do not, you will not realize that fear is all that needs to be left behind. You will still *think* you have more to learn because you are angry, depressed, in a state of denial contrary to the denial asked of you, or because you still feel like bargaining with God. These things are only reactions to faulty perceptions, only the steps *toward* acceptance until they are accepted.

4.53   As we move into full access and awareness of unity, love is all that is required. Acceptance has been the means chosen, by us, to move you through the layers of illusion that have disguised your fear, to move you beyond false learning to the truth that only needs to be accepted. If you can move forward without fear, you can move forward. If you can move forward without fear, you will move forward only with love. If you move forward only with love, you will have realized there is nothing unacceptable about who you are except fear.

4.54   You but think that you can wholeheartedly desire to move forward with love and without fear and that there is still anything that can hold you back. This is what the time of acceptance was meant to show you! Nothing can hold you back except fear! You do not have to be perfect—perfect is but a label, and all labels of any type cause is delay. You only have to be accepting. Accepting of all that you are. Fear is not a part of what you are, which is why it cannot remain with you as the way opens for you to fully know the Self of unity. You are about to achieve your first glimpse of wholeness, of oneness with God. To know the truth of your inheritance.

4.55   Think a moment of the story of the prodigal son. All that the prodigal son was asked to do was to accept his own homecoming. Do you think he would have considered himself perfect as he approached his father's presence? Surely he would not have. You are asked but to accept your own homecoming. To leave behind the time of wandering, seeking, learning. To leave behind fear for the embrace of the love and safety of your true home.

4.56   This choice has come before you might have expected it to. It does not come at the end but at the beginning of our time together for a reason. This is simply because this choice is the beginning. This is the choice that allows us to continue our dialogue as one. To talk heart to heart. To have the kind of discourse that can only be had without fear. To truly experience relationship. It is from this beginning that you will come to be as I am.

4.57　We are here for the final stage of your becoming, not because you have reached some ideal of enlightenment or what you might think of as perfection. If this were asked of you, how many of you would have felt free to join me? Yet in your acceptance is your perfection realized without judgment. In your becoming is your enlightenment realized without judgment. These things become not achievements, but the acknowledgments of the accomplishment that has always existed within you and all of your brothers and sisters.

4.58　Here is the beginning point from which we continue to burn away the remnants of attachment to the old, the attachments that cause some of you to continue to feel sadness, anger, depression, or nostalgia for the way things were. These things will not leave you before you leave them. But you will leave them.

4.59　Join me in this choice, and we will leave behind the old and continue our movement toward creation of the new. There are many discussions still to be had. We are only at the beginning of our time together.

4.60　Our forward movement must be achieved, however. But one is needed to begin this movement. Followers will naturally succeed the first although this will occur with no fanfare and no "one" to follow. The first will create a series. Thus will the secret of succession be returned to you and put behind us forever the temptations of the human experience.

Day 5

Access to Unity

5.1   A point of access will no longer be needed once full entry is attained, just as a key is no longer needed once a door has been unlocked and passed through. Even though it will not be permanently needed, however, this point of access will remain crucial as long as you *maintain* rather than *sustain* the state of unity. This point of access will thus now be discussed, both as an initial entry point and as a continued entry point so that it is available to you until it is no longer needed.

5.2   For each of you this access point will in truth be the same, but perhaps quite different in the action which you use in order to enter it. For those of you who have felt the point of entry to be the mind in experiences already registered, there is no need to combat this feeling. For those of you who have felt the state of unity through experiences of the heart, there is again, no need to struggle against this. Let me elaborate.

5.3   For many of you, "thoughts you did not think" are among your first experiences of unity. Thus, just as when you might look up when trying to remember something, or tap a finger at your temple, there is, in a certain sense, a "place" to which you turn for these experiences. This does not mean that these experiences come from your mind or from a place just beyond your physical concept of the mind but, since *you* are not your body, the idea of what originates "within" coming from a point beyond the body is not now too unbelievable to contemplate.

5.4   As we said yesterday, our form of meditation, a meditation that is not a tool but a function of your natural Self, is a focus on access. Thus we begin with what feels natural to you. We give access a focal point in the realm of form.

5.5   This focal point must be of your own choosing. Your point of access may be your head, or a place just above or to the right or left of your head. It may be your heart, or some mid-point just beyond the body. It may, for some, feel like a connection that arises from the earth and as if it is just below the form of the physical body. Some could feel it in their hands and others as if it comes directly from their mouths as speech is enabled that bypasses the realm of thought completely. Do not fight any of these feelings or others that I have not named. Just consider them givens and choose what feels most natural to you as a focal point for your focus on access.

5.6   What we have focused on for some time now is love. Love never changes. It thus is the same for each of us. Yet not one of us expresses love in exactly the same way as another. This is important to remember now as you begin to work with your access to unity.

5.7   Unity and Love—as we have within this work shown them to be—are the same.

5.8   Thus, access too is the same. It exists. It is there for you. It is given. It cannot be denied unless you deny it. It is only because you have not known this that we speak of it in this way here.

5.9   Just as it is helpful in some instances to associate love with your heart even though we have identified heart as the center of the Self rather than the pump that functions as part of your body, it will be helpful to have identified this chosen access point for unity even while remembering it is not of the body alone.

5.10   While the purpose of this work was to have you identify love and thus your Self, correctly, there is still fine-tuning to your understanding to be done, and this will be done as you come to know what unity is, and so more fully come to know your Self and love.

5.11   There would seem to be one major difference between unity and love and that difference would seem to be love's ability to be given away.

5.12   Access to unity will seem, at first, a quite individual accomplishment, something one may have and another may not. While this remains the case, you may desire to give others what you have and feel unable to do so. Yet, like love, unity is known through its effects. All the benefits of union can be given away to any willing to receive.

5.13   While you do not consider yourself as having or needing an "access" point to love, and while you may treat love still as an individual attribute intimately associated with the Self you are, you know love is not an attribute and that all love comes from the same Source. You know you have been able to "give" love only when you have felt you "have" love to give. You thus have long known the truth of giving and receiving as one within your own heart. You might think of access in the same way—as enabling you to realize that you "have" the benefits of union to give.

5.14   Like love, unity has one source and many expressions. It will be in your unique expression of union that your Self will come to wholeness and you will be fully who you are and able to express love fully.

5.15   Realize here that although you are now a part of a community seeking the same goal, the realization, or "making real" of your accomplishment, and its expression, will not look the same way twice. What you each desire from union most will be what finds the greatest expression through you.

5.16   A "healer" for instance, might, thus, feel her access point as being the hands and express what is gained through unity by a laying on of hands. Similarly, you might say healing is one of the ways the healer expresses love. In truth healing and love are the same.

5.17   Who you are now, what your desires are, and where your talents have been recognized, are as given as the goal you now desire to realize. Again I remind you that the sameness of union is not about becoming clones or one specific type of idealized holy person. Union is being fully who you are and expressing fully who you are. This is the miracle, the goal, the accomplishment that is achieved through the reign of love, the maintenance and finally the sustainability of union.

5.18   Realize here that while you want to know the specifics of how this thing called access to unity will work, you are also impatient with specifics. You want immediate results, not more practice. You want relief and an end to effort, not another lesson to learn that you will be told is not a lesson. Not another cause for seeming effort in order to arrive at the effortless. But realize also that this effort that you rail against is still of your own choosing. The realization of a "way" to make things as they are is never effortful in and of itself.

5.19   As you may seem to pause here in your movement in order to understand the way in which that movement is achieved, you will almost surely once again have doubts. Doubts are never more pronounced than when specifics are being dealt with. Yet you continue to desire specifics. This is because you are still entrenched in the pattern of learning, as your earnest effort to leave effort behind implies. Remember that union cannot be learned, for if it could be, the time of learning would be perpetuated rather than ended.

5.20   Remember that you are tired of learning. You are tired here, after your climb. You simply want to rest and have whatever transformation is to come to you to come. If you could indeed give in to this desire fully, it would speed the transformation along quite nicely. So please, listen to your weariness and to your heart's desire to rest. Listen to the call to peace and let yourself recline in the embrace of love, feeling the warm earth beneath you and the heat of the sun above you. Let languor enfold you and apply no effort to what you read here. Just accept what is given. All that is being given is the helpful hints you have desired from an older brother who has experienced what you, as yet, have not.

5.21   In this frame of mind, we can return more specifically to our focus on access. Wherever your chosen point of access lies, imagine now the needle that was discussed as passing through the onion in the Course chapter "The Intersection," and imagine the point of intersection connecting with your chosen access point. Imagine this now, not as a needle but as the wisdom you seek. Imagine this wisdom not as being stopped by the layers of thinking and feeling that we used the onion to illustrate, but as a point of entry and pass-through. What comes of unity enters you and passes through you to the world. This is the relationship you have with unity while in form—a relationship of intersection and pass-through.

5.22   No longer will what enters you get stopped by layers of defenses. No longer will it meet the road-block of your thinking, your effort, your attempts to figure out how to do it and what it all means. There is no cause for such effort. Effort is only a layer of defense, a stop gap between what you would receive and what you would give in which the ego once made its bid to claim ownership. Effort, as translated by the ego, was about turning everything that was given into what "you" could only work hard to attain, and thereby claim as your individual accomplishment. Obviously, union is not about this. While the ego is gone, effort remains, and while it remains, you will not realize full access to what you are given. We are speaking here of letting your form serve union and union serve your form. This service is effortless for it is the way of creation. Again, this is why the "effort" of learning must cease.

5.23   Let's return to the image of the healer that was discussed earlier. While many will heal, all attempts to teach or learn "how to" heal must be thwarted, for if not, the pattern of learning will remain. This is why there have always seemed to be "secrets" held among the great healers and spiritual guides. They have understood that what they have gained access to cannot be taught. This has not meant that they were not eager to share, only that the means of sharing was not one of teaching or learning.

5.24   Each expression of union must remain as what it is—untaught and unlearned. Each gain from unity will only, in this way, be seen as the new givens come to replace learning.

5.25   Remember this as well as you focus on the your access to unity. Focus does not mean thinking. Focus does not mean learning. Remember the example of how your breathing becomes unnatural when you think about it, and contrast this with the increase in awareness of breath that comes from the focus of meditation. A focus point is a point of convergence. A focal point is a point of intersection that gives rise to a clear image.

5.26   The intersection spoken of here is that of pass-through. Although we have spoken of this focal point as an entryway, this does not imply that something that is not of you is entering you, and it does not imply entry without exit. When you think of breathing, you may think of inhaling as taking in air, and of air as something that is not "of" you. But the air you breathe is "of" you. You may think of the air you exhale as being more "of" you, but there is no more or less to the relationship of entry and exit. You are in continual relationship with the air you breathe and in continual relationship with unity. It is a constant exchange. When you are fully aware of this is when full access is attained. So we will continue our work now in releasing you from those things that would still block your full awareness.

Day 6

The Time In Between

6.1   We now will discuss *being* the true self while *becoming* the true self—the time in between your awareness of and access to Christ-consciousness, or unity, and your sustainability of Christ-consciousness, or unity, in form. As was said earlier: To realize the state of becoming is to realize that an in-between exists between the time of learning and the time of being the elevated Self of form. This is what our time on this holy mountain is largely comprised of. We are in an in-between state of time. We stand at the intersection point of the finite and the infinite in order to complete the creative act of becoming.

6.2   While you know this is the focus of our time together, few, if any of you, feel as if you have truly taken leave of the every-day world of your "normal" existence and feel fully present on the holy mountain. This is not a second-best situation. Although it is being handled in this way partially because to ask you to walk away from your "normal" life for forty days and forty nights would cause too much anxiety and exclude too many, this is not the only, or even the major reason for this chosen method.

6.3   Before we can continue to expand on your awareness of the difference you have chosen, we thus must address this time so that any confusion it seems to be causing will not delay your progress.

6.4   Since we have often discussed the similarity between the creation of art and the work we are doing here, we will return to this example. We have spoken of becoming as the time of movement, being, and expression coming together. We have further spoken of your point of access to unity as one of convergence, intersection, and pass-through. Can you see the similarities between these actions despite the difference in language used?

6.5   Movement, Being, Expression; Convergence, Intersection, Pass-through.

6.6   How might these things be linked to the example of creating art? I choose this particular example to address this particular time of being in-between.

Let us consider the creation of a piece of music. The creation of a piece of music, like the creation of a painting or a poem, takes place in stages.

6.7   At one time the creation of a piece of music is only an idea in the mind and heart of the creator. The creation of a song or a symphony may begin as simply as with a few notes "running through the mind" or a particular turn of phrase that inspires the creator to see these words as lyrics. At some point after this gestation within the mind and heart, the artist puts pen to paper, or picks up a guitar, or sings into a tape recorder. Much starting and stopping may be done, or the piece may find its expression easily, in a way that the artist might describe as flowing. Depending on the disposition of the artist, the piece of music might be shared with others at each step of the process, or only late in its development. But at some point, the sharing will take place, and the reactions of those with whom the music is shared will impact the artist and the piece. Positive reactions might validate the artist's instinct and encourage even more boldness. Negative reactions might cause the artist to doubt her instincts, to make changes, or to be more determined than ever to see the piece through to the point where it will be appreciated. Finishing touches will be put on the piece. Some collaboration might take place to get it just right. By the time the artist has completed the piece of music she began, it may have little resemblance to the piece originally intended, or it might be quite true to the original idea.

6.8   Every creative piece of art that comes to completion includes a choice. At some point along the way a commitment is made between the artist and the piece of art. A commitment to see it through. This commitment may come because the artist knows it is "good enough" to deserve the time and attention, or the commitment may come as a recognition that a relationship of love has developed, and "good enough" or not, completion is necessary. It may even be a commitment simply to practice, with the artist feeling no certainty about the value of the piece, but determining to see the project through, knowing that it will make the next piece or the next a better piece of music.

6.9   In all stages of its creation, the piece of music exists in relationship to its creator. Be it only an idea, a partially completed rhythm, lyrics without notes, or a completed work that will qualify more as practice than as art, the piece exists. In each stage of creation it is what it is. Only when it is a complete, and full, and true expression of the artist's idea, however, will it and the artist be one.

6.10　You are a work of art headed for this oneness of full and true expression. No stage you pass through to reach this oneness is without value. Each stage contains the perfection of that stage. Each stage contains the whole and each whole contains each stage.

6.11　You have been told you are in the final stage of becoming. You have committed to completion of the becoming that will create oneness between Creator and created. You have developed the creative relationship that is union. You are *in* and *within* the movement of the creative process where there is no distinction between Creator and created. You are being who you are right now and eliciting the expression that will take you to the final stage of being who you will be in oneness.

6.12　You are not separate now from who you will be when you reach completion! You are *in* and *within* the relationship of creation in which created and creator become one.

6.13　Now, in returning to one of the main themes of this chapter—the simple truth that you are having to go about this creative process while remaining embroiled in daily life—I want to acknowledge the difficulty some of you will seem to be experiencing even while pointing out to you that *life is life*.

6.14　Let's begin with the seeming difficulty. It may take on many forms, but its main source is almost surely a desire to focus on the relationship developing between us, and a corresponding desire not to have to focus on the details of daily life. You may be thinking that the ease so often spoken of in our conversations would be there *if only* you could be truly "taken away" from it all and experience nothing but our relationship, focus on nothing but your point of access, have a chance to really begin to invite abundance without having to look at the bills that arrive by daily mail or worry about the many other aspects of your simple survival.

6.15　Yet realize that if you were told to leave these worries behind and get away from it all, you would likely rebel and find many reasons not to make it so. And so, abundance will have to come first, lack of cause for worry will have to come first, an ability to focus on other than daily life will have to come first. These are what these continuing dialogues will facilitate.

6.16   They will facilitate this by facilitating the acceptance of life as it is. This is why this dialogue is occurring on the holy mountain *without* taking you away from life as you know it. We are, after all, speaking of the elevation of the self of form. This elevation must occur in life, in *your* life *as it is*, rather than in some idealized situation *away* from what you consider normal life.

6.17   This does not, however, mean that this elevation can be postponed, put off, or can wait for some convenient time. Quite the contrary. We are having our dialogue on the holy mountain while you remain within your life for the very purpose of not allowing this to happen.

6.18   It also does not mean that many of you will not have changed or will be changing the very fabric of your daily life. Changes you feel called to make are not discouraged here. The point being made is simply that removal from life is not possible or desirable.

6.19   Learning takes the student away from "normal" life and creates a place for teaching and only calls this place elevated. Awareness, acceptance, and discovery cannot occur in a place set apart from "normal" life. Believe me when I tell you that the elevation you are currently experiencing is the only elevation you would want. *As within, so without* is the operative phrase here. It is not the other way around. You cannot find a place outside of yourself that will allow for the elevation of which we speak. There are no hallowed halls of learning that will accomplish this. There is no mountain top in any location on Earth that can accomplish this. It is only the relationship we are developing in this elevated place *within* that will bring to your full realization and manifestation *without* the accomplishment that already exists.

6.20   I know it doesn't always seem so. Give your attention for a moment to the temptations associated with the mountain top of my own experience. They were temptations of the world, of the normal, daily life of my time. They were attempts to distract me from my purpose, to change my focus, to engage me in debate, to lure me from the place of elevation I knew I had attained. The temptations of the human experience are the same now as they were then. They are the same on the mountain top as they are on level ground. A "place" that seems externally removed from them cannot remove them. Only a created place within can do so.

6.21   This place within is what we are creating here. It is a truly elevated place. It is as real as a mountain top, in fact much more real. Were your scientists to know what to look for, they would find it. It is being created to exist both within the body and beyond the body. It is, in truth, the portal of access we have spoken of, a connection with the state of union as real as if a tether were stretched from here to there.

6.22 The point here, however, is this: Quit trying to remove yourself from life! If this were required it would be done! Think not that I cannot arrange the ideal environment for our dialogue. This is it!

6.23 Think a moment about a new job or some other endeavor in which you apprenticed. In such a situation a person is taught and shown the skills and activities needed for the accomplishment of the tasks he or she is to perform. But often it is only when the teacher steps aside, and the apprentice is able to gain experience, that the apprentice is in a position to be able to begin to perform with any certainty. Even learning is accelerated by hands-on activities, by *doing* what one has previously only learned.

6.24 You have done your learning and your teacher has stepped aside as a teacher and become a companion. Would you desire to prolong your time as an apprentice by being removed from the performance of your tasks? Perhaps you would. But as has been stated from the beginning, there is an urgency to your task.

6.25 Thinking of our relationship as that of colleagues as well as companions, as fellow workers or work-mates with a task to accomplish, as well as conversationalists, is not an erroneous way to think of our relationship. We are both friends and co-workers. Colleagues as well as companions.

6.26 Our dialogue is not without purpose. You know this or you would not be here. You know this or you would not feel the devotion to me and to what we do here that you do. And what's more, you feel the eagerness of your brothers and sisters. If you felt our goal was unlikely to be accomplished, or that it would elevate only a few and leave all others behind, you would not feel this devotion. You *know* our task is holy and incomparable. You know there is nothing more important for you to be involved in. All other areas where you might previously have placed your devotion pale in comparison to our task.

6.27 As your belief grows in our ability to accomplish together our given task, you are almost surely feeling this devotion extend to others, particularly those who, along with us, work toward its accomplishment. In doing so you are not creating new special relationships but the true devotion that will replace special relationships forever.

6.28   But this very knowing of the sanctity and incomparability of our task is what seems to create the difficulty so many of you are currently experiencing in one way or another. Your desire is where it belongs—here—in the passionate acceptance of our work together. And so the lack of desire you are experiencing for other areas of the life you still seem so deeply involved in is disturbing to you. Yet why should this be disturbing? Why should you continue to desire the life you have had?

6.29   Now let's address this seeming paradox. You have been told to do only what you can feel peaceful doing, to do only what allows you to be yourself, and yet here are you told not to try to remove yourself from life.

6.30   Do you need to feel desire for what you do in order to do it peacefully? Do you need to be other than yourself in order to navigate your daily life? What you are being shown here is that you do not. What you are going to realize from this time of seeming difficulty is an end to difficulty and the growth of your ability to do whatever you do peacefully and to be who you are in any situation in which you find yourself. There is no time to wait while you learn, or think you learn, the qualities that will allow this. This is the point of movement, being, and expression coming together. The point of convergence, intersection, and pass-through. This is it! Right here in your life as it is right now.

6.31   There is, thus, no call to be discouraged. This is not delay, but what you might think of as trial by fire. Be encouraged rather than discouraged that you are able to embrace this dialogue and remain in your life. Realize that this is just what we work toward! This difficulty will pass through you as you allow for and accept where you are right now and who you are right now.

6.32   Does this work of acceptance seem never ending? It is until it is replaced by reverence, just as learning was unending until it was replaced by acceptance. The conditions, however, of this time of acceptance are not the conditions of the time of learning, and so you will soon see that the difficulty of the time of learning truly is behind you.

6.33   Let us speak now of the conditions of the time of acceptance, for these will cheer you.

Conditions of the Time of Acceptance

7.1   What does the idea of only now coming to acceptance imply but that you were previously unaccepting? And what does being unaccepting imply but the very denial of yourself that you have come to see as your former state?

7.2   Denial of yourself was the precondition that set the stage for the time of learning. The time of learning would not have been needed had you not denied your Self. When you saw yourself as separate and alone, you could not help but suffer fear, loneliness, and all the ills that came from the base emotion of fear. Fear is degenerating. Nothing about fear is life giving. You thus were given life only to have it become degenerated by fear.

7.3   Acceptance of your Self is the precondition for the *time* of acceptance. You are no longer denying your Self. You are no longer denying unity. You have replaced fear with love. Love is life giving and life *supporting*. There is thus nothing now degenerating about life.

7.4   Life is now supported. Support is thus a condition of the time of acceptance.

7.5   You must realize here that the pattern of learning is now all that is left that can be degenerating to you. While you always were supported, the *idea* of learning that you accepted during the *time* of learning was not one of support but one of effort. You must accept, now, that the pattern of learning is an extension of fear and be willing and vigilant in replacing it with a pattern of acceptance. I say this because so many of you still do not feel supported in your daily life. You may feel supported in your spiritual life, in your progress toward full awareness and the elevation of the self of form, but as in the discussion of abundance, you may still feel unsupported in form. Realize now, that this makes no sense when our goal is the elevation of form. If for no other reason, begin to accept this support of form because it makes sense. It is logical. And realize further that love is not opposed to logic but returns true reason to the mind and heart.

7.6   Love replaces fear and is life-generating rather than life-degenerating. Your bodies will thus regenerate rather than degenerate. Love is, of course, not a condition, as it is not an attribute, but the *effect* of living from love rather than from fear will have a major transformative effect on form in this time of acceptance. Regeneration is a condition of the time of acceptance.

7.7   Another condition of the time of acceptance that will be of great service to you now is that of the different relationship that you will have with time. This is a time of convergence, intersection, and pass-through of the finite and the infinite, of time and no time. Time has not yet ceased to be, but as you are in a state of transformation, so too is it. Again I remind you, *as within, so without.* As you let go of time's hold on you, it will let go of you. Time will seem to expand but will actually be contracting into nothingness. Time is replaced by presence, by your ability to exist in the here and now in acceptance and without fear.

7.8   Again let me remind you that you are in an in-between time. Thus these conditions I have spoken of and those I have yet to speak of, are also in an in-between state. They exist along with the new you. They exist in acceptance and union. They do not exist in learning and separation. They exist in love. They do not exist in fear. Like with Christ-consciousness, you are moving from a place of maintenance of these conditions to one of sustainability of these conditions. They do not come about from changes in your external circumstances but from changes in your internal perspective.

7.9   The conditions that affect life are conditions that affect the body. Yet it was only your mind's acceptance of the condition of fear that led the body to exhibit the conditions of fear in the time of learning. Thus it is the mind's acceptance of love that will lead the body to exhibit the effects of love in the time of acceptance.

7.10   A further condition of the time of acceptance is that of expansion. The singular self you once believed yourself to be was not capable of true expansion and true sharing. The singular self withdrew into its own little world and created its own universe. The elevated Self of form will expand into the world and create a new universe. This condition of expansion is operative now and beginning to find manifestation through the sharing we are doing here.

7.11   Conditions of the time of acceptance are conditions of creation and include those we have already spoken of as movement, being, and expression; and convergence, intersection and pass-through.

7.12   There are many lesser conditions that are nonetheless extremely transformative, such as the replacement of special relationship with the devotion of holy relationship that we have already spoken of. Another replacement is that of control with grace. This occurs as you give up the control you have but thought you exerted over your life and its circumstances, and live in a state of grace, meeting grace with grace by accepting what is given for your regeneration.

7.13   It is easy to see from here how the dominoes fall and each condition of learning is replaced, always by a far gentler and more compassionate alternative. Thus there is no need for me to list every new condition here. As you become increasingly aware of your relationship with union, each of these new conditions and your relationship with each of these new conditions will become clear to you.

7.14   Obviously your relationship or access to union is of supreme importance, since all else will come of this. However, this is not an *if this, then that* situation even if it may seem so. Is the process of breathing an *if this, then that* situation, just because breathing sustains life? Your access to union sustains real life, the life of the Self, and will come to sustain the elevated Self of form in a way as natural to you as breathing.

7.15   *Access to unity* is a phrase that will only be used in this in-between time. You have always existed in unity and once this is fully realized you will no more need access to unity than you need access to breathing. Unity will be your natural state.

7.16   When your natural state is fully returned to you and sustained within Christ-consciousness, the conditions of the time of acceptance, like the conditions of the time of learning, will pass. There are no conditions in the state of union as there are no attributes to love. The natural created Self is all that is. Reverence prevails.

7.17   There will be, however, a new stage following the time of acceptance in which the elevated Self of form will be created and come into full manifestation.

7.18   And yet what we are concerned about now is the present. It is here, in this present and given time on the mountain that you must realize that the conditions of the time of acceptance, like the conditions of the time of learning, arise from within. Life has always existed within the conditions of the time of acceptance. The conditions of the time of learning were but imposed conditions that also arose from within.

7.19   The conditions of the time of acceptance that we have spoken of are thus not new conditions. They are conditions natural to your Self, to a mind and heart joined in union. It was the disjoining of mind and heart, of the real Self from the ego-self, that created the need for learning and the imposition, from *within*, of the conditions of the time of learning.

7.20   The condition of the time of acceptance that will most clearly reveal to you your status in regard to maintaining or sustaining your access to union will be that of the replacement of doubt with certainty. Certainty is a condition of the present. Realize you may say you are certain of the future or the past but that you cannot make it so. Thus your ability to maintain and then sustain your access to union and thus your certainty, goes hand-in-hand with your ability to live in the present. This ability is also contingent upon your recognition of what certainty really is.

7.21   There is an acceptance of the present that some of you are finding difficult and a false sense of certainty that some of you may be experiencing. Thus these will be the subject of our next dialogue.

Accept the Present

8.1 Some of you have felt, once again, a bit of disappointment or resignation as a result of our dialogue concerning not removing yourself from life. Your whole purpose in pursuing the course of this dialogue may have been, at least subconsciously, the idea of removing yourself from normal life. Even the conditions of the time of acceptance may not have cheered you fully. Now, with the ideas of the conditions of the time of acceptance fresh in your minds and hearts, let's return to that earlier discussion.

8.2 If you can't remove yourself from life, what choice have you but to join with it? Love it. Love yourself. Love yourself enough to accept yourself. Love will transform normal, ordinary, life into extraordinary life. Loving exactly who you are and where you are in every moment is what will cause the transformation that will end your *desire* to remove yourself from life. All those frustrations you currently feel have a purpose: To move you through them and beyond them—to acceptance.

8.3 But here is the point that needs clearing up. This is *not* about acceptance of what you do not like. Do you really think you are being called to accept "normal life?" Called to accept those conditions that have made you feel unhappy? No! You are being called to an acceptance of new conditions!

8.4 Realize that your desire for your life to be different, your desire for your unhappiness to be gone, is very unlikely, in truth, to stem from the details of your life. Even so, you are not called to accept what you do not like, but to accept that you don't like whatever it is you don't like. Then, and only then— when you have accepted how you *feel*—can you respond truly. Only when you have accepted how you feel do you quit labeling good or bad; only then can you deal with anything from a place of peace.

8.5 Does accepting that you don't like something cause a judgment to occur? Do you judge peas if you do not like them? And yet, do you not accept that you are at the mercy of situations of all kinds? A job you do not like? You may not like it, and you may say often that you do not like it, but you may just as often say that you accept it. You may, in fact, need a job that you do not like, but in acceptance of the simple truth that you do not like your job, you have accepted your Self and where you are now, rather than the external circumstance. We are not, when talking of acceptance, talking of externals, but of internals. We are not talking of the old adage or prayer that calls you to "accept what you cannot change" but of acceptance—absolute, unconditional, acceptance—of your Self.

8.6   Yet to state that you do not like your job is to pre-judge your job, to assume that the conditions you did not like yesterday will be the same today.

8.7   Now you may have been thinking—again, at least subconsciously— that your "real" Self has no feelings of dislike, and in this confusion have been "trying" and even "struggling" to accept what you do not like in order to be more true to an ideal self. Yet this ideal self is not the self you are right now. You cannot accept only an ideal self. This is nonsense. Can you not see this?

8.8   All power to effect change comes from acceptance—not acceptance of the way *things* are, but acceptance of who *you* are *in the present*. Not through acceptance of the way you want to be but of the way you are now. There will be many things within your life that will take some time to change, but many others that can change instantly through this radical acceptance. You will find, once you have begun to practice acceptance of the present, that there will be far fewer things you do not like, and that you will be shown, in the relationship you have in the present, the response to those you still do.

8.9   Gossip would be an easy example. Gossip goes on in many environments. You are highly unlikely to like gossip, but you may have felt that to say you do not like it is to judge it, or that to accept what *is*, is to accept that people gossip. These false ideas about acceptance may then have blocked your own true feelings and true response. However, a simple acceptance that *you* do not like the gossip taking place in a present moment situation, will enable you not to participate, judge, or appear to accept that which you do not truly find acceptable.

8.10   Not all situations will seem as easy as this example. Acceptance does not require any specific action but it will lead to action that is consistent with who you are when you are fully comfortable in your acceptance of who you are. Understand, however, that this eventual outcome will never occur without the initial acceptance.

8.11   This acceptance is the only thing that will truly prevent judgment, for it does not require you to be your brother's keeper but only your own. It requires you to know yourself without judging yourself.

8.12   Will knowing your dislikes cause you to be intolerant? This is an important question. You have been intolerant of yourself and it was easy to extend this intolerance to others. Once acceptance of the Self begins to be practiced, you will realize that the self of intolerance was the self of fear. Acceptance of yourself, in love, leads to acceptance of others. Knowing this aspect of how you feel, what we are here calling your dislikes, is but a first step in this beginning stage of acceptance and only of importance *because* of your intolerance of your own feelings.

8.13   Remember that you have been told that your real Self will be intolerant only of illusion and that this intolerance will take the form of seeing only the truth rather than attempting to combat illusion. Thus when you see others gossiping, you are called to see only the truth of who they are—to see beyond the illusion, what would seem to be the "fact" of their gossip—to the fear that feeds it, and beyond the fear to the love that will dispel it. You are not called to walk away in disgust, showing your righteous contempt for the actions of others, but to accept who you are within the relationship of that present moment.

8.14   Even this type of seeing will have remnants of righteousness attached to it if you do not accept the feelings generated by it. You may know that you dislike gossip only because you have been both a participant and a victim of it. It may still call up feelings of shame or irritation. It may even still intrigue you if you are interested enough in the subject of the gossip. To walk away from gossip, accepting that you do not like it without accepting the feelings associated with it, will make of it a mental construct, a rule you have set up for your new self to follow. If this becomes the case, you will find yourself adhering to a standard rather than acting from who you are. You will, in fact, have returned to judgment because you will have made a predetermination, just as in saying you do not like your job, you predetermine a continuing dislike. Soon, you might see a group of people who often gossip and *assume* that they are gossiping rather than observing the situation for what it is and responding in the present.

8.15   If you replace the act of gossiping with a mental construct or rule that says you do not tolerate it, then you will become intolerant. And because you will then act from a predetermined standard rather than feeling the feelings associated with gossip in the present moment, you will soon find that a bit of gossip will crop up in your own speech, couched as something else, something even worse than gossip. You will sigh, and reference something someone said or did that but shows that they are not yet as "advanced" as you, only revealing, through your reference, that it is you who are not as "advanced" as you think you are.

8.16   This is the importance now of accepting yourself in the *present* and of understanding certainty. Certainty cannot be predetermined, just as you cannot predetermine either your likes or dislikes. Being aware of how you feel *in the present moment* is the only way to certainty. Thus to say that you are certain that you do not like gossip, or certain that you do not like your job, or even certain that you do not like peas, is an inaccurate use of the term of *certainty*. It may have been consistent with the term or word *certainty* as it was used in the past, but you will not want to confuse the *term* and the *condition*. You may think that taking away the type of certainty associated with the "term" of certainty will cause you to be even less certain than you were before. You will be less certain in your judgments and opinions, but this is highly appropriate and much needed practice for true certainty.

8.17   We have talked little of feelings here, and there has been a reason for this discussion coming so late in our time together. To accept the feelings of the self of illusion would have been to accept the feelings generated by the fear of the ego thought system or the bitterness of your heart. It would have been to accept the feelings of a personal self who had not yet unlearned the lessons of the past or taken these steps toward elevation. Now, however, it is crucial that you come to acceptance of yourself—in the present, as you are—for only by doing so will you come to *full* acceptance of who you are and be able to allow the Self of unity to merge with the self of form, thus elevating the self of form. You will also, only in this way, come to true expression of the elevated Self of form. Access and expression are both conditions of the present.

8.18 Another error can occur if you deny your feelings in favor of the perceived higher path to enlightenment. In denying your own feelings you will tend also to deny the feelings of others. You will think that you know the real from the unreal, truth from illusion, and so will disregard the feelings of others as if they do not matter. This will only happen if you allow yourself to deny and thus become distanced from your own feelings.

8.19 Does this seem confusing? To be called to see only the truth, to see beyond illusion, and then to be told to accept the feelings of others? It should not. While true compassion sees only the truth, this does not mean it holds the feelings of anyone—not those living in truth, or those living in illusion—in disregard. This disregard is a temptation of those who live in peace, a temptation unlike the more pleasant temptations that were spoken of earlier. This temptation stems from one thing only—from not living in the present. Distancing, or non-acceptance of your own feelings, *is* not living in the present and will create an attitude that will not be compassionate. This is why we talk specifically here of dislikes. While you are prone to acceptance of that which you "like," to those feelings you think of as "good" feelings, you are still prone to non-acceptance of that which you do not like in yourself and others and even to, at times, the false sense of certainty about your non-acceptance that we have spoken of.

8.20 When you develop a false sense of certainty, you see not the true Self and the holiness of the true Self being expressed in the feelings of a present moment situation, but see a future where the true Self will be more evolved, evolved enough not to feel the anger or hurt, the bitterness or guilt that you do not like. You hold others to the "standards" you hold for yourself, thus the only "standard" that is consistent with the time of acceptance is that *of* acceptance.

8.21 Now you must realize that you no longer have cause to fear your feelings. They will no longer be the source of the misdirection of the past *if* you accept your feelings in present time and begin to be aware of your natural ability to respond truly *because* you have accepted your feelings in present time. This is a recognition that by being in the present you know your feelings are of the truth. This is certainty. This is all that will prevent you from "reacting" to feelings out of your previous pattern.

8.22 If anger arises in you now, it does not mean that you will react in whatever way anger once called you to react and it does not mean that something is wrong with you or that you are not spiritual enough! It simply means that you are involved in a situation or relationship that has called forth that feeling. It is in the expression of that feeling that who you are is revealed, not in the feeling itself. The feeling is provided by the body, a helpmate now in your service as a route to true expression.

8.23 Remember always that we work now to unite the Self of union with the self of form. The self of form cannot be denied now. This is a continuation of the reversal of some of the ideas of yourself that began in A Treatise on the New.

8.24 Let me repeat a passage from that Treatise here, a passage about the power to observe what is. "It is not about observing a potential for what could be if your brother or sister would just follow in the way that has been shown to you. It is about observing what *is*. The power to observe what is, is what will keep you unified with your brothers and sisters rather than separating you from them. There is no power without this unity. You cannot see 'others' as other than who they are and know your power."

8.25 Non-acceptance in any form is separating.

8.26 The very idea of potential, you may recall, is a product of the ego thought system that would keep your true Self hidden. You are used to hiding the self of the past about whom you are not well pleased, and you are used to hiding the self of potential, the future self you think you can only dream of being. The ego-self was the self you felt safe presenting to the world, the self you believed the world would find acceptable. If you are still presenting this self, you are still in a state of non-acceptance and whatever peace you are feeling will not last. Whatever access to unity you have experienced will not last because you will not be choosing the time of acceptance.

8.27 I have called this time both the time of unity and the time of acceptance because you cannot only focus on unity when you are still in need of this full acceptance or you will not reach the place of sustainability. Every situation and every feeling that you do not like will pull you from union toward separation. All feelings of non-acceptance lead to a feeling of needing to learn "how to" reach acceptance of that which you do not like, or "how to" create a situation that you will like. It is the by-passing of this "how to" function—a function of the time of learning—that we are heading toward.

8.28 Realize how freeing it will be to not go through the gyrations of attempting to figure out "how to" reach acceptance of what you do not like! How freeing it will be to realize you have no need to do this! How freeing it will be to accept *all* of your feelings and not to puzzle over which are true and which are false! To realize that you no longer have false feelings. That your feelings are not misleading you but supporting you! That they are but calling you to expression of your true Self! To true representation of who you are—who you are now!

8.29 Remove all thinking that says that you can err in following your feelings. This is the thinking of the old thought system, not the new. This is thinking comprised of the time-delay of the time of learning—of a time when you used your feelings, opinions, and judgments interchangeably and either "thought" about them in order to know how to react or suffered the consequences of reacting without "thought." Judgment has been left behind and with it the need for opinions and for "thinking" about "how to" react. Reaction has been replaced by response, calculated mental constructs have been replaced with true expression. It does not seem so only if you have not allowed yourself to enjoy the freedom of the new, the freedom of being your true Self.

8.30 I call you now to embrace this freedom.

Freedom

9.1 Freedom from want, freedom from lack, freedom from repression, are what we will now enjoy together on our mountain top retreat. We have not removed ourselves from life in any way, and yet we have reached a place of retreat, a place of safety and of rest, a place away from "normal" life and the lack of freedom you have experienced there. I am your refuge from the past, your gate of entry to the present. You have fled the foreign land, where freedom was merely an illusion, and arrived at the Promised Land, the land of our inheritance.

9.2 Allow yourself, now, to experience your arrival, your return to your true home, your return to your Self. Laugh. Cry. Shout or wail. Dance and sing. Spin a new web. The web of freedom.

9.3 In other words, express your Self!

9.4 You who do not feel confident in your feelings, who do not feel confident in your ability to respond, who do not as yet feel the freedom of the new, allow yourself now, to do so. Allow freedom to reign, for it is your allowance, your choice, your permission, that will make it so. The only one who can stop you now is yourself. The only permission you ever needed was your own.

9.5 We will practice here to build your confidence, a confidence sorely lacking. What confidence is it of which we speak? The confidence to be yourself. This confidence is what must precede true certainty in this time of elevation of the self of form. The certainty that arises from unity is different from this confidence in the self of form and they must be realized together for the elevation of the self of form to take place. What good will be the certainty of unity if the self of form has no confidence in its ability to express it? *Expression* of the certainty of unity is what the elevated Self of form is all about. Certainty of mind and heart has been realized by many. The *expression* of that certainty in form has not.

9.6 Freedom is nothing other than freedom of expression. No one can block the freedom of what your mind would think or heart would feel. But take away the ability to *express* what the mind would think or heart would feel, and freedom is no more. Yet it is not an outward source that you must fear or protect your freedom against. It is none other than yourself who has not allowed you the freedom of expression.

9.7   Realize now the truth of what you have just heard. While you know you have not allowed yourself freedom of expression, you believe you have allowed yourself freedom of thought. You believe you have allowed yourself freedom of feeling. And yet if the truth be admitted, you know that even this is not quite true. You know that you censor your own thoughts and feelings, accepting some and not others. You know you have repressed your emotions. You know you have lived in a state in which you believed yourself to be lacking. You know you have never known freedom from want.

9.8   Today, I would like you to know freedom.

9.9   Let's begin this day with a consideration of the idea that you may have an inaccurate idea of an ideal self.

9.10   Where might your notion of what an ideal self is have come from? It may have come from your ideas of right and wrong, good and bad. It may have its source in your religious beliefs. It may have come from someone you have idolized, someone you believe to be the spiritual titan you still but hope to be. Your image of an ideal self may have sprung from your reading, from descriptions of those the world has come to see as enlightened ones. It may be linked to your ideas of being able to express wisdom or compassion. The image of the ideal self you hold in your mind, no matter what form it takes, is still an image, and must now be done without if you are going to realize freedom.

9.11   As was said earlier, all of your images are false images. Isn't it possible that none are more false than this image of an ideal self? Not having false idols is an ancient commandment. An ideal image *is* an idol. It is symbolic rather than real. It has form only within your mind and has no substance. To work toward, or to have as a goal, the achievement of an ideal image is to have created a false god.

9.12   Realize now that your ideal image, no matter how it was formed, is a product of the time of learning. It became an image in your mind, and maybe even within your heart, through the process of learning. It arose from the learning of right from wrong, good from bad. It arose from the learning of moral and religious beliefs. It arose from comparison. It arose from seeking. It arose from your perception of lack.

9.13   This ideal image is intimately related with the time of learning in another way as well. It is the epitome of learning, what you have seen learning as being *for*. While other learning goals may have receded, this one seems a learning goal worthy of your *effort*. It seems to be a true goal amidst many illusory goals. Just as you may have believed that if you worked hard enough you would achieve a position of status within your profession or material wealth, you have believed that if you work hard enough you can maybe, someday, if you are blessed or lucky, achieve this ideal image.

9.14   But this ideal image is as much a product of illusion as have been all of your worldly goals.

9.15   As with most goals of the time of learning, it was an ego-centered goal, a carrot of fulfillment the ego but dangled before you in the place it called the future. As with all messages of the ego, it but says that who you are is not good enough.

9.16   The idea of your "potential" was a useful learning tool and one that served the purposes of the Holy Spirit as well as those of the ego. The idea of your "potential" and your ability to be "more" than what your limited view of yourself would have you be, was a necessary tool to call you to the learning that would return you to your true identity. But the time for such tools is over.

9.17   How will you ever realize, or make real, the Self you are when you strive to be something else? Just as "finding" brought "seeking" to an end, accomplishment brings striving to an end.

9.18   An idealized image, like a rule, is a mental construct. All mental constructs are pre-determinations.

9.19   All ideas such as those of advancement or enlightenment are mental constructs. They are pre-determinations.

9.20   While language cannot be completely stripped of usages such as these, and while some use of similar terms, like our use of the term *elevated*, are still necessary, it is only in your understanding that our use of these terms is not a cause for predetermination that we can proceed. For if you believe that we are proceeding to some predetermined ideal state, we will not succeed in the work we are doing here together. For if you believe this, you will not accept your Self as you are. If you do not accept your Self as you are, you will not move from image to presence. If you do not move from image to presence you will never realize your freedom. If you do not realize your freedom, you will not realize your power.

9.21   To *represent* an image is to *become* an image. To become an image, even an idealized image, is to still become a false idol or even what is referred to in more common usage as a spiritual leader or guru. True spiritual leaders or gurus have no need nor desire to be seen as such and are often made into images such as these only within the minds of those who would seek to follow their teachings. This desire of "followers" to accept an image is less prevalent now but still a common danger.

9.22   What an image does is separate. The holder of an image, precisely because he or she holds an image as a goal, holds him or herself separate. They realize not that they are the same as the one they idolize, but realize only that they are different. In "wanting" to be the same and not realizing sameness, they fail to celebrate their own difference and do not bring the gift of their sameness, or of their difference, to the world, but hold it in waiting for such a time as the ideal is reached.

9.23   You are the "same" or "as" accomplished as every enlightened one who has ever existed. Without realizing this, however, your unique expression of your accomplishment will not be realized.

9.24   Your freedom is contingent upon your ability to give up your images, particularly the image you hold of an ideal self. It is contingent upon your ability to accept that you are your ideal self. Yes, even right now, with all your seeming imperfections.

9.25   What are these imperfections but your "differences?" Have we not spoken of these differences as givens, as gifts? These are not just the givens of talents or inspired ideas, but all the givens that combined create the wholeness and the holiness of who you are. A creator who desired only sameness would not have created a world of such diversity. You are a creator who created this diversity. It was and is a choice meant to release the beauty of expression in all its forms. You have a *given* form that is perfect for your expression of the beauty and truth of who you are. You cannot express the beauty and truth of who another is. You cannot express the beauty and truth of a future self. You can only express the beauty and truth of who you are now, in the present. And you do. You just have not realized that you do. You have not desired to do so but desired to do something else! Desired to wait, desired to learn, desired to imitate.

9.26   What might happen if you change what you desire? You might just realize your freedom.

9.27   Nothing, not even the ego, has been able to keep you from expressing the beauty and truth of who you are. You came into the world of form incapable of not expressing the beauty and truth of who you are. That you *are* is an expression of beauty and truth. You express the beauty and truth of who you are by being alive. It has only been your inability to accept this that has caused your grief and pretensions. In a certain sense, your ability to express the beauty and truth of who you are has been taught out of you by learning practices that sought for sameness, and saw not your differences as the gifts they are.

9.28   All of these learning practices were the product of false images of the way things—and *you*—should be! Can you not see the extreme urgency of not perpetuating such a practice?

9.29   All you need do is look at a young child to see the joy, beauty, and truth of expression. You, too, were once a young child. You are still the same self you were then. You are, however, a self in whom the freedom of expression has been diminished. Diminished, but not extinguished.

9.30   Now we must return to you the freedom and the *will* to fan the flames of your desire to be, and to express, who you are in truth.

9.31   Thus you can see that a key step in doing this is the debunking of the myth of an ideal self. An ideal self, like a god seen as "other than" puts all that you would long for in a place outside of, or beyond, the self you are now.

9.32   You might ask here what is wrong with desiring to have the freedom to strive to be more and to do more. You might ask what life would be *for* without this type of freedom to strive, to achieve, to accomplish, to work toward and realize goals. This is the second myth that must be shattered if you are to know true freedom. It begins with the simple realization that you do still *desire*, or *think* you desire, learning challenges of this type and with the realization that this is all these are—learning challenges. You seek learning challenges now only because of the consistency with which you did so in the past. In the past you moved quickly from one learning challenge to another. You have just completed a monumental learning challenge and so your natural pattern would be to keep going now, to use the momentum of this learning success to achieve another.

9.33   This pattern will be easily replaced, however, as your acceptance of yourself as you are, the *real* challenge of this time, begins to grow and to build your confidence. Unity and your access to unity will be your certainty. Trust in your own abilities—the abilities of the self of form joined with the Self of union—will be your confidence. Only these *combined* abilities will release your power.

Day 10

Power

10.1   Power is the ability to *be* cause and effect. It is the ability to harness the cause and effect power of love. It is a quality of form as well as a quality of union. Form *is* the ultimate expression of the power of creation. The power of creation, harnessed *by* form in the service *of* form is the next step in the expansion of the power of creation. It is the power of the elevated Self of form.

10.2   See you now why the certainty of union must be combined with the confidence of the self of form? Certainty is knowing that this power exists. Confidence is the expression of your reliance upon it. To rely on your own power is to rely on the connection that exists between the self of form and the Self of union and to, through this reliance, tie the two together so that there is no seam, no boundary, no remaining separation.

10.3   We have talked before of conviction and your willingness to, like the apostles, let your conviction spring from your willingness to experience its cause and its effect. I am asking you now to be willing to move from conviction to reliance. I am not asking you to do this today any more than I am asking you to move from maintenance to sustainability today, I am merely making you aware of this difference, just as I made you aware of the difference between the states of maintenance and sustainability. As with the states of maintenance and sustainability, I am giving you cause for movement, the effect of which will be the movement from conviction to reliance.

10.4   Conviction is tied to belief, and to a former lack of belief that has been overcome. Reliance is not tied to belief nor to the overcoming of disbelief and thus releases you from the need for belief. Certainty is complete lack of doubt and any perceived need for doubt.

10.5   Realize that in the time of learning, you felt a need for your doubt just as you felt a need for your beliefs and for the reassurances that were important to your self-confidence. These needs are tied to your feelings and thus we will return to a discussion of feelings in connection with the ideas of confidence, reliance, and certainty.

10.6   Confidence in your *feelings* will lead to confidence in your Self. While you think it is your access to unity that will be the more difficult to achieve and sustain, this will not be the case for most of you, for the simple reason that the certainty that comes from union will seem to come, at least initially, from a place other than the self. Because certainty seems to come from a place "other than" or beyond the self of form, you will instinctively have greater trust in it. You will believe it comes from a place "other than" or beyond the self of form *because* it comes in the form of certainty.

10.7   The feelings that lead you to either a state of confidence or to a state of lack of confidence could be spoken of most succinctly by considering your concept of intuition. You all understand intuition and each of you have had intuitive moments. You may have felt, for no good reason, as if you shouldn't do something you were about to do. You may have trusted the intuition and then learned that had you done what you planned to do, an accident or some other event you would not have welcomed might have occurred. You may have never had any proof that following your intuition was the correct thing to do but still felt as if it was. Or you may have doubted your intuition and had something occur that made you think back and wish that you had not doubted it.

10.8   This intuition came as a feeling, but not necessarily as a feeling of certainty. You may have reacted to the intuition with confidence or with lack of confidence.

10.9   There are other instances of intuition that come, not as these seeming warnings, but as what you might call intuitive flashes of insight—intuition that causes you to make connections between point A and point B, be point A and point B distinct points in a scientific puzzle or murky points about relationships between lovers.

10.10   This type of intuition seems to come more as thought than as feeling, but even so, it is your feelings about such thoughts that will often determine how you act upon them. Do you trust in your intuition or do you doubt it?

10.11   What you have trusted in the most is rational thought, and intuition is different than rational thought, as are feelings of all kinds. You think of feelings either as that which comes to you through your five senses or as emotions, and you have not trusted in these feelings as much as you have trusted in rational thought. This lack of trust works both for you and against you now. It works for you in that you do not have to resist and reject an existing trust as you do with the thoughts of the mind you call rational. It works against you because all feelings are capable of providing what you have called intuitive knowledge or insights and your distrust of this knowledge and insight will need to be overcome.

10.12 Feelings come from the innate knowing of the self of form—in short, from the body. The body is the "given" form and while it was the perfect vehicle for learning in the time of learning, it is now being transformed into the perfect vehicle for the realization of the elevated Self of form. During this transformation, we work with what *is* as well as with the new and the forgotten. This is why it has been said that the certainty that comes from access to unity may be less difficult for you to become aware of and accept than the confidence in the self of form that must accompany it. In developing the confidence of the self of form, we work with what has been in a new way, and as you all know from the time of learning, it is often more difficult to become adept in doing something in a way different than you have done it before than to do something completely new. This is because old patterns or habits must be done away with before achievement of a new way is possible.

10.13 This also relates to our discussion of image versus presence and to the image of your personal self that was discussed at the beginning of our dialogue. While you still hold an image of your personal self, you still hold inaccurate ideas about the feelings of the personal self. This is because your image of the personal self is based on the past and the feelings of the past. This is also because your image of the personal self is a mental construct, and not a simple mental construct but a whole set of thoughts, beliefs, and mental pictures.

10.14 Because you believe that your feelings have misled you in the past, you now still doubt your feelings. Because you have doubted yourself in the past, you now still look for reassurances and proof that you are "right" before you feel confidence and the ability to act. To "know" before you act is wise. But to think that doubting your feelings or seeking outside assurances of what you know will lead to either confidence or certainty is foolish.

10.15 Pause a moment here and consider our need for a distinction between the certainty you feel from unity and the confidence you need to feel in the self of form. Reflect further on your idea of certainty coming from a place "other than" the self. Realize in these reflections that you are still reliant on means "other than" the self, including your image of the state of unity and including your image of me. Although you have been called to union you still hold an image of the state of unity as separate from yourself. Although I have removed myself from the role of teacher and entered this dialogue with you as an equal, you still hold an image of me as "other than" yourself. You will never fully rely upon your Self while you hold these images.

10.16 When I call you to replace conviction with reliance, I call you to replace belief in an outside source with reliance upon your Self.

10.17 Part of the difficulty you find in accepting reliance on your Self is what you have "learned" within this Course. As you "learned" to remove the ego and deny the personal self, you transferred your reliance to me and to the state of unity. This was purposeful. Now, however, you are asked to return to wholeness, a state in which you are not separate from me or from the state of union.

10.18 You have "learned" the distinction between Christ-consciousness and the man Jesus. You have "learned" the distinction between your Self and the man or woman you are. Now you are called to forget what you have "learned" and to let all distinctions slip away. You are called to forget what you have learned and to realize what you know.

10.19 Thus I will speak to you from this point onward as the voice of Christ-consciousness, the voice of your own true consciousness, the consciousness that we truly share. I came to you in the form of the consciousness of the man I once was because you were, prior to this point, unready to give up image for presence, the individual for the universal, reliance on an outside source for reliance on yourself, Jesus for Christ-consciousness. You needed the reference point of a "person," of a being who had lived and breathed and met challenges similar to your own. You have been unable to see the two as the same for you have not realized this sameness in yourself. This sameness of the person you are and Christ-consciousness, of union and presence, of the individual and the universal, is what the elevated Self of form must encompass.

10.20 I ask you not to give up your relationship with me as the man Jesus, but to accept that the man Jesus was simply a representation, in form, of Christ-consciousness. I do, however, ask you to give up your identification of the voice of this dialogue as that belonging to the man Jesus who lived two thousand years ago. To continue to identify this voice with that man is to be unable to recognize this voice as the voice of your own true consciousness—the voice of Christ-consciousness. Yet to realize that this is the same voice that animated the man Jesus two thousand years ago will aide you in realizing that this is the voice that will now animate the elevated Self of form, or in other words, you.

10.21 I have spoken with you throughout this time as the man Jesus so that you realize that man and Christ-consciousness can be joined. That you, as man or woman, existing in this particular time and space, can join with Christ-consciousness. You can be both/and, rather than either/or. As I speak to you now as the voice of Christ-consciousness—as your own true Self— you will not have lost Jesus as your companion and helpmate but will only know more fully the content of the man Jesus. As you join with Christ-consciousness in this dialogue, you will realize you have not lost your Self but will only know more fully the content of your Self.

10.22 Remember that you have been told since the beginning of *A Course of Love* that the answers that you seek lie within, and that their source is your own true identity. You have been told since the beginning of this Course that this is the time of the second coming of Christ. What we have just discussed is what both of these statements mean. This is the culmination point of these two great objectives coming together in you and your brothers and sisters.

10.23 I will still be with you to point the way, but if you can cease to think of this as the wisdom of an outside source, if you can hear it and feel it and think of it as a true dialogue, a true sharing in relationship in which an exchange is taking place, you will further your progress greatly.

10.24 Let us talk a moment of this exchange, for it is a key to your understanding of your Self and your power. This dialogue, as one-sided as it may seem when presented in this way, *is* an exchange and will only become more so as we proceed. I am not imparting wisdom that you are unaware of but reminding you of what you have forgotten. I am not having a monologue, but we are having a dialogue in which you are a full participant. As much of what you read in these dialogues comes from your own heart and those of your brothers and sisters in Christ as it does from me. It comes, in truth, from our union, from the consciousness we share. This shared consciousness is the source of wisdom *because* it is shared—shared in unity and relationship.

10.25 Before we move on to the all-important discussion of unity and relationship, let me spend my final time with you as the man Jesus talking more of feelings.

10.26 It is highly unlikely that in your image of an ideal self you left much room for feelings of the type you currently experience. This is why we have recently spoken of anger and of those things which you dislike—why we have spoken, in short, of the feelings you would think would have no place within the ideal self or the elevated Self of form.

10.27 I asked you once before to review your ideas about the afterlife, a life in which most of you believe peacefulness reigns and the spirit is free of the body. Yet if you were to think now of a person whom you know who has died, you would not be likely to think of them much differently than they were in life, even while you are able to imagine them being peaceful and free of the constraints of the body. This is as good an idea as I can give you of how to imagine the elevated Self of form, as not much different than you are now, but peaceful and free of the constraints of the body.

10.28 Let's continue with this idea a while longer as you consider a particular person you fondly remember from life and how you have thought of him or her since death. Do you not occasionally think that this person would be happy or sad to see you in the state you are in when you think of them? Do you not at times shake your head and think that a dead loved one was lucky not to have lived to see the current state of affairs of the world because you know they would not have liked it? And do you not, in all honesty, think that even in whatever form or lack of form they now occupy, they do not like it, even now, even beyond the grave?

10.29 And do you not, when thinking of idolized spiritual leaders, see them as *world* leaders as well, leaders not only capable but bound to taking a stance against the many situations there are to dislike in the world? Do they not feel for the suffering? Do they not dislike poverty? Are they not called upon at times to take unpopular stands against popular leaders? Do not even your ideas of saints and angels include concepts of their feeling compassion and mercy, and of their acting upon those feelings by championing the cause of good over that of evil or of the powerless over the powerful? Isn't history replete with idols who have done just this?

10.30 I am not calling you to be as these people are or were or to act as these people have, but I am calling you to acknowledge that feelings are involved at every level of every being you can imagine. Consciousness is about what you are aware of, not about what you think. And you are very much aware of your feelings.

10.31 If you are being called to acknowledge these feelings, what are you being called to do with them? You are being called to respond to them with acceptance and love. As a man, I took a stand for the powerless and called them to power. I am still doing so. Not because any of you are powerless but because you do not know your power. If there is one thing associated with my life more so than any other, it was this. I was an advocate for all to know their power. Do you think that my advocacy was a social statement for the times in which I lived? Or do you not see that it is the same now as then?

10.32 All the issues those you would call spiritual leaders are called to champion or censor have their roots in timeless and universal spiritual truths. It is the timeless and universal that you are called, in unity, to respond to and with. But this response will not be generated without the feelings that precede them! When speaking of gossip we used a simple example of a relatively harmless situation. When speaking of the many issues facing your world in this time, we are speaking of situations that would seem to be extreme and to call for extreme measures. The only extreme measure called for now is the same extreme measure that I called for during my life. It is the call to embrace your power.

10.33 My dear brothers and sisters in Christ, turn your thoughts not to ideals of social activism, to causes, or to championing any one side over another. Turn not to your thoughts but to your feelings and go where they lead. And everywhere they lead you, remember one thing only. Remember to embrace your power. The power of love is the cause and effect that will change the world by returning you, and all your brothers and sisters, to who they are in truth. This cannot be done from without but must be done from within. It is the transformation that is caused within that will affect the world without.

10.34 The power you must come to rely upon is the power of your own Self to create and express the cause and effect that is the power of love.

10.35 Although I need no awareness of the issues facing your time in order to speak to you of such things, I am aware of them. So is every other living thing because all that lives exists in relationship. What I have often referred to as the urgency of this time has been partially because of these issues and partially because of your readiness. It is no accident that these two aspects of urgency are converging. When your reliance on all that exists apart from your Self—your reliance on science and technology and medicine and military might—has been shown to be unfounded, a new source of reliable power is finally sought with the tenacity with which these other sources of seeming power have been sought. This is what has occurred. This is the time at which we stand.

10.36 All of the solutions to the issues facing the world and those who live upon it have been pursued separately from one another and from God—until recently. Now unity is being sought and unity is being found.

10.37 But these issues, when removed from feelings, still remain issues. They remain social causes, environmental causes, political causes. The cause of all these issues is fear. The cause and effect of love is all that will replace these causes of fear with the means and end that will transform them along with you. You are means and end. It is within your power to be saviors of the world. It is from within that your power will save the world.

10.38 As you can see, it is difficult for me, even now, even in this final address to you as the man Jesus, to speak of feelings without addressing the grand scheme of things. I want to comfort and reassure you in this final message. I want to tell you to be embraced by love and to let all the feelings of love flowing through you now find their expression. I desire, more than anything, your happiness, your peace, and your acceptance of the power that will cause these things to come to be. Yet I know you and what you want to hear. I know you have long waited for your feelings to be addressed in a more personal way. But please remember than none of the approaches that have been used to "address" your feelings in the way you might desire have worked. This will work.

10.39 This is the secret of succession, your promised inheritance. This is the gift of love I came to give and give newly now, to you. Blessed brother and sister, we feel the same love, the same compassion, the same tenderness for each other and the world. This is unity. This will save us. This will save the world.

Christ-Consciousness

11.1 We are one Self. How else could we be capable of receiving what we give? How else could our lives be capable of experiencing no loss but only gain? Why else would we have to share ourselves to know ourselves?

11.2 Because we are one heart, one mind, one Self, we can only know our selves through sharing in unity and relationship. We could only share in unity and relationship through a seeming separation from the oneness in which we exist. This is the great paradox that unites the world of form and the world of spirit, the world of separation with the world of union, even while it does not unite the world of illusion with the world of truth. Sharing in unity and relationship is the way and the means to see past the world of illusion to the truth of the union of form and spirit, separate selves and the One Self.

11.3 The elevation of the self of form is nothing but the recognition of the One Self within the Self.

11.4 The One Self exists within the many in order to know Its Self through sharing in union and relationship.

11.5 All the benefits you might want to bring to the world are brought about in only one way: The way of sharing in union and relationship. It is only in relationship that the oneness of the self separates from oneness and so knows oneness. It is only through the means of separate relationships joining in union that the One Self is capable of being either the observer or the observed. This is as true of God as it is of the self of form. God is the oneness and the separation. Life is the relationship. God is what is. Life is the relationship of what is with Its Self.

11.6 Separation, of itself, is nothing. What is separate *and* joined in relation-ship is All because it is all that is knowable. The All of Everything cannot be known anymore than can nothingness. The All of Everything is unknow-able. Thus you are the knowable of God. You are the knowable because you are the relationship of All with Its Self. Separation is as unknowable as the All of Everything. To be separate in truth would be to not exist. To be the All of Everything would be to not know existence. Only what exists in relationship knows that it exists. Thus relationship is everything. Relationship is the truth. Relationship is consciousness.

11.7   Christ-consciousness is the awareness of existence through relationship. It is not God. It is not man. It is the relationship that allows the awareness that God is everything. It has been called wisdom, Sophia, spirit. It is that without which God would not know God. It is that which differentiates all from nothing. Because it is that which differentiates, it is that which has taken form as well as that from which form arose. It is the expression of oneness in relationship with Its Self.

11.8   Life is the connecting tissue of the web of form with the divine All. Life is consciousness. Christ-consciousness is awareness of what *is*. It is the awareness of connection and relationship of All to All. It is the merging of the unknowable and the knowable through movement, expression, and being.

The Spacious Self Joined in Relationship

12.1　Now we listen to feelings. Now we listen to feelings and understand what they have to say to us. Now we listen with a new ear, the ear of the heart. Now we recognize the thoughts that would censor our feelings, calling them selfish, uncaring, or judgmental. We examine. And we realize it is our thoughts and not our feelings that are selfish, uncaring, or judgmental. We realize this because we realize the sacred *space* we have become. Our space is the space of unity. It is the space of ease because thoughts are no longer allowed their rule.

12.2　Imagine the air around you being visible and your form an invisible *space* within the visible surroundings. This is the reality of Christ-consciousness. Consciousness may seem to be embodied by form but the reverse is true and has always been true. The body is now ready to know that it is embodied, enclosed, surrounded, taken up, by consciousness. It is your feelings that now will be the sense organs of this spaciousness. Not feelings of sight or sound, smell or touch, but feelings of love of Self. Feelings of love of Self are now what hold open the space of the Self, allowing the space to be.

12.3　The merging of form with Christ-consciousness is this merging of the Self with the unconditional love of the One Self. The One Self loves Its Self. There is nothing else to love. The One Self is the All.

12.4　The space of the One Self is everything. Space is neither divided nor separated nor occupied by form. Space is all that is. Christ-consciousness is the space of all that is.

12.5　Navigating this endless space as an expression of love is the simplest thing imaginable. All you must do is listen to your Self. Your Self is now a feeling, conscious space, unhindered by any obstacles of form.

12.6　When an obstacle of form, be it human or material in nature, seems to present itself, all you must do is remind yourself that space has replaced what was once your self of form. Feel the love of the space that is you. All obstacles will vanish.

12.7　All obstacles of form are only real in the world of form, a world that is perceived rather than known. Christ-consciousness replaces perception with knowing, form with space.

12.8　Not all forms will be met as obstacles. Forms are only as real as the perceiver perceives them to be. Thus your space will effortlessly join with the space that is free and open to joining. There is no boundary between space and space. There are only perceived boundaries. When a perceived boundary is perceived as solid, it is an obstacle, for it has no space available for joining. What is a boundary to a perceiver is met as an obstacle by the spacious self. Obstacles need not be avoided for space encompasses all obstacles, making them invisible. The mind would say that making obstacles invisible is uncaring. The spacious Self knows no obstacles for it knows no uncaring. It knows only love for the One Self. It feels the obstacle but does not know it. The feeling that is the sense organ of the spacious Self then remembers its spaciousness and calls upon it. The obstacle is thus enfolded in the space, becoming one with it. The perceiver knows not of the enfolding but feels no hurt nor lessening of spirit by becoming invisible within the space. The solidity of the perceiver is, in this manner, deflected from the One Self, becoming not an obstacle. The open space of the perceiver who sees not with perception only, and holds not his or her boundaries solid, is joined rather than deflected. The open perceiver may or may not know of this enfolding, but may realize a sense of comfort or of safety, a feeling of love or of attraction.

12.9　Non-human obstacles have no need of being deflected for their boundaries have not been made solid by perception. A seeming obstacle of non-human form is easily enfolded in the space of the One Self and can be moved or passed through.

12.10　This is joining in relationship.

Union with the Spacious Self

13.1   Once the One Self became form and knew Its Self, it knew separate thought. The separate thoughts of the one self, rather than the form of the one self, allowed for the knowing of the self that created the many selves. The many selves who have come and gone since the beginning of time now know themselves as the many and the one, the individual and the collective. This is the knowing in relationship that is available to you *now*.

13.2   The "one" self of form is the self you were born into. The one self of form comes to know the One Self through relationship with other selves experiencing oneness through being selves of form.

13.3   You are thus not meant to lose the experience of the self of form but to integrate it so that you are both the many and the one. The oneness that your individual self represents in this life is the oneness of the Holy One who is both one—somewhat in the way you think of the individual self—and All.

13.4   The love that is found in the relationships of the one Self with the many is the love of God. There is no other love. God's love is constantly being given, received, and felt in relationship. God's love is your love. Your love is the love of God. God is love.

13.5   Thus is explained the relationships and the forms emptied of love. Where there is no love there is no God present. Where there is no love there is a lack of godliness or what you have defined as evil. A complete lack of love creates formidable obstacles, or in other words, obstacles of solid form that contain no spaciousness. Solid form is actually a void, a substance devoid of spaciousness, a form that is form only. These forms are still encompassed by the loving space of Christ-consciousness and thus are easily rendered ineffective.

13.6   Imagine the spacious Self as an invisible Self, a Self whose form is transparent. Through this transparency, the reality of the One Self being also the many, or the all, is apparent. The spaciousness of love, the lovely complexity of form, the awesome majesty of nature, all are visible within the One Self because of the invisibility of the one boundary-less Self of form. All of creation is present and apparent in this boundary-less Self of form. This Self is everything and everyone. Because it is everything and everyone it is also the self of the void, the void of the loveless self. As long as the void of the loveless self exists within the spacious Self, they exist in harmony. It is only in attempting to eject the loveless self from the Spacious self that disharmony occurs. Thus holding the loveless self within the spacious Self of love is the answer to the question of evil and the final lifting of the last veils of fear.

13.7 The same is true of all you would fear, such as the suffering self. A suffering self, held within the spacious Self, exists in harmony with the spacious Self. Attempts to eject the self of suffering from the spacious Self create disharmony. It is only by this holding within that the loveless self and the suffering self are rendered ineffective. It is only in this way that you realize that all exist within. It is only in this way that you become completely fearless and totally spacious, for fear is part of the density of form, being a lack of love.

13.8 Once fear is gone, true relationship is not only possible but inevitable. True relationship exists naturally in the state of harmony that is the spacious Self. This is the state of union.

DAY 14

Healing

14.1   All time is included in the spacious Self. Acceptance is necessary because escape is not possible. Everything that is, is with us, which is why we are the accomplished as well as the void, the healed as well as the sick, the chaos and the peace. Thus we heal now by calling on wholeness, accepting the healed self's ability to be chosen while not encountering resistance or any attempts at rejection of the sick or wounded self. It is your acceptance that escape is not possible that will lead you out of forgetfulness to remembrance. It is in the equality of all that is realized with the acceptance of the spacious Self, the One Self, and the many, that full acceptance is actually achieved and complete transformation begun.

14.2   The spacious Self realizes that the outer world is a projection and most often a rejection rather than an extension of what is within. Thus, sickness is a rejection of feelings. All that causes fear is rejection of feelings. All that causes loneliness is rejection of feelings. All that causes violence is rejection of feelings.

14.3   What is ejected from the self becomes separate and in the separation willfully forgotten. The Spacious self no longer ejects or forgets because all feelings are accepted as those of the One Self.

14.4   All feelings are accepted as those of the many as well. It is by holding all feelings of others within the spacious Self, by not forgetting that the one and the many are the same, by willfully remembering that the feelings of the many can be "held" and not projected into the world as sickness, violence, and so on, that acceptance occurs. It is in accepting all feelings as the feelings of the many that the feelings of "others" are accepted as one's own and held within the spaciousness of the One Self, the whole Self.

14.5   Further, it is in willful remembering that extension replaces rejection both in the self and in "others." Extension of health can, in this way, replace rejection of illness and woundedness.

14.6 This is why, after learning to disclaim all that you have called your "own," you are now given the task of claiming your power as your own. All that is within your power is *within your power.* Your power is the power of the many and the one that exist in wholeness within the spacious Self.

14.7 Once you fully realize that you cannot escape, whatever remains that was brought to a stop within you must pass through for the self to be the fully invisible or spacious Self described earlier. What you once stopped and held in a "holding pattern" to return to later, is the opposite of the *holding within* you are asked to do now because those things that were held in a "holding pattern" were based on fear. You feared them because you did not understand them and could not assign meaning to them. Being inexplicable the "holding pattern" that you entered into with them was one of willful forgetting and escape. They were "shelved" like museum pieces and collected solidity within you. Like stones thrown into a clear pool, they made ripples and then settled.

14.8 The invisible or spacious Self is the Self through which pass-through naturally occurs because there are no blocks or boundaries, no holding patterns, no mental interferences.

14.9 Pass through was never about escape or rejection. Pass through is about releasing the particular while maintaining the relationship. It is what happens in oneness as opposed to the stopping and holding "apart" that occurred in separation. What the spacious Self holds within is the relationship of all to all. Relationship is the invisible reality only expressed through form.

14.10 Only now, in your realization of your invisibility and spaciousness, do you look within and see the stones that settled in your clear pools. They are as specks of sand to the ocean. And yet we do not choose to keep them. Spaciousness is spaciousness. Invisibility is invisibility. We are no longer collectors but gatherers. We hold within only what is real and in our realization of the reality of relationship, we accept our relationship to the unexplainable.

14.11 All, *all* you are doing here is accepting your relationship to the unexplainable. Acceptance is the creator of invisibility, the creator of the spacious Self. God has been described as the "all knowing" for God is the relationship. Relationship is the known. The unknown, like the unexplainable, becomes known through the relationship of acceptance. Acceptance of your relationship with the unknown is the only way to arrive at acceptance of your relationship with your means of coming to know.

14.12 Your acceptance of these words is a form of acceptance of the unknown and as such a means of coming to know. These words are only one means, which is why this is called a dialogue. Realize now that this is but one voice of the many. You have entered into the dialogue with the many as well as the one. This dialogue is going on all around you. Have you been listening to but one voice? Or have you begun to hear the one voice in the many?

14.13 You must now own this dialogue—own it as you own the power that is yours. This one voice of the many will continue to point the way for only a short time longer. Thus the voice of the many must be heard as the voice of the one. You are not on this mountain top alone! Can you not hear your own voice? Can you not hear the voices of the many who join us here?

14.14 Entering the dialogue is the means of sustaining the one voice within the many, the means of sharing your access to unity, the manifestation, in form, of the healed and whole and thus spacious Self.

Entering the Dialogue

15.1   When you fully realize that sharing is necessary you will have *entered the dialogue*. When you have fully surrendered to the fact that you can't come to know *on your own* you will have *entered the dialogue*. When you fully accept that the voice of the one can be heard in the voice of the many you will have *entered the dialogue*. When you fully realize that you are in-formed by everything and everyone in creation, you will have *entered the dialogue*.

15.2   To inform is to make known. Thus *you* can be made known by everything and everyone in creation just as everything and everyone in creation can be made known by you. We have just spoken of the *unknown* and your willingness to accept your relationship with it in order for you to come to know it. The unknown and the known exist together in everything and everyone. Thus your willingness to be made known and to know exists alongside your willingness to embrace the unknown.

15.3   The spirit that animated all things is the spirit that is in all things and that is the great informer. As you are more fully able to maintain Christ-consciousness you begin the movement away from being observed to being in-formed by the spirit which animates all things. You begin the movement away from observing to informing.

15.4   How can the invisible be observed? From within Christ-consciousness, you begin to be able to know and to make known without observation or observance *of the physical*. This occurs *through your relationship with the unknown*. You begin to be informed by what *is* without any regard for your level of understanding or knowing. You do this by taking what *is* into your spacious form rather than observing it as separate from you.

15.5   Previously, what you did not observe, or see, was not real to you. Through the practice of observance of the physical and the obvious, you began to be able to see beyond the physical and the obvious to what could not be observed physically. This practice had two purposes. The first purpose was the establishment of a new kind of interaction and relationship between observer and observed. The second purpose was your preparation to move beyond observation.

15.6   It has been in the relationship of observation that you have interacted with all other life forms as well as with inanimate forms. In the relationship generated by observation, those forms have been perceived as real. That observation produced the solidity and mass of the forms you observed. Yet it is the spirit that animates form that is real. Informing could be understood as making the spirit known in the form of physicality. It is not simply the bringing of spirit into form but the making known of spirit in form. What you made known through judgment-free observation was but the precursor to what is made known through informing.

15.7   The difference between simply bringing spirit into form and making spirit known through form is the difference for which the time has come. The observation you have practiced has prepared you to move from observation to informing and being informed.

15.8   The animation of form with spirit is an ongoing aspect of creation. It is thus not time bound. It did not take place at the birth of creation and then cease to be. It did not take place at the birth of the body and then cease to be. It is not about life and making form alive but about spirit and informing spirit. It is about making spirit known through the form of physicality.

15.9   In practicing observation without judgment, you learned to be neutral observers. Being neutral observers allowed cause and effect to occur naturally rather than having your judgment alter natural cause and effect. This practice will continue to serve you and will not be replaced, but supplemented by the new practice of informing, until the practice of observation is no longer needed.

15.10   This is the new realm of power that few in physical form have practiced and that has never been practiced by many at one time. It is a major shift because it is not neutral but creative. It is of creation and can only flow through those who have mastered neutral observation because the intent of creation, rather than the intent of the observer, is the creative force, the animator and informer. Yet informing is a quality of oneness and thus the joining of the self with the spacious Self in oneness and wholeness must precede this step. This power cannot be misused because it is unavailable to those who have not realized their oneness with the creative force. Thus while it is not the self who informs and is informed by the creative force, it is the Self joined in union with the creative force that informs and is informed. In other words, in union there is no distinction between the Self and the creative force of the universe, the animator and informer of all things.

15.11 Engaging in dialogue with those who join you on the mountain top is necessary to this next step. One reason is that it allows a starting point for your practice. While it is possible to practice observance in every situation, it is necessary to practice the ability to inform and be informed with others who have reached this level of neutrality along with you. This is why observation is not being replaced. Observation is needed until this level of neutrality is reached by a much greater number. This greater level of neutrality will not be reached until those who are the forerunners have practiced and mastered this interaction with the creative force long enough to realize their oneness with it. While there is division remaining between the self and the spacious Self, the self and the creative force, you remain in the state of maintenance rather than sustenance of Christ-consciousness. This is an acceptable state for this time of limited practice with those with whom you are engaged in this specific mountain top dialogue. It is not an acceptable state for full-scale interaction with the world. Although this power cannot be misused, to have access to this power in one instance and not another as you move in and out of the state of Christ-consciousness will not serve the purpose of creation.

15.12 What does it mean to practice informing and being informed? It means to join together with others who have the ability to maintain Christ-consciousness in your company. This creates the joining together of spacious Selves. It is a joining without boundaries. You become clear pools flowing into each other. You make your spirits known.

15.13 This cannot be explained in great detail, which is why it must be practiced. It is to your own authority only that you must appeal for guidance. The first step is to access your own readiness. Are you able to be a clear pool? If not, what prevents you? Do not be too hard on yourself now, for as has been said, the stones within your pools are like flecks of sands within the ocean. Observe these stones with neutrality and see if they do not wash away. Your willingness to have them gone is all that is required. If doubts of your readiness continue to persist, remember that doubt is caused by fear.

Examine what you fear. Is it really the stones within your pool, or is it the challenge of moving with the current that you know will be generated by the joining of spacious Selves? Do you fear your power even though you have been told it cannot be misused? Do you feel unworthy and seek to keep your unworthiness hidden? Do you still fear being known?

15.14 If so, enter the dialogue with the purpose of your final preparations in mind. Bring your fears into the light of oneness and see how the light dispels the darkness. This is what we are here for. There is no time to waste and no protracted length of time will be required if your willingness is true.

15.15 You are here to make one another known and in so doing to know oneness. It will be less difficult to know this voice as the voice of oneness once you have listened to the voice of oneness in each other and benefited from its healing properties. To heal is to make whole. To make whole is to become the spacious Self. To become the spacious Self is to become ready to be informed and to inform with the spirit of creation.

15.16 This is a very "individual" stage in the creative process. "Group think" does not replace the consciousness of the One Self with the "one group self." This is not a time of being judged or of adopting the beliefs of others but one of finally conquering judgment with neutrality or acceptance. Allowing others to accept you as you are is a gift that releases them from judgment and any notion that may have remained within them that Christ-consciousness is a form of "group think." Never will you feel more like an individual than when you are made known through the informing of spirit!

15.17 Realize how necessary dialogue is. Many resist this stage of development because they feel they have achieved inner knowing. They may still consider themselves to be capable of growing and changing, but feel, in a certain sense, that it is unnecessary. They have achieved a goal consistent with their concept of inner knowing and mistaken this as knowing the self. Movement is necessary to know the self. The on-going informing or animation of the physical with the spiritual is just that—on-going. The easiest way of all to slip from knowing to not knowing is through stagnating in a "known" place. To cease to accept the unknown is to cease to come to know.

15.18 Entering the dialogue keeps you in constant contact with the unknown and with unceasing coming to know.

15.19   You thus are not to come together as the known but as the unknown. You dialogue about the unknown, not the known. By keeping in constant contact with the unknown you stay in constant dialogue for you have not claimed a knowing that disallows coming to know. You are in dialogue because in dialogue, coming to know is a fluid exchange.

15.20   Imagine the current of the energy, or clear pools of the spacious selves, coming together. This current washes some stones clean and washes others away. It changes the clear pool by dredging up sediment that has settled on the bottom. As the clear pool merges with the current of other clear pools it is able to change directions, see new sights, gain new insights. While this is only an initial, or practice stage of movement, it is obvious that movement will always be needed for the clear pool to not become a stagnant pond.

15.21   To be engaged in dialogue with certain others is different than entering the dialogue, but entering the dialogue is not different than engaging in specific dialogues. This is so because entering the dialogue is an all-encompassing state in which everything and everyone interacts with you through the exchange of dialogue. While you are asked to promote wholeness and the sustainability of Christ-consciousness with others sharing this specific means of coming to know with you, you are not asked to disregard any other means of coming to know or to see any others differently than you see those with whom you are engaged in this specific dialogue for this specific purpose or practice.

15.22   However, knowing that you have entered the dialogue does not mean that you will not have an awareness of those who would infringe upon, rather than join with, your boundary-less state. You must but remember that those who still have boundaries have a need for those boundaries. Thus you are not depriving them of anything when you slip into observable states of being. There is a purpose for this time in which both informing and observing, being informed and being the observed coexist. You must respect the boundaries of those who are still in need of them and not offer more than can be received. This is why practice among those who are ready to be boundary-less and spacious selves is appropriate and acceptable.

15.23   To practice, as to inform, is to make known. To practice, as to inform, does not mean, however, that you know nothing. Practice is the merging of the known and the unknown through experience, action, expression, and exchange. It alters the known through interaction with the unknown. It allows the continuing realization that what you knew yesterday was as nothing to what you know today, while at the same time, aiding in the realization that what you come to know has always existed within you in the realm of the unknown that also exists within you.

15.24 While you have not been asked to remove yourself from life during this time on the mountain, you have been asked to be here and to join with others here for a purpose. As such, this time is also a beginning to the practice of realizing and being able to accept a certain duality. Without necessarily realizing it, your consciousness has been in two places at once without being divided. As you re-enter life on level-ground, this ability to carry an undivided but spacious consciousness with you will be paramount and will have many practical as well as spiritual applications.

15.25 One of the practical aspects has just been discussed—that of engaging in dialogue with some and entering the dialogue with all. This is a demonstration of levels of consciousness at work. It is important to be able to hold the spacious consciousness of the One Self and also to be able to focus—to not exclude while also making choices about where your attention is given. Just as you respect the boundaries of those who are still in need of boundaries, you also must respect your own boundary-less space.

15.26 As you engage in dialogue as the spacious Self and are made known, your purpose here will become more clear. Thus your ability to embrace all while focusing on your own purpose in being here, will begin a new process of individuation. The distinctness of your own path will be made visible and you will see that it may be quite different from the others with whom you are coming to know, and perhaps quite different than you thought it would be. You will be shown that you can enter the dialogue with all and still focus, or place your attention, on areas that might not interest others in the slightest.

15.27 You may, thus, find that there is a time of walking alone approaching, or a time of gathering with many. You will realize that you have felt cocooned by the time on the mountain and by those who have joined you, and that you may have grown less eager to strike out *on your own*. You may have thought the joining being done here was the joining with a specific group rather than a joining with yourself and with all. This fallacy needs to be brought to your attention now so that as you join in true spaciousness with those coming to know along with you, you do not create false ideas concerning what this is about.

15.28 Remember that this journey has not been about becoming self-less but about realizing your true identity. We have now debunked your myths about your true identity being an idealized form of the self. Now are you ready, through your ability to view your own Self as well as that which you observe with a neutrality that embraces the unknown as well as the known, to reclaim your Self and your purpose here.

DAY 16

Paradise Re-Found

16.1   Everything that can't be seen but *is*, is consciousness. Accepting everything that can't be seen, including the unknown, is full consciousness. Acceptance is key. You can't accept what you fear.

16.2   Because all that is not physical exists only in consciousness, it simply exists. It is simply "there" within consciousness. All that you "know" because you have felt it, is still there because consciousness is eternal. All that you have learned that has touched your heart is there because you felt it. All that you have thought is still there because you thought it.

16.3   What is of form comes and goes and is impermanent. What is of spirit, or consciousness, is eternal.

16.4   Sickness has been defined as rejected feelings, feelings about which consciousness was not chosen. With this rejection, these feelings became physical. What is not of consciousness is of physical form. The rejected feelings that became physical were made separate from the self and yet were maintained within the body, thus interrupting the body's natural means of functioning. Sickness is not sickness but rejected feelings. The rejected feelings exist as separate and forgotten physical manifestations until they are willfully remembered and accepted back into the spacious Self. Rejected feelings are those for which you blame yourself. Sickness is the form of manifestation of rejected feelings. These manifestations come to you to prove to you what you think you know—that you are responsible for the sorry circumstances of your life.

16.5   Ejected feelings are projected outside of the body. These are the unwanted feelings that are blamed on others. These manifest in your interactions with the world, taking on form in the actions of others, in instances where acts of nature or accidents seem to thwart plans, or in "situations" or crises of all kinds. These manifestations also come to you to prove what you think you know—that others, or the world in general, are to blame for the sorry state of your life.

16.6   This is what is meant by no escape. No escape does not mean that anyone is bound to the past and to their former pain but that each is still bound to, and affected by, all that has been rejected or ejected. All that has been expelled is part of the wholeness of the self. As what was ejected or rejected and became "real" is returned to the Self, the physical manifestation dissolves, because the source, which was separation, is no more. In other words, illness is no longer observable once what was rejected rejoins the spacious Self. The illness was but is no more. Because it was physical it came only to pass. Because the feeling that generated the physical manifestation was not physical to begin with—was not of the physical world—it returns to its non-physical nature within the spacious Self. Thus it was not escaped but reintegrated into the oneness of the Self.

16.7   This reintegration requires, of course, a change in what you want to prove to yourself. All you may now continue to seek proof of is that your feelings, rather than your thoughts about your feelings, reflect who you are, and that by acting on them, you will act in accord with who you are and thus in accord with the universe. The reintegration is the process through which you discover this proof, proof of the benevolence of your feelings and of the benevolence of the universe itself.

16.8   What happens when feelings of loneliness or despair, anger or grief join with the spacious Self? This joining occurs only through acceptance. Without acceptance, the separation remains along with the physical manifestation.

16.9   It is only in the present that acceptance can occur. There is no "going back" or reliving of the past required. There is also no escape, however, because in Christ-consciousness, you must become fully aware of the present. The present is the time of no time, wholeness, where all that is real and all that was ever real exists. While the physical manifestations of all that you feared and expelled were not real because they were projections rather than creations, the feelings were real because you felt them. Had you not feared and expelled them, you would have seen that they were nothing to fear.

16.10   You have no feelings that are bad. Fear is not a feeling but a response to a feeling. Emotions are responses. You have been told there are but two emotions, love and fear. What this is really saying is that there are but two ways to respond to what you feel —with love or with fear. If you respond with fear you expel, project, and separate. If you respond with love you remain whole. You realize that you have no feelings that are bad. You embrace sadness, grief, anger, and all else that you feel because these feelings are part of who you are in the present moment. When you remain in the present moment you remain within Christ-consciousness where all that *is* exists in harmony. To embrace is the opposite of to escape. To hold all within your-self in the embrace of love is the opposite of holding onto what you have already responded to with fear and made separate. There is no escape for there is only the embrace. The embrace *is* Christ-consciousness.

16.11 This relates to everything, not only your response to sickness or crisis situations, because it relates to whether or not you are able to remain in a state of constant coming to know. What you expel is what you do not want to know. What you try to control is what you do not want to know. You do not want to know every time you predetermine, in advance of knowing, what something is or will be. You predetermine, or decide, for instance, that a physical symptom is bad, and then choose to find out what is "wrong," in which case your "decision" rather than your "feeling" is only confirmed. When you feel uneasy or uncomfortable about a situation, you determine that you already know that the situation is bad or is most likely going to be bad, and then you "think" that through your effort or control you can alter the situation for the better. Only when you accept that no feelings are bad will you allow yourself to come to know what they truly are.

16.12 When you feel an "intuition" you respond differently than you do to unwanted feelings that you are quick to want to "do something" about. If all feelings were treated more like intuition is treated—with a "knowing" that the feeling has come to tell you something that is as yet *unknown* to you, but nevertheless for your benefit, you would go a long way toward acceptance.

16.13 All that you predetermine you have come to know will be cause only for suffering, arrogance, and righteousness if you attempt to hold onto it as the "known" and do not remain in a constant state of coming to know. What you would hold onto is based on fear and expelled into solidity where you can keep your eyes upon what you have "formed" an opinion about. What you hold within the embrace is held in love and so exists along with you in the spacious state of constant coming to know.

16.14 Consciousness, or the spacious Self, thus includes feelings of sadness, loneliness, and anger as well as feelings of happiness, compassion, and peace. Consciousness does *not*, however, include your responses. Consciousness thus does not include either love or fear. This is because love is everything and fear is nothing.

16.15 Consciousness began as all feeling and all thought, all of which were of love because love is everything. All feeling and all thoughts of love extended into the paradise of creation. This was the Garden of Eden, the Self, the All of All. Unwanted feelings that you attempted to expel from the Garden of Eden were not expelled from consciousness, but from your awareness. This created the separate and the unloved in your perception, and your perception created an unreal reality of the separate and unloved, often referred to as hell or hell on earth. Love and fear existed simultaneously as did paradise and hell. This became your world, which slowly grew from a world primarily made up of paradise and love, to a world primarily made up of hell and fear because as more was expelled from paradise, more was perceived as hellish or fearful. Less of love was extended. More of fear was projected.

16.16 The expelled feelings that seemed to cause this duality still exist in consciousness. Once these expelled feelings are returned to the spacious Self and the spacious Self embraces them with love, the spacious Self will be whole, for it will embrace everything—as love, which *is* everything—embraces it. This is paradise re-found.

The Fulfillment of the Way of Jesus

17.1 Just as the creation story had to start somewhere—so you had to start somewhere. We have spoken of the spirit that animated all things as the movement or cause of movement that began the creation story. We have spoken of Christ-consciousness as the awareness of existence through relationship. We have spoken of life-consciousness and Christ-consciousness as the merging of the human and the divine into observable form. Thus there must be a difference between life-consciousness and Christ-consciousness, since you have been life-conscious without being Christ-conscious. You have been the created without being the creator. Something has been missing. What is Christ? What is Christ-consciousness? Are they different or the same?

17.2 You have been told Christ-consciousness is neither God nor man but the relationship that allows the awareness that God is everything. You have been told Christ-consciousness has also been known as wisdom, Sophia, spirit. Christ-consciousness thus obviously predates the man Jesus, and creation itself. It is both the feminine and masculine, the "identity" of God, or in other words, the All of All given an identity. God holds you within Himself. Christ is held within you as the center or heart of yourself—as your identity and God's identity. Christ is the "I Am" of God, the expression of "I Am" in form, the animator and the animated, the informer and the informed, the movement, being, and expression of creation. Christ is that which anointed form with the "I Am" of God. In many religious traditions, life is ritually or sacramentally anointed in its coming and its going in remembrance of the original anointing.

17.3 Why do we return to this now, repeating what has been said before? Because we have reached the time, once again, for you to claim your identity. Although being who you are has been discussed in many ways, many of you still await being different than who you are. This is because you realize that being your true self is being in union, undivided and inseparable from God, the All of All. God is only the all-knowing because God is in everything and everyone. Consciousness itself is not knowing but awareness. God is the creator of knowing because God created a means of coming to know. This "part" of God, the animator and informer, is Christ-consciousness.

17.4   What is the drive that kept you reading this Course, caused you to enter this dialogue, kept you examining, kept you attempting to move beyond learning to a new means of knowing? Christ-consciousness. This is why it was said in the beginning pages of the Course that the Christ in you was the learner. The Christ in you is what was created to inspire movement beyond simple awareness to knowing. You have always been aware that you exist and always been in search of an answer as to why you exist. You have always been aware of the world around you and always been in search of answers to what the world around you is all about. An approach to knowing, which was called learning, was previously the predominant approach. As this approach became more and more centered in the mind and more and more about coming to know what others had already learned and were capable of teaching, learning began to fail the cause of knowing.

17.5   There have always been individuals who challenged the predom- inant patterns of learning because of the strength of their connection to Christ-consciousness. While no one has more access to Christ-conscious- ness than another, some exhibited more willingness to let that consciousness be their guiding force—that by which their being gained movement and expression. Those like Jesus, who fully expressed Christ-consciousness in form, did so as individuals, by not negating their being as they realized this connection. Many others with realization of Christ-consciousness as strong as that of the man, Jesus, did not express that realization but negated the individual in favor of the "spiritual."

17.6   This is why we return now to your identity and the individuation of your identity.

17.7   Christ-consciousness is not the second coming of Christ but the first coming—the movement of being into form. This being was fully expressed by Jesus Christ, who represented, in form, the first coming and who began the movement from maintenance to sustenance of Christ-consciousness. Let's consider why this representation should be necessary.

17.8   As the universe is not comprised of the unnecessary, nor are human beings. The universe, as well as human beings, are comprised of nothing that is superfluous, but only of the necessary in the sense that all the given components are necessary for wholeness. Representation of the power of Christ-consciousness in human form was necessary to complete the cycle of birth, death, and rebirth.

17.9   Christ-consciousness was represented not only by Jesus, but by his mother, Mary. Mary, like Jesus, realized full Christ-consciousness and full expression of Christ-consciousness in form. Each did so in individual ways, ways that revealed the choices available to those who would follow after them. One way, that of Jesus, was the way of acceptance, teaching by example, and preparing a way for those who would approach Christ-consciousness through teaching and learning and leading example lives. Another way, that of Mary, was the way of creation, and was a representation and preparation for those who would approach Christ-consciousness through relationship.

17.10   The way of Jesus represented full-scale interaction with the world, demonstrating the myth of duality, the death of form, the resurrection of spirit. The way of Mary represented incarnation through relationship, demonstrating the truth of union, the birth of form, and the ascension of the body. Both ways were necessary. Both ways were necessarily represented or demonstrated. Both ways were represented and demonstrated by many other individuals as well. The way was a choice. The main ability of the individual is the ability to represent what God created, the means of coming to know—which *is* Christ- consciousness—through individual choice or will.

17.11   Christ-consciousness is your will to know, to be, and to express. The time of Christ, and the second-coming of Christ, are expressions meant to symbolize the completion of the cycle of birth, death, and re-birth as a means of coming to know.

17.12   What Jesus represented or demonstrated has now been realized, which is why this is called the time of Christ. The "time" of Christ, whom so many associate with Jesus Christ, represents the "time" of fulfillment of the way of Jesus. What could be taught and learned has been taught and learned. Now it is time to move beyond what could be taught and learned to what can only be realized through relationship. Now is the time of the final revelation of what can be realized, or made real, through following the example life of Jesus.

17.13 Thus we enter the ending stage of what can be realized through fulfillment of the way of Jesus and the beginning of the fulfillment of the way of
Mary. This ending stage of the fulfillment of the way of Jesus is the stage of
interaction with the world, the time of miracles, the death of the old way and
the birth of the new.

The Way to Paradise

18.1 You have been preparing for this final stage of the fulfillment of the way of Jesus. You have also been preparing for the beginning of the fulfillment of the way of Mary. Many of you will follow the way of Jesus to completion, beginning a stage of interaction with the world, an interaction with the miracles that will aide in the dismantling of the old and with preparing the way for the birth of the new. Others of you will follow your hearts to a by-passing of the final stage of the old and to anchoring the new within the web of reality. Still others will participate in both, following their innate desire to facilitate the creation of change through a specific function even while moving into the new as they do so. Each way is as needed now as it was two thousand years ago.

18.2 One way is active. One way is receptive. Yet the ways are not separate any more than Jesus was separate from Mary—or any mother separate from her child. The ways are rather complimentary and symbiotic. Together they return wholeness and will bring about the completion of the time of Christ. This symbiotic working together will be essential for the birth of the new and in truth symbolizes it in form and process. As within, so without. Mary represents the relationship that occurs within, Jesus the relationship that occurs with the world. So do each of you. These two ways also represent God and Christ-consciousness, the extension of God. God is everything in heaven and on earth and is in everything on heaven and on earth. Thus, God represents the world without. Christ-consciousness is God within *you*, your particular manifestation of God and relationship with the God within.

18.3 As has been said, the time of teaching and learning is over. If the way of Jesus was a way of acceptance, teaching, learning, and leading an example life, then the remaining ways of Jesus that are still applicable and appropriate in this final period are those of acceptance and of being an example life.

18.4   Only those who have fully accepted who they are, are capable of being example lives. These example lives are evidenced through the individuation of the One Self among the many. In other words, to choose to be an example life is to choose to be made known by, and to, the many. It is full acceptance of the Self in a form that can be distinguished, or individuated from the rest. It is full acceptance of difference as well as sameness and of the necessity of each. It is a choice many will be called to so that sameness is seen in difference, the one is seen in the many, and the many seen in the one. It is a way of service through action. It is a way of joy and harmony for only through joy and harmony can true service become true action. It is the way for those who desire to bring expression to a calling they feel within to "do" something. It is the way for those whose fulfillment and completion is interlaced with bringing this expression to fulfillment. If the call is there, the need is there. Have no question in your mind about this. The universe is comprised of no superfluous elements. What you feel called to is needed.

18.5   To be an example life is to be what you represent in truth. Followers of all faiths are called to example lives and to representation of the same truth. All faith is faith in the unknown through knowing, as a glimpse of fleeting light in darkness provides for a knowing of light. Those who accept completion of the way of Jesus accept their power to be generators of light in darkness without judging or expelling darkness. They accept their power to represent both the known and the unknown and to reveal the unknown through the known. They accept the death of the self and the resurrection of the One Self, the end of the individual and the individuation of the One Self amongst the many. They find renewed pleasure in being who they are because they have been renewed through resurrection. They follow the calling of their hearts without attachment to previous concerns, for in their renewal they fully realize the necessity of what can be given only through expression of what is within them. They realize that what is needed now is needed in order to renew or resurrect the world and all who abide within it.

18.6   Resurrection lays aside death's claim and with it the claim of all that is temporary. This is why we have spent time on the idea of sickness and other unwanted states as temporary manifestations. Your separated state *was* a sickness, an unwanted state, and thus a temporary manifestation. The joining of mind and heart provided reunion of the human and divine and thus accomplished the resurrection of the eternal in form. Your virgin state, the state unaltered by the separation, has been returned.

18.7 The truth represented by Jesus and Mary was represented as a visual pattern that would aide understanding of the invisible. This is what you are now called to do. Whether you demonstrate the myth of duality or the truth of union, you are demonstrating the same thing. The *way* in which you do this must be chosen, and for this choice to be made with full consciousness, you must rely on your feelings.

18.8 Feelings are your awareness of the present and thus of the truth. They are your means of coming to know. They arise from Christ-consciousness. They come not in response but as creations. Often science and religion have puzzled over the "beginning" of life, over what *causes* the formation of life, over what tells the brain what to do, over the organizing factor of DNA, of tissues and cells that do know exactly how to interact. Where does this knowing come from? When something appears to go wrong, what is the source of the malfunction?

18.9 You have been told that although you believed yourself to be separate this separation never actually occurred and that you have always been the accomplished. If this had not been true, the *cause* of life would not have been a cause of truth. Just as neither brain nor heart alone provide for a functioning body, mind and heart in separation could not truly exist and allow for a functioning state of life or consciousness. Thus there was only a degree of separation that was able to occur to allow for a certain type of experience. Now a new degree of union is occurring to allow for a new type of experience.

18.10 The new visual pattern is that of spirit resurrected in form. It is the ascension of the body, or elevation of the self of form. You are called to demonstrate this pattern. The choice is to demonstrate this pattern through interaction with the world, or through incarnation through relationship. Neither is exclusive. Both are contained within the other. But the way of discovery and demonstration is different.

18.11 You are called to demonstrate this new visual pattern. What is meant here by the word *demonstrate*, is to show your feelings, to make them visible. They are the creations unique to you through your interaction with the Christ-consciousness that abides within you. One *way* of doing this is through individuation and becoming known. One *way* of doing this is incarnation through relationship in which the relationship, rather than the individuated self, becomes the known. Both ways are ways of creation. When feelings are shown, or made visible, the new is created. This has always been the way of creation. Each blade of grass, each flower, each stone, is a creation of feelings. All you need do is look about you to know that feelings of love still abound. Beauty still reigns.

18.12 Both the self and the relationship of self to all must become known in order for the paradise that has been re-found to be re-created for everyone. What else would life be for but to make the invisible paradise of love visible and livable for all?

The Way of Mary

19.1   Those of you who are the forerunners of the way of Mary may have felt confusion over your sense of calling. You know you are called to something, and something important, but it does not have a form within your mind and so you see not how it can become manifest in the world. In other words, you know not what to do. You perhaps see no "specific" accomplishment in your future, but see instead a way of living as the ultimate accomplishment. You see living as who you are in the world as the accomplishment that is needed from you and yet at times you compare yourselves to those who are able to live as who they are in the world *and* accomplish certain functions within the world. You perhaps feel function-less and purposeless at times, while at other times, you feel as if you are being exactly as you are meant to be.

19.2   The key here is discernment between true contentment and denial. Although this is overly simplified, you might think of this as the artist being content in creating art, the musician in creating music, the healer in creating health. Those of the way of Mary are content with a way of living. Yet everyone has a function to fulfill in creation of the new world. Only those who express themselves are truly content.

19.3   You can see right away, however, that if the artist, musician, or healer were content *only* in their expression of their specific gifts, their contentment would not be complete. Neither would it be complete without that expression.

19.4   Being content is being fulfilled by the *way* in which you express who you are—by the way you express your content—your wholeness. Those who use their gifts to create the truth they see are those who in "doing" find their way to true contentment and true creation. They become who they are to be through their acts of creation. Those called to the way of Mary are called to be what they want to see reflected in the world and to the realization that this reflection is the new way of creation. In their being they become what they want to create.

19.5   The ultimate accomplishment *is* living as who you are within the world. But in what kind of world? This is the catch that causes feelings of purposelessness in those who are content to live as who they are within the world. Until they realize the power of reflection, they wonder why they, unlike their brothers and sisters called to "do," do not have a specific part to play in establishing the world in which all are able to be content with who they are.

19.6   The answer lies in the simple statement of *as within, so without*. By living as who you are in the world, you create change in the world. You create change in the world through relationship. All live and create in relationship. Those called to the way of Mary, however, are called to the creation and anchoring of the new relationship in the new world. Their relationship of union, upon which their contentment is based, is the birthplace, the womb of the new. Their *expression* is expression of this union.

19.7   To be called to a specific function that creates change is really to be called to a function of preparing one or many for the change that must occur within. The function of those called to the way of Jesus is to call others to the new through means so widespread, varied, and remarkable that they cannot be ignored.

19.8   Just as Jesus would not have been literally birthed without Mary, the way of Mary cannot be reborn without the way of Jesus. Both ways arose from Christ-consciousness as demonstrations of ways. Those who have thought of Mary as an intermediary are as inaccurate in this belief as are those who thought of Jesus in such a way. Neither demonstrated intermediary functions but demonstrated direct union with God. Each demonstrated the creative aspect of that function in different ways. But the function remained one of direct union with God. This is quite literally the function of all in this new time. When we speak of functions unique to each, we speak of expressions of this one ultimate function. Together, the way of Mary and the way of Jesus demonstrate the truth of *as within, so without* and the *relationship* between the inner and outer world.

19.9   The way of Mary is not a place or state of non-interaction however. This is not the state or place of the monks, nuns, or the contemplatives of old. It is not solitary nor isolated, nor confined to a specific community. It is a way of existence in which relationship is paramount. It is not listening to a calling to "do" but a calling to "become."

19.10 All are called to become, but some must "do" in order to "become." Those called to the way of Mary are not required to do in the sense of fulfilling a specific function that will become manifest in the world, but are required to do in the sense of receiving, sharing, and being what they are asked to become. This is an act of incarnation, and is a new pattern, a pattern of what can be imagined being made real, not through doing, but through the creative act of incarnating in union with spirit. It corresponds with the end of the way of Jesus in that the way of incarnation is the way of miracles. It corresponds with the end of the way of Jesus in that an example is provided. It differs only in that the example is not an example of an individuated life but an example of the union and relationship that is all life.

19.11 This is not to say that those called to the way of Jesus will find acclaim and those called to the way of Mary will find obscurity. Many called to the way of Mary will "do" much that is greatly desired in the world but what they do will be a byproduct of their way of being rather than a means of facilitating that way of being. Many of the way of Mary will find acclaim, yet neither acclaim nor obscurity will matter to those following these ways. Being true to the self and the calling of the One Self is all that matters. Eventually all will follow the way of Mary and such ideas as acclaim and obscurity will be no more. But at this time of transition, both ways are needed to demonstrate the means of coming to know, which are what all true expression is about.

19.12 The fear of losing the self is still the primary fear, even among those who have never found the self. They fear losing the known to the unknown. The two ways of demonstration make the unknown known. One makes the unknown known through individuated example lives. One makes the unknown known through creation of the new so that the unknown is no longer unknown but made available to be experienced.

19.13 This availability is what is meant by the anchoring of the new. Those who, in relationship with the unknown, through unity and imagination, create the new by means other than doing, open a way previously unknown, and as all forerunners do, anchor that way within consciousness by holding open this door to creation. They, in truth, create a new pattern and begin to weave it into the web of reality, anchoring it for discovery by their brothers and sisters.

19.14 The truth of this way is not discovered through the passing on of knowledge in form but through relationship. Those following the way of Mary become mirrors of the truth they discover, reflecting the way to their brothers and sisters. This is why this is not a place or state of non-interaction but of great interaction. It is a state that facilitates knowing through relationship. This occurs through the one Self of form.

19.15 In this action of joining in union and relationship is contained the key to creation of the new. It was spoken of earlier as the act of informing and being informed, as the step beyond that of observing and being observed. It is where creation of the new can begin because it is the intent of creation, rather than the intent of the observer, that is the creative force, the animator and informer. Being joined in union and relationship allows for the channeling of creation through the one Self because the one Self is joined in union and relationship.

19.16 This is very tricky for those who reach highly individuated states and it is necessary for those of the way of Mary to support, encourage, and reflect the new to those being examples of the way of Jesus. This too is tricky for it can lead to judgment. When there is more than one way, there is always room for comparison and judgment. Thus it is realistic to see the two ways as intertwined circles existing in support and harmony with one another. As those given specific functions fulfill those functions, they move naturally to the way of Mary.

19.17 Without those pursuing the way of Jesus, those pursuing the way of Mary would have a much more difficult task. There would be little space in which to anchor the new. Those following the way of Jesus create the openness of the spacious Selves who allow for the anchors of the new to be cast and thus to ride out the many storms of this time of transition.

DAY 20

The First Transition

20.1 Now we begin preparation for your transition to level ground. We depart even farther here from the guidance you have relied upon so that you begin to rely more and more fully on the truth of this dialogue.

20.2 You have realized now your relationship with the unknown and ceased to fear it. You are, perhaps, even eager now, to move beyond the known to the unknown. You are perhaps eager without fully realizing that this eagerness symbolizes a true ending—an ending within you and within your reality—an ending within your conscious awareness. A true end of learning.

20.3 This is the first transition, the transition in which you really "get it" that the unknown cannot be taught, laid out on a map, or shown to you by another.

20.4 When you read what has been written here, you perhaps think this is a contradiction, for surely you have been told much here that you did not previously know. This isn't quite accurate however. What has happened here is that words have been put on the feelings and remembrances that you have within your minds and hearts and have been sharing in this dialogue. The way of saying this perhaps is new, but the *way* of saying this is the expression of the human being receiving it. The way in which you are hearing and responding to these truths is perhaps new, but that way too is of the human being receiving it, in this case, you.

20.5 The truth is the truth. It doesn't change. It is the same for everyone.

20.6 What, then, is the unknown? The reception and expression of truth.

20.7 This is why you can "know" while always coming to know. Why you can know yourself and constantly be coming to know. The only thing there is to know is the One Self in its many expressions. You are the known and the unknown. Everything is both the known and the unknown.

20.8 You *are* the expression of the unknown and the *only* means of the unknown becoming known.

20.9 In other words, all the truth and all the wisdom that is available but *unknown* to you, takes *you* to make it known. And if this is the only way that the beauty, truth, and wisdom of the One Self can be made known, then *you* are the source and the power of coming to know and making known.

20.10 Apply the art of thought to this idea and you will complete the first transition.

Day 21

The Reversal

21.1   The first transition, as you have probably already realized, is about a letting-go of any of the ideas that you may still have that an outside source exists. There is no such thing as an outside source. There are no outside sources of wisdom, guidance, or even information.

21.2   This was true even within the pattern of learning you have been so familiar with, for in order to learn, the source of wisdom, even though you may have seen it as existing outside of yourself, had to function as what it was—a channel through which the wisdom, guidance or information moved. If it did not do so, learning did not occur. In traditional learning patterns, the wisdom, guidance, or information sought moved from a teacher—whether that teacher was an actual teacher, or a parent or a friend—to a student, or in other words, from a giver to a receiver.

21.3   Nothing was capable of being taught or learned without the reception of what the giver gave. The giver could make available but could not really teach, guide, or even make information coherent without the action of the receiver. Thus it has always been the action of the receiver that made learning possible. The receiver was thus also the source because the receiver had to accept or "give" what was offered, to herself.

21.4   The channel is the means, not the source. The source is oneness or union, a state you now realize that you share and have access to.

21.5   What you allow yourself to receive and what you do with what you receive is all that matters.

21.6   You realize now that life itself is a channel and that you are constantly receiving. You still perhaps think in terms of receiving meaning that there is something given from a source beyond the self, but this is the "thought" that has to change. If giving and receiving are one, then giver and receiver are also one. It is only you who can do anything with the wisdom, guidance, or information that you receive in union as a channel of the divine

life force that exists in everything and everyone. There is nothing channeled to one that isn't channeled to all. The old notions of teaching and
learning but made it seem as if some had more and others less. But even the
pattern of learning had as its outcome the sameness of teacher and learner—
the transfer of knowledge that would eventually make teacher and learner
equal. Means and end have always been the same.

21.7   Now, however, there is no longer an "eventually." Teacher and learner
are equal and thus neither are needed any longer. The "transfer" of knowledge is now an act of giving and receiving as one. No intermediary is needed
when you exist in union. It is recognized that the knowledge, wisdom, guidance, or information that is needed in each moment is available within each
moment and that the interaction, rather than being one of taking something
from an outside source into the self where it is learned and then regurgi-
tated or even applied, has given way to an interaction that begins within and
extends outward.

21.8   This will seem like an incredible reversal and thus it is. This is the
reversal that will make of you a creator. But it can only happen if you make
the first transition.

21.9   You began your mountain top experience with a companion who had
offered himself as a teacher in order to bring you to the place of being
willing to accept that a teacher was not needed. He joined you on the mountain top in order to prepare you for his departure, a departure from reliance
upon him that would allow you to arrive at reliance upon yourself. This reliance upon yourself has been expressed as a dialogue taking place within
Christ-consciousness, the consciousness you share in union and relationship with all. You have now been told to own this dialogue and to realize
that its wisdom is your own. Are you accepting this? Are you beginning
to ready yourself to hear this voice as your own? To express the voice of
Christ-consciousness as only you can express it?

21.10   Realize that this is the aim of our final time together. Concentrate on
making the first transition and on the reversal of thought that it requires.
Thus will you carry this time forward with you into creation of the new.

DAY 22

Channeling

22.1　If we have spoken little of channeling here, it is only because you have been coming to know yourself as channels without the need for these words. Now we must speak of this, however, for there is a confusion that can occur in regards to channeling. Yesterday we spoke of teachers being channels during the time of learning. It was also noted that you realize that all of life is a channel. There is a big difference between seeing a teacher as a channel, all of life as a channel, and the Self as a channel or channeler.

22.2　Let's look at the idea of channeling as simply an idea of expressing, but an idea of expression that is given and received, received and given. When the word channeling has been used in reference to spirituality, it has often been used to indicate an intermediary function. The channeler was perhaps seen as a mediator between the living and the dead or the world of spirit and the world of humanity. This idea separated the living and the dead, the spiritual and the human into two states—states that could, at their most basic levels—be seen as known and unknown states. The teacher in the example used was also an intermediary with the separation being between the known and the unknown. Thus, a channel could be seen as that through which the unknown moves into the state of knowing. This is the way in which life itself can be seen as a channel. Since the first transition involves realizing that *you* are the expression of the unknown and the *only* means of the unknown becoming known, it is important to discuss this in as many ways as possible to make this idea clear to you. You are life, and you are also surrounded by living forces channeling to you constantly.

22.3　Channeling, in the commonly understood spiritual sense, can either promote a sense of separation or a sense of unity. The sense of separation comes when the channeler is seen as having something unavailable to everyone rather than being seen as a means to provide, or channel, availability to everyone. What each person channels is unique and only available through their expression. The availability is there for everyone. The means of expression is there for everyone. What is expressed is different because it is a combination of the universal (what is available) with the individual (what is expressed). Whether one chooses to avail oneself of the channeled or expressed universality of another is a choice and another indicator of the uniqueness of channeling. The universal is everything. The channel is what, from among everything, is allowed reception and expression. Some will find many avenues of channeling available to them, both through themselves and through spiritual channels, without realizing that both are the same because both require a choice, a choice to allow entry or union. In this choice, the universe (what is available) is channeled through the expression of (the individual) desires.

22.4   Every choice is thus a means of channeling. It is taking the infinite number of experiences or information available and channeling only what one desires to know. Thus, it is prudent to repeat once again, that *you* are the expression of the unknown and the *only* means of the unknown becoming known. You, in other words, are the channel, the conduit, of the unknown becoming known. What you choose to know and how you choose to know it is an act of channeling.

22.5   There is also, however, the idea of a channel as a passage to take into consideration. This we have spoken of previously as your access to union— as a place or state of consciousness through which your awareness of unity passes through your self of form. It is clear, when looked at in terms of process, that there is no intermediary function involved in channeling, but a function of union. This is the very function that you have waited to have revealed to you, the function you have known you are here to fulfill, the function of direct union with God.

22.6   It does not matter that everyone's function is the same because no one expression of this same function produces the same results. No one who is in union with God is in union with the known. Yet it is as if through this union you have learned a great secret that you long to share. But what is it? And how do you share it? How do you convey it? How do you channel it? Through what means can you express it? Can you put it into words, make it into images, tell it in a story? You will feel as if you will burst if you cannot share the union that you touch when you fulfill your function of direct union with God. How do you let it pass through you to the world?

22.7   The most simple, direct, and uncomplicated answer is that of living love. The simple answer is that you must express the unknown that you have touched, experienced, sensed, or felt with such intimacy that it is known to you *because* the knowing becomes real in the making known. It is the only way it remains real. You know union in order to sustain and create union by channeling the unknown reality of union into the known reality of separation. You realize that you know the unknown and you desire to make the unknown knowable. You realize that you have known a place where nothing but love exists, where there is no suffering, no death, no pain nor sorrow, no separation or alienation. You sense that if you could fully express this place of union, if you could abide there, if you could share this place in an aware and conscious state, that you would bring this state into existence in the reality in which you exist.

22.8   This awareness of union with God is what is now within you awaiting your expression. Awareness of union with God exists in everything. It is there in every tree and every flower, in every mountain stream and every blowing wind. It is there in each and every human being. It is now time to quit acting as if it is not. It is time to be a channel for the awareness that exists in every tree and every flower, in each mountain stream and in the blowing wind. It is time to be a channel for the awareness of union with God that exists in every living being.

22.9   This awareness is what we have been calling Christ-consciousness, but what you call it now matters not. All the words that have been expressed here, that say so many similar things in so many different ways, are words that are simply calling you to realization of your union with God and to the new world you can create once you accept and make real this union.

22.10 You might think of yourself as a channel through which union with God is expressed and made real here and now. There is no other time. There is no "higher" self waiting to do what only you can do. There is no one else who knows what you know the way you know it or who can express the unknown in the way that you can express it. The unknown can only be made known through reception and expression. Call it what you will for what you call it matters not. Throw out all the words that express the unknown in ways that you would not, and find your own. Each way is needed.

22.11 Remember only the feeling that a place of union exists in which you know God, in which you know love, in which you know of joy without sorrow, and life everlasting. This is the great unknown that you can make known.

DAY 23

Carrying

23.1 Forget not that who you are is what you are here to make known and thus you must be a being who knows love without fear, joy without sorrow, and life everlasting. You must *be* this. *A Course of Love* gave you the understanding you needed in order to realize that you *are* this. The Treatises gave you a way to apply this understanding. This dialogue is meant to give you the means to carry what you have been given.

23.2 As air carries sound, as a stream carries water, as a pregnant woman carries her child, this is how you are meant to carry what you have been given. What you have been given is meant to accompany you, propel you, and be supported by you. You are not separate from what you have been given, and you *do* carry what you have received within you.

23.3 As we spoke earlier of being a channel, today we speak of being a carrier. Your instruction has been given. Now the task before us is to come to understanding of the means by which you will carry what you have been given down from the mountain and onto level ground, the ground of the earth, the place where you are connected and interconnected to all that lives and breathes along with you. We are coming metaphorically and literally out of the clouds, out of the illusion, surrendering the mist that was all that separated one world from another.

23.4 The clouds of illusion, even those that have gently surrounded our time together on the mountain top must now be surrendered, much as a woman surrenders her body to the growth of a child within. This is a willing but not an active surrender. It is a surrender to the forces that move inside of you. It is a knowing surrender to the unknown. It is a willingness to carry the unknown into the known and the known to the unknown.

23.5 Surrendering to the forces that move inside of you is surrendering to your own will. It requires full acknowledgment that you hold within yourself a will to know and to make known. This will is divine will, your will,

Christ-consciousness. It is alive within you. All that is required is that you carry it with awareness, honor, willingness. From this will the new be birthed.

Potential

24.1 You are the caterpillar, the cocoon, and the butterfly. This is the way that you are many Selves as well as one Self. You are a Self with many forms. The form you occupy contains all of your potential manifestations as the form of the caterpillar contains all of its potential manifestations.

24.2 You are the virgin, the pregnant, the birth, and the new life. This is the way of the world as well as the way of creation. What is unaltered remains unaltered despite its many manifestations. Wholeness exists in every cell, in each of every smallest particle of existence. Wholeness exists in you. Nothing can take wholeness from you. It is as natural to you as it is to all of creation. It does not exist only once potential is realized or made manifest, but always in all things.

24.3 Potential is that which exists. It exists as the power and energy, the spirit within you. It does not await. It simply is. It can remain as the untapped power of transformation, or it can be released. The choice is and is not yours. This power is a force of nature that exists, not separately from you, but not separately from nature either. It is triggered in any number of ways, only one of which is by your choice. When it was said that *A Course of Love* was a trigger, it was meant that the Course is both a trigger of choice and a trigger of nature. It was meant to convey the action of a catalyst. Now it is up to you whether you allow your true nature to be revealed.

24.4 To struggle against your nature is what you have spent a lifetime doing. Stop. If you allow your potential to be released, your true nature in all its wholeness will be revealed.

24.5 You might think of the caterpillar as the unaltered self with which you began your journey. You might think of your body as the cocoon, the carrier of your potential. You might think of the butterfly as your spirit, revealed only after the potential has matured and been released. There is, in other words, a necessity for each step in the accomplishment of wholeness, even while wholeness has always existed as potential. Do not forget, however, that wholeness has always existed, that potential is that which exists, or that potential does not await.

24.6   To attempt to remain within the cocoon of the body, to attempt to contain the spirit within that cocoon, is to attempt the impossible. It is the nature of spirit to become. Its wings poke and prod from within as its potential is triggered. Only with release from its container can it become.

24.7   Yet the body is not left behind. The caterpillar, the cocoon, and the butterfly have always been one and remain one. Each form is but a different stage in the becoming of the spirit. Without release, it must die to its present form in order to begin again. Thus spirit is always becoming, even when it must die to begin again.

24.8   Will activates potential. It is the greatest of all triggers. An activated will realizes that you are the carrier of all the potential that exists. An activated will releases the power that is potential. Remember potential is that which exists, that which is. It is not that which is not, not that which is in the future, not that which could come to be, but that which is.

24.9   Potential is what you carry, as air carries sound, a stream water, a pregnant women her child. You carry your potential to the place of its birth through an activated will, a will that is also carried within you. This merging of will and potential is the birth of your power and the birth of the new.

Tending Your Garden

25.1 Emptiness of mind will now be something that may seem to plague many of you. Where once the mind was searching, yearning, questioning, now it is likely to become still. From the stillness comes its emergence as what it is.

25.2 You need not be content within this stillness, however. As it envelopes you, there is a part of you that will fight back. If there is nothing new to record, nothing new to learn, no new divine inspiration, a part of your mind will attempt to create from this nothingness. Allow this to happen. Allow the stillness when you can. Allow the mind to fight back when you cannot. Resist nothing.

25.3 You are not what you once were. You need not guard against an over-zealous ego-mind. Your ideas in this time may sound crazy, even to your own ears. Let them come. Your feelings may be confused in one moment, crystal clear in the next. Let them all come. Your thoughts will slip from the sublime to the mundane. Let them come.

25.4 You need not, in this time, seek either questions or answers. You need rather, in this time, to come into the practice of letting the new come. It is in the new pattern of stillness combined with non-resistance that the new will come.

25.5 Rather than a time of questions and answers, you might think of this time as a time of sorting and culling. Become used to letting what comes to you come to you without judgment. Let it come. Enjoy your silly thoughts as much as your wise thoughts. Let go your resistance to thoughts that seem of the old pattern. That you know they are of the old pattern is enough. Let them come. Let them go.

25.6 When feeling reflective, sort and cull. Do not do this with an attitude of looking for something. What has come has already come. It does not require seeking. Be a gardener in such times. Separate the harvest from the weeds. Do this as much by rote as you would weed a garden, recognizing that you know the harvest from the weeds. Think of yourself as stockpiling this harvest. It is not yet time for the harvest celebration. It is, rather, a time for gathering.

25.7   This is a time of preparation, not a time of waiting. What you need to know now cannot be gathered except by your own hands. It cannot be sorted except by your own will. I remind you not to attempt this as a task to which you apply the mind or the question of "What am I looking for?" You are looking for nothing. You are tending your garden.

Self-Guidance

26.1　It has been said that *you* are the source and the power of coming to know and making known. It naturally follows, then, that you are capable of self-guidance.

26.2　Let us talk a moment of the concept of guidance. When you have sought guidance, you have sought because you have not known. You have sought externally because you have not known of a source of internal guidance. You have been guided by teachers, counselors, and leaders of all kinds, through words spoken and read, through dialogue, through example. If you had known, you would not have sought guidance. Thus your idea of guidance is likely to hinge upon this concept of the unknown.

26.3　Now let's speak a moment of the Self as guide. This simply means that you turn to the Self as the source of coming to know of the unknown. While simple, this idea can be expanded upon.

26.4　A guide shows the way, creates movement, gives direction. These things too the Self can do if allowed to do so. The Self *will* guide you if you will allow it to. Your Self will lead you down from the mountain top and through the valleys of level ground. There is no other guide. We are One Self.

26.5　You *can* trust in your Self. Will you? By tending your garden you will develop this trust and prepare for your descent to level ground.

26.6　Your self-guidance can be thought of as an internal compass. It will not necessarily know the answers as each answer is sought, but if paid attention to, it will show you the way to knowing.

26.7　This alchemical transition, this passing of the unknown into the known, this moment when the unknown becomes the known *within the Self,* is the birth of creation. It is the culmination of all that has come before, the All of Everything realized in a single heartbeat, a single instant of knowing. This is the One Self knowing itself. This is not knowing that comes with a great ah ha, but knowing that comes with the awe of reverence. Creator and created are one and the homecoming experienced is that of union.

26.8   Self-guidance is the propulsion, the fuel, for the One Self to know itself. You are ready to be so known.

The Apprehension of Levels of Experience

27.1 Think now not of being apprehensive in terms of being fearful of the rest of your life, but apprehensive in terms of taking hold of the rest of your life, of keeping it within your understanding, within your ability to come to know, within your own grasp of it. You have been asked to let go of much, but not of life.

27.2 You have been asked to let go of uncertainty, not certainty. You have been assured of a certainty you never before believed you were capable of. This certainty is beginning to form within you but will not come into its fullness except through experience. This certainty has only been able to begin to form within you because you have agreed to this mountain top experience while remaining engaged in life. You have thus begun to experience on two levels. This has been a goal of the time we have spent together in this way.

27.3 Experiencing life without the insight of spirit was to experience external life. Life itself showed you the way, pointed you in differing directions, taught you what you needed to know. This was the external experience of life. Most of you have had well-examined external lives. You have looked for causes behind the direction in which life led you, but your life was not inner-directed because it was devoid of inner-sight. While you looked outwardly for signposts to guide you, the self-guidance of inner-sight was not developed.

27.4 Inner-sight made an appearance on occasion, showing up as flashes of insight. These flashes of insight might be thought of as brief views from the mountain. The obstacles confronted on level ground suddenly gave way and you saw clearly, if only for an instant. You saw as if from a great distance, and because of that great distance, your view was expanded.

27.5 This is the quality of the inner-sight you now will carry with you to level ground because you have practiced during our mountain top time together the ability to *experience* on two levels.

27.6   Coming to know is not an aspect of the mind alone. It is not an aspect of the spirit alone. Coming to know is a quality of inner-sight, of wholehearted human experience combined with spiritual experience. You are and always have been both human and spirit, both form and content. Now you contain within you the ability to combine both levels of being through the experience of life. You have already been doing this. You are, in fact, becoming well-practiced.

27.7   Now you are asked to apprehend—to understand, and to hold within your conscious mind—this situation that you find yourself in, this new relationship that you have with yourself and with life. You quite literally have a new way of seeing. You might think of this initially as having two perspectives, an internal and an external perspective, a human perspective and a spiritual perspective, a perspective from level ground and a mountain top perspective. Your descent from the mountain top will not mean that you no longer have the perspective gained there. You did not "go" to the mountain. The mountain came to you.

27.8   As you continue to practice your apprehension of this new situation, it will become more than a concept. As was spoken of in A Treatise on the Nature of Unity and Its Recognition, it will become a trusted ability and, through practice, lose its dualistic seeming nature and become as intrinsic to who you are as is breathing. In this same way, the dualistic seeming nature of all of life will be revealed to only seem to be so.

27.9   The two levels of experience which you have been participating in are the joint cornerstones for the biggest revelations yet. All that is now seen as dualistic in nature can be experienced as different levels of experience of one whole. You might consider this by again picturing the mountain-top. Looking in one direction, you might see only darkness. Looking in another, you might see the dawning of light. Opposites exist only as different aspects of one whole. Different aspects exist only as different levels of experience.

27.10   To be able to hold onto, apprehend, and carry with you the ability to experience both levels of experience, the internal and the external, the form and the content, the human and the divine, is to elevate the self of form, or, in other words, to be what you have always been: Whole.

27.11 As darkness and light, hot and cold, sickness and health are each just opposite ends of the same continuum, you can now see that they are only distinguished by degrees of separation. So too have you been.

27.12 The degree of your separation from wholeness can be seen much as the degree of separation between hot and cold. If you were to perceive of wholeness as an ideal temperature, you might think for a moment, just as an illustration, of your experience of separation always taking place at a certain number of degrees away from the ideal. The "temperature" was thus never perfect, but rather always either too hot or too cold. Yet the perfect temperature always existed, you just did not experience it. You were, in other words, separate from it because of the degree of separation that you chose. Because you never chose union, or wholeness, you did not experience lack of body temperature or the effects of weather, but it is as if you denied your body the ideal 98.6 degrees internally and 78 degrees externally. There is no living body that does not exhibit a temperature, no environment that does not do so. Some kind of temperature is thus a constant. A constant is an aspect of wholeness. A variable is an aspect of separation. The constant does not become variable because variability exists.

27.13 That you are who you are and that you have always been the accomplished is a constant and an aspect of wholeness. The variability of how you experience who you are is also a constant within the aspect of separation. Merge the two, however, into one level of experience and the whole formula changes.

27.14 This is what we move toward as we practice participating in two levels of experience simultaneously. We practice experiencing the constant and the variable as one. We practice experiencing the constant and the variable together. We practice in order to move toward an experience of variability within wholeness rather than within separation. It can be done.

27.15 Life, your humanity, is the variability. Spirit, your oneness, is the constant. Life is oneness extended into separation and variability through experience. The elevated Self of form will be the expression of new life lived within the constant of wholeness but continuing to experience the variability of separation. This is what you practice as you gather on the mountain top while remaining on level ground.

27.16 Separation, as well as the variability of the experience of the separate self, have always been variables that exist within the constant of wholeness.

What you have experienced, however, has not been wholeness or the experience of wholeness, but the experience of separation. What we are speaking of now is being able to experience wholeness *and* the variability of experience that has come through the separated self of form. This is what you are beginning to do through your practice. Your proficiency will change your experience, and your experience will change the world.

From Externally to Internally Directed Life Experience

28.1 At one time there seemed to be little or no choice between staying engaged in an externally directed life and removing oneself from life. This may have seemed to be an either/or proposition and thus one of limitation. Moving from an externally directed to an internally directed experience of life creates unlimited choices. The unlimited choices of internally directed experience are what you must begin to face as we begin our descent from the mountain top. To wait until level ground is reached to begin to view the choices available would be to put off coming to know the difference between externally and internally directed life experiences.

28.2 Most of you have experienced several stages of awareness, and we will speak here of those experienced during the years of what is called adulthood, coming of age, or the age of reason. These have been discussed before so this will be kept brief and illustrate only what is needed for our discussion of the next stage.

28.3 The first stage of awareness is a stage of simple external movement through life. Many people, especially young adults, have little experience other than this. Their lives are directed almost totally by external forces, from parents, to mandatory schooling, to somewhat voluntary schooling.

28.4 As the time of schooling is left behind, the next stage of movement begins, that of external movement toward independence. With this movement, the number of choices increase and the level of awareness increases with the increase in choices available. As young people do not usually move away from the home of their parents until they are at least college age, the opportunity to move away, move out, become more independent increases the awareness of self as self. As the self matures beyond school age, the choices become those of degrees of independence, moving away, moving into one's own sphere of friends, colleagues, relationships. For some these choices include commitments to partnerships of a personal or professional nature. For some these choices include marriage and starting a family. Some follow a more standard pattern than others, with schooling, career, marriage, and family seen as an almost inescapable as well as desirable norm. Others pursue dreams or adventures.

28.5   All of these choices are externally directed. They may include a great deal of inner reflection in order to be made, but they are still *directed* at external outcome. By living the experiences of these externally directed life situations, growth occurs, changes happen, new avenues to explore at times open up, leading to the next level of experience: That of external movement toward a chosen type of life.

28.6   At this level, some people reach a crossroad that feels like a choice that will move their lives in such a different direction that it is both exciting and at times excruciatingly difficult. Others reach a plateau of sorts and just keep following the opportunities that are presented along one path. They may have chosen one career, for instance, and made choices within that career path, but never really consider a different career path. Many simply reach a state of reasonable comfort and will make no choices that will effect that comfort level.

28.7   All of these stages may be associated or accompanied by religious or spiritual experiences that seem to help guide the choices, but the choices remain the same: Externally directed choices.

28.8   Now something new awaits you. It is a choice so different and a means so revolutionary that it will take some getting used to. This change is predicated on all the changes that have come before it, including, and most particularly, on that which was most recently spoken of, that of apprehending the new reality of wholeness. It is not wholeness that is new, but the reality of wholeness that is new. The reality of being able to experience the variability of separation from within the state of wholeness is what is new.

28.9   This must be kept foremost in your mind. The reversal spoken of recently, the reversal from believing in a giver and a receiver to knowing that giver and receiver are one, is also of paramount importance.

28.10   You and your life are one. Your life is not the giver and you the receiver.

28.11   You and God are one. God is not the giver and you the receiver.

28.12 This is wholeness.

28.13 Depending on the circumstances of your life, one of these two attitudes will have a reverse side that will have a greater hold on you. Your life may have shown you that you are not in control in many ways and at many times. Therefore, you think that you must take what life has to "give." This is most likely the attitude of those whose major life dilemmas have been of a monetary or career nature, where success or failure "in life" is seen as the most crucial element of a happy life.

28.14 If the attitude you will have greater need of reversing is that of God determining the circumstances of your life, you have probably been more affected by the relationships of life, by loss or death of loved ones, by accidents, or illness, or "natural" disasters, by the unexplainable forces that have affected you with sadness more so than with ideas of success or failure. Therefore, you think that you must take what God has to "give."

28.15 Most people feel at least some combination of these two attitudes, but will find that one is prevalent. You must now get past all such notions or attitudes.

28.16 Acceptance has been a main theme of this dialogue and was revisited and defined as acceptance of internal rather external conditions. It makes no sense, however, to accept what is not the truth. Most of what is not the truth has been identified as old thought patterns. This is all that the notion of a giver and a receiver is: An old thought pattern.

28.17 Thought patterns exist within thought systems that have been externalized and are part of the world on level ground. These external systems are based, as are all that you have made, on the externalization of what is within. At the same time however, what is within has been based upon what was previously externalized. This is what now must change, and as can be seen, this change is essential to changing the world.

28.18 This change, this transformation, can only take place within time because only within time is the experience of separation possible, and experience is where the power of transformation lies. This transformation will, however, take you beyond time, because once experience is moved out of the realm of separation and into the realm of union or wholeness, new conditions will apply. This is why it has been said that the changes that are to come are not about time-bound evolution. Only this first change, this first transformation, must take place in time.

28.19 This is the change, the transformation, we have been working on by changing your experience of time to one of experiencing two levels of "time." Our "time" on the mountain would be more rightly described as "time outside of time."

28.20 "Time outside of time" by itself will not cause the shift that needs to occur, however. What will create the shift is the ability to experience "time outside of time" and "time" simultaneously. Thus is the "wholeness" of time, or eternity, experienced and made real. Eternity might thus be seen as the unchanging constant that has not been affected by the variable of time. Said in another way, eternity and time are part of the same continuum as are properties such as hot and cold. They are part of the same whole that is the constant of all that is whole...all that is one.

28.21 So too are giving and receiving and giver and receiver.

28.22 To move to internally directed experience is to make the move into wholeness that will cause the "shift of the ages," the experience of variability within wholeness.

28.23 The key to this movement is the simple realization that it is possible. This is what our time on the mountain has provided you with: The experience required in order to realize a new possibility.

28.24 As you move toward wholeness, all the pieces of all that we have talked about will begin to fit together. A whole will form within your mind much as if you have been following a thread and now can see the tapestry. This tapestry will bear the mark of your experiences and will be like no other. The thread represents your own journey to truth, your own journey to wholeness.

28.25 Separation is desired no longer, but experience is. Your will and God's are one and thus it is being made so.

28.26 Presently it is as if you follow two threads, the thread that has led you to the mountain and the thread of the life from which you have not removed yourself. Now you must begin to weave these two threads together into the tapestry of your new life. This weaving will take place as you continue to intertwine the two experiences that you are simultaneously holding within your conscious awareness.

28.27 This is what we will continue to speak of as we conclude this dialogue.

The Common Denominator of Experience

29.1 This is where we begin to really lose sight of concepts of duality—where they cease to be real for us. Wholeness and separation, God and man, life and the individuated self, what you do and who you are, the eternal and the temporal, joy and sadness, sickness and health, all cease to have the limited power that all such concepts have formerly held. When they cease to be held as separate concepts in your mind, they cease to be separate. Remember that you have already realized the ability to participate in two levels of experience simultaneously and that duality is really just a matter of different levels of experience. If you can be having the experience of the mountain top and the experience of level ground simultaneously, then you can also have the experience of all other "opposites" in this same, simultaneous way. If you can integrate all that opposes wholeness into one level of experience, you will be able to experience life from within the reality of wholeness rather than from within the reality of separation.

29.2 Your "self" will no longer be divided into a spirit Self and a human self, living under different conditions, at times complimenting and at times opposing one another. Just as mind and heart became one in wholeheartedness and ended the conflict induced by their seeming separation, the spirit and the human self must now do so also.

29.3 Mind and heart joined as you let go of judgment and re-learned or remembered wholehearted desire—the source of your power. Now this power is available to assist you in accomplishing the final joining, the joining that will end duality and return you to wholeness—to who you truly are—in the reality in which you truly exist.

29.4 This is no more complicated than ending the rift between mind and heart. You have accomplished that and you can accomplish this—in your reality. As you realize by now, all this talk of accomplishment is merely about bringing forward what already exists into the reality in which you exist. Another way of saying this is bringing who you are into wholeness, which can be interpreted both as bringing all that you are into existence and as bringing all that you are into existence in union.

29.5   Your access to union, so newly discovered and yet always existing within you, has been a part of the process that has allowed you access to two levels of experience. It *is* your access to two levels of experience—the experience of wholeness and the experience of separation. While you may have seen it as access to information or sensory experiences of another kind, it is, in actuality, access to a state of being.

29.6   Your familiarity with your spacious self has also been part of the process and part of the experience of merging wholeness and separation. While you may have seen it as a new means of interaction, it has been, in actuality, access to a new state of being.

29.7   A new state of being is a new reality. It is linked with your notion of who and where you are, for who you are and where you find yourself, and experience yourself, are your reality. This is why experience has needed to find a place in which it could become the common denominator between wholeness and separation. Once you experience yourself in wholeness and find yourself in union, you have made of *yourself* the common denominator upon which experience can find anchor in wholeness and union.

29.8   *You* are thus, as always, the creator of your reality.

Yielding to Wholeness

30.1 What is held in common is shared and is a characteristic representation of the whole. Just as simple fractions can be added together to achieve wholeness once a common denominator is found, your own fractiousness can yield to wholeness through the common denominator of the self. A common denominator is simply that which yields to wholeness. This yielding is a natural process. To yield is to give up, surrender, but also to produce and bear fruit.

30.2 The two levels of experience we have spoken of might be seen as the process, much like in math, through which the common denominator is found. The common denominator is not by itself the whole, but is, in combination, the whole. In order for a common denominator to be found, more than one (fraction, part, or variable) must exist. The purpose of finding a common denominator is to translate what is more than one into one. An assumption of wholeness is "common" in every denominator.

30.3 A denominator is a named entity. To denominate is to name. "In the beginning" the separate expressions of the whole were named. This naming was an act of creation, stating simply the existence of what was named or denominated. Existence and wholeness are the same. Thus *your* existence, the existence of the self, is, or can be, a common denominator of wholeness. In our act of saying it is so, we name or denominate the Self as what is common to wholeness. Despite unlimited variations being available, commonality is also always available. Thus no matter how fractious are the separate selves, commonality and wholeness always exist and have always existed.

30.4 Wholeness cannot be achieved without joining, thus the commonly known injunction of "where two or more are joined together." If you would think of this in terms of "God" or the state of "Wholeness" or "Beingness" separating into more than one in order to know Itself, you would see that knower and known are one. You would see that two or more are needed in order for knowing to occur. To not know wholeness would be to be in a state of nothingness. Thus the joining of two or more are needed in order for wholeness to be known and thus to exist as a state of conscious awareness.

30.5 Now let us consider this in terms of experience. As knower and known are one, experience and experiencer are one. In other words, one must experience in order to know. It follows then that what is experienced is what is known. It also follows then, that to not experience joining is to not experience wholeness. Stated another way, the *self* cannot know the *Self* without *joining* with the Self. The Self must be the knower and the known, the experience and the experiencer. The quest to join with God is this quest. The quest to be the knower and the known, the experience and the experiencer. The culmination of this quest then, is joining.

DAY 31

Joining

31.1 Joining is both about union and about relationship. Let us consider this by considering the two levels of experience—that of the mountain top experience—and that of the experience on level ground.

31.2 While you have been immersed in one level of experience you have been either knower or known. This is why experience has seemed to exist apart from you. You say, "I had this experience" or "I had that experience," as if you have "had" contact and interaction with circumstances or events that are separate from the self. In saying this, you express your realization of relationship but no realization of the unity in which relationship exists. You "know" the experience because you have "had" the experience. The truth that you *are* the experience escapes you.

31.3 What the mountain top experience is helping you to see is that you *are* the experience. The mountain top experience did not happen to you or happen separately from you. It has happened and is happening *within* you. You are the experience and the experiencer, the knower and the known. This joining is the point of the experience and the key to *experiencing* wholeness.

31.4 As has already been stated, wholeness could not be *experienced* without division. Wholeness and oneness are the same. You are one in being with your Father, your Creator, the originator and denominator of life.

31.5 To have experienced only separation is to have known only half of any experience, to have seen every experience in only one dimension—in short, to have seen experience as happening to you rather than as you. By realizing the unity of the relationship in which experience becomes manifest, you not only realize oneness, but realize that you are a creator and that you always have been.

31.6 All experience is a product of knower and knowee. It is the One Self knowing itself as one individuated Self.

31.7　Joining is differentiated from union only by experience. Union is the realm of the One. Joining is where the realm of the One unites with the realm of the many. In each of the many is the One—the common denominator. By knowing the One in the many, experience can be achieved within wholeness.

31.8　The beginning of this knowing occurs within, with the knowing, or experiencing, of the One within the individuated Self. Notice the link here of knowing and experiencing. To know experience as the Self is to know the Self as creator, or in other words, to know the One Self within the individuated Self. To know the One Self within the individuated Self is to join the two. The two are thus joined in the relationship of experience. Experience is not known separately from the Self. Self and God are one and experiencing together in wholeness. For the individuated Self to experience separately from God is to negate the purpose of the experience of the Self which is God. To negate is to deny what *is*. The denial of what *is* is the source of separation. The acceptance of what *is* is the Source of union and the ability to experience in wholeness.

The Experience of the Self and the Power of God

32.1 The experience of the Self is God. It is not from God. It is not of God. It *is* God.

32.2 If all of life is the oneness that is God and God has chosen to experience that oneness through relationship, then you are also that experience and are in relationship with God through that experience.

32.3 Here we must revisit the concepts of oneness and manyness for if you retain any notions of God that are inaccurate, they will arise here.

32.4 Let us discuss, for a moment, the concept of God because everyone has at least some sort of concept of God.

32.5 First we will look at the concept of God as Supreme Being—God as *one* being, *one* entity. When thought of in such a way, it is somewhat easier to relate to God than when God is thought of in broader terms. You might think of God as you think of yourself. When thinking of the ideas put forth here, you might think of God deciding to know Himself. You might think of God deciding to create. You might think of God creating. You might think of God granting free will to His creations. Then, perhaps, you might think of God resting, or standing back and witnessing the unfolding of all that He created.

32.6 What would the purpose of this be? Would God be standing back, judging Himself on the goodness of what He created? Thinking that He'd like to make adjustments here or there, perhaps, but no, He has already granted free will so He can't do that? If the original purpose was knowing Himself, what kind of knowing would this provide? Wouldn't this suggest a situation similar to a parent thinking he or she could know him- or herself through observation of the children they produced?

32.7 Another concept of God is that of Creator. This concept might have nothing to do with the notion of God wanting to know Himself. This concept may be quite amorphous and not tremendously different than scientific notions of the source of life. Whether it be called God or the Big Bang or evolution, this notion presents the concept of something being begun and then turned loose, proceeding from its beginnings under scientific or natural laws.

32.8 Another idea of God within the concept of a Creator God is of God existing in all of what has been created. God is, within this concept, seen as the spirit within all that lives and also seen as an overriding spirit, a force, a unifying factor. God is closer, within this idea, to being a participatory being, but still falls short. Man lives and has free will. Animals abide by the laws of nature. God is still a concept.

32.9 Yet most religious beliefs encompass the concept of a living God. How might God live? Could He live in time and space in a dimension we know not? Does He live as the spirit within us, and as such have some small role, perhaps akin to that of what we refer to as our conscience? What kind of life would this be? A difficult to imagine life at the very least.

32.10 A *concept* of God is not necessary. False concepts of God, however, are compromising to God and to Self.

32.11 Jesus spoke to you of his life as an example life. Jesus was called the Son of God and also God. Those who understand the meaning of any or all of the example lives that have come as revelations of who God is, understand that those lives were not separate from God.

32.12 Yet to believe that God is everyone can still make you feel as if you are not God. How can this be? This can be only because in your contemplation of this idea, you lose your sense of self. There is a rebellion, a negation of either the self or God that occurs when these two concepts—concepts of the self and of God—cannot be reconciled or joined in harmony. Either the self or God takes precedence in all lives. *All* lives. There is no other choice as long as the self and God are seen as separate.

32.13 Whether God is seen as Creator or Supreme Being, God is still seen as the All Powerful. While God is seen as the All Powerful, man is disenfranchised. Even while God is perhaps seen in all things, or as the spirit by which all that lives, lives, God is still seen as having what man has not. The list of what one can imagine makes God powerful and man not could be endless, just as one could make an endless list of what they believe differentiates God from man. The example lives in which the power of God was demonstrated in the lives of men and women are seen as little more than pass-through situations in which the power of God passed through men and women to other men and women.

32.14 Only Jesus was known as the Son of God and *as* God. This is why Jesus came as your teacher and was used as the example life for this work. This is the point that this work has striven to get across. That man and God are one. Not only is man God. But God is man and woman and child. God is.

32.15 And yet, God could not be all that is, or God would not be in relationship. If the natural world around you has revealed anything to you of the nature of life and God, it has revealed to you the truth of relationship. As has been said before, if separation had severed relationship, then separation would truly exist. Each entity or being would be singular and alone. Yet God has been referred to as the All of All. How could God be the All of All and not also be man? How can God be all that is and at the same time not all that is? How can God be the All Powerful and Living God and also be lowly and powerless man?

32.16 God has also been referred to within this work as relationship itself. Let us consider this idea newly by considering God's relationship to Jesus.

32.17 The claimed relationship of God to Jesus was that of Father to Son but also as one in being. One in being, but different in relationship.

32.18 Could God be one in being, but different in relationship, to each of us? Could not God's oneness of being be the consciousness we all share? Could not God's relationship to everything be what differentiates God from us and us from God? So that we are both one in being *and* different? Could it be that while we are one in being with God we can also become more god-like through the practice of holy relationship? Could not the instructions that you have been given—such as those of access to unity, and becoming a spacious Self, and the means that have been used—such as the two levels of experience you have achieved during the days and nights of our time together, be attempts to show you how you can be more like unto God in relationship, even while you *are* God in being?

32.19 Would this answer your questions concerning how God is both different and the same? Would this answer your questions concerning God's great power when compared to your own? Could you see that God's power stems from His relationship to everything rather than from His being? This is the easiest way to say this, if not quite accurate. Being *is* power. But being, like oneness, cannot know itself without relationship. You *are* one in *being* with your Father, with God, with the Creator and with all of creation. You are also, however, a *being* that exists in relationship. The extent of your ability to be in relationship is the extent of your ability to be god-like.

32.20 God is the being and the relationship. You are capable of all the power of God's being but you are powerful only as God is powerful—in relationship. Because God is in relationship with everything, God is All Powerful. Because you are in a state of limited relationship, you have limited power. This is the difference between God and man. This difference, however, can be diminished as you embrace holy relationship. As you embrace holy relationship you can become powerful as God is powerful.

Being in Relationship

33.1   As we begin to speak of power, we must return to the initial idea put forth in A Treatise on the New: That all are chosen. To embrace an idea of some having power while others remain powerless is to embrace an idea laden with conflict. The power of God exists within everyone because all are one in being with God. And yet this power cannot be used. It can only serve. What does it serve? The cause of holy relationship.

33.2   Relationship is the interconnective tissue that is all life. The *answer* of how to respond to each and every relationship—and remember, here, that situations and events are relationships too—lies within your own being. Being in relationship. This is what you are and what your world is. *Being* in relationship.

33.3   All relationship is holy because it is within relationship that *being* is found and known and interacted with. Relationship is thus the route or access to being and being the route or access to relationship. One cannot exist without the other and thus both are one in truth. This is the divine marriage, the divine relationship of form and being.

33.4   While these may seem like simple words, or like a theory being proposed, these words are at the heart of the new way of seeing yourself—a way of seeing that will create a new world.

33.5   Say to yourself, as you confront the events and situations of your world, that you are *being* in relationship. It is to your *being* that the people, places, events and situations that make up your world appeal. It is in your response that *who* you are being is revealed.

33.6   You are *being a who*. Your *who* is your individuated self. But your *who* is also your representation of *being*. The two becoming one—the individuated self becoming one in being—is the aim toward which we have journeyed together.

33.7   You might think of *being* as *what* you are, and responding as *who* you are. You have been told that these words are being given to you so that you do not respond to love in the same way again. This wording may make love sound as if it is an event, something that comes to you or happens to you. Yet if relationship and being are one, and you are one in being and different in relationship, what is being said is that being and relationship are of one piece, one whole, and that whole is love. In other words, every relationship, everything that comes to you, every event, every situation, is *of* being, which *is* God, which *is* love.

33.8   How, then, do you respond? If you respond as *who* you truly are, you respond with love. Love is the only response.

33.9   Yet the response of love can look as different as the events, situations, people, and places that populate your world. How can this be? And how can you look at each event, no matter how horrific, as a response of love?

33.10   The *only* way that you can do this is by always knowing and never forgetting *who* you are. You are *being* in relationship: The creator of events as well as the experiencer of events, the creator of relationship as well as the relationship itself. You either know this or you don't. It is not about "believing" that this is so, but knowing that this is so. It is when you *know* that this is so, and you also know *who* you are, that you know with certainty that the only response is love.

33.11   All relationship is with love because all relationship is with God, who is one in being with you.

33.12   Being is power. Relationship is powerful. In other words, relationship is the expression of power—all the different expressions of power. In the time of Jesus, the powerful were seen as being blessed by God and the powerless as not being so blessed. This way of seeing has gone much unchanged. All are powerful. But, since all are powerful only in relationship, your relationship to power must be realized. Those who are powerful have realized their relationship to power. Those who see themselves as powerless have not realized their relationship to power. They have not made it real and so it has not served them.

33.13   And yet, since no one can exist outside of relationship and relationship is where power is expressed, everyone does have a relationship with power. Power is one in being with each and every one of us. Every single individual has within them the power to affect, change, or recreate the world. Every single individual does so to the extent to which they realize their power. A baby realizes the power of its cry within moments of being born. Many a teenager develops full realization of the power of their independence. In other words, you each have claimed some type of power for yourself, some means of exerting that power, which is the same as saying some means of individuating the self.

33.14 This is the power of being. The power to individuate the Self. The power to be who you are. This is power and the source of power. This is the force of creation, the *only* true power.

33.15 But again, despite that we each hold the power of creation within us, it is only in relationship that it is expressed and that we become powerful. To realize that you are in relationship with everything and everyone all of the time, is to realize the full extent of your power. You *cannot* realize that you are in relationship with everything and everyone all of the time and retain the desire to *use* your power. This is impossible. The realization that you are in relationship with everything and everyone all of the time is the realization of oneness and unity, the realization that you are one in being, creator and created. This is a realization that only comes of love because love is the only "condition" of union.

33.16 Thus when you realize your relationship to all, you are all powerful.

Saying Yes to Power

34.1 Power is of creation, not of destruction. Yet creation and destruction are two sides of the same continuum as are hot and cold, darkness and light. Seeing in wholeness includes seeing the opposites that seem to exist at these two ends of the same spectrum. If the new way of seeing the Self just spoken of—seeing the Self as *being* in relationship—is key to creating a new world, how does this relate to the seeming opposite of creation? How does this new way of seeing relate to destruction? Does creation of the new have to include destruction of the old?

34.2 Creation simply does include destruction in much the same way *all* includes *nothing.* Without relationship, *all* and *nothing* are the same. In relationship, the difference between all and nothing is everything. So too is it with creation and destruction. Without relationship, creation and destruction are the same. In relationship, the difference between creation and destruction is everything.

34.3 Relationship is needed to create difference. However, relationship with everything creates sameness—or the very oneness in being that we have been talking about.

34.4 The wholehearted desire that is upon you now is the desire to know and experience this oneness of being in relationship rather than the difference of being in relationship—the wholeness of being in relationship rather than the separation of being in relationship.

34.5 This wholehearted desire can be fulfilled in you—it *is* being fulfilled in you. As it is fulfilled in you, you will create a new world—a world based on sameness rather than difference. You have faced and admitted your willingness to leave striving for specialness and differences behind. Now you need only realize that your wholehearted desire has made it so and begin to see and create this change in the world around you.

34.6 This is your world and your experience. This is your life and your experience of life. Now you must believe that you are its creator and powerful in your relationship to it.

34.7   If *you* do not make real your power, *you* will experience yourself as powerless. If you experience your being as powerless, you are negating the power of God who is one in being with you.

34.8   Thus we continue to draw to the close of our time together by asking each other to experience our power—the power of sameness of being. Are you willing to experience the power of God? To let it flow through you? Realize how many have said no to this request. Realize the importance and the power of your willingness to say yes.

Being a Creator in Unity and Relationship

35.1 In your relationship to God, who is your being, you can know relationship to everything, because in this *one* relationship, you are in relationship with all. Thus you need not become a world traveler, a joiner, an activist. You simply must become aware of all that you are.

35.2 In this fullness of being there is only love. In this fullness of being is found the means for the extension of love. In this fullness of being is found the cause for love. Means and end are one. Cause and effect the same. Fullness of being is thus the answer that you have sought and that you have always possessed.

35.3 This fullness of being is different for each one of you because it is the cause and effect, the means and end of relationship. You have always existed in relationship with God who is your being. But while it has been said that you are *one* in being and *different* in relationship, relationship is also God. God is the relationship of everything to everything.

35.4 You have known yourself in relationship to yourself and others, without realizing that your being is God, that others are one with you, that God is the relationship of everything to everything, or that you are the relationship of everything to God. Everything that is shared with God is shared with all because God is in relationship with everything. It has been said that when you reach awareness of the state of unity, you can't not share. This is why.

35.5 So you might ask, was it once possible for you to be so unaware of your being that you were not sharing the relationship of everything with God? As long as you have known that you are a self, as long as you have been aware of your own existence, you have been aware of God. Your awareness of Self is God. God's awareness of you is Self. This awareness exists in reciprocal relationship.

35.6   How is knowing this going to be of practical benefit to you as you leave the mountain top experience behind? This question has been asked in this way in order to remind you that while you will return to level ground, you will also retain the mountain top experience. As was said before, the mountain came to you. You will thus always have the power to call upon the mountain top experience and the view of wholeness we have achieved here. You will carry it within you, and when you feel not its power, you will be able to call it forth simply by asking for it to be so.

35.7   What we speak of when speaking of your return to level ground is returning in a calm, even, and equal manner, to the most elemental and fundamental aspects of being human, while carrying within you a very elemental and fundamental idea—the idea that you are one in being and different in relationship. The idea that you return to your humanity with is an idea of oneness come to replace an idea of separation, an idea of sameness come to replace an idea of specialness, an idea of accomplishment and union here and now come to replace all ideas of life after death.

35.8   These are ideas that take the way in which you once related to life and shift it entirely. Because the way in which you relate to life is what has caused life to be as it has been, this shift will cause life to be different, or in other words, new.

35.9   Ideas are neither learned nor accomplished. They simply are. They thus take no time to learn and require no steps to accomplishment. They can be lived immediately. No intermediary is needed. No tools are needed. All that is needed is that you carry them within you in the way we have previously spoken of carrying. Carry them as a pregnant woman carries her child. Let them grow. Let them live. And give them life.

35.10   Giving ideas life is the role of creatorship.

35.11   As a creator of life, new life, your first creation is, in a sense, creation, or re-creation of yourself. This is why you return to the ground-level of humanity with the heights of divinity fresh in your minds and hearts. This is why you return accepting of yourself rather than in a quest for self or with a desire to know a higher self. You return knowing you are one in being with your Creator and accepting your power to create. You return to create unity and relationship, through unity and relationship.

35.12   Only through unity and relationship are you able to be a creator. A new world can be *created* only in this way. A new world can *only* be created. To proceed relying upon anything other than your power to create would be to only attempt to repair or replace.

35.13 Unity is oneness of being. Relationship is different expressions of oneness of being.

35.14 Being a creator must begin with full realization of oneness of being, which is unity, because without this full realization the potential exists for conditions other than love to exist. It should not take much consideration to know that to create from anything but love could have disastrous effects. This has been seen time and time again as you have "created" in separation.

35.15 To create without the possibility of many expressions of creation would negate the purpose of creation, which is life in relationship, life in harmony, the experience and the expression of the one in, and within, the many.

35.16 Creation has produced life through union and relationship. Humankind's unawareness of the union and relationship in which it exists has produced the idea of separation, while at the same time, humankind's desire for separation produced unawareness of union and relationship. Now humankind's desire for union and relationship has led to awareness of union and relationship while at the same time union and relationship has led to this desire. Creation itself, which stands apart from particulars but united with wholeness, has led to this time of opposites becoming one and wholeness becoming actual rather than probable. Wholeness is actual. All that is left to be created is awareness that this is so.

35.17 If creation only occurs through unity and relationship, then the original creation must have occurred in this way. We will not return to previous discussions of original creation, but it must be thought of so that you understand creation. It has been said before that creation is continuous and ongoing. It is continuous and ongoing in everything that has been created, including you. This does not mean, however, that you have been a creator.

35.18 Being a creator, and creating anew, is different than being affected by the ongoing nature of creation. Saying that you have been affected by creation, however, is also not the entire story, for as has been said many times, means and end are one, cause and effect the same. You have been "creating" but relating to creation in separation. You have seen yourself as separate from creation and separate from all others. Thus what you have "created" has stood apart from wholeness. What is not created in unity could be said to have been *made* rather than *created*. The world as you know it is what you have made. Your life as you know it is what you have made. You will only fully realize the difference between what you have made and what you can create when you have accepted your power and begin to create in unity and relationship.

35.19 Because you *are* a creator, you could, however, not create. The word distinction between *made* and *create* thus does not fully do justice to the power you have always retained. But creating in separation is as different from creating in unity as has been your concept of God and man. Few of you have even thought of creating as God creates. You have barely been able to accept the thought of the miracle!

35.20 And yet you are not being called upon to create as you have been, but to create as who you truly are being. You are called to nothing short of creating a new heaven and a new earth. This does not, however, entail specificity any more than the miracle does. It does not entail choice. It is a way of being. When you are fully aware of your oneness of being and begin to create in unity and relationship, you will do so by simply being who you are being, just as you have "created" during the time of your separation by being who you have thought yourself to be.

35.21 Most of you are aware of having at least some role in the creation of your life. You may feel that at times God has intervened, or that at times you have been a victim of fate, but you are also aware of the role you have had in your own life, primarily as you have reached maturity and begun to make choices. While it has just been said that you will create in unity and relationship much as you "created" during the separation, your creation in unity and relationship will be free of choice. Creation in unity and relationship is creation within the embrace of the All of All. How can you choose when what you create is everything?

Who You Are in Unity
and Relationship

36.1 The exercise of your power is in the creation of your experience.

36.2 As an ego-self, you created an experience for yourself that was separate from all others. You made choices concerning how you would live your life from within the realm of what you considered possible. You did so continuously. This was the way in which you created your experience of a separate existence.

36.3 Your experiences in their totality you call your life. Yet you have stood apart from these experiences—all of them. You can look back on your life and see its form. You could write an autobiography describing every experience you encountered between your earliest memory and the present moment and it would say nothing about you if it related the experiences only as physical events. Your experiences may, in their totality, be called your life, but they cannot be called you. You stand apart. And yet in your choice of, and response to your experiences were you revealed, because, in this way only, were you a creator.

36.4 Powerlessness is moving through life as a being without the power to create.

36.5 You have felt like the creator of your life in the choices you have made. The experiences of consequence to you were the experiences of choice. Experiences that were "of" your choice are those that would move the story of your life along as a "personal" experience rather than as experience itself. Even experiences dictated by "fate" were of consequence only in your response after the fact. The story of your life, in short, would be a story of how you chose to respond, day-in and day-out, to the world around you. You, in short, created your life through chosen responses. You created your life through your responses to the circumstances of your birth, your opportunities or lack of opportunities, the fateful incidents that you encountered, the people you met. You started with what you believed you had been given, the self that you saw yourself to be—the self you considered immutable and unchangeable—and proceeded from there. Yet you created in *response* to "reality" rather than *creating* reality. Now you are called to create reality—a new reality.

36.6   This is where you begin again. Begin again with the Self you now know yourself to be.

36.7   When you start over, knowing that what you have been given is everything, your creatorship of your experience is a totally different exercise. You realize that your life is not you but that your life is an exercise in creatorship. Creator and creation are one. You are one in being with the power of creation and different in your relationship to and expression of that power.

36.8   Can you not see that if you can create your experience you can create a new reality—a new world? Can you not see the difference between creating as a separate self in response to a "given" set of circumstances in a "given" world and creating your experience as a creator who has realized oneness and unity—who has realized a new reality? The old reality was that of separation. The new reality is that of union. It is new only in that it has gone uncreated.

36.9   This is a true starting over with the true realization that giving and receiving are one and that both are within your power. This is starting over with the realization that you can give yourself a new set of circumstances and a new world by creating it as your experience. This is starting over with the realization that you are now the creator of your experience. You have always been creating because you have always been one in being with God who is endlessly creating. But you are only now a creator in union and relationship.

36.10   The difference here is all the difference in the world. It is the difference between all and nothing in relationship to one another. Recall the example used earlier. There is no difference between all and nothing without relationship. In relationship, the difference is everything. This same difference is what is meant when it is said that you are one in being and different in relationship. Without your awareness of unity and relationship, it was as if God was everything and you were nothing, or as if you were everything and God was nothing. But just as with all and nothing, there was no difference between your being and God's being without relationship. You could conceive of self and God in different ways, but you could not truly create difference but only perceive of difference. You thus always remained one in being with God, yet continued to relate only to a world and to experiences you perceived as being either created by a separate God or created by your separate self. You experienced the power of being because you were a being who existed, but you did not experience being powerful.

36.11 There is only difference between your being and God in relationship. This is the example that the ideas of Father, Son, and Holy Spirit as a trinity representing one God were meant to portray. The Son could only be God in relationship to God. The Holy Spirit could only be God in relationship to God. The Father could only be God in relationship to God. God could only be the Father, Son, and Holy Spirit in relationship. Without relationship, God is simply all—being. Without relationship, what is not God is simply being—simply existing at the opposite end of the continuum of everything that is creation.

36.12 What we have called illusion *is* this simple nothingness of existence without relationship to God, and thus existence without relationship to the power of creation. The illusion is an illusion of simply being. Is this not how you have seen yourself? As a simple *being* doing your best to live the life you've been given? All the choices in the world save this one before you now, have made no difference to your state of being. You have just kept being, kept making choices between one illusion and another in your separate reality. A separate reality that cannot exist in truth but only in illusion.

36.13 Despite all of this, you have always had some remembrance of yourself as a creator. Despite all of this, you have loved and feared, grown and evolved, made choices of integrity and courage, responded with nobility or doubt, boldness or timidity, all within a frame of thought and feeling that has felt completely real to you and is completely real to the separate being you have been being.

36.14 Because you have always been one in being with God, this power—this power of being—has always been yours. The power to feel—love, hate, anger, compassion, greed, humility, and longing—have always been yours. The power to think—rationally or passionately, logically or instinctively—has always been yours. The power to create—everything from weapons of mass destruction to cathedrals of towering majesty—has always been yours. The power to know or perceive—even an unreal reality—has always been yours.

36.15 To be a being of feeling, thought, creativity and knowing or perception is to be one in being with God. Accept this, for this is what God is and what you are. This is being. To be one in being with God and yet to exist outside of the powerful state of relationship and union has been a challenging choice. A god-like choice. A choice for a new kind of experience that has led to the creation of an unreal reality so populated by the god-like and the god-less, so near to replacing creation with destruction, so joyous and loving, and so hate- and pain-filled, that you have been moved to a new choice.

36.16 When you realize that you are one in being with God and different in relationship you accept the power of being, or individuating God. You accept the power of God. You become powerful.

36.17 God remains God who is one in being with all, and God also is given form, or is, in other words, differentiated. God is All in All. And God is also All in One and All in Many. God is still the Creator of All, but God is also now the Creator of One, the Creator of the experience of one life, or many lives, the experience and the experiencer of life. Through differentiation, God is you as you are God. God retains oneness of being and also becomes a being in union and relationship—in short—a being in union and relationship with you.

36.18 Yet you do not disappear or cease to be. You are not replaced by God whom you have always been one with in being. You simply accept the truth of being *and* the truth of being in union and relationship. Both at the same time. Both/and rather than either/or. Cause and Effect. Means and End. You accept the end of choice and the beginning of creation.

36.19 You can see, now, perhaps, why we have had to build your awareness slowly in order for you to be able to reach this place where you may be able to accept this new idea which is simply the truth. It is the same truth that has been stated here in many different ways to allow you to become accustomed to the idea of a truth that may seem heretical to some of you when it is stated as directly as it is being stated here. But our time together is coming to an end and your acceptance of the truth of who you are and who you can be is essential to the accomplishment of our mission—to the creation of a new heaven and a new earth. The only way to create it is to experience it. The only way to experience it is to create it. All that stands in the way of your creatorship is your final acceptance of who you are in unity and relationship.

A New Idea of God

37.1   What we have just done is replaced an old idea of God with a new idea of God.

37.2   If you no longer believe in God as a supreme and separate being, why should it be difficult to see that God *is* being? This is not much different than saying that the most basic truth about you is that you are being—and that the most basic truth about God is that God is being. Yet the fact that you are being does not define who you are any better than the earlier example of your experiences would define who you are, because being, by itself, does not differentiate or individuate you.

37.3   Recall that creation begins with movement. Being is only being in relationship. Movement nor experience exist without relationship. Thus the world does not exist without relationship—as nothing exists without relationship. But relationship, like being and experience, does not differentiate or individuate you in separation as it does in union. Separation and the contrast of the separate define every relationship with either/or rather than both/and thinking: that is, you are a woman and *not* a man, you are a human being and *not* a divine being, you are a person and *not* a tree. As a separate being, you only relate to other separate things. In short, who you are being is all predicated, first and foremost, by the relationship that you see yourself as having to the world around you. Since you see yourself as separate from it, all that you experience with your being is separation. All that you represent with your being is a separate being or a separate self.

37.4   This could not help but be your perception since you came into being in a known world, where you were told that you are a person with a certain name, that you belong to a family, all of whom are separately named and have separate roles, and that you live in a household, in a city, in a state, in a country, in a world, wherein everything has a separate name and purpose. In a sense, this is the end of the story, or the beginning of a story already written—a story of separation. You were not alone in this story, and yet you were taught to experience only in separation from the being you were being. And thus, not knowing your union and relationship with your being, but only your separate relationships with "others," you saw yourself as a separate being, and incapable of creating anything except, just possibly, the relationship you would choose to have with others and the world around you.

37.5   You have thus experienced relationship in a very defined and separate way—a way that does not represent the truth of who you are, or what relationship is—a way that represents separation rather than differentiation or individuation.

37.6   Relationship *and* union are the way of God. The way of heart and mind, body and soul, heaven and earth. God is being in unity and relationship. So are you.

37.7   How then, you might ask, are you distinct from God? Is your body distinct from your aliveness? You keep looking for distinction from God as if distinction means separation—as if God is a separate being. If this were all this idea was, it would not be so difficult to dislodge, but the difficulty lies in that you think of God in *your* image, and the image you hold of yourself has been inaccurate. Because you believe you are separate, you created God as a particular and separate being.

37.8   You keep striving for differentiation in a way that simply will not work—through separation! And what's more, you keep striving for differentiation while wanting to continue a certain reliance. Your differentiation from the being of God can only come through the relationship and unity that you would deny in your quest for separation! This would be like demanding to be a body and not a mind! Your reliance on God can only come through the relationship and unity that you would deny in your quest for separation! This would be like demanding that the mind send the body the signals it needs while proclaiming their separation.

37.9   One of the reasons you have been as intent as you have been on your idea of a separate and particular God is that you want to believe that there is a compassionate being in charge of everything, looking out for you, there to help when you are in need. God is all compassionate being everywhere—not one being of compassion! In union and relationship you realize this. And you realize that all compassionate being everywhere is a consciousness or beingness that you share. And further, you realize that what is possible is for you to become the one being of compassion that you already are in God.

37.10 And then you realize that Jesus was being God and was called Jesus Christ because he lived within Christ-consciousness, or the compassionate consciousness that you share. You realize that the man, the God, the historical figure who has been called Jesus Christ was not only Jesus but Christ. Not only Christ but Jesus. Not separated but individuated. You realize that the call for the second coming of Christ has sounded and that it is a call to the difference you have always desired while not requiring you to remain separate!

37.11 Subtract any sum from another and you will realize that subtraction results in a new number, a remainder, that when added to the previous number returns it to its original value. Think further of a problem in division that results in something left undivided, something called a remainder. To remain is to continue to exist. It is what is left when parts have been taken away. It is what was not destroyed by the removal of the parts. You "remain" one in being. You "remain," just as the numbers of simple mathematics remain, one with the whole. You have seen yourself as capable of being divisible from that which is your Source, but division, like differentiation or individuation, is only possible in union and relationship. Two separate numbers, with no relationship, no interaction, no division and no subtraction, simply remain what they are.

37.12 Let us look for a moment at what and who you have been being and what and who God has been being.

37.13 You have, quite simply, been being. The simple truth that you are a being makes you one with God, who *is* being. This truth, however, has escaped you. So you have been being the particular self you have "known" or perceived yourself to be—the self you were defined as at birth—a *human* being—something you have seen as *separate* rather than *distinct* from the *divine* being who is God. Because you are being, however, (and note here that you are being, and God is being, and that it is not being said that either you or God are "a" being) you have power—the power of being which is the power of thought, feeling, creating, and perceiving or knowing.

37.14 You have known that power only in relationship to the separate reality in which you believe yourself to exist. You have exercised that power by making choices as and for your separate self, at times in relationship with loved ones, at times seeing the connectedness of your life with that of others, but even then, only on a limited scale. You have often not exercised even this limited power, believing that life just "happens" to you, and then responding to what happens. You believe either that you are in complete control of your life, or that God or fate have as much control as you do. You may believe yourself, God, and fate to be benevolent, or you may believe that everything, including yourself, works against you. You may rely more on your thoughts, or more on your feelings. You may see yourself as creative, or you may not. You may realize the extent to which your perception of the world shapes your life, or you may not.

37.15   But more fundamentally than even all of this, you might ask, if you are one in being with God, is it being said that you are being God? That you have been being God even within the limited parameters of life as you have known it?

37.16   Unfortunately, this is not what is being said. What is being said is that you are simply being. You are being a feeling, thinking, creating, perceiving *human* being because this is what you believe yourself to be. You may see yourself as a separate human being having a separate and distinct relationship with God, by which you mean a relationship like no other. And if you see yourself in such a way, then you do have a relationship in separation. It might be somewhat like your relationship with a deceased relative in that you feel a bond, a link between heaven and earth, and even some possibility of communication through prayer or other experiential means. But this is still a relationship in separation—between your separate self and the separate and now dead self of the relative. This is not only a relationship in separation but a perceived relationship only —and only because you do not believe that you can "know," truly know, what you do in truth know. You know that you know, but you do not believe that you know, because you believe you are separate and so cannot know anything for certain save that for which you have experiential or scientific proof. As a separate being unable to know, you have been forced, or so you think, to rely on "external" proof.

37.17   Perception and knowing have been used together here in describing the conditions of being because you must be able to perceive in order to be a being. But knowing is also used because you are, as a being, just as capable of knowing as you are of perceiving. In separation, however, the only known can be the self. How could you possibly "know" anything from which you are separate? You can imagine what it means to "know" another person, to be a tree blowing in the wind, what it would be like to know God, but you cannot know, and your separate being "knows" of this impossibility. This is why this Course has had, as its main objective, returning you to true knowing of your Self. A separate being can only truly know itself. Yet in knowing yourself, you can come to know that you are not separate. If you can come to know that you are not separate, you can return to union and relationship and through union and relationship to true individuation and true knowing.

37.18 Certainly you "feel" like an individuated being, a unique being. You "feel" love and you feel pain, and both feel quite unmistakably like "your" love and "your" pain and no one else's. You feel like a "you." This too is "who" you have been being, because as a being you feel. But here again, you have felt only as a being in separation can feel. You know that despite how often someone says they "know how you feel" that they really do not. They cannot know because they are not you. You cannot know how another feels because you are not them. You can join in relationship with others who feel similarly and can find great joy in feeling "as if" someone knows how you feel and who you are. But you have felt doomed to never being known and to never really sharing how you feel.

37.19 This is "who" you have been being.

37.20 Now let us talk of God.

37.21 God is being in unity and relationship with everything. Thus God knows you. God is one in being with you because you are one aspect of everything. As one being in unity and relationship with everything God is one with every thought and every feeling. God is one with every creation. God is all knowing. God is, in short, the collective consciousness and the collective consciousness is that which links every being with every other being in unity and relationship.

37.22 This "link" is very powerful. Where willingness is demonstrated, this link can be moved to be, rather than "just" a link, a cooperative relationship. This cooperative relationship, accessed through willingness, could also be called the "being" that you appeal to when you appeal to God. Knowing what you are coming to know about the true nature of God should thus not leave you feeling bereft of a God you can feel close to, appeal to, thank and praise. But doing so can also be confusing if it leads to thoughts of God as a particular being. Yet the idea of God as Father, introduced and championed by Jesus Christ, was also created by Jesus Christ. Thus is the power of man and God together, the power of creation. What this is saying is that there is a God the Father to relate to and that this God the Father does not negate God, nor does God negate God the Father.

37.23 God the Father is an idea that was created and thus exists much as other ideas of God were created and thus exist. But this creation, like the creation of Jesus Christ himself, is not all of God, while at the same time it is all of God just as Jesus was and *is* all of God. In union and relationship, God is all *and* God is differentiated.

37.24 Jesus, the example life used throughout this Course, was both man and God. He was being in unity and relationship. Being God did not negate his being Jesus. And being Jesus did not negate God being God. Jesus could create God the Father, could create a being consistent with his being, because he was a creator. He was, in short, being in union and relationship

37.25 Jesus was all of God and God was all of Jesus while *at the same time* each was different or individuated by being in union and relationship.

37.26 The only real difference that exists or has ever existed between God and man is that man sees difference in a way that makes no sense. Like the faulty ideas of creation that shaped your "creation" of your separate world spoken of early in this Course, your quest for differentiation has been caused by your faulty memory of creation. To differentiate in union and relationship is to be God in form—to give expression to "all" that exists in union and relationship through your being.

37.27 By simply being, you have been "part" of God but you have not seen this as what it really means either. You have seen this as being separate, or at most as being "a" part of God—as if you are a drop of water in the ocean—and in this example reemphasized the mightiness of God and the lowliness of man. The "part" of God you have been being is being. You have been a feeling, thinking, creating, perceiving being. The "part" of God you have not been being is union. Remember, God is being in union and relationship. This is what God is. God is being. God is relationship. God is union.

37.28 Holy relationship is relationship with the Christ in you—the bridge to unity.

37.29 Like heart, mind, and body is to your form, being, union, and relationship is to God's "form."

37.30 You have been being, and you have been being in relationship because you could not "be" otherwise, but you have not been being in union.

37.31 The divineness of your being is most revealed in relationship. The divineness of your being is most revealed when you cooperatively join with another or even with yourself. When you cooperatively join, you move the particular self aside and sometimes glimpse the divine being in relationship. But because you have so clung to separation, you have rarely, until recently, glimpsed union.

37.32 Glimpses of the being you are being when you are in unity and relationship have been offered to everyone. They have been afforded by willingness. They come from observation of self and they come from observation of others. They come from what you are willing to observe. They become more than glimpses only when they become what you are willing to be.

Day 38

Who I Am

38.1 My beloved,

38.2 We have not spoken much recently of love, but now it is time to return to love. Do you know, can you feel as yet, how much I love you? How full of love I am for you?

38.3 Now we set aside once again the "we" of Christ-consciousness, of our shared being, and enter into relationship with one another. I ask you to turn your attention, I ask you to be attentive, to the relationship that you feel with God.

38.4 Being full of love for one another is the beginning of extension, the end of withdrawal. It is the mutuality of our love that causes this fullness. Remember briefly here the feelings of withdrawal you have experienced when you believed you loved more or that you were loved less by a friend or lover. Remember briefly here the feelings of withdrawal you experienced when you felt loved for being something other than that which you are. Know, through your brief contemplation of these feelings that this is behind us now. Know that we can be known and loved equally for who we are.

38.5 Call me God the Father, call me God the Mother, call me Creator, or Great Spirit, Yahweh or Allah, but call me yours. For this is who I Am.

38.6 Call yourself daughter or son, sister or brother, co-creator or friend. But call yourself mine. For we belong to one another.

38.7 And realize that as I call upon you, I call you who I Am.

38.8 This is the meaning of the embrace—the possession, the ownership of belonging—of carrying, or holding relationship and union within one's own Self. This has been called the tension of opposites, of being one's own Self and being one in union and relationship. These opposites, like all others, are held within the embrace of love and belonging.

38.9 You are ready now to return to this ownership, this possession of relationship and union. Possession and ownership are words that have become faulty ideas in separation. They mean an entirely different thing in union and relationship. They mean union and relationship. That you own it. That you possess it. That you hold it and carry it within your own Self. That you make it yours. As you make me yours and as I make you mine. I Am your own. You are my own. We are the beloved when we are the beloved to one another, when we are who I Am to one another.

38.10 Relationship and union are not other than this. Being in relationship and union means just that. It means a love deeper than any love you have known, for in not owning and possessing, in not being owned and possessed by, and in, union and relationship, you have not fully known love. To claim something as your own is simply to claim possession for your own Self. Now it is time to see me as your own God as well as God of all. Now it is time to call me who I Am.

38.11 There is a subtle and loving difference between *I Am* and *who I Am*. *Who* is an acknowledgement of individuated or differentiated being in union and relationship.

38.12 Community, or union with, can never replace or replicate ownership and possession in union and relationship. It cannot replace who I Am, or who I Am to you.

38.13 Who I Am to you, and who you are to me, is all that matters. Our relationship can only be thus in union and relationship with each other because we are in union and relationship with each other. We are not two beings who are separate but relating in union. We are each other's own being. We are one and we are many. We are the same and we are different. In "own"-ership we are full of one another's own being. We are each other's own.

38.14 Fullness comes only from love, which is the source and substance of who we are being. I Am being you. You are being me. In this equation is fullness of being, which is love.

Day 39

Who I Am to You

39.1 My beloved,

39.2 It is time now to come to your own discovery of who I Am to you. No one can give you this answer, not even me, because this is the nature of who we are. Individuated beings are who we are in relationship to one another.

39.3 You have heard of life spoken of as a projection. Because we are all one being, we must either extend or project in order to individuate and be in relationship. You are an extension of I Am into form. Through *your* extension, you can become who you are to me, instead of who I have been to you.

39.4 You may find it difficult to give yourself an answer to who I Am to you in words, and even if you are able to do so, you may not be able to share this answer in a way that makes sense to anyone else. Let this tell you something.

39.5 We are going to speak again of contradiction here. Of the importance of your knowing who I Am to you, and of the importance of being able to continually discover who I Am to you. Of your embrace of knowing, and your embrace of mystery. Of knowing me as your God and as God of all. Of knowing you are no longer being *on your own* and yet of having to come to this realization of who I Am to you *on your own*.

39.6 This is the beginning of individuation in union and relationship. This is the beginning of wholeness. What you strive for here is revelation. For only through revelation can you know all and still hold the mystery. This revelation is not something being withheld from you. But it is a revelation that can only come to you as an individuated being in union and relationship. This is what makes it a true revelation. Because true revelation is between you and me.

39.7 "Between" you and me is the presence of Christ. Remember we have talked about the Christ "in" you. Remember that you have been told of Christ being a bridge. When you relate to anyone, Christ is there, bridging the distance that would keep you separate and holding you in relationship.

Christ has provided the necessary link between the separate and each other, between all and God. Yet if the time of Christ is about the end of the need for the intermediary, what becomes of the intermediary relationship Christ seems to offer? Are you ready to hold relationship *on your own?*

39.8   Contemplate the "buffer" nature of all that is intermediary. An intermediary stands between as well as links. It is a totally unnecessary requirement in unity because the boundaries of separation have fallen. To be individuated being in union and relationship is to *be* Christ, to realize that what we call Christ is the integration of relationship into the Self.

39.9   Being in union is being all. Being in union *and* relationship requires individuation, and individuation requires relationship. Thus you must now accept yourself as Christ, or as the bridge of relationship between all that is individuated in union and relationship.

39.10   This is why you must discover your own relationship with me. Discovering your own relationship with me is discovering the Christ in you. When you have discovered your own relationship with me is when you have discovered that you are who I Am because you realize—or make real—your oneness with Christ. When you have discovered your own relationship with me is when an intermediary is no longer needed—because you have realized and made real your oneness with Christ. When relationship is established you realize that relationship *is* the intermediary link between individuated beings and that you hold this link, through relationship with me, within yourself. Christ is direct relationship with me.

39.11 Establishing this relationship with me may sound lofty and difficult, but it is simple. It is as simple as relationship is within your everyday life. You may not think that relationship within everyday life is simple, but you also know it as a constant. You know that you have had "good" relationships and "bad" relationships, love relationships and work relationships, and that being in relationship with "others" is an inescapable truism of your life. Even these relationships of separation, the types of special and not-so-special relationships you have chosen to leave behind, are not done away with but only transformed. Relationship is part of life. Inescapable. Acceptance that our relationship *is* and that it is a determinant of who we both are, is all that is required. The relationship that you accept with me is the relationship of union, for union is no more than this, as we are one in being and when you have discovered relationship, we are one in union as well.

39.12 Relationship itself is intermediary, it is what you carry, the connection between one thing and another. In this instance it is the connection between two individuated beings in union and relationship. You and me. In order for this link of relationship to exist there must be two beings for it to link *(where two or more are joined together)*. In other words, there must be a you and a me. In other words, as you are individuated, so too am I. We jointly individuate rather than separate. We can only do this in relationship. We can only have relationship as individuated beings.

39.13 Thus, both must occur as one.

39.14 This is like the big bang, the explosion of creation. It is all at once. All of Everything. Yet in relationship.

39.15 What must occur now must occur between you and me. Your willingness is all that is required.

39.16 Let me tell you what has occurred in the past so that you know not to respond to love in the same way again.

39.17 Who I have been to you is who you have been to yourself. Remember the idea of projection. This is what projection does. It projects outward. It is different from extension in that extension is like a projection that remains at one with its source. Projection separates.

39.18 You have separated me from you through your projection. And yet what you projected and called God, just as what you projected and named thousands of other "things," you separated from yourself only in time and space. In time and space your projections became separate and other than you. This is what the world of time and space is. A world that is a projection that you have made, a world that has the shape and form, the character and value, the image and meaning, that you would give it. This is your universe. I have been, to you, the God of this universe.

39.19 Thus your ideas of the universe and your ideas of me have been inseparable projections. As have your ideas of the universe and your ideas of your own self.

39.20 Have I been a benevolent God in your universe? Then you have been benevolent and seen your universe as a benevolent universe.

39.21 Have I been a judgmental God in your universe? Then you have been judgmental and lived in a judgmental world.

39.22 Have I been a powerful God who can work miracles? Then you have been a powerful miracle worker.

39.23 Have I been a distant God who does not show his love for you or others? Then you have been distant from yourself and those you love.

39.24 Have I been a God you have sought and never found? Then you have not found yourself.

39.25 Have I been a fair God? Then you have been fair and the world has treated you fairly.

39.26 Have I been the God of your religion? Then you have been religious.

39.27 Have I been a God of vengeance? Then you have been vengeful.

39.28 Have I been a God of love? Then you have been loving.

39.29 Have I been all of these? So, too, then, have you, and so too has your universe been.

39.30 Has your God not been a god at all, but science, money, career, beauty, fame, celebrity, intellect? Then these things have become the content of who you are. Science, money, fame, celebrity, intellect or any other concept that has become your God can be a tough task master, or a fair friend, loving or unloving, distance you from yourself and others or bring you closer to yourself and others. No god who has been projected is without attributes, even gods such as these.

39.31 Have you had no god, no science, no beauty, no wealth, but only a meager and hopeless life? Then your god has been the god of defeat.

39.32 Have you had no god, no science, no career, no fame, but only a life of hate and violence? Then your god has been the god of bitterness.

39.33 Everyone has a god because everyone has a being and an identity for that being. Everyone carries the memory of I Am.

39.34 What memory of I Am will you carry with you now that you know that I Am is who I am and who you are? What memory has this Course and this Dialogue returned to you? What memory is without attributes because it is who I Am and not a projection? Only love. What memory is not a memory, but your identity? Only love.

39.35 Only that which is by nature without attributes can be one in being in union and relationship *and* individuate. Could you become your sister or your brother? A tree become a frog? The sun the moon? Yet love could become all of these, because love, by its nature, has no attributes. Love is creation's genesis, the unattributable given the attributes of form.

39.36 Who Am I to you? Only who you are to yourself. Now it is time for you to be not who you have been to yourself, but who you are, and have been, to me.

39.37 Here is where we must return to paradox, to knowing who you are and who I Am and to constantly discovering who you are and who I Am, because who you are and who I Am are the same being in the constant creative tension of differentiating from one another.

39.38 This is a time of knowing who you are and who I Am while at the same time, holding, or carrying, the mystery within you. That mystery is the tension of opposites. It is time and eternity. Love and hate. Good and evil. In other words, All and Nothing. It is the tension of individuation, a tension that has existed since the beginning of time, *between* time and eternity, between the attributeless love and the attribute laden being. Between the one being of love and the many beings of form, between love's extension and form's projection.

39.39 This is a time of knowing you are not *on your own* but that you must come into direct relationship with me *on your own* and of your own free will.

39.40 All of these aspects of what stand between are also an aspect of the Christ in you.

39.41 But breathe a sigh of relief, my beloved, for you do not have to learn all that the Christ in you learned. This is why we have had to enter the time of non-learning—so that you accept that you do not have to try to learn the unlearnable. This is why we have left the time of becoming behind, why you stand ready to enter the time of being in union and relationship. The Christ in you is the accomplished. The Christ in you is that which, upon this final acceptance, returns your wholeness to you.

39.42 Realize your own expansion, the expansion that has taken place under the tutelage of Jesus, within the dialogue with Christ-consciousness, within the recesses of your heart where your relationship with love has never been severed. Realize your readiness. Proclaim your willingness.

39.43 Realize that I love your smile, your teeth, the hair upon your head, the warm, smooth shape of your skull. Realize that I love your hands and that as you take another's hand, you hold my own, and that I am with you as well as within you. Realize that I love all that you are, and that as you snarl in anger, cry in despair, hang your head in weariness, howl with laughter, I am with you and within you.

39.44 You will realize as you enter union by means of the bridge of our direct relationship that you will not leave your humanity behind. You will realize that as you enter union by means of the bridge of our direct relationship that you will no longer see me as an inhuman God. You will know I am as human as are you and that you are as godly as am I.

39.45 Do not expect perfection, only union. Do not expect sainthood, only Godhood. Do not expect the world, expect heaven. Do not expect answers, only knowing. Do not expect learning, only revelation. Do not expect all, without also expecting nothing. Expect to know that you hold both within yourself and that you hold me as I hold you.

39.46 You will realize as you enter union that the tension of opposites *is* the individuation process and that you are the bridge. You are the bridge to me. I am the bridge to you. You are the bridge to your brothers and sisters. They are your bridge to yourself. You will also be the bridge between war and peace, sadness and joy, evil and good, sickness and health. You will turn anger to gladness, tears to laughter, and replace weariness with rest. But you will still *know* all of these. You will *know* the All of Everything and the emptiness of nothing and our *relationship* will bridge the distance and become cause and effect, means and end.

39.47 You will realize that as we individuate we are in a constant state of creation as well as of creative tension. As we become individuated beings in union and relationship, we continuously create one another. We create from the field of the possible which must include everything.

39.48 Do you not realize yet, that this is what we do and who we are? That we are creators? That we think, feel, know, and *create*. Creation is the manifestation of all we think, feel, know and come to know. Because we are constantly creating, we are constantly coming to know anew. This is eternity. A being in time wants to be known in time but can only be known in eternity. You now are the bridge between time and eternity.

39.49 And so am I. As the Christ in you ceases to be a bridge, the Christ in you is not only integrated into you but integrated into me. I could no more reach across time and space without this relationship than could you. Only with our willingness joined, are we able to negate the need for intermediaries and be in relationship. Only with our willingness joined do we both become, welcome, and share, the Christ relationship to and with each other.

39.50 This is who I know you to be and who you, in union with me, know me to be.

Who You Are to Me

40.1 Through your extension of your being into union, you complete a circuit, a circle of wholeness, and I become who you are to me. Thus giving and receiving are one. Cause and effect complete.

40.2 All that being *is* was extended into who you are.

40.3 Although this is a difficult concept to get across with the words that are available, I would like you to understand that when I am love being, I am being without attributes—love being in union and relationship. I am the anchor that holds all that has taken on attributes within the embrace of the attributelessness of love. This is why my being has been capable of accepting your projections—because I am attributeless being. I am love, being.

40.4 I did not make you in my image. I created you in love because it is the nature of a being of love to extend. Realize that it is only when being is added to love—only when love is in relationship with being—that love is given its nature. Realize that it is only when love is in relationship with being that it attains this quality that we are calling extension.

40.5 Love of itself has no nature. It does not *do* anything. It just *is*, and its *isness* is what I hold, or anchor within myself, and that which Christ bridges through relationship. Your attributes are the attributes of being in relationship. You came into the world, into form, as a being in relationship. The application of your being to relationship, like the application of being to love, gives relationships their nature, including your relationship with yourself.

40.6 Through the application of your being to relationship you have taken on distinguishers through which you became a *different* or *distinct* being, a being *different* or *distinct* from who I am, and who others are. These are the attributes of your being, what you might call your personality or even who you are. As has been said before, you saw these attributes of being as making you separate rather than *distinct* from who I am being and who others are being. Your attempt at individuation and extension, an attempt consistent with the nature of your being, failed only because you experienced separation rather than differentiation, and fear rather than love.

40.7 When I created, I extended my being, a being of love, into form. Through that extension, I became *I Am*. I became instantly because there was no opposing tension—only love and an idea that entered love, of love's extension. As soon as I became *I Am* there also became all I am not, the Christ connection between all I Am and all I am not, and an *I Am*, called the son, who could become who I Am and continue to extend who I Am.

40.8 When you create, you create as my relation. You extend your being into form. That form then becomes. It becomes who you are. Both beings and thus both extensions are the same. The differences have arisen through becoming. For with the birth of *I Am* came the birth of all I am not and the need to differentiate. In separation you have striven against the "opposing" force of union in order to *become* separate. In seeing the self as separate you have known fear and have been forced to reconcile fear with love. Now, in coming back to relationship and union with me you have realized that you are not separate and now have striven against the "opposing" force of separation. With the acceptance of the Christ in you, you are returned to relationship and need no longer strive against the "opposing" force of separation, for you no longer know it. The creative tension that now remains in our relationship is the tension of individuation or the individuation and differentiation process.

40.9 This tension, or process, is not *bad*. There is nothing *wrong* with this individuation process or the creative tension that has been in existence since the beginning of *time*. It is creation in the making. What will be created now, and the individuation that will occur now, will hold all the power of your experience as well as all the power of your longing for return. This will be a great power that you carry within you as you return to love and to level ground as who I Am being.

40.10 Lest you do not fully understand, this might be more easily grasped if we talk for just a moment of specifics, such as art or music or literature, religion or politics or science. Jesus or Martin Luther or Muhammad may have been said to have created religions, but these creations, in their *becoming* took on attributes, as all creations do once they are extended into form and time. This is the nature of creation. Creation is about giving attributes to the attributeless. Giving form to the formless. An artist might be moved to her art by a feeling of love so intense she could never put words, music, or paint together in such a way as to express it—she knows as she begins that she but tries to bring form to the formless. Why? Because the nature of a being of love is to extend. The nature of a being of love is to bring form to the formless—to bring love into form.

40.11 Love has no attributes, no form, no conditions, no nature. It simply is. It was said earlier that being *is* as Love *is*. This was a reference to my being, to my being love. I have reconfirmed this statement and said I am the anchor that holds all that has taken on attributes within the embrace of the attributelessness of love. This is why my being has been capable of accepting your projections...because I am attributeless being. I am love, being. But in being God, as in being human, being takes on attributes. As was said earlier, this was meant to provide for the individuation process rather than the process of separation. In being God, I Am. In being love there is no I Am, but only love being.

40.12 Does this help you understand? Help you understand that you are being, and that you are also being some *one*? You have been being separate—a separate being with attributes. Now you are being in union and relationship—an individuated being with attributes. As a separate being, your attributes were based on fear. As a being in union and relationship, your attributes are based on love.

40.13 Recall what was said earlier: Christ-consciousness is the awareness of existence through relationship. It is not God. It is not man. It is the relationship that allows the awareness that God is everything. It has been called wisdom, Sophia, spirit. It is that without which God would not know God. It is that which differentiates All from nothing. Because it is that which differentiates, it is that which has taken form as well as that from which form arose. It is the expression of oneness in relationship with Its Self.

40.14 The difference between you and me is that I am being God and also love, being. This is why I am all and nothing, the attribute-laden God and the attributeless love. This is why it can be rightly said that God is Love and Love is God. But I am also an extension of love, just as you are. This is all *I Am* means. There is no *I Am* except through love's extension. How does love extend? Through relationship.

40.15 Only in my relationship to you am I God. Only in your relationship to me are you who you are in truth.

40.16 Just as you have had many "separate" relationships that in their totality would define your life, so have I, as God, had many "separate" relationships with you and your brothers and sisters, relationships that define who you have thought me to be. Because these relationships are so different, many of you have gone on quests to find the "one, true, God." Do you not see that this would be like going on a quest to find the "one, true, relationship" in your own life? As if you could only be mother or father, daughter or son, husband or wife, sister or brother, friend or foe? You are who you are in relationship. I Am who I Am in relationship as well.

40.17 You would perhaps beg to differ now, and ask of me, "Are you not who you are 'separately' from relationship?" Separately from relationship, there is no I Am, but only love, being.

40.18 You would perhaps beg to differ here, and say that regardless of what I say, you are who you are outside of your relationships. You are not *just* the relationships that you hold. You are more than a mother, daughter, sister, friend. You are an "I" that stands separate from these relationships.

40.19 This is true. You know this "I" because you have a relationship with yourself. If you did not have a Self to have a relationship with, you would not know that you have an identity apart from the separate identities of your separate relationships.

40.20 This Self with whom you have a relationship is love's extension. It is the Self you long to be as well as the Self you are. This paradox has kept you as intrigued with the idea of self as with the idea of God. You have searched for a "one, true, self" as you have searched for a "one, true, God." This search only makes sense to the separated self, who believes all things are separate and thus believes that its self, as well as its God, must be separate from what it is being. It doesn't understand, until joining with the Christ Self, before becoming one with holy relationship itself, that relationship is an identity.

40.21 God is a relationship with love. This relationship with love is all that provides for the I Am of God.

40.22 As a separate being, you have been in a relationship with fear. This relationship with fear is all that has provided the "I" of the separated self. But because you exist as an extension of love, you have always held within you the Christ, who *is* the relationship with love. This is why individuation has become the conflict between, or the tension of, opposites. Because you have relationship with both fear and love.

40.23 Now, as you recognize, acknowledge, and accept the Christ as the Self you have been in relationship with, you are returned to relationship with me and with love. You end your separated state and become for the final time. You "become" being in union and relationship.

40.24 But what does this mean?

40.25 How often have you said or felt, when confronted with some insensitivity toward yourself, especially that of being "left out," unrecognized, or unwelcome: "Don't you know that I am an individual? That I have feelings?" Are you saying this now, as you contemplate leaving behind who you have been for being who you are to me?

40.26 Perhaps you have noticed that in yesterday's discussion of who I Am to you and today's discussion of who you are to me, that one has not been discussed without the other. This would be impossible. Because we are who we are in relationship to one another.

40.27 Is this really so difficult, so improbable, so discomfiting to accept? Does it become less difficult if you remember who I Am? That I Am everything being love? This is not the same as saying you are who you are in relationship to your mother, and your mother who she is in relationship to you. This is saying that you are who you are in relationship to all that is love. This is saying that this is who you are and that this is who I Am.

40.28 Further, this is saying that who you are being in relationship to all that is love is up to you. That through the application of your thinking, feeling, creating, and knowing being to all that you are in relationship with, you extend who you are. This is saying that through the application of your being to all that you are in relationship with you create. You give attributes and you take on attributes. You individuate your being in union and relationship. And in union and relationship, you create only from love.

40.29 Who you are being in union and relationship with me, is me, as well as you. This is the power of differentiation in union and relationship, the demonstration of oneness that was heralded in the time of Jesus Christ.

40.30 With this ability to individuate in unity and relationship comes the greatest gift of all. It is the end of becoming and the beginning of being who you are. With this gift comes the ability to be known and to know. Can you give up the ideal of your separated self in order to be known? In order to know?

40.31 What has been the strongest feeling that you have had as you have read this Course and the related materials? Has it not been a feeling of being known? Has this Course not addressed the questions, the longing, the doubts that you would have, before now, called uniquely yours? Has it not spoken to you as if it knows the secrets of your heart? As if it were written just for you? So it was.

40.32 You are my beloved. We have just shared a dialogue. Your heart has spoken to me, and I have responded. Love has responded. How, now, will you respond to love?

40.33 When you turn the last page, will you cry tears of sadness that our dialogue is complete, that you will hear my voice no more? Or will you brave your *own* relationship with me? Will you turn to your brother and hear my voice in him? Will you be my voice as you turn to your sister? Will you carry the fullness of our relationship within you? Will you be one with me, and in being one with me never feel alone again? Will you let the emptiness of separation leave you once and for all?

40.34 Will you continue this dialogue with me and with each other? Will you carry it with you to level ground—to the place of completion and demonstration of who you are being?

40.35 Will you be the relationship that returns love to all who share this world with you?

EPILOGUE

A Note on Being

E.1　Ah, imagine now what it will be like to have nothing left to learn, nothing left to become. The pressure is off. The alchemy has occurred. The coal has become a diamond. Ah, imagine now being able to forget all ideas of self-improvement, imagine how much time will be saved by this quest coming to an end. But what now will you do? What now will you be?

E.2　Believe it or not, you will find these questions arise less and less until soon, and very soon, they will be entirely gone, never to be asked again. Why? Because now that you are being who you are in unity and relationship, these questions will make no sense to you. They already have far less power. Can you not feel it? The questions remain only as questions of the old patterns of thought, patterns that you need only be aware of before choosing to have them gone from you. This is the only choice you will still have to make—the choice to leave behind the old in order to *be*.

E.3　You are in relationship now only with love, and so nothing will be hard for you. Desire an old pattern to be gone and it will be gone. This little note added to the end of our mountain top time together is only here to help you realize and accept that this will be so. Do not expect difficulties and they will not arise.

E.4　You have returned to your true nature. Perhaps you will remember that within *A Course of Love* you were once asked to "Imagine the ocean or the cheetah, the sun or the moon or God Himself, attempting to learn what they are. They are the same as you. All exist within you. You are the universe itself."

E.5　You are returned to your natural Self, and as you begin to move more fully back into your life, you will realize where the differences between this natural Self and your former self lie. You will realize that you know what to do. You will realize that there is no "will be." That you are and that you will respond as easily to your surroundings as does the cheetah to his.

E.6   This little note is just included to tell you to expect this. Expect heaven on earth you were told. This is what it is. There will be no doubt, no indecision. Your path will be so clear to you it will be as if it is the only path in the world and you will wonder why you didn't see it all along. Expect this. And it will be. So be it.

E.7   There is no becoming. As you are no longer becoming there will be no becoming projected from you onto the world. There will be no projections at all and this is why you will see so clearly. You will see what is. You will create what will be through the extension of love. This is all. So be it.

E.8   You no longer have a universe of projection to maintain but a universe of love to enjoy and a universe of love to create. So be it.

E.9   For as long as you know that what I am telling you is true, for as long as you carry this knowing within yourself, this is how long the eternity of being will be for you. There is no one to turn out the lights but you. Drift from knowing to unknowing, close your eyes, and you can experience the stillness of not knowing, the rest and calmness of nothingness. You can experience non-being and in a similar fashion, drift as gently and as your own desire arises, into all-being. Mainly you will enjoy being—being who you are. You will be happy. You will be content. And you will know, unerringly, how to act naturally from your being.

E.10   You can do everything you did before, or nothing you did before, all with the total confidence of being. You need not worry about this joy being selfish for there is no such thing in unity. You will share your joy continuously just by sharing yourself.

E.11   You will not realize that everything has changed until you "realize" or "make real" that change. Let this revelation come to you. All you need do is expect it to come and it will come. So be it.

E.12   You will also not realize that you have chosen nothing until and unless you realize that everything has not changed. Let this realization come too if it must. And make a new choice. The future is up to you.

E.13   What you "realize" now you truly "make real" as your being applies love's extension to all with whom you are in relationship.

E.14   You will no longer need to "think" about who you are and what you will do, and your willingness to give up this thinking will be paramount to your realization that everything has changed or that nothing has changed.

E.15   These are both possibilities, as all possibilities are yours. Which do you choose?

E.16   There is no longer an in-between unless you create it. You have taken the step of accepting the relationship of the between, the relationship of Christ, into your own being. The cooperative relationship of all with everything abides within you now. You do not, and cannot decide what to do with it, you can only be it. This is the choice you have made. To be. So be it.

E.17   You do not as yet think you know how to just be, and this is why, in a sense, this dialogue, in this form, must come to an end. The dialogue you will carry forward with you, with your realization of being, will be a different dialogue.

E.18   This dialogue has been your final quest. It is the final quest in the quest for being because the quest has been accomplished, fulfilled, completed.

E.19   Leave these words behind now, and bring only the dialogue with you. You will unerringly find those who can engage in the new dialogue, those who have chosen the new, those who seek to share and exchange in harmony. Thus will you begin and your numbers increase.

E.20   Do not be afraid now to be who you are. Do not think you need to be something different, something other than you have been. Leave all thinking behind. Leave all notions of being better, smarter, kinder, more loving behind. Realize that these were all thoughts and notions of becoming. If you hang on to them, your being will not have the chance to realize and make real its being. You will *be* different, only if you allow and will yourself to realize and make real this difference. It is a difference between becoming and being. It is all the difference in the world. It is the difference between separation and differentiation in union and relationship.

E.21   This difference, if you will allow it to come, will take away all worry, all thought about how you could be better, more, greater. If you still possess some things that you would consider character flaws or faults, forget about them now. In being they will be yours or they will not. You will be happy that you have these aspects of humanness or you will not and they will be gone. Do not expect the same unhappiness with yourself. You are fine. You are being. You are being fine. So be it.

E.22   If you will but let it come, you will see that you are being who you are being for a reason, for a purpose, a purpose that will be so clear to you that you will joyously accept yourself for who you are being. So be it.

E.23 It will be possible for you, for a while, to drift between being and becoming if you are not vigilant of your thought processes. This will not take long, however, to overcome, for once you have begun to realize that everything is different, you will not desire to turn back, not even for the familiar thought processes that, although they have bedeviled you, you have held dear.

E.24 When you meet what you would have before seen as difficulties, as you encounter a world where love still does not seem to reign, when you meet that which would oppose love, remember that you are now the bridge between this creative tension of opposites becoming one. Remember that this is creation in the making. Remember that you are a creator. Never forget that in being who I Am being, you extend only love.

E.25 This one note, this tone, this canticle of joy, this celebratory alleluia, is all you need return to, all you need keep in hand should doubt arise. This one note is so full of love, so powerful, that it will be dear to you forever more.

E.26 You will remember, just briefly, as you re-read it, in your quickly passing times of doubt, how different you are. You will recall with poignancy who you once were, but you will not turn back. You will know that all turning back would be but a retracing of the circular route you have traveled from yourself to yourself.

E.27 What will there be to strive for? What quest will replace this quest for being? The quest for love's expression—the quest to see, experience, and share, as many of love's expressions as the world needs to be returned, along with you, to its own Self.

E.28 Does this seem like a long and harrowing road? An endless quest? An endless quest for love's expression is eternity itself.

E.29 Be happy that there is no end in sight to this road you travel now. It is simply the road of what *is* endlessly creating like unto itself.

E.30 You now know how to respond to love, for you are love, being. So be it.

Learning in the Time of Christ

In 2003, about a year after the scribing of A Course of Love *was completed, Mari additionally received "Learning in the Time of Christ." It is evidently intended as an aid to the reader. It also anticipates the formation of discussion groups. For clarity, the parts that correspond to the three Books—The* Course (I), The Treatises (II), *and* The Dialogues (III)—*are indicated.*

I

A.1   A major difference between *A Course in Miracles* and *A Course of Love* has to do with the movement into the Time of Christ, a time of direct learning in union and relationship with God. The word *learning* is loosely used here for no learning is needed in union and relationship.

A.2   Yet, as your work with *A Course of Love* begins, learning and unlearning continue. It continues for the sole purpose for which learning has always existed—that of returning you from self-doubt to self-love. This could also be expressed as returning you from your perceived state of separation to your true state of union. Learning is needed only until perception is cured. The perception of your separated state was the illusion for which a cure was needed—and within *A Course in Miracles* offered.

A.3   Perception is the result of learning. Perception is learning.

A.4   Since the mind is the realm of perception we have taken a step away from the realm of perception by appealing to the heart and the heart's ability to learn in a new way. You are thus instructed not to apply your thought and your effort, your usual means of learning, to this Course of Love. This Course is not for the mind but for the heart. It is not a way of thought and effort but a way of feeling, of ease, and of direct relationship. Again I say to you, in the direct relationship achieved in union, no learning is required. Until you have truly recognized unity, which may come before or after completing the "Treatise on the Nature of Unity and Its Recognition," you continue to perceive of yourself as a learning being. This is the only reason for this continuation of the coursework provided in *A Course in Miracles*. While you continue to put effort into learning what cannot be learned, as you continue to see yourself as a student seeking to acquire what you do not yet have, you cannot recognize the unity in which you exist and be freed from learning forever.

A.5 This is not to say that you will find this Course or the end of learning to be easy. Yet it is your difficulty in giving up your attachment to learning through the application of thought and effort that creates the perception of this Course's difficulty. Thus it is said to you to take this Course with as little attachment to your old means of learning as is possible for you. If you do not understand, accept that you do not understand and go on. Listen to the words as if they are spoken to you, for such they are. Listen as you would listen to a friend in conversation. Listen simply to hear what is being said. Listen simply to let the words enter you.

A.6 This is recommended for your first reading of the Course.

A.7 When you succeed at listening without seeking for understanding, without grasping for meaning, without applying the effort you are used to applying to study, you begin the transformation that is the movement from head to heart and from their separation to their union.

A.8 In wholeheartedness, then, you are ready to return to a second reading of the Course. In wholeheartedness you will find difficulty falling away and understanding arising. You are beginning to know yourself in a new way. You are beginning to know yourself without the perceptions and the judgments of the mind. You are beginning to know yourself as you truly are and you will begin to hear the language of the Course as the language of your own heart.

A.9 Now you may feel quite compelled to share your experience of the Course with others. What might you expect to find?

A.10 Often you will find a desire to read the Course again—to read it aloud—to hear it spoken. This is a natural desire to let the words of the Course enter you in yet another way—the way of voice. Again it is not required nor even recommended that these readings be interrupted by a search for meaning. Listen. Respond. Let meaning be revealed.

A.11 What you will find yourself accepting through this method is precisely what cannot be taught. What you are learning through this method is precisely what cannot be sought after and attained through your seeking. What you are finding through this method is receptivity. You are coming home to the way of the heart. What you gain by sharing with others is a situation in which you "learn" in unity through the receptivity of the heart.

A.12   Am I telling you not to question? Not to enter discussion? I am only telling you to receive before you seek to perceive. I ask you not to receive as one who does not have what another has, as this is not a passing on of information that you do not possess. I ask you merely to receive in order to learn receptivity, the way of the heart. I ask you only to pause, to give the mind a rest, to enter a realm foreign to the mind and yet beloved to the heart. I ask you but to give yourself a chance to let the relief of not having another task to apply your effort to fill you. I ask you but to give yourself a chance to forget about approaching this as one more self-improvement exercise, or one more objective to accomplish. Only in this way do you come to realize you are already accomplished.

A.13   Through receptivity, what your mind finds difficult to accept, your heart accepts with ease. Now you are ready to question what you must. Now you are ready to hear the answer that arises in your own heart or from the voice of the man or woman sitting next to you. Now you are ready to hear all the voices around you without judgment, to enter discussion without an agenda to attend to, to not be so anxious to say what you are thinking that you forget to listen. Now you are ready to let understanding come without the aggressiveness of going out to get it.

A.14   You are patient, loving, and kind. You have entered the time of tenderness. You begin to hear what your feelings are saying to you without the interferences and cautions of your thinking mind. You begin to trust and as you begin to trust you begin to extend who you are. True giving and receiving as one begins to take place. You have entered Holy Relationship.

A.15   The task of facilitators of such meetings of open hearts is to direct the reader away from ego mind and back to wholeheartedness or Christ-mind. "How do you feel?" is a more appropriate question than, "What do you think?" The sharing of experience is more appropriate than the sharing of interpretation. The sharing of process is more appropriate than the sharing of outcome. Facilitators will keep readers from attempting one correct interpretation, as the only correct interpretation is that which comes from each reader's own internal guidance system. Group attendees will find themselves feeling less competitive or interested in asserting their beliefs as it becomes clear to them that unlike in other learning situations, there is no correct answer or specific set of beliefs to be adopted. The student begins to move beyond the need for shared belief to personal conviction and authority.

A.16 Can students be misguided? Is there, in other words, perhaps no "right" answer or correct interpretation, but "wrong" answers and inaccurate interpretations? This is a matter of unity versus separation rather than a matter of right and wrong. In unity and relationship, each is not only capable but will inevitably receive the answer and come to the understanding or interpretation that is "right" for them.

A.17 Those who do not enter unity and relationship cannot be helped, fixed, or shown the inaccuracies of their perceptions. Their perceptions will remain true for them because their minds have told them they are true and their belief in the supremacy of the mind has temporarily overridden the openness of their hearts. The need for some to remain within the teaching and learning situation of "right" and "wrong" answers will be strong. Many will not be dissuaded from the logic that tells them they must work hard to attain anything of value.

A.18 Let me be clear. The seeming lack of difficulty in this Course is where its difficulty lies. To give up difficulty for ease is more than some egos are willing to accept. To give up effort for receptivity is more than some *can* accept. Why? Because it is too difficult. It goes against all you have learned and the nature of the reality in which the mind has functioned. In turning to the heart we seek to bypass this difficulty as much as possible, but each will feel it to some degree, the precise degree to which they are capable of giving up reliance on what they but think has worked for them in the past.

A.19 The way of the heart is the way of the Time of Christ. The time of the Holy Spirit has passed. The time of the intermediary is over. The greatest intermediary of all has been the mind. It has stood between you and your own inner knowing, caught in a dream of perception.

A.20 Collectively and individually, you have come to a level of frustration with what can be taught that has exceeded its limits. Your readiness is felt as impatience. Many can ride the wave of this impatience to a new way. Others need to battle against it a while longer.

A.21　For those ready for a new way the time of battles has ended. They care to engage in no more debates, care not to be proven right or proven wrong, care not to hear the evidence for this approach or that. They have grown weary of the ways of the mind. They are ready to come home to the way of the heart.

A.22　The way of learning in the Time of Christ brings with it a new kind of evidence, an evidence demonstrated clearly and plainly with every willingness to end reliance on the ego-mind and to leave the hell of the separate self behind. What will be demonstrated and shared is the perfect logic of the heart, and that abandonment of the old way will not bring forth ruin but will bring instead the wisdom that each one knows she or he has always possessed.

A.23　Facilitators can rely on this demonstration even when many in a group may remain attached to the ways of the thinking mind. The demonstration will work for those who observe from a place of unity even if it works not at all for the reader who cannot find it within him- or her-self to accept union. There is no cause to delay the movement of the group or to feel anything but gentleness toward those who cannot at this time accept the new way. No harm will come to anyone from the demonstration that will be provided of just how little gain comes to those who cannot receive.

A.24　Through receptivity is the wisdom inherent in being who you truly are revealed. Being who you truly are, accepting your true identity, is the goal of this Course and of this beginning level of what I only loosely call a curriculum. It is appropriate to remember and to be reminded at this level, that being true to your Self is not about reaching an ideal state or a state of identity exactly the same as another's. It is also not about being selfless. These ideas too are part of the unlearning of this Course and are to be discouraged.

A.25　Readers then naturally may wonder what there is left to strive for and in doing so reach again the very difficult transition away from striving. In unity, perfection is the reality. Your reality is union. Thus no striving for either unity or perfection is necessary. The "answer" for those in need of challenges, is the challenge presented in the call to reside in unity and to express the divinity of their nature through sharing in union and relationship. This call is addressed further in the work of the Treatises.

II

A.26 Readers who have not moved away from their desire to learn something that will feed their minds or egos will seldom continue to this next level. The next level brings with it the same situation the reader encountered in receiving the Course, but the reader will now encounter these situations in life. The reader is no longer only a reader. Their experience of this Course has extended beyond reading and beyond the classroom situation. Now a time may come when studying truly seems to be in order. The guidance provided by their reading may seem to come and go and their desire to rely on what they have "learned" will grow. They may desire to backtrack, review, or begin to highlight passages to return to again and again. New questions may arise and a desire for feedback or discussion grow stronger. This may also be precisely the time when the reader is so caught up in experience and learning "in life" that return to a group or classroom situation feels next to impossible.

A.27 Rather than being in a standard learning situation, what the reader who is now experiencing life in a new way is doing is attempting to reinforce what he or she already knows and has already accepted. The "language" is returned to, as a helpful friend would be turned to for judgment-free advice. What those who begin to experience life in a new way begin to discover are the patterns of thoughts and behavior that are most deeply entrenched in them. They feel in need of assistance!

A.28 At this point, groups may need to become more flexible, meet less frequently, or even disband in favor of former "classmates" meeting in more casual and spontaneous encounters. It remains important for facilitators and group members to be available to one another if at all possible during this time, for what is being gained through experience is still in need of being shared. This sharing can offer a rich and rewarding opportunity for differences to be revealed and for the welcome realization that differences do not make separate.

A.29 The forward motion, regardless of a group's configuration, is still the same. It is one movement away from learning and toward acceptance of what is. While differences may be highlighted in this time, what will be revealed through sharing is that while experiences may differ greatly and seem to be offering diverse "learning" situations, the individuals will actually be coming to many very similar new insights and truths.

A.30   The impatience of the earlier level may seem to have increased as these experiences will be moving each individual along at her own pace. Comparisons may arise and some may feel they are not advancing as quickly as others, while those moving quickly may feel in need of time to catch their breath!

A.31   Now, despite the rapidity of movement or lack thereof, to read the Treatises together will likely feel as if it is almost a waste of valuable time. Thus, gatherings of those working with the Treatises will naturally include more sharing of experiences. The facilitator's task is now one of placing these experiences in context. After giving the group time to talk, the facilitator might choose a brief passage that will fit within the content of the sharing. Always it is the facilitator's role to guide the individual group members away from inclinations, which may be strong during this time, to "figure things out." Problem solving is to be discouraged. Trust is to be encouraged. Often a discussion can be facilitated greatly by the question, "How might we be able to look at this situation in a new way?" To encourage the gentleness of the Art of Thought over the relentless stridency of the thinking mind is always helpful. Obsessive thinking is always ruthless, judgmental, and wearing on the thinker. He or she needs help in breaking its grip and should never be allowed to suffer.

A.32   Assisting individuals with the recognition of patterns is also a highly valuable service that facilitators and other group members can provide. The entrenched patterns of the past are difficult to dislodge even when they have been recognized. Individuals can be encouraged here to "watch the parade go by" as what has gone unhealed is brought forward for acceptance, forgiveness, and letting-go. With the letting-go of each old pattern or situation that seems fraught with peril, a cloud of despair will lift, a little more of darkness recedes, and a little more light is available to show the way.

A.33   Often here the facilitator will meet as well individual assessments and self-doubts. Group members may wonder if they are missing something. They may feel as if they have not experienced unity or as if they are no closer to knowing themselves or God. They may feel as if this Course of study that seemed to be working so well for a while now is letting them down. They may wonder where and when the peace, ease, and abundance promised by this Course will arrive. These need help in staying grounded in the present and reminders that they are no longer seeking. They need your reassurance that this time of engagement with life is just what is needed to integrate what has been learned. A return to the simple words that begin the Treatise on Unity would be appropriate: "A treasure that you do not as yet recognize is going to be recognized. Once recognized it will begin to be regarded as an ability. And finally, through experience it will become your identity."

A.34   The achievements of the past, achievements that awarded credentials, certificates and degrees, admiration, respect, and status, are now a thing of the past. What individuals may well be looking for is their reward for the investment they have made in this coursework. While they are looking for it to show up in an old way they will miss the new ways that are being revealed to them. Remind them gently that the achievements of the past were not lasting and that they are not what they would truly want now. Remind them that the goal is reached in being who they are at last. It is present—not in the future. It is with them—not beyond them. The treasure is them.

III

A.35   Beyond the coursework of the Treatises lies direct relationship—direct relationship with me. Entering the dialogue is the way this is expressed; yet this is not merely about entering spoken dialogue. As was said in A Treatise on the Art of Thought, "Creation is but a dialogue to which you have not responded."

A.36   Creation is a dialogue.

A.37   Creation is an unending act of giving and receiving as one. So too is dialogue.

A.38   "Listen and you will hear." But to what are you listening? Entering the dialogue is akin to residing in the present moment and to hearing all that is being spoken in all the ways it is being spoken. Now is the time to truly begin to "hear" my voice in every aspect of creation and to respond with your own voice in all of your own acts of creation. It is time to realize that you are a creator.

A.39   This is a time of great intimacy. This is a time that is between you and I more so than has been the coursework up to this point. It is a time of realizing that "I" am speaking to "you" directly in every moment of every day, in all that you encounter, in all that you feel. It is a time of true revelation in which you are revealed to your Self.

A.40 This is what dialogue, particularly the dialogue that is an exchange between "two or more gathered together" reveals. It reveals Who You Are.

A.41 This relationship between Self and Other, Self and Life, Self and God, Humanity and Divinity, is the dialogue of which we speak. It may seem to suggest duality but it suggests relationship. The idea of unity and relationship must fully enter you now.

A.42 You are not a "student" of The Dialogues but a full participant in The Dialogues. You have entered the final stages of revelation of Who You Are. When Who You Are is fully revealed you will realize that it is time to leave the classroom and live as Who You Are in the world. You will realize that your participation in the world as Who You Are is part of an on-going dialogue, and that it is an on-going aspect of creation by which the new will be created.

A.43 What now will be your relationship to this work that has returned you to Who You Are? Your relationship to this work continues as you live and express Who You Are being in the world. For some of you this may mean continued involvement with this coursework and a direct sharing of it with others. For many more of you it will not.

A.44 For each, being Who You Are will be an expression of unity and oneness that only you are able to express. As each expresses who they are being in unity and relationship, creation of the new will proceed and wholeness and healing renew the world in which you live.

A.45 This Course becomes a beloved alma mater, honored and returned to as a giver of new life. It offers no walls to confine you. It becomes not dogma to restrict you. It is new life come to extend the way of creation, the way of love, the way of living, the new way. It will be with you in every dialogue and will not leave you comfortless. It has no end point in its benefits and associations.

A.46 What continues of this Course is its dialogue. It is on going.

A.47 Gather still with those with whom you learned and grew and became new, but gather in ever-wider configurations. This dialogue is going on all around you. I am with you and will never leave you comfortless. Call on me, for I am here. Talk to me, and I will hear you. Listen, and I will respond. I am in each voice that responds to you and your voice is mine as you respond to others.

A.48 Go forth not as completed works of art but as permeable energy, ever changing, ever creating, ever new. Go forth with openness for revelation to happen through you and through all you encounter. Go forth joyously on this adventure of discovery. Be ever new, ever one, ever the beloved.

A.49 Bring your voice to this continuing dialogue. This is all that is asked of you. This is the gift you have been given and the gift you bring the world: your own voice, the voice of Who You Are. This is not a voice of separation or of the separated self but a voice of union and of the One Self. It is how union is expressed and made recognizable in form. It is what will usher in the new and change the world. It cannot be accomplished without you— without your ability to stand in unity and relationship as The Accomplished.

A.50 Beloved brothers and sisters, You are The Accomplished.

Referencing Guide

References to specific text within this Combined Volume generally follow the pattern of Book:Chapter.Paragraph with Book One being referenced as the "Course" (C), Book Two as the "Treatises" (T), and Book Three as the "Dialogues" (D).

Thus within the Course, C:20.30 refers to chapter 20, paragraph 30. References to paragraphs within The Preludes or the Introduction would be, for example, C:P.8 or C:I.9.

References to paragraphs within the Treatises must identify the number of the Treatise, for example T2:10.1, or T3:13.6.

References to paragraphs generally within the Dialogues would be, for example, D:12.4, but references to paragraphs within the "Forty Days and Forty Nights" require special treatment, as for example D:Day1.23.

References to paragraphs within the Epilogue or the Addendum may be referenced simply as, for example, E.6 or A.4.

Related Works

The Grace Trilogy, by Mari Perron, Julieanne Carver, and Mary Love (1997), is the story of the experiences of three close friends that paved the way for Mari Perron to receive *A Course of Love* (see the Foreword, pages x-xi). It is now available as an ebook.

Creation of the New, by Mari Perron (2007), is a mystical "post-apocalyptic vision" of the death of the old and the birth of the new. It is a rumination on the "new" that the mind cannot take hold of, but rather is held and immersed in. It invites the reader to stop talking about the sea of God and to dive into it.

The Given Self: Recovering Your True Nature, by Mari Perron (2009), is a highly personal yet universal exploration of breaking the trance of convention, moving toward wholeness through one's own humanity, and embracing the authentic self: the Given Self.

Resources

Support for the ACOL community, including Mari Perron's blog and a variety of resources, can be found at www.acourseoflove.com. Readers are also invited to view the publisher's website, www.takeheartpublications.com.